THE GREEN GUIDE

Châteaux of the Loire

Château d'Ussé Photo: © A.J.Cassaigne/Photononstop

MICHELIN

THE GREEN GUIDE **CHÂTEAUX OF THE LOIRE**

Editors	Clive Hebard
Principal Writers	David Holland, Mike Pedley
Production Manager	Natasha G. George
Cartography	Stéphane Anton, John Dear
Photo Editor	Yoshimi Kanazawa
Photo Researcher	Sean Sachon
Interior Design	Chris Bell
Layout	Michelin Apa Publications Ltd. John Higginbottom
Cover Design	Chris Bell, Christelle Le Déan
Cover Layout	Michelin Apa Publications Ltd.

Contact Us

The Green Guide
Michelin Travel and Lifestyle
One Parkway South
Greenville, SC 29615, USA
www.michelintravel.com

Michelin TravelPartner
Hannay House
39 Clarendon Road
Watford, Herts WD17 1JA, UK
✆01923 205240
www.ViaMichelin.com
travelpubsales@uk.michelin.com

Special Sales

For information regarding bulk sales, customized editions and premium sales, please contact our Customer Service Departments:

USA 1-800-432-6277
UK 01923 205240
Canada 1-800-361-8236

HOW TO USE THIS GUIDE

PLANNING YOUR TRIP

The blue-tabbed PLANNING YOUR TRIP section at the front of the guide gives you **ideas for your trip** and **practical information** to help you organize it. You'll find tours, practical information, a host of outdoor activities, a calendar of events, information on shopping, sightseeing, useful words and phrases, and more.

INTRODUCTION

The orange-tabbed INTRODUCTION section explores the **Region Today**, including food and drink. The **History** section spans Roman times through the Revolution and World Wars, exploring the development of the region and the châteaux. The **Art and Culture** section covers architecture, art and literature, while the **Nature** section delves into landscape, flora and fauna.

DISCOVERING

The green-tabbed DISCOVERING section features Principal Sights by region, featuring the most interesting local **Sights**, **Walking Tours**, nearby **Excursions**, and detailed **Driving Tours**. Admission prices shown are normally for a single adult.

ADDRESSES

We've selected the best hotels, restaurants, cafés, shops, nightlife and entertainment to fit all budgets. See the Legend on the cover flap for an explanation of the price categories. See the back of the guide for an index of where to find hotels and restaurants.

Sidebars

Throughout the guide you will find blue, peach and green-colored text boxes with lively anecdotes, detailed history and background information.

A Bit of Advice

Green advice boxes found in this guide contain practical tips and handy information relevant to your visit or to a sight in the Discovering section.

STAR RATINGS★★★

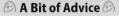

Michelin has given star ratings for more than 100 years. If you're pressed for time, we recommend you visit the ★★★, or ★★ sights first:

- ★★★ **Highly recommended**
- ★★ **Recommended**
- ★ **Interesting**

MAPS

- Principal Sights map.
- Region maps.
- Maps for major cities and villages.
- Local tour maps.

All maps in this guide are oriented north, unless otherwise indicated by a directional arrow. The term "Local Map" refers to a map within the chapter or Tourism Region. A complete list of the maps found in the guide appears at the back of this book.

© Spila Riccardo/Sime/Photononstop

© Bertrand Rieger/hemis.fr

PLANNING YOUR TRIP

INTRODUCTION TO CHÂTEAUX OF THE LOIRE

DISCOVERING CHÂTEAUX OF THE LOIRE

CONTENTS

Welcome to Châteaux of the Loire

The Loire Valley is one of France's most beautiful regions. Its magnificent châteaux, cultural riches and eventful history have earned the Val de Loire its place on the list of UNESCO World Heritage Sites – a label which covers a 280km/170mi stretch of the river from Sully-sur-Loire in the east, to Chalonnes-sur-Loire, near Angers, in the west. Between the two lies a rich and fertile land known as "the garden of France" offering a wealth of unrivalled attractions including the majestic châteaux and towns of Amboise, Angers, Blois, Chinon, Saumur and Tours. *Bienvenue!*

THE LOIRET *(pp90–115)*

The Loiret is one of the original 83 *départements* created at the time of the administrative reorganisations of the French Revolution. The area is largely agricultural with grain production on the plains of the Beauce to the north, horticulture in the Val d'Orléans and livestock in the south. Although known more as the gateway to the Val de Loire, the Loiret has a number of attractions which are well worth discovering before venturing deeper into châteaux country. Orléans Forest, the largest natural forest in France, offers walking trails along with opportunities for fishing and water sports.

THE LOIRE BLÉSOISE *(pp116–140)*

Blois is very much the focal point of the region, renowned for its splendid château which proudly displays the architectural styles to be seen throughout the Loire Valley from the Middle Ages to the 17C. The Forest of Russy to the south is a reminder of how the landscape would once have looked, while the area's many other magnificent châteaux, led by Chambord, Cheverny, Beauregrad, Talcy and Fougères-sur-Bièvre, offer an architectural and historical feast.

THE SOLOGNE *(pp141–154)*

The Sologne is a peaceful, wild and untamed area, abounding in game-filled forests and harbouring almost 3 000 ponds, making this a popular area with walkers, fisherman and hunters. The Domaine du Ciran in Ménestreau-en-Villette is dedicated to explaining the flora and fauna of Sologne, and, like the château de la Ferté-Saint-Aubin, is a must-see. Elsewhere, the Maison des Étangs in Saint-Viâtre gives a splendid interpretation of the aquatic life of Sologne.

EAST TOURAINE *(p155–186)*

The Touraine is a former province of France, with its capital at Tours; today it is renowned for its wine production and its celebrated châteaux, notably on the east coast at Chenonceau, Loches and Amboise, where Leonardo da Vinci spent the last three years of his life.

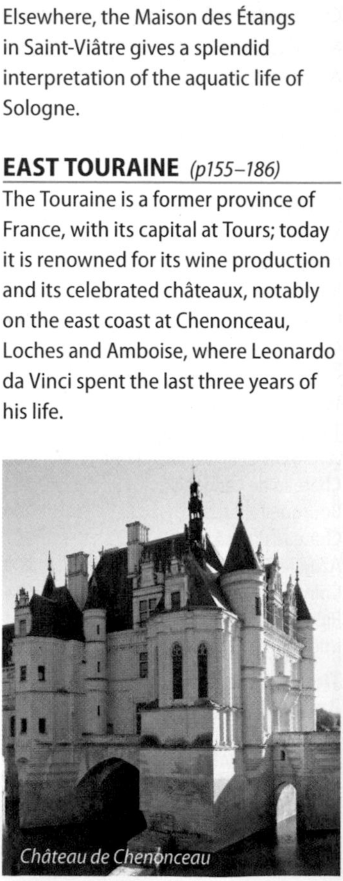

Château de Chenonceau

WEST TOURAINE *(pp187–223)*

The western part of Touraine has its fair share of stunning châteaux, from the splendid Azay-le-Rideau and wonderland Château d'Ussé, to the stark ruins of Chinon and the breathtaking gardens at Villandry. The main city, Tours, is famous for the many bridges spanning the Loire, but it is especially noteworthy for its medieval district, Le Vieux Tours, a place of splendid half-timbered houses. With its excellent TGV links, Tours is a logical starting point for visits to the Loire Valley.

THE SAUMUR AND BAUGÉ REGIONS *(pp224–248)*

The historic château town of Saumur lies between the Loire and Thouet rivers, surrounded by extensive vineyards that produce some of the finest wines in France, Including Chinon, Bourgueil and Coteaux du Layon. Baugé by comparison has a fine 15C château, and it was here that a major battle against the English was fought in 1421. The annual Opéra de Baugé, modelled on England's Glyndebourne Festival, draws over 3 000 visitors, and is justly popular.

ANJOU AND THE MAUGES COUNTRY *(pp249–274)*

Anjou, an ancient county, duchy and province, centres on the city of Angers in the lower Loire Valley. Best known for its castle and the Tapestry of the Apocalypse, Angers can trace its pedigree to Roman times and occupies both banks of the Maine river, which is spanned by six bridges. Today, the corner of Angers that flanks the river is renowned for its nurseries and market gardens. Several dolmens and menhirs in the countryside of Mauges testify to a prehistoric presence more than 12 000 years ago. The Menhir de Saint-Macaire-en-Mauges is an impressive highlight.

LAVAL AND THE MAYENNE VALLEY *(pp275–288)*

An agreeable mix of nature and tradition reigns in Mayenne, with much to delight lovers of countryside, Romanesque churches, castles and beautiful villages. Flanking the Mayenne River, the main community is the market town of Laval. 17km/10.5mi north of Angers the valley boasts the 15C Château du Plessis-Bourré and its vast moat.

THE SARTHE VALLEY AND PERCHE-GOUËT *(pp289–316)*

Le Mans, straddling the Sarthe river, will be forever associated with the famous 24-hour motor races, but historically its significance rests on its well-preserved old town, the *Cité Plantagenet*, where this English dynasty was founded by Henry II of England, son of Geoffrey V of Anjou. It is a delightful part of the city, where the inspiring architecture is imbued with great sense of place. The countryside of the Sarthe Valley is comprised of woodland, meadows and fields of cereal; orchards and dairy farms dot the Perche-Gouët.

THE LOIR VALLEY *(pp317–351)*

Everyone knows the Loire, France's longest and wildest river, but few are acquainted with Le Loir, a place of more modest but no less beautiful villages and castles.

Le Loir rises in the little village of Fruncé, to the west of Chartres, and along its course runs by numerous troglodytic sites and dwellings, many still used today as homes, shops and restaurants.

Gardens of the Château de Villandry
© Spila Riccardo/Sime/Photononstop

PLANNING YOUR TRIP

Michelin Driving Tours

The following is a brief description of possible driving tours in the region covered by this guide.

1 HAUT-ANJOU

170km/102mi starting from Angers

Begin this tour in "Good King René's" city, and discover the surrounding region of Anjou Noir. Hedgerows and sunken paths cut across the landscape, abbeys and châteaux abound. The River Mayenne offers opportunities for pleasant cruises and waterside picnics. There are many lovely manor houses and impressive properties along this route.

The region is renowned for its mellow, fecund landscapes, and for the warm welcome of its people, helped, undoubtedly, by the balmy maritime climate, which does much to support the production of crops and age-old vineyards, and a gentle way of life.

2 LE MANS, SARTHE AND LOIR

240km/144mi starting from Le Mans

Head for the hills, starting from the city of Le Mans, host to the 24-hour motor race since 1923, and famous as the cradle of the Plantagenet dynasty. The rolling landscape sparkles with good fishing streams; meadows and woods form a patchwork. You may prefer to take your time and spend more than a day on this itinerary.

Le Mans is a vibrant, bustling town situated on the Sarthe river, and a vital part of any itinerary. Its inhabitants are called Manceaux and Mancelles, and it is the capital of the Sarthe *département*.

The Sarthe *département* was created during the French Revolution in 1790, and in Roman times the province contained the city of Mans, of which a number of ruins are still standing. The driving tour provides ample opportunity to visit vineyards producing the delightful Jasnières white wine.

3 THE LOIR VALLEY AND THE VENDÔME REGION

170km/102mi starting from Châteaudun

The landscapes along the enchanting Loir Valley are a peaceful and harmonious succession of meadows, woods and vineyards. This natural beauty is dotted with Romanesque churches, romantic ruined castles and houses built in the distinctive white stone of the region. The château at Châteaudun is the northernmost of the châteaux of the Loire *(La Loire)*; from there follow the tributary Loir *(Le Loir)* south to Vendôme – a charming, lively town. Continue on to Lavardin, one of the prettiest villages in France, dominated by the ruins of a giant medieval fortress. The route continues to Montoire-sur-le-Loir, then Trôo, where cave dwellings have been carved into the stone cliffs. Visit the Renaissance château in Poncé-sur-le-Loir or the manor of La Possonnière. This itinerary then veers north again, going through Mondoubleau, perched on a hillside. In St-Agil, the château is watched over by two magnificent lime trees, nearly 300 years old. The Knights Templar established the Commanderie at Arvillé. Return to Châteaudun via Courtalain.

4 ORLÉANS AND SOLOGNE

180km/108mi starting from Orléans

Follow La Loire as it meanders through Sologne. Much of the farmland was once an uninhabitable flood plain. Over time, fields have been recovered for farming; since the 19C, the woodlands have been a favoured hunting ground. Today, there are still wild animals roaming the pine forest, and waterfowl on the many ponds. Along the riverside, great châteaux welcomed many historic figures. From Orléans, travel to Châteauneuf-sur-Loire, where a museum presents a history of navigation on the river. Then carry on to St-Benoît, site of one of the most beautiful abbeys in France. The château at Sully was rebuilt after the Second World War, and in Gien the brick château is now home to a hunting museum. Lamotte-Beuvron is famous for its *tarte tatin* (apple upside-down cake). Finish your tour with a relaxing stroll in the gardens of La Source.

5 BLOIS AND THE GREAT CHÂTEAUX OF THE RENAISSANCE

120km/72mi starting from Blois

In the heart of the Centre-Val de Loire region, not far from Paris and easily accessible by road or high-speed train, Blois is the gateway to the kingdom of castles. Here, between the Cher and the Loire, stand some of the most elegant Renaissance buildings in the world, in such abundance that their grace and beauty are almost overwhelming. Visit the royal palaces of Chambord and Blois (once occupied by King Louis XII); the sumptuous châteaux of the nobility at Beauregard, Chaumont and Cheverny; and the manor house of Villesavin. Blois is of ancient origin, but does not appear in records to any extent until the 6C. In the 9C it became the seat of a powerful countship, and in the 16C, Blois was frequently the location of the French court.

6 VAL DE TOURAINE: DRINK IN THE BEAUTY

150km/90mi starting from Tours

This is the land the French dream of when they reflect on all that is good in their country: the roots of history, the fruit of the vine and unequalled *savoir vivre.* Begin in Tours and stop in Vouvray, home to the wine of the same name. Then on to Amboise, where François I held court, and to Clos-Lucé, where Leonardo da Vinci came to live at the King's request. In Montrichard, make time to see a demonstration of birds of prey. Then head for the beautiful Château de Chenonceau, gracefully arcing over the Cher. A visit to Loches carries the imagination back to the Middle Ages. Return to Tours via the valley of the River Indre and the town of Monbazon.

7 THE MOST BEAUTIFUL CHÂTEAUX IN TOURAINE

130km/78mi starting from Tours

Discovering the Val de Touraine is like opening a jewellery box lined in lush green velvet, fragrant with the scent of summer roses. The jewels on the green field are royal castles. Start out from Tours and drive to the Château de Luynes, perched upon a rocky spur. Then visit Cinq-Mars-la-Pile – the name derives from a slender tower *(pile)* dating from Gallo-Roman times. Langeais presents the severe façade of a feudal fortress, but inside the decoration is evocative of life at court in ages past. In Bourgeuil, stop and visit a local vintner to taste his light-hearted wines; continue on to Chinon to compare with the slightly more robust red wines made there. Enter the Château d'Ussé quietly, so as not to disturb Sleeping Beauty!

The image of Azay-le-Rideau reflected in the waters of the Indre is a model of Renaissance elegance. Villandry is especially loved for the beauty of its carefully restored gardens: the garden of love, the water garden, the herb garden and the kitchen garden.

8 THE SAUMUR REGION AND THE LAYON VALLEY

140km/84mi starting from Saumur

This lovely region south of the Loire is a garden of delights – or a vineyard of delights, if you prefer!

As you leave the town of Saumur, the sunny hillsides are covered in the vines that produce Anjou wines; the region is also renowned for some excellent cheeses, too. Farther on you encounter a wooded landscape, and at every stage culinary pleasures await. There are many interesting monuments and sights to visit: Brissac and its enormous eight-storey château, Doué-la-Fontine, the "City of Roses", the Minières zoo, the medieval ramparts of Montreuil-Bellay, and the marvellous royal abbey of Fontevraud. In the Layon Valley, keep an eye open for the curious *moulins à cavier*, hut-like windmills on conical platforms.

When and Where to Go

WHEN TO GO

CLIMATE

Visitors to the Loire Valley will be impressed by the beauty and diversity of the landscape all year round. When planning your visit, it is worth noting that the weather can be very hot and the various places of interest draw large crowds of visitors at the height of the **summer** (July–August).
Spring comes early to the Loire Valley, especially in the western Loire, which seems to enjoy its own microclimate, creating a pocket of mild weather conditions. Trees burst into blossom as early as the beginning of April in the Angers region and local plant life thrives in May and June, with green fields and orchards stretching away on either side of the roads. The River Loire is at its most scenic during this period. By July, the river is reduced to a narrow stream in places, winding between golden sandbanks. Tempting as it is to go for a swim, bathers should first check that the river bed is safe, as the sandbanks can be quite treacherous in some places.
In **autumn**, the month of September, which is characteristically mild, heralds the wine harvest, in honour of which there are lively traditional harvest processions held throughout the Loire Valley.

WHAT TO PACK

As little as possible! Laundry services are available everywhere. Most personal items can be replaced at reasonable cost.
Try to pack everything in one suitcase and small back pack. Take an extra back pack for new purchases, shopping at the open-air market, carrying a picnic, etc., but, if you are flying, check how much carry-on baggage is permitted by airlines. Be sure luggage is clearly labelled.
Do not pack medication in checked luggage, but keep it with you.

WEATHER FORECAST

Météo-France offers recorded information at national, departmental and local levels. This information is updated three times a day and is valid for up to seven days.

- **National and departmental forecast:**
  ☎3250 followed by
  1 – for all the information about the *département* for the next 7 days, or
  2 – for information about towns.
- **Local forecast:** ☎08 92 68 02 followed by the number of the *département* – *see below.*

12-day weather forecasts in English available at http://france.lachainemeteo.com.

THEMED TOURS

Travel itineraries on specific themes have been mapped out to help you discover the regional architectural heritage and the traditions which make up the cultural heritage of the region. You will find brochures in tourist offices, and the routes are generally well marked and easy to follow (signs posted along the roads).

HISTORICAL TOURIST ROUTES

The Val de Loire has been on UNESCO's World Heritage list since the end of the year 2000.
To allow tourists to discover France's architectural heritage in a historical context, local authorities have set up a number of routes focusing on local architectural, cultural and traditional themes. These **routes historiques** are indicated by road signs. Each of them is detailed in a brochure available from tourist information offices. Several interesting itineraries are found in the regions covered in this guide.

- **Route historique du Roi René** – This circuit takes in the most important châteaux in the Anjou area; most of which are occupied, but still open to the public.

Château de Plessis-Bourré *(49460 Écueillé; ℘02 41 32 06 01).*

- **Route historique de la Vallée des Rois** – The route once used by the Kings of France, on the way from Gien to Saumur via Orléans, Blois and Tours.
Château des Réaux *(37140 Chouzé-sur-Loire; ℘02 47 95 14 40).*
Thematic Michelin map 226 *La Vallée des Rois.*

- **Route historique des Dames de Touraine** – Dedicated to the great ladies who showed both talent and determination in building, renovating, embellishing or simply enjoying their splendid estates, this route winds its way among the towns of Amboise, Beauregard, Montpoupon, Le Grand-Pressigny, Valençay, Chenonceau, etc.
Château de Montpoupon *(Céré-la-Ronde, 37460 Montrésor; ℘02 47 94 21 15).*

- **Route historique François-Ier** – Runs from the Blois region down to the banks of the River Cher, evoking the many visits François I and his retinue paid to the region.
14 r. St-Julien-le-Pauvre, 75005 Paris, ℘01 43 29 48 44.

- **Route historique du patrimoine culturel québécois en France** – This route links places with French immigration to Quebec.
Comité Chomedey-de-Maisonneuve, Centre Culturel Maisonneuve *(10190 Neuville-sur-Vannes; ℘03 25 40 68 33; http://perso.orange.fr/comite.maisonneuve).*

- **Les routes de Jeanne d'Arc** – Four itineraries illustrate Joan of Arc's mission: *Les débuts* (beginnings), *La campagne de Loire* (the Loire campaign), *La campagne du sacre* (the coronation campaign) and *La capture* (taken prisoner). Locations in this guide include the towns of Beaugency, Chinon, Chécy, Gien, Loches, Orléans, Patay and Sainte-Catherine-de-Fierbois.
Association des villes Johanniques, Mairie *(88630 Domrémy-la-Pucelle).* The association has an office in the town hall at Orléans.

- **Société historique des Plantagenêts** – The society aims to promote a better knowledge of 12C European civilisation through the discovery of monuments and sites which testify to the wealth of the period.
Société historique des Plantagenêts, Archives Nationales *(Hôtel de Soubise, 60 r. des Francs-Bourgeois, 75141 Paris Cedex 03; ℘01 40 27 63 50).*

PARKS AND GARDENS

- **Route des Parcs et Jardins** – The art of formal gardens, which came to characterise French châteaux and parks, was born in the Loire Valley in the early 16C. This tourist route leads through some of the most beautiful and ingeniously designed gardens from the Renaissance up to the present, including Château de **Villandry**, Château de **Chamerolles**, Château de **Villeprévost**, the floral park at **Orléans-la-Source**, Château de **Beauregard**, Château de **Chaumont-sur-Loire**, Château de **Cheverny**, Château de **Valmer** and the priory of **St-Cosme**.

DÉPARTEMENTS IN THE CHÂTEAUX OF THE LOIRE REGION

Cher	18	**Eure-et-Loir**	28
Indre	36	**Indre-et-Loire**	37
Loir-et-Cher	41	**Loiret**	45
Maine-et-Loire	49	**Mayenne**	53
Sarthe	72		

What to See and Do

OUTDOOR FUN

CANOEING AND KAYAKING

This method of exploring local waterways need not be exclusively reserved for seasoned canoeing experts. Sometimes this sport can be a pleasant way to discover secluded spots inaccessible by any other means. The main difference between a canoe and a kayak is that the former is propelled by a single-bladed paddle and the latter by a double-bladed paddle. Canoeing trips of half a day, a whole day or more can be organised for individuals or a group (allowing for brief training and certain safety measures). The most suitable rivers are the Cisse, Conie, Cosson, Huisne, Indre, Le Loir, Sauldre, Thouet, Vienne and, of course, La Loire. For detailed information, contact the Loisir Accueil section in each *département*, or the:

- **Fédération Française de Canoë-Kayak (FFCK),** 87 quai de la Marne, BP 58, 94340 Joinville-le-Pont, ✆01 45 11 08 50.
- **Comité Régional de Canoë-Kayak du Centre, Maison des Sports,** 1240 r. de la Bergeresse, 45160 Olivet, ✆02 38 49 88 80.
- **Ligue Canoë-Kayak des Pays de Loire, route d'Angers,** 49080 Bouchemaine, ✆02 41 73 86 10.

CYCLING

The **Loire à Vélo** cycling trail features 700km/435mi of signposted routes across the Pays de la Loire and Loire Valley as well as the Loire-Anjou-Touraine Regional Nature Park.
For full details of packages, bike hire and practical information see **www.loire-velo.fr.**
The Loire countryside is fairly flat, so presents few difficulties to the average cyclist. The Indre Valley, the Sologne, the numerous forest tracks and the banks of the Loire, away from the main roads, are particularly pretty. The ever-changing scenery and the rich heritage of the Loire Valley add greatly to the pleasure of a cycling tour.
Contact the Fédération Française de Cyclotourisme *(12 r. Louis-Bertrand, 94200 Ivry-sur-Seine, ✆01 56 20 88 88)* for suggested itineraries covering most of France, with information on mileage, difficult routes and sights to see. There is an IGN map (1:50 000) of cycle routes around Orléans *(1,000km à Vélo autour d'Orléans)*. Lists of bicycle rental firms are also available from the Tourist Information Centres.
For information on mountain biking *(VTT, standing for vélo tout terrain)* in the Layon region, apply to the Anjou tourist office in Angers.

FISHING

Recent French surveys reveal that freshwater fishing is the second most popular national leisure pastime after football! Swift-flowing or not, the waters of the Loire offer anglers numerous attractive possibilities.
All authorised types of fishing are open to the angler, whether fishing for gudgeon, roach and dace, or trying for pike or the striped mullet which come upstream as far as Amboise in summer. Other options include going after the catfish, tench and carp which lurk in dips in the river bed of the Loire, the Indre and the Loir and in the pools of the Sologne which are also teeming with perch.
Trout are to be found in the Creuse, the Sauldre, the streams of Anjou or the tributaries of the Loir, whereas the Berry, Briare, or Orléans canals are home to eels and sometimes freshwater crayfish which can be caught with a net.
For salmon fishing it is necessary to have a flat-bottomed boat; professionals possess specialist equipment such as nets stretched across the river, held in place by poles fixed in the river bed.
Regulations and open seasons – These differ according to whether the water is classified as first category (contains trout and salmon) or second category (coarse fish). Stricter

rules apply to fish needing special protection, so salmon fishing in particular may be forbidden outright during some years, or permitted for a restricted period only between March and June. Likewise, pike may only be tackled between July and January. Generally speaking, in the case of first category rivers, the **fishing season** starts on the second Saturday in March and ends on the third Sunday in September. As for rivers belonging in the second category, fishing is authorised throughout the year. Regional and national regulations should be observed. Anglers will need either to buy a special holiday fishing permit, valid for two weeks between June and September, or take out annual membership of an officially approved angling association. These officially stamped permits cover fishing with up to four lines on second category waterways administered by an angling association or one line on all public waterways. Only one line is allowed on first category waters and a supplementary tax is payable.
On **private property**, where the fishing rights belong to the owner of the bank, the owner's permission must be obtained. In the case of certain private lakes, which are excluded from the angling legislation, the owner's permission (annual, monthly or daily permit) is the only formality required and can be granted at any time of year.
Minimum size of catch – National regulations state that anglers must return to the water any fish they catch below the minimum permitted length (50cm/20in for pike, 40cm/16in for pike-perch, 23cm/9in for trout, 50cm/20in for salmon, 9cm/4in for crayfish).
Useful brochures and folding maps Fishing in France *(Pêche en France)* are published and distributed by the **Conseil Supérieur de la Pêche**, 134 av. Malakoff, 75116 Paris, ✆01 45 02 20 20; also available from local angling organisations.
Délégation régionale du Conseil Supérieur de la Pêche, 112 faubourg de la Cueille, 86000 Poitiers, ✆05 49 41 29 88.
For information about regulations contact the Tourist Information Centres or the offices of the *Eaux et Forêts* (Water and Forest Authority).

Federations for fishing and the protection of rivers:

- **Indre-et-Loire:** 25 r. Charles-Gilles, 37000 Tours, ✆02 47 05 33 77.
- **Loir-et-Cher:** 11 r. Robert-Nau, Vallée Maillard, 41000 Blois, ✆02 54 90 25 60.
- **Loiret:** 49 rte. d'Olivet, BP 8157, 45081 Orléans Cedex 2, ✆02 38 56 62 69.
- **Maine-et-Loire:** 14 allée du Haras, 49100 Angers, ✆02 41 87 57 09.
- **Mayenne:** 78 r. Émile-Brault, 53000 Laval, ✆02 43 69 12 13.
- **Sarthe:** 40 r. Bary, BP 17, 72001 Le Mans Cedex, ✆02 43 85 66 01, www.unpf.fr/72.

Aquariums and angling centres

- Aquarium de Touraine at Lussault-sur-Loire (Indre-et-Loire)
- Aquarium Tropical at Tours (Indre-et-Loire)
- Aquarium de Sologne, Aliotis, at Villeherviers (Loir-et-Cher)
- Carrefour des Mauges at St-Florent-le-Vieil (Maine-et-Loire)
- Centre Piscicole at Brissac-Quincé (Maine-et-Loire)
- Observatoire de la Loire at Rochecorbon (Indre-et-Loire)
- Observatoire Fédéral at Champigny-sur-Veude (Indre-et-Loire)

GOLF

The popularity of golf, which took off in the early 1980s, is steadily increasing. There are more than 280 000 golf players officially registered in France, indulging in their favourite sport on around 500 golf links.
The map *Golfs, les Parcours Français*, published by Éditions Plein Sud and based on Michelin map no 721,

provides useful information on the location, address and type of golf course open to players throughout the country. The *Peugeot Golf Guide*, published by D and G Motte in Switzerland, offers a selection of 750 courses in 12 European countries. A whole page is devoted to each site; the guide lists all the necessary information (location on Michelin map, rates, clubhouse, nearby hotels, level of skills required) and gives its opinion on each establishment.

- Fédération Française de Golf 68 r. Anatole-France, 92309 Levallois-Perret, ✆01 41 49 77 00, www.ffgolf.org.
- Ligue du Centre, Golf de Touraine 37510 Ballan-Miré, ✆02 47 67 42 28.
- Ligue de Golf des Pays de la Loire 9 r. du Couëdic, 44000 Nantes, ✆02 40 08 05 06.

HUNTING

The varied terrain of the Loire countryside makes it very popular with hunters for stalking, beating, coursing or shooting. The plains of the Beauce and the meadows of Touraine and Anjou provide plenty of food for partridge, quail, thrush and lark. Hares find cover in the copses and the fields of maize and sugar beet. Wild rabbits and partridge breed in the sterile marshland, whereas pheasants favour wooded countryside. Red deer and roe deer are to be found in the thick woods around Baugé, in the forests of Château-la-Vallière and Loches and around Valençay. Wild boar favour the deep forests of Orléans and Amboise and the grounds of Chambord. The islands and banks of the Loire provide nests for teal and mallard.
The Sologne is a favourite haunt for game: duck, teal and woodcock on the lakes and rivers, pheasant by the roadside, wild boar in the marshy brakes and deer in the woods.
Address all enquiries to **Union Nationale des Fédérations Départementales des Chasseurs**, 48 r. d'Alésia, 75014 Paris, ✆01 43 27 85 76.
During the rutting season, which lasts from mid-September to mid-October, the stags are known to behave in a curious way and it is interesting to observe them in action. It is possible to do so in Chambord Forest – contact the **Office National des Forêts** for details, ✆02 54 78 55 50.

WALKING

Short, medium and long distance footpath *Topo-Guides* are published by the **Fédération Française de la Randonnée Pédestre (FFRP)**. These give detailed maps of the paths and offer valuable information to the rambler; they are on sale at the information centre: 14 r. Riquet, 75019 Paris, ✆01 44 89 93 90. For further information apply to the **Comité de Touraine pour la Randonnée Pédestre** (Office de Tourisme de Tours, 78 r. Bernard-Palissy, 37042 Tours Cedex; ✆02 47 70 37 35).
The **Comité Départemental du Tourisme de l'Anjou** has published five IGN maps (Institut Géographique National, 1:50 000) showing routes for ramblers. There is a network of long-distance footpaths *(sentiers de grande randonnée – GR)* covering the area described in the guide:

- **GR 3** along the Loire Valley through the forests of Orléans, Russy and Chinon.
- **GR 3c** running westwards across the Sologne from Gien to Mont-près-Chambord.
- **GR 3d** through the Layon vineyards.
- **GR 31** linking Mont-près-Chambord, on the southeast edge of Boulogne Forest, to Souesmes, south through Sologne Forest.
- **GR 32** north-south through Orléans Forest.
- **GR 335**, from the Loir to the Loire, north-south between Lavardin and Vouvray.
- **GR 35** along the Loir Valley.
- **GR 36**, the footpath from the English Channel to the Pyrenées

route, crossing the region described in this guide between Le Mans and Montreuil-Bellay.
- **GR 46** along the Indre Valley.

RIDING AND PONY TREKKING

Not surprisingly, in view of the number of highly reputed local stud farms and the National Riding School at St-Hilaire-St-Florent near Saumur, the Loire region has numerous riding centres which are open to visitors. Some of these also serve as an overnight stop for those on pony-trekking holidays. Guides indicating suitable routes and overnight stops for those travelling on horseback are available from the regional and national riding associations, and details of local equestrian centres can be obtained from the Tourist Information Centres.
Contact the Comité nationale de tourisme équestre, 9 bd. Macdonald, 75019 Paris, t01 53 26 15 50, which publishes an annual brochure on exploring France on horseback. Other useful contacts include:
- **Association régionale de tourisme équestre des Pays de la Loire**; 3 r. Bossuet, 44000 Nantes, ✆02 40 48 12 27 (départements of Maine-et-Loire, Mayenne and Sarthe);
- **Association régionale de tourisme équestre Centre-Val de Loire**; Maison des Sports, 32 r. Alain-Gerbault, BP 719, 41007 Blois Cedex, ✆02 54 42 95 60 ext 411 (départements of Cher, Indre, Indre-et-Loire, Loir-et-Cher and Loiret).

ACTIVITIES FOR KIDS

In this guide, sights of particular interest to children are indicated with a KIDS symbol. Some attractions may offer discount fees for children.
Angers, Blois, Chinon, Loches, Le Mans, le Perche-Sarthois, Saumur, Tours, the Loir Valley and Vendôme offer family-oriented activities with the **Entrez dans la cour des Grands** programme which is designed to encourage children (aged 7–12) to discover the heritage and history of the region. More details at www.entrezdanslacourdesgrands.com and www.tourism-touraine.com.
The Châteaux de la Loire pass gives reduced admission and other advantages at the 19 participating châteaux between Sully-sur-Loire and Nantes. Several options are available depending on the length of your stay and the number of châteaux you wish to visit. Information from tourist offices and at www.valdeloire.org.

SHOPPING

BUSINESS HOURS

Most of the larger shops are open Mondays to Saturdays from 9am to 6.30 or 7.30pm. Smaller, individual shops may close during the lunch hour. Food shops – grocers, wine merchants and bakeries – are generally open from 7am to 6.30 or 7.30pm; some open on Sunday mornings. Many food shops close between noon and 2pm and on Mondays. Bakery and pastry shops sometimes close on Wednesdays. Hypermarkets usually stay open non-stop until 9pm or later.

VALUE ADDED TAX

There is a Value Added Tax in France (TVA) on almost every purchase (books and some foods are subject to a lower rate). However, non-European visitors who spend more than 175€ (amount subject to change) in any one participating store can get the VAT amount refunded. Usually, you fill out a form at the store and have to present your passport. Upon leaving the country, you submit all forms to customs for approval (they may want to see the goods, so if possible don't pack them in checked luggage). The refund is usually paid directly into your bank or credit card account, or it can be sent by mail. Big department stores that cater to tourists provide special services to help you; be sure to mention that you plan to seek a refund before you pay for goods (no refund is possible for tax on services). If you are visiting two or more countries within the European Union, you submit the forms only on departure from the last EU country. The refund is worthwhile for those visitors who would like to buy fashions, furniture or other fairly expensive items, but remember, the minimum amount must be spent in a single shop.

SOUVENIRS

Wine is the obvious choice, and wine tasting at roadside "shops" will help you choose from the many excellent wines produced in the Loire Valley. Note, however, that *en vrac* means that they sell in larger quantities than you would find in supermarkets, i.e. not by the bottle.

Cheese – The best of the region's array of different varieties are Ste-Maure-de-Touraine, Valençay, and Selles-sur-Cher goat's cheese.

If your car boot doesn't get over 50 °C/122 °F in the sun, the local cheeses keep and travel well!

Tempting **confectionary and delicacies** from the region include **Cointreau**, a liqueur from St-Barthélémy d'Anjou; apricot-filled prunes from Tours and the **livre tournois**, a rich creation of pure chocolate; **muscadin**, a delicious mix of cherry, ground chestnut and black chocolate from Langeais; **cotignac**, quince jelly from Orléans sold in round wooden pots; smooth honey from the Gâtinais and **praslines** from Montargis; **moinillons**, shaped like tiny monks, are coloured sweets that come in five different flavours and can be found alongside other souvenirs with a monastic theme at the shop run by the Benedictine community at St-Benoît-sur-Loire.

Blois is home to the Poulain chocolate factory. **Quernons d'ardoise**, produced in Angers, are nougat bars covered in slate-coloured chocolate which recalls the city's rooftops.

The symbol of the town of Sablé-sur-Sarthe is its **sablés**, pure butter shortbread biscuits that are the ideal accompaniment with a tea-time drink in a local café.

Terrines and **pâtés** are popular souvenirs and can be found in and around the region's many game-filled forests and parks. Some are made from often unexpected ingredients such as bison (at Cerqueux-sous-Passavant) or ostrich.

In Angers, Blois, Tours, Vendôme and Vouvray pork is king with a huge variety of preserved and potted meat specialities and pâtés to choose from including *rilles*, *rillauds*, *rillons* and *rillettes* – all variations on the theme of porkmeat and fat in differing preparations. Try them at one of the many fine *traiteurs* (delicatessens) in the region.

Markets – The region's best, and biggest, open-air market is held every Sunday morning in Amboise with up to 150 stalls. Most towns and villages have their own markets once or twice a week.

For the home – Among non-perishable goods, high-quality handicrafts, such as wicker work from Villaines-les-Rochers and Gien earthenware, is well worth taking home.

Cholet is famous for its handkerchiefs and throughout the Loire Valley you are sure to come across a wealth of antiques shops, flea markets and village fairs where you can pick up a bargain.

SIGHTSEEING

BIRDWATCHING

See the Introduction for information on the Loire Valley's bird population.

The French National Association for the Protection of Bird Life – **Ligue pour la Protection des Oiseaux (LPO)** – has its headquarters at 8-10 r. du Docteur Pujos, BP 90263, 17305 Rochefort Cedex 05 46 82 12 34, www.lpo.fr.

It is a not-for-profit organisation set up to protect species of wild bird as well as their environment. Its aim is to educate the general public and make people more aware of nature by organising visits, excursions and conferences on the subject of natural reserves.

- **LPO Touraine:** ✆02 47 51 81 84
- **LPO Anjou:** ✆02 41 44 44 22
- **LPO Loire-Atlantique:** ✆02 51 82 02 97

The **Carrefour des Mauges** (a permanent centre whose role is to provide information about the Loire and Mauges environment, Ferme abbatiale des Coteaux, BP 44, 49410 St-Florent-le-Vieil, ✆02 41 71 77 30) stages a number of one-day programmes, including on-the-spot visits, during which you can identify the different bird species, study their behaviour and see them in their natural habitat (*telescopes and binoculars are supplied by the organisations*).

Other useful addresses:

- **Maison de la Nature et de l'Environnement d'Orléans** 64 rte. d'Olivet, 45100 Orléans ✆02 38 56 69 84.

This association is responsible for other sites including the Réserve naturelle de l'île de St-Pryvé-St-Mesmin and the Maison forestière d'Ouzouer-sur-Loire.

- **SEPN 41** *(Société d'étude et de protection de la nature en Loir-et-Cher)* 17 r. Roland-Garros, 41000 Blois; ✆02 54 42 53 71.

If you find an injured bird, please contact the LPO who will direct you to the nearest Centre de sauvegarde de la faune sauvage (Wildlife protection centre).

BUS TOURS

Organised bus tours are available through **Discover France** and include Loire Valley castles day trips, or visits to vineyards.

Two-day Châteaux Country tours are available from Paris. Other packages are available, ranging from 2-hour introductory tours to week-long excursions. Online booking available at http://tours.discoverfrance.net.

FROM THE AIR

Weather permitting, there are various ways of getting an aerial view of the Loire Valley, from microlights (ULM, standing for *ultra-légers motorisés*), gliders, helicopters or light aircraft. Trips leave from the airport at Tours-St-Symphorien, flying over Chinon, Chambord, Chenonceau and Azay-le-Rideau, and from Blois-le-Breuil or Orléans aerodrome to fly over Amboise, Cheverny and Beaugency.

Hot air balloon over Château d'Amboise

It is also possible to take a trip in a hot-air balloon (allow about half a day for 1hr–1hr30min in the air; prices vary considerably, from 145€ to 250€ per person).

Microlights

- **Aérodrome d'Amboise-Dierre:** ☎02 47 57 93 91.
- **Aérodrome de Tours-Sorigny:** ☎02 47 26 27 50.
- **Fédération Française de Planeur Ultra-Léger Motorisé:** 96 bis r.Marc-Sangnier, BP 341, 94709 Maison-Alfort Cedex ☎01 49 81 74 43, www.ffplum.com.

Hot-Air Balloons

Travelling by hot-air balloon adds an old-world charm to the discovery of the Loire Valley from above. Balloons take off from almost anywhere (except towns, of course), usually in the early morning or late evening; landing, on the other hand, greatly depends on the strength and direction of the wind and the landing spot is sometimes unpredictable. Flights last between 1hr and 1hr 30min, but it is wise to allow three times that amount of time for the flight preparation and the drive back to the starting point in the vehicle that follows the balloon *(France Montgolfières, 24 r. Nationale, 41400 Montrichard; ☎02 54 32 20 48, www.france-montgolfière.com).*

LOCAL INDUSTRIES/CRAFTS

The following workshops or factories are open to the public, giving an insight into local crafts and industry:

- **Chinon** – nuclear power station
- **Gien** – potteries
- **Montrichard** – J M Monmousseau's Champagne-method wine cellars
- **Poncé-sur-le-Loir** – arts and crafts centre *(see Vendôme)*
- **St-Barthélemy-d'Anjou** – Cointreau distillery *(see Angers)*
- **St-Cyr-en-Bourg** – Saumur cooperative wine cellar *(see Saumur)*
- **St-Hilaire-St-Florent** – Bouvet-Ladubay sparkling Saumur wines *(see Saumur)*
- **Saut-aux-Loups** –mushroom beds *(see Chinon)*
- **Turquant** – Troglo des Pommes Tapées (dried apples) *(see Chinon)*
- **Vaas** – Rotrou corn mill *(see Vendôme)*
- **Villaines-les-Rochers** – basketwork cooperative *(see Azay-le-Rideau)*

MILL TOURS

The particular geographical and climatic conditions of Anjou account for the presence of many different mills in the region.
The **Association des Amis des Moulins de l'Anjou** (AMA) publishes brochures and organises visits to local mills. For information apply to 17 r. de la Madeleine, BP 725, 49007 Angers Cedex 01, ☎02 41 43 87 36.

See the Introduction for the history and types of mills in Anjou.

RIVER TOURS

River cruising

For cruise information, contact the **Comité départemental de tourisme**, Tourisme fluvial Pays de La Loire, 1 pl. Kennedy, 49000 Angers, ☎02 41 23 51 30. Small private barges can be taken on the **Loire**, **Maine**, **Mayenne**, **Oudon** and **Sarthe** rivers, as well as on the canalised stretch of the **Cher** and the **Canal de Berry**. Houseboats can also be hired for one or several nights in order to explore the Anjou region via its waterways. Day cruises on piloted boats are also available.

River passenger boats

There exist two types of river passenger boat: the *bateau-mouche* and the *coche d'eau*. They usually leave at set hours (often at 3pm and 5pm) between mid April and mid October. Some trips include the passing of locks or a fascinating and instructive commentary on local birds species or water transport in the Loire region. Discovering the tracks of small animals like beavers and bird spotting add to the pleasure of these charming, peaceful cruises.

- Starting from **Briare**, along the canal with the company Les Bateaux Touristiques (☏02 38 37 12 75); from **Chisseaux**, 1hr 30min cruise along the Cher, gliding beneath the arches of the Château de Chenonceau and beyond.
- From **Fay-aux-Loges**, along the Orléans canal, Syndicat du canal d'Orléans ☏02 38 46 82 90.
- From **Montrichard**, 1hr 30min cruise along the Cher aboard the *Léonard-de-Vinci*.
- From **Olivet**, 1hr 30min cruise along the Loiret aboard the *Sologne* ☏02 38 51 12 12.
- From **Saint-Aignan**, 1hr 30min cruise along the Cher aboard the *Val-du-Cher*.

Along the rivers of **Anjou** and **Maine**:

- **Batellerie Promenade,** 2 r. de Beauvais, 49125 Cheffes ☏02 41 42 12 12;
- **Sarth'Eau, Halte Nautique**, r. du Port, 72210 La Suze-sur-Sarthe ☏02 43 77 47 64;
- **Féérives, Le Moulin**, 49220 Chenillé-Changé ☏02 41 95 10 83
- **Le Duc des Chauvières**, Parc St-Fiacre, 53200 Château-Gontier ☏02 43 70 37 83.

SOUND AND LIGHT SHOWS AT THE CHÂTEAUX

These polished evening spectacles, which developed from an original idea of the magician Jean-Eugène Robert-Houdin (*see Blois*), were inaugurated as a feature of the Loire Valley tourist season at Chambord in 1952.
By combining characters dressed in period costume with firework displays, illuminated fountains and image projection on huge screens, the *son et lumière* shed quite a different light on some of the Loire Valley's most famous châteaux. Nocturnal illuminations enhance the architecture of the buildings, offering a different scene from that seen during the day. Special effects using film and staging techniques, laser beam projections and an accompanying soundtrack lend ancient walls a surprisingly different aura. From time to time the theme of the *son et lumière* is changed.

Admiring Château Chambord on board a boat

The Art of Drinking Wine

To identify and describe the qualities or defects of a particular wine, both wine buffs and wine experts use an extremely wide yet precise vocabulary. Assessing a wine involves three successive stages, each associated with a particular sense and a certain number of technical terms:

The eye (general impression) – Crystalline (good clarity), limpid (perfectly transparent, no particles in suspension), still (no bubbles), sparkling (effervescent wine) or *mousseux* (lots of fine, Champagne-type bubbles).

Colour and hues – A wine is said to have a nice robe when the colour is sharp and clean; the main terms used to describe the different hues are pale red, ruby, onion skin, garnet (red wine), salmon, amber, partridge-eye pink (rosé wine) and golden-green, golden-yellow and straw (white wine).

The nose – Pleasant smells: floral, fruity, balsamic, spicy, flinty.

Unpleasant smells: musty, corked, woody, hydrogen sulphide, cask.

The mouth – Once it has passed the visual and olfactory tests, the wine undergoes a final test in the mouth. It can be described as agreeable (pleasant), aggressive (unpleasant, with a high acidity), full-flavoured (rich and well-balanced), structured (well-constructed, with a high alcohol content), heady (intoxicating), fleshy (producing a strong impact on taste buds), fruity (flavour evoking the freshness and natural taste of grapes), easy to drink, jolly (inducing merriness), round (supple, mellow), lively (light, fresh, with a lowish alcohol content), etc.

Quality control – French wines fall into various official categories indicating the area of production and therefore the probable quality of the wine. AOC *(Appellation d'Origine Contrôlée)* denotes a wine produced in a strictly delimited area, stated on the label, made with the grape varieties specified for that wine in accordance with local traditional methodology. VDQS *(Vin Délimité de Qualité Supérieure)* is also produced in a legally controlled area, slightly less highly rated than AOC. Vin de pays denotes the highest ranking table wine after AOC and VDQS.

You will find information about these events in the following chapters: Amboise, Azay-le-Rideau, Blois, Château de Chenonceau, Le Mans, Loches and Château de Valençay; it is advisable to check each programme with the local tourist office.

TOURIST TRAINS

A number of charming old steam trains are operated along parts of the Loire Valley, generally by groups of volunteers, with the result that they usually only run on weekends.

- **Pithiviers tourist train** (Loiret): contact Pithiviers tourist office ℘02 38 30 50 02.
- **Lac de Rille historical railway** (Indre-et-Loire): AECFM, ℘02 47 96 42 91, www.trains-fr.org/unecto.
- **Touraine steam train** (Indre-et-Loire): TVT, 13 av. de la Gare, 31720 Richelieu, ℘02 47 58 12 97.
- **Loir Valley tourist train** (Loir-et-Cher): Town Hall (attention M. Claude Germain) ℘02 54 72 80 82.
- **Compagnie du Blanc Argent** (Loir-et-Cher): Compagnie du Blanc Argent, gare de Romorantin-Lanthenay ℘02 54 76 06 51.
- **Sarthe steam train**: TRANSVAP, www.transvap.fr.

- **Semur-en-Vallon tourist train**: ✆02 43 93 67 86.

WINE COUNTRY

Like all wine-growers, the *vignerons* from the Loire region are extremely hospitable and eager to welcome visitors to their cellars and storehouses in order to offer tastings, talk about their profession, show their working equipment, explain winemaking techniques and sell their wine.

The Loire Valley is France's third largest wine-producing region, and the second largest region for sparkling wine. Loire wines are commonly regarded as the most popular in the restaurants of France, and include white, red, rosé, sparkling, still, dry and sweet. The most famous are Sancerre, Vouvray, Bourgueil and Chinon. The principal grape varieties are Cabernet Franc, Pineau, Gamay and Chardonnay.

The wine producers, merchants and cooperatives willing to accept visitors are too numerous for us to draw up a complete list. However, all the tourist information centres and the Maisons du Vin (especially those in Amboise, Angers, Bourgueil, Chinon, Montlouis-sur-Loire, Saumur and Vouvray) will supply the necessary details:

- **La Maison du Vin de l'Anjou**
  5 bis pl. Kennedy, 49100 Angers
  ✆02 41 88 81 13.
- **Comité interprofessionnel des vins du Val de Loire**
  Hôtel des Vins La Godeline
  73 r. Plantagenêt, 49100 Angers
  ✆02 41 87 62 57.
- **La Maison des vins de Nantes**
  Bellevue, 44690 La-Haye-Fouassière
  ✆02 40 36 90 10.
- **La Maison du vin de Saumur**
  quai Lucien-Gautier, 49400 Saumur ✆02 41 38 45 83.
- **Interloire**
  12 r. Étienne-Pallu,
  BP 1921, 37019 Tours Cedex 1
  ✆02 47 60 55 10.

BOOKS

REGIONAL HERITAGE

A Wine and Food Guide to the Loire - Jacqueline Friedrich. Henry Holt (1998).
This is an award-winning guide to the Loire, its wines and cuisine. It covers the 60 or so appellations in the five wine regions of the Loire, describing the history, soil and vintners of each, and rates more than 600 wineries; sections on local cheeses, sausages and fish dishes. This book is very complete and entertaining too. It will really add pleasure to your trip!

Châteaux of the Loire - Thorston Droste, Axel M Mosler (Contributor) - St Martins Press (1997). This over-sized book is a collection of lavish photographs of the architecture, interiors, and gardens of the Loire châteaux, including previously unpublished photos illustrating life in the châteaux during the 19C and early 20C. Each château is accompanied by a text that describes architectural, historical, and travel details.

Châteaux of the Loire Valley - Jean-Marie Perouse De Montclos, Robert Polidori (Photographer) - Konemann (2007).
This is a beautiful book, filled with high quality photographs, portraying natural beauty of the region as well as highlighting the architecture of the famous châteaux.

Loire Valley Sketchbook - Fabrice Moreau & Jean-Paul Pigeat - St Martin's Press (2003).
A delightful collection of watercolours, history and travel writing which makes this book the perfect souvenir volume to remember your trip.

Loire - Hubrecht Duijker - The Wine Lover's Touring Guides Series (March 1995).
The author of this book was appointed *Officier de l'Ordre du Mérite Agricole* by the French Government for sharing his wealth of information on local treasures, from little-known villages to Gérard Depardieu's castle. Plenty

of practical touring advice for an enjoyable trip, especially if you are interested in wine!

Gardens of the Loire Valley - Marie-Francoise Valery - Garden Art Press (2008). This lovely and beautifully illustrated book is one of the most attractive and well-informed books on the subject of the gardens of the Loire Valley.

A Little Tour in France - Henry James Elibron Classics (2005). A facsimile of the 1900 American edition in which the novelist describes his travels among the towns and châteaux of the Loire before heading further south.

Wine Regions of France - Michelin (2010). This completely revised edition of the Green Guide for wine lovers features an overview of the history, geography and climate of the wine-growing regions and appraisals of the wines. It includes established wine routes and suggested Michelin Driving Tours.

UNDERSTANDING THE FRENCH

Our Man in Paris: A Foreign Correspondent, France and the French - John Lichfield, Signal Books (2010). A collection of serious and light-hearted dispatches from the *Independent*'s Paris correspondent who gives a great insight into the country and its people.

French Impressions: The Loire Valley - George East - La Puce Publications (2011). The latest in a series by this colourful expat who provides a humorous and bracingly honest account of living and travelling in France. He tackles the culture, history, food and drink of the Loire with a sprinkling of odd characters encountered along the way and some tasty local recipes.

Crossing the Loire - Heidi Fuller-Love France Pronde Publications (2004). Written by a travel journalist living in France, *Crossing the Loire* recounts the trials, tribulations and joys of moving to live in France, including battles with the infamous French bureaucracy. Packed with twisted humour, sticky camembert and plumbing tales to make your hair stand on end.

France on the Brink - Jonathan Fenby - Arcade Publishing (1999). The author has culled 30 years of experience living in or writing about France into this book, which has met with both high praise and keen criticism. From Brigitte Bardot to the baguette, from the integration or exclusion of foreign cultures to hot political scandals, this portrait of contemporary France is personal, perceptive and instructive.

Savoir-Flair: 211 Tips for Enjoying France and the French - Polly Platt - Distribooks Intl (2000). Useful communication and travel tips if your French is rusty or outdated. Handy phrases and explanations of cultural particularities that are easily misinterpreted by foreign visitors.

French or Foe? - Polly Platt - Culture Crossings Ltd. (1994). Explores the cultural hurdles to understanding the French, and outlines the essence of Frenchness.

HISTORY

Recent books covering the most noteworthy episodes in the region's eventful history:

The Virgin Warrior: The Life and Death of Joan of Arc - Larissa Juliet Taylor - Yale (2010). A well-balanced critical biography that attempts to get behind the myths and explore the facts of the remarkable story of the teenage girl who inspired a king and country.

The Valois: Kings of France 1328–1589 - R.J. Knecht, Hambledon Continuum (2006). From Philip VI to Henry III, an account of the dynasty that ruled France through some of the most troubled years of its history from the Middle Ages, the Hundred Years War to the dawning of the modern age.

Martyrs and Murders: The Guise Family and the Making of Europe - Stuart Carroll - Oxford (2011).

Traces the fortunes and intrigues of the House of Guise, one of the most powerful families in 16C Europe, renowned for the muder of its Duke at the Château de Blois in 1588.

Conquest: The English Kingdom of France in the Hundred Years War - Juliet Barker - Abacus (2010).

The respected historian focuses on the last 40 years of the conflict from Henry V's invasion of France in 1417 by way of Joan of Arc to the English withdrawal from all but Calais in 1453.

FICTION

Five Quarters of the Orange - Joanne Harris, William Morrow & Co (2001).

The narrator of this novel is writing from the restored Loire farmhouse where she grew up and lives under an assumed identity. 65-year-old Framboise recounts her life and the terrible memories of the Second World War. The heroine is devoted to deciphering and preserving her mother's notebook of recipes and jottings. The texture, shape and aroma of bread and cakes, fruit and wine, thyme and olive become characters in this compelling and complex story.

CLASSIC FICTION

The following novels are set in the Loire region:

Honoré de Balzac: *Eugénie Grandet, Le Curé de Tours, La Femme de Trente Ans, L'Illustre Gaudissart, Le Lys dans la Vallée*

François Rabelais: *Gargantua and Pantagruel* comprising *Pantagruel, Gargantua, Tiers Livre, Quart Livre.*

Émile Zola: *La Terre (1887).*

Alain-Fournier: *Le Grand Meaulnes (1913).*

FILMS

The following films have historical and cultural associations with the places and people that have played a part in the region:

Le Grand Meaulnes (1913). Alain-Fournier's haunting tale of youth, yearning, loss and love in the Sologne has twice been adapted for film. Jean-Gabriel Albicocco's 1967 version is widely considered to be a classic, with a remake by Jean-Daniel Verhaeghe in 2006.

La Princesse de Montpensier (2010). Based on the novella by Madame de Lafayette. Set during the Wars of Religion, the story follows the tragic destiny of Marie de Mézières who is forced into a marriage with the Prince de Montpensier yet remains in love with the Duke of Guise. Filmed partly on location at the Château de Blois.

La Reine Margot (1994). Lavish costume drama based on events in life of Margeurite de Valois, daughter of Catherine de' Medici. It traces her marriage to Henry of Navarre (later Henri IV), her love affairs and the various plots, political tensions and intrigues of 16C courtly life during the Wars of Religion and the St. Bartholomew's Day massacre of Protestants.

Joan of Arc: the Messenger (1999). Luc Besson's spectacular take on the story of the Maid of Orléans from her early visions, to battles against the English, her trial, and burning at the stake.

Calendar of Events

The regional tourist offices publish brochures listing local festivals and fairs. Most places hold festivities for France's National Day (14 July) and many organise events on 15 August, also a public holiday.

JANUARY

Angers

Film festival
☏02 41 88 92 94

MARCH-APRIL

St-Benoît-sur-Loire

Great Easter Saturday Vigil
☏02 38 35 72 43

APRIL

Saumur

Performance by the Cadre Noir in the dressage arena of the École Nationale de l'Équitation
☏02 41 53 50 60
www.cadrenoir.fr

Le Mans

24-hour motorcycle race
☏02 43 40 24 24
www.lemans.org

Cholet

Harlequin Festival
☏02 41 49 26 00
www.ville-cholet.fr/arlequins
Evening Carnival Parade
☏02 41 62 28 09
www.ville-cholet.fr/carnaval

MAY

Orléans

Joan of Arc Festival
☏02 38 24 05 05
www.tourisme-orleans.fr

Le Mans (Abbaye de l'Épau)

Festival
☏02 43 81 72 72

Château-Gontier

Horse Show at Château de la Maroutière
☏02 41 21 18 28

Le Mans

Les Nocturnales: street theatre in Old Le Mans (2nd and 3rd weeks)

Châteauneuf-sur-Loire

Whitsun Rhododendron Festival
☏02 38 58 44 79 (Sat and Sun)

Saumur

International 3-Day Event (end of month)
☏02 41 67 36 37
www.cadrenoir.fr

Tours

Florilège Vocal: Choral Festival
☏02 47 21 65 26
www.florilegevocal.com

Le Mans 24-hour motorcycle race

JUNE

Le Mans
24-hour motor race
✆02 43 40 24 24
www.lemans.org

Chambord
Game Fair: National Hunting and Fishing Festival (3rd weekend)
✆01 41 40 32 32

Sully-sur-Loire
International Festival of Classical Music
✆02 38 36 29 46

Tours and around
Touraine Summer Music Festival
✆02 47 21 65 08

MID-JUNE TO MID-OCTOBER

Chaumont-sur-Loire
International Garden Festival
✆02 54 20 99 22
www.chaumont-jardins.com

Orléans
Jazz Festival
✆02 38 24 05 05
www.tourisme-orleans.fr

Anjou
Anjou Festival in the historical sites of Maine-et-Loire
✆02 41 88 14 14
www.festivaldanjou.com

JULY

Le Mans
Les Nocturnales: street theatre in Old Le Mans (Wednesday and Saturday evening, July–August)
✆02 43 28 17 22

Loches
Festival of Musical Drama
✆02 47 91 82 82
www.loches-tourainecotesud.com

Doué-la-Fontaine
Rose Show in the amphitheatre
✆02 41 59 20 49

St Lambert du Lattay
Festival of Wine and Anduoillette (2nd weekend)
✆02 41 78 49 07

St Aubin de Luigné
Displays on the theme of air, fire, water and earth
✆02 41 78 59 38

La Ménitré
Head dress and old-fashioned costume parade with examples from the region's folkloric traditions
✆02 41 45 63 63

Saumur
Military tattoo with mounted, motorised and armoured divisions
✆02 41 40 20 60

AUGUST

Molineuf
Bric-a-brac fair; with antique dealers, enthusiasts and buyers
✆02 54 70 05 23

Sablé-sur-Sarthe
Festival of Baroque Music
✆02 43 62 22 22
www.sable-sur-sarthe.fr

Bourgueil
Wine Festival
✆02 47 97 91 39

SEPTEMBER

Amboise
Melon Festival (1st Wed)

Angers
(Les Accroche-couers)
'Kiss-Curl' Festival and spectacles in the streets
✆02 41 23 50 00

Orléans
Loire Festival – boats and barges, music and culture on the quays of Orléans
✆02 38 24 05 05
www.tourisme-orleans.fr

Château-Gontier
Horse Show at Château de la Maroutière
✆02 41 21 18 28

Varrains
Yew tree Festival (2nd weekend)
✆02 41 21 18 28

Saumur
Horsemanship performance by the Cadre Noir
✆02 41 53 50 60
www.cadrenoir.fr

OCTOBER

Le Lion-d'Angers

International Horse Show: demonstrations by the best riders in the world representing 20 nations
℘02 41 95 86 51

St-Aignan

Town fair – stalls, entertainment
℘02 38 24 05 05

NOVEMBER

Tours

"Les Soirées d'automne" classical music festival
℘02 38 35 72 43

Montrichard

Touraine primeur wine fair (3rd weekend in month)
℘02 54 32 05 10

24 DECEMBER

Anjou

Messes des Naulets (held in a different country church every year). Groups in traditional Anjou costume sing Christmas carols in the local dialect
℘02 41 23 51 11

St-Benoît-sur-Loire

Christmas Eve midnight Mass (begins 11pm)
℘02 38 35 72 43
www.abbaye-fleury.com

MAIN WINEMAKING EVENTS

All year round, a great many wine fairs and wine festivals are staged at set dates in order to promote the different types of local *appellations.*

MARCH

Wine fair, Bourgueil
℘02 47 97 91 39

APRIL

Onzain Wine Fair, Onzain
℘02 54 20 78 52

MAY

Wine Fair, Saumur
℘02 41 83 43 12

Annual Saumur Wine Competition, Saumur
℘02 41 51 16 40

JUNE

Champigny Biennial, Montsoreau
℘02 41 51 16 40

JULY

Wine Harvest Festival, St-Lambert-du-Lattay
℘02 41 78 30 58

Saumur-Champigny Festival, Varrains
℘02 41 87 62 57

Vintage Wine Festival, St-Aubin-de-Luigné
℘02 41 78 33 28

NOVEMBER

Touraine primeur wine fair (3rd weekend in month) Montrichard
℘02 54 32 05 10

Champigny Biennial, Montsoreau
℘02 41 51 16 40

Know Before You Go

USEFUL WEBSITES

www.franceguide.com
The French Government Tourist Office/ Maison de la France site is packed with practical information and tips for those travelling to France. The homepage has a number of links to more specific guidance, for American or Canadian travellers for example, or to the FGTO's London pages.

www.FranceKeys.com
This site has plenty of practical information for visiting France. It covers all the regions, with links to tourist offices and related sites. Very useful for planning the details of your tour in France.

www.ambafrance-uk.org
The French Embassy's website provides basic information (geography, demographics, history), a news digest and business-related information. It offers special pages for children, and has pages devoted to culture, language study and travel. You can reach other selected French sites (regions, cities, ministries) with hypertext links.

www.fr-holidaystore.co.uk
The French Travel Centre in London has gone online with this service, providing information on all of the regions of France, including updated special travel offers and details of available accommodation.

www.F-T-S.co.uk
The French Travel Service specialises in organising holidays in France using the rail network. Let FTS organise your travel and hotels anywhere in France.

www.fngi.fr
The Federation of Licenced Tour Guides has a membership of more than 700 guides working in 32 languages.

TOURIST OFFICES ABROAD

For information, brochures, maps and assistance in planning a trip to France:

Australia – New Zealand

Sydney
Level 13, 25 Bligh Street, Sydney, New South Wales 2000
✆(02) 9231 5244
Fax: (02) 9221 8682

Canada

Montreal
1800 Avenue McGill College
Suite 1010, Montreal, Quebec
H3A 3J6
✆(514) 288-2026
Fax: (514) 845-4868

Ireland

No office ✆+15 60 235 235
(Irish information line)
http://ie.franceguide.com

South Africa

3rd floor, Village Walk, Office Tower, cnr Maude and Rivonia, Sandton
✆(0) 11 523 82 92
http://za.franceguide.com

United Kingdom

London Maison de France
Lincoln House, 300 High Holborn, London WC1V 7JH
✆09068 244 123
Fax: 020 7061 6646
http://uk.franceguide.com

United States

http://us.franceguide.com

New York –
825 Third Avenue, 29th floor (entrance on 50th Street), New York NY 10022
✆France-on-Call Hotline (514) 288 1904

Los Angeles –
9454 Wilshire Blvd, Suite 210, 90212 Beverly Hills, CA
✆310-271-6665

Chicago – Consulate General of France, 205 N Michigan Ave., Suite 3770, 60601 Chicago, Illinois
✆312 327 0290

Information can also be requested from: **France on Call** ℘(514) 288 1904. **Maison de la France** website: www.franceguide.com/us

TOURIST OFFICES

Visitors may also contact local tourist offices for more precise information, to receive brochures and maps. The addresses and telephone numbers of tourist offices in the larger towns are listed after the symbol 🅸. Below, the addresses are given for local tourist offices of the departments and regions covered in this guide. The index lists the *département* after each town. At regional level, address enquiries to:

SEM Régionale du Tourisme des Pays de la Loire (Loire-Atlantique, Maine-et-Loire, Mayenne, Sarthe, Vendée), 2 r. de la Loire, BP 20411, 44204 Nantes Cedex 02 ℘02 40 48 24 20 www.enpaysdelaloire.com

Comité Régional du Tourisme du Centre-Val de Loire (Cher, Eure-et-Loir, Indre, Indre-et-Loire, Loir-et-Cher, Loiret), 37 av. de Paris, 45000 Orléans ℘02 38 79 95 00 or 02 38 79 95 28 www.loirevalleytourism.com

For each *département* within the region, address enquires to the **Comité Départemental du Tourisme (CDT):**

- **Anjou (Maine-et-Loire Département):** pl. Kennedy BP 32147, 49021 ANGERS Cedex 02 ℘02 41 23 51 51 www.anjou-tourisme.com
- **Cher:** 5 r. de Séraucourt 18000 BOURGES ℘02 48 67 00 10 www.berrylecher.com
- **Eure-et-Loir:** 10 r. du Docteur Maunoury, BP 67, 28002 CHARTRES Cedex ℘02 37 84 01 00 www.tourisme28.com
- **Indre:** Centre Colbert, 1 pl. Eugène Rolland, BP 141, 36003 CHÂTEAUROUX Cedex ℘02 54 07 36 36 www.berrylindre.com
- **Touraine-Val de Loire (Indre-et-Loire Département):** 30 r. de la Préfecture, BP 3217, 37032 TOURS Cedex ℘02 47 31 47 48 www.tourisme-touraine.com
- **Loir-et-Cher:** 5 r. de la Voûte-du-Château BP 149 41005 BLOIS Cedex ℘02 54 57 00 41 www.tourismeloir-et-cher.com
- **Loiret:** 8 r. d'Escures, 45000 ORLEANS, ℘02 38 78 04 04 www.Tourismloiret.com
- **Mayenne:** 84 av. Robert-Buron, BP 0325, 53003 LAVAL Cedex, ℘02 43 53 18 18 www.tourisme-mayenne.com
- **Sarthe:** 19 bis, r. de l'Etoile 72000 LE MANS ℘02 43 40 22 50 www.tourisme-en-sarthe.com

🅸 **Tourist Information Centres** – The addresses and telephone numbers of the local tourist offices *(Syndicats d'Initiative)* appear in the green "orient panels" of the Principal Sights in the *Discovering* section of this guide. These offices provide information on itineraries with special themes, such as wine tours, history tours and artistic tours.
Eleven cities and areas, labelled *"Villes et Pays d'Art et d'Histoire"* by the Ministry of Culture, are mentioned in this guide (Angers, Blois, Bourges, Chinon, Loches, Loire Touraine, Loire Valley, Le Mans, Saumur, Tours and Vendôme). These cities are particularly active in promoting their architectural and cultural heritage and offer guided tours by highly qualified guides, as well as activities for 👪6–12-year-old children.

🅸 More information is available from local tourist offices and from www.vpah.culture.fr.

EMBASSIES AND CONSULATES IN FRANCE		
Australia	Embassy	4 r. Jean-Rey, 75724 Paris 01 40 59 33 00. www.france.embassy.gov.au
Canada	Embassy	35 av. Montaigne, 75008 Paris 01 44 43 29 00. www.international.gc.ca
Eire	Embassy	4 r. Rude, 75116 Paris 01 44 17 67 00. www.embassyofireland.fr
New Zealand	Embassy	7 r. Léonard-de-Vinci, 75116 Paris 01 45 00 24 11. www.nzembassy.com/france
South Africa	Embassy	59 quai d'Orsay, 75343 Paris 01 53 59 23 23. www.afriquesud.net
UK	Embassy	35 r. du Faubourg St-Honoré, 75363 Paris 01 44 51 31 00. http://ukinfrance.fco.gov.uk/en
	Consulate	16 r. d'Anjou, 75008 Paris 01 44 51 31 01 (visas, passports, living in France).
USA	Embassy	2 av. Gabriel, 75382 Paris 01 43 12 22 22. http://france.usembassy.gov
	Consulate	2 r. St-Florentin, 75001 Paris 01 42 96 14 88.
	Consulate	15 av. d'Alsace, 67082 Strasbourg 03 88 35 31 04 – Fax: 03 88 24 06 95.

INTERNATIONAL VISITORS
EMBASSIES AND CONSULATES

See the chart opposite.

DOCUMENTS

Passport – Nationals of countries within the European Union entering France need only a national identity card; in the case of the UK, this means your passport. Nationals of other countries must be in possession of a valid national **passport**. In case of loss or theft, report to your embassy or consulate and the local police.

Visa – No **entry visa** is required for Canadian, US or Australian citizens travelling as tourists and staying less than 90 days, except for students planning to study in France. If you think you may need a visa, apply to your local French Consulate.

US citizens should obtain the booklet *Safe Trip Abroad* (US$1), which provides useful information on visa requirements, customs regulations, medical care, etc. for international travellers.

Published by the **Government Printing Office**, it can be ordered by phone ((202) 512-1800) or consulted on-line (www.access.gpo.gov). General passport information is available by phone toll-free from the **Federal Information Center** (item 5 on the automated menu), 800-688-9889. US passport application forms can be downloaded from http://travel.state.gov.

DUTY-FREE ALLOWANCES	
Spirits (whisky, gin, vodka, etc.)	10l/2·6gal
Fortified wines (vermouth, port, etc.)	20l/5·2gal
Wine (not more than 60l sparkling)	90l/23·7gal
Beer	110l/29gal
Cigarettes	800
Cigarillos	400
Cigars	200
Smoking Tobacco	1kg/2·2lb

CUSTOMS REGULATIONS

Apply to the Customs Office (UK) for a leaflet entitled *A Guide for Travellers* on customs regulations and the full range of duty-free allowances. **HM Customs and Excise**, Thomas Paine House, Angel Square, Torrens Street, London EC1V 1TA, ℘08450 109 000. For the nearest office, consult the telephone book under Federal Government, US Treasury. The **US Customs Service** *(PO Box 7407, Washington, DC 20044, ℘202-927-5580)* offers a free publication *Know Before You Go* for US citizens.

Americans can take home, tax free, up to US $400 worth of goods (limited quantities of alcohol and tobacco products). Canadians up to CAD$300; Australians up to AUS $400 and New Zealanders up to NZ $700.

People travelling to the USA cannot import plant products or fresh food, including fruit, cheeses and nuts. It is acceptable to carry tinned products or preserves.

Residents from a member state of the European Union are not restricted with regard to purchasing goods for private use, but there are recommended allowances.

HEALTH

First aid, medical advice and chemists' night service rota are available from chemists/drugstores *(pharmacie)* identified by the green cross sign.

You should take out comprehensive insurance coverage as the recipient of medical treatment in French hospitals or clinics must pay. **Nationals of non-EU countries** should check with their insurance companies about policy limitations. All prescription drugs should be clearly labelled; it is essential that you carry a copy of prescriptions.

British and Irish citizens (and all EU citizens) should apply for a European Health Insurance Card (EHIC), which has replaced the old E111 form, and entitles the holder to free or reduced-cost treatment for accident or unexpected illness in EU countries.

British citizens apply online at www.dh.gov.uk/travellers, or telephone 0845 606 2030.

Irish citizens should consult; www.ehic.ie.

Americans and Canadians can contact the **International Association for Medical Assistance to Travelers**, which can also provide details of English-speaking doctors in different parts of France: ℘for the US (716) 754-4883; for Canada (416) 652-0137. www.iamat.org.

The **American Hospital of Paris** is open 24hr for medical and dental emergencies, as well as consultations, with English-speaking staff *(63 bd. Victor-Hugo, 92200 Neuilly-sur-Seine, ℘01 46 41 25 25; www.american-hospital.org)*. Accredited by major insurance companies.

The **Hertford British Hospital** is just outside Paris *(3 r. Barbès, 92300 Levallois-Perret; ℘01 46 39 22 22; www.britishhospital.org)*.

ACCESSIBILITY

The sights described in this guide which are easily accessible to people of reduced mobility are indicated in the admission times and charges by this symbol: ♿.

Since 2001, the designation **Tourisme et Handicap** has applied to a thousand sites accessible to the disabled: go to www.franceguide.com. The principal French source

for information on facilities is the **Association des Paralysés de France:** www.apf.asso.fr.
On **TGV and Corail trains**, operated by the national railway (SNCF), there are special wheelchair slots in 1st class carriages available to holders of 2nd-class tickets. On **Eurostar** and Thalys, special rates are available for accompanying adults. All **airports** are equipped to receive passengers with access needs.
You can find information for slow walkers, mature travellers and others with special needs at www.access-able.com. For information on museum access for the disabled, contact **La Direction** *(Les Musées de France, Service Accueil des Publics Spécifiques, 6 r. des Pyramides, 75041 Paris Cedex 1; ✆01 40 15 35 88).*
The **Michelin Guide France** and the **Michelin Camping & Caravanning France** indicate hotels and campsites with facilities suitable for people with physical disabilities.

PETS

After years of strict quarantine rules, the UK has come into line with the rest of the European Union and introduced new regulations which make it much easier travelling with pets between the UK and mainland Europe. All animals must be microchipped, vaccinated against rabies (at least 21 days prior to travel) and have the EU Pet Passport. Full details are available from the website of the **Department for Environment, Food and Rural Affairs**, www.defra.gov.uk/pets. Check also with the **Animal Health and Veterinary Laboratories Agency (AHVLA)** for details of the export certification requirements if travelling further afield, email: lab.services@vla.defra.gsi.gov.uk.

Getting There and Getting Around

BY PLANE

The various international and other independent airlines operate services to **Paris** (Roissy-Charles de Gaulle and Orly airports), **Tours** and **Nantes**. Check with your travel agent, however, before booking direct flights, as it is sometimes cheaper to travel via Paris.
Air France (✆0820 820 820), the national airline, links Paris to Nantes and Tours several times a day.
Contact airline companies and travel agents for details of package tour flights with a rail or coach link-up as well as fly-drive schemes.
Discount flights within Europe offer wide choice, but conditions change often, so check the websites. Top discounters include **Ryanair** (www.ryanair.com); **easyJet** (www.easyjet.com; **Flybe** (www.flybe.com) and **Jet2.com** (www.jet2.com).
Within France, air travel generally compares unfavourably with rail, both for price and time, especially when you consider transport to and from airports, and check-in times.

PRACTICAL ADVICE

Practical advice for travelling by plane, specifically as regards carrying liquids, gels, creams, aerosols, medicines and food for babies is provided on www.franceguide.com. Some countries impose restrictions on liquids bought in duty-free shops when transferring to a connecting flight. Aéroports de Paris recommends that passengers contact individual airline companies for further information.
www.aeroportsdeparis.fr.

AIRPORT TRANSFERS

Visitors arriving in **Paris** who wish to reach the city centre or a train station may use public transportation or reserve space on the Airport Shuttle

(for Roissy-Charles-de-Gaulle ✆01 45 38 55 72, for Orly, ✆01 43 21 06 78. You can reach the Loire Valley by TGV direct from Roissy-Charles-de-Gaulle. From Orly, an Air France bus links to Paris-Montparnasse TGV station.
For **Nantes Airport**, the TAN (Nantes Area Transport Company) links the centre of Nantes to the airport via the Tan Air Service. At **Tours Val-de-Loire Airport**, there is a bus shuttle to and from the city centre.

BY SHIP

There are numerous **cross-Channel services** (passenger and car ferries) from the United Kingdom and Ireland, as well as the rail Shuttle through the Channel Tunnel (**Le Shuttle-Eurotunnel,** ✆08705 35 35 35, www.euro-tunnel.com).
To choose the most suitable route between your port of arrival and your destination use the **Michelin Tourist and Motoring Atlas France**, **Michelin map 726** (which gives travel times and mileages) or **Michelin Local maps** from the 1:200 000 series.

For details apply to travel agencies or to:

- **P&O Ferries** ✆08716 645 645 (UK dialling), or 0825 120 156 (in France), www.poferries.com. Dover–Calais.
- **Norfolk Line** ✆0844 847 5042 www.norfolkline-ferries.co.uk. Dover–Dunkerque.
- **Brittany Ferries** ✆0871 244 0744 (in UK); 0825 828 828 (in France). www.brittany-ferries.com. Portsmouth–St-Malo, Caen and Cherbourg; Poole–Cherbourg; Plymouth–Roscoff; Cork–Roscoff.
- **LD Lines**, ✆0844 576 8836, www.ldlines.co.uk. Portsmouth–Le Havvre; Dover–Boulogne; Newhaven–Dieppe; Rosslare–Cherbourg.
- **Condor Ferries**, ✆01202 207216, www.condorferries.co.uk. Weymouth and Poole–St-Malo; Portsmouth–Cherbourg.
- **Seafrance** ✆0871 22 22 500. www.seafrance.com. Dover–Calais.

BY TRAIN

All rail services throughout France can be arranged through **Rail Europe** in the UK, online (www.raileurope.co.uk), by telephone ✆0844 848 4070, or call into the Rail Europe Travel Centre at 1 Regent Street, London SW1. Rail Europe can also book Eurostar travel.
Eurostar runs from **London** (St Pancras) to **Paris** (Gare du Nord) in under 3hr (up to 20 times daily). In Paris it links to the high-speed rail network (TGV) which covers most of France. There is fast inter-city service from **Paris** (Gare Montparnasse) to **Vendôme** *(45min)*, **Le Mans** *(50min)*, **Tours** *(1hr)* and **Angers** *(1hr 30min)* on the TGV.
Bookings and information ✆08705 186 186 (£5 booking fee applies) in the UK, www.eurostar.com.
Citizens of non-European Economic Area countries will need to complete a landing card before arriving at Eurostar check-in. These landing cards can be found at dedicated desks in front of the check-in area and from Eurostar staff. Once you have filled in the card please hand it to UK immigration staff.
Eurailpass, **Flexipass**, **Eurailpass Youth**, **EurailDrive Pass** and **Saverpass** are travel passes which may be purchased by residents of countries outside the European Union. In the US, contact your travel agent or **Rail Europe** 2100 Central Ave. Boulder, CO, 80301, ✆1-800-4-EURAIL or **Europrail International** ✆1 888 667 9731. If you are a European resident, you can buy an individual country pass, if you are not a resident of the country you where you plan to use it. Information on schedules can be obtained on websites for these agencies and the **SNCF,** respectively: www.raileurop.com.us, www.eurail.on.ca, www.sncf.fr. At the SNCF site, you can book ahead, pay with a credit card, and receive your ticket in the

mail at home. There are numerous **discounts** available when you purchase your tickets in France, from 25–50% below the regular rate. These include discounts for using senior cards and youth cards, and seasonal promotions. There are a limited number of discount seats available during peak travel times, and the best discounts are available for travel during off-peak periods. Tickets for rail travel in France must be validated (*composter*) by using the (usually) automatic date-stamping machines at the platform entrance (failure to do so may result in a fine).
The French railway company **SNCF** operates a telephone information, reservation and prepayment service in English from 7am to 10pm (French time). In France call ☎08 36 35 35 39 (when calling from outside France, drop the initial 0).

BY COACH/BUS

Regular coach services operate between **London** and **Tours** or **Nantes**: **www.eurolines.com** is the international website with information about travelling all over Europe by coach (bus). From the **UK** telephone ☎08717 71 71 71 for travel advice and ticket information.
A **Disabled Persons Travel Helpline** is available on ☎08717 818170.
A textphone is provided for customers who are deaf or hard of hearing on ☎0121 455 0086.

LOCAL SERVICES

Information about shuttle services operating from the airports is included in the section on travelling by air (*see pp33–34*).
All towns and cities have internal public transport services, sometimes using trams, but more generally buses. These are primarily to serve the local population and are rarely geared to tourism, so be sure to check timetables if you intend to use public transport; this is, however, an excellent way to gain local experience. Attraction-specific transport often

Water bus on the Loire River, Nantes
©Bertrand Rieger/ hemis.fr

operates between the town or city centre and the attraction, and information about this is given in the relevant section of the guide.

BY CAR

PLANNING YOUR ROUTE

The area covered in this guide is easily reached by main motorways and national roads.
Michelin map 726 indicates the main itineraries as well as alternate routes for avoiding heavy traffic during busy holiday periods, and gives estimated travel times. **Michelin map 723** is a detailed atlas of French motorways, indicating tolls, rest areas and services along the route; it includes a table for calculating distances and times.
The latest route-planning service is available on **www.ViaMichelin.com**. Travellers can calculate a precise route using such options as shortest route, route avoiding toll roads or the Michelin-recommended route.
In addition to tourist information (hotels, restaurants, attractions), you will find a magazine featuring articles with up-to-the-minute reports on holiday destinations.
The roads are very busy during the holiday period (particularly weekends in July and August) and, to avoid traffic congestion it is advisable to follow the recommended secondary routes (signposted as *Bison Futé – itinéraires bis*). The motorway network includes

rest areas *(aires)* and petrol stations, usually with restaurant and shopping complexes attached, about every 40km/25mi, so that long-distance drivers have no excuse not to stop for a rest every now and then.

IN AND ON THE CAR

Since 2008, it has been compulsory for all vehicles to carry a **safety jacket** for each passenger, and a **warning triangle** in line with numerous other European countries that have already implemented this measure. It is advisable to have both.

For the vehicle, an international distinguishing sign plate or sticker should be displayed as near as is reasonable to the national registration plate at the rear of the vehicle.

DOCUMENTS

Travellers from other European Union countries and North America can drive in France with a valid national or home-state **driving licence.** An **international driving licence** is useful because the information on it appears in nine languages (keep in mind that traffic officers are empowered to fine motorists). For **visitors from the US**, a permit is available from the **National Automobile Club**, ✆650-294-7000 or www.nationalautoclub.com; or contact your local branch of the **American Automobile Association**.

You must carry with you the original of the vehicle's **registration document**, and a **current insurance certificate** (plus a letter of authorisation from the owner, if the vehicle is not registered in your name).

BREAKDOWN AND INSURANCE

Certain motoring organisations (AA, RAC) offer accident **insurance** and breakdown service schemes for members. Check with your current insurance company in regard to coverage while abroad. Be aware that European Breakdown Cover does not apply to emergencies on the autoroutes, which are privately owned. If you break down on an *autoroute* you must use the emergency call phones, or drive off the *autoroute* if you are able to do so and want to use your own insurance. In the case of a **breakdown,** a red warning triangle or hazard warning lights are obligatory.

ROAD REGULATIONS

The minimum driving age is 18. Traffic drives on the right. All passengers must wear **seat belts.** Children under the age of 10 must ride in the back seat. Headlights must be switched on in poor visibility and at night; use sidelights only when the vehicle is stationary. In the absence of stop signs at intersections, cars must **give way to traffic approaching from the right.** Traffic on main roads outside built-up areas (priority indicated by a yellow diamond sign) and on roundabouts has right of way. There are many **roundabouts** located just on the edge of towns; you must slow down when you approach one and give way to the cars in the circle. Vehicles must stop when the lights turn red at road junctions and may filter to the right only when indicated by an amber arrow.

The regulations on **drinking and driving** (limited to 0.50g/l) and **speeding** are strictly enforced – usually by an on-the-spot fine and/or confiscation of the vehicle.

SPEED LIMITS

Although liable to modification, these are as follows:

- **Toll motorways** *(autoroutes)* 130kph/80mph (110kph/68mph when raining);
- **Dual carriageways and motorways** without tolls 110kph/68mph (100kph/62mph when raining);
- **Other roads** 90kph/56mph (80kph/50mph when raining) and in towns 50kph/31mph;
- **Outside lane on motorways** during daylight, on level ground and with good visibility – minimum speed limit of 80kph/50mph.

PARKING

In town there are zones where parking is either restricted or subject to a fee; tickets should be obtained from the ticket machines (*horodateurs* – small change necessary) and displayed inside the windscreen on the driver's side; failure to display may result in a fine, or towing away. Other parking areas in town may require you to take a ticket when passing through a barrier. To exit, you must pay the parking fee (usually there is a machine located by the exit – *sortie*) and insert the paid-up card in another machine which will lift the exit gate. In France, most motorway sections are subject to a **toll** *(péage)*. You can pay in cash or with a credit card.

PETROL/GASOLINE

French service stations dispense:

- *sans plomb98* (super unleaded 98)
- *sans plomb95* (super unleaded 95)
- *diesel/gazole* (diesel)
- *GPL* (LPG).

Prices are listed on signboards on the motorways, although it is usually cheaper to fill up before joining or after leaving the motorway. Check the large hypermarkets on the outskirts of towns for the lowest prices.

RENTAL CARS – CENTRAL RESERVATION NUMBERS IN FRANCE	
Avis	✆08 02 05 05 05
Europcar	✆08 03 35 23 52
Budget France	✆08 00 10 00 01
Hertz France	✆01 39 38 38 38
SIXT-Eurorent	✆01 40 65 01 00

CAR RENTAL

There are **car rental** agencies at airports, railway stations and in all large towns throughout France. European cars have manual transmission; automatic cars are available in larger cities only if an advance reservation is made. Drivers must be over 21; between ages 21–25, drivers are required to pay an extra daily fee; some companies allow drivers under 23 only if the reservation has been made through a travel agent. It is relatively expensive to hire a car in France; Americans in particular will notice the difference and should make arrangements before leaving, take advantage of fly-drive offers, or seek advice from a travel agent, specifying requirements.

In addition to standard vehicles, National/citer (www.citer.fr) offers electric, hybrid and reduced CO2-emitting cars.

Where to Stay and Eat

For Hotel & Restaurant listings, see the **Addresses** *within the Principal Sights in Discovering the Châteaux of the Loire.*

WHERE TO STAY

FINDING A HOTEL

Turn to the **Addresses** within individual sight listings for descriptions and prices of typical places to stay (**Stay**) and eat (**Eat**) with local flair.

The key at the back of the guide explains the symbols and abbreviations used in these sections. To enhance your stay, hotel selections have been chosen for their location, comfort, value for the money, and in many cases, their charm. Prices indicate the cost of a standard room for two people in peak season. For an even greater selection, use the red-cover **Michelin Guide France**, with its well-known star-rating system and hundreds of establishments throughout France. The **Michelin Charming Places to Stay** guide contains a selection of 1 000 hotels and guest houses at reasonable prices. Be sure to book ahead, especially for stays during the high season.

For further assistance, **Loisirs-Accueil** *(280 bd. St-Germain, 75007 Paris; ☎01 44 11 10 44; www.loisirs-accueil.fr)* is an online booking service. You can also contact the tourist offices for further information on all kinds of accommodation in their respective areas, such as hotel-châteaux, bed-and-breakfasts, etc.

Another resource, which publishes a catalogue listing holiday villas, apartments or chalets in each *département* is the **Fédération Nationale des Locations de France Clévacances** *(54 bd. de l'Embouchure, BP 52166, 31022 Toulouse Cedex 2; ☎05 61 13 55 66, www.clevacances.com).*

For good-value, family-run hotels, **Logis de France**, is one of the best organisations to contact (*☎01 45 84 83 84; www.logis-de-france.fr*).

Relais & Châteaux provides information on booking in luxury hotels with character: ☎0825 32 32 32; within the UK: ☎00 800 2000 00 02; within the US: ☎1 800 735 2478; www.relaischateaux.com.

These days, there are many websites which offer discount hotel accommodation.

Try **www.hotels.com**, **www.wotif.com** or **www.lastminute.com**.

If you know where you want to stay, do a price comparison at **www.travelsupermarket.com** or **www.comparethemarket.com**.

ECONOMY CHAIN HOTELS

If you need a place to stop en route, these can be useful, as they are inexpensive and generally located near the main road. Breakfast is available, but there may not be a restaurant; rooms are small, with a TV and bathroom.

Central reservation numbers:

- **Akena** ☎01 69 84 85 17
- **B&B** ☎0892 78 29 29 (inside France); +33 2 98 33 75 00 (from outside France)
- **Etap** ☎0892 68 89 00
- **Mister Bed** ☎01 46 14 38 00
- **Villages Hôtel** ☎03 80 60 92 70

The hotels listed below are slightly more expensive, and offer a few more amenities and services.

Central reservation number:

- **Campanile** ☎01 64 62 46 46
- **Kyriad** ☎0825 003 003
- **Ibis** ☎0825 882 222

Many chains have online reservations:
www.etaphotel.com
www.ibishotel.com

COTTAGES, BED AND BREAKFAST

Gîtes de France is an information service on self-catering accommodation in the Loire Valley (and the rest of France). Gîtes usually take the form of a cottage or apartment decorated in the local style where visitors can make themselves at home, or bed and breakfast accommodation *(chambres d'hôtes)* which consists of a room and breakfast at a reasonable price.

Contact the **Gîtes de France** office in Paris (*59 r. St-Lazare, 75439 Paris Cedex 09, ☎01 49 70 75 75*), or their representative in the UK, **Brittany Ferries** (*Millbay Docks, Plymouth, Devon PL1 3EW, ☎0990 360 360, www.brittany-ferries.com*).

The Internet site, *www.gites-de-france.com*, has a good English version. From the site, you can order catalogues for different regions illustrated with photographs of the properties, as well as specialised catalogues (bed and breakfasts, farm stays, etc.). You can also surf on *www.loire-valley-holidays.com* to view and book cottages in Touraine and contact the local tourist offices which may have lists of available properties and local bed and breakfast establishments.

www.westernloire.com comprises thousands of short descriptive texts on accommodations and activities.

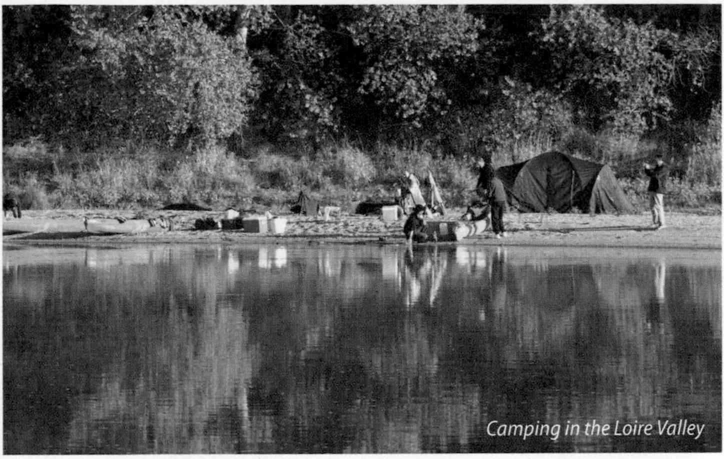

Camping in the Loire Valley

©Hervé Lenain/hemis.fr

HOSTELS, CAMPING

To obtain an **International Youth Hostel Federation** card (no age requirement; senior card available), contact the IYHF in your own country for information and membership applications *(UK ✆01727 855215; US ✆202 783 6161)*. There is a booking service on the internet *(iyhf.org)*, which you may use to reserve rooms as far as six months in advance. There are two main youth hostel associations *(auberges de jeunesse)* in France, the **Ligue Française pour les Auberges de la Jeunesse** *(67 r. Vergniaud, 75013 Paris, ✆01 44 16 78 78, www. auberges-de-jeunesse.com)* and the **Fédération Unie des Auberges de Jeunesse** *(4 bd.Jules-Ferry, 75011 Paris, ✆01 43 57 02 60, Fax 01 43 57 53 90)*.

There are numerous officially graded campsites with varying standards of facilities throughout the Loire Valley. The **Michelin Camping France** guide lists a selection of campsites. The area is very popular with campers in the summer months, so it is wise to reserve in advance.

WHERE TO EAT

A selection of places to eat in the different locations covered in this guide can be found in the **Addresses** throughout *Discovering Châteaux of the Loire*. The key at the back of the book explains the symbols and abbreviations. We have highlighted an array of eating places primarily for their atmosphere, location and regional delicacies. Prices indicate the average cost of a starter, main dish and dessert for one person.

Use the red-cover **Michelin Guide France**, with its well-known star-rating system and hundreds of establishments throughout France, for an even greater choice. If you would like to experience a meal in a highly rated restaurant from The Michelin Guide, be sure to book ahead. In the countryside, restaurants usually serve lunch between noon and 2pm and dinner between 7.30 and 10pm. It is not always easy to find something in between those two mealtimes, as the "non-stop" restaurant is still a rarity in the provinces. However, a hungry traveller can usually get a sandwich (usually a filled baguette) in a café, and ordinary hot dishes may be available in a brasserie. Throughout France, the culture leans more towards sitting and eating than to grabbing a sandwich on the go, so it's worth planning ahead if you're unsure.

In French restaurants and cafés, a service charge is included. Tipping is not necessary, but French people often leave the small change from their bill on their table, about 5% for the waiter in a nice restaurant. *See p46.*

MENU READER

agneau	lamb
alose	shad
anguilles	eels
bavette aux échalottes	sirloin with shallots
blanquette de veau	veal in cream sauce
boudin blanc	chicken sausage
boudin noir	blood sausage
brioche	sweet egg-and-butter bread
canard	duck
cèpes	wild mushrooms
chapon	capon
charcuterie	pork meats
chipirones/seiches	squid
choux	cabbage
confits (canard)	(duck) cooked and preserved in fat
coq au vin	chicken in red wine sauce
côtes d'agneau	lamb chops
crevettes	shrimp / prawns
crudités	raw vegetable salad
dorade aux herbes	sea bream with herbs
éclade	mussels cooked over pine needles
escargots	snails
esturgeon	sturgeon
faux filet au poivre	sirloin with pepper sauce
fèves	broad beans
foie	liver
filets de sole	sole fillets
frites	French fries
fromage de brebis	sheep's milk cheese
fruits de mer	seafood
garbure	hearty vegetable and meat soup
haricots	beans
homard	lobster
huître	oyster
jambon	ham
jus de fruits	fruit juice
langouste/ langoustines	spiny lobster
lapin	rabbit
loukinos	garlic sausage
magret	duck fillet
marrons	chestnuts
menu enfant	children's menu
mojettes	white beans
moules	mussels
mouton	mutton
noix	walnuts
nos viandes sont garnies	our meat dishes are served with vegetables
oie	goose
omelette aux morilles	wild-mushroom omelette
palombe	wood pigeon
pastis	anise-flavoured liqueur
pêche	peach
pibales	young eels
poule/poulet	chicken
poule au pot	chicken stew with vegetables
prune	plum
pruneau	prune
ravigote	seasoned white sauce
salmis	stew of roast fowl and game
saumon grillé	grilled salmon
sorbet: trois parfums	sorbet: three flavours
steak haché	minced beef
tarte aux pommes	apple pie
terrine de lapin	rabbit pâté
tournedos	fillet steak
tourteau fromager	sweet cake made with cheese
tourtière	flaky pastry with prune filling
tripotcha	mutton sausage
ttoro	Basque fish stew
vin rouge, vin blanc, rosé	red wine, white wine, rosé wine

well-done, medium, rare, raw = *bien cuit, à point, saignant, cru*

Useful Words and Phrases

Sights

	Translation
abbey	abbaye
belfry	beffroi
bridge	pont
castle	château
cemetery	cimetière
chapel	chapelle
church	église
cloisters	cloître
courtyard	cour
convent	couvent
covered market	halle
fountain	fontaine
garden	jardin
gateway	porte
house	maison
lock (canal)	écluse
market	marché
monastery	monastère
museum	musée
park	parc
port/harbour	port
quay	quai
ramparts	remparts
square	place
statue	statue
street	rue
tower	tour
town hall	mairie
windmill	moulin

Natural Sites

	Translation
beach	plage
beacon	signal
cave	grotte
chasm	abîme
coast, hillside	côte
dam	barrage
forest	forêt
lake	lac
ledge	corniche
pass	col
river	rivière
spring	source
stream	ruisseau
swallow-hole	aven
valley	vallée
viewpoint	belvédère
waterfall	cascade

On The Road

	Translation
car park	parking
driving licence	permis de conduire
east	Est
garage (for repairs)	garage
left	gauche
motorway/highway	autoroute
north	Nord
parking meter	horodateur
petrol/gas	essence
petrol/gas station	station essence
right	droite
south	Sud
toll	péage
traffic lights	feu rouge
tyre	pneu
west	Ouest
wheel clamp	sabot
zebra crossing	passage clouté

Time

	Translation
today	aujourd'hui
tomorrow	demain
yesterday	hier
autumn	automne
spring	printemps
summer	été
winter	hiver
week	semaine
Monday	lundi
Tuesday	mardi
Wednesday	mercredi
Thursday	jeudi
Friday	vendredi
Saturday	samedi
Sunday	dimanche

Numbers

	Translation
0	zéro
1	un
2	deux
3	trois
4	quatre
5	cinq
6	six
7	sept
8	huit
9	neuf
10	dix
11	onze
12	douze

13	treize
14	quatorze
15	quinze
16	seize
17	dix-sept
18	dix-huit
19	dix-neuf
20	vingt
30	trente
40	quarante
50	cinquante
60	soixante
70	soixante-dix
80	quatre-vingt
90	quatre-vingt-dix
100	cent
1000	mille

Shopping

	Translation
bank	banque
baker's	boulangerie
big	grand
butcher's	boucherie
chemist's	pharmacie
closed	fermé
cough mixture	sirop pour la toux
cough sweets	cachets pour la gorge
entrance	entrée
exit	sortie
fishmonger's	poissonnerie
grocer's	épicerie
newsagent, bookshop	librairie
open	ouvert
post office	poste
push	pousser
pull	tirer
shop	magasin
small	petit
stamps	timbres

Food and Drink

	Translation
beef	bœuf
beer	bière
butter	beurre
bread	pain
breakfast	petit-déjeuner
cheese	fromage
dessert	dessert
dinner	dîner
fish	poisson
fork	fourchette
fruit	fruits
glass	verre
chicken	poulet
ice cream	glace
ice cubes	glaçons
ham	jambon
knife	couteau
lamb	agneau
lunch	déjeuner
lettuce salad	salade
meat	viande
mineral water	eau minérale
mixed salad	salade composée
orange juice	jus d'orange
plate	assiette
pork	porc
restaurant	restaurant
red wine	vin rouge
salt	sel
spoon	cuillère
sugar	sucre
vegetables	légumes
water	de l'eau
white wine	vin blanc
yoghurt	yaourt

Personal Documents and Travel

	Translation
airport	aéroport
credit card	carte de crédit
customs	douane
passport	passeport
platform	voie
railway station	gare
shuttle	navette
suitcase	valise
train ticket	billet de train
plane ticket	billet d'avion
wallet	portefeuille

Clothing

	Translation
coat	manteau
jumper	pull
raincoat	imperméable
shirt	chemise
shoes	chaussures
socks	chaussettes
suit	costume
tights	collants
trousers	pantalon

Useful Phrases

	Translation
goodbye	au revoir
hello/good morning	bonjour
how	comment
excuse me	excusez-moi
thank you	merci
yes/no	oui/non
I am sorry	pardon
why	pourquoi
when	quand
please	s'il vous plaît

Do you speak English?
Parlez-vous anglais?
I don't understand
Je ne comprends pas
Talk slowly
Parlez lentement
Where's...?
Où est...?
When does the ... leave?
A quelle heure part...?
When does the ... arrive?
A quelle heure arrive...?
When does the museum open?
A quelle heure ouvre le musée?
When is the show?
A quelle heure est la représentation?
When is breakfast served?
A quelle heure sert-on le petit-déjeuner?
What does it cost?
Combien cela coûte?
Where can I buy a newspaper in English?
Où puis-je acheter un journal en anglais?
Where is the nearest petrol/ gas station?
Où se trouve la station essence la plus proche?
Where can I change traveller's cheques?
Où puis-je échanger des chèques-voyage?
Where are the toilets?
Où sont les toilettes?
Do you accept credit cards?
Acceptez-vous les cartes de crédit?

Useful to Know

On national and departmental roads, there are often roundabouts (traffic circles) just outisde the towns, which serve to slow traffic down.
At a French roundabout (**rond point**), you are likely to see signs pointing to the **Centre Ville** (town centre) or to other towns (the French use towns as directional indicators, rather than cardinal points).
You are also likely to see a sign for **Toutes Directions** (all directions – this is often the bypass road to avoid going through the town) or **Autres Directions** (other directions – in other words, a place that isn't indicated on one of the other signs on the roundabout!).

„Couteau" and „fourchette"

Basic Information

DISCOUNTS

Almost all attractions offer discounted admission prices for children, seniors, students and (sometimes) family groups. The age bands across which children's discounts apply vary considerably, and, where these relate to sites that are noted as specific attractions for children, then the price and age range for children is given. Student discounts tend as a rule to be for French students only, on presentation of a student ID card, but this rule is quite often freely interpreted.

ELECTRICITY

The electric current is 220 volts. Circular two-pin plugs are the rule. Adapters and converters (for hairdryers, for example) should be bought before you leave home; they are on sale in most airports. If you have a rechargeable device (video camera, portable computer, battery recharger), read the instructions carefully or contact the manufacturer or shop. Sometimes these items only require a plug adapter, in other cases you must use a voltage converter as well or risk ruining your appliance.

EMERGENCIES

If you are driving on an *autoroute*, there are emergency telephones at regular intervals, and these will connect you with a service that will either repair the problem or get you off the autoroute.

EMERGENCY NUMBERS	
Police:	**17**
SAMU (Paramedics):	**15**
Fire (Pompiers):	**18**
European-wide Emergency number	**112**

MAIL/POST

Main post offices open Monday to Friday 8am to 7pm, Saturday 8am to noon. Smaller branch post offices generally close at lunchtime between noon and 2pm and at 4pm.

Postage via air mail:

- **UK:** letter (20g) 0.77€
- **North America:** letter (20g) 0.89€
- **Australia and NZ:** letter (20g) 0.89€

Stamps are also available from newsagents and *bureaux de tabac*. Stamp collectors should ask for *timbres de collection* in any post office.

MONEY

CURRENCY

There are no restrictions on the amount of currency visitors can take into France. Visitors carrying a lot of cash are advised to complete a currency declaration form on arrival, because there are restrictions on currency export.

NOTES AND COINS

The **euro** is the only currency accepted as a means of payment in France, as in the other European countries participating in the monetary union. It is divided into 100 cents or centimes. Notes in French francs can be exchanged at the Banque de France only until 2012.

BANKS

Although business hours vary from branch to branch, banks are generally open from 9am to noon and 2pm to 4pm and are closed either on Monday or on Saturday. Banks close early on the day before a bank holiday. A passport is necessary as identification when cashing traveller's cheques in banks. Commission charges vary and hotels usually charge more than banks for cashing cheques.
One of the most economical ways to obtain money in France is by using ATM machines to get cash directly from your bank account (with a debit

American Express ✆01 47 77 72 00	
Visa ✆08 36 69 08 80	
MasterCard/Eurocard ✆01 45 67 84 84	
Diners Club ✆01 49 06 17 50	

card) or to use your credit card to get a cash advance. Be sure to remember your PIN number, you will need it to use cash dispensers and to pay with your card in shops, restaurants, etc. Code pads are numeric; use a telephone pad to translate a letter code into numbers. PIN numbers have 4 digits in France; enquire with the issuing company or bank if the code you usually use is longer. Visa is the most widely accepted credit card, followed by MasterCard; other cards, credit and debit (Diners Club, Plus, Cirrus, etc.) are also accepted in some cash machines. American Express is more often accepted in premium establishments. Most places post signs indicating which cards they accept; if you don't see such a sign, and want to pay with a card, ask before ordering or making a selection. Cards are widely accepted in shops, hypermarkets, hotels and restaurants, at tollbooths and in petrol stations.

Before you leave home, check with the bank that issued your card for emergency replacement procedures. At the same time, inform the bank that you will be using your credit card abroad – it can save potential embarrassment at cash desks if your card is refused.

Carry your card number and emergency phone numbers separate from your wallet and handbag; leave a copy of this information with someone you can easily reach. If your card is lost or stolen while you are in France, call one of the following 24-hour hotlines:

You must report any loss or theft of credit cards or traveller's cheques to the local police who will issue you with a certificate (useful proof to show the issuing company).

It may be a good idea to carry some traveller's cheques in addition to your cards, and to keep them in a safe place in case of emergency.

PUBLIC HOLIDAYS

See the box above for a list of major public holidays in France. There are other religious and national festivals days, and a number of local saints' days, etc. On all these days, museums and other monuments may be closed or may vary their hours of admission. In addition to the usual school holidays at Christmas and in the spring and summer, there are long mid-term breaks (ten days to a fortnight) in February and early November.

1 January	New Year's Day *(Jour de l'An)*
Mon after Easter Sun	Easter Day and Easter Monday *(Pâques)*
1 May	May Day *(Fête du Travail)*
8 May	VE Day *(Fête de la Libération)*
Thurs 40 days after Easter	Ascension Day *(Ascension)*
7th Sun-Mon after Easter	Whit Sunday and Monday *(Pentecôte)*
14 July	France's National Day *(Fête de la Bastille)*
15 August	Assumption *(Assomption)*
1 November	All Saint's Day *(Toussaint)*
11 November	Armistice Day *(Fête de la Victoire)*
25 December	Christmas Day *(Noël)*

SMOKING

In February 2007, France banned smoking in public places such as offices, universities and railway stations. The law became effective for restaurants, cafés, bars, nightclubs and casinos in January 2008.

TELEPHONES

PUBLIC TELEPHONES

Most public phones in France use pre-paid phone cards *(télécartes)*, rather than coins. Some telephone booths accept credit cards (Visa, Mastercard/Eurocard). *Télécartes* (50 or 120 units) can be bought in post offices, branches of France Télécom, *bureaux de tabac* (cafés that sell cigarettes) and newsagents and can be used to make calls in France and abroad. Calls can be received at phone boxes where the blue bell sign is shown; the phone will not ring, so keep your eye on the little message screen.

NATIONAL CALLS

French telephone numbers have ten digits. Paris and Paris region numbers begin with 01; 02 in northwest France; 03 in northeast France; 04 in southeast France and Corsica; 05 in southwest France.

Local directory enquiries

℘118 218
Available online at **www.118218.fr**. **www.pagesjaunes.fr** gives business and private numbers and includes listings of recommended bars, restaurants, films, exhibitions and other leisure activities.

INTERNATIONAL CALLS

To call France from abroad, dial the country code (+33) + 9-digit number (omit the initial 0). When calling abroad from France, dial 00, then dial the country code followed by the area code and number of your correspondent.

International Dialling Codes

Dial 00 before the country code minus the first 0, then the full number.
To use your **personal calling card** dial:

- **AT&T** ℘0800 99 00 11
- **Sprint** ℘0800 99 00 87
- **MCI/Verizon** ℘0800 99 00 19
- **Canada Direct** ℘0800 99 00 16
- **BT** ℘0800 99 02 44
- **International information**, US/Canada: ℘00 33 12 11
- **International operator** ℘00 33 12 + country code

MOBILE/CELL PHONES

France has an efficient mobile phone service with several networks to choose from including SFR, Orange and Bouygtel. Check with your network provider that your phone is set up for International roaming before you go – your phone will automatically switch to the local network when you get to France. Bear in mind that calls are more expensive than those made within the UK or US and you also pay to receive a call. If you're going to be making and receiving a lot of calls, it might be worth getting a global sim card (*www.0044.co.uk* or *www.gosim.com*), which will give you a local number and lower calling rates. If you're going to be making a lot of calls in France, you should consider buying a pay-as-you-go *(sans abonnement)* phone from a high-street shop or supermarket. Alternatively, you could hire a phone (delivery or airport pick-up provided):

- **World Cellular Rentals** www.worldcr.com

TIME

France is 1hr ahead of **Greenwich Mean Time (GMT)**. France goes on Daylight-Saving Time from the last Sunday in March to the last Sunday in October. In France "am" and "pm" are not used but the 24-hour clock is widely applied.

TIPPING

Since a service charge is automatically included in the price of meals and accommodation in France, any additional tipping is up to the visitor, generally small change, and generally not more than 5 percent. Taxi drivers and hairdressers are usually tipped 10–15 percent.
As a rule, the cost of staying in a hotel, eating in a restaurant or buying goods and services is significantly lower in the French regions than in Paris.

CONVERSION TABLES

Weights and Measures

1 kilogram (kg)	**2.2 pounds (lb)**	**2.2 pounds**	*To convert kilograms to pounds, multiply by 2.2*
6.35 kilograms	14 pounds	1 stone (st)	
0.45 kilograms	16 ounces (oz)	16 ounces	
1 metric ton (tn)	**1.1 tons**	**1.1 tons**	
1 litre (l)	**2.11 pints (pt)**	**1.76 pints**	*To convert litres to gallons, multiply by 0.26 (US) or 0.22 (UK)*
3.79 litres	1 gallon (gal)	0.83 gallon	
4.55 litres	1.20 gallon	1 gallon	
1 hectare (ha)	**2.47 acres**	**2.47 acres**	*To convert hectares to acres, multiply by 2.4*
1 sq kilometre (km²)	**0.38 sq. miles (sq mi)**	**0.38 sq. mlles**	
1 centimetre (cm)	**0.39 inches (in)**	**0.39 inches**	*To convert metres to feet, multiply by 3.28; for kilometres to miles, multiply by 0.6*
1 metre (m)	**3.28 feet (ft) or 39.37 inches or 1.09 yards (yd)**		
1 kilometre (km)	**0.62 miles (mi)**	**0.62 miles**	

Clothing

Women			
	35	4	2½
	36	5	3½
	37	6	4½
Shoes	38	7	5½
	39	8	6½
	40	9	7½
	41	10	8½
	36	6	8
	38	8	10
Dresses & suits	40	10	12
	42	12	14
	44	14	16
	46	16	18
	36	6	30
	38	8	32
Blouses & sweaters	40	10	34
	42	12	36
	44	14	38
	46	16	40

Men			
	40	7½	7
	41	8½	8
	42	9½	9
Shoes	43	10½	10
	44	11½	11
	45	12½	12
	46	13½	13
	46	36	36
	48	38	38
Suits	50	40	40
	52	42	42
	54	44	44
	56	46	48
	37	14½	14½
	38	15	15
Shirts	39	15½	15½
	40	15¾	15¾
	41	16	16
	42	16½	16½

Sizes often vary depending on the designer. These equivalents are given for guidance only.

Speed

KPH	10	30	50	70	80	90	100	110	120	130
MPH	6	19	31	43	50	56	62	68	75	81

Temperature

Celsius (°C)	0°	5°	10°	15°	20°	25°	30°	40°	60°	80°	100°
Fahrenheit (°F)	32°	41°	50°	59°	68°	77°	86°	104°	140°	176°	212°

To convert Celsius into Fahrenheit, multiply °C by 9, divide by 5, and add 32.
To convert Fahrenheit into Celsius, subtract 32 from °F, multiply by 5, and divide by 9.

NB: Conversion factors on this page are approximate.

Château de Cheverny

INTRODUCTION TO CHÂTEAUX OF THE LOIRE

The Region Today

POPULATION AND LIFESTYLE

The population of the Pays de la Loire is in excess of 3.2 million, with the greatest concentrations being in

- Nantes (406 000)
- Angers (208 000)
- Le Mans (190 000)

The population density is in the region of 100 persons per sq km.

The Loire region is a prime tourist destination and wine-producing area, and as a result its inhabitants enjoy a comfortable and prosperous lifestyle based on these principal activities. Some branches of the region's economy (such as industry, property building and tourism) have had problems with providing new jobs in recent years, or even with keeping pre-existing employment. But on the whole, the general economic trend of the Pays de la Loire region is quite similar to the economic situation of the rest of France.

Unemployment issues have persisted since the 1970s, and the Pays de la Loire has an unemployment rate of 6%, although a number of attempts have been made since to curb the unemployment rate. As France is the most-visited country in the world, with over 75 million visitors a year, tourism is a significant contributor to the French economy.

RELIGION

In matters of religion, the region is not dissimilar to the rest of France: Catholicism is the primary religion. During the Ancien Régime, France had traditionally been considered the Church's eldest daughter, and the King of France always maintained close links to the Pope. Roman Catholicism, however, is no longer considered a state religion as it was before the 1789 Revolution.

ECONOMY AND GOVERNMENT

France is the fifth largest economy in the world in USD exchange-rate terms. With a GDP of $US2.58 trillion (2010 data), the seventh largest by purchasing power parity, it shows the lowest poverty rate among the large economies (6.2 percent), the lowest income inequality rate and has some of the world's strongest social services (such as health care, education, retirement systems) and public service sectors (such as public transport and public security). According to World Bank and IMF figures, it is the second largest in Europe after Germany.

France is the European Union's leading agricultural producer, accounting for about one third of all agricultural land within the EU: Northern France is characterised by large wheat farms; dairy products, pork, poultry and apple production are concentrated in the western region; beef production is located in central France; while the production of fruits, vegetables and wine ranges from central to southern France.

France is a large producer of many agricultural products and is currently expanding its forestry and fishery industries. The implementation of the Common Agricultural Policy (CAP) has resulted in reforms in the agricultural sector of the economy.

Nicolas Sarkozy was elected President of the French Republic on 6 May 2007 after defeating Socialist Party contender Ségolène Royal. Before his presidency, Sarkozy was leader of the UMP right wing party.

Sarkozy is known for his conservative stance on law and order issues and his admiration for a new economic model for France. In foreign affairs, he has promised higher profile involvement internationally.

LOCAL GOVERNMENT

According to its constitution, France has three levels of local government: 22 *régions* and four *régions d'outre-mer* or overseas regions (Réunion, Martinique, Guadeloupe and French Guiana); 96 *départements* and four *départements d'outre-mer* (Réunion, Guadeloupe, Martinique and French Guiana). There are 36 679 *communes* (municipalities).

FOOD AND DRINK

The following menu lists a few local specialities and the wines best suited to accompany them.

Hors-d'œuvre: various types of potted pork; sausage stuffed with chicken meat *(boudin blanc)*.

Fish: pike, salmon, carp or shad with the famous *beurre blanc* (white butter) sauce; small fried fish from the Loire, rather like whitebait *(friture)*; stuffed bream and casserole of eels simmered in wine with mushrooms, onions and prunes (in Anjou).

Main course: game from Sologne; pork with prunes; veal in a cream sauce made with white wine and brandy; casserole of chicken in a red wine sauce or in a white wine and cream sauce with onions and mushrooms; spit-roasted capon or pullet.

Rillauds, rillons and rillettes: all three words derive from the French 16C term *rille*, meaning small dice of pork. *Rillons*, sometimes referred to as *grillons*, are made with pork meat, both lean and fat, which is cut into small morsels. These are then sautéed in fat until they are golden brown and served cold. To make *rillettes*, take some *rillons*, slice them finely and put them back to cook on a low heat. They are kept in a pot where the fat rises to the surface, ensuring perfect conservation. *Rillettes* can also be made with goose meat. Anjou *rillauds* are chunks of belly of pork cooked in a vegetable stock enhanced with aromatic herbs for several hours. When the sauce has been reduced, some lard can be added for the final stages of cooking. The dish is best served with a glass of Vouvray.

Vegetables: green cabbage with butter; Vineuil asparagus; mushrooms – stuffed or in a cream sauce; lettuce salad with walnut oil dressing.

Cheese: St-Benoît, Vendôme and St-Paulin are made from cows' milk. Chavignol, Valençay, Selles-sur-Cher, Ste-Maure and Crémets d'Anjou are made from goats' milk (the latter are small fresh cream cheeses); Olivet is factory made with a coating of charcoal.

Fruit: plums, prunes and melons from Tours; strawberries from Saumur; apricots and pears from Angers; Reinette apples from Le Mans.

Dessert: macaroons from Cormery; apple pastries; quince and apple jelly *(cotignac)*; preserves from Orléans and pastries from Tours; caramelised upside-down apple tart.

Liqueurs: there are excellent marcs and fruit liqueurs, including the famous Cointreau.

Marcs: pure white spirit obtained from pressed grape skins and pips.

Bottle of Bourgueil

S. Sauvignier/MICHELIN

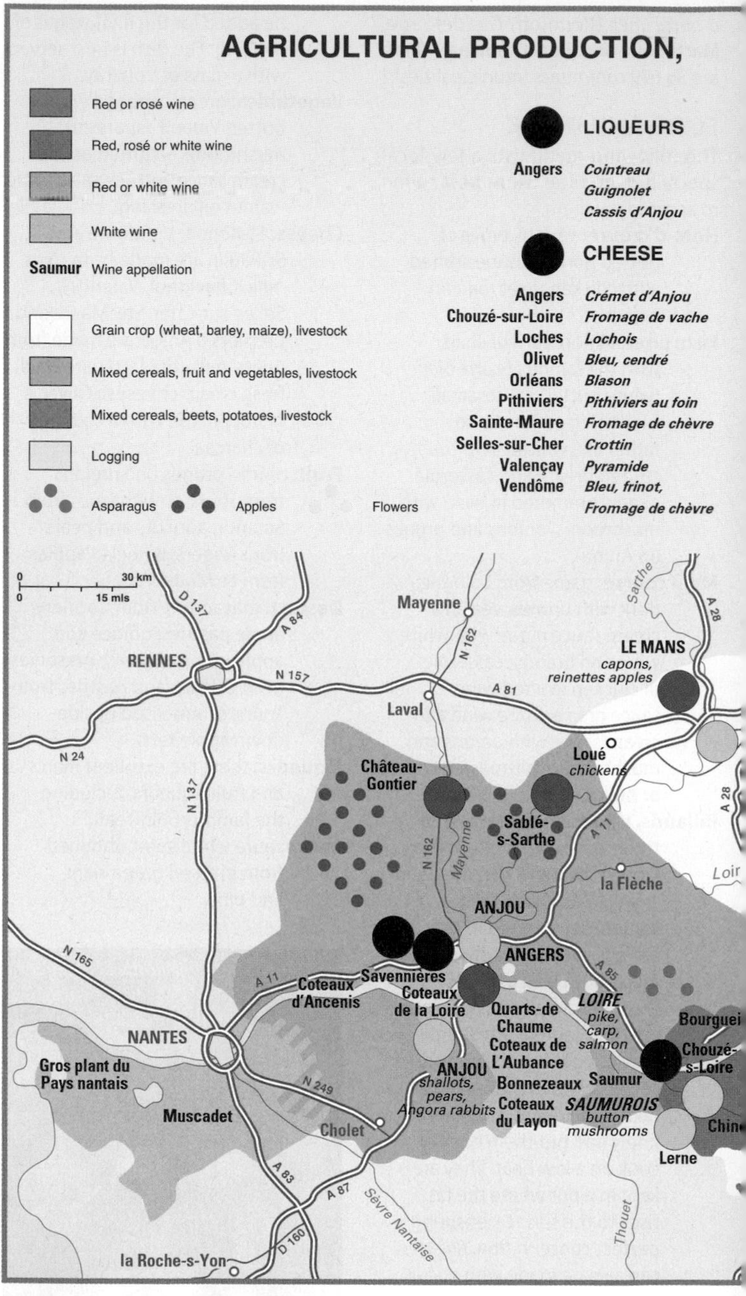

WINE

See also "Wine Country" in Themed Tours in the Planning Your Trip section.

For a guide to the best years and advice on the best combinations of foods and wines, see the list printed in the Michelin Guide France.

For more in-depth wine-related touring information, consult *The Green Guide Wine Regions of France.*

SPECIALITIES AND VINEYARDS

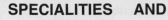

CONFECTIONERY

Angers	*Quernons d'ardoise*
Beaugency	*Liquorice*
Blois	*Chocolate, chocalate buttons*
Château-Gontier	*Croquets*
Cormery	*Macaroons*
Gâtinais	*Honey*
Le Mans	*Bugattises*
Orléans	*Apple Jelly*
Pithiviers	*Pithiviers almond tart*
Romorantin-Lanthenay	*Liquorice*
Sablé-sur-Sarthe	*Shortbread*
Saint-Benoît-sur-Loire	*Moinillons*
Sologne	*Tarte tatin, palet solognot*
Tours	*Livre tournois* *Sucres d'orge* *Stuffed prunes* *Muscadines*

OTHER SPECIALITIES

Angers	*Crêpes, veal chump chop, rilletes, rillons*
Blois	*Pâtés, rillettes, rillons*
Chinon	*Fouace bread, eel stew*
Jargeau	*Smoked pork sausage*
Lerné	*Fouace*
Le Mans	*Fricassée de poulet, rillettes, rillons*
Orléans	*Mustard, vinegar*
Tours	*Rillettes, rillons*
Vendôme	*Andouille, poulet à la ficelle, rillettes, rillons*
Vouvray	*Andouillettes, rillettes, rillons*

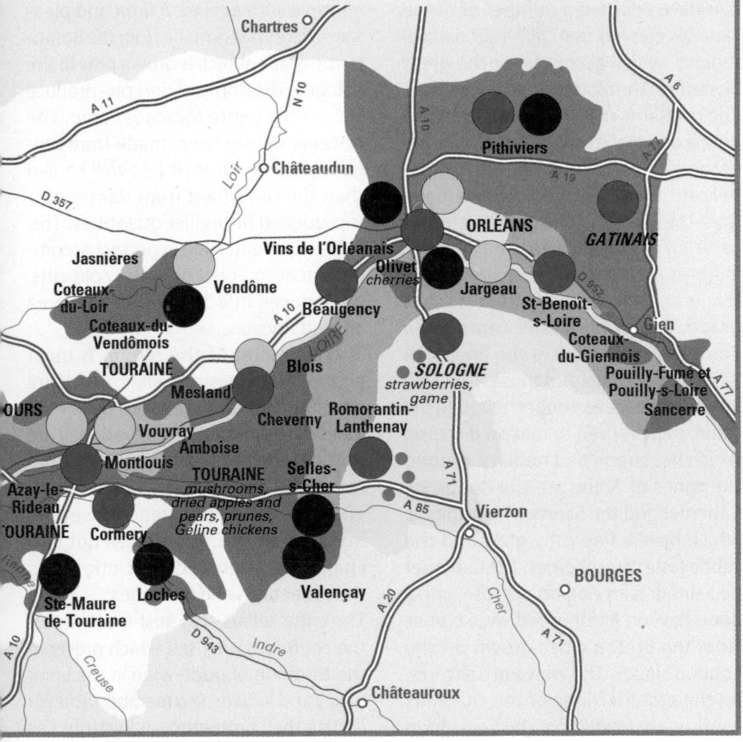

Local wines

The vestiges of an early stone winepress were discovered at Cheille, near Azay-le-Rideau, testifying to the existence of winemaking in the Loire Valley under Roman rule, around AD 100. It is believed that the great St Martin himself ordered vines to be planted on the slopes of Vouvray in the 4C. From then onwards, this activity became firmly

In the Temple of Bacchus

Picture the scene: the owner of the vineyard fills the glasses and the ruby-red nectar is held up to the light. The wine should be savoured first for its bouquet and then, after a knowing glance at one's neighbour, tasted in small sips. On emptying the glass, a simple click of the tongue is enough to signal appreciation. The owner, his eyes shining, will say *"ça se laisse boire"*.

Once inside the cellar, all round, projecting from recesses in the rock, are coloured bottle tops – red, yellow, blue and white: full-bodied Sancerre; Vouvray, among the most famous white wines from Touraine and said to "rejoice the heart" (you will notice the motto etched on the glasses there); heady Montlouis from the terraced tufa slopes abutting the river Loire; Chinon with its aftertaste of violets; Bourgueil with its hint of raspberries or wild strawberries; and their Angevin brothers, sparkling Saumur, lively and spirited, white Saumur, dry and sprightly, wines from La Coulée de Serrant and the Layon.

established in the area. Over the centuries, Anjou, Touraine and the Orléanais have adopted a number of grape varieties coming from different natural regions, which accounts for the great diversity of the *cépages* (grape varieties). The best-known white wines are Vouvray, a dry, mellow wine tasting of ripe grapes, and Montlouis, known for its delicate, fruity flavour. Both are made from the Chenin Blanc grape, referred to locally as Pineau de la Loire.

The best-known red wine, known as Breton, is made from the Cabernet Franc grape, which originally came from Bordeaux and produces the fine, light wines of Bourgueil and those from Chinon, which have a stronger bouquet; the same grape is used to make a dry rosé, which has charm and nobility. Among the wines of Anjou are the Rouge de Cabernet and the Saumur-Champigny, which have a fine ruby glow and the subtle taste of raspberries. The Cabernet de Saumur is an elegant dry rosé with a good flavour. Another red wine comes from the Breton vines grown on the Loudun slopes. The wines of Sancerre, on the eastern fringe of the châteaux country, are made from the Sauvignon grape and are known for their gunflint flavour. Less famous wines are the *gris meuniers* from the Orléanais and the *gascon*, which are pale and have a low alcohol content.

The slopes of the Loire produce a dry white and an acid-tasting red which improve with ageing. A light and pleasant white wine is made from the Romorantin grape, which is grown only in the Sologne. The slopes of the Loire produce 15% of the entire Muscadet crop. The Ancenis-Gamay wine, made from Burgundy Gamay vines, is less well known than the Gros Plant from Nantes as it is produced in smaller quantities. This light, dry, fruity wine, a perfect accompaniment to pork and other cold cuts, is produced in a 350ha/865-acre area around Ancenis.

The character of the region is most apparent in the wine cellars, which are often old quarries hollowed out of the limestone slopes at road level. They are therefore easily accessible so that the owner can drive his vehicles straight in. The galleries often extend for several hundred metres. Some open out into chambers where local societies hold their meetings and festivities.

The wine cellars also host meetings of the *confréries vineuses*, which preserve the tradition of good wine in the Loire Valley and initiate new members *(chevaliers)* to their brotherhoods joyously: Les Sacavins in Angers, Les Bons Entonneurs Rabelaisiens in Chinon, La Chantepleure in Vouvray and La Côterie des Closiers in Montlouis.

History

TIME LINE

GALLO-ROMAN ERA AND THE EARLY MIDDLE AGES

52 BC Carnutes revolt. Caesar conquers Gaul.
AD 1C–4C Roman occupation of Gaul.
313 Constantine grants freedom of worship to Christians (Edict of Milan).
372 St Martin, Bishop of Tours (dies at Candes in 397).
573–594 Episcopacy of Gregory of Tours, author of the *History of the Franks*.
7C — Founding of the Benedictine abbey of Fleury, later to be named St-Benoît.
late 8C Alcuin of York's school for copyists *(see Tours)*. Theodulf, Bishop of Orleans.
768–814 Charlemagne.
840–877 Charles the Bald.
9C Vikings invade Angers, St-Benoît and Tours. Rise of Robertian dynasty.

THE CAPETS (987–1328)

987–1040 Fulk Nerra, Count of Anjou.
996–1031 Robert II, the Pious.
1010 Foundation of the Benedictine abbey at Solesmes.
1060–1108 Philippe I.
1101 Foundation of Fontevraud Abbey.
1104 First Council of Beaugency.
1137–1180 Louis VII.
1152 Second Council of Beaugency. Eleanor of Aquitaine marries Henry Plantagenet.
1154 Henry Plantagenet becomes King of England as Henry II.
1180–1223 Philippe Auguste.
1189 Death of Henry II Plantagenet at Chinon. Struggle between Capets and Plantagenets.
1199 Richard the Lionheart dies at Châlus and is buried at Fontevraud.
1202 John Lackland loses Anjou. The last of the Angevin kings, he dies in 1216.
1215 Magna Carta.
1226–1270 Louis IX (St Louis).
1285–1314 Philippe IV, the Fair.
1307 Philippe the Fair suppresses the Order of the Knights Templars.

THE VALOIS (1328–1589)

1337–1453 Hundred Years' War: 1346 Crécy; 1356 Poitiers; 1415 Agincourt.
1380–1422 Charles VI.
1392 The King goes mad *(see Le Mans)*.
1409 Birth of King René at Angers.
1418 The Massacre at Azay-le-Rideau.
1422–1461 Charles VII.
1427 The Dauphin Charles establishes his court at Chinon.
1429 Joan of Arc delivers Orléans, but she is tried and burnt at the stake two years later *(see Chinon and Orléans)*.
1453 Battle of Castillon: final defeat of the English on French soil.
1455–1485 Wars of the Roses: Margaret of Anjou leader of Lancastrian cause.
1461–1483 Louis XI.
1476 Unrest among the powerful feudal lords.
1477 The region's first printing press is set up in Angers.
1483 Death of Louis XI at Plessis-lès-Tours.
1483–1498 Charles VIII.
1491 Marriage of Charles VIII and Anne of Brittany at Langeais.
1494–1559 The Campaigns in Italy.
1496 Early manifestations of Italian influence on French art *(see Amboise)*.
1498 Death of Charles VIII at Amboise.
1498–1515 Louis XII. He divorces and marries Charles VIII's widow.
1515–1547 François I.
1519 French Renaissance: work on Chambord starts. Da Vinci dies at Le Clos-Lucé.

1539 Struggle against Emperor Charles V. He visits Amboise and Chambord.

1547–1559 Henri II.

1552 The sees of Metz, Toul and Verdun join France. Treaty signed at Chambord.

1559–1560 François II.

1560 Amboise Conspiracy. François II dies at Orléans.

1560–1574 Charles IX.

1562–1598 Wars of Religion.

1562 St-Benoît Abbey is pillaged by the Protestants. Battles at Ponts-de-Cé and Beaugency.

1572 The St Bartholomew's Day Massacre in Paris.

1574–1589 Henri III.

1576 Founding of the Catholic League by Henri, Duke of Guise to combat Calvinism. Meeting of the States-General in Blois.

1588 The assassination of Henri, Duke of Guise and his brother, the Cardinal of Lorraine (*see Blois*).

THE BOURBONS (1589–1702)

1589–1610 Henri IV.

1589 Vendôme recaptured by Henry IV.

1598 Edict of Nantes. Betrothal of César de Vendôme (*see Angers*).

1600 Henri IV weds Marie de' Medici.

1602 Maximilien de Béthune buys Sully.

1610–1643 Louis XIII.

1619 Marie de' Medici flees from Blois.

1620 Building of the Jesuits college at La Flèche.

1626 Gaston d'Orléans, brother of Louis XIII, is granted the County of Blois.

1643–1715 Louis XIV.

1648–1653 Civil war against Mazarin. The Fronde.

1651 Anne of Austria, Mazarin and young Louis XIV take refuge in Gien.

1669 Première of Molière's play *Monsieur de Pourceaugnac* at Chambord.

1685 Revocation of the Edict of Nantes by Louis XIV at Fontainebleau.

1715–1774 Louis XV.

1719 Voltaire exiled at Sully.

1756 Foundation of the Royal College of Surgeons at Tours.

1770 The Duke of Choiseul in exile at Chanteloup.

THE REVOLUTION AND FIRST EMPIRE (1789–1815)

1789 Storming of the Bastille.

1792 Proclamation of the Republic.

1793 Execution of Louis XVI. Vendée War. Fighting between the Republican Blues and Royalist Whites (*see Cholet and Les Mauges*).

1803 Talleyrand purchases Valençay.

1804–1815 First Empire under Napoleon Bonaparte.

1808 Internment of Ferdinand VII, King of Spain, at Valençay.

CONSTITUTIONAL MONARCHY AND THE SECOND REPUBLIC (1815–1852)

1814–1824 Louis XVIII.

1824–1830 Charles X.

1830–1848 July Monarchy: Louis-Philippe.

1832 The first steamboat on the River Loire.

1832–1848 Conquest of Algeria.

1848 Internment of Abd El-Kader at Amboise.

1848–1852 Second Republic. Louis Napoleon-Bonaparte, Prince-President.

THE SECOND EMPIRE (1852–1870)

1852–1870 Napoleon III as Emperor.

1870–1871 Franco-Prussian War.

1870 Proclamation of the Third Republic on 4 September in Paris. Frederick-Charles of Prussia at Azay-le-Rideau. Defence of Châteaudun. Tours made headquarters of Provisional Government.

1871 Battle of Loigny.

THE THIRD REPUBLIC (1870–1940)

1873 Amédée Bollée completes his first car, L'Obéissante (*see Le Mans*).
1908 Wilbur Wright's early trials with his aeroplane.
1914–1918 First World War.
1919 Treaty of Versailles.
1923 The first 24-hour sports car race at Le Mans.
1939–1945 Second World War.
1940 Defence of Saumur. Historic meeting at Montoire.
1945 Reims Armistice.

CONTEMPORARY TIMES

1946 Fourth Republic.
1952 First *Son et Lumière* performances at Chambord.
1958 The Fifth Republic came into being. On 8 January, Charles de Gaulle became the first President of the new era.
1963 France's first nuclear power station at Avoine, near Chinon.
1972 Founding of the Centre (later called Centre-Val-de-Loire) and Pays de la Loire regions.
1989 Inauguration of the *TGV Atlantique* (high-speed train).
1993 Opening of the International Vinci Congress Centre in Tours.
1994 The Centre region is renamed Centre-Val de Loire.
1996 Pope John Paul II visits the city of Tours.
1999 The euro was introduced in France to replace the franc.
2000 The Val de Loire (between Sully-sur-Loire and Chalonnes-sur-Loire) is placed on the UNESCO World Heritage List.
2007 Nicolas Sarkozy is elected President of France: he took office on 16 May; the 6th President of the French Fifth Republic, the 23rd President of the French Republic and Co-Prince of Andorra.
2007 Opening of the final section of the A 85 linking Vierzon and Angers.
2008 France holds the rotating 6-month presidency of the EU.
2009 France assumes full membership of NATO.
2011 France holds the presidency of the G7 and G20 economic groups.

AN EVENTFUL PAST

ANTIQUITY AND THE EARLY MIDDLE AGES

During the Iron Age the prosperous and powerful people known as the **Cenomanni** occupied a vast territory extending from Brittany to the Beauce and from Normandy to Aquitaine. They minted gold coins and put up a long resistance to both barbarian and Roman invaders.

The Cenomanni reacted strongly to the invasion of Gaul by the Romans and in 52 BC the **Carnutes**, who inhabited the country between Chartres and Orléans, gave the signal, at the instigation of the Druids, to raise a revolt against Caesar. It was savagely repressed but the following year Caesar had to put down another uprising by the Andes, under their leader Dumnacos.

Peace was established under Augustus and a period of stability and prosperity began. Existing towns such as Angers, Le Mans, Tours and Orléans adjusted to the Roman model with a forum, theatre, baths and public buildings. Many agricultural estates *(villae)* were created or extended as the commercial outlets developed. They reached their peak in the 2C. By the end of the 3C instability and danger were so rife that cities had been enclosed behind walls.

At the same time Christianity was introduced by St Gatien, the first bishop of Tours; by the end of the 4C it had overcome most opposition under **St Martin**, the greatest bishop of the Gauls, whose tomb later became a very important place of pilgrimage (St Martin's Day: 11 November).

In the 5C the Loire country suffered several waves of invasion; in 451 Bishop

Aignan held back the Huns outside Orléans while waiting for help. Franks and Visigoths fought for domination until the Frankish King Clovis was finally victorious in 507.

His successors' endless quarrels, which were recorded by Gregory of Tours, dominated the history of the region in the 6C and 7C while St Martin's Abbey was establishing its reputation. In 732 the Saracens, who were pushing north from Spain, reached the Loire before they were repulsed by Charles Martel. The order achieved by the Carolingians, which was marked by the activities of **Alcuin** and **Theodulf**, did not last. In the middle of the 9C the Vikings came up the river and ravaged the country on either side, particularly the monasteries (St-Benoît, St-Martin). **Robert**, Count of Blois and Tours, defeated them but they continued their depredations until 911 when the Treaty of St-Clair-sur-Epte created the Duchy of Normandy.

During this period of insecurity the Robertian dynasty (the forerunner of the Capet dynasty) gained in power to the detriment of the last Carolingian kings. A new social order emerged which gave rise to feudalism.

PRINCELY POWER

The weakness of the last Carolingian kings encouraged the independence of turbulent and ambitious feudal lords. Although Orléans was one of the favourite royal residences and the Orléans region was always Capet territory, Touraine, the county of Blois, Anjou and Maine became independent and rival principalities. This was the age of powerful barons, who raised armies and minted money. From Orléans to Angers every high point was crowned by an imposing castle, the stronghold of the local lord who was continually at war with his neighbours.

The counts of Blois faced a formidable enemy in the counts of Anjou, of whom the most famous was **Fulk Nerra**. He was a first-class tactician; little by little he encircled Eudes II, Count of Blois, and seized part of his territory. His son, Geoffrey Martel, continued the same policy; from his stronghold in Vendôme he wrested from the house of Blois the whole county of Tours. In the 12C the county of Blois was dependent on Champagne, which was then at its peak.

At the same period the counts of Anjou reached the height of their power under the **Plantagenets**, a dynasty founded in Le Mans; when Henri, Count of Anjou, became King Henry II of England in 1154 his kingdom stretched from the north of England to the Pyrenées. This formidable new power confronted the modest forces of the kings of France but they did not quail under the threat of their powerful neighbours and skilfully took advantage of the quarrels which divided the Plantagenets.

In 1202 when King John of England, known as **John Lackland**, lost all his continental possessions to **Philippe Auguste**, the Loire country returned to the French sphere of interest.

In accordance with the wishes of his father Louis VIII, when Louis IX came to the throne he granted Maine and Anjou as an appanage to his brother Charles, who abandoned his French provinces, including Provence, and tried to establish an Angevin kingdom in Naples, Sicily and the Near East, as did his successors. Nonetheless, Good **King René**, the last Duke of Anjou, earned himself a lasting place in popular tradition.

CRADLE OF FEUDALISM

Feudalism flourished in France in the 11C and 12C in the region between the Seine and the Loire under the **Capet** monarchy. The system was based on two elements: the fief and the lord. The **fief** was a beneficium *(benefice)*, usually a grant of land made by a lord to a knight or other man who became his vassal.

The numerous conflicts of interest which arose from the system in practice produced a detailed code of behaviour embodying the rights of the parties. During the 12C the services due were defined, such as the maximum number of days to be spent each year in military service or castle watch. Gradually the fiefs became hereditary and the lord retained only

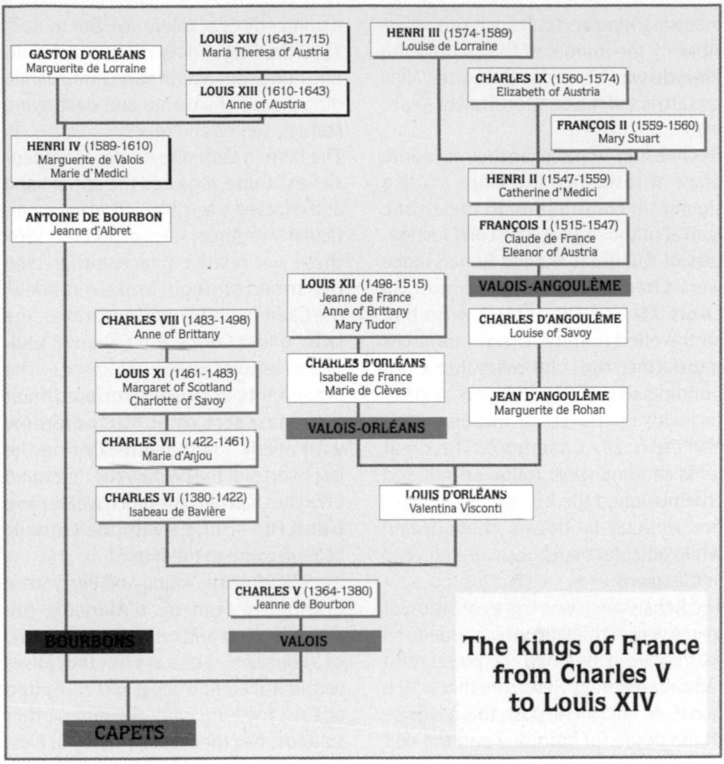

The kings of France from Charles V to Louis XIV

overall ownership. In the case of multiple vassalage, liege homage was paid to one lord and this was more binding than homage to any other.

An almost perfect hierarchical pyramid was created descending from the king to the mass of simple knights. The more important vassals had the right of appeal to the king in the event of a serious dispute with their suzerain; it was by this means that King John (John Lackland) was deprived of his French fiefs by Philippe Auguste early in the 13C.

All the inhabitants of an estate were involved in the economic exploitation of the land; the estate had evolved from the Carolingian method of administration and was divided into two parts: the domain, which was kept by the lord for himself, and the holdings, which were let to the tenants in return for rent.

The authority exercised by the lord over the people who lived on his estate derived from the royal prerogative of the monarch to command his subjects which passed into the hands of powerful lords who owned castles.

This unlimited power enabled them to impose military service, various duties (road mending, transport, etc.) and taxes on their tenants.

16TH CENTURY

The 16C saw in the Renaissance, an explosion of new ideas in the fields of art and architecture, resulting in one of the liveliest periods in the history of the Loire region.

The Renaissance

The University of Orléans, with its long-established reputation, attracted a number of **humanists**: Nicolas Béraud, Étienne Dolet, Pierre de l'Estoile, Anne du Bourg. The world of ideas was greatly extended by the invention of printing – the first printing press in the Loire Valley was set up in Angers in 1477 – which made learning and culture more accessible. By the middle of the century the **Pléiade** was formed in the Loire Valley and attracted the best local talent (*see p80*).

By choosing Touraine as their favourite place of residence the kings made a significant contribution to the artistic revival of the region. The chief instigators of the great French Renaissance were **Charles VIII** and even more so **Louis XII** and **François I**, who had all travelled in Italy. These monarchs transformed the Loire Valley into a vast building site where the new aesthetic ideals flourished at Amboise, Blois and especially Chambord. The great lords and financiers followed suit and commissioned the building of elegant houses (Azay-le-Rideau, Chenonceau) while graceful mansions were erected in the towns.

The Renaissance was the expression of a new way of thinking which redefined man's place in the world and presented a radically different view from that which had been held in the past; this gave rise to the desire for harmony and the cult of beauty in all fields: poetry, music, architecture as an expression of nature shaped by man.

Religious Tumult

The Renaissance excited not only intellectual activity, but also the need for a moral and religious revival. Despite several local experiments (e.g. Le Mans), the Roman Church did not succeed in satisfying these aspirations. Naturally the ideas of **Luther** and **Calvin** (who stayed in Orléans between 1528 and 1533) were well received in cultivated circles. In 1540 the Church responded with repression; several reformers died at the stake but the Reform movement continued to grow; nor was support confined to the elite but extended to the mass of the people, craftsmen and tradesmen. The dispute between Protestants and Roman Catholics inevitably led to armed conflict. In 1560 the **Amboise Conspiracy** failed disastrously and ended in bloodshed. Catherine de' Medici tried to promote conciliation by issuing edicts of tolerance, but in April 1562 the Huguenots rose up, committing numerous acts of vandalism: damaging places of worship and destroying statues, tombs and relics.

The Roman Catholics, under Montpensier and Guise, regained the upper hand and exacted a terrible vengeance, particularly in Angers. From 1563 to 1567 there was relative peace, but in 1568 the armed struggle broke out anew; the Catholic and Protestant armies, the latter under Condé and Coligny, indulged in regular waves of violence. The inhabitants of Orléans suffered their own **massacre of St Bartholomew** with nearly 1 000 deaths. During the last quarter of the century the Reformed Churches had become much weaker and **Henri III**'s struggle with the Catholic League came to the fore.

In 1576 Touraine, Anjou and Berry were granted to François d'Alençon, the King's brother and head of the League, as a conciliatory gesture but the Guises would not compromise and conspired against the King who, seeing no other solution, had them assassinated at Blois in December 1588. The population divided into Royalists and Leaguers, who were powerful in the Loire region. Henri III, who had been forced to withdraw to Tours, allied himself with Henri of Navarre and was marching on Paris when he himself was assassinated on 2 August 1589.

It took Henri IV nearly 10 years to restore peace to the region. The brilliant period in the history of the Loire valley, which coincided with the last years of the Valois dynasty, ended in tragedy.

17C–18C: PEACE RESTORED

The Loire country ceased to be at the centre of political and religious ferment. There were admittedly a few alarms during the minority of Louis XIII and the Fronde uprising, in which the indefatigable conspirator, Gaston d'Orléans, played a significant role. Order was restored under Louis XIV with centralisation under the crown stifling the slightest sign of autonomy: the districts of Orléans and Tours were administered by energetic treasury officials while the towns lost the right to self-government.

As far as religious life was concerned, the Roman Catholic Church re-established itself: a growth in the number of convents and seminaries, the reform of the old monastic foundations and the suppression of sorcery went hand in hand with an improvement in the intellectual level of the clergy. Protestantism struggled to survive, except in Saumur thanks to the Academy, and was dealt a devastating blow by the **Revocation of the Edict of Nantes** in 1685.

A Developing Economy

Human enterprise benefited from the general stability. Agriculture developed slowly: cereals in the Beauce, raw materials for textiles (wool, linen, hemp), market gardening together with fruit growing and winemaking in the Loire Valley, were a considerable source of wealth whereas cattle raising remained weak. Rural crafts played an important role together with urban manufacturing: hemp cloth around Cholet, cheesecloth in the district of Le Mans, sheeting in Touraine and Anjou, bonnets in Orléanais. The silk weavers of Tours earned themselves a good reputation.

Nevertheless in the 18C, except for sheets from Laval and Cholet, the textile industry fell into decline. Orléans, the warehouse of the Loire, specialised in sugar refining and the finished product was distributed throughout the kingdom. The Loire, under the control of the community of merchants, was the main axis for trade: wine from Touraine and Anjou, wool from the Berry, iron from the Massif Central, coal from the Forez, wheat from the Beauce, cloth from the Touraine and cargoes from exotic countries – everything travelled by water. On the eve of the Revolution these activities were waning but the region featured two million inhabitants and several towns: Orléans (pop. 40 000), Angers (pop. 30 000), Tours (pop. 20 000) and Le Mans (pop. 17 000).

THE REVOLUTION

The Touraine and Orléanais regions accepted the Revolution, but Maine and Anjou rose in revolt.

Social Conflict

At first it was social conflict in which the country peasants were opposed to the townspeople and the weavers from the villages. Townspeople, who had been won over by the new ideas, were enthusiastic about the new political order, while peasants became increasingly disillusioned. Religious reform upset parish life and the administrative reforms aroused criticism and discontent because they favoured the townspeople. The national guards in their blue uniforms were increasingly disliked: they were sent out from the towns to impose revolutionary decisions on the populace, if necessary by force.

The decree imposing mass conscription in March 1793 was seen as an unacceptable provocation in rural areas and the peasants rose in a body. Les Mauges in particular was immediately in the forefront of the battle.

The Vendée War

The Angevin rebels appointed leaders from among their own class: countrymen like Stofflet and Cathelineau, as well as noblemen like Bonchamps. For four months their armies won several important engagements in support of the Church and the King; they captured Cholet, Saumur and then Angers. The Convention, the Republican government of France between September 1792 and November 1795, replied by sending in several army units. The royalist Whites were severely defeated at Cholet on 17 October by General Kléber and General Marceau and compelled to retreat. As they fled, they were pitilessly massacred and the remnants of the great Catholic and Royal Army were exterminated in the Savenay Marshes beyond Nantes. By way of reprisal against the local population the Convention appointed General Turreau in January 1794 to clean up the country. From February to May his **infernal columns** converged on the centre, killing women and children and setting fire to villages.

The Chouans

The war was followed by sporadic outbursts of guerrilla activity: daring exploits, ambushes and even assassinations. **Jean Cottereau**, also known as Jean Chouan, was the leading figure who gave his name to the movement. The country people maintained a relentless resistance. At the end of August a faint peacemaking gesture was made under the authority of **General Hoche**. Charette and Stofflet, who continued the struggle, were arrested and shot in February and March 1796. The insurrection in the Vendée came to an end under the Consulate, a triumvirate including a certain General Bonaparte set up in 1799 to provide stronger government than the existing Republican regime with its divided factions. The war left in its wake widespread ruin and an entrenched bitterness which was revealed later in the very rigid political attitudes of the people of Maine and Anjou.

FROM WAR TO WAR

October 1870–January 1871

After the fall of the Empire, France recovered its balance under the stimulus of Gambetta who arrived in Tours by balloon on 9 October, having escaped the Paris siege. The Bavarians, who were victorious at Artenay, had already captured Orléans (11 October) and indicated that they would link up with the Prussian army at Versailles via the Beauce. Châteaudun put up a heroic resistance for ten hours on 18 and 19 October and was bombarded and set on fire in reprisal.

The army of the Loire was formed under the command of **General d'Aurelle de Paladines**; two corps, the 15th and 16th (Chanzy), formed in the Salbris camp, set out from Blois for Orléans. The engagement took place at Marchenoir and then at Coulmiers on 9 November: the French were victorious and General Von der Thann was forced to evacuate Orléans. Meanwhile the 18th and 20th Corps tried to check the advance of the Duke of Mecklenburg on Le Mans and Tours but they were beaten on 28 November at Beaune-la-Rolande by Prince Frederick-Charles who had hastened south from Metz. On 2 December the 16th and 17th Corps were defeated at Patay and Loigny where the Zouaves under Lt Col de Charette, the great-nephew of the famous Vendéen Royalist, fought with distinction. Although cut in two the first army of the Loire survived. Orléans had to be abandoned while the government retreated to Bordeaux (8 December).

A second Loire army was formed under **General Chanzy**; it resisted every enemy attack and then retrenched on the Loir. On 19 December the Prussians captured Château-Renault and two days later arrived in front of Tours but did not besiege the town. The decisive battle was fought between 10 and 12 January on the Auvours plateau east of Le Mans. Chanzy was forced to retreat towards Laval; Tours was occupied and Prince Frederick-Charles took up residence at Azay-le-Rideau. The armistice was signed on 28 January 1871.

1917–1918

The Americans set up their headquarters in Tours while the first Sammies disembarked at St-Nazaire and were billeted along the Loire.

1940–1944

On **10 June 1940** the French Government moved to Tours, and Cangé Château, on the southeast edge of the town, became the temporary residence of the President of the Republic. On 13 June the Franco-British Supreme Council met in Tours; at Cangé the Council of Ministers decided to transfer the government to Bordeaux. During that week of tragedy the bridges over the Loire were machine-gunned and bombarded; floods of refugees choked the roads. The towns were badly damaged. Two thousand cadets from the Cavalry School at Saumur excelled themselves by holding up the German advance for two days along a 25km/15.5mi front (*see Saumur*). On 24 October 1940 Marshal Pétain met Hitler at **Montoire**

Tours-La Riche railway bridge bombed by the Allies to paralyse the German operations during the Second World War

(see *Montoire-sur-le-Loir*), and agreed to his demands; collaboration was born. The Gestapo in Angers unleashed a reign of terror in the region.

The Resistance was born in 1941; the information and sabotage networks, the underground forces and the escape agents (the demarcation line followed the River Cher and ran between Tours and Loches) hampered the movements of the occupying forces who responded with torture, deportation and summary execution. In August and September 1944 the American army and the forces of the Resistance achieved control of the area with heavy losses.

DEVELOPMENT OF THE CHÂTEAUX

THE FIRST CHÂTEAUX (5C–10C)

In the Merovingian period the country was protected by isolated strongholds: some had evolved from Gallo-Roman villas (country estates), which had been fortified; others were built on high ground (Loches, Chinon). Generally they covered a fairly large area and served several purposes: residence of important people, place of worship, place for minting money, agricultural centre and place of refuge for the population. This type of stronghold continued under the Carolingians but the growing insecurity in the second half of the 9C introduced a wave of fortification in an attempt to counter the Viking threat.

The early castles, which were built in haste, rested on a mound of earth surrounded by a wooden palisade; sometimes a central tower was erected as an observation post. The structure contained very little masonry. Until the 10C castle building was a prerogative of the king but thereafter the right was usurped by powerful lords; small strongholds proliferated under the designation of towers – the keep had been invented.

THE MOTTE CASTLE (11C)

The motte was a man-made mound of earth on which was erected a square wooden tower, the keep. An earth bank protected by a ditch supported the perimeter fence, which consisted of a wooden palisade and enclosed an area large enough to contain people from the neighbourhood. The **keep** was built either as the last place of refuge or at the weakest point in the perimeter fence; some castles had more than one motte. In several of the Angevin castles built by Fulk Nerra the keep protected a residential building erected at the end of a promontory, as at Langeais, Blois and Loches, which are typical of the Carolingian tradition.

THE STONE CASTLE (12C–13C)

By the 11C some castles had defensive works built of stone. The keep was still the strongest point and took the form of a massive quadrangular structure. The keeps at Loches, Langeais, Montbazon, Chinon (Coudray) and Beaugency are remarkable examples of 11C architecture.

The 12C keep overlooked a courtyard which was enclosed by a stone curtain wall, gradually reinforced by turrets and towers. Within its precincts each castle comprised private apartments, a great hall, one or more chapels, soldiers' barracks, lodgings for the household staff and other buildings such as barns, stables, storerooms, kitchens, etc.

The tendency grew to rearrange the buildings more compactly within a smaller precinct. The keep comprised a storeroom on the ground floor, a great hall on the first and living rooms on the upper floors. The compact shape and the height of the walls made it difficult to besiege and only a few men were needed to defend it.

In the 13C, under the influence of the crusades and improvements in the art of attack, important innovations began to make their presence felt. Castles were designed by experts to be even more compact with multiple defensive features so that no point was unprotected. The **curtain wall** bristled with huge towers and the keep was neatly incorporated into the overall design.

A circular plan was adopted for the towers and keep; the walls were splayed at the base; the depth and width of the moat were greatly increased.

Sometimes a lower outer rampart was built to reinforce the main rampart; the intervening strip of level ground was called the lists. Improvements were made to the arrangements for launching missiles: new types of loophole (in a cross or stirrup shape), stone machicolations, platforms, brattices, etc.

The 13C castle, which was more functional and had a pronounced military character, could be built anywhere, even in open country.

At the same time a desire for indoor comfort began to express itself in tapestries and draperies and furniture (chests and beds), which made the rooms more pleasant to live in than they had been in the past.

THE LATE MEDIEVAL CASTLE

In 14C and 15C castle-building the accent moved from defence to comfort and decoration. The living quarters were more extensive; large windows to let in the light and new rooms (state bedrooms, dressing rooms and lavatories) appeared; decoration became an important feature.

In the military sphere there were no innovations, only minor improvements. The keep merged with the living quarters and was surmounted by a watchtower; sometimes the keep was suppressed altogether and the living quarters took the form of a rectangular block defended by huge corner towers. The entrance was flanked by two semicircular towers and protected by a barbican (a gateway flanked by towers) or by a separate fort.

The top of the curtain wall was raised to the height of the towers which were crowned by a double row of crenellations. In the 15C the towers were capped by pointed, pepper-pot roofs.

OTHER FORTIFIED BUILDINGS

Churches and monasteries, which were places of sanctuary and therefore targets of war, were not excluded from the fortification movement, especially during the Hundred Years War.

The towns and some of the villages also turned their attention to defence and built ramparts round the residential districts. In 1398, 1399 and 1401 Charles VI issued letters and ordinances enjoining the owners of fortresses and citizens to see that their fortifications were in good order.

From the end of the 13C fortified houses were built in the country districts by the lords of the manor; they had no military significance but are similar in appearance to the smaller **châteaux**.

SIEGE WARFARE

The attackers' first task was to besiege the enemy stronghold. The defences they constructed (moat, stockade, towers, forts or blockhouses) were intended both to prevent a possible

Studio 3Bis/MICHELIN

sortie by the besieged and to counter an attack from a relief army.
In the great sieges a fortified town grew up in its own right to encircle the site under attack. In order to make a breach in the defences of the besieged place the attackers used mines, slings, battering rams and siege towers. For this they had specialist troops who were experts in siege operations.
The advent of the cannon altered siege technique. Both attackers and defenders used artillery: the firing rate was not very high and the aim was even less accurate. Military architecture was completely transformed; towers were replaced by low thick bastions and curtain walls were built lower but much thicker. This new system of defence was perfected by Vauban.

THE RENAISSANCE CHÂTEAU

In the 16C military elements were abandoned in the search for comfort and aesthetic taste: moats, keeps and turrets appeared only as decorative features, like at Chambord, Azay-le-Rideau and Chenonceau. The spacious attics were lit by great dormer windows in the steep pitched roofs. The windows were very large. The spiral turret stairs were replaced with stairs that rose in straight flights in line with the centre of the main façade beneath coffered ceilings. The gallery – a new feature imported from Italy at the end of the 15C – lent a touch of elegance to the main courtyard.

Whereas the old fortified castle had been built on a hill, the new château was sited in a valley or beside a river where it was reflected in the water. The idea was that the building should blend in with its natural surroundings, although these were shaped and transfigured by human intervention; the gardens, laid out like a jewel casket, were an integral part of the design. Only the chapel continued to be built in the traditional style with ogive vaulting and Flamboyant decoration.

THE COURT IN THE LOIRE VALLEY

A BOURGEOIS COURT

The court resided regularly in the Loire Valley under **Charles VII** whose preference was for Chinon and Loches. These visits ended with the last of the Valois, Henri III. Owing to the straitened circumstances to which the King of France was reduced, Charles VII's court was not particularly glittering; but the arrival of Joan of Arc in 1429 won the castle of Chinon a place in the history books. **Louis XI** disliked pomp and circumstance. He installed his wife Charlotte of Savoy at Amboise but he himself rarely went there. He preferred his manor at Plessis-lès-Tours where he lived in fear of an attempt on his life. According to writer and diplomat Commines, his only interests were hunting and dogs.
The queen's court consisted of 15 ladies-in-waiting, 12 women of the bedchamber and 100 officers in charge of various

Daily Life in the Châteaux

The Medieval Household: In the 10C and 11C life in a castle was thought to be somewhat primitive. The whole family lived, ate and slept in the same room on the first floor of the keep. Furniture was sparse and tableware rudimentary. When the lord was out hunting or fighting his neighbours or off on a crusade, his lady would take over the administration of his affairs.

The Great Hall: The finest room in the castle was the Great Hall, where the lord held audience and dispensed justice, and where feasts and banquets were organised. The earlier loopholes were replaced by windows, fitted with panes and shutters.

The walls were hung with paintings and tapestries; the floor tiles were covered with rush mats or carpets on which one could sit or lie; flowers and greenery were strewn on the floor and, in summer, in the fireplaces.

The Bedchamber: Except in royal or princely households, a married couple slept in the same room. Over the centuries the furnishings grew richer; the bed was set on a dais and surrounded with sumptuous curtains; there were Venetian mirrors, tapestries, costly drapes, benches with backs, a princely chair, a *prie-dieu*, library steps and cushions, a dresser, a table, chests and a cupboard. To entertain the ladies there was an aviary, often with a parrot. Near the bedchamber was a study which was also used for private audiences, a council chamber and an oratory or chapel. A special room was set aside for the guards. In the larger houses there was also a stateroom where the ceremonial clothes were on display.

Food: Food at court was good and the meals gargantuan. When eaten in private, meals were served in the bedchamber or in the Great Hall. Before and after eating, basins and ewers of scented water were provided for the diners to rinse their hands since fingers often took the place of forks. The plates were made of silver.

Bathing and Hygiene: Near the bedchamber or in a separate building was the bathhouse. Until the 14C bathing was the fashion in France. The common people used to go to the public baths once a week; the upper classes often took a daily bath. The bathhouse contained a sort of pool which was filled with warm water and a chamber for the steam bath and massage. A barber or a chambermaid was in attendance, for it was the fashion to be clean shaven. In the absence of a bathhouse, baths were taken in a tub made of wood or bronze or silver. Men and women bathed together without being thought immoral. These habits of cleanliness disappeared from the Renaissance until the Revolution. In the 13C there were 26 public baths in Paris; by the time of Louis XIV's reign there were only two. In other respects medieval castles were well enough provided with conveniences.

Entertainment: Castle life had always had plenty of idle hours and a variety of distractions had developed to fill them. Indoors there was chess, spillikins, dice, draughts and, from the 14C, cards. Outdoors there was tennis, bowls and football, wrestling and archery. Hunting with hounds or hawks and tournaments and jousts were the great sports of the nobles. The women and children had dwarfs to entertain them; at court the jester was free to make fun of people, even the king. There were frequent festivities. Performances of the Mystery Plays, which sometimes lasted for 25 days, were always a great success.

functions including the saddler, the librarian, the doctor, the chaplain, the musicians, the official tasters and a great many butlers and manservants. Charlotte was a deep-thinking woman and a great reader; her library contained over 100 volumes, a vast total for that time. They were works on religious thought, ethics, history, botany and domestic science. A few lighter works, such as the *Tales of Boccaccio*, relieved this solemnity. In fact, compared with that of Charles the Bold, the royal lifestyle seemed homely rather than princely.

A LUXURIOUS COURT

In the late 15C, **Charles VIII** acquired a considerable amount of furniture and numerous other decorative objects in order to embellish the interior of the Château d'Amboise. He installed hundreds of Persian carpets, Turkish woollen pile carpets, Syrian carpets, along with dozens of beds, chests, oak tables and dressers. The rooms and sometimes the courtyards (in the case of prestigious events) were hung with sumptuous tapestries from Flanders and Paris. He also endowed the château with an extensive collection of beautifully crafted silverware, and a great many works of art, mainly from Italy. The Armoury (note the inventory dating back to 1499) contains several sets of armour and outstanding weapons having once belonged to Clovis, Dagobert, St Louis, Philip the Fair, Du Guesclin and Louis XI.

A GALLANT COURT

Louis XII, who was frugal, was the "Bourgeois King" of Blois. But under **François I** (1515–47) the French court became a model of elegance, taste and culture. The Cavalier King invited men of science, poets and artists to his court. Women, who until then had been relegated to the Queen's service, were eased by the King into a more prominent role in public life as focal points of a new kind of society. He expected them to dress perfectly and look beautiful at all times – and gave them the means to do so. The King also ensured that these

S. Sauvignier/MICHELIN

Salamander (François I) – Nitrusco et Extinguo (I Nourish the Good and Destroy the Bad)

ladies were treated with courtesy and respect. A code of courtesy was established and the court set an example of good manners.

François I divided his time between Amboise and Blois. The festivities he organised were of unprecedented brilliance. Weddings, baptisms and the visits of princes were lavishly celebrated. Sometimes these celebrations took place in the country, as on the occasion when the reconstruction of a siege was organised; a temporary town was built to be defended by the Duke of Alençon while the King led the assault and capture. To increase the sense of realism, the mortars fired huge balls. Hunting, however, took pride of place; 125 people were employed in keeping the hounds while 50 looked after the hawks.

Upon his return from Italy, he had Chambord built and spent the rest of his life there.

THE LAST VALOIS

Under **Henri II** and his sons, Blois remained the habitual seat of the court when it was not at the Louvre palace in Paris. It was **Henri III** who drew up the first code of etiquette and introduced the title His Majesty, taken from the

Roman Emperors. The Queen Mother and the Queen had about 100 ladies-in-waiting. Catherine de' Medici also had her famous **Flying Squad** of pretty girls, who kept her informed and assisted her in her intrigues. About 100 pages acted as messengers. In addition there were 76 gentlemen servants, 51 clerks, 23 doctors and 50 chambermaids.

The King's suite included 200 gentlemen-in-waiting and over 1 000 archers and Swiss guards. There was a multitude of servants. Princes of the blood and great lords also had their households. Thus, from the time of François I, the royal entourage numbered about 15 000 people. When the court was on the move, 12 000 horses were needed. By way of comparison, in the 16C only 25 towns in the whole of France had more than 10 000 inhabitants!

QUEENS AND GREAT LADIES

Whether they were queen or the current royal mistress, women at court played an increasingly important political role, while the lively festivities with which they surrounded themselves made a major contribution to the sphere of cultural and artistic influence of the royal court.

Agnès Sorel graced the court of Charles VII at Chinon and at Loches. She gave the King good advice and reminded him of the urgent problems facing the country after the Hundred Years War, while the Queen, Marie d'Anjou, moped in her castle.

Louise of Savoy, mother of François I, was a devout worshipper of St Francis of Paola. This religious devotion, mingled with the superstitions of her astrologer Cornelius Agrippa, was barely enough to keep her insatiable ambition in check. She lived only for the accession of her son to the throne and to this end she upset the plans of **Anne of Brittany** by making him marry Claude, daughter of Louis XII.

The love life of François I featured many women, including Françoise de Châteaubriant and the **Duchess of Étampes**, who ruled his court until his death.

Diane de Poitiers, the famous favourite of Henri II, was a remarkably tough woman. She retained her energy, both physical and mental, well into old age, to the amazement of her contemporaries. She made important decisions of policy, negotiated with the Protestants, traded in Spanish prisoners, distributed honours and magistracies and, to the great humiliation of the Queen, saw to the education of the royal children. Such was her personality that almost every artist of the period painted her portrait.

The foreign beauty of **Mary Stuart**, the hapless wife of young King François II, who died at the age of 17 after a few months' reign, lent an all too brief lustre to the court in the middle of the 16C. She is recalled in a drawing by Clouet and some verses by Ronsard.

A different type altogether was **Marguerite de Valois**, the famous Queen Margot, sister of François II, Charles IX and of Henri III. Her bold eyes, her exuberance and her amorous escapades caused a great deal of concern to her mother, Catherine de' Medici. Her marriage to the future King Henri IV did little to calm her down and was in any case later annulled.

Catherine de' Medici married the Dauphin Henri in 1533 and was a prominent figure at court for 55 years under five different kings. Although eclipsed for a while by the beautiful Diane de Poitiers, she had her revenge on the death of Henri II by taking Chenonceau from her and building the two-storey gallery across the River Cher. With the accession of Charles IX she became regent and tried to uphold the authority of the monarchy during the Wars of Religion by manoeuvring skilfully between the Guises and the Bourbons, making use of diplomacy, marriage alliances and family intrigue.

Art and Culture

ARCHITECTURE AND ART

GOTHIC PERIOD

In addition to the castles built for the dukes of Anjou, such as Saumur, manor houses and mansions were constructed in the 14C for merchants who had grown rich through trade. The 15C saw a proliferation in the lively ornate Gothic style of châteaux built of brick with white stone facings, such as the château at Lassay, of manor houses such as Le Clos-Lucé near Amboise, of town mansions with projecting stair turrets and high dormers, and of half-timbered houses. The finest examples of Gothic houses are to be found in Le Mans, Chinon and Tours.

Gardens

Monastic gardens, such as those belonging to the abbeys in Bourgueil, Marmoutier and Cormery, consisted of an orchard, a vegetable patch with a fish pond and a medicinal herb garden.

In the 15C they were succeeded by square flower beds, created by King René at his manor houses in Anjou and by Louis XI at Plessis-lès-Tours. A fresh note was introduced with shady arbours and fountains where the paths intersected; entertainment was provided by animals at liberty or kept in menageries or aviaries.

RENAISSANCE PERIOD

The Renaissance did not spring into existence at the wave of a magic wand at the end of the Italian campaigns. Before the wars in Italy, Italian artists had been welcomed to the French court and the court of Anjou; Louis XI and King René had employed sculptors and medallion makers such as Francesco Laurana, Niccolo Spinelli and Jean Candida. New blood, however, was imported into local art by the arrival of artists from Naples in 1495 at the behest of Charles VIII.

At Amboise and Chaumont and even at Chenonceau, Azay or Chambord, the châteaux still looked like fortresses but the machicolations assumed a decorative role. Large windows flanked by pilasters appeared in the façades, which were decorated with medallions; the steep roofs were decorated with lofty dormers and carved chimneys. Italian influence is most apparent in the low-relief ornamentation. At Chambord and Le Lude the decor was refined by local masters such as Pierre Trinqueau.

The Italian style is most obvious in the exterior of the François I wing at Blois where Il Boccadoro copied Bramante's invention of the rhythmic façade which featured alternating windows and niches separated by pilasters. Later, as in Beaugency town hall, came semicircular arches and superimposed orders, then the domes and pavilions which mark the birth of Classical architecture.

The Italians created new types of staircases: two spirals intertwined as at Chambord, or straight flights of steps beneath coffered ceilings as at Chenonceau, Azay-le-Rideau and Poncé.

The Renaissance also inspired a number of towns halls – Orléans, Beaugency, Loches – and several private houses – Hôtel Toutin in Orléans, Hôtel Gouin in Tours and Hôtel Pincé in Angers.

Gardens

In his enthusiasm for Neapolitan gardens, Charles VIII brought with him from his kingdom in Sicily a gardener called **Dom Pacello de Mercogliano**, a Neapolitan monk, who laid out the gardens at Amboise and Blois; Louis XII entrusted him with the royal vegetable plot at Château-Gaillard near Amboise. Pacello popularised the use of ornate flower beds bordered with yew and fountains with sculpted basins. The gardens of Chenonceau and Villandry give a good idea of his style.

The extraordinary vegetable garden at Villandry, whose decorative motifs were highly popular during the Renaissance, has retained a number of traditional and monastic features dating from the Middle Ages; the rose trees planted in a symmetrical pattern symbolise the monks, each digging in his own plot.

CLASSICAL PERIOD (17C–18C)

Following the removal of the court to the Paris region (Île-de-France), architecture in the Loire Valley fell into decline. Handsome buildings were still constructed but the designers came from Paris. In the more austere climate of the 17C the pompous style of the Sun King displaced the graceful fantasy of the Renaissance and the picturesque asymmetry of medieval buildings. The trend was towards pediments, domes (Cheverny) and the Greek orders (Gaston-d'Orléans wing at Blois). Tower structures were abandoned in favour of rectangular pavilions containing huge rooms with monumental fireplaces decorated with caryatids and painted ceilings with exposed beams; they were covered with steep roofs in the French style.

There was a new wave of château building, but the main legacy of the 18C is in the towns. Great terraces were built in Orléans, Tours and Saumur with long perspectives aligned on the axis of magnificent bridges with level roadways.

ROMANESQUE (11C–12C)

Orléanais

The church in Germigny-des-Prés, which dates from the Carolingian period, and the Benedictine basilica of St-Benoît are particularly fine examples of Romanesque art in the Orléans area. There are two pretty churches in the Cher valley at St-Aignan and Selles.

Touraine

Various influences from Poitou are evident: apses with column buttresses, domed transepts, doorways without pediments. The bell-towers are unusual: square or octagonal with spires surrounded at the base by turrets.

Anjou

Angevin buildings are clustered round Baugé and Saumur. The church in Cunault shows the influence of Poitou in the nave buttressed by high aisles with groined vaulting. The domes roofing the nave of the abbey church at Fontevraud and the absence of aisles are features of the Aquitaine School.

FROM ROMANESQUE TO GOTHIC

The **Plantagenet style**, which is also known as **Angevin**, takes its name from Henry Plantagenet. It is a transitional style which reached the height of its popularity in the early 13C and died out by the end of the century.

Angevin Vaulting

Unlike standard Gothic vaulting in which all the keystones are placed at the same level, Angevin vaulting is domical so that the central keystones are higher than the supporting arches. The best example is the cathedral of St-Maurice in Angers. This type of vaulting evolved to feature an ever finer network of increasingly fragile-looking ribs, which were eventually adorned with sculptures.

The Plantagenet style spread from the Loire valley into the Vendée, Poitou, Saintonge and the Garonne Valley. At the end of the 13C it was introduced into southern Italy by Charles of Anjou.

GOTHIC (12C–15C)

Gothic art is characterised by the use of intersecting vaults and the pointed arch. The triforium, which originally was blind, is pierced by apertures which eventually give way to high windows. The tall, slender columns, which were crowned by capitals supporting the vaulting, were originally cylindrical but later flanked by engaged columns. In the final development the capitals were abandoned and the roof ribs descended directly into the columns.

The **Flamboyant style** follows this pattern; the diagonal ribs are supplemented by other, purely decorative, ribs called liernes and tiercerons.

The Flamboyant style (15C) of architecture is to be found in the façade of La Trinité in Vendôme and of St-Gatien in Tours, in Notre-Dame-de-Cléry and in the Sainte-Chapelle at Châteaudun.

RENAISSANCE AND CLASSICAL STYLES (16C–17C–18C)

Italian influence is strongly evident in the decoration of **Renaissance** churches: basket-handle or round-

headed arches, numerous recesses for statues. Interesting examples can be seen at Montrésor, Ussé, Champigny-sur-Veude and La Bourgonnière.
In the **Classical** period (17C–18C) religious architecture was designed to create a majestic effect, with superimposed Greek orders, pediments over doorways, domes and flanking vaulting. The church of Notre-Dame-des-Ardilliers in Saumur has a huge dome whereas the church of St-Vincent in Blois is dominated by a scrolled pediment.

STAINED GLASS

A **stained-glass window** is made of pieces of coloured glass fixed with lead to an iron frame. The perpendicular divisions of a window are called **lights**. Metal oxides were added to the constituent materials of white glass to give a wide range of colours. Details were often drawn in with dark paint and fixed by firing. Varied and surprising effects were obtained by altering the length of firing and by the impurities in the oxides and defects in the glass.
The earliest stained-glass windows to have survived date from the 12C (The Ascension in Le Mans Cathedral).
In the 12C–13C the colours were vivid with rich blues and reds predominating; the glass and leading were thick and smoothed down with a plane; the subject matter was naïve and confined to superimposed medallions.
The Cistercians favoured grisaille windows, which were composed of clear-to-greenish glass with foliage designs on a cross-hatched background, giving a greyish effect.
The master-glaziers of the 14C–15C discovered how to make a golden yellow; lighter colours were developed, the leading became less heavy as it was produced using new tools and techniques, the glass was thinner and the windows larger. Gothic canopies appeared over the human figures.
Windows became delicately coloured pictures in the 16C in thick lead frames, often copied from Renaissance canvases with strict attention to detail and perspective; there are fine examples at

S. Sauvignier/MICHELIN

14C stained-glass window, Abbaye de la Trinité, Vendôme

Champigny-sur-Veude, Montrésor and Sully-sur-Loire.
In the 17C–19C traditional stained glass was often replaced by vitrified enamel or painted glass without lead surrounds. In the cathedral of Orléans there are 17C windows with white diamond panes and gold bands, along with 19C windows portraying Joan of Arc.
The need to restore or replace old stained glass stimulated a revival of the art in the **20C**. Representational or abstract compositions of great variety emerged from the workshops of the painter-glaziers: **Max Ingrand, Alfred Manessier, Jean Le Moal, M Rollo**.

MURAL PAINTING AND FRESCOES

In the Middle Ages the interiors of ecclesiastical buildings were decorated with paintings, motifs or morally and spiritually uplifting scenes. A school of mural painting akin to that in Poitou developed in the Loire region. The surviving works of this school are well preserved owing to the mild climate and low humidity. The paintings are recognisable by their weak matte colours against light backgrounds. The style is livelier and less formalised than in Burgundy or the Massif Central whereas the composition is more sober than in Poitou. Two techniques were used: **fresco work**, which was done with watercolours on fresh plaster thus making it impossible to touch it up later; and **mural painting**, where tempera colours were applied to a dry surface, producing a less durable work of art.

Romanesque Period

The art of fresco work with its Byzantine origins was adopted by the Benedictines of Monte Cassino in Italy, who in turn transmitted the art to the monks of Cluny in Burgundy. The latter used this art form in their abbeys and priories, from where it spread throughout the country.

Technique

The fresco technique was the one most commonly used, although beards and eyes were often added once the plaster was dry with the result that they have since disappeared. The figures, drawn in red ochre, were sometimes highlighted with touches of black, green and the sky-blue so characteristic of the region.

Subject Matter

The subjects were often inspired by smaller-scale works. The most common theme for the oven vaulting was Christ the King Enthroned, majestic and severe; the reverse of the façade (at the opposite end of the church from the apse) often carried the *Last Judgement*; the walls depicted scenes from the New Testament whereas the Saints and Apostles adorned the pillars. Other subjects portrayed frequently are the Conflict of the Virtues and Vices, and the Labours of the Months.

Good examples of fresco painting are to be found throughout the Loire Valley in Areines, Souday, St-Jacques-des-Guérets, Lavardin and best of all in the chapel of St-Gilles at Montoire. There is also a fine work in St-Aignan in the Cher valley. The crypt of the church in Tavant in the Vienne valley is decorated with lively paintings of high quality.

In Anjou a man called Fulk seems to have supervised the decoration of the cloisters in the abbey of St-Aubin in Angers. His realistic style, although slightly stilted in the drawing, seems to spring from the Poitou School. More characteristic of the Loire valley are the Virgin and Christ the King from Ponginé in the Baugé region.

Gothic Period

It was not until the 15C and the end of the Hundred Years' War that new compositions were produced on themes which were to remain in fashion until the mid-16C. These were really more mural paintings than frescoes and new subjects were added to the traditional repertoire; a gigantic *St Christopher* often appeared at the entrance to a church (*see Amboise*), whereas the legend of the Three Living and Three Dead, represented by three proud huntsmen meeting three skeletons, symbolised the brevity and vanity of human life. In the Loire Valley such paintings are to be found in Alluyes, Lassay and Villiers. Two compositions with strange iconography adorn the neighbouring churches in Asnières-sur-Vège and Auvers-le-Hamon.

Renaissance

In the 16C paintings in churches became rarer. There are, however, two surviving examples from this period: the Entombment in the church in Jarzé and the paintings in the chapter house of Fontevraud Abbey.

SECULAR PAINTING

During the 15C and 16C, the French School asserted itself, first through the work of Jean Fouquet (c. 1420–80), a portrait painter and miniaturist native of Tours who travelled to Italy, and later through the paintings of the Master of Moulins (late 15C), sometimes identified with Jean Perréal (c. 1455–1530).

The Flemish artist Jean Clouet, commissioned by Louis XII and François I, and his son François Clouet (1520–72), who was born in Tours, became famous for their portraits of the Valois.

Last but not least, Leonardo da Vinci (1452–1519) spent the last three years of his life at the court of François I.

TAPESTRIES FROM THE LOIRE WORKSHOPS

Hanging tapestries, which had been in existence since the 8C to exclude draughts or divide up huge rooms, became very popular in the 14C. The weavers worked from cartoons or preparatory sketches using wool woven with silk, gold or silver threads on horizontal (low warp – *basse lisse*) or vertical (high warp – *haute lisse*) looms.

Their value made tapestries ideal for use as investments or diplomatic gifts; as well as those commissioned for châteaux or even specific rooms, some were hung in churches or even in the streets. The most famous is the 14C Apocalypse tapestry *(see Angers)*.

The *mille-fleurs* (thousand flowers) tapestries evoked late medieval scenes – showing an idealised life of enticing gardens, tournaments and hunting scenes – against a green, blue or pink background strewn with a variety of flowers, plants and small animals. These are attributed to the Loire Valley workshops (c. 1500). Good examples can be seen in Saumur, Langeais and Angers.

THE RENAISSANCE TO THE 20C

The use of cartoons (full-scale designs, usually in reverse) instead of paintings, and more sophisticated weaving techniques and materials rendered greater detail possible. The number of colours increased and panels were surrounded by wide borders. In the 18C the art of portraiture was introduced into tapestry work.

In the 20C Jean Lurçat, originally a tapestry renovator, advocated the use of natural dyes. Contemporary weavers started to experiment with new techniques in order to create relief and three-dimensional effects.

GEMMAIL

Gemmail is a modern art medium consisting of assembling particles of coloured glass over a light source. The inventor of this art form was **Jean Crotti** (1878–1958). The Malherbe-Navarre brothers, an interior decorator and a physicist, provided the technical expertise; they discovered a bonding agent which did not affect the constituent elements.

Moulin de la Herpinière, Turquant

S. Sauvignier/MICHELIN

RURAL ARCHITECTURE

Mills of Anjou

Very early on, the extensive network of waterways encouraged the construction of a great many watermills of all kinds (barge-mills, bank-mills, mills with hanging wheels). But the region is furthermore exposed for most of the year to strong winds blowing from the southwest to the northwest – a fact which led to the proliferation of various types of windmills as early as the 13C. Some of these have been restored or converted and are still standing today. The region still features many structures sometimes open to the public during the summer season or on request. They fall into three categories:

CORN MILLS

Characteristic of the Anjou landscape, the corn mill consists of a conical stone base called the cellar, surmounted by a wooden cabin bearing the shaft and sails. The cellar was used for storing grain, flour and spare parts; in some cases, it also housed stables and a shed.

ABC OF ARCHITECTURE

Ecclesiastical architecture

LE MANS – Ground plan of St-Julien Cathedral (12C-15C)

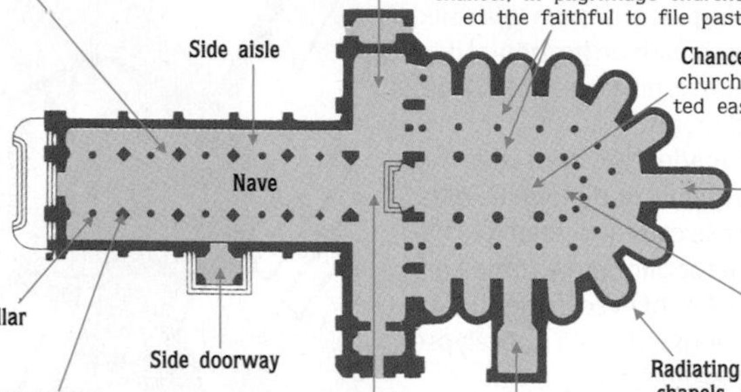

ST-AIGNAN – Longitudinal section of the collegiate church (11C-12C), transept and chancel

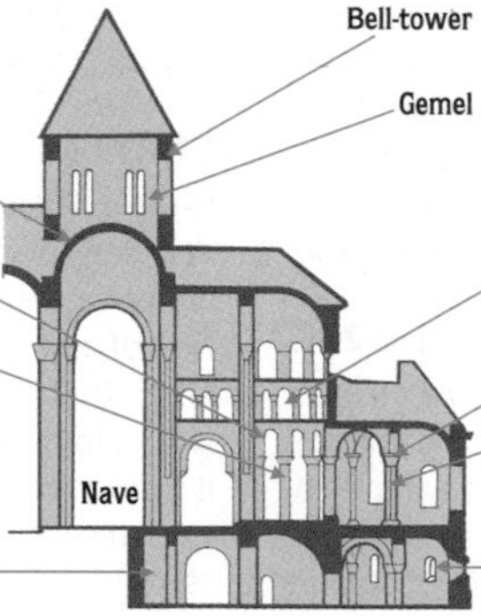

ANGERS – Vaulting of St-Serge Church (early 13C)

This type of domical vaulting is known in France as **Angevin** or **Plantagenet vaulting.** It is curved so that the central keystone is higher than the supporting arches, unlike ordinary Gothic vaulting where they are at the same level. Towards the end of the 12C, Angevin vaulting became lighter, with slimmer, more numerous ribs springing from slender round columns. Early in the 13C, church interiors became higher, beneath soaring lierne vaulting decorated with elegant sculptures.

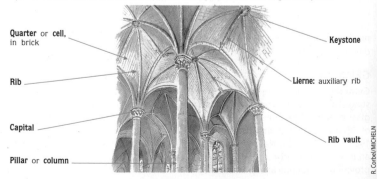

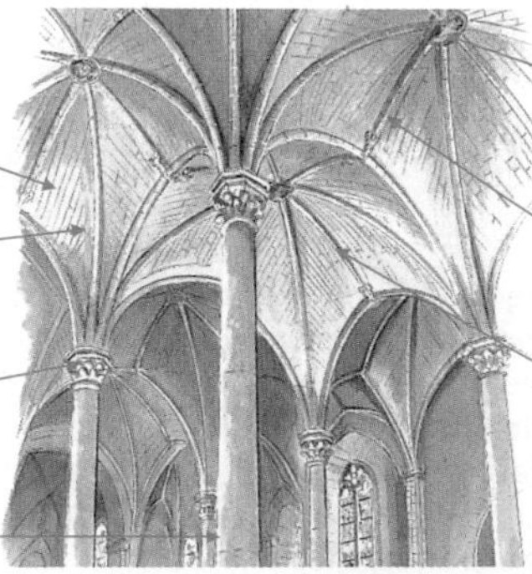

ST-BENOÎT-SUR-LOIRE – Basilique Ste-Marie (11C-12C)

Romanesque church. Ground plan with double transept is rare in France; the small, or false, transept crosses the chancel.

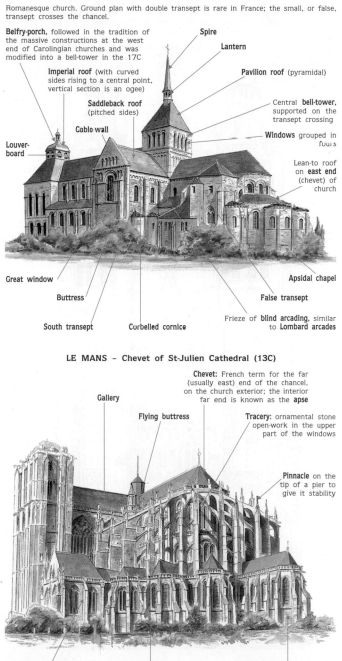

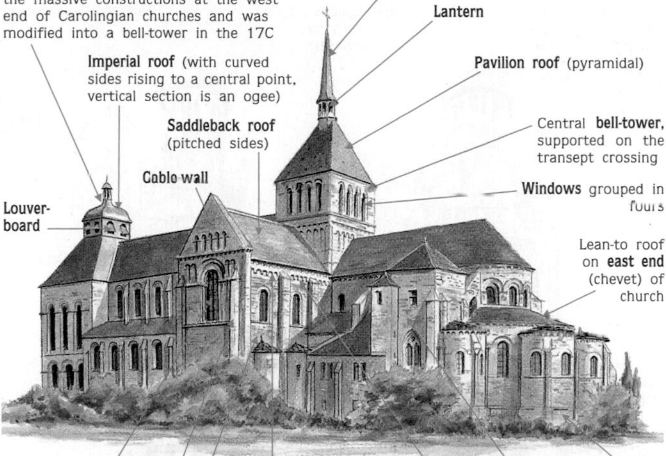

LE MANS – Chevet of St-Julien Cathedral (13C)

TOURS – Façade of St-Gatien Cathedral (13C-16C)

St-Gatien is a fine example of a harmonious combination of styles: Romanesque at the base of the towers, Flamboyant Gothic on the façade, and Renaissance at the top of the bell-towers which are crowned with **lantern-domes**.

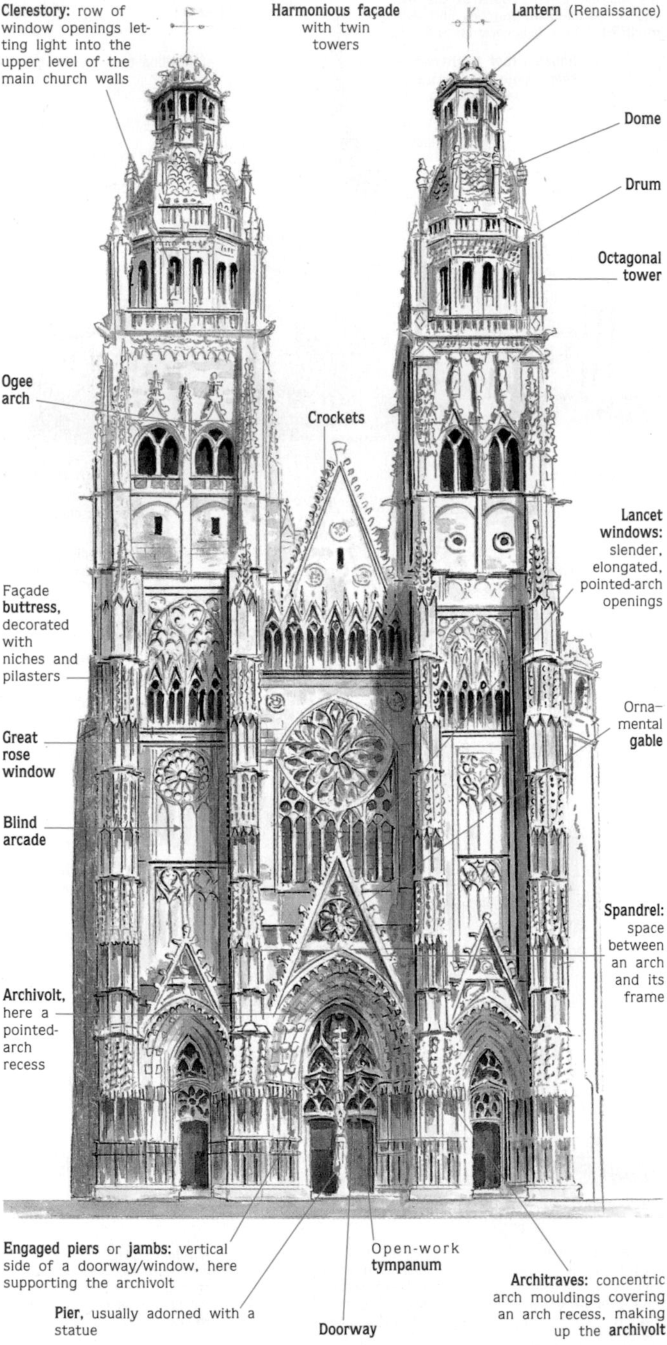

LORRIS – Organ case (15C) in Notre-Dame Church

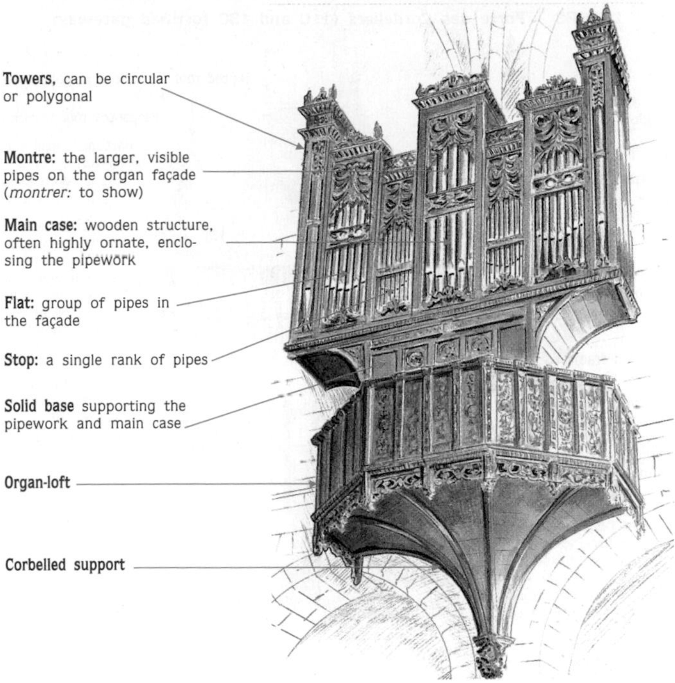

ANGERS – Monumental 19C pulpit in St-Maurice Cathedral

This work by Abbé René Choyer is a pastiche (1855) of 13C Gothic art. As a whole, the pulpit embodies an in-depth knowledge of medieval architecture and sculpture.

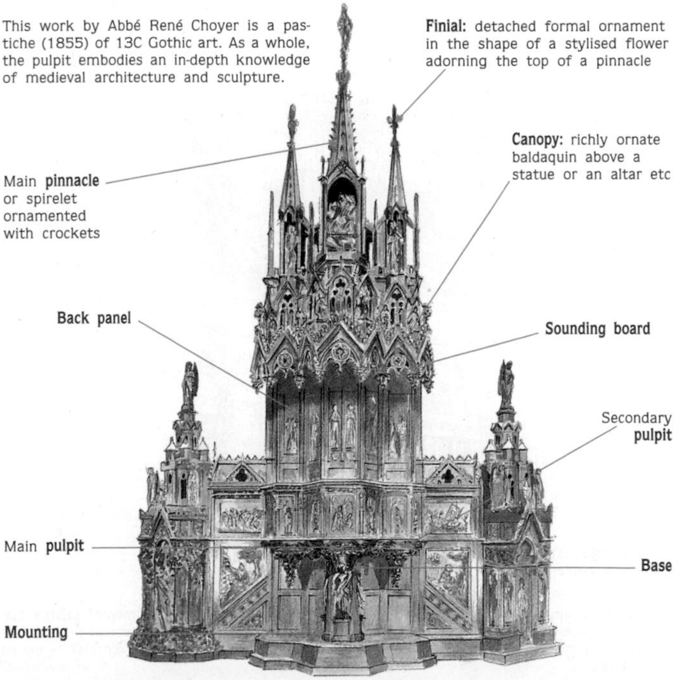

R. Corbel/MICHELIN

Military architecture

LOCHES – Porte des Cordeliers (11C and 13C fortified gateway)

Civil architecture

BLOIS – Château, François-1er staircase (16C)

The spiral stairway is built inside an octagonal staircase half set into the façade. It opens onto the main courtyard in a series of balconies which form loggias. The king and his court would view all sorts of entertainment from here: the arrival of dignitaries, jousting, hunting or military displays.

SERRANT - Château (16C-17C)

Brown schist, white tufa and grey-blue slate lend great character to this luxurious residence in which Renaissance and Classical styles are harmoniously combined.

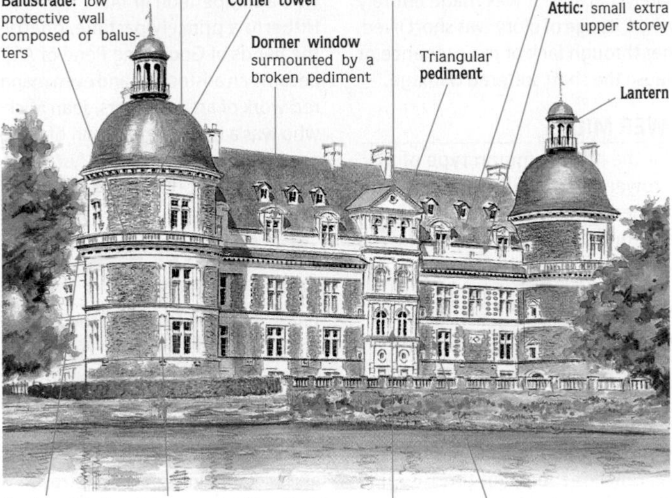

VILLANDRY — Layout of the Jardins d'Amour (Renaissance style)

The four gardens on the theme of love consist of box borders punctuated by clipped yews and filled with flowers. Each box parterre is laid out in the form of symbolic images: tragic love is represented by sword blades and daggers; unfaithful love by cuckolds' horns, ladies' fans and love letters etc

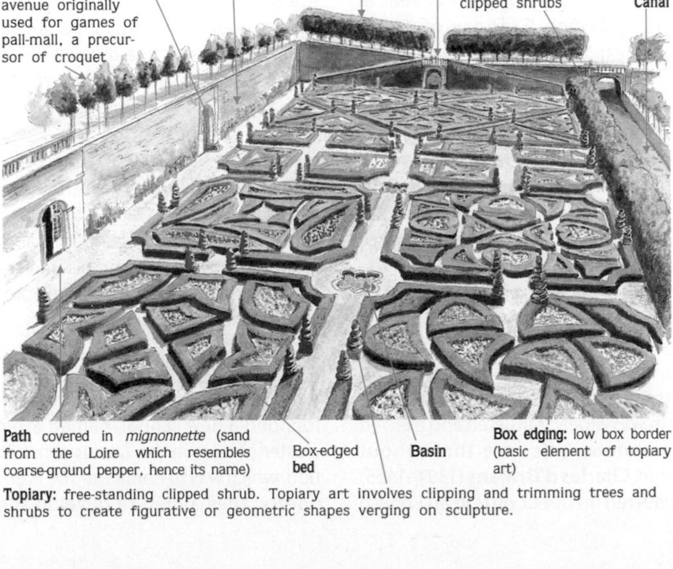

R. Corbel/MICHELN

POST MILLS

The post mill was a huge wooden structure supporting the sails, the millstone as well as the whole mechanism. Unfortunately, because it was made entirely of wood, its age of glory was short lived, either through lack of maintenance or because the shaft suffered damage.

TOWER MILLS

By far the most common type of mill, the tower mill – built in stone – has remained comparatively intact over the centuries. The conical roof, with its rotating cap, carries the sails.

LITERATURE

"LE BEAU PARLER"

Since the Loire Valley was the cradle of France, it is here that old France is recalled in the sayings which have shaped the French language. It is said that the best French is spoken in the Touraine region; though this does not mean that you hear nothing but the most sophisticated, high-brow language. However, the French language has certainly found some of its finest expression in the Loire Valley, where the peace and beauty of the countryside have fostered many leading French writers.

MIDDLE AGES

In the 6C, under the influence of St Martin, Tours became a great seat of learning. Bishop **Gregory of Tours** wrote the first history of the Gauls in his *Historia Francorum* and **Alcuin of York** founded a famous school of calligraphy at the behest of Charlemagne, while art in the 11C came under the influence of courtly life in the Latin poems of **Baudri de Bourgueil**. At the beginning of the 13C Orléans witnessed the impact of the popular and lyrical language of the *Romance of the Rose*, a didactic poem by two successive authors – the mannered **Guillaume de Lorris**, who wrote the first 4 000 lines, and the realist **Jean de Meung**, who added the final 18 000. The poem was widely translated and exerted tremendous influence throughout Europe. **Charles d'Orléans** (1391–1465) discovered his poetic gifts in an English prison. He was a patron of the arts and author of several short but elegant poems; at his court in Blois he organised poetic jousts – **François Villon** won a competition in 1457.
Hitherto a princely pastime, poetry in the hands of Good King René of Anjou became an aristocratic and even mannered work of art. In Angers, Jean Michel, who was a doctor and a man of letters, produced his monumental *Mystery of the Passion*; its 65 000 lines took four days to perform.

RENAISSANCE AND HUMANISM

When the vicissitudes of the Hundred Years War obliged the French court to move from Paris to Touraine, new universities were founded in Orléans (1305) and Angers (1364). They very soon attracted a vast body of students and became important centres in the study of European humanism.
Among those who came to study and to teach were Erasmus and William Bude, Melchior Wolmar, a Hellenist from Swabia, and the reformers Calvin and Theodore Beza; **Étienne Dolet**, a native of Orléans, preached his atheist doctrines for which he was hanged and burned in Paris.
François Rabelais (1494–1553), who was born near Chinon, must be about the best-known son of the Touraine. After studying in Angers, he became a learned Benedictine monk and then a famous doctor. In the adventures of Gargantua and Pantagruel he expressed his ideas on education, religion and philosophy. He was very attached to his native country and made it the setting for the Picrocholine war in his books. His comic and realistic style, his extraordinarily rich vocabulary and his universal curiosity made him the foremost prose writer of his period.

THE PLÉIADE

A group of seven poets from the Loire founded a new school, named after a cluster of stars in the Taurus constellation, which was to dominate 16C French poetry; they aimed to develop their language by imitating Horace and the Ancients. Their undoubted leader was **Pierre de Ronsard**, the Prince of Poets from near Vendôme, but it was **Joachim du Bellay** from Anjou who wrote the manifesto of the group, *The Defence and Illustration of the French Language*, which was published in 1549.

The other members of the group were **Jean-Antoine de Baïf** from La Flèche, Jean Dorat, Étienne Jodelle, Marot and Pontus de Tyard who all held the position of Court Poet; their subjects were nature, women, their native country and its special quality, *la douceur angevine*.

CLASSICISM AND THE AGE OF ENLIGHTENMENT

At the end of the Wars of Religion, when the king and the court returned north to the Paris region (Île-de-France), literature became more serious and philosophical. The **Marquis of Racan** composed verses on the banks of the Loir and the Protestant Academy in Saumur supported the first works of **René Descartes**. In the following century, **Néricault-Destouches**, from Touraine, followed in Molière's footsteps with his comedies of character; Voltaire stayed at Sully; Rousseau and his companion Thérèse Levasseur lived at Chenonceau; Beaumarchais, who wrote *The Barber of Seville,* settled at Vouvray and visited the Duke of Choiseul in exile at Chanteloup.

ROMANTICISM

The pamphleteer **Paul-Louis Courier** (1772–1825) and the songwriter **Pierre-Jean de Béranger** (1780–1857), both active during the second Bourbon restoration, were sceptical, witty and liberal in politics. **Alfred de Vigny** (1797–1863), a native of Loches who became a soldier and a poet, painted an idyllic picture of Touraine in his novel, *Cinq-Mars*.

The greatest literary genius of Touraine was however **Honoré de Balzac** (1799–1850). He was born in Tours and brought up in Vendôme; he loved the Loire Valley and used it as a setting for several of the numerous portraits in his vast work, *The Human Comedy*.

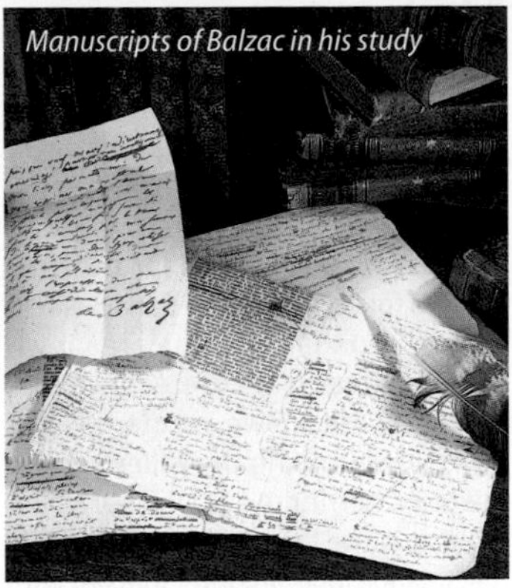
Manuscripts of Balzac in his study

J.-B. Darrasse/MICHELIN

CONTEMPORARY WRITERS

The poet **Charles Péguy**, born in Orléans, wrote about Joan of Arc and his beloved Beauce. **Marcel Proust** also returned to the Beauce in his novel *Remembrance of Things Past*. Another poet, **Max Jacob** (1876–1944), spent many years in work and meditation at the abbey of St-Benoît-sur-Loire.

The Sologne calls to mind the young novelist, **Alain-Fournier**, and his famous work, *Le Grand Meaulnes (The Lost Domain)*. The character of Raboliot the poacher is a picturesque evocation of his native country by the author **Maurice Genevoix** (1890–1980), a member of the Academy. The humourist **Georges Courteline** (1858–1929) was born in Touraine which was also the retreat of several writers of international reputation: Maeterlinck (Nobel Prize in 1911) at Coudray-Montpensier; Anatole France (Nobel Prize in 1921) at La Béchellerie; Bergson (Nobel Prize in 1927) at La Gaudinière. **René Benjamin** (1885–1948) settled in Touraine where he wrote *The Prodigious Life of Balzac* and other novels.

Angers was the home of **René Bazin** (1853–1932), who was greatly attached to the traditional virtues and his home ground, and of his great-nephew, **Hervé Bazin** (1911–96), whose violent attacks on conventional values were directly inspired by his native town.

Nature

LANDSCAPES

GEOLOGICAL FORMATION

The Loire region is enclosed by the ancient crystalline masses of the Morvan, Armorican Massif and Massif Central and forms part of the Paris Basin.

In the Secondary Era the area invaded by the sea was covered by a soft, chalky deposit known as **tufa**, which is now exposed along the valley sides of the Loir, Cher, Indre and Vienne. A later deposit is the limestone of the sterile marshlands *(gâtines)* interspersed with tracts of sands and clays supporting forests and heathlands. Once the sea had retreated, great freshwater lakes deposited more limestone, the surface of which is often broken down into loess or silt. These areas are known as **champagnes** or *champeignes*.

During the Tertiary Era, the folding of the Alpine mountain zone created the Massif Central, and rivers running down from this new watershed were often laden with sandy clays, which, when they were deposited, gave rise to areas such as the Sologne and Orléans Forest. Later subsidence in the west permitted the ingress of the **Faluns Sea** as far as Blois, Thouars and Preuilly-sur-Claise, creating a series of shell marl beds *(falunières)* on the borders of Ste-Maure plateau and the hills to the north of the Loire. Rivers originally flowing northwards were attracted in a westerly direction by the sea, thus explaining the great change in the direction of the Loire at Orléans. The sea finally retreated for good, leaving an undulating countryside with the river network the most important geographical feature. The alluvial silts *(varennes)* deposited by the Loire and its tributaries were to add an extremely fertile light soil composed of coarse sand.

The limestone terraces, which provided shelter, and the naturally fertile soil here attracted early human habitation, of which there are traces from the prehistoric era through the Gallo-Roman period (site of Cherré) to the Middle Ages (Brain-sur-Allonnes). This substratum is immediately reflected in the landscape: troglodyte dwellings in the limestone layers, vineyards on the slopes, cereals on the silt plateaux, vegetables in the alluvial silt. The marshy tracts of the Sologne were for many centuries untilled since they were unhealthy and unsuitable for any sort of culture.

THE RIVER LOIRE

The longest French river (1 013km/629mi) springs up beneath the Mont Gerbier de Jonc, in the Vivarais region, on the southern edge of the Massif Central mountain range. The flow of the Loire is somewhat erratic: in summer it is reduced to a few meagre streams meandering along the wide, sandy river bed, but in autumn, during the rainy season, or in spring, when the thaw comes, the

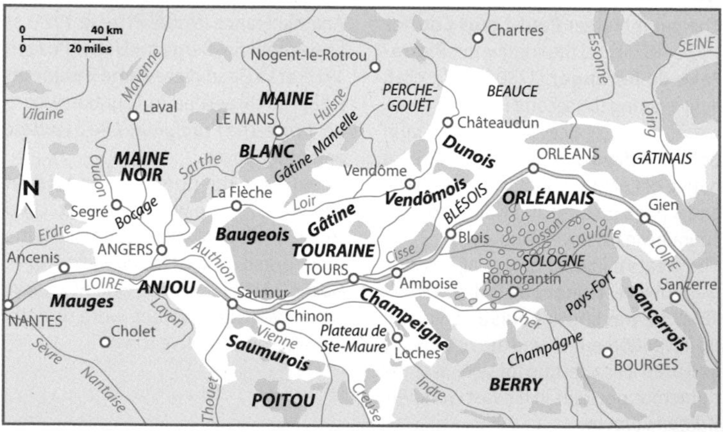

Marshland of the Sologne

S. Sauvignier/MICHELIN

river is in spate, sometimes causing memorable floods (the worst recorded floods took place in 1846, 1856, 1866, 1910 and 1980).

Until the end of the 19C, the Loire was a busy waterway in spite of its unpredictable behaviour: flat-bottomed boats rigged with square sails used to sail up and down the river and its tributaries, in particular the Cher, carrying cargo and passengers between Orléans and Nantes (even horse-drawn carriages were placed on rafts).

In 1832, the first steam-powered regular service between Orléans and Nantes was inaugurated, but the development of railways soon struck a decisive blow to boat transport.

LANDSCAPES

The Garden of France

From whatever direction you approach the Loire region – across the immense plains of the Beauce, through the mysterious Berry countryside or the green wooded farmland *(bocage)* of the Gâtine Mancelle – you are always welcomed by the sight of vineyards, white houses and flowers. For many foreigners this peaceful, fertile countryside is a typically French landscape. But make no mistake, the Garden of France is not simply a sort of Eden laden with fruit and flowers.

The historian Michelet once described it as a "homespun cloak with golden fringes", meaning that the valleys – the golden fringes – in all their wonderful fertility, bordered plateaux whose harshness was tempered only by occasional fine forests.

Northern Berry

This region, lying between the Massif Central and the Loire country, includes the **Pays Fort**, an area of clay soil sloping down towards the Sologne. The melancholy atmosphere of the landscape is described by Alain-Fournier in his novel *Le Grand Meaulnes (The Lost Domain)*. Between the Cher and the Indre is the Champeigne, an area of limestone silt pock-marked with holes *(mardelles)*.

Orléanais and Blésois

Below Gien the valley opens out, the hills are lower and a refreshing breeze makes the leaves tremble on the long lines of poplars and willows. This is the gateway to the Orléanais, which covers the Beauce, the Loire Valley (i.e. the Dunois and Vendômois), the Sologne and Blésois (Blois region). In the vicinity of St-Benoît, the valley, commonly known as the **Val**, is a series of meadows; beyond, horticulture predominates with the growing of seedlings and rosebushes on the alluvial deposits known locally as *layes*. There is a proliferation of greenhouses, some with artificial heating. Orchards and vineyards flourish on the south-facing slopes.

From Orléans to Chaumont along its northern bank, the Loire eats into the Beauce limestone and then into the flinty chalkland and tufa. On the south the river laps the alluvial sands brought along by its own waters. This area, where asparagus and early vegetables are grown, features large expanses of dense brushwood full of game where the kings of France once used to hunt. The great châteaux then begin: Blois, Chambord, Cheverny, Chaumont, and so on.

The **Beauce**, the granary of France, a treeless plain covered with a thin layer (2m/6ft maximum) of fertile silt or loess, extends into the area between the Loire and Loir known as the Petite Beauce, where silt gives way to clay in Marchenoir Forest. In the **Sologne** and the **Forest of Orléans** meagre crops alternate with lakes and woodland.

Touraine

The comfortable opulence of the **Loire Valley** will delight the visitor already charmed by the dazzling quality of the light. The blue waters of the Loire, which flow slowly between golden sandbanks, have worn a course through the soft tufa chalk. Channels abandoned by the main river are divided into backwaters *(boires)* or occupied by tributary streams such as the Cher, Indre, Vienne and Cisse.

From Amboise to Tours the flinty chalk soil of the valley slopes is clad with vineyards producing the well-known Vouvray and Montlouis wines. **Troglodyte** houses have been carved out of the white tufa. The **Véron**, lying between the Loire and the Vienne, is a patchwork of small fields and gardens bordered by rows of poplars.

The **Gâtine** of Touraine, between the Loir and Loire, was once a great forest; the area is now under cultivation, although large tracts of heath and woodland have survived (Chandelais and Bercé forests). The main features of the Touraine Champeigne, where the fields are studded with walnut trees, are the forests of Brouard and Loches and the Montrésor Gâtine. The plateaux of Montrichard and Ste-Maure are similar in many ways to the **Champeigne**.

Anjou

The north bank of the Loire consists of a fertile alluvial plain (**varenne de Bourgueil**) where spring vegetables thrive, surrounded by the famous vineyards planted on warm, dry gravels lying at the foot of the pine-covered hills. Between the Loire and the Authion, lined with willows, green pastures alternate with rich market gardens growing vegetables, flowers and fruit trees. The land below Angers is covered with vineyards, especially the famous Coulée de Serrant vineyard.

The pleasant **Saumurois**, which lies south of the Loire and extends from Fontevraud and Montsoreau to Doué-la-Fontaine and the Layon Valley, has three differing aspects: woods, plains and hillsides – the slopes of which are often clad with vineyards, producing excellent wine including the white wine to which the town of Saumur has given its name. The many caves in the steep, tufa valley sides of the Loire around Chênehutte-les-Tuffeaux are now used for mushroom growing. North of the river lies the sandy **Baugeois**, an area of woods (oak, pine and chestnut) and arable land.

Angers marks the border between the schist countryside of Black Anjou and the sharply contrasting limestone of White Anjou.

The countryside is greener, heralding an area of wooded farmland – the Bocage Segréen and **Les Mauges** – which is characterised by a patchwork of small fields surrounded by hedge-topped banks criss-crossed by deep lanes leading to small farmsteads. Around Angers, nursery and market gardens specialise in flowers and seedlings.

Maine

Only the southern part of this region is included in the guide.

The Lower Maine (**Bas-Maine**) otherwise known as Black Maine, is a region of sandstones, granites and schists and wooded farmland. Geographically this area is part of the Breton Armorican Massif. The Upper Maine (**Haut-Maine**), covering the Sarthe and Huisne basins, is known as the White Maine because of its limestone soils.

EARTH'S BOUNTY

A well-disposed lie of the land, fertile soil and temperate climate make the Loire Valley ideal for the cultivation of trees and market gardens. Fruit and vegetables make a significant contribution to the economy of the Centre-Val de Loire and Pays de la Loire regions, accounting for around 20 percent of domestic production. The cultivation of many of the varieties found in the Loire Valley dates from as early as Roman rule, whereas others introduced to the region during the Renaissance continue to thrive.

FRUIT

Ripening well in the local climate, the succulent fruits of the region are renowned throughout France. The most common are apples, pears and, more recently, blackcurrants. Many have a noble pedigree: Reine-Claude greengages are named after Claude de France, the wife of François I; Bon-chrétien pears originated from a cutting planted by St Francis of Paola in Louis XI's orchard at Plessis-lès-Tours. They were introduced into Anjou by Jean Bourré, Louis XI's Finance Minister. Rivalling the latter are the following varieties: Monsieur, Williams, a speciality of Anjou; Passe-crassane; and autumn varieties such as Conférence, Doyenné du comice and Beurré Hardy. Melons were introduced to the region by Charles VIII's Neapolitan gardener. Already in the 16C the variety and quality of the local fruit and vegetables were much praised, namely by Ronsard. The walnut and chestnut trees of the plateaux yield oil and much-prized wood (in the former case) and edible chestnuts (in the latter), often roasted during evening gatherings.
Alongside traditional varieties like the Reinette apple from Le Mans are more prolific varieties better adapted to market demands such as the Granny Smith and Golden Delicious.

EARLY VEGETABLES

A wide variety of vegetables is grown in the Loire Valley. There are two main areas of production: the stretch of valley between Angers and Saumur and the

Anjou pear orchard

Orléans region. Vegetables cultivated under glass or plastic include tomatoes, cucumbers and lettuces, especially around Orléans. Early vegetables are a speciality in the Loire Valley since, in general, they are ready two weeks before those of the Paris region. Asparagus from Vineuil and Contres, potatoes from Saumur, French beans from Touraine, onions and shallots from Anjou and Loiret and artichokes from Angers are dispatched to Rungis, the main Paris market.
One of the region's more unusual crops is mushrooms; over 60 percent of button mushrooms cultivated in France come from the Loire Valley. They are grown in the former tufa quarries near Montrichard, Montoire, Montsoreau, Tours and particularly in the Saumur area.

FLOWERS AND NURSERY GARDENS

Pots of geraniums or begonias, borders of nasturtiums and climbing wisteria with its pale mauve clusters adorn the houses. The region of Orléans-la-Source, Olivet and Doué-la-Fontaine is famous for its cultivated flowers – roses, hydrangeas, geraniums and chrysanthemums – which are grown under glass. Tulips, gladioli and lilies are grown (for bulbs) near Soings.

Beef cattle, Maine

© Champa/Fotolia.com

Nursery gardens proliferate on the alluvial soils of the Loire. The lighter soils of Véron, Bourgeuil and the Angers district are suitable for the growing of artichokes, onions and garlic for seed stock. The medicinal plants that were cultivated in the Chemillé region during the phylloxera crisis (a severe blight which destroyed many French vineyards in the 19C) are attracting renewed interest.

LIVESTOCK

Dairy stock are generally reared outdoors in the fields, except in winter, when they are kept inside and given corn silage. However, in the case of beef cattle, the animals spend most of the year feeding on pastures in the Maine, Anjou and Touraine valleys.

The main dairy cattle breeds are Prim'Holstein, Normandy and Pie-Noire, whereas the best-known beef breeds are Normandy, Maine-Anjou and especially Charolais. Dairy production is concentrated in Maine, Anjou, the Mayenne Valley, Les Mauges and in the west of the Sarthe Valley. Sheep rearing is confined to the limestone plateaux of the Upper Maine where the black-faced Bleu du Maine and Rouge de l'Ouest prosper.

Pigs can be found everywhere but particularly in Touraine, Maine and Anjou; the production of potted pork specialities – *rillettes* and *rillons* – is centred in Vouvray, Angers, Tours and Le Mans. Recently, in the Sarthe *département* a *label rouge* (red label), guaranteeing the highest quality, was awarded to free-range pigs raised on farms.

The ever-growing demand for the well-known goats' cheeses, in particular the *appellation d'origine contrôlée* (AOC) brands, Selles-sur-Cher and, more recently, Sainte-Maure, have led to an increase in goat keeping. Market days in the west country are colourful occasions: the liveliest are the calf sales in Château-Gontier and the cattle and goat sales in Cholet and Chemillé.

Poultry – Poultry rearing, firmly established in the Loire region, has developed quite considerably; its expansion is linked to the food industry and local co-operatives. This sector has two main characteristics: the high quality of its produce, thanks to many labels, in particular the most prestigious ones recommending the free-range poultry of Loué, and variety – chickens, capons, ducks, guinea fowl, turkeys, geese, quails, pigeons and, generally speaking, all game birds.

FAUNA

The Loire is frequently referred to as the "last untamed river in Europe". During the summer months, along some of its banks, the local climate can tend to resemble more that of African climes. This phenomenon, known as a topoclimate, favours the growth of many tropical plants. The Loire is also inclined to overflow, flooding the surrounding meadows and filling the ditches with water. When it eventually withdraws, leaving the gravel pits and sandbanks to dry out, it creates many natural niches and shelters, the perfect environment for myriad animal and plant species. Consequently, the banks of the Loire are home to many forms of wildlife and especially bird life attracted by the relative peace and calm of the river's waters, which are well stocked with food (water insects, larvae, tiny shellfish and amphibians).

More than 220 species of bird live in, nest in or migrate to the Loire valley every year. To get the most out of birdwatching, without disturbing the birds while respecting their nesting places, you need to identify the particular habitat associated with each species.

Along the banks of the Loire, suitable habitats include islets, gravel banks, tributary channels or *boires*, alluvial plains and marshes.
In addition to its healthy bird population, the Loire region is home to developing populations of **otter**, **European beaver**, **wild boar**, **polecat**, **pine marten**, **snakes**, **badger**, **European pond tortoise**, and **red deer**.

ISLETS AND GRAVEL BANKS

The islets, long sandbanks and high grasses found in midstream, provide safe refuges for the **common heron**, the **kingfisher**, the **great crested grebe** and the **cormorant**, who can rest peacefully, protected from intruders by a stretch of water. The irregular flow of the Loire appears to suit their reproductive pattern, as it offers many open shores suitable for building nests.
Downstream from Montsoreau, the **Île de Parnay** (a protected site closed to the public from 1 April to 15 August) alone is home to more than 750 pairs of birds between March and late June, including **black-headed gulls**, **common gulls**, **Icelandic gulls**, **common terns** and **little ringed plovers**. The **Île de Sandillon**, 15km/10mi upstream of Orléans, is home to 2 500 such pairs.

BOIRES

This is the name given to the networks of channels filled with stagnant water which line either side of the Loire, and which flow into the river when it is in spate. These channels, teeming with roach, tench and perch, provide shelter to the bittern, the moorhen, the coot, the garganey, and small perchers like the great reed warbler, which builds its nest 50cm/20in above the water, solidly attached to three or four reeds.

ALLUVIAL PLAINS

Meadows and pastures which can sometimes be flooded after heavy rains offer hospitality either to migratory birds like the whinchat and the gregarious black-tailed godwit, or to more sedentary species such as the corncrake (March to October).

Little ringed plover

Grey heron

Black-tailed godwit

MARSHES AND POOLS

Among the many migratory birds, the **osprey**, which feeds on fish, had practically disappeared from French skies in the 1940s; fortunately, its population is now on the increase. It is an impressive sight to see it skimming over the water while it looks for its prey, then darts forward, claws open, to pounce on a 30–40cm/12–15in long fish. The **water rail** is another breed which finds comfort in the long reeds and bulrushes surrounding the marshes.

Château de Chaumont-sur-Loire

DISCOVERING CHÂTEAUX OF THE LOIRE

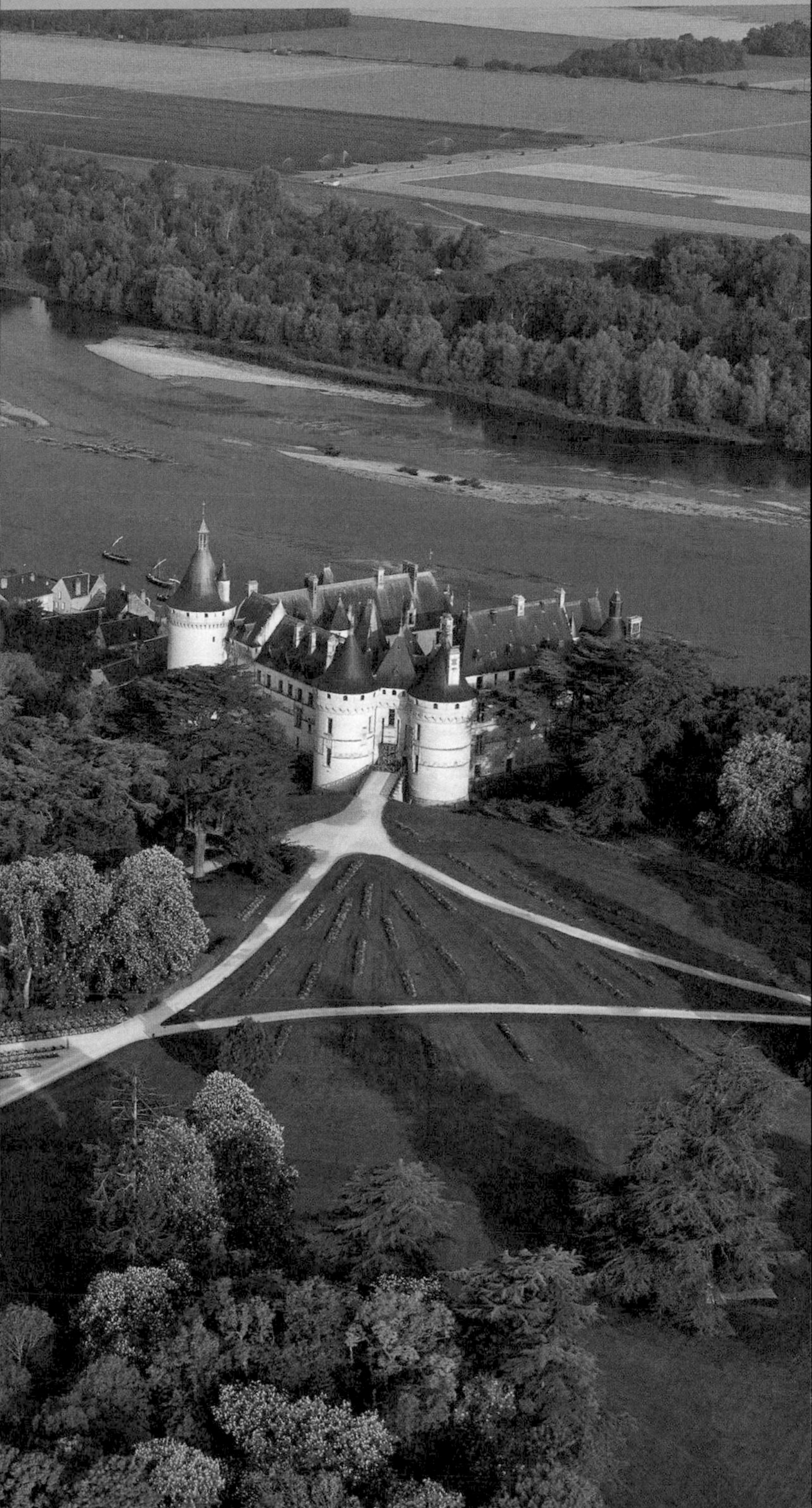

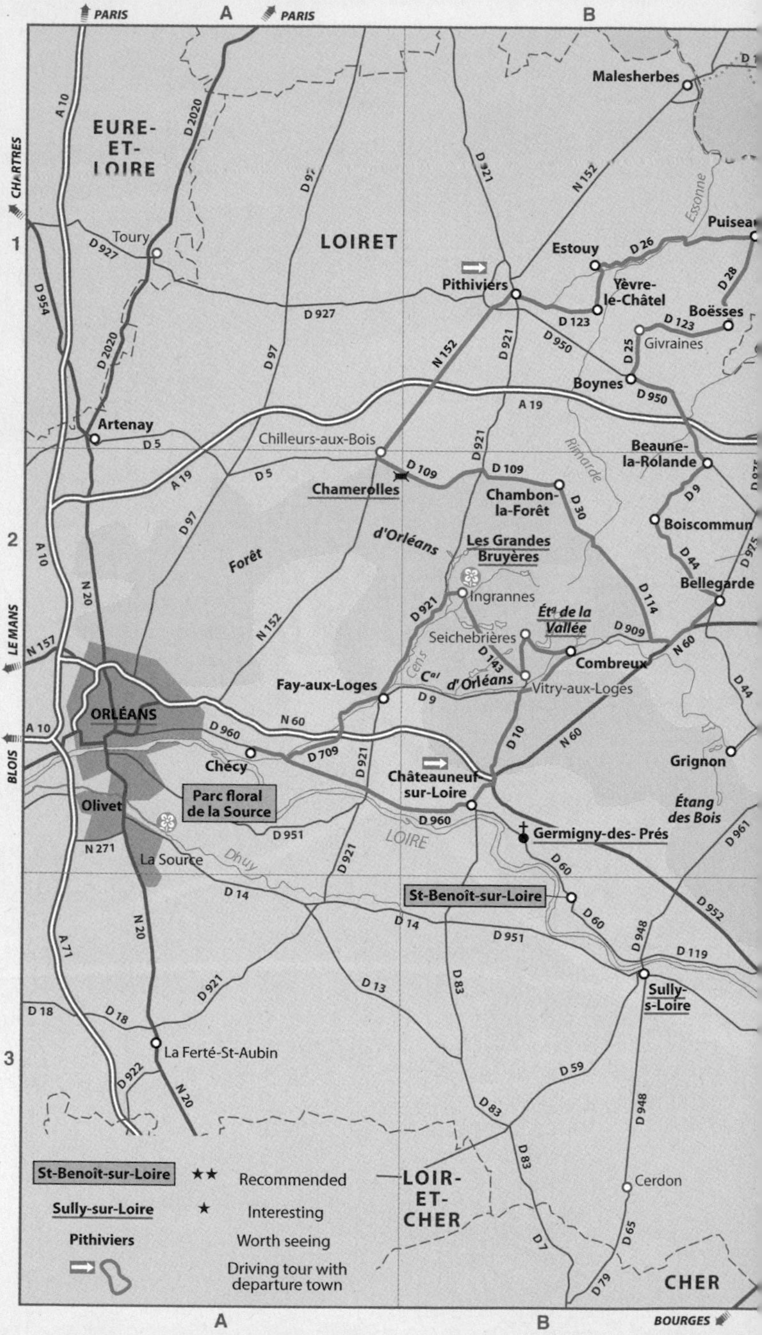
PARIS
A
PARIS
B
EURE-
ET-
LOIRE
LOIRET
CHARTRES
LE MANS
BLOIS
BOURGES
Malesherbes
Puiseaux
Estouy
Yèvre-
le-Châtel
Boësses
Givraines
Pithiviers
Toury
Boynes
Artenay
Chilleurs-aux-Bois
Chamerolles
Beaune-
la-Rolande
Chambon-
la-Forêt
Boiscommun
Bellegarde
Forêt
d'Orléans
Les Grandes
Bruyères
Ingrannes
Étg de la
Vallée
Seichebrières
Combreux
Vitry-aux-Loges
Cal d'Orléans
Fay-aux-Loges
ORLÉANS
Chécy
Châteauneuf-
sur-Loire
Parc floral
de la Source
Olivet
La Source
Dhuy
LOIRE
Germigny-des- Prés
St-Benoît-sur-Loire
Grignon
Étang
des Bois
Sully-
s-Loire
La Ferté-St-Aubin
Cerdon
LOIR-
ET-
CHER
CHER
Essonne
Rimarde
Cens
1
2
3
A 10
A 19
A 71
N 20
N 60
N 152
N 157
N 271
D 2020
D 927
D 954
D 97
D 921
D 123
D 950
D 25
D 26
D 28
D 5
D 109
D 30
D 9
D 44
D 114
D 909
D 143
D 960
D 709
D 951
D 14
D 13
D 18
D 922
D 83
D 59
D 60
D 948
D 119
D 952
D 961
D 65
D 7
D 79
St-Benoît-sur-Loire
★★
Recommended
Sully-sur-Loire
★
Interesting
Pithiviers
Worth seeing
Driving tour with
departure town

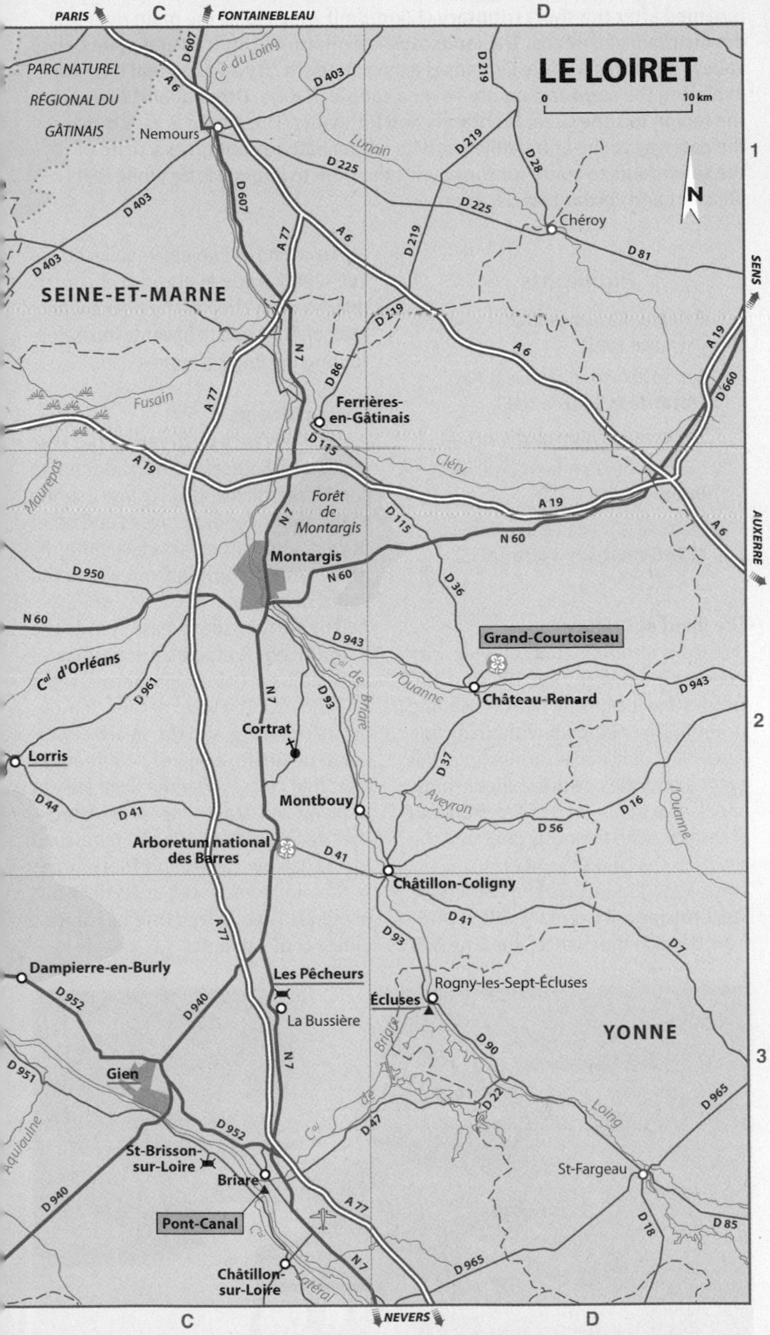
LE LOIRET
0
10 km
N
PARIS
FONTAINEBLEAU
C
D
1
2
3
SENS
AUXERRE
NEVERS
PARC NATUREL
RÉGIONAL DU
GÂTINAIS
Nemours
Cal du Loing
Lunain
Chéroy
SEINE-ET-MARNE
Fusain
Ferrières-
en-Gâtinais
Cléry
Forêt
de
Montargis
Montargis
Grand-Courtoiseau
Château-Renard
Cal d'Orléans
Lorris
Cortrat
Montbouy
Aveyron
Arboretum national
des Barres
Châtillon-Coligny
l'Ouanne
Dampierre-en-Burly
Les Pêcheurs
La Bussière
Rogny-les-Sept-Écluses
Écluses
YONNE
Gien
Loing
St-Fargeau
St-Brisson-
sur-Loire
Briare
Pont-Canal
Châtillon-
sur-Loire
Latéral
Aquiauline
A 6
A 19
A 77
N 7
N 60
D 607
D 403
D 219
D 28
D 225
D 81
D 86
D 115
D 660
D 950
D 943
D 961
D 93
D 36
D 37
D 44
D 41
D 56
D 16
D 7
D 952
D 940
D 951
D 90
D 22
D 47
D 965
D 18
D 85

THE LOIRET

Although dominated by the great arc in the Loire as it changes direction and heads southwest on its long journey to the Atlantic, the Loiret *département* is named after the short tributary (12km/8mi) which joins the main river just downstream of Orléans. The landscape is a mixture of agricultural plains, river valleys and forests while Orléans is a busy modern city and an ideal base for exploring the surrounding area over a couple of days. Other quaint towns in the region include Gien, Montargis and Pithiviers. The region is very much the gateway to the Loire Valley and its great châteaux but gives a taste of the splendours to come for those with the time to linger a little while in its pleasant and verdant landscapes.

Highlights

1. **Orléans**, former capital of France (p93)
2. Spring flowers in bloom at **Parc Floral de la Source** (p99)
3. The canals of **Montargis** (p104)
4. Gustave Eiffel's **Pont-Canal de Briare** (p109)
5. Impressive Romanesque basilica at **St-Benoît-sur-Loire** (p113)

The Maid of Orléans

Orléans is a combination of wide, airy avenues lined with fine 18C and 19C façades and the quaint, narrow winding streets of the old town with many fine Renaissance and medieval buildings. But everywhere, the one unavoidable presence is that of the Joan of Arc, the Maid of Orléans, who famously liberated the city from the English in 1429.

The main sights include the Cathédrale Ste-Croix and its remarkable woodwork décor in the chancel, the Fine Arts Museum and its impressive collection of 16C–20C European art and, of course, the reconstruction of the house where Joan of Arc is said to have stayed before routing the English armies.

Spring blooms

A short distance upstream is the Parc Floral de la Source which, in addition to superb seasonal displays of irises, spring bulbs, rhododendrons, roses and other flowers, also features a popular butterfly house and the spring from which the Loiret river flows.

A little further south-east stands the magnificent Romanesque basilica of St-Benoît-sur-Loire, built between the 11C and 13C. The town of Gien, famous for its ceramics, and the nearby Pont-Canal de Briare, a 662m/2 180ft aqueduct that crosses over the Loire are not to be missed. Make time for Montargis, the "Venice of the Gâtinais", renowned for its narrow canals and footbridges in the old town as well as its delicious praslines from Mazet, one of France's oldest confectioners.

Garden at Parc Floral de la Source

Orléans★

Once the capital of France, Orléans is today the capital of the Centre region and an important administrative and university town. In spite of having no castle, Orléans has a lot to offer visitors: its cathedral, its old town and Classical façades, its splendid fine arts museum, and its beautiful parks and rose gardens.

- **Population:** 263 292
- **Michelin Map:** 318: I-4
- **Info:** 6 r. Albert-Ier, 45000 Orléans. ℘02 38 24 05 05. www.ville-orleans.fr.
- **Location:** Along with Tours and Angers, Orléans is one of the three large cities in the Loire valley. One hour from Paris by A 10, unless you prefer to idle leisurely through the many back roads of the Île-de-France.
- **Don't Miss:** The Fêtes de Jeanne d'Arc, held every spring.
- **Kids:** The Maison Jeanne d'Arc.
- **Timing:** Allow 1 day for exploring the city.

A BIT OF HISTORY

The Carnutes to Joan of Arc

The Gauls considered the land of the Carnutes to be the centre of their territory, Gaul; each year the Druids held their great assembly there and it was at Cenabum *(Orléans)* that the signal was given to revolt against Caesar in 52 BC. A Gallo-Roman city soon rose from the Gaulish ruins. In June 451 it was besieged by Attila the Hun, but the inhabitants succeeded in driving off the invaders.

THE SIEGE OF 1428–29

This memorable siege was one of the great episodes in the history of France; it marks the rebirth of a country and a people sinking into despair.

The Forces Engaged – From the early 15C the defences of Orléans had been set up to repel English attack. The city wall was divided into six sections, each defended by 50 men. All the townspeople took part in the defence of the city either by fighting as soldiers or by maintaining the walls and ditches.

During the summer of 1428 the commander of the English army, the **Earl of Salisbury**, had destroyed the French strongholds along the Loire and gained control of the river downstream from Orléans.

The struggle began on 17 October when the English began pounding the city with heavy cannon fire. On the south side of the town there was a bridge spanning the Loire defended at its southern end by the Tourelles Fort. On 24 October, the English captured Tourelles, but as Salisbury was inspecting the grounds, he was killed by a cannon-ball.

Orléans was now cut off from the rest of the French Kingdom. On 8 November the majority of the English forces withdrew to Meung-sur-Loire and the French took the opportunity to raze the other suburbs to prevent the English from re-establishing themselves there.

The two sides settled down to a war of attrition punctuated by skirmishes outside the gates. From time to time feats of arms raised the morale of the besieged. The prowess and cunning of Master-Gunner Jean de Montesclerc became legendary: he killed many English soldiers and would often pretend to die so that when he reappeared the dismay and alarm of the English were redoubled.

However, food grew scarce and in February 1429 part of the garrison left. It seemed that the English were close to victory and in Orléans, Dunois was the only person to remain optimistic.

The Arrival of Joan of Arc – In April 1429 Joan of Arc persuaded the future **Charles VII** to rescue Orléans. She left Blois with the royal army, crossed the river and approached Orléans along the south bank, meaning to take the English by surprise, but the river was too high and the army had to return to the bridge at Blois. Meanwhile, Joan and a few companions crossed by boat a few miles upstream of Orléans and entered the town on 29 April through the Porte de Bourgogne. She was greeted by an enthusiastic crowd and issued her famous ultimatum to the English, that they should surrender to her, the young girl sent by God to drive them out of France, the keys of all the French towns that they had captured.

The people of Orléans rallied and prepared for battle while Joan found herself up against the hostility of the captains and the Governor. On 4 May the royal army, which Dunois had rejoined, attacked the Bastille St-Loup without warning Joan. When she learned of it she made a sortie, raising her banner, and the French were victorious. On the morning of 6 May, Joan herself led the attack against the Augustins Fort. For a second time her spirited intervention threw the English into confusion as they were engaged in pursuing the retreating French troops. This second victory increased her popularity. Joan went on the offensive again on 7 May against the advice of the Governor who tried to bar her way.

While fighting in the front line outside Les Tourelles she was wounded in the shoulder by a crossbow bolt. The English thought she was done for and Dunois suggested postponing the attack until the following day, but Joan returned to the attack with her standard raised high. With renewed vigour the French hurled themselves into the fray against the English defence.

The English garrison in the fort were caught in crossfire, forced to abandon the fort and surrender. On Sunday 8 May the English withdrew from the last fort and raised the siege. Joan was carried into Orléans in triumph after her victory.

SIGHTS

The town centre owes its stately character to the vast expanse of place du Martroi, to the elegant arcades along rue Royale, to the 18C and 19C façades of the buildings and private mansions. However, the old town nearby offers a striking contrast with its medieval and Renaissance houses lining the lively pedestrianised streets right to the edge of the River Loire.

Hôtel Groslot

Built in 1550 by the bailiff of Orléans, Jacques Groslot, this large Renaissance mansion in red brick was subject to extensive remodelling in the 19C.

This was the King's residence in Orléans: François II, who died here after opening the States-General in 1560, Charles IX, Henri III and Henri IV all stayed here.

Place Ste-Croix, a symmetrical esplanade, bordered by neo-Classical façades and arcades, was laid out c, 1840 when rue Jeanne-d'Arc was opened up.

Hôtel Groslot

Place du Martroi

This square marks the symbolic centre of the town and is adorned with a statue of Joan of Arc. On the west corner of rue Royale stands the old **Pavillon de la Chancellerie**, built in 1759 by the Duke of Orléans to house his archives.

Rue Royale

This broad street, lined with arcades, was opened c. 1755 when the Royal Bridge (**Pont George-V**) was built to replace the old medieval bridge which had stood upstream in line with the main street of the old medieval city. Beyond the house and the two adjoining Renaissance façades on the right there is an arch leading into square Jacques-Boucher. Standing alone in the garden is the **Pavillon Colas des Francs**, an elegant little Renaissance building, where Boucher's grandson conducted his business; a room on the ground floor houses the archives, another upstairs is where the silver was kept.

Quai Fort-des-Tourelles

Opposite a statue of Joan of Arc standing in a small square are a commemorative cross and an inscription on the low wall beside the Loire which mark the site of the southern end of the medieval bridge and of the 15C Tourelles Fort, the capture of which by Joan of Arc led to the defeat of the English and the lifting of the siege.

Quai du Châtelet provides a quiet shaded walk beside the river. In Sully's time, early in the 17C, this was one of the busiest parts of town, from where goods bound for Paris were transferred from river to road, and the six-day voyage downstream to Nantes began.

Rue de Bourgogne

This was the main east-west axis of the old Gallo-Roman city. Now largely pedestrianised, it is ideal for window shopping. There are several old façades: no. 261 is a 15C stone house with a half-timbered gable. Along the street is the **préfecture**, housed in a 17C Benedictine convent. Opposite in rue Pothier is the façade of the old **Salle des Thèses**, a 15C library, the only remnant of the University of Orléans where **Jean Calvin**, the religious reformer, studied law in 1528.

Cathédrale Ste-Croix★

This cathedral was begun in the 13C and construction continued until the 16C, although the building was partly destroyed by the Protestants in 1568. Henri IV, the first Bourbon king, being grateful to the town for having supported him, undertook to rebuild the cathedral in the Gothic style. The **west front** has three large doorways with rose windows above them crowned by a gallery with open-work design.

Interior

Splendid early-18C **woodwork**★★ adorns the chancel and the stalls. In the **crypt** are traces of the three buildings which predated the present cathedral, and two sarcophagi; one belonged to Bishop Robert de Courtenay (13C) who collected the most precious items in the **treasury**.

North transept and east end

In the north transept is a rose window with the emblem of Louis XIV at the centre. Excavations at the base have revealed the old Gallo-Roman walls and part of a tower. The **east end** with its flying buttresses and pinnacles is clearly visible from the gardens of the former episcopal palace, an 18C building which now houses the municipal library.

Campo Santo

To the left of the modern Fine Arts School (École Régionale des Beaux-Arts) is a graceful Renaissance portal and on the north side of this same building is a garden edged with an arcaded gallery.

Musée des Beaux-Arts★★

The variety and high standard of the collections displayed in this Fine Arts Museum, the oldest of which date back to the days of the French Revolution, make it one of France's most outstanding cultural venues. The paintings, sculptures and objets d'art provide a

WHERE TO STAY

Chambre d'hôte Les Courtils.. ①
Hôtel de l'Abeille.................... ④
Hôtel des Cèdres...................... ⑦
Hôtel D'Orléans........................ ⑩
Hôtel Marguerite....................... ⑬
Jackotel................................ ⑯

WHERE TO EAT

Chez Jules.............................. ①
Eugène................................... ②
L'Eldorado.............................. ④
La Dariole............................... ⑦
Le Nextdoor............................. ⑫
Le Viking................................ ⑬
Les Plantes.............................. ⑯

STREETS INDEX

Ducerceau (R.)........................ 2
Sainte-Catherine (R.).............. 5
Tabour (R. du)........................ 8

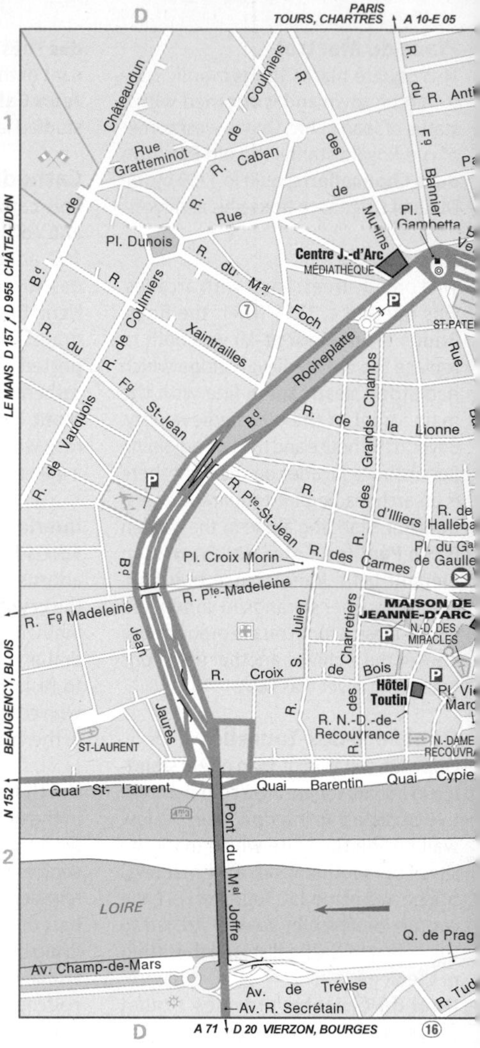

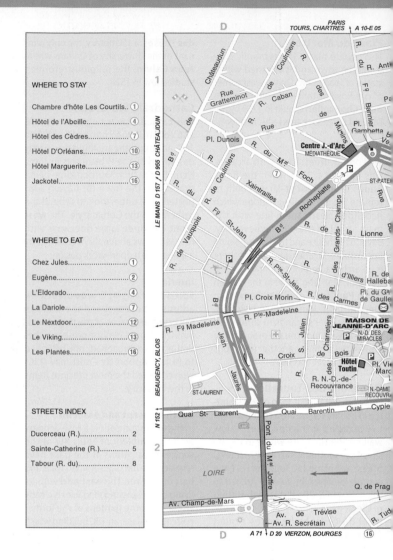

fascinating insight into European art from the 16C–20C.

The **second floor** is devoted to the Italian, Flemish and Dutch Schools, represented by works by Correggio *(Holy Family)*, Tintoretto *(Portrait of a Venetian)*, Annibale Carracci *(Adoration of the Shepherds)*, Van Dyck, Teniers and Ruysdael. On the **first floor**, there are works from the 17C–18C French School. In the **Pastel Gallery** there are 18C portraits including works by Perronneau, Quentin La Tour, Chardin *(Self-Portrait with Spectacles)* and Nattier.

The rooms devoted to the 19C offer a wealth of interesting collections covering Neoclassicism, Romanticism, Realism and pre-Impressionism. The modern art section, housed in the basement, concentrates above all on sculpture.

Musée historique et archéologique★

Open Jul–Aug Tue–Sun 9.30am–12.15pm, 1.30–5.45pm (Sun 2–6pm). May–Jun and Sept Tue–Sun 1.30–5.45pm (Sun 2–6pm). Oct–Apr Wed

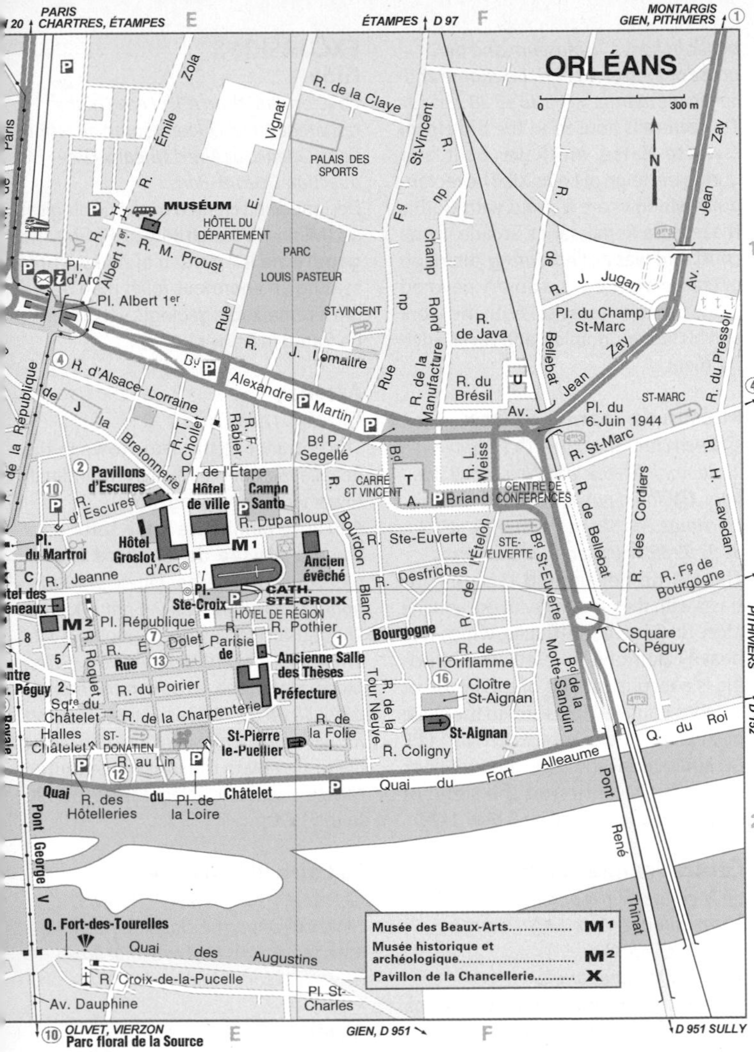

1.30–5.45pm, Sun 2–6pm. Closed 1 Jan, 1 and 8 May, 14 Jul, 1 and 11 Nov, 25 Dec. 3€, no charge 1st Sun in the month. 02 38 79 21 55. www.musees.regioncentre.fr.

The Museum of History and Archaeology is housed in an elegant little mansion, **Hôtel Cabu** (1550), next to another Renaissance façade.

On the ground floor is the astonishing **Gallo-Roman treasure**★ from Neuvy-en-Sullias which consists of a series of expressive statues, a horse and a wild boar in bronze as well as a number of statuettes of great artistic value.

The first floor is devoted to the Middle Ages and the Classical period, as well as typical local ceramic ware. The second floor is occupied by local folklore, pewter ware, gold and silverware and clocks. Another room presents the history of the port of Orléans, describing the various industries associated with river traffic in the 18C–19C.

Centre Charles-Péguy

Museum and interior courtyard: *Open Mon–Fri 2–6pm. Closed*

public holidays. Museum and the house of Joan of Arc: 2€, no charge 2nd Sun in the month. 02 38 53 20 23.
This centre is housed in the old **Hôtel Euverte-Hatte**, which was built later during the reign of Louis XII. The rectangular windows are framed with Gothic friezes; the Renaissance arcade in the courtyard was added during the reign of François I. There is a library devoted to the poet and essayist Péguy, his work and his literary, political and social environment.

Maison de Jeanne d'Arc★

Open (Tue–Sun) May–Oct 10am–12.30pm, 1.30–6.30pm, Nov–Apr 1.30–6pm. Closed public holidays. 2€; no charge 2nd Sun in the month. 02 38 52 99 89. www.jeannedarc.com.fr.
The tall timber-framed façade contrasts with the modernity of the square, place du Général-de-Gaulle, which was heavily bombed in 1940. The building is a reconstruction of the house of Jacques Boucher, Treasurer to the Duke of Orléans, where Joan stayed in 1429. An audiovisual show on the first floor recounts the raising of the siege of Orléans by Joan of Arc on 8 May 1429.

Centre Jeanne-d'Arc

Open Tue–Sun & public holidays 10am–noon, 2–6pm. No charge. 02 38 65 45 33. www.jeannedarc.com.fr.
The centre's resources include a book library, a film library and microfilm and photographic archives.

Museum★

Open 2–6pm. Closed 1 Jan, 1 and 8 May, 1 Nov, 25 Dec. 3€. 02 38 54 61 05.
The old museum houses displays of a scientific and cultural nature. The four upper floors of the museum are devoted to the marine world, aquatic ecosystems (aquarium), reptiles and amphibians, higher vertebrates (diorama on the Sologne region), mineralogy, geology, palaeontology and botany (greenhouses of temperate and tropical plants on the top floor).

EXCURSIONS

Gidy

12km/8mi N via A 10. Leave at the rest areas Aire d'Orléans-Saran direction Paris-Orléans or Aire d'Orléans-Gidy direction Orléans-Paris.
Designed and created by the Geological and Mining Research Bureau (BRGM), the **géodrome** is a garden of rocks representing an enormous relief map of the most remarkable geological features to be found in France.

Artenay

20km/12.4mi N on N 20.
The entrance to this large town in the Beauce region is marked by a windmill-tower with a revolving roof (19C).
A Beauce farmhouse is the setting for the **Musée du Théâtre forain** (*open Wed–Mon; Jun–Sept 10am–noon, 2–6pm, Oct–May 2–5pm; closed 2nd and 4th weekends in the month, 1 Jan, 1 May, 14 Jul, 15 Aug, 1 and 11 Nov, 25 Dec; 3€, no charge 1st Sun in the month; 02 38 80 09 73; www.museetheatre-forain.fr.com)*, a museum devoted to the life of travelling theatre, which toured French towns and villages from the 19C to the 1970s.

La Loire Blésoise★★

From Orléans to Blois – 84km/52mi. Leave Orléans on av. Dauphine (S of the town map); cross the Loiret that flows between wooded banks.

Olivet

Like the southern suburbs of Orléans, the greater part of Olivet is given over to growing flowers, roses and ornamental plants. It is also a pleasant summer resort on the south bank of the Loiret, composed of elegant houses and old watermills, where people come for the fishing and canoeing.

Promenade des moulins

5km/3mi round trip from the bridge along the north bank of the Loiret going W; returning on D 14 going E.
At the far end of the loop, two old mills straddle the river over their mill-races between the wooded banks of the

Loiret, while ducks and swans glide up and down on the quiet river.

In Olivet take D 14 E to the Source Floral Park.

Parc Floral de la Source★★
Open end Mar–early Oct 10am–7pm. Rest of year 2–5pm. Closed 1 Jan, 25 Dec. 4€ (6–16 years: 2.50€). ***Small train:*** *May–mid-Sept afternoons; rest of year call for information. 2€. 02 38 49 30 00. www.parc-floral-la-source.fr.* This park was laid out in the wooded grounds of a 17C château to host the 1967 Floralies Internationales horticultural exhibition. As the seasons change, so does the display: in spring, the flower beds are in bloom with tulips, daffodils, then **irises**★, rhododendrons and azaleas; mid-June to mid-July is when the rose bushes are at their best; in September the late-flowering rose bushes come into bloom with the dahlias. The **butterfly house** is a great attraction.

The **Loiret spring**★ can be seen bubbling up from the ground. The spring is the resurgence of the part of the river which disappears underground near St-Benoît-sur-Loire. Throughout the year, flocks of cranes and emus and herds of deer roam the park, while flamingoes stalk by the banks of the Loiret.

ADDRESSES

STAY

Chambre d'hôte Les Courtils – *r. de l'Ave, 45430 Chécy. 10km/6mi E on N 460. 02 38 91 32 02. www.les-courtils.com. 4 rms.* This lovely village house overlooks the Loire. The rooms are named after climbing plants and are furnished with floral fabrics, a blend of old and modern furniture and Sologne floor tiles.

Hotel Jackotel – *18 cloître St-Aignan. 02 38 54 48 48. Closed Sun and public holidays at lunch. P. 61 rms. 6€.* Near the river in the old town, this hotel is set in the lovely peaceful St-Aignan Cloister, shaded by horse chestnut trees.

Hôtel de l'Abeille – *64 r. d'Alsace-Lorraine. 02 38 53 54 87. www.hoteldelabeille.com. 31 rms. 11€.* Located in the town centre, this hotel offers small, nicely spruced-up rooms with personalised colour schemes and selected period furniture.

Hôtel des Cèdres – *17 r. Mar.-Foch. 02 38 62 22 92. www.hoteldescedres.com. Closed 24 Dec–4 Jan. 32 rms. 8€.* This hotel, enjoying a quiet location, offers gradually renovated bedrooms. The veranda, where breakfast is served, overlooks the garden planted with cedar trees.

Hôtel Marguerite – *14 pl. du Vieux-Marché. 02 38 53 74 32. www.hotelorleans.fr. Closed 22–30 Dec. 25 rms. 7€.* Renovated entrance hall and corridor, increased soundproofing and new bedding: this centrally located hotel is improving its level of comfort. Simple yet spacious rooms.

Hôtel d'Orléans – *6 r. Adolphe-Crespin. 02 38 53 35 34. www.hoteldorleans.fr. 18 rms. 7.50€.* This establishment consists of two buildings surrounding a courtyard and linked by the breakfast room. The simple yet practical rooms are well kept.

EAT

Chez Jules – *136 r. de Bourgogne. 02 38 54 30 80. Closed 23 Feb–1 Mar, 7–20 Jul, Sat lunch, Sun.* This small, rustic and inexpensive restaurant stands apart from the neighbouring establishments on account of its warm welcome and generous, updated, traditional cuisine.

La Dariole – *25 r. Étienne-Dolet. 02 38 77 26 67. Closed 1–7 Apr, 4–26 Aug, 23–28 Dec, Wed lunchtime, Sat–Sun. Reservation recommended.* This half-timbered house is near the elegant Hôtel Cabu (1550), now home to the Museum of History and Archaeology. The old-fashioned dining room is quite attractive, and in the summer months there is alfresco dining in the back garden. Traditional French fare.

L'Eldorado – *10 r. Marcel-Belot. 45160 Olivet. ☎02 38 64 29 74. www.camus-eldorado.com. Closed Feb hols, 31 Jul–16 Aug, Mon–Tue.* The charming terrace on the bank of the Loiret and a pretty garden rolling down to the river are the two assets of this former "guinguette".

Les Plantes – *44 r. Tudelle. ☎02 38 56 65 55. www.lesplantes.neu.fr. Closed 10 days in Feb, Aug, Sat lunch, Sun eve, Mon. Reservation advisable.* It's not easy to find this small restaurant located on the left bank of the Loire, close to the George V bridge. Inside, the yellow and salmon colour scheme, the pictures and the photo prints create a cosy atmosphere. On the menu: cuisine from the Loire valley and fish specialities.

La Veille Auberge – *2 fg St-Vincent. ☎02 38 53 55 81. Closed Sat lunch, Mon in Jul–Aug and Sun eve.* New team serving contemporary cuisine based on simple, fresh ingredients in the quiet garden or cosy dining room.

Le Viking – *233-235 r. de Bourgogne. ☎02 38 53 12 21. www.viking-resto.com. Closed Sun–Mon. Dinner reservation advisable.* This restaurant is a must: traditional cuisine, ***crêpes*** and gastronomic pancakes. The décor is cosy and the produce used is fresh.

Eugène – *24 r. Ste-Anne. ☎02 38 53 82 64. Closed 1–10 May, 1–16 Aug, 26 Dec–3 Jan, Sat lunch, Sun–Mon.* The size of the restaurant is irrelevant when the fare is so good: this is what you'll say when you've tasted Alain Gérard's delicious cuisine which successfully blends trendy recipes and Southern flavours.

Le Nextdoor – *6 r. au Lin. ☎02 38 62 40 00. www.nextdoor45.com. Closed Sun.* Contemporary décor supervised by a leading antique dealer: flat screen, special lighting effects, design furniture and colourful chandeliers. Contemporary dishes.

SHOPPING

Martin Pouret – *236 fg Bannier. 45400 Fleury-les-Aubrais. 3km/2mi N on D 97. ☎02 38 88 78 49. www.martin-pouret.com. Closed Sat–Sun.* Founded in 1797, this is the only establishment in town which still makes wine vinegar according to the authentic Orléans method.

LEISURE ACTIVITIES

Base de loisirs de l'Île Charlemagne – *45650 St-Jean-le-Blanc. 2km/1mi E. ☎02 38 51 92 04.* The outdoor recreation area offers swimming (May–Aug), windsurfing boards, catamarans, sailing dinghies and kayaks for hire. Beach-ball, pony club and mountain bike trails.

ENTERTAINMENT

L'Absinthe – *133 r. Marcel-Belot. 45160 Olivet, 3.3km/2mi S. ☎02 38 63 76 36. Tue–Fri 7pm–1am, Sat 7pm–3am. Closed 8–22 Aug. Reservation recommended Sat–Sun.* A very fashionable place to go for a beer. Choice of over 200 brews, of which 90 percent are Belgian.

La Chancellerie – *27 pl. du Martroi. ☎02 38 53 57 54. www.lachancellerie.fr. Closed Sun.* A high-class café-restaurant run by the Erta family since 1957 and specialising in fine wines. A popular place to meet in town.

Mc Ewan's Café – *250 r. de Bourgogne. ☎02 38 54 65 70. Closed Sun.* A lively Irish pub, run by a native of Marseille, where the most popular drinks are beer and Ricard. Rock and Breton music concerts three times a month. Friendly atmosphere.

Plisson – *4 r. du Tabour. ☎02 38 53 59 25. www. plisson-patissier.fr. Mon–Sat 8am–7.30pm. Closed Sun, 1 week Feb, 1 week Easter, 3 weeks Aug.* Try original flavoured macaroons: glacé raspberries in Orléans vinegar, rose petal jam, pear and ginger preserve, etc. and the Loiret gourmand, a hazelnut cake with pear and cherry filling smothered in hazelnut cream. Other specialities include delicious pastries and huge meringues.

Pithiviers

Pithiviers is situated on the border between the Beauce and the Gâtinais regions. Its main economic activities are related to local products – cereals and sugar beet (sugar refinery at Pithiviers-le-Vieil) – but other industries are currently being introduced. The town of Pithiviers has given its name to a delicious cake found in most French boulangeries, consisting of oblong squares of light puff pastry with an almond paste filling.

- **Population:** 9 242
- **Michelin Map:** 318: K-2
- **Info:** 1 mail Ouest, maison Les Remparts, 45300 Pithiviers. ☎02 38 30 50 02.
- **Location:** 43km/27mi NE of Orléans along the N 152, and 100km/63mi S of Paris.
- **Timing:** Allow 1hr to explore the town.
- **Don't Miss:** St George's Fair in April if you're a gourmet.
- **Kids:** Transport Museum.

SIGHTS

Musée des Transports

Open Jun–Aug Sat–Sun and public holidays 2.30–5pm; May and Sept Sun and public holidays 2.30–6pm. 7€ (children 5€). ☎02 38 30 48 26.

The Railway Museum was founded by volunteer workers in the old terminus of the Tramways à Vapeur du Loiret line. The 0.6m/2ft wide tracks designed by Decauville, who promoted this particular width for French railways, would carry passengers and sugar beets from Pithiviers to Toury until 1951. The museum contains several steam locomotives, two electrical tramways and a rail car running on both electricity and oil (1923).

Musée municipal

Open Sat–Sun and public holidays 2.30–5pm. ☎02 38 30 00 64. www. ville-pithiviers.fr.

Predominantly local memorabilia are displayed on the first floor. The first room, on the South Sea Islands, adds a touch of the exotic. Another room is devoted to famous local people, to the more or less legendary origins of the culinary specialities of Pithiviers and to saffron, the strongly coloured aromatic derived from the crocus, which the west Gâtinais was one of the first places in Europe to cultivate.

EXCURSIONS

Malesherbes

18km/11.2mi NE along N 152.

Situated along the Essonne Valley, this small town is entirely surrounded by woods. The **Buthiers** leisure park lies close to the river, in a forest setting dotted with sandstone boulders.

Château

Open end of Mar to mid-Nov Sat–Sun 2.30–6.30pm. Closed 1 Jan, 1 May. 8€. ☎02 38 34 41 02. www.ville-malesherbes.fr.

The 14C round towers are all that remains of the feudal castle rebuilt in the 15C. The courtyard leads to the former outbuildings: 14C tithe barns where wheat was stored four floors high; Tour des Redevances; and a pavilion known as Châteaubriand's House in memory of the famous poet who stayed in it.

The 14C dovecote could accommodate 8 000 pigeons. Inside, the ground-floor reception rooms have been refurbished as they were before the Revolution and the visit ends with the bedroom and vaulted oratory of **Henriette d'Entragues**, who succeeded Gabrielle d'Estrées as Henri IV's official mistress. However, the King soon tired of Henriette's bad temper and she was forced to retire to Malesherbes where she spent her time plotting.

DRIVING TOUR

95km/59mi round trip. Allow half a day.

Leave Pithiviers E along D 123.

Malesherbes

This tolerant man, who became one of Louis XVI's ministers, encouraged the introduction and circulation throughout France of Diderot's *Encyclopédie*. Having retired from public service on the eve of the Revolution, he requested the honour of defending the King before the Convention. He was later guillotined together with his daughter, his son-in-law, as well as one of his granddaughters and her husband the Marquess of Châteaubriand, the eldest brother of the writer.

Yèvre-le-Châtel

Perched on its promontory, Yèvre overlooks the Rimarde, a tributary of the River Essonne. The ramparts date from the 13C. A fortified gate under the elm trees in the main square opens into the outer bailey of the castle.

Château fort

Open Apr–Oct 2–6pm; rest of year by appointment. 3€. 02 38 34 25 91.

The stronghold, recently restored, is diamond-shaped with a round tower at each corner containing hexagonal rooms with ogive vaulting.

The northwest and south towers provide a **view** of the Beauce and the Gâtinais regions. To the south the treetops of Orléans Forest darken the horizon.

Église St-Lubin

On the south side of the village among the tombstones stands the unfinished stone shell of a huge Gothic church. Its vast size seems to have been dictated by the need for a place of refuge rather than a place of worship.

Drive to Estouy and turn right onto D 26 which follows the River Essonne.

Puiseaux

This busy cereal centre of the Gâtinais region developed round a priory belonging to the Parisian abbey of St-Victor, a famous theological centre in medieval times.

The twisted spire of the 13C church can be seen from afar.

Drive S out of Puiseaux along D 948 then turn right onto D 28.

Boësse

This once fortified village stretches its winding streets on the hillside; the church is preceded by an impressive porch reminiscent of part of a cloister.

Take D 123 on the right to Givraines then turn left onto D 25 to Boynes.

Boynes

Seeing it today, it is difficult to imagine that Boynes remained the world capital of saffron for 300 years (16C–19C). Drastic changes in the agricultural world brought with them the decline of saffron and of wine-growing, but the town recalls its prosperous past at the **Maison du Safran** (*open Apr–Oct Sat–Sun and public holidays 2.30–6pm, last admission 30min before closing; guided tours possible; 3€; 02 38 33 13 05 or 02 38 33 10 09; www.coeur-de-france.com).*

Beaune-la-Rolande

Lying on the banks of the River Rolande, Beaune is a market town where sugar beets and cereals have replaced saffron and vines.

Source of Saffron

S. Sauvignier/MICHELIN

The 15C–16C **church** features an elegant north side in the Renaissance style: there are pilasters bearing medallions, recesses and doorways with pediments decorated with busts.

Boiscommun

5.5km/3.4mi SW on D 9.

Of the castle only two towers and other ruins remain and these can be seen from the path which now follows the line of the former moat. The 13C **church** with its Romanesque doorway has a Gothic nave with a majestic elevation. It is relatively easy to discern the different periods of construction by looking at the changes in the capitals, the form of the high windows and openings of the triforium.

Bellegarde

The town's colour-washed houses are grouped round a huge square and surrounded by rose nurseries, market gardens and wheat fields.

Château★

Grouped round the old keep, this unusual and picturesque ensemble, built in the 14C by Nicolas Braque, Finance Minister to Charles V, stands on a platform surrounded by a moat. The brick **pavilions** with stone dressings which frame the courtyard were built by D'Antin to house the château staff and his guests; from left to right they comprise the Steward's pavilion surmounted by a pinnacle turret, the Captain's massive round brick tower, the kitchen pavilion, the Salamander pavilion, which houses the town hall – **Hôtel de ville** – (*open Mon–Fri and public holidays 1.15–5pm (Fri 1–6pm); no charge 02 38 90 10 03)* and contains the **Regency Salon** with wood panelling, and, on the other side of the gate, the D'Antin Pavilion with a mansard roof. A rose garden has been laid out round the moat.

Church

The façade of this Romanesque building is a combination of balanced proportion and harmonious decoration. Note the ornamentation of the central doorway: wreathed and ringed engaged piers support carved capitals depicting imaginary foliage and animals.

The nave contains an interesting collection of 17C **paintings**: *St Sebastian* by Annibale Carracci and *The Infant Louis XIV as St John the Baptist* by Mignard (right wall) and *The Deposition* by Lebrun (*right chapel*); Louise de la Vallière may have been the model for the two female characters in these pictures.

Drive SW through Bois de la Madeleine then turn right onto D 114.

Chambon-la-Forêt

This lovely flower-decked village lies on the edge of Orléans Forest.

Drive out along D 109.

Château de Chamerolles★

Open Apr–Sept 10am–6pm; Oct–Dec and Feb–Mar Wed–Mon 10am–5pm. Closed 25 Dec. 5€. 02 38 39 84 66. www.loiret.com.

On the edge of Orléans Forest, stands this sumptuous Renaissance building and its formal gardens restored to their former glory. The Dulac family moved here in the 15C, when Lancelot I (named after the hero immortalised in the story of the Knights of the Round Table) commissioned the construction of the present château. Lancelot, who was acquainted with Louis XII and François I, designed a medieval stronghold with an elegant, comfortable interior.

Promenade des parfums★

The Chamerolles estate is given over to perfume and other olfactory delights. The south wing of the château houses a chronological exhibition of different scents from the 16C up to the present day, taking the visitor through a series of rooms decorated with objects related to perfume. A small bridge spanning the moat allows you to continue an aromatic exploration by visiting the **garden★**. The flower beds have been painstakingly restored to the layout they would have had during the Renaissance, reflecting the threefold purpose of gardens in those days: ornamentation, leisure and utility.

Return to Pithiviers along N 152.

Montargis

More than 130 bridges and footbridges over a maze of canals have earned Montargis its nickname the "Venice of the Gâtinais." It invites visitors to stroll among its old half-timbered houses and fine Renaissance residences, discover the ruins of the châteaux and the gardens at nearby Grand-Courtoiseau.

- **Population:** 15 755
- **Michelin Map:** 318: N-4
- **Info:** 10 r. Renée-de-France, 45200 Montargis, 02 38 98 00 87. www.montargis.fr.
- **Location:** 56km/35mi SW of Sens, 60km/38mi west of Joigny.
- **Don't Miss:** Old Montargis and views of the Canal de Briare.
- **Kids:** The Beekeeping museum.
- **Timing:** Allow 1–2hrs to discover the town.

WALKING TOUR

THE OLD TOWN

Some streets in the old town enjoy fine views of the Canal de Briare which has encircled the north and east of Montargis since 1642 linking the river Loing to the Loire. The canals in the town were dug to regulate the water level in a region that was subject to constant danger of flooding. These, and the many bridges and footbridges that now span the channels, give the historic part of the town its unique and charming appeal.

Take r. du Port, then bd. du Rempart and, from the canal bridge, bd. Durzy, to the musée Girodet

Musée Girodet

2 r. du Fg-de-la-Chaussée. Open 9am–12pm, 1.30–5.30pm, Fri 9am–12pm, 1.30–5pm (last entry 30min before closing). Closed Mon, Tue and bank holidays. 3€ (children 2€). 02 38 98 07 81.

Dedicated to painter **Anne-Louis Girodet-Trioson** (1767–1824), born in Montargis, and favourite pupil of Jacques-Louis David, the pre-eminent Neoclassical artist during the Revolution and First Empire. The museum is housed in the 19C **Hôtel Durzy** set in pleasant grounds on the banks of the Loing. In the first part of the picture gallery don't miss the extraordinary *Flood (Déluge)*, a painting that took Francisco de Zurbarán four years to complete.

The **Girodet collection★** is the main attraction with a score of pitcures including portraits (Dr Trioson and Mustapha Sussen), a copy by the artist of his most famous work (in the Louvre) inspired by Chateaubriand's novel, *The Funeral of Atala*, and the charming *Geography Lesson* (1803).

Part of the rich collection of sketches is displayed in a rotating exhibition in the salon Girodet. The painted ceiling featuring the monuments of the region is the work of one of his pupils. The library, with furniture by Romantic sculptor **Henri de Triqueti** (1804–74), houses a large collecion of small Romantic sculptures by Girodet's contemporaries: Feuchère, Barre, Gechter, Pradier, etc. There are some delightful terracotta pieces upstairs.

Boulevard Durzy

Shady avenue lined with plain trees running between the canal and the jardin Durzy. At the end a tall and elegant metallic humpback footbridge, the work of the Eiffel factories in 1891, completes the perspective. The bridge gives pretty **views** of two canal locks.

Take the footbridge over the canal and continue straight on.

Boulevard Belles-Manières

With a narrow channel to the north, footbridges lead to houses built on the levelled towers of the old ramparts.

Walk back to the beginning of bd. Belles-Manières, turn left into r. du Moulin-à-Tan, then, with pl. de la République on your left, take r. Raymond-Laforge.

Rue Raymond-Laforge

Old dwellings with wash-houses overlook two canals you cross. Decorative little boats are used as window boxes along the canal banks.

Retrace your steps and take r. de l'Ancien-Palais.

At the end of the street, turn right into an alley with a bridge at the end which gives views over the canal you have just crossed.

Turn right into r. de la Pêcherie.

Walk through the renovated district where there are several remaining half-timbered houses. From place Jules-Ferry, rue Raymond-Tellier leads, after about 50m/55yd, to another impressive view of the water channels as far as the Canal de Briare.

Turn left into r. du Loing, then r. du Gén.-Leclerc along the south side of the Église Ste-Madeleine, and turn left into r. du Château.

Musée du Gâtinais

7 r. du Château. Call for details of opening times. Closed bank holidays, 25 Dec–1 Jan and at 4.30pm on the eve of bank holidays. 2.80€ (children 1.70€). 02 38 93 45 63.

Set in a former tannery (15C), the museum features a collection of archaeological finds from the Gallo-Roman settlements at Sceaux-en-Gâtinais and Les Closiers (where a temple, an amphitheatre and a necropolis were unearthed) including a beautiful plaque dedicated to the goddess Segeta. Note also artefacts from Merovingian tombs at Le Grand Bezout, several Egyptian and Ancient Greek pieces, objects from traditional tanneries and some 19C local headdresses.

Musée des Tanneurs

Carr. Henri-Perruchot. Open Sat 2.30–5.30pm (last entry 30 min before closing). 2€ (children free). 02 38 98 00 87.

Quite close to the Musée du Gâtinais, in the renovated historic Ilot des Tanneurs district. This 16C house displays the craft, methods and tools of tanners from the last century. The first floor features a display of local costumes and headdresses including the fanchon (checkered scarf) for everyday wear, the caline (bonnet) for going out and about in the town and embroidered headdresses for special occasions.

Return to pl. du 18-Juin-1940 by the pont du Québec.

EXCURSIONS

Ferrières-en-Gâtinais

Best route is along D 315 through the Forest of Montargis (18km/11mi).

The town is a maze of narrow winding streets at the foot of the former Benedictine abbey, an important centre of Carolingian civilisation and monastic life in the Gâtinais.

Ancienne abbaye St-Pierre-et-St-Paul – *Leave your car on the shady esplanade.* The Gothic **church** stands out for its **transept crossing★** (12C), built as a rotunda on eight high columns. A 9C Carolingian edifice built here probably inspired this canopy style. Note the unusual liturgical accessory in the transept arm: a gilded palm leaf adorned with grapes used to exhibit the Holy Sacrament. The 13C chancel is illuminated by five Renaissance stained-glass windows. In the left transept arm note the collection of 14C and 17C statues. From the terrace below the courtyard of the old cloister there are **views** of the southern wall of the church and the chapel .

Château-Renard

17km/10.5mi SE on D 943.

This small town, which owes its name to a château built in the 10C on the hill overlooking the river Ouanne, and Count Renard de Sens, has kept some of its historic half-timbered houses with sculptured features (the finest dates from the 15C on place de la République). On the left bank of the Ouanne, the 17C Château de la Motte *(private)* stands in pretty grounds.

The **church** is on the site of the former chapel (11C and 12C) of the château. A fortified doorway between two towers leads to the building set among the ruins. A deep well stands in front of the bell-tower façade which is crowned by a lantern. The nearby terrace, with a 12C oil mill, gives interesting **views** of the town below.

Learn all about the fascinatng life of bees at the **Musée vivant de l'Apiculture gâtinaise de La Cassine**, towards Chuelles (D 37; *open Jul–Aug 10am–6pm; Apr–Jun, Wed and weekends 10am–6pm; rest of the year on appointment; 5€ (children 3.50€); 02 38 95 35 56; www.museevivant.com*). Follow the discovery tour and then spot the queen bee in the glass-sided hives. Animated displays and videos show how life is organised inside the hive. The visit concludes with the extraction of the honey and a tasting session.

Jardins du Grand-Courtoiseau★★

18km/11mi E of Montargis, between Château-Renard and Triguères, on D 943.

(in fine weather). Open mid-Apr–mid-Oct Thu–Mon and bank holidays 2.30–6pm. Closed mid-Oct–mid-Apr. 8€ (children under 11 years free). 06 80 24 10 83. www.grand-courtoiseau.com.

Designed by talented landscape gardener Alain Richert, this 6ha/14acre award-winning garden combines an orchard, kitchen garden and flower garden around a 17C manor house.

ADDRESSES

STAY

Hôtel Dorèle – *222 r. Émile-Mengin. 02 38 07 18 18. les-hotels-dorele@wanadoo.fr.* Modern building near the station. The rooms, although not too big, are well soundproofed. Comfortable lounge.

Hôtel Ibis – *2 pl. Victor-Hugo. 02 38 98 00 68. www.ibishotel.com.* The rooms are modern and practical and up to the usual standard of this economy chain. The 3rd floor rooms are ideal for families. Nice restaurant with a retro atmosphere, glass roof, wall lights, benches. Brasserie cuisine.

Hôtel Central – *2 r. Gudin. 02 38 85 03 07. www.hotel-montargis.com.* In the town centre, this hotel set in a former convent has been fully restored. The rooms vary in size but are simple and well kept.

Hôtel Le Belvédère – *192 r. J.-Ferry, 45200 Amilly. 02 38 85 41 09. Closed 9–23 Aug and 20 Dec–3 Jan.* This family hotel with a pleasant flower garden stands opposite the village school. The small, character rooms are quiet and comfortable.

EAT

La Péniche – *Quai du Pâtis. 02 38 98 93 02. www.lapeniche.fr. Closed 1st week Jan.* This brasserie-style restaurant set on a barge serves tasty meals in pleasant surrounds. In summer ask for a table on the deck to make the most of the atmosphere.

Les Dominicaines – *6 r. du Dévidet. 02 38 98 10 22. www.restaurant-lesdominicaines.com. Closed last 2 weeks Aug, Sat lunch, Sun and bank holidays.* Mimosa-yellow walls, lavender landscapes and mirrors make up the décor of the three small dining rooms in this restaurant nestling in a pedestrian street in the town centre. Fish and seafood specialities.

Châtillon-Coligny

On the banks of the river Loing and the Canal de Briare, dotted with old wash-houses, Châtillon-Coligny, with its unusual church and ruined château still bears the scars from the Wars of Religion as an important centre of Protestantism. It is the gateway to the southern reaches of the Gâtinais, a popular terrain for hunting and fishing.

- **Population:** 1 912
- **Michelin Map:** 318: O-5
- **Info:** 2 pl. Coligny, 45230 Châtillon-Coligny. 02 38 96 02 33.
- **Location:** 22km/13.6mi SE of Montargis on D 93, and 31km/19.5mi NW of St-Fargeau.
- **Kids:** The Henri Becquerel displays at the museum.
- **Timing:** Allow time for a stroll on the banks of the Loing.

THE TOWN

Château

In the early 16C, the marshal of Châtillon (Gaspard I de Coligny) built a luxurious home by the medieval castle and polygonal Romanesque keep (1180–90), a highly unusual edifice put up by the Count of Sancerre.

The Revolution spared only the keep (originally almost 50m/150ft high) and the cellars. Three monumental terraces and a well attributed to sculptor Jean Goujon are all that remain from the fine Renaissance building. Below lies the **church** (16C and 17C).

Museum

Open Apr–Oct 2–5.30pm, weekends 10am–noon, 2–5.30pm; Nov–Mar weekends 2–5pm. Closed Mon, 1 Jan, 1 May, 25 Dec. 2.40€ (children under 12 years 1.30€). 02 38 92 64 06.

Set in the former Hôtel-Dieu (15C), the museum features portraits and documents relating to the Coligny and Montmorency families, successive owners of the estate, and the violent history of Protestantism in France. One section recounts the amazing story of Henri Becquerel, the discoverer of radioactivity alongside Marie and Pierre Curie. Note the jaw-dropping advert from 1905 vaunting the merits of radium as a cure for hair loss!

EXCURSIONS

Montbouy

6km/3.7mi NW on D 93.

The remains of a Gallo-Roman amphitheatre (1C) can be seen north of the village.

Cortrat

12km/7.5mi NW via Montbouy and Pressigny-les-Pins.

Small country **church** and cemetery. The sculpted **tympanum★** (11C) features a primitive portrayal of people and animals representing the Creation.

Arboretum National des Barres

8km/5mi NW. Guided tours (1hr30). Phone for opening times. 7€. 02 38 97 62 21. www.arboretumdesbarres.com.

At the heart of a vast forest domain, it features some 3 000 plant species and varieties set in 35ha/86acres and divided into three collections.

Rogny-les-Sept-Écluses★

10km/6mi S.

Henri IV ordered the construction of the Rogny locks in 1605 as part of a vast project to link the Mediterranean to the Atlantic and the English Channel. 12 000 workers toiled on the canals which were opened for navigation in 1642. Six other locks are now open for craft using the Canal de Briare.

La Bussière

10km/6mi NE on D 622.

This village is renowned for the Château des Pêcheurs, a fortress rebuilt in the 17C on the banks of a pond and which houses a collection of art and artefacts related to fishing.

Lorris★

Lorris is located in the southernmost area of the former Gâtinais region. The town is famous for the Freedom Charter, which was granted to it in 1122 by Louis VI. The town was a hunting seat for the Capet kings and a place of residence for Blanche of Castille and her son Louis IX of France. In 1215 it became the birthplace of Guillaume de Lorris, who wrote the first part of the ***Romance of the Rose (Roman de la Rose)*****, a poem of courtly love which influenced Geoffrey Chaucer in his writings.**

- **Population:** 2 777
- **Michelin Map:** 318: M-4
- **Info:** 2 r. des Halles, 45260 Lorris. ☎02 38 94 81 42. www.ville-lorris.fr.
- **Location:** Lorris is midway between Montargis and Châteauneuf-sur-Loire, at the eastern extremity of the Orléans forest.
- **Don't Miss:** Resistance and Deportation Museum.
- **Timing:** Allow around 2hrs to explore the town.

SIGHTS

Église Notre-Dame★

An elegant Romanesque door leads into a well-lit Gothic nave. In the nave are a **gallery** and the early-16C **organ loft**★ *(see Architecture in Introduction)*, both ornately carved. The late-15C **choir stalls**★ are decorated with the Prophets and Sibyls on the cheekpieces and scenes from The Golden Legend, the New Testament and everyday life on the misericords.

A **museum** dedicated to the organ and old musical instruments in general has been set up under the eaves.

Musée départemental de la Résistance et de la Déportation

Open Jul–Aug 10am–noon, 2–6pm; rest of year one weekend per month; call for details. Closed Christmas school holidays–3 Jan. 4€. ☎02 38 94 84 19.

This museum is housed in the old station. Its collections relate the history of the Second World War and its consequences in this region. The course of events, from the underlying causes of the war until the liberation of France, is illustrated with the aid of documents, dioramas (the exodus of refugees and a reconstruction of a camp of members of the Resistance movement in a forest).

Musée Horloger Georges Lemoine

4 r. des Marchés (entry via the Tourist Office). Open 9am–noon, 2–6pm, 4–6pm; Sun and bank holidays 10am –noon (except Sept–May during exhibitions). ☎ 02 38 94 85 75. www.musee-horloger-lorris.fr.

Displays the working environment of a rural clock and watchmaker in the 1930s–60s. Interesting collection of tools and timepieces.

EXCURSIONS

The **Canal d'Orléans**, which was in its heyday in the 18C, was finally closed to traffic in 1954. It is currently being dredged and restored with the aim of having 78km/48mi navigable by 2020.

Grignon

5km/3mi W on D 44 then left at Le Coudroy on D 444.

An attractive hamlet with three canal locks. Cross **Vieilles-Maisons** (pretty church with half-timbered porch).

Étang des Bois

5km/3mi SW on D 88.

Oak, beech and chestnut trees stand on the banks of this small lake which is popular in fine weather (fishing, swimming, pedal boats).

Briare

This quiet town on the banks of the Loire is the meeting point of two canals, which connect the basins of the Seine and Loire. The Briare Canal, completed in 1642, 38 years after its conception, was the first canal in Europe designed to link up two different canal networks in this way. Along its 57km/36mi path, six locks move the waters from the Loire Lateral Canal to the Loing Canal. At Rogny-les-Sept-Écluses, the seven original locks, no mean feat of engineering at the time, form a sort of giant's stairway, in an impressive, natural setting.

- **Population:** 5 660
- **Michelin Map:** 318: N-6
- **Info:** 1 pl. Charles-de-Gaulle, 45250 Briare, 02 38 31 24 51
- **Location:** 80km/50mi SW of Orléans and 10km/6mi SE of Gien by the D 952.

SIGHTS

Pont-Canal★★

The canal bridge, completed in 1890 and inaugurated in 1896, may no longer fulfil an important economic role, but it does transport the visitor who takes the time to stroll along the towpaths.

Musée de la Mosaïque et des Émaux

Open Feb–Dec 2–6pm (Jun–Sept 6.30pm). Closed Jan, 25 Dec. 5€. 02 38 31 20 51.

Devoted to local enamel crafts, the main theme is the history of Jean Félix Bapterosses, inventor of the first machine able to produce buttons in industrial quantities. The museum also presents late-19C mosaic work typical of the town, and in particular the work of Art Nouveau precursor Eugène Grasset.

Gien★

Built on a hillside overlooking the north bank of the Loire, Gien, a small town with many a pretty garden, is well known for its glazed blue-and-yellow earthenware, or faïence, and for its splendid hunting museum housed in the castle, said to have been built by Charlemagne.

- **Population:** 15 300
- **Michelin Map:** 318: M-5
- **Info:** Pl. Jean-Jaurès, 45501 Gien. 02 38 67 25 28. www.gien.fr.
- **Location:** 67km/42mi E of Orléans, 45km/28mi S of Montargis, and 76km/47mi NE of Bourges.
- **Don't Miss:** The Hunting museum: Musée International de la Chasse.
- **Timing:** 2hrs for the town.

A BIT OF HISTORY

It was here, in 1410, that the Armagnac faction was set up in support of Charles d'Orléans against the Burgundians in the civil war, which led up to the last episode in the Hundred Years War.

The castle was later rebuilt by **Anne de Beaujeu** (1460–1522), the Countess of Gien, who was Louis XI's eldest daughter. Aged 23 when her father died, she was appointed regent during the minority of her brother Charles VIII (1483–91).

SIGHTS

Musée International de la Chasse★★

Open Jul–Aug 10am–6pm, Apr–Jun and Sept Wed–Mon 10am–6pm, Feb–Mar and Oct–Dec Wed–Mon 10am–noon, 2–5pm. Closed Jan, 25 Dec. 5€. 02 38 67 69 69.

Gien **château**★ stands on the eastern fringe of Orléans Forest and the Sologne, a region abounding in game, making it an ideal setting for a Hunting Museum. The château, which dominates the town, was rebuilt shortly before 1500 with red brick and a slate roof. The decoration is restrained: a pattern of contrasting dark bricks and bands of white stone and a few stair turrets.

The rooms of the château with their beamed ceilings and fine chimney-pieces form an attractive backdrop to the exhibition of fine art inspired by hunting as well as weapons and accessories used in hunting since the prehistoric era. Particularly noteworthy is the collection of some 4 000 blazer buttons decorated with hunting motifs. There is also a collection of hunting horns as well as 500 antlers, given to the museum by the great hunter, Claude Hettier de Boislambert.

Faïencerie

Open Mar–Dec 9am–noon, 2–6pm (Sun and public holidays 10am). Jan–Feb Mon–Fri 2–6pm, Sat 9am–noon, 2–6pm. Closed 1 Jan, 1 May, 1 and 11 Nov, 25 Dec. 4€. 02 38 05 21 06.

An old paste store has been converted into a **Faïence Museum**; some of the very large pieces were made for the Universal Exhibition in 1900. There is also a display of the current production and a shop where factory pieces can be purchased at reduced prices.

EXCURSIONS

St-Brisson-sur-Loire

6km/3.7mi SE along D 951.

Here in the borderlands between Berry and the Orléans region stand the remains of a 12C hilltop **fortress** deprived of its original keep and crenellated south wall. The east wing and the staircase tower were restored in the 19C. The cellars of the old castle are open to the public, as is a suite of rooms with mementoes from the D'Estrades and Séguier families.

In the library is a letter written by Jean-Jacques Rousseau. Replicas of medieval weaponry (mangonel, swivel gun) have been set up in the moat. Archery demonstrations are regularly staged on Sunday afternoons from mid-June to mid-September.

Dampierre-en-Burly

13km/8mi NW along D 952.

The flat-tiled roofs of Dampierre present an attractive spectacle to anyone approaching from the west on D 952 from Ouzouer-sur-Loire; as the road crosses the tree-lined lake by a causeway, the ruins of a château loom into sight. Beyond what remains of the towers and curtain wall of the castle rises the church tower. In the square by the church stands one of the château gatehouses, an elegant early-17C building, in brick and stone, decorated with bossed pilasters beneath a pyramidal roof.

Musée du Cirque et de l'Illusion

Outside Dampierre-en-Burly, on D 952, on the right. Open Jul–Aug 10am–7pm; rest of year 10am–12.30pm. Closed 24, 25 and 31 Dec, early Jan–early Feb. 6€ (children 4–13 years 4.50€). 02 38 35 67 50. www.museeducirqueetdelillusion.com.

Learn the surprising history of the circus and discover the tricks of master magicians. Artefacts, models and displays.

Centre Nucléaire de Production d'électricité CNPE

3km/S of Dampierre-en-Burly. Centrale nucléaire de Dampierre-en-Burly, BP 18, 45570 Ouzouer-sur-Loire. Open Mon–Fri and 1st Sat of month 2–5.30pm. Closed bank holidays. Proof of identity must be shown. Free guided tours at 3pm. 02 38 29 70 04.

Learn about the workings of the Dampierre nuclear power station which was commissioned in 1980–81. Its four cooling towers rise 165m/540ft above the banks of the Loire and it houses four 900 MW pressurised water reactors. The **Henri-Becquerel information centre** is named after the local scientist who helped to disocver radioactivity. The family lived 30km/18.6mi from the site of the plant at Châtillon-Coligny.

Sully-sur-Loire★

The Château de Sully commanded one of the Loire crossings. Its history is dominated by four great names: Maurice de Sully, Bishop of Paris who commissioned the building of Notre-Dame; Joan of Arc; statesman duc de Sully and Voltaire. Today an agreeable charm pervades the mellow stones of the fortress reflecting in the still waters of the moat and bathed in the soft light of the Loire Valley.

- **Population:** 5 830
- **Michelin Map:** 318: L-5
- **Info:** pl. du Général-de-Gaulle, BP 12, 45600 Sully-sur-Loire. 02 38 36 23 70. www.sully-sur-loire.fr.
- **Location:** On the left bank of the Loire at an important crossroads between Gien and Orléans.
- **Don't Miss:** The international music festival which takes place in June.

A BIT OF HISTORY

The determination of Joan of Arc – In 1429 Sully belonged to Georges de la Trémoille, a favourite of Charles VII. The King was living in the castle when Joan of Arc defeated the English at Patay and captured their leader, the famous Talbot, Earl of Shrewsbury. Joan hastened to Sully and eventually persuaded the indolent monarch to be crowned at Reims. She returned to the castle in 1430 after her check before Paris, and there felt the jealousy and hostility of La Trémoille gaining influence over the King. She was detained and almost made prisoner but escaped to continue the struggle.

Sully's capacity for work – In 1602 **Maximilien de Béthune**, the Lord of Rosny, bought the château and the barony. Henri IV made him Duc de Sully, and it was under this name that the great Minister passed into history.
Sully had begun to serve his King at the age of 12. He was a great soldier, the best artilleryman of his time and a consummate administrator. A glutton for work, Sully began his day at 3am and kept four secretaries busy writing his memoirs. Fearing indiscretions, he had a printing press set up in one of the towers of the château and the work was printed on the spot.

CHÂTEAU★

Open Jul–Aug 10am–6pm, Apr–Jun and Sept Tue–Sun 10am–6pm, Feb–Mar and Oct–Dec Tue–Sun 10am–noon, 2–5pm. 5€. Guided tours (1hr) 7€. 02 38 36 36 86. www.loiret.com.
This imposing feudal fortress dates largely from before 1360. The keep, which faces the Loire, was built at the end of the 14C by Guy de la Trémoille. The huge main hall on the first floor, was the part of the seigneurial residence used during the Middle Ages for dispensing justice and holding feasts. An iron door concealed in the panelling leads to the old exercise room from where the guards operated the drawbridge and the trapdoor. Nowadays called the **oratory**, this room was also the Duke's treasury in the 17C.

Timber roof

The upper half of the keep has one of the finest timber roofs to have survived from the Middle Ages.
It was built towards the end of the 14C and is impressive in size. Its good state of preservation is due to the infinite pains taken by its builders, both in treating the timber and in the way it was put together.

Petit Château

This part of the château was built some years after the keep and houses the Duke of Sully's apartments, notably his bedchamber and its coffered ceiling adorned with mottoes and motifs related to his title of Grand Master of the Artillery reflecting the high esteem in which the Duke held his king, Henri IV.

St-Benoît-sur-Loire★★

The basilica of St-Benoît-sur-Loire is one of the most famous Romanesque buildings in France. Visitors are enthralled by its harmonious proportions and its elaborate carvings steeped in golden light.

- **Population:** 1 876
- **Michelin Map:** 318: K-5
- **Info:** 44 r. Orléanaise, 45730 St-Benoît-sur-Loire. ✆02 38 35 79 00. www.saint-benoit-sur-loire.
- **Location:** At the intersection of the meridian of Paris and the Loire, between Gien and Orléans, you can get to St-Benoît by taking D 60, which hugs the curve of the river.
- **Timing:** Spend half a day at St-Benoît, allowing 45min for the basilica.

A BIT OF HISTORY

Foundation (7C) – According to Celtic tradition St-Benoît-sur-Loire was the place where the local Carnute druids assembled. In 645 or 651 a group of Benedictine monks led by an abbot from Orléans came to this spot and founded a monastery which very soon gained the favour of the great. Around 672 the **Abbot of Fleury** learned that the body of **St Benedict**, the father of western monasticism who died in 547, was buried beneath the ruins of the abbey of Monte Cassino in Italy. He gave orders for the precious relic to be transported to the banks of the Loire where it attracted great crowds of people and brought success to the monastery.

Theodulf, **Odo**, **Abbo and Gauzlin** – Charlemagne gave Fleury to his adviser and friend, **Theodulf**, the Bishop of Orléans, who founded two famous monastic schools, an external one for secular priests and an internal one for postulant monks. The scriptorium produced some beautiful work.

In the 10C the situation underwent a spectacular change. In 930, **Odo**, a monk from Touraine, became Abbot of Cluny; he imposed the Cluniac rule at Fleury and reopened the abbey school. St-Benoît regained its prosperity. Students flocked to the school, particularly from England, and the French king and princes offered gifts and extended their patronage. The late 10C was dominated by **Abbo**, a famous scholar and teacher, who enjoyed the favour of the Capets. He entered Fleury as a child, studied in Paris and Reims where he was under the celebrated Gerbert, who had himself been at Fleury, and then returned c. 975 to Fleury as Head of Studies. He added to the already extensive **library** and enlarged the area of study. During his reign as abbot (from 988), the abbey was at the forefront of western intellectual life with a particularly strong influence in England and the west of France. Abbo was very influential with Robert II and commissioned a monk called Aimoin to write a History of the Franks, which became the official chronicle expounding the ideology of the Capet monarchy. Abbo was assassinated in 1004.

The reign of Abbot **Gauzlin**, the future Archbishop of Bourges, early in the 11C is marked by the production of the so-called Gaignières **Evangelistary**, an illuminated manuscript – gold and silver lettering on purple parchment – the work of a Lombard painter, and by the construction of the porch belfry.

The present church (crypt, chancel, transept) was built between 1067 and 1108; the nave was not completed until the end of the 12C.

From the Middle Ages to the present – In the 15C St-Benoît passed *in commendam*. This meant that the revenues of the abbey were granted by the monarch to commendatory abbots, often laymen, who were simply beneficiaries and took no active part in the religious life of the community. The monks did not always make such abbots welcome. Under François I they refused to receive

Theodulf, a dignitary at Charlemagne's court

Theodulf was a Goth, probably originally from Spain or the Ancient Roman province of Gallia Narbonensis (modern southwest France). This brilliant theologian, scholar and poet, well-versed in the culture of Classical Antiquity, came to Neustria after 782 and joined Charlemagne's erudite circle. After a long time spent journeying round the south of France as the emperor's *missus dominicus,* he was made Bishop of Orléans, then Abbot of Micy and of St-Benoît-sur-Loire.
Theodulf had a villa (country estate) not far from Fleury; all that now remains is the oratory, or church of Germigny-des-Prés. The villa was sumptuously decorated, with murals depicting the Earth and the World, marble floors and superb mosaics in the oratory which date from about 806. On Charlemagne's death, Theodulf fell into disgrace, accused of plotting against Louis the Pious. He was deposed in 818, exiled and finally died in an Angers prison in 821.

Cardinal Duprat and shut themselves up in the tower of the porch. The King had to come in person, at the head of an armed force, to make them submit. During the Wars of Religion (1562–98) one of these abbots, Odet de Châtillon-Coligny, the brother of the Protestant leader Admiral Coligny, was himself converted to Protestantism. In 1562, St-Benoît was looted by Condé's Huguenot troops. The treasure was melted down, the marvellous library was sold and its precious manuscripts were scattered across Europe, now to be found in Berne, Rome, Leyden, Oxford and Moscow.
The celebrated Congregation of St-Maur, introduced to St-Benoît in 1627 by Cardinal de Richelieu, restored its spiritual and intellectual life.
The abbey was closed at the Revolution, its archives transferred to Orléans and its property dispersed. At the beginning of the First Empire the monastic buildings were destroyed and the church fell into disrepair. In 1835 it was registered as a historical monument, and restored on various occasions between 1836 and 1923. Monastic life was revived there in 1944.

BASILICA★★

Open 6.30am–10pm (closed 7–9pm Nov–Mar) Guided tours (1hr 30min) Easter–Oct by arrangement one month in advance. Closed 1st Fri of the month. 3€. 02 38 35 72 43. www.abbaye-fleury.com.

This imposing basilica was built between 1067 and 1218. The towers were originally much taller.

Belfry-porch★★

The belfry originally stood by itself, and is a fine example of Romanesque art. It is worth taking a close look at the richly decorated Corinthian capitals with their abaci and corbels beautifully carved in handsome golden stone from the Nevers region. Stylised plants and flowing acanthus leaves alternate with fantastic animals, scenes from the Apocalypse, and events in the Life of Christ and the Virgin Mary.

Basilica of St-Benoît-sur-Loire
©Schütze/Rodemann/age fotostock

Nave
This was rebuilt in the early-Gothic style during the 12C. It is suffused with light thanks to its white stonework and high vaulting. The organ was added c. 1700.

Transept
Completed in 1108; the dome carries the central bell-tower. Under the dome are the stalls dated 1413 and the remains of a choir screen in carved wood presented in 1635 by Richelieu, when he was Commendatory Abbot of St-Benoît. In the north transept is the 14C alabaster statue of Notre-Dame-de-Fleury.

Chancel★★
The long Romanesque chancel was built between 1065 and 1108; note the decor of blind arcades with sculpted capitals forming a triforium. The ambulatory with radiating chapels is typical of a church built for crowds and processions. The floor is paved with a Roman mosaic transported from Italy in 1531 by Cardinal Duprat; it is similar to the style popular in the eastern part of the Roman Empire. The recumbent figure is Philippe I, the fourth Capet king, who died in 1108.

Crypt★
This impressive masterpiece of the second half of the 11C has kept its original appearance. Large round columns form a double ambulatory with radiating chapels round the large central pillar containing the modern shrine of St Benedict, whose relics have been venerated here since the 8C.

EXCURSION
Église de Germigny-des-Prés★
The little church in Germigny is a rare and precious example of Carolingian art; it is one of the oldest in France and can be compared with the Carolingian octagon in the cathedral at Aachen, Germany. The original church, with a ground plan in the form of a Greek cross reminiscent of Echmiadzin Cathedral in Armenia, among other places, had four very similar apses.

Châteauneuf-sur-Loire

On the site of the old fortified castle to which the town owes its name, where Charles IV, the Fair, died in 1328, Louis Phelypeaux de la Vrillière, Secretary of State to Louis XIV, built a small-scale imitation of the château of Versailles. After the Revolution the château was sold to an architect from Orléans who had it demolished; only the 17C rotunda and gallery, the outbuildings and the pavilions in the forecourt, some of which are used as the town hall, remain.

- **Population:** 7 032
- **Michelin Map:** 318: K-4
- **Info:** pl. A.-Briand, 45110 Châteauneuf-sur-Loire. ☎02 38 58 44 79. www.briare-le-canal.com.
- **Location:** 25km/15.5mi E of Orléans, on the Loire's right bank.
- **Timing:** Allow 1–2hrs to explore the town.
- **Kids:** Make the most of the Étang de la Vallée, W of Combreux: fishing, swimming, windsurfing, picnics.

VISIT
Château grounds
The park is bordered by a moat; the western section filled with water and spanned by a stone footbridge.

Musée de la Marine de Loire
Open Apr–Oct Wed–Mon 10am–6pm, Nov–Mar Wed–Mon 2–6pm. Closed 1 Jan, 1 May, 25 Dec. 3.50€. ☎02 38 46 84 46. www.musees.regioncentre.fr.

The museum contains collections that testify to the importance of the Loire through the ages. Among the displays are carpentry tools as well as garments, jewellery and a collection of faïence.

CANAL D'ORLÉANS: LOIRE REACH

For Seine Reach, see LORRIS.

The Orléans Canal was built between 1677 and 1692, and was the scene of intense activity, mainly the transport of timber and coal, for 250 years.

DRIVING TOUR

64km/40mi round trip. Allow 3hrs.

Pays de la Forêt d'Orléans

The Forest of Orléans is the largest national forest in France stretching over 60km/37mi between Gien and Orléans. Leave Châteauneuf to the NE on D 10. In Vitry-aux-Loges, take D 9 to Combreux.

Combreux

13km/8mi NE along D 10 and D 9.

The town clusters on the south bank of the Orléans Canal. On the north side of the town and the canal stands an eye-catching **château** (16C–17C).

Étang de la Vallée★

2km/1mi W of Combreux.

The reservoir feeding the Orléans Canal is on the eastern fringe of Orléans Forest in a wild setting where there are facilities for swimming, fishing, sailing and picnics.

Arboretum des Grandes Bruyères à Ingrannes★

Open late Mar–1 Nov, Sun and bank holidays 10am–6pm, Mon–Sat 10am–12.30pm, 2–6pm (ring the bell at the entrance). Closed Easter, last week in Jul–1st week Aug. 10€ (children 5–12 years 5€). Dogs not admitted. 02 38 57 12 61. www.arboretumdesgrandesbruyeres.fr.

In the heart of the Forest of Orléans, this remarkable 5ha/12acre park was laid out in 1972, bringing together plants from different climates in the northen and southern hemispheres. To preserve the ecosystem no herbicides, fertilisers or chemicals are used. Dogwood, magnolias, old roses and heather form the core of the four main collections. After the French-style garden visitors discover the informal English park with its grass paths winding between copses, a lake before reaching the maze, the rose garden and the organic vegetable garden.

Take D 921 S to Fay-aux-Loges.

Faye-aux-Loges

9km/5.5mi NW on D 11.

Village on the banks of the Canal d'Orléans with a stoutly built **church** *aux lignes dépouillées* – 'bare in style' (11C–13C). Behind the church, the presbytery occupies a fortified house.

Chécy

15km/9mi W along N 960.

The church of St-Pierre-St-Germain, with its 12C belfry-porch, offered hospitality to Joan of Arc on the eve of the Orléans siege. Behind the church the small **Musée de la Tonnellerie** *(guided tours; open Jun–Sept Wed–Sun 2.30–6.30pm; May and Oct Sat–Sun and public holidays 2.30–6pm; closed 1 May; 2.50€; 02 38 86 95 93; www.checy.fr)* and a restored farmhouse remind you that in days gone by most of the local people were wine-growers.

ADDRESSES

STAY

Chambre d'hôte La Ferme du Grand Chesnoy – *Lieu-dit Grand-Chesnoy, 45260 Chailly-en-Gâtinais. 02 38 96 27 67. Closed Dec–Mar. 4 rooms.* The rooms are in a tower dating from 1896 and are decorated in a rustic style. Kitchen and dining room available. The garden and dovecote are charming. Tennis and footpaths.

THE LOIRE BLÉSOISE

Lying between the Sologne and the Touraine, the Loire Blésoise is home to some of the region's most spectacular châteaux, all located within a relatively small area around the main town of Blois. Perched high in the centre, the château gives an insight into French history from the 15C to 17C and is complemented by the palatial contours of the monumental Château de Chambord, the largest and most impressive of the Loire's royal residences.

Highlights

1. **Château de Blois**, one of France's most prestigious Renaissance monuments (p118)
2. Flamboyant **Château de Chambord** (p127)
3. Walking tour of **Beaugency**'s Medieval centre (p133)
4. Galleries des Illustres at **Château de Beauregard** (p138)
5. Elegant **Château de Cheverny** amid rolling parkland (p138)

Courtly Life

Standing on the northern bank of the Loire, the Château de Blois impresses with its unique combination of medieval, Renaissance and Classical architecture. Although surrounded by the busy modern town, it gives a glimpse of courtly life through the ages. Chambord, by contrast, rises seemingly from nowhere in the midst of the nearby forest, a symbol of François I's taste for splendour echoed only in the following century by Louis XIV's grandiose dreams for Versailles. The Forest of Russy, south of Blois, and the Chambord estate offer a wealth of opportunities for walking, cycling and other outdoor pursuits. Travelling downriver from Orléans, Meung-sur-Loire and Beaugency are deligthful stopovers with their attractive old towns and historic civic buildings while the Château de Talcy, inland north of the Loire, is a delightful Renaissance manor house.

Portraits and Tintin

The Château de Beauregard, south of Blois on the edge of the Forest of Russy, is unique for its fascinating portrait gallery which features over 300 historical figures, including all the kings of France from 1328 to 1643 along with their queens, courtiers and foreign contemporaries, including Elizabeth I. The spacious park and curious Jardin des Portraits in the kitchen garden are also not to be missed. Cheverny, a gem of 17C Classical architecture, will be familiar to admirers of Tintin as the inspiration for Marlinspike Hall (Château de Moulinsart in the original French) in the *Adventures of Tintin* series.

Gallery, Château de Beauregard

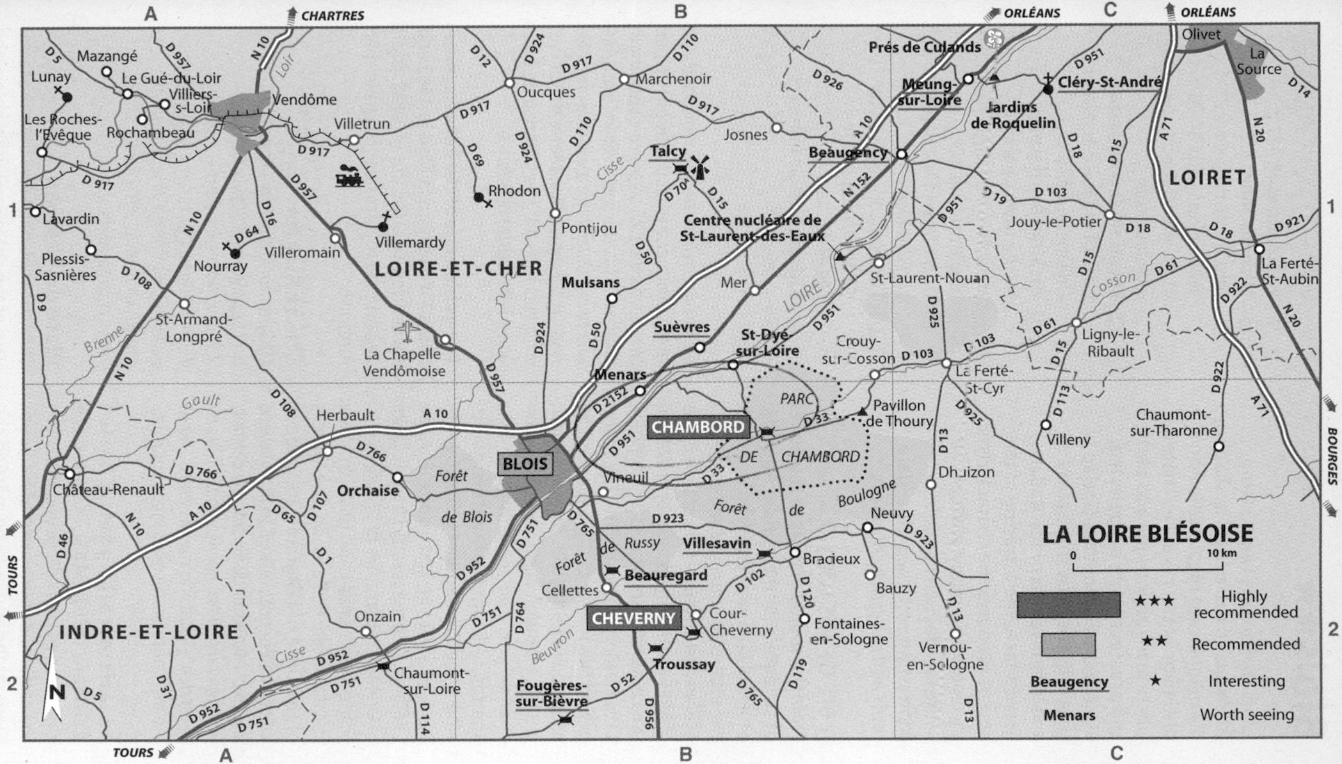
LA LOIRE BLÉSOISE
0
10 km
★★★ Highly recommended
★★ Recommended
Beaugency ★ Interesting
Menars Worth seeing
LOIRE-ET-CHER
LOIRET
INDRE-ET-LOIRE
CHARTRES
ORLÉANS
ORLÉANS
BOURGES
TOURS
TOURS
BLOIS
CHAMBORD
CHEVERNY
PARC DE CHAMBORD
Forêt de Blois
Forêt de Russy
Forêt de Boulogne
LOIRE
Loir
Cisse
Cosson
Beuvron
Brenne
Gault
Lunay
Mazangé
Le Gué-du-Loir
Villiers-s-Loir
Les Roches-l'Évêque
Rochambeau
Vendôme
Villetrun
Lavardin
Plessis-Sasnières
Nourray
Villeromain
Villemardy
St-Armand-Longpré
La Chapelle Vendômoise
Herbault
Château-Renault
Orchaise
Onzain
Chaumont-sur-Loire
Oucques
Marchenoir
Rhodon
Pontijou
Mulsans
Talcy
Josnes
Centre nucléaire de St-Laurent-des-Eaux
Mer
Suèvres
Menars
St-Dyé-sur-Loire
Vineuil
Cellettes
Beauregard
Fougères-sur-Bièvre
Troussay
Cour-Cheverny
Villesavin
Bracieux
Bauzy
Fontaines-en-Sologne
Neuvy
Crouy-sur-Cosson
Pavillon de Thoury
La Ferté-St-Cyr
Dhuizon
Vernou-en-Sologne
St-Laurent-Nouan
Beaugency
Meung-sur-Loire
Prés de Culands
Jardins de Roquelin
Cléry-St-André
Jouy-le-Potier
Ligny-le-Ribault
Villeny
Chaumont-sur-Tharonne
La Ferté-St-Aubin
Olivet
La Source
A 10
A 71
N 10
N 20
N 152
D 951
D 952
D 751
D 957
D 924
D 917
D 766
D 765
D 925
D 923
D 2152
D 103
D 33
A
B
C
1
2
N

Blois★★

Louis XII, François I and Gaston d'Orléans all had a hand in shaping the magnificent royal castle into the image of their era. The château, where many an intrigue was plotted and a famous crime perpetrated, illustrates a Flamboyant Gothic style influenced by the fantasy and inventiveness of the Italian Renaissance. The terracing of the houses produces the characteristic tricoloured harmony of Blois, the white façades of its buildings contrasting with their blue-slate roofs and red-brick chimneys.

- **Population:** 48 487
- **Michelin Map:** 318: E-F 6
- **Info**: 23 pl. du Château, 41006 Blois. 02 54 90 41 41. www.loiredeschateaux.com.
- **Location:** On the north bank of the Loire, between Orléans and Tours.
- **Parking:** See the map for the town's parking areas; two are fairly near the château.
- **Don't Miss:** The château, and Old Blois.
- **Timing:** 2hrs to visit the château, plus 2hrs for Old Blois.
- **Kids:** The magic museum.

A BIT OF HISTORY

From the counts of Blois to the dukes of Orléans – In the Middle Ages the counts of Blois were powerful lords with two estates: Champagne and the region of Blois and Chartres. One of the counts of Blois married the daughter of William the Conqueror and their son, Stephen, became King of England in 1135. In this period the House of Blois reached its peak under Thibaud IV. After his death in 1152, attention was concentrated on Champagne, and the Loire area was abandoned together with England, where the Plantagenets took over in 1154. In 1392 the last count, Guy de Châtillon, sold the county to Louis, Duke of Orléans and brother of Charles VI. Fifteen years later Louis d'Orléans was assassinated in Paris on the orders of the Duke of Burgundy. His widow, Valentina Visconti, retired to Blois where she expressed her disillusion by carving on the walls: *"Rien ne m'est plus, plus ne m'est rien"* ("Nothing means anything to me any more"); she died inconsolable.

An aristocratic poet: Charles d'Orléans (1391–1465) – Charles, the eldest son of Louis d'Orléans, inherited the castle and spent some of his youth there. At the age of 15 he married the daughter of Charles VI, who later died in childbirth. At 20 he married again but soon departed to fight the English. He proved a poor general at the Battle of Agincourt, where he was wounded and taken prisoner, but his poetic gift helped him to survive 25 years of captivity in England. He returned to France in 1440 and being once more a widower he married, at the age of 50, Marie de Clèves, who was then 14. The Château de Blois was his favourite residence.

The golden age of the Renaissance – **Louis XII** was born at Blois in 1462 and succeeded Charles VIII in 1498. Blois became the royal residence rather than Amboise.

CHÂTEAU★★★

Open Jul–Aug 9am–7pm; Apr–Jun and Sept 9am–6.30pm; Oct 9am–7.30pm; Nov–Mar 9am–12.30pm, 1.30–5.30pm. Closed 1 Jan, 25 Dec. 7.50€; no charge first Sun of the month Oct–Mar. 02 54 90 33 33. www.chateaudeblois.fr.

Place du Château

This vast esplanade was once the farmyard of the château. Slightly below, the terraced gardens offer a wide view of the bridge spanning the Loire beyond the rooftops and place Louis XII at the foot of the retaining wall; to the right are

The Assassination of the Duke of Guise (1588)

A. Cassaigne/MICHELIN

Bedroom of Henri III where the Duke of Guise was assassinated

The historical interest of the château reached its peak under **Henri III**. In 1588 **Henri de Guise**, the Lieutenant-General of the kingdom and all-powerful head of the League in Paris, supported by the King of Spain, forced Henri III to call a second meeting of the States-General, which was then the equivalent of Parliament. Five hundred deputies, nearly all supporters of Guise, attended. Guise expected them to depose the King. The latter, feeling himself to be on the brink of the abyss, could think of no other means than murder to get rid of his rival.

It is the morning of the 23 December 1588. Of the 45 impoverished noblemen who are Henri III's men of action, 20 have been chosen to deal with the Duke. Eight are waiting in the Chambre du Roi (King's Chamber), with daggers hidden under their cloaks, sitting on chests and seeming innocently to be swapping yarns. The 12 others, armed with swords, are in the Cabinet Vieux (Old Cabinet). Two priests are in the oratory of the Cabinet Neuf (New Cabinet), where the King is making them pray for the success of his enterprise.

The Duke of Guise is in the Salle du Conseil (Council Chamber) with various dignitaries. Henri III's secretary tells Guise that the King would like to see him in the Old Cabinet. To reach this room Guise has to go through the King's chamber as, only two days previously, the door between the council chamber and the old cabinet had been walled up. The Duke enters the King's chamber and is greeted by the men there as if nothing were amiss. He turns left towards the old cabinet but, as he opens the door leading into the corridor outside it, he sees men waiting for him with swords drawn in the narrow passage. He tries to retreat but is stopped by eight men, who are now clearly assassins, in the King's chamber. They fall upon their victim, seizing him firmly by his arms and legs and trapping his sword in his cloak. The Duke, who is an exceptionally strong man, manages to strike down four of his assailants and wound a fifth with his comfit box. He gives his murderers a run for their money for the entire length of the King's chamber, but with the odds so heavily stacked against him his valiant efforts are in vain and he finally collapses, riddled with stab wounds, by the King's bed. Henri III emerges from behind the wall hanging where he has been hiding and ventures up to the corpse of his rival. According to some accounts, he slapped his face, marvelling at the dead man's size and commenting that he seemed almost bigger now than he did when alive.

Afterwards, Henri III is reported to have gone down to his mother, Catherine de' Medici, and told her joyfully, "My comrade is no more, the King of Paris is dead!" His conscience apparently clear, Henri goes to hear Mass in the chapel of St-Calais as an act of thanksgiving.

The next day, the Duke of Guise's brother, the Cardinal de Lorraine, imprisoned immediately after the murder, was also assassinated. His body was put with Guise's somewhere in the château – speculation surrounds the precise location of the room where the bodies were kept. Finally, the bodies were burned and the ashes thrown into the Loire. Eight months later Henri III himself succumbed to the dagger of Jacques Clément.

Royal Castle of Blois courtyard
©Press department Royal Castle of Blois

the spires of the church of St-Nicolas and to the left the cathedral with its Renaissance tower.

The **façade** of the château – "one of the most beautiful and elaborate of all the old royal residences in this part of France" (Henry James) – on the esplanade has two main parts: the pointed gable of the Salle des États-Généraux (Chamber of the States-General), relic of the former feudal castle (13C), on the right and then the pretty building of brick and stone erected by Louis XII. In keeping with the endearing whimsicality which characterises buildings from the Middle Ages, this has a random, asymmetrical arrangement of window openings.

The great Flamboyant **gateway** is surmounted by an alcove containing an equestrian statue of Louis XII, a modern copy (made in 1857 by Seurre) of the original. The window consoles are adorned with spirited carvings. The coarse humour of the period is sometimes displayed with great candour (first and fourth windows to the left of the gateway).

The inner courtyard

Cross the courtyard to reach the delightful terrace (good **view** of the church of St-Nicolas and the Loire) on which stands the 13C **Tour du Foix**, a tower which formed part of the medieval fortified wall.

Galerie Charles-d'Orléans

Although it is named after Charles d'Orléans, this gallery probably dates from the Louis XII period. Until alterations were made in the 19C the gallery was twice its present length and connected the two wings at either end of the courtyard. Note the unusual basket-handle arches.

Aile Louis-XII

The corridor or gallery serving the various rooms in the wing marks a step forward in the quest for greater comfort and convenience. Originally rooms opened into one another. At each end of the wing a spiral staircase gave access to the different floors. The decoration is richer and Italianate panels of arabesques adorn the pillars.

Aile François-I

The building extends between the 17C Gaston-d'Orléans wing and the 13C Salle des États-Généraux (Chamber of the States-General). Only 14 years passed between work finishing on the Louis-XII wing and beginning on the François I wing, but in this time an important milestone had been passed, heralding the triumphant arrival of the Italian decorative style.

French originality, however, persisted in the general composition. The windows were made to echo the internal arrangement of the rooms, without regard for

symmetry; they could be close together in some places and far apart in others; their mullions might be double or single; and pilasters might flank the window openings or occupy the middle of the opening.
A **staircase** was added to the façade. Since Mansart demolished part of the wing to make room for the Gaston d'Orléans buildings, this staircase is no longer in the centre of the façade. It climbs spirally in an octagonal well, three faces of which are recessed into the building.

Royal apartments (Aile François-I) and museums

Inside the Gaston-d'Orléans wing, a projecting gallery runs round the base of the cupola crowning the grand staircase, sumptuously decorated on all but the lower level with trophies, garlands and masks. Many plans displayed on the ground floor illustrate the various alterations of the château.

Musée Archéologique

Same hours as the château.
Château admission ticket includes entry to the museum. 02 54 90 33 33.
The archaeological museum presents artefacts resulting from digs carried out in the Loir-et-Cher *département*, laid out in the rooms which served as kitchen quarters under François I. A great many exhibits were uncovered on the medieval site of the castle, a small hillock.

Apartments in the François-I Wing

The François-I staircase leads up to the Royal apartments on the first floor, where a succession of rooms containing fireplaces, tapestries, busts, portraits and furniture can be seen. The interior decoration was restored by Duban in the 19C.
The most interesting room on the **first floor** is that of Catherine de' Medici. It still has its 237 carved wood panels concealing secret cupboards which may have been used to hide poisons, jewels or State papers, or may simply have been made to cater for the then prevalent taste for having wall cupboards in Italian-style rooms. They were opened by pressing a pedal concealed in the skirting board.
The **second floor** was the scene of the **murder of the Duke of Guise** (*see box p119*). The rooms have been altered and the old cabinet demolished to make way for the Gaston-d'Orléans wing. It is therefore rather difficult to follow the phases of the assassination.

Salle des États-Généraux

This is the oldest (13C) part of the château, the feudal hall of the old castle of the counts of Blois. From 1576 to 1588 the States-General, the French Parliament, used to convene in this hall. The twin barrel vaults are supported by a central row of columns.

Musée des Beaux-Arts★

Same hours as the château.
Château admission ticket includes entry to the museum. 02 54 90 33 33.
The main interest of this Fine Arts Museum lies in the 16C and 17C paintings and portraits. The **portrait gallery** contains paintings from the Château de St-Germain-Beaupré *(Creuse département)* and Château de Beauregard; there is an outstanding collection of 50 terracotta **medallions** by Jean-Baptiste Nini. The Guise Gallery houses several works on the theme of the events of 1588, such as *Meeting of the Duke of Guise* and *Henri III* by Pierre-Charles Comte. Finally, the wrought-iron and locksmithing gallery contains the Frank collection in which one of the star exhibits is the remarkable fire-pan destined for the Count of Chambord, executed by local ironsmith Louis Delcros.

WALKING TOUR

OLD BLOIS★

Follow route on map. Allow at least 2hrs.
Every street corner of this fascinating town has something to offer the dedicated visitor prepared to stroll through the old districts.

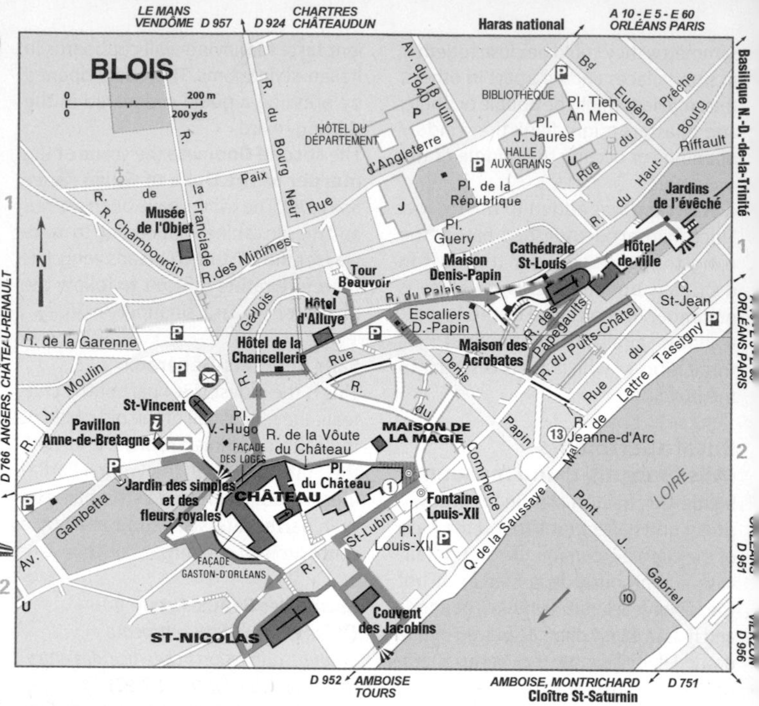

Pavillon Anne-de-Bretagne★

This graceful little building of stone and brick, crowned by a high slate roof, once the belvedere of the Royal Gardens, is now the tourist centre. Note the cable mouldings which emphasise the corners, and the open-work sculptured stone balustrade with the initials of Louis XII and Anne of Brittany, his wife. On the right along avenue Jean-Laigret, the pavilion extends into a long half-timbered wing, also built under Louis XII, which was later used as an **orangery** *(now a restaurant)*. Walk along place Victor-Hugo, which is lined on the north by the façade of the 17C church of **St-Vincent** built in the style known as Jesuit, and on the south by the beautiful **Façade des Loges** of the château.

Jardin des Simples et des Fleurs Royales

This small terraced garden is all that remains of the vast château gardens. Standing near the balustrade one has an excellent **view**★ to the left over the Pavillon Anne-de-Bretagne, the church of St-Vincent and place Victor-Hugo; on the right rises the Façade des Loges (François-I wing of the château) and the end pavilion of the Gaston-d'Orléans wing. Down below, a modern garden (1992) is a delightful tribute to Renaissance gardens.

Façade des Loges

The interior part of François I's initial construction backed on to the medieval rampart wall and had no outside view. This troubled the King and so he decided to add a second building with as many openings as possible against the outside of the ramparts. Following the King's wish to copy the most recent Roman buildings, the architect drew his inspiration from the Vatican palace; however, the loggias do not communicate and the addition of bartizans adds a somewhat medieval note to the overall effect. The top storey is underlined by fine gargoyles.

Église St-Nicolas★

This fine 12C and 13C church formed part of the Benedictine abbey of St-Laumer whose monastic buildings stretch down to the river bank. It features a vast chancel and ambulatory with aspidial chapels and delicately sculpted capitals. In the left of the chancel is a retable dedictaed to St Mary of Egypt.

Couvent des Jacobins

r. Anne-de-Bretagne.

As early back as the 15C–16C, these convent buildings already housed the **Musée d'Art religieux** *(first floor; open Tue–Sat except public holidays 2–6pm; no charge; 02 54 78 17 14)* devoted to religious art collections on the first floor and, on the second floor, beneath a fine timber roof shaped as an inverted hull, the **Muséum d'Histoire naturelle** *(second floor; open Tue–Fri Jul–Aug 10am–noon, 2–6pm, Sat–Sun and public holidays 2–6pm; rest of year Tue–Sun 2–6pm; closed 1 Jan, 1 May, 1 Nov, 25 Dec; 2.80€; 02 54 90 21 00; www.ville-blois.com)*, where stuffed and mounted animals vividly portray the wildlife of the region.

Fontaine Louis XII

This Flamboyant Gothic fountain is a copy of the monument erected during the reign of Louis XII. The weather-worn original is kept in the Château.

Maison de la Magie Robert-Houdin★

Open Apr–mid-Sept 10am–12.30pm, 2–6.30pm; Oct–Mar Mon in school holidays only. 7.50€ (children 6–11 years 5€). 02 54 55 26 26. www. maisondelamagie.fr.

Set up in a 19C *hôtel particulier* facing the château, the Maison de la Magie enlightens visitors on the history of magic and serves as a national centre for the art of illusionism *(open to professional conjurers and researchers only)*. The museum is dedicated to the great Robert-Houdin. A six-headed dragon, operated by a highly sophisticated computer system, welcomes visitors to this attractive mansion made with tufa and painted bricks. The tour starts with a guided visit through the history of conjuring, illustrating the chronological developments in this fascinating world. Visitors then become part of the exhibition, walking through a giant kaleidoscope and stepping into a picture gallery before they reach the foyer devoted to magicians of international renown such as Georges Méliès, who was to pave the way for special effects in the film industry.

On the first floor, set against an elegant and theatrical backdrop, the **Cabinet fantastique Robert-Houdin** displays exhibits relating to the world of magic. Posters, engravings, manuscripts and miscellaneous accessories evoke Houdin's performances, which would attract large crowds of Parisian socialites to the Palais-Royal Theatre.

The **Théâtre des Magiciens**★ (400 seats set up under the château esplanade) has been especially designed for high-class conjuring acts and offers a 20min show of dazzling expertise, performed by some of the world's leading illusionists.

Hôtel de la Chancellerie

At the corner of rue Chemonton and rue du Lion, this late 16C mansion is one of the largest in Blois. In the courtyard notice the superb staircase.

Hôtel d'Alluye

8 r. St-Honoré.

This fine private mansion was built in 1508 for **Florimond Robertet**, treasurer successively to Charles VIII, Louis XII and François I. When accompanying Charles VIII on his expedition to Naples, the financier took a liking to Italian art. Behind the façade of the mansion with its delicate Gothic Renaissance sculptures, a large courtyard opens up with pure Renaissance Italianate **galleries**★. The building now houses the head office of a group of insurance companies founded in 1820.

Tour Beauvoir

Group visits only. 02 54 71 82 77.

This square keep (11C) belonged to a separate fief from the château and was later incorporated into the town's fortifications. The cells which can be visited today were used until 1945.

From the terrace there is a fine **view**★ of Blois and the surrounding area.
Old half-timbered façades line rue Beauvoir (nos. 3, 15 and 21), surrounding a 15C stone house (no. 19).
Escalier Denis-Papin – This steep staircase gives fine views to the south. At the top stands a statue of Denis Papin (1647–1712) recognised (posthumously) as the father of the steam engine.

Maison des Acrobates

3 pl. St-Louis.
This is a typical medieval house, with its half-timbered façade, its two corbelled storeys, its posts carved with acrobats and jugglers, and its foliage ornamentation.

Cathédrale St-Louis

The cathedral was almost entirely destroyed by a storm in 1678. It was rebuilt in the Gothic style and features contemporary stained glass windows in the nave which contrast with the highly decorative 19C windows in the chancel.

Hôtel de Ville and Jardins de l'Évêché

Access through the gate to the left of the cathedral.
Situated behind the cathedral, the town hall lies in the former bishop's palace, built at the beginning of the 18C by the father of the architect of place de la Concorde in Paris.
Further towards the east, the gardens of the bishop's palace form a terrace overlooking the Loire, with a lovely **view**★ (*stand near the statue of Joan of Arc*) over the river, its wooded slopes and the roofs of the town; to the south is the pinnacle of the church of St-Saturnin and on the north bank, the pure spires of the church of St-Nicolas. Lovely view also of the cathedral chevet.
Maison Denis-Papin is a Gothic house perched at the top of rue Pierre-de-Blois, **Rue des Papegault** features attractive Renassiance houses at nos.15, 13, 10, 8 and 4, while no. 7 **Rue du Puits-Châtel** is worth seeing for its Renaissance arcaded courtyard.

ADDITIONAL SIGHTS

Musée de l'Objet

r. Franciade. Open Jul–Aug Wed–Sun 1.30–6.30pm; Mar–Jun and Sept–Nov Sat–Sun 1.30–6.30pm (during the week by arrangement). Closed public holidays except 14 Jul and 15 Aug. 4€. 02 54 55 37 40. www.museedelobjet.org.
The collections presented in the former Couvent des Minimes are unusual in that they were made with extremely simple, mundane objects designed for everyday use. They are the work of contemporary artists who have deliberately chosen these materials in order to turn them into something different: this novel approach based on manipulating matter has given birth to a new art form. A ready-made composition by Marcel Duchamp (1887–1968) welcomes visitors, who may then explore a series of curious or striking exhibits laid out on three levels, executed by leading names such as César, Christo or Isou.

Mur des Mots

On the corner of rue Franciade and rue de la Paix, one of the walls of the Conservatoire is covered with graffiti stating axioms and proverbs.

EXCURSIONS

Boat trips

Sailing along the Loire in a traditional boat will offer you the opportunity of observing at leisure the local fauna and flora. For information, apply to the tourist office.

Orchaise

9km/5.6mi W on D 766.
Situated near the church, the **Priory Botanical Gardens** (*open Apr–Oct Sat–Thu 3–7pm, last admission 30min before closing; 6€; 02 54 70 03 92; http://prieure.orchaise.free.fr*), covering an area of 3ha/7 acres, boast a superb collection of rhododendrons, azaleas, camellias and peonies, as well as numerous evergreen plants.

Mulsans

14km/8.7mi NE along D 50.

Mulsans is a small farming village on the edge of the Beauce, heralded by the village's traditional walled-in farmyards which are characteristic of this region. The charming **church** (*visit by appointment; 02 54 87 34 73)* has Flamboyant windows and a fine Romanesque bell-tower decorated with blind arcades and twin round-arched window openings. There is a Renaissance gallery supported by carved wooden columns extending the full width of the nave and incorporating the porch; this is a regional feature known as a *caquetoire* where people would pause to talk after Mass.

Suèvres★

11km/7mi NE along N 152.

The ancient Gallo-Roman city of Sodobrium hides its picturesque façades below the noisy main road on the north bank of the Loire. The **church of St-Christophe** beside the road is entered through a huge porch *(caquetoire)* where the parishioners could pause to engage in conversation. The stonework is decorated with various fishbone and chevron patterns characteristic of the Merovingian period.

The houses at no. 9 and no. 14 bis in rue Pierre-Pouteau date from the 15C. Turn right into a picturesque cul-de-sac, rue des Moulins, running beside the stream which is spanned by several footbridges. The washing place is at the corner of rue St-Simon; on either side of the street are traces of an old fortified gate. Further on through the trees *(left)* emerges the two-storey Romanesque tower of the **Église St-Lubin** with its attractive south door (15C).

ADDRESSES

STAY

Chambre d'hôte les Salamandres – *1 r. de St Dyé, 41350 Montlivault. 10km/6mi SE of Blois. 02 54 20 69 55. www.salamandres.fr. 5 rms.* This former wine-producing building has been tastefully restored in styles, ancient, rustic and contemporary. The bedrooms are housed in the former barns.

Chambre d'hôte La Villa Médicis – *1 r. Médicis, Macé, 41000 St-Denis-sur-Loire. 4km/2.5mi NE of Blois on N 152 towards Orléans. 02 54 74 46 38. www.lavillamedicis.com. 6 rms. . Evening meal .* Marie de Medici came to take the waters at the springs in the park in which this 19C villa was built, as a hotel for spa patrons.

Hôtel Anne de Bretagne – *31 av. J.-Laigret. 02 54 78 05 38. www.annedebretagne.free.fr. Closed 9 Jan–6 Feb. 28 rms. 7€.* This small family hotelis near the castle and the terraced Jardin du Roi.

Hotel Holiday Inn Garden Court – *26 av. Maunoury. 02 54 55 44 88. www.holiday-inn.fr. 10€. Restaurant .* Well-equipped and good-sized rooms. Just out from the centre, but still convenient.

Hôtel Ibis – *3 r. Porte-Côté, in the town centre. 02 54 74 01 17. www.ibishotels.com. 56 rms. 8€.* Central location, with some adjoining, all well soundproofed, rooms.

Hotel le Monarque – *61 r. Porte-Chartraine. 02 54 78 05 38. Closed 4 Dec–8 Jan. 6.50€. Restaurant .* Newly renovated and soundproofed hotel, and decorated in pastel shades.

Chambre d'hôtel Le Plessis – *X195 r. Albert-1er. 02 54 43 80 08. www.leplessisblois.com. 5 rms.* A pretty renovated vineyard: reading room and brunch-style breakfast served in the main house (18C), carefully appointed rooms in the old wine-press building.

EAT

Au Bouchon Lyonnais – *25 r. des Violettes. 02 54 74 12 87. Closed Jan, Sun–Mon except public holidays. Reservation recommended.* Located just at the bottom of the hill crowned by the château, this restaurant is a favourite with residents of Blois, who enjoy the rustic decor with exposed beams and stone walls. Regional fare.

Restaurant de la Poste – *11 av. de Blois, 41190 Molineuf. 02 54 70 03 25. www.restaurant-podiras.com. Closed 16*

Nov–4 Dec, 8–19 Feb, Tue Oct–Apr, Sun eve Sept–June, Wed. On the edge of the Forest of Blois, this country inn features a brightly coloured dining room and conservatory. Contemporary cuisine with a touch of sophistication.

Au Rendez-vous des Pêcheurs – *27 r. Foix. ℘02 54 74 67 48. www.rendezvousdespecheurs.com. Closed 2–11 Jan, 29 Jul–20 Aug, Mon lunch, Sun. Reservation recommended.* A provincial-style bistro in the old part of Blois. Stained-glass windows filter the light in the quiet dining room. Fish features prominently.

Les Banquettes Rouges – *16 r. des Trois-Marchands. ℘02 54 78 74 92. Closed 10 days in Jun, 10 in Aug, Christmas, Sun–Mon.* This pretty little restaurant has a red façade. Warm furnishings, bistro chairs and red benches. Good food.

Côté Loire – *2 pl. de la Greve. ℘02 54 74 07 86. www.coteloire.com. Closed 2–10 May, 1–7 Sept, 16–29 Nov, 5 Jan–3 Feb. 9€. Restaurant (Closed Sat lunch Jul–Aug, Sun–Mon).* The charm of this country inn derives from the original 16C beams, varnished wooden tables, an antique dresser and a set blackboard menu prepared from seasonal market produce. Guest rooms.

Le Bistrot de Léonard – *8 r. Mar.-de- Lattre-de-Tassigny. ℘02 54 74 83 04. www.lebistrotdeleonard.com. Closed 24 Dec–1 Jan, Sat lunch, Sun.* This bistro, with a Parisian ambiance, is behind an attractive wood façade on the embankment. Specials chalked up on the board, stylish table layout and references to Leonardo da Vinci throughout.

Le Médicis – *2 allée François-1er. ℘02 54 43 94 04. www.le-medicis.com. Closed 9–15 Nov, 5–31 Jan, Sun eve Nov–May, Mon Nov–Mar.* This house dating from 1900 offers good contemporary cuisine in a luxurious dining room/veranda (moulded ceilings, Second Empire furniture). Ten modernised guest rooms.

NIGHTLIFE

Le Boulot – *9 r. Henri-Drussy. ℘02 54 74 20 20. Closed Sun.* The moustachioed owner opened his first pizzeria over 20 years ago. He offers a different choice of wines by the glass every week, to be enjoyed with the dish of the day or a snack.

Rond-point de la Résistance – There are three cafés near this roundabout by the river. It is more pleasant to go late in the evening, to avoid the car exhaust fumes: L'Époque, Le Maryland and Le Colonial Café. Nearby are tobacconists and newsagents which stay open late.

Rue Foulerie – In this narrow street on the edge of the old part of town you will find a disco, a piano bar and a couple of pubs.

SHOPPING

Rue du Commerce – Rue du Commerce and the adjacent streets in this pleasant pedestrian-only district offer all kinds of shopping.

TAKING A BREAK

Le Bistrot – *12 r. Henry-Drussy. ℘02 54 78 47 74.* Attractive, slightly old-fashioned décor, eclectic music and a long terrace set among the acacias in place Ave-Maria popular on fine days.

La Salsa – *4 ruelle Ronceraie. ℘02 54 78 28 67. Closed Mon.* The atmosphere is very easy-going, to the beat of salsa and African music.

SON ET LUMIÈRE

Enormous projectors combine photographs with special sound and lighting effects to give a lively show of the history of Blois.
Performances mid Apr–May and Aug 10pm, Jun–Jul 10.30pm, Sept 9.30pm. ℘02 54 90 33 32. www.ville-blois.fr.

PRACTICAL INFORMATION

TOURS – Discovery tours *(2hrs)*. Information at the tourist office or on www.vpah.culture.fr.

Château de Chambord★★★

The writer Henry James elegantly summed up this great castle: "Chambord is truly royal – royal in its great scale, its grand air, its indifference to common considerations."
The largest by far of the Loire châteaux, Chambord is built on a scale that foreshadowed the château at Versailles. It looms into sight suddenly, and as the view of its white mass gradually expands on approaching, its detail becoming ever clearer. At sunset especially, it makes a striking impression on the viewer. The magnificent building also owes its impact to its fine architectural unity and sumptuous Renaissance decoration, dating from the period when this style was at its most splendid.

- **Michelin Map:** 318: G-6.
- **Location:** An hour-and-a-half drive SW of Paris, the château is situated between Beaugency and Blois. It sits back from the the Loire, off the south bank, at the end of a long avenue. Visitors enter through the Porte Royale. Brochures with a detailed map of the château are available from the reception desk.
- **Don't Miss:** Two particularly outstanding features of the château: the great staircase and the roof terrace. Tapestries in the State Rooms.
- **Timing:** Allow a full day to enjoy Chambord, alloting at least 2hrs for the castle. The vast grounds, with their deer and wild boar, are worth visiting as well. Stay to see the castle's floodlights at nightfall.
- **Kids:** Boating on the moat.

A BIT OF HISTORY

Grandiose creation of François I (16C) – The counts of Blois had built a small castle in this isolated corner of the forest of Boulogne, which was excellent hunting country. As a young man François I liked to hunt in the forest and in 1518 he ordered the old castle to be razed to make room for a sumptuous palace. Several designs were put forward and no doubt Leonardo da Vinci, the King's guest at Le Clos-Lucé, drew up a plan which was made into a model by Le Boccador.

As work progressed, the original plans were altered and large sums of money were swallowed up, but the King refused to cut corners. Even when the Treasury was empty and there was no money to pay the ransom for his two sons in Spain, work went on. It suffered only one interruption, from 1524 to 1525, during the Italian campaign which resulted in the defeat of Pavia. In his enthusiasm the King even proposed in 1527 to divert the course of the Loire so that it should flow before the château, but in view of the enormity of this task a smaller river, the Cosson, was chosen instead.

By 1537 the major construction work was completed. Only the interior decoration remained to be done. In 1538 the King commissioned a pavilion linked to the keep by a two-storey building, and a second symmetrical wing to be added to the west side. The whole complex measured 117m/380ft by 156m/510ft. In 1539 the King was able to receive **Charles V** at Chambord. In 1545 the royal pavilion

Touring Tip

All year round, from sunset to midnight, a sophisticated system of floodlighting allows visitors to feast their eyes on the château's outstanding architecture, set off by a dazzling kaleidoscope of red, white, yellow and blue.

was finished, but François I, who until then had lived in the north-east tower, leaving him little time to enjoy it as he died two years later.
Henri II continued his father's work by building the west wing and the chapel tower while the curtain wall was completed. At his death in 1559 the château was still unfinished.

Louis XIV and Molière – François II and Charles IX came frequently to hunt in the forest. Henri III and Henri IV hardly put in an appearance at Chambord, but Louis XIII reforged the royal link. Louis XIV stayed at Chambord nine times between 1660 and 1685.
Molière wrote *Monsieur de Pourceaugnac* at Chambord in a matter of a few days. During the première the King did not seem at all amused. Lully, who had written the music and was playing the role of an apothecary, had an inspiration; he jumped feet first from the stage on the harpsichord and fell through it. The King burst out laughing and the play was saved. *Le Bourgeois gentilhomme* caused Molière renewed anguish. The King was icy at the first performance. The courtiers who were made fun of in the play were ready to be sarcastic. But after the second performance the King expressed his pleasure and the whole court changed their criticism into praise.

The Affair of the White Flag (1871–73) – In 1871, Henri, Count of Chambord and, since the fall of Charles X in 1830, legitimate heir to the French throne, was close to achieving his goal. This was the year when, following the disruption of the Franco-Prussian War, the French elected a monarchist assembly in favour of restoring the monarchy. However, the monarchists were divided into two groups: the legitimists who supported the traditional conception of absolute monarchy and the Orléanists, more modern in their outlook, who upheld the principles of 1789. Eventually both parties agreed on the name of the heir; **Henri V**, the last of the Bourbon line. As he had lived in exile for 40 years, Henri was not well-informed of the realities of French politics when he returned to his native soil. He went to live at Chambord where on 5 July 1871 he proclaimed his convictions in a manifesto which ended with these words "Henri V will not give up the white flag of Henri IV". The effect of this declaration on public opinion was a disaster: the Royalists lost the elections. The Count of Chambord stubbornly refused to reconsider the matter

Maréchal de Saxe (18C)

Louis XV presented the estate, with a revenue of 40 000 *livres,* to the Maréchal de Saxe as a reward for his victory over the Dutch and English at the Battle of Fontenoy in 1745. The extravagant, proud and violent Maréchal entertained a lively, exciting lifestyle. To satisfy his taste for arms, he made room to accommodate two regiments of cavalry composed of Tartars, Wallachians and natives of Martinique. These unconventional troops rode high-spirited horses from the Ukraine which were trained to assemble at the sound of a trumpet. The Maréchal imposed iron discipline on his entourage. If the slightest offence was committed, the culprits would be hanged from the branches of an old elm. More by terror than by courtship, Maurice de Saxe won the favours of a well-known actress, Mme Favart, and compelled her to remain at Chambord. He re-erected Molière's stage for her amusement. Monsieur Favart played the triple role of director, author and consenting husband.

The Maréchal died at 54, some said, in a duel with the Prince de Conti, whose wife he had seduced. Others ascribed his death to a neglected chill. Vainglorious even in death, Maurice de Saxe had given orders that the six cannon, he had placed in the main courtyard of the château should be fired every quarter of an hour for 16 days as a sign of mourning.

©Sylvaine Poitau/Apa Publications

and returned to Austria. Two years later in October 1873 a final attempt to compromise – a tricolour flag dotted with fleur-de-lis – failed. The National Assembly accepted the situation and voted for the Republic. Henri did not succeed to the throne and died in 1883. The Château de Chambord, which had witnessed the final hours of the monarchy, was handed down to his nephew, the Duke of Parma. In 1932 his descendants sold it to the State for about 11 million francs.

VISIT

Open mid-Jul–mid-Aug 9am–7.30pm; Apr–mid-Jul and mid-Aug–Sept 9am–6.15pm; Oct–Mar 9am–5.15pm (last admission 30min before closing). Closed 1 Jan, 1 May, 25 Dec. 9.50€ in Jul–Aug, rest of year 8.50€. 08 25 82 60 88. www.chambord.org.

Although the ground plan of Chambord is feudal – a central **keep** with four towers, which qualifies as a château in its own right, set in an enclosed precinct – the architecture is Renaissance and makes no reference to war. The château is a royal palace built for pleasure. During the construction two wings were added, one containing the royal apartments and the other the chapel. Chambord is the personal creation of François I. The name of the architect has not been recorded, but the architecture seems to have been inspired by the spirit of Leonardo da Vinci who had been staying at the French court and died in the spring of 1519 just as work on the château began.

Double Staircase

The famous double staircase, undoubtedly conceived by Leonardo da Vinci, stands at the intersection of the cross formed by the four guard-rooms. The two flights of steps spiral round each other from the ground floor to the roof terrace. The stonework at the centre and round the outside is pierced by many openings so that you can see from one flight to the other.

State Apartments

The State Rooms on the ground floor and on the first floor contain a superb collection of French and Flemish tapestries.

François I's rooms were in the north tower on the **first floor**. In the King's Bedchamber the bedspread and hangings are made of gold embroidered velvet (16C Italian). In François I's dressing room the salamander, the King's emblem, and the letter F alternate in the coffers of the barrel-vaulted ceiling. The Queen's Bedchamber in the Tour François-Ier is hung with Paris tapestries relating the History of Constantine, after cartoons by Rubens. The King's Suite which follows is decorated with tapestries and historic portraits. The Royal or State Bedchamber has the original Regency style panelling fitted

48 for the Maréchal; the room next or, at the exact centre of the building, gives a remarkable view of the park. The Dauphin's Suite in the East Tower, contains many mementoes of the Count of Chambord.

Musée de la Chasse et de la Nature★
The museum displays the hunting techniques of the Renaissance and explains how important the Château's location was to François I as a keen huntsman. The hunting art on show includes the remarkable *Diana and her nymphs* (a joint work by Rubens and Jean Bruegel) and scenes such as the *Salon de Chasse* and the *Chambre des chasseurs* by Mark Dion, a contemporary artist. A gallery leads to the rectangular **chapel★** which occupies the West Tower. The initials of François I, Henri II, Louis XIV and the Count of Chambord testify to its different stages of construction and decoration.

Roof terrace
The terrace, a direct inspiration from castles such as Méhun-sur-Yèvre and Saumur, is unique: a maze of lanterns, chimneys, stairs and dormer windows, all intricately carved and decorated with a mosaic of inset slates cut in various shapes – lozenges, circles and squares – in imitation of Italian marble. It was here that the court spent most of its time watching the start and return of the hunts, military reviews and exercises, tournaments and festivals.

The Château in Numbers

The Château de Chambord is a jewel of the Renaissance, comprising 440 rooms, 365 fireplaces, 13 main flights of stairs and 70 backstairs. 1 800 workmen toiled for 28 years at the site (1st phase: the keep and royal wing), François I stayed for just 72 days, the Count of Chambord 3 days and the Maréchal de Saxe 10 years. 2 000 people could be accommodated in the Château.

The thousands of nooks and crannies of the terrace invited the confidences, intrigues and assignations which played a great part in the life of that glittering society.

Sport of Kings

The château estate was richly stocked with game and lent itself to hawking. At one time there were more than 300 falcons. Hunting was the favourite medieval sport and princes were brought up to it from their earliest days.

The Park

Visit of the park is free. Guided tours of the park are in tune with each season. ℘02 54 50 50 40 or 02 54 50 50 41.

Since 1948 the park has been a national hunt reserve covering 5 500ha/13 591 acres of which 4 500ha/11 120 acres are taken up by forest; it is enclosed by a wall, the longest in France, 32km/20mi long and pierced by five gates at the end of six beautiful drives.

Écuries du Maréchal de Saxe

A display of **horsemanship** (*45min equestrian show Jul and Aug 11.45am and 4.30pm; May, Jun and Sept Mon–Fri 11.45am, Sat–Sun 11.45am and 4.30pm; 9.50€, children 7€; ℘02 54 20 31 01; www.ecuries-chambord.com)* is held in the ruins of the former stables belonging to the Maréchal de Saxe.

It retraces the history of the château from the Renaissance period to the days of the Comte de Chambord.

For tired tots, why not suggest a ride in a **horse-drawn carriage** (*open May-Sept 45min tour of the grounds in a horse-drawn carriage by request 10am-6pm; 8.50€, children 6€; ℘02 54 20 31 01)* as a way of enjoying the scenery and relieving tired feet?

EXCURSION

Château de Villesavin★

11km/7mi S by D112 and D 102; turn right at Bracieux. Guided tours (75min). Open Jun–Sept 10am–7pm; Oct–mid-Nov 10am–noon,

Pigeons as a Status Symbol

The right to keep pigeons – held essentially by large land the privileges that disappeared with the Revolution. The size o depended on the size of the estate: there was one pigeon-hole containin couple of birds for each acre of land. In the Middle Ages, dovecotes were built to attract pigeons and doves for two reasons: not only did the birds provide meat, but their droppings were also highly prized as a fertilizer – though it was so rich in nitrates that it could be used only in the rainy season, when it would be naturally diluted. It is thought that the practice of keeping pigeons was brought back by the Crusaders from the Middle East where the land has always been fertilized with pigeon manure.

2–6pm; mid-Nov–Dec Sat-Sun 2–5pm; mid-Feb–May 10am–noon, 2–7pm. Closed 25 Dec. 7.50€. 02 54 46 42 88. www.chateauvillesavin.com.
Villesavin derives from Villa Savini, the name of a Roman villa, which stood beside the Roman road that passed through Ponts-d'Arian (Hadrian's Bridges).

The **château** was built between 1527 and 1537 by Jean Le Breton, Lord of Villandry and superintendent of works at Chambord. It is a charming Renaissance building with certain Classical tendencies and consists of a central block flanked by symmetrical pavilions.

Left of the château stands a large 16C **dovecote** with 1 500 pigeon-holes.

ADDRESSES

STAY

Chambre d'hôte la Giraudière – *256 r. de la Giraudière, 41250 Mont-Près-Chambord. 02 54 70 84 83. 3 rms.* Not far from the forest of Boulogne, this chambre d'hôte provides a rural, wooded setting at reasonable prices.

Chambre d'hôte la Grange aux Herbes – *4 r. du Pavillon, 41220 Thoury. 02 54 87 55 79. www.lagrangeaux herbes.fr. 5 rms.* This former farm has been elegantly restored, giving onto a shaded parc with a small pond.

Hôtel Grand St-Michel – *pl. St-Michel, 41250 Chambord. 02 54 20 31 31. Closed 12 Nov–20 Dec and Wed Dec–Mar. 40 rms. 8€. Restaurant* This regional-style building opposite the castle benefits from the peace of its magnificent park.

EAT

La Table d'Armelle – *8 pl.de l'Hôtel-de-Ville, Bracieux. 0254 46 03 53. Closed 2 weeks Mar, 2 weeks Oct, Sun in low season, Mon.* A hugely popular restaurant run by three generations of the same family serving delicious crêpes and salads. Bookings strongly advised.

Auberge du Bon Terroir – *20 r. 8-Mai, 41500 Muides-sur-Loire. 02 54 87 59 24. Closed 23 Nov–8 Dec, 4–26 Jan, Mon–Tue.* Traditional cuisine and Loire Valley specialities inside or on the terrace under a shady lime tree.

LEISURE ACTIVITIES

Boating – *St-Michel Bridge. 02 54 56 00 43. Mid-Mar–Oct 10am–nightfall.* A leisurely trip in a boat on the Cosson river, along the castle's moat and on the grand canal.

Cycling – Apr–Nov 10am–nightfall. Bikes can be rented at the landing dock. *02 54 33 37 54.*

SON ET LUMIÈRE

Penetrate the intimacies of Château de Chambord, its images and sounds. Virtual settings and personnages bewitch you in this evening show wherein you become the actor. *Jul–Sept. 02 54 50 40 00.*

…âteau de Talcy★

This austere-looking château on the borders of the Loire Valley and Beauce region stands well off the beaten track. Once inside the courtyard, however, visitors discover a charming, Renaissance manor house.

- **Michelin Map:** 318: F-5
- **Info:** Office du Tourisme de Blois, 23 pl. du Château, 41006 Blois, 02 54 90 41 41. www.loiredeschateaux.com.
- **Location:** Between Beaugency (18km/11mi to the E) and Vendôme (36km/22.4mi to the W).
- **Timing:** Allow 1hr30min for the Château.

VISIT

Open May–Aug 9.30am–noon, 2–6pm; Sept–Apr 10am–noon, 2–5pm (Oct–Mar Wed–Mon). Closed 1 Jan, 1 May, 25 Dec. 5€. 02 54 81 03 01.

The keep, part of which dates from the 15C, has a double doorway (postern and carriage gate), two corner turrets and a crenellated sentry walk which looks medieval although it dates from 1520. The first courtyard owes its charm to a graceful gallery and an attractive well. In the second courtyard is a large 16C **dovecote**, with 1 500 pigeon-holes in a good state of preservation.

The house itself is furnished as it would have been in the 17C and 18C.

Fine furniture (17C–18C) and Gothic **tapestries** adorn the guard-room, office, kitchen, bedrooms and salons which are roofed with French-style ceilings (with decorated exposed beams).

Beaugency★

Beaugency certainly recalls the Middle Ages and was an important town in the 11C–13C. Due to its proximity to the Loire, the town was commerically important when trade was conducted on the river. It is best to enter the town from the south, crossing the River Loire by the age-old multi-arched bridge (attractive view). The oldest parts of the bridge date from the 14C but an earlier bridge used as a toll was already in existence in the 12C.

- **Population:** 7 584
- **Michelin Map:** 318: G-5
- **Info:** 3 pl. Dr-Hyvernaud, BP 44, 45190 Beaugency. 02 38 44 54 42. www.beaugency.fr.
- **Location:** Beaugency is 20km/12mi S of Orléans, and 29km/18mi N of Blois, and the right bank of the Loire.
- **Parking:** There are areas to park (fee) on the river front.
- **Don't Miss:** The medieval houses in the centre.
- **Timing:** A leisurely half-day, or whiz around the town in an hour.
- **Kids:** Check with the tourist office for activities including walks, water sports and horse riding during the summer months.

A BIT OF HISTORY

The two councils of Beaugency (12C) – Both councils were called to deal with the marital problems of Philippe I and Louis VII. While visiting **Fulk IV** in Tours, Philippe seduced his host's wife, the Countess Bertrade, and shortly afterwards repudiated Queen Bertha. The King thought that he would easily obtain the annulment of his marriage by raising a vague claim of consanguinity, but Pope Urban II refused to comply with his request. The King persisted and was excommunicated so he was unable to join the First Crusade (1099). Eventually the excommunication was lifted by the **Council of Beaugency** in 1104 and four years later the King died at peace with the church. Far more important was the **Council of 1152** which annulled the marriage of Louis VII and **Eleanor of Aquitaine**.

The beautiful and seductive Eleanor had married Louis in 1137. For 10 years the royal couple lived in perfect harmony. In 1147 they set out on the Second Crusade, but once in Palestine their relationship took a turn for the worse. Divorce became inevitable and on 20 March 1152 the Council of Beaugency officially dissolved the union of Louis and Eleanor for prohibited kinship. Eleanor was not without suitors; she married **Henry Plantagenet**, the future King of England, so that her dowry, a large part of southwest France, passed on to the English crown.

WALKING TOUR

Known as the "Princess de la Loire", the Medieval centre and riverside is on the UNESCO World Heritage list.

Petit Mail

This tree-lined avenue overlooks the Loire and commands fine views of the valley. The **porte Tavers** (12C) is a vestige from the town's defensive walls.

r. de la Porte-Tavers leads to pl. St-Firmin.

Tour St-Firmin

A street used to run under this tower, which is the sole remaining feature of a 15C church destroyed during the Revolution. You can hear the chimes of the Angelus bell at noon and 7pm.

Cross pl. St-Firmin into the short rue de la Sirènes.

Maison de Templiers

Note the Romanesque windows in this 12C house at the corner of rue du Puits-de-l'Ange and rue du Traîneau.

Follow r. du Traîneauback to pl. du Dr-Hyvernaud and, on the left, r. des Chevaliers.

Clock Tower

This was originally the Exchange Tower. In the 12C it became one of the main gateways in the town wall.

Take r. du Change back to pl. du Dr-Hyvernaud, at the foot of the hôtel de ville, on your left.

Hôtel de Ville

Guided tours (20min) daily 3pm, 4pm, 4.30pm; May–Sept Mon–Sat; Oct–Apr Tue–Thu. Closed public holidays. 1.80€. 02 38 44 54 42. www.beaugency.fr.

The Council Chamber on the first floor is hung with eight beautiful pieces of **embroidery**★, executed with remarkable skill. Four of them, depicting the four continents known at that time, are 17C.

*Take r. du Pouët-de-Chaumont to the delightful r. du Pont. Turn right and stroll along the Rû, the flower-lined brook that flows into the Loire. Turn right, walk under the **voûte St-Georges**, otherwise known as the "porte de la Barrière" as the only gateway into the town, the château and the abbey church.*

Château Dunois

The medieval fortress was converted into a typical 15C residence by Dunois, Lord of Beaugency, one of Joan of Arc's followers. At the back, the painstakingly re-created medieval garden is a fitting backdrop to the restored façade. *Closed for restoration until 2012.*

Musée Daniel-Vannier★ set in the château, displays the arts, traditions and crafts of the Orléanais region. Climb up to the attics to see the 15C roof frame.

Take r. du Traîneau back to pl. du Dr-Hyvernaud and, on the left, r. des Chevaliers

Église Notre-Dame★

This restored 12C Romanesque abbey church was badly damaged by fire during the Wars of Religion. In the chancel, the windows and main arcades are separated by gemelled arches. Don't miss the *Assumption* by Michel Corneille. Next to the church are the 18C buildings of the former abbey of Notre-Dame.

At night, old street lights illuminate the charming **place Dunois**, in front of the church and the keep, and **place St-Firmin.**

Tour César★

This recatangular 36m/118ft tower, supported by buttresses , is a good example of 11C military architecture. The interior, which covered five floors, is a ruin.

Donjon★

This keep is a fine example of 11C military architecture. At this period, keeps were rectangular and buttressed; later they became circular.

Tour du Diable

At the bottom of the narrow rue de l'Abbaye stands the Devil's Tower which was part of the fortifications defending the bridgehead; in the Middle Ages the Loire flowed at its foot.

Cross place de la Motte, the town's old river harbour. Before going up r. de l'évêché – where offloaded goods were carried to the town centre - note the pretty street to your left, r. Ravelin, previously r. des Pêcheurs. Pl. St-Firmin, r. de la Porte-Tuvers lead you back to the tree-lined Petit Mail.

ADDRESSES

STAY

Chambre d'hôte Le Clos de Pontpierre – *115 r. des Eaux-Bleues, 45190 Tavers. 2km/1mi SW towards Blois 02 38 44 56 38. 4 rms. . evening meal* . Don't worry about being near the road, as behind this old farmhouse is a swimming pool set in a huge garden. The simple rooms overlook the countryside. In fine weather dinner is served in the shade of a century-old horse chestnut tree.

EAT

Le P'tit Bateau – *54 r. du Pont. 02 38 44 56 38. www.le-petit-bateau.com. Closed 24 Feb–4 Mar, 28 Oct–5 Nov, Sun eve, Tue eve, Mon.* In the two rustic dining rooms, the chef serves delicious traditional cuisine at moderate prices.

Meung-sur-Loire★

This fortified village stretches from the Loire, which laps at the roots of the tall trees lining the avenue up the slope, to the main road (N 152) on the plateau.
From the old market a narrow and twisting street, rue Porte-d'Amont, climbs up to an archway; little lanes skirt Les Mauves, a stream with many channels that runs between the houses.

- **Population:** 6 152
- **Michelin Map:** 318: H-5
- **Info:** 7 r. des Mauves, 45130 Meung-sur-Loire. 02 38 44 32 28.
- **Location:** 14km/8.7mi from Orléans, via the N 152.
- **Timing:** Allow around 2hrs.
- **Don't Miss:** The Château.
- **Kids:** The outdoor spaces of the Jardins de Roquelin and Arboretum des Prés de Culands, criss-crossed by canals.

A BIT OF HISTORY

The town has put up a statue in honour of its most famous son, Jean de Meung. In about 1280 he added 18 000 lines to the *Romance of the Rose (Roman de la Rose),* which had been written some 40 years earlier by Guillaume de Lorris and consisted of 4 000 lines.

The allegorical narrative was the greatest literary achievement of a period in which readers certainly had to have stamina.

SIGHTS

Collégiale St-Liphard★

This slightly austere collegaite church (11C–13C) features a bold bell-tower with a stone spire and a triple apse. At the far end of the chancel, note the fine views of the church and château.

Château

Open Mar–Oct daily 10am–7pm; Nov–Feb Sat–Sun and public holidays 2–6pm. Closed 1 Jan, 25 Dec. 7€. 02 38 44 36 47. www.chateaudemeung.com.

This old building reflects a curious mixture of styles, having partly retained its medieval aspect, for instance in the entrance façade (12C–13C).

Until the 18C the château belonged to the bishops of Orléans, who administered justice in their diocese.

Musée Van-Oeveren

Le Clos de Bel Air, rte. d'Orléans, 45130 Meung-sur-Loire. 02 38 45 35 82. www.musee-escrime.com. Guided tours (1hr) Jul–Aug: 2–6pm, rest of year: upon application Closed Mon; 7€ (children 4.50€).

Museum dedicated to fencing, duelling and weaponry set in the Château de Bel Air (17C). Impressive armoury where the fencing master gives lessons.

Espace culturel La Monnaye

Musée municipal, 22 r. des Remparts. 02 38 22 53 36. Open Wed and Fri, 2.30–6pm, Sat 9.30am–12.30pm, 3–6pm. Free admission.

On the site of a former mint where copper coins, *liards,* were minted in the 17C. The museum displays a collection of rare works and texts including books by François Villon, Jehan de Meun, etc. One of the highlights is an illustrated facsimile of the *Roman de la Rose* which is kept in New York. Other rooms are given over to the collection of archaeological items, fossils and coins put together by François Quatrehomme. Visitors can discover the work of another local artist Gaston Couté (1880–1911), poet and songwriter who made his name in the taverns of Montmartre

EXCURSIONS

Jardins de Roquelin

Towards Cléry-St-André, cross the bridge and head immediately left, follow the signs (500m/545yd). Open end April–mid-July and early Sept–mid-Oct 10am–6pm and on appointment. Closed Tue. 5€ (under 18 free). 06 70 95 37 70. www.lesjardinsderoquelin.com.

The 1ha/2.5acre garden at this working nursery features old roses, a vegetable garden, aquatic plants, medieval style trellises and a "jardin à l'anglaise."

Arboretum des Prés de Culands

Towards Orléans, beyond the Nivelle Mill. Guided tours only Apr–Sept. 02 38 63 10 49.

This romantic site, famous for its display of holly, is criss-crossed by canals that form tiny islands planted with maple trees, oaks and alders.

ADDRESSES

STAY

Chambre d'hôte La Mouche – *02 38 44 34 36. 3 rooms.*

On the banks of the Loire, this beautiful place has an orchard and vegetable garden, as well as a small pond. Tastefully decorated rooms, and guests have access to a bbq and fridge in case you want to cook for yourself.

Basilique de Cléry-St-André★

The present Notre-Dame de Cléry is a church dating from the 15C with the exception of the 14C square tower that abuts the north side of the basilica. It remains as the only part of the original structure to have escaped destruction by the English.

- **Michelin Map:** 318: H-5
- **Info:** 111 r. du Mar.-Foch, 45370 Cléry-St-André. ✆02 38 45 94 33. www.clery-saint-andre.com.
- **Location:** 13km/8mi from Orléans via the D 951, on the Loire's left bank.
- **Timing:** Allow 30–45min. If visiting in July, time your visit to coincide with the *son et lumière*, when a meal is served before the show. ✆ 02 38 45 94 06. www.cleryraconte.com.

A BIT OF HISTORY

In 1280 labourers set up a statue of the Virgin Mary they had found in a thicket in a humble chapel that was to become the present-day **church**. Worship of this statue spread throughout the district, and the chapel, too small to accommodate the pilgrims, was transformed into a church served by a college of canons. In 1428 the church was destroyed by the English commander Salisbury during his march on Orléans.

Charles VII and Dunois supplied the first funds for rebuilding, but the great benefactor of Cléry was **Louis XI**. During the siege of Dieppe, while still only the Dauphin, he vowed to give his weight in silver to Notre-Dame de Cléry if he were victorious. His prayer was answered and he kept his vow. When he became King, Louis XI dedicated himself to the Virgin Mary and in doing so strengthened his attachment to Cléry. He was buried there at his request and the building was completed by his son, Charles VIII. The house (now a school) in which Louis XI stayed during his visits to Cléry is on the south side of the church opposite the transept entrance.

Every year a popular pilgrimage is held on 8 September and the following Sunday.

VISIT★

30min. Enter through the transept.

Although somewhat austere, the interior of the church is suffused with light and conveys great elegance.

Basilique de Cléry-St-André

Tomb of Louis XI

The tomb stands on the north side of the nave and is aligned with the altar dedicated to Our Lady, so that it lies at an oblique angle to the axis of the church. The marble statue of the King is the work of an Orléans sculptor, Bourdin (1622). It took the place of the original bronze statue, which was melted down by the Huguenots.

Funerary vault of Louis XI – Louis XI's bones and those of his wife, Charlotte de Savoie, are still in the vault, which opens onto the nave near the tomb. The two skulls, sawn open for embalming, are in a glass case.

Tanguy de Châtel, who was killed during a siege while saving the life of Louis XI, is buried under a flagstone alongside the royal vault. Further to the right, another stone covers the urn containing the heart of Charles VIII.

Chapelle St-Jacques★

The church dean, Gilles de Pontbriand, and his brother built this chapel, dedicated to St James, to serve as their tomb. The chapel's Gothic decoration is highly ornate. The vaulting is decorated with girdles and pilgrims' purses, for Cléry is on the pilgrimage route to St James' shrine in Santiago de Compostela, Spain. The walls are studded with ermines' tails and bridges (the arms of the Pontbriands). The Breton-style wooden grille in front of the chapel was donated by Louis XIII in 1622.

Chapelle de Dunois

From the Chapelle St-Jacques, the second door on the left. Dunois and his family are buried here (*see Châteaudun*). The church at Cléry was already finished when this chapel was added (1464), hence the construction of the vaulting was complicated by the presence of a buttress.

Son et lumière

During the first fortnight of July, visitors to the basilica can enjoy a traditional meal (7pm) followed by the sound and light show from 10.30pm.

Stalls

These were presented by Henri II. Their seats are carved with a variety of human masks and the initials of the donor and his mistress, Diane de Poitiers.

Chancel

On the 19C high altar is a statue in wood of Notre-Dame de Cléry. In the central window a fine piece of 16C stained glass – the only one from this period in the church – represents Henri III founding the Order of the Holy Spirit.

Sacristy and oratory of Louis XI

In the second ambulatory bay on the right is the beautiful door to the sacristy, in pure Flamboyant style. Above it, a small window opens into an oratory from which Louis XI could follow Mass.

EXCURSION

Orléans Wine Route

A signposted route lined by vines and fruit trees between Saint-Hilaire, Saint-Mesmin and Cléry-Saint-André takes in most of the Orlénas-Cléry winegrowing region.

Orléans wine and the coveted AOC

After 20 years of effort from local winemakers and fans of the light whites and pale and fragrant reds and rosés, Orléanais wine joined the Appellation d'origine contrôlé "club" in 2007, henceforth to be known as AOC orléans-cléry. Grapes grown on the plateaux bordering the Loire around Orléans that fall under this appellation are principally Pinot Noir, Gris Meunier, Auvernat Blanc and Auvernat Gris. The redcurrent and blackcurrent flavours are often paired with charcuterie and game from Sologne.

Château de Beauregard★

The château stands in a vast park overlooking the Beuvron Valley. The building has kept its Renaissance appearance despite 17C additions and the 20C roof extension.

- **Michelin Map:** 318: F-6
- **Info:** ✆02 54 70 36 74. www.beauregard-loire.com
- **Location:** 9km/6mi from Blois on D765, 7km/4.3mi from Cour-Cheverny.
- **Kids:** Quiz during the tour.
- **Timing:** Allow 1–2hrs to explore the château and grounds.

SIGHTS

Cabinet des Grelots★

Open Jul–Aug 9.30am–6.30pm; Apr–Jun and Sept 9.30am–noon, 2–6.30pm. Oct–Mar Tue–Thu 9.30am–noon, 2–5pm. Closed early Jan–early Feb, early Dec–25 Dec. 6.50€ (park only 4.50€) ✆02 54 70 36 74. www.beauregard-loire.com.

This charming little room, was fitted out towards the middle of the 16C for Jean du Thier, Secretary of State to Henri II and then Lord of Beauregard.

His coat of arms decorates the coffered ceiling; the bells reappear as a decorative motif on the oak panelling lining the room and conceals the cupboards where the château archives are kept.

Galerie des Illustres★★

The long room has retained its splendid old Delft tiling depicting an army on the march. The ceiling was covered in 1624 with a rich blue paint made from ground lapis lazuli.

The most interesting feature of the gallery is the collection of over 327 historical portraits. They are arranged in bays, each devoted to a different reign making a complete succession of monarchs from the first Valois, Philippe VI, to Louis XIII.

Château de Cheverny★★★

Standing on the edge of Sologne Forest, not far from the châteaux of Blois and Chambord, Cheverny owes its charm to the harmonious proportions of its symmetric design, and to its sumptuous interior decoration. Crowned by a splendid slate roof, its Classical façade is built of attractive white stone from the Bourré quarries (28km/17mi SW).

- **Michelin Map:** 318: F-7
- **Info:** Office de tourisme – 12 r. du Chêne-des-Dames, 41700 Cour-Cheverny. ✆02 54 79 95 63.
- **Location:** 17km/10.5mi S of Blois via the D 765.
- **Timing:** Allow 1-2hrs to visit the château, but if the weather is good, consider taking a walk or a picnic in the gardens.
- **Kids:** The permanent exhibition about the adventures of Tintin and Captain Haddock.

VISIT

Open Jul–Aug 9.15am–6.45pm. Apr–Jun and Sept 9.15am–6.15pm. Oct 9.45am–5.30pm. Rest of year 9.45am-5pm. 7€ (château and park), 11.80€ (château and permanent exhibit), 11.70€ (château and discovery of unusual sights in the park and canal). ✆02 54 79 96 29. www.chateau-cheverny.com.

Château

17c

Construction work was carried out uninterrupted between 1604 and 1634; consequently, the château displays a rare unity of style, both in the architecture and the decoration. The symmetric design and harmonious grandeur of the façade are characteristic features of the period of Louis XIII. At first-floor level there are oval niches housing the busts of Roman emperors, whereas the Hurault coat of arms above the main doorway is surrounded by two concentric collars, one symbolising the Order of the Holy Ghost, the other, the Order of St Michael.

Dining room

To the right of the hall is the dining room hung with a fine 17C Flemish tapestry. The room has retained its French-style painted ceiling and small murals depicting the story of Don Quixote; both are by Jean Mosnier (1600–56), a native of Blois.

Private Apartments

Access to the west wing is via the splendid main staircase with its straight flights of steps and rich sculptural decoration. The private apartments consist of eight rooms, all magnificently furnished.

Armoury★

The ceiling, the wainscots and the shutters were painted by Mosnier. A collection of arms and armour from the 15C to the 17C is displayed on the walls.

King's Bedchamber★★

The King's Bedchamber is the most splendid room in the château. The ceiling is in the Italian style, gilded and painted by Mosnier. The walls are hung with tapestries from the Paris workshops (1640) after Simon Vouet.

Grand Salon★★

Back to the ground floor.

The Grand Salon is decorated with 17C and 18C furniture and paintings. The ceiling is entirely covered, as is the wall panelling, with painted decoration enhanced with gilding. The paintings on either side of the mirror include a portrait of Cosimo de' Medici by Titian, another of Jeanne d'Aragon from the School of Raphaël and, on the chimney-piece, a portrait by Mignard of Marie-Johanne de Saumery, Countess of Cheverny.

Gallery, Petit Salon, Library

The **Gallery** is furnished with magnificent Régence chairs and contains several paintings, including three splendid **portraits by François Clouet**★★, a portrait of Jeanne d'Albret by Miguel Oñate and a Self-Portrait by Rigaud. The **Petit Salon** is hung with 16C, 17C and 18C pictures.

Tapestry Room

The smaller salon is hung with five 17C Flemish tapestries after cartoons by Teniers. Both rooms contain Louis XIV and Louis XV period furnishings, including a Louis XV Chinese lacquered commode and a magnificent Louis XV **clock**★★ decorated with bronzes by Caffieri.

The Park

The château is surrounded by a lovely 100ha/247-acre park.

Visitors of all ages will enjoy a tour of the grounds aboard an electric car and a boat trip. Fans of Tintin and Captain Haddock will delight in the permanent exhibition displayed in the château's former smithy.

Outbuildings

There are **kennels**★ for about 90 hounds, cross-breeds from English foxhounds and the French Poitou race, and the **Trophy Room** displays 2 000 deer antlers.

L'Orangerie

Some 200m/220yd from the northern steps, on the way out of the château grounds, stands a magnificent early-18C orangery, now entirely restored.

EXCURSION

Château de Troussay

3.5km/2mi W skirting the Cheverny park as far as D 52; turn left and take the first fork on the right. Guided tours (35min) available. Phone for times. 5.50€. 02 54 44 29 07.

This small Renaissance château was refurbished in the late 19C by the historian Louis de la Saussaye.

Note particularly the stone carving of a **porcupine**, the emblem of Louis XII, on the rear façade taken from the Hurault de Cheverny mansion in Blois and the beautiful **chapel door**★ carved with delicate scrollwork. The tiles on the ground floor date from the reign of Louis XII, the Renaissance windows came from the Guise mansion in Blois and the grisaille on the ceiling in the little salon are attributed to **Jean Mosnier**.

The château, which is lived in, is furnished with fine pieces dating from the 16C to the 18C. The outbuildings round the courtyard house a small **museum** evoking past domestic and agricultural life in the Sologne.

Château de Fougères-sur-Bièvre★

In the charming village of Fougères, surrounded by nursery gardens and fields of asparagus, stands the austere north façade of the feudal-looking château of Pierre de Refuge, Chancellor to Louis XI. It is easy to imagine the original moats, drawbridge and arrow slits – replaced in the 16C by windows – and the keep's battlements, which disappeared when the roof was added.

- **Michelin Map:** 318: F-7
- **Info:** Office du tourisme de Blois-Pays de Chambord, 23 pl. du Château, 41006 Blois. 02 54 90 41 41. www.loiredeschateaux.com.
- **Location:** 21km/13mi S of Blois, on the D 52 between Pontlevoy and Cheverny.
- **Timing:** Allow 1hr to explore the château.

VISIT

Open mid-May–mid-Sept 9.30am–12.30pm, 2–6.30pm; mid-Sept–mid-May Wed–Mon 10am–12.30pm, 2–5pm. Closed 1 Jan, 1 May, 1 and 11 Nov, 25 Dec. 5€.

The present building was begun in 1450 with the construction of the two wings giving onto the courtyard, dedicated to Jeanne de Faverois, the wife of Jean de Refuge. In 1470, Pierre de Refuge was granted royal permission to fortify his castle and, shortly afterwards, he erected the north wing, whose defensive features were aimed to impress, playing a purely symbolic role in times of peace. However, when completed by his grandson, Jean de Villebresmes, the château acquired a certain grace: the east wing in the main court has a gallery of arcades with lovely dormer windows; the attractive turreted staircase in the northwest corner has windows flanked by pilasters with Renaissance motifs; the large windows added in the 18C to the south wing made it ideal as a spinning mill in the 19C. The size of the rooms seen from within is impressive; so are the wooden roof-frame of the main building which is shaped like a ship's hull, and the conical roof-frame of the towers.

The Medieval-themed garden, east of the château, features herbs and plants that were used for dyes and traditional medicines. The garden enjoys pretty views of the nearby **Église St-Éloi,** just behind the château. Note the quarter-sphere vault and finely carved choir stalls in the early 12C chancel and the Villebresmes coat of arms on the vaulted roof of the family chapel.

Bordered by the Loire to the north and the Cher to the south, the Sologne is a largely unspoilt region of forests, lakes and farmland where time seems to have stood still in its sleepy red-brick and half-timbered villages. It offers the perfect combination of nature, picturesque hamlets, a couple of remarkable châteaux, a range of outdoor activities, wildlife spotting and some truly delicious local specialities in goats' cheese and the famous tarte tatin.

Country Life

The best way to appreciate the Sologne is on a walking tour from the Domaine du Ciran in Ménestrau-en-Villette, especially early in the morning or at dusk which are the best times to spot deer, wild boar, foxes and pine martens. The visitor centre provides explanations of local history, flora and fauna. The region also features two remarkable châteaux: Valençay, once home to Napoleon's wily minister Talleyrand, is best viewed during one of the candlelit tours in summer with carriage rides in the park, hunting horns and other attractions. La Ferté Saint-Aubin has a superbly restored estate which offers a wealth of family attractions including the working stables and Orient Express railway station in the grounds complete with its own steam engine and carriage.

Highlights

1 Driving tour through the **Sologne** woods in autumn (p144)

2 The **Domaine du Ciran** nature trail, particularly at dawn or dusk (p146)

3 Tasting home-made madeleines in the kitchens of **La Ferté-Saint-Aubin** château (p149)

4 A unique combination of architectural styles at **Selles-sur-Cher** (p152)

5 *Son et Lumière* show at **Château de Valençay** (p153)

Ambitions of François I

The main town in the Sologne is Romorantin-Lathenay. In 1517 François I had great plans for the locality and asked Leonardo da Vinci to start drawing up grandiose plans for a magnificent palace and town centre. Sadly, the project came to nothing as the King's famous guest was to die at Amboise in 1519. The main attraction today is the local history museum, the Musée de Sologne. Visitors seeking a lasting impression of the Sologne should read Alain-Fournier's classic novel *Le Grand Meaulnes*. Indeed, no other work better captures the atmosphere of the region's flat expanses as early morning mists linger over still ponds and bird calls are the only sounds to break the silence.

Mill on the river Sauldre, Romorantin-Lanthenay, the Sologne

©Jean-Marc Charles/age fotostock

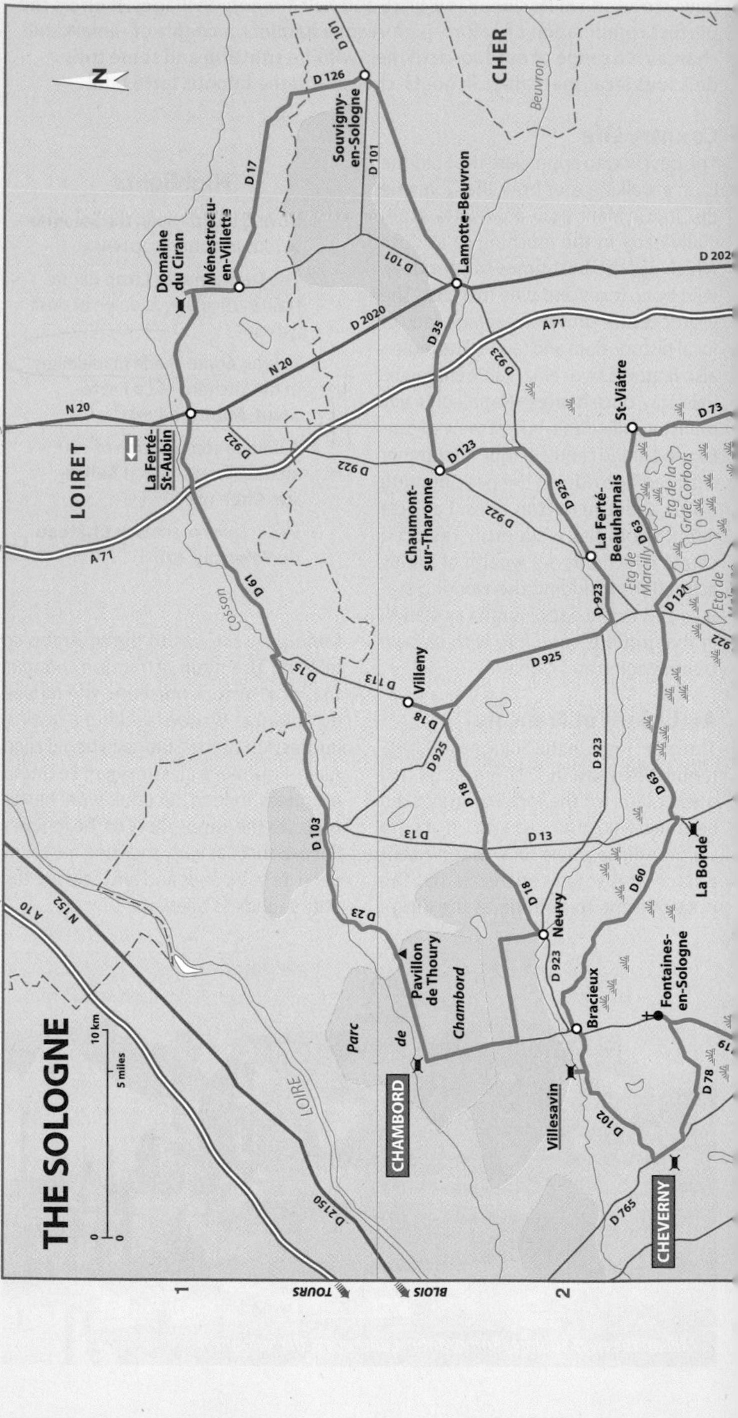
THE SOLOGNE
10 km
5 miles
LOIRET
CHER
ORLÉANS
TOURS
BLOIS
CHAMBORD
Parc de Chambord
CHEVERNY
LOIRE
Cosson
Beuvron
La Ferté-St-Aubin
Domaine du Ciran
Ménestreau-en-Villette
Souvigny-en-Sologne
Lamotte-Beuvron
Chaumont-sur-Tharonne
La Ferté-Beauharnais
St-Viâtre
Villeny
Neuvy
La Borde
Pavillon de Thoury
Bracieux
Fontaines-en-Sologne
Villesavin
Etg de Marcilly
Etg de la Grde Corbois
A 10
A 71
N 20
N 152
D 2020
D 2150
D 922
D 923
D 925
D 101
D 126
D 17
D 35
D 61
D 15
D 113
D 18
D 103
D 13
D 23
D 60
D 63
D 73
D 121
D 123
D 102
D 78
D 765

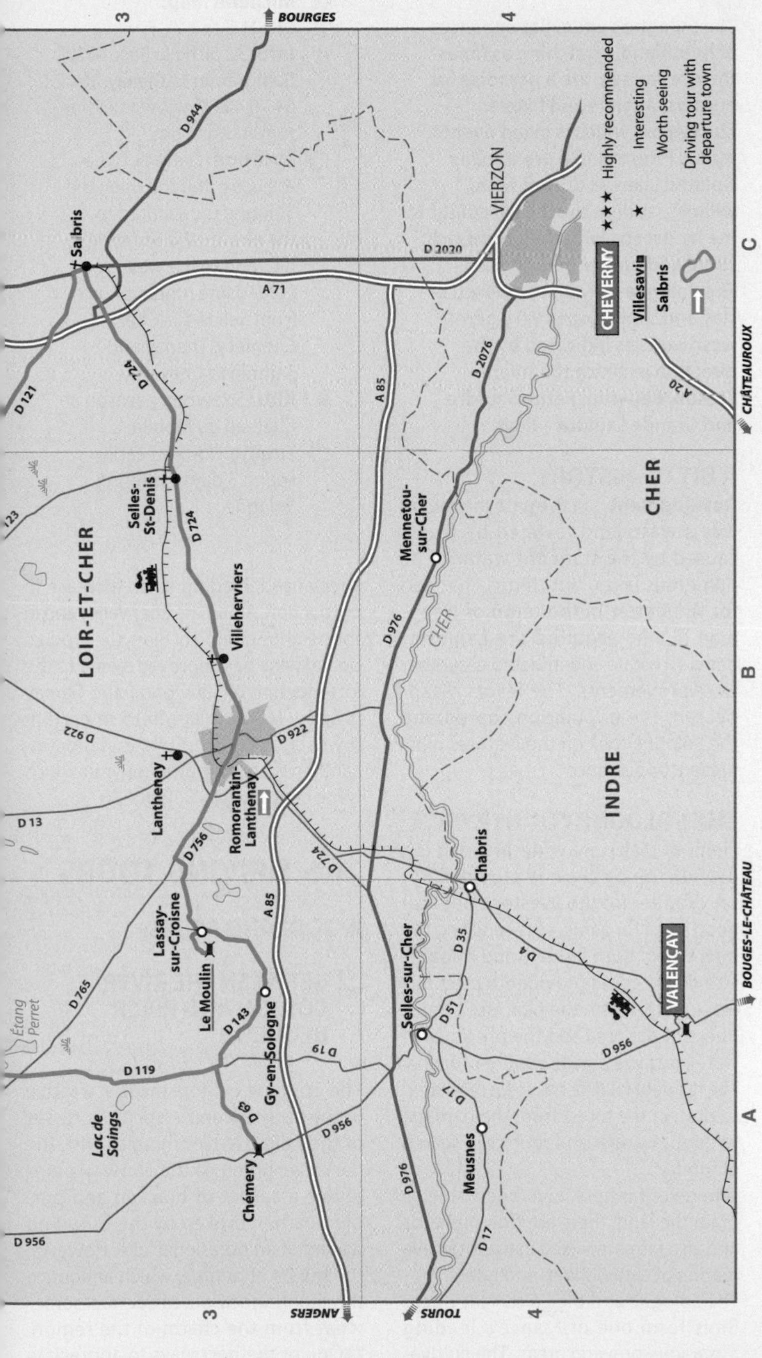

LOIR-ET-CHER
CHER
INDRE
BOURGES
ANGERS
TOURS
CHÂTEAUROUX
BOUGES-LE-CHÂTEAU
Salbris
VIERZON
Selles-St-Denis
Villeherviers
Lanthenay
Romorantin-Lanthenay
Lassay-sur-Croisne
Le Moulin
Gy-en-Sologne
Chémery
Lac de Soings
Étang Perret
Mennetou-sur-Cher
Chabris
Selles-sur-Cher
Meusnes
VALENÇAY
CHER
D 944
D 121
D 724
A 71
D 2020
A 85
D 2076
A 20
D 976
D 922
D 13
D 756
D 765
D 143
D 119
D 19
D 956
D 63
D 35
D 4
D 51
D 17
CHEVERNY ★★★ Highly recommended
Villesavin ★ Interesting
Salbris Worth seeing
Driving tour with departure town
A
B
C
3
4

La Sologne★

The Sologne's wide, flat expanses of heathland, stretching as far as the eye can see, are a paradise for hunters, anglers and hikers.
The region, which is given over to farms, forests and a great many isolated lakes, is dotted with villages, adding touches of colour to the landscape with their red-brick, stone and timber buildings.
The Sologne terrain, composed of clay and sand, slopes very gently westwards as indicated by the direction in which the rivers – Cosson, Beuvron, Petite Sauldre and Grande Sauldre – flow.

- **Michelin Map:** 318: H-5 to J-7
- **Info**: 32 pl. de la Paix, 41200 Romorantin-Lathenay. ℘02 54 76 43 89. www.tourisme-romorantin.com.
- **Location:** Lying between the Loire and the Cher, the Sologne is delimited to the east by the Sancerre hills and to the west by a curved line running north from Selles-sur-Cher via Chémery, Thenay and Sambin to Cheverny.
- **Kids:** Strawberry season at Château du Moulin.
- **Timing:** You can easily spend 3 days exploring Sologne.

A BIT OF HISTORY

Development – In the past the region was a wasteland ravaged by fevers caused by the stagnant water of its numerous lakes, but things changed for the better in the reign of Napoleon III who acquired the Lamotte-Beuvron estate and initiated a number of improvements. The fevers disappeared, the population soared and the Sologne took on the features of its present appearance.

THE SOLOGNE COUNTRYSIDE

Fields of maize are widespread; it is a useful crop because it provides not only fodder for the livestock but also good cover for game, so reconciling the interests of both farmers and hunters. The dense cover provided by the forest, together with the peaceful atmosphere of the area and the presence of water, attracts a wide variety of fauna. The resident wildlife has to be regulated to protect the forest from the damage wrought by deer and rabbits in search of food.
Wherever farmers have been able to drain the land, there are fruit orchards and also farms involved in the intensive rearing of cattle, sheep and goats.
The Sologne and the Loire Valley near Blois form one of France's leading asparagus-growing areas. The cultivation of strawberries has become very specialised, leading to an increase in production. Along the Cher Valley and in the neighbourhood of Blois, the production of wine has improved owing to the introduction of Sauvignon and Gamay grapes. Markets are held in certain towns such as Gien, Sully, Romorantin-Lanthenay and Lamotte-Beuvron, which is the centre of the Sologne.

DRIVING TOURS

WOODLAND AREAS★

1 BETWEEN THE RIVER COSSON AND RIVER BEUVRON

The Sologne is at its most attractive in the early autumn, when the russet of the falling leaves mingles with the dark evergreen of the Norway pines above a carpet of bracken and purple heather, broken by the brooding waters of an occasional lake. However, the bursts of gunfire, which announce the shooting season, can detract somewhat from the charm of the region. One of the best ways to appreciate the natural beauty of the Sologne is to take a walk. Owing to the many enclosures, prohibited areas and animal traps, it is advisable to keep to the waymarked footpaths.

La Ferté-Saint-Aubin

See LA FERTÉ-SAINT-AUBIN

Drive NW out of La Ferté along D 61 towards Ligny-le-Ribault.

D 61 then becomes D 103; in Couy-sur-Cosson, turn left onto D 33.

The **Pavillon de Thoury** marks the entrance to the Chambord estate.

Hikers and visitors are welcome along footpaths. An observation area is available for keen picture hunters wishing to catch a glimpse of deer and wild boar on the move.

Château de Chambord★★★

See CHÂTEAU DE CHAMBORD

Follow D 112 S, turn left at the Chambord intersection, then right at King Stanislas crossroads onto the forest road to Neuvy.

Neuvy

Apply to the town hall to visit. 02 54 46 42 69.

Neuvy is located on the southern edge of Boulogne Forest on the north bank of the River Beuvron.

The village church stands on its own in a graveyard near a half-timbered farmhouse with brick infill on the opposite bank. It was partially rebuilt in 1525. The rood beam supports 15C statues.

Villeny

The **Maison du cerf** reveals all the secrets of the stag, the "king" of the forests of the Sologne *(pl. de l'église; open Jul–Aug 10am–12pm, 2.30–6.30pm, closed Mon; school holidays 2.30–6.30pm, closed Mon; rest of year Wed, Sat–Sun and bank holidays 2.30–6.30pm; closed mid-Dec–mid-Feb; 4.50€ (children 7–12 years 3€); 02 54 98 23 10; www.coeur-de-france.com).*

La Ferté-Beauharnais

The village has retained several old houses (Maison du Carroir, Cour à l'Écu, Relais du Dauphin) worth a detour.

Drive E along D 922 then turn left onto D 123.

Chaumont-sur-Tharonne

The line of the old ramparts can be traced in the layout of the town which is situated round its 15C–16C church on a bluff in the centre of the Sologne.

Lamotte-Beuvron

Soon after Napoleon III acquired the château, this simple hamlet got its own railway station and promptly became the rendezvous of hunters in the Sologne region.

Souvigny-en-Sologne

The 12C–16C church, preceded by a vast timber porch (known as a *caquetoir* or gossip place), is surrounded by timber-framed houses.

The immediate surroundings are criss-crossed by 80km/50mi of marked footpaths (detailed map available in the local shops).

Ménestreau-en-Villette

7km/4.3mi E from La Ferté-St-Aubin.

In this Sologne village, the **Domaine du Ciran** (Conservatoire de la Faune Sauvage de Sologne *open Jul–Aug 10am–12.30pm, 2–7pm; Apr–Jun and Sept 10am–noon, 2–6pm; Oct–Mar Wed–Mon 10am–noon, 2–5pm; closed 1 Jan, 25 Dec; 5€; 02 38 76 90 93; www.domaineduciran.com*) is devoted to the Sologne region, its flora and its fauna, both past and present. Here you get an insight into the natural resources of the area thanks to a discovery trail featuring around 20 display cases framed with wood. Observation points have been set up all along, providing opportunities for chance photographs of deer, wild boar, foxes, martens and roe deer, especially at sunrise or sunset.

The Domaine du Ciran is criss-crossed by discovery trails. For a closer look at the natural environment, take advantage of walking tours, which last several days, and witness the astonishing variety of the Sologne flora and fauna. *Don't forget to bring your camera, binoculars and sturdy shoes!*

Lakes and Moors★

2 ROUND TRIP FROM ROMORANTIN-LANTHENAY

Romorantin-Lanthenay★
See ROMORANTIN-LANTHENAY

Drive E out of Romorantin along D 724.

Villeherviers
Weekdays: ask at the town hall to visit. 02 54 76 07 92.
The village is set among asparagus fields in the broad valley of the Sauldre. There is Plantagenet vaulting in the 13C church.

Selles-St-Denis
This village lies on the north bank of the Sauldre. The chapel, which dates from the 12C and 15C and has side chapels and an apse in the Flamboyant style, is decorated with 14C murals of the Life of St Genoulph to whom it is dedicated.

Salbris
Salbris, on the south bank of the Sauldre, is a busy crossroads and a good centre for excursions into the forest.
The stone and brick **church of St-Georges** was built in the 15C and 16C. The transept chapels have coats of arms of the donors on the keystones of the vault and attractive pendant sculptures representing the Three Wise Men and the Virgin and Child and the symbols of the Evangelists.
At Salbris station, you can take the **petit train du Blanc-Argent** *(Le Blanc-Argent; gare de Romorantin-Lanthenay; 02 54 76 06 51)* a metric-gauge railway, which goes up to Luçay-le-Mâle, offering a pleasant tour of the Sologne region.

Drive N out of Salbris along N 20, turn left onto D 121 then right 10km/6.2mi farther on towards St-Viâtre on D 73.

St-Viâtre
This smart little town was formerly a place of pilgrimage containing the relics of St Viâtre, a hermit who retired here in the 6C. At the chancel step stands a remarkable carved wood desk (18C) of surprising size. In the south transept are four **painted panels★** dating from the early 16C. **Maison des Étangs** – The site occupies two houses and presents the ecology, fauna and fish life in the Sologne, as well as a display of traditional crafts *(guided tours (1hr15) Apr–Oct 10am–noon, 2–6pm; rest of year Wed and weekends 2–6pm; 5€ (children 2.50€); 02 54 88 23 00; www.maison-des-etangs.com).*
Reposoir St-Viâtre – Small 15C brick building at the north entrance.

Continue W along D 63 to Vernou-en-Sologne.

South of the village stands the beautiful Château de Laborde *(closed to the public)*. Note the slate inlays underlining the openings.

Drive to Bracieux along D 60 via Bauzy.

Bracieux
Bracieux is a smart village on the border of the Sologne and the region round Blois. The houses are grouped round the 16C market on the south bank of the Beuvron which is spanned by a bridge.

Château de Villesavin★
2km/1mi from Bracieux along D 102.
See CHAMBORD: Excursion

Château de Cheverny★★★
See CHÂTEAU DE CHEVERNY

Drive out of Cheverny along D 765 then turn left onto D 78.

Fontaines-en-Sologne
The **church**, which largely dates from the 12C, was fortified in the 17C. Beside

the church there are half-timbered houses with roofs of smallflat tiles, commonly found in the region.

Take D 119 S along Perret Lake then along Soings-en-Sologne Lake.

The water level of the lake is liable to change abruptly without any apparent reason; in the past, this gave rise to many local legends!

Continue along D 119. Just before Rougeiu take D 63 right.

Château de Chémery

Open Apr–Nov 10am–dusk; Dec–Mar Sat–Sun and public holidays 2–6pm. 6€. 02 54 71 82 77.

The château (15C and 16C) is a mixture of medieval and Renaissance architecture. It was built on the site of a 12C fortress. In the grounds is a dovecote with spaces for 1 200 birds.

In Rougeou, turn onto D 143.

Gy-en-Sologne

The typical Sologne cottage here, **Locature de la Straize** (*open Apr-Oct Sat-Mon and Wed-Thu 10-11.30am, 3-6pm; 4€; 02 54 83 82 89*), dates from the 16C.

Lassay-sur-Croisne

Lassay is a village in the Sologne, a region of woodland and vast lakes. A cluster of old houses, crowned with long slate roofs, add a colourful touch to the urban landscape thanks to their stone and brick architecture.

Église St-Denis

This charming little 15C church has a beautiful rose window and a slender spire. In the left transept, above the recumbent figure of Philippe du Moulin, there is an attractive early-16C **fresco** depicting St Christopher.

Château du Moulin★

1.5km/0.9mi W on a track beside the River Croisne. Guided tours (1hr) Apr–Sept 10am–2.30pm, 2–6.30pm. 8€. 02 54 83 83 51. www.chateauxfrance.com/chateaudumoulin.

The Château du Moulin stands in a rural setting, its red-brick walls reflected in the water of the moat. It was built between 1480 and 1506 by **Philippe du Moulin**, a prominent nobleman devoted to the service of Charles VIII and Louis XII.

The original castle was built on the square ground plan typical of fortresses, surrounded by a curtain wall reinforced with round towers.

The keep or seigneurial residence features large mullioned windows and is furnished in the style contemporary with the period in which it was built: the bedrooms contain tester beds and Flemish tapestries. However, 19C comfort is represented by the chimney plaques which provided central heating.

Château du Moulin

ADDRESSES

STAY

Chambre d'hôte Le Petit Clos – *6 r. de la Folie. 41600 Chaumont-sur-Tharonne. ℘02 54 88 28 17. 5 rms. Evening meal*. A brick-built house at the heart of the village, with an enclosed garden.

Hotel du Parc – *8 av. d'Orléans, 41300 Salbris. ℘02 54 97 18 53. 23 rms.* An elegant old Sologne-style hotel in a rural setting, with renovated rooms, and rustic restaurant.

Domaine de Valaudran – *41300 Salbris. 1.5km/0.9mi SW of Salbris on D 724. ℘02 54 97 20 00. www.hotelvalaudran.com. Closed 3 Jan–15 Mar - 32 rooms. 13€. Restaurant*. This fine brick house with its own park is a good place to relax and find peace and quiet. Follow the tree-lined drive to the house, where the rooms have views over the countryside.

EAT

Les Copains d'Abord – *52 av. d'Orléans, 41300 Salbris. ℘02 54 97 24 24. Closed 1–13 Jan, 7–25 Aug, Sun eve, Tue.* All the locals know this bistro with its happy, convivial atmosphere. You'll find good traditional cooking, and every weekend there is live jazz.

Auberge le Creussard – *6 pl. de l'Eglise, 41210 St-Viâtre. ℘02 54 88 91 33. Closed Mon, Tue eve and 3 weeks in March. 5 rooms. 6€.*In the heart of the village, a good address for traditional country cuisine.

Au Fil du Temps – *11 pl. de la Halle, 41250 Bracieux. ℘02 54 46 03 84. Closed Thu in summer; Thu–Fri lunch in winter.* Sets up in the marketplace (every Sat). Best for eating outdoors on fine days. Traditional cuisine, excellent welcome.

Le Relais de la Sologne – *63 pl. 8 mai 1945, 45240 Ménestreau-en-Villette. ℘02 38 76 97 40. www.lerelaisdesologne.com. Closed 22–28 Dec, 23 Feb–11 Mar, Sun–Tue eve, Wed.* In the heart of the village, this traditional restaurant features a rustic dining room and terrace. Don't miss the nearby Domaine du Ciran (2km/1.2mi) nature conservatoion centre.

Auberge du Prieuré – *41230 Lassay-sur-Croisne. ℘02 54 83 91 91. Closed 15 days in Jun, 3 weeks in Nov, Sun eve, Tue eve, Wed.* This restaurant has a lovely setting, opposite a gothic church. Simple and refined decor with exposed beams and a fine carved wooden mantelpiece.

La Grenouillère – *rte. d'Orléans, 41600 Chaumont-sur-Tharonne. ℘02 54 88 50 71. Closed Mon and Tue.* Nestling on the edge of the forest, a traditional Sologne red-brick house with conservatory. Welcoming rustic interior. Refined local cuisine with an up-to-date touch.

Tatin – *5 av. de Vierzon. 41600 Lamotte-Beuvron. ℘02 54 88 00 03. Closed 2 weeks in winter, 2 weeks in Aug, Sun eve, Mon in Feb (except public holidays).* This is where the Tatin sisters invented their eponymous apple tart.

SHOPPING

Bergeries de Sologne – *Feme de Jaugeny, 41250 Fontaines. ℘02 54 46 45 61. www.bergeries-de-sologne.com. Visitor centre and tastings: open Jul and Aug on Tue from 10.45am.* Smallholding specialising in raising sheep and chickens. The "discovery and gastronomy" days include tours of the farm, sheepdog displays and sheep shearing. Shorter programmes also available. Preserved meat dishes for sale.

Frizot –*54 av. de l'Hôtel-de-Ville, 41600 Lamotte-Beuvron. ℘02 54 88 08 81. Open Mon, Thu–Sat: 8am–12.30pm, 3–7.30pm; Tue, Sun and bank holidays: 8am–12.30pm. Closed 15 Aug–8 Sept, and other school holidays.* Since the Sologne is hunting country, this butcher naturally decided to make his own wild boar slicing sausage. He also makes other award-winning produce such as game pâtés and terrines, black pudding with wild mushrooms, sausages, foie gras as well as the local rillettes and rillons potted meat specialities.

La Ferté-Saint-Aubin

The old district has a few typical local houses: low, timber-framed constructions with brick infill and large roofs of flat tiles. A splendid château stands among greenery, on the banks of the River Cosson.

- **Population:** 7 028
- **Michelin Map:** 318: I-5
- **Info:** r. des Jardins, 45240 La Ferté-St-Aubin. ☎02 38 64 67 93.
- **Location:** On the N 20, 15km/9mi S of Orléans.
- **Kids:** The Orient Express railway station.
- **Timing:** Allow 1hr.

La Ferté-Saint-Aubin

©Jason Langley/age fotostock

VISIT

Château★

Open Easter–Sept 10am–7pm; mid-Feb–Easter 2–6pm. 8.50€. ☎02 38 76 52 72.

Built in brick relieved with courses of stone, this is an impressive edifice; to the left is the Little Château with its 16C diamond-patterned brickwork and, to the right, the Big Château, built in the mid-17C with a Classical façade topped by sculpted dormers. Inside, the Dining Hall and the Grand Salon have 18C furnishings and a number of portraits including one of the Marquis de la Carte attributed to Largillière. The Marshal's Room is devoted to the memory of **Maréchal de la Ferté**, who distinguished himself in battle. The Château is particularly renowned for its magnificent working stables and tack room. In the fully-functioning kitchens, madeleines are baked and can be sampled.

The Park

To round off the tour, visit the **menagerie** and its little model farm with hens, geese, dwarf goats, sheep and donkeys, or else take a walk through the English-style parkland with its charming network of islets. There is also a reconstruction of a 1930s railway station complete with steam engine, carriage and Orient Express restaurant.

ADDRESSES

STAY

Chambre d'hôte La VeilleForêt – *rte. de Jouy-le-Potier, 45240 La Ferté-St-Aubin. 5.5km/3.5mi NW of La Ferté-St-Aubin on D18. ☎02 38 76 57 20. www.ravenel@numero.fr. 2 rooms.*
A Solognote farmhouse at the end of a forest path. Ideal for families and walkers. The rooms are in the converted stable block. Fishing pond.

EAT

Auberge de l'Écu de France – *6 r. du Gén. Leclerc, 45240 La Ferté-St-Aubin. ☎02 38 64 69 22.*
Small 17C inn close to the Château. Cosy half-timbered interior and traditional cuisine.

La Sauvagine – *53 r. du Gén. Leclerc, 45240 La Ferté-St-Aubin. ☎02 38 76 62 23. www.restaurant-la-sauvagine.com. Closed Sun eve and Mon, booking advised.*
Stylish town centre restaurant: soft décor, pale green tablecloths, amusing collection of miniature ducks. Cuisine based on fresh local produce.

Romorantin-Lanthenay

The point where the River Sauldre divides into several arms is the site of the former capital of the Sologne, with its pine forests, moorlands, numerous lakes, and gastronomic specialities including pumpkin pâté.

- **Population:** 17 572
- **Michelin Map:** 318: H-7
- **Info:** 32 pl. de la Paix, 41200 Romorantin-Lanthenay. ℘02 54 76 43 89. www.tourisme-romorantin.com.
- **Location:** 40km/25mi SE of Blois; almost all the routes of Sologne converge on Romorantin.
- **Don't Miss:** The Old Town.
- **Timing:** Allow 1–2hrs to explore the town.

SIGHTS

Old Houses★

On the corner of rue de la Résistance and rue du Milieu stands the **chancellerie**, a corbelled Renaissance house, of brick and half-timber construction, where the royal seals were kept when the King resided in town. The corner post features a coat of arms and a musician playing the bagpipes.

Standing at the junction of rue du Milieu and rue de la Pierre is the **Maison du Carroir doré** with its remarkable carved corner posts showing the Annunciation and St George killing the Dragon.

View from the bridges★

From the north branch of the river there is a **view** of the **Château royal**, opposite the Sologne museum complex, which dates from the 15C and 16C and now houses the sub-Prefecture. Along the narrow southern branch of the river there is a row of half-timbered houses.

Square Ferdinand-Buisson

This is a pleasant public garden with tall trees and footbridges over the river.

Chapelle St-Roch

CLosed to the public.

On the edge of the St-Roch suburb this graceful chapel features a façade framed by small towers: the attractive semi-circular windows are typical of the Renaissance

Église St-Étienne

Above the transept crossing of the church rises a Romanesque tower with finely executed sculptures.

ADDITIONAL SIGHTS

Espace automobiles Matra

Open Wed–Fri and Mon–Tue 9am–noon, 2–6pm, Sat–Sun and public holidays 10am–noon, 2–6pm. Closed 1 Jan, 1 May, 25 Dec. 5€. ℘02 54 94 55 58. www.museematra.com.

Housed in disused factory premises, this Motor Racing Museum presents an exhibition of Matra cars, including the Formula 1 car which won the world championship in 1969, and a series of display cases retracing the technical developments in racing car construction. Established in 1968, Matra is the biggest employer in the town.

Musée de Sologne★

Open Wed–Sat and Mon 10am–noon, 2–6pm, Sun and public holidays 2–6pm. Closed 1 Jan, 1 May, 25 Dec. 4.50€. ℘02 54 95 33 66. www.museedesologne.com.

The museum is in the heart of the old quarter of Romorantin-Lanthenay, spanning the river; three buildings house the museum collections.

The **Moulin du Chapitre**, whose exterior still reveals traces of its former activity as a 19C flour mill, consists of exhibition areas laid out over four floors: the history, flora and fauna of the Sologne region; life in the châteaux and the rural community.

The **Moulin de la Ville** presents the history of Romorantin, focusing on Leonardo

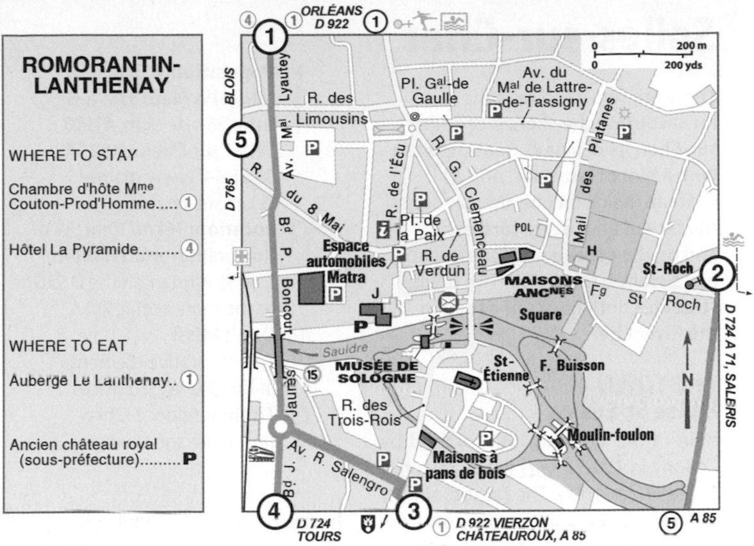

da Vinci's plans to build a new city and royal residence. The **Jacquemart Tower** is the oldest building in town, and used to house temporary exhibitions.

EXCURSIONS

Lanthenay

4km/2.5mi N.

The Chapelle St-Aignan here contains a painting of the Virgin Mary between St John the Baptist and St Sebastian, dating from 1523 and attributed to Timoteo Viti from Urbino who influenced Raphael in his early days.

Mennetou-sur-Cher

20km/12.4mi SE along D 922 and N 76.

This medieval town is enclosed within its original ramparts which were built in the 13C. On the side of town towards Vierzon, En-Bas gateway can boast that Joan of Arc once passed through its portal, and features pointed supporting arches, and its guard-room contains the original fireplace complete with hood. **Old houses** – Grande-Rue, the steep and winding main street, leads from Bonne-Nouvelle gateway to that of En-Haut, past most of Mennetou's interesting old houses. These embody a variety of architectural styles, dating from the 13C to 16C.

ADDRESSES

STAY

Chambre d'hôte Mme Couton–Prod'Homme – *41320 Langon. 11.6km/7.2mi SE. 02 54 98 16 21. 4 rms.* Small establishment in a lovely rural setting. Visit Langon's 16C church.

Hôtel La Pyramide – *r. Pyramide, by ①. 02 54 76 26 34. www.hotellapyramide.com. 66 rms. 10€. Restaurant. Closed 21 Dec–6 Jan, Fri lunch).* Modern building near a cultural complex. Functional rooms, which are all identical, in a modern style. Traditional meals are served in the simple dining room or on the terrace behind the restaurant.

EAT

Auberge Le Lanthenay – *9 r. Notre Dame du Lieu. 2.5km/1.5mi by ① and D 922. 02 54 76 72 91. Closed 2–26 Jan, Fri lunch, Sun eve, Mon. Restaurant (pre-book).* Pleasant place to spend the night in a picturesque hamlet, where you'll discover good cuisine combined with quiet surroundings. The dining room is more intimate than the veranda.

Selles-sur-Cher

There are two good reasons for savouring the charms of Selles-sur-Cher: its delicious goats' cheese with a hint of hazelnut, and a château which on one side presents the face of an austere fortress, and on the other a gracious Italian Renaissance residence. The town straddles both banks of a loop in the River Cher.

- **Population:** 4 666
- **Michelin Map:** 318: G-8
- **Info:** 26 r. de Sion, 41130 Selles-sur-Cher. ℘02 54 95 25 44. www.mairie-selles-sur-cher.fr.
- **Location:** 16km/10mi SW of Romorantin and 15km/9mi E of St-Aignan on the D 976 or the more scenic D 17.
- **Don't Miss:** The decorative elements in the church St-Eusice.
- **Timing:** Allow 1–2hrs to explore the town.

THE TOWN

Église St-Eusice

Built in the 12C and 15C, torched by Coligny in 1562, it was partly restored in the 17C and 19C. The façade, almost entirely Romanesque, includes columns and capitals from an earlier church.

The **end of the chancel** is finely constructed with two Romanesque friezes: one, under the windows, illustrates scenes from the New Testament with naively sculpted figures; the other, higher and more elegant, relates incidents from the saint's life.

By the north wall, the bas-reliefs represent work during the different months of the year; higher up to the right is a Visitation, sheltered and protected by the transept chapel.

The late 13C north wall is broken by a delightful doorway with scuplted capitals and a garland of wild rose flowers and leaves. The crypt houses the 6C tomb of Saint Eusice.

Château

The remains of the stout 13C fortress stand opposite two 17C buildings joined by a long wall. Four bridges span the wide moat.

EXCURSION

Meusnes

6.5km/4mi SW on D 956 towards Valençay, then right on D 17.

The **church** is pure Romanesque style. In the transept, a triumphal arch is surmounted by three charming arcades. The statues are 15C and 16C.

The town hall houses the small **musée de la Pierre à fusil** which recounts the history of the local gunflint industry over three centuries *(guided tour (1hr) on request; 2€; ℘02 54 71 33 74).*

ADDRESSES

STAY

Hôtel Le Grand Chêne – *ZA le Grand-Chêne. 41130 Gièvres. A 85 exit Romorantin. ℘02 54 98 61 70. www.legrandchene.fr. 21 rms. 6€.* Near the RN 76, this quiet budget hotel offers comfortable rooms (2 and 3 beds) including 1 for disabled guests, all with bathrooms. Good value for stopovers.

EAT

Le Pont de la Saudre – *2 r. Nationale, rte. de Tours, 41130 Billy. ℘ 02 54 97 48 84.* Recently taken over by the proprietors of the renowned Quatre-Saisons in Aurillac.

SHOPPING

La Fromagerie –*2 r. du Dr-Massacré. ℘ 02 54 88 57 60. Open daily except Mon 9am–12.30pm, 3–7pm, Sun 9.30am–noon, closed first week Jan.* Proposes a full selection of regional goats' cheese including Selles-sur-Cher, Pyramides de Valençay, Pouligny-Saint-Pierre, an unusual blue cheese and a selection of Loire wines.

Château de Valençay★★★

Geographically speaking, Valençay is in the Berry region but the château can be included with those in the Loire Valley because of the period of its construction and its huge size, in which it resembles Chambord. A *Son et Lumière* show enhances the château's beautiful setting.

- **Michelin Map:** 318: G-9
- **Info:** Office du tourisme du pays de Valençay, 2 av. de la Résistance, 36600 Valencay. ✆02 54 00 04 42. www.pays-devalencay.fr.
- **Location:** 56km/35mi south of Blois and 23km/14mi southeast of St-Aignan.
- **Kids:** The animal park and Napoléon's vast maze.
- **Don't Miss:** The park; wine and cheese tasting.
- **Timing:** Getting the most out of your visit will take at least 3hrs.

A BIT OF HISTORY

A Financier's Château – Valençay was built c. 1540 by Jacques d'Estampes, the owner of the existing castle. He had married the daughter of a financier, who brought him a large dowry, and he wanted a residence worthy of his new fortune. The 12C castle was demolished and in its place rose the present sumptuous building.

Charles-Maurice de Talleyrand-Périgord, who had begun his career under Louis XVI as Bishop of Autun, was Minister of Foreign Affairs when he bought Valençay in 1803 at the request of Napoleon, so that he would have somewhere to receive important foreign visitors. Talleyrand managed his career so skilfully that he did not finally retire until 1834.

VISIT

Open Julug 9.30ampm; Junept 10ampm; end Maray 10.30ampm; Oct 10.30am.30pm. 9€, includes a show (children 6€). ✆02 54 00 10 66. www.chateau-valencay.fr.

The **entrance pavilion** is a huge building, designed like a keep, but for show not defence, with many windows, harmless turrets and fancy machicolations. The **west wing** was added in the 17C and altered in the 18C. At roof level mansard windows alternate with small circular apertures. The tour of the ground floor includes the great Louis XVI vestibule; the gallery devoted to the

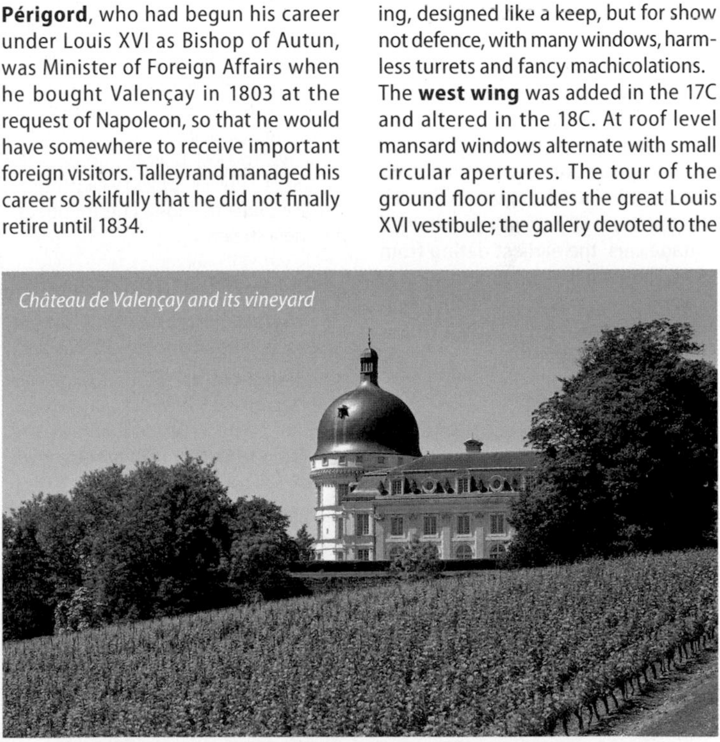
Château de Valençay and its vineyard

Talleyrand-Périgord family; the Grand Salon and the Blue Salon which contain many works of art and sumptuous Empire furniture including the famous Congress of Vienna table; and the apartments of the Duchess of Dino.

On the first floor the bedroom of Prince Talleyrand is followed by the room occupied by Ferdinand VII, King of Spain, when he was confined to Valençay by Napoleon from 1808 to 1814; the apartments of the Duke of Dino and those of Mme de Bénévent (portrait of the princess by Élisabeth Vigée-Lebrun); the great gallery (with a Diana by Houdon) and the great staircase.

Park

Black swans, ducks and peacocks strut freely in the formal French gardens near the château. Under the great trees in the park deer, llamas, camels and kangaroos are kept in vast enclosures.

Musée de l'Automobile du Centre

av. de la Résistance. Open Jul–Aug 10.30am–2.30pm, 1.30–7pm; Jun 10.30am–2.30pm, 2.30–6.30pm; Apr–May and Sept–Oct 10.30am–12.30pm, 2–6pm. 5€. 02 54 00 07 74. www.cc-valencay.fr.

The Car Museum contains the collection of the Guignard brothers, the grandsons of a coachbuilder from Vatan (Indre). There are over 60 perfectly maintained vintage cars, the earliest dating from 1898. The 1908 Renault limousine was used by presidents Poincaré and Millerand; there are also old Michelin maps and guides predating 1914.

EXCURSION

Chabris

14km/8.7mi NE along D 4.

This ancient Roman town lying on the south bank of the Cher is renowned for its wines and goats' cheese.

Église

The church is dedicated to St Phalier, a 5C anchorite who died in Chabris and was at the origin of a pilgrimage. Two naive panels in the chancel illustrate the life and miracles of St Phalier. The 11C **crypt** contains the saint's sarcophagus.

ADDRESSES

STAY

Hotel le Relais du Moulin – *94 r. Nationale, 36600 Valençay. 02 54 00 38 00. 54 rms. 7€. Restaurant.* Recent establishment with functional, well soundproofed rooms. The restaurant serves traditional cuisine.

EAT

Le Lion d'Or – *14 pl. de la Halle. 02 54 00 00 87. Closed Jan–Feb, Mon.* This old coaching inn is ideally situated oposite the covered market. The dining room has charming 1930s decor. Enjoy the terrace in summer. Nine guest rooms available.

Auberge St-Fiacre – *36600 Veuil. 6km/3.7mi S of Valencay on D 15 and minor road. 02 54 40 32 78. Closed 6–27 Jan, 1–14 Sept, Sun eve, Mon except public holidays.* This low-built 17C house in the centre of a flower-decked village has a terrace under the horse chestnut trees, beside a stream.

LEISURE ACTIVITIES

The **château** hosts a number of live shows to illustrate the life of Talleyrand.

Candlelight tours – In summer, 2 000 candles light up the château and gardens for three evenings only *13.50€. (Children 10€). Dinner at the Orangerie (bookings compulsory).*

Enjoy getting lost in the **Grand Labyrinthe de Napoléon**, a maze covering over 2 000 sq m/2400 sq yds.

The eastern part of the Touraine region boasts some of the Loire Valley's finest châteaux in Amboise, Chenonceau and Chaumont. Further inland stands the medieval stronghold town of Loches while Montrésor, Montpoupon and Montrichard are home to other châteaux lying off the beaten track that are well worth discovering. This is where the history of the French monarchy in the Loire Valley really comes to life as witnessed by the marks left by kings, queens and favourites on the region's stunning châteaux and charming towns.

Queens and Favourites

Many of the châteaux in the region are dominated by the role that women have played in their lives. Diane de Poitiers, mistress of Henri II, was the chatelaine of Chenonceau before being given her marching orders by Catherine de' Medici upon the King's death in 1559.

The favourite moved a short distance up the Loire to Chaumont while the queen settled in and set about reshaping Chenonceau. The medieval castle and town of Loches are remembered for Agnès Sorel, mistress of Charles VII, whose tomb lies in the collegiate church. Despite recent forensic work on her remains when they were returned to the church, there are still questions as to the circumstances of the royal mistress' death and a new exhibition explains how the enquiry was carried out. The château also bears witness to the passage of Joan of Arc who came to urge the King to go to Reims for his coronation during the struggle to rid France of the English armies in 1429.

Leonardo da Vinci

The main town in the region is Amboise, renowned for its imposing hilltop château where Charles VIII met an untimely end. Le Clos Lucé is the nearby manor house where Leonardo da Vinci spent the last years of his life and which features an exhibition of models of his famous machines including the first helicopter, automobile and parachute. The displays are always popular with children.

In addition to the fine views it affords of the Loire, the Château de Chaumont hosts an international garden festival every year which draws crowds of landscape gardeners, architects, designers and enthusiasts from all over the world. Montrichard and St-Aignan are pleasant small towns on the banks of the Cher with some fine medieval buildings, Romanesque churches and, of course, their own châteaux.

Highlights

1. The *Son et Lumière* show in the château at **Amboise** (p157)
2. **Chaumont**'s International Garden Festival (p165)
3. A tour of Montrichard's **Caves Monmousseau** wine cellars (p168)
4. Fairy-tale perfection of **Château de Chenonceau** (p170)
5. Walking tour of **Loches**' Medieval core (p179)

Replica of Leonardo da Vinci's helicopter, Le Clos-Lucé

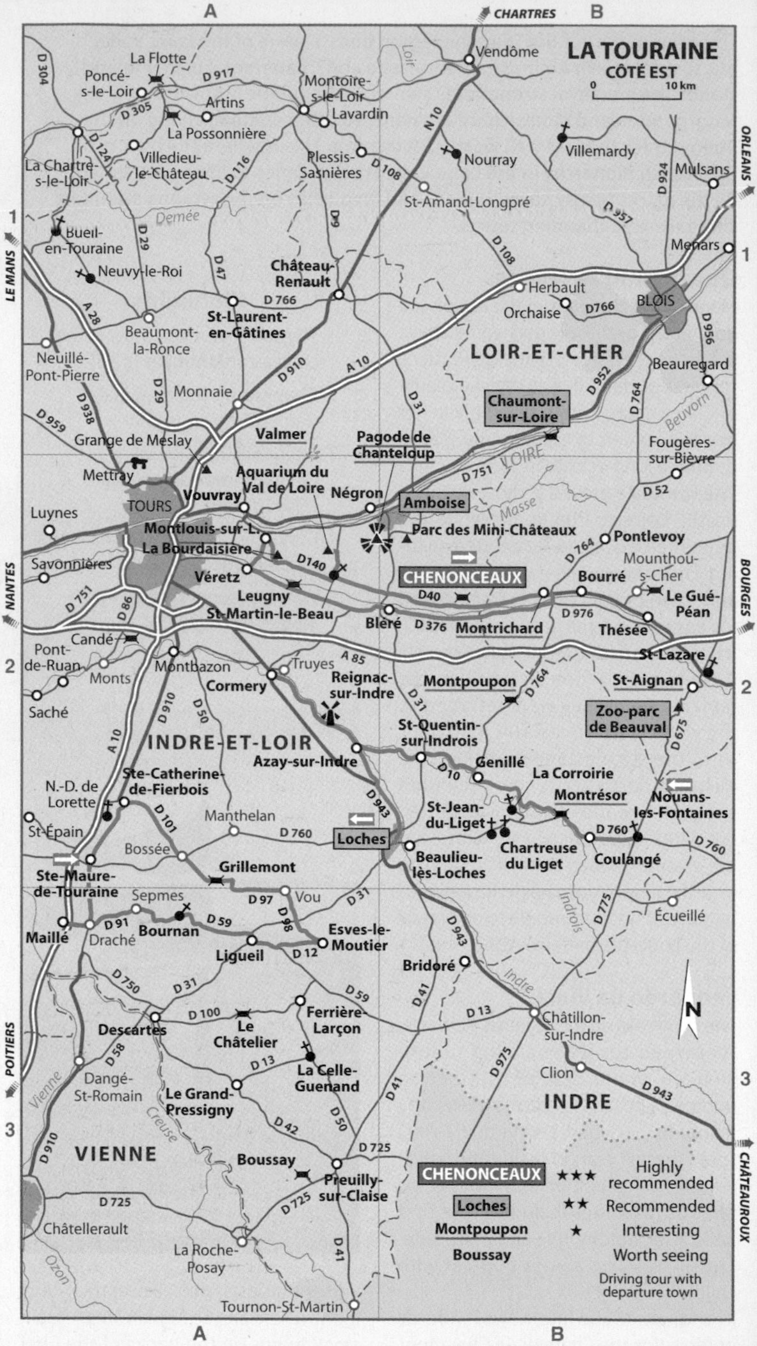
LA TOURAINE
CÔTÉ EST
0 10 km
A
B
1
2
3
CHARTRES
ORLEANS
BOURGES
CHÂTEAUROUX
POITIERS
NANTES
LE MANS
Vendôme
La Flotte
Poncé-s-le-Loir
Montoire-s-le-Loir
Lavardin
Artins
La Possonnière
La Chartre-s-le-Loir
Villedieu-le-Château
Plessis-Sasnières
Nourray
St-Amand-Longpré
Villemardy
Mulsans
Menars
Bueil-en-Touraine
Neuvy-le-Roi
Château-Renault
St-Laurent-en-Gâtines
Beaumont-la-Ronce
Herbault
Orchaise
BLOIS
Neuillé-Pont-Pierre
LOIR-ET-CHER
Beauregard
Monnaie
Chaumont-sur-Loire
Valmer
Pagode de Chanteloup
Grange de Meslay
Fougères-sur-Bièvre
Mettray
Aquarium du Val de Loire
Vouvray
Négron
Amboise
TOURS
Luynes
Montlouis-sur-L.
Parc des Mini-Châteaux
Pontlevoy
La Bourdaisière
Savonnières
Véretz
CHENONCEAUX
Mounthou-s-Cher
Bourré
Le Gué-Péan
Leugny
St-Martin-le-Beau
Bléré
Montrichard
Thésée
Candé
Pont-de-Ruan
Monts
Montbazon
Truyes
St-Lazare
Cormery
Reignac-sur-Indre
Montpoupon
St-Aignan
Saché
Zoo-parc de Beauval
INDRE-ET-LOIR
St-Quentin-sur-Indrois
Azay-sur-Indre
Genillé
Ste-Catherine-de-Fierbois
La Corroirie
N.-D. de Lorette
Montrésor
Nouans-les-Fontaines
St-Jean-du-Liget
St-Épain
Manthelan
Loches
Chartreuse du Liget
Coulangé
Bossée
Beaulieu-lès-Loches
Ste-Maure-de-Touraine
Grillemont
Sepmes
Vou
Écueillé
Maillé
Draché
Bournan
Esves-le-Moutier
Ligueil
Bridoré
Ferrière-Larçon
Descartes
Le Châtelier
Châtillon-sur-Indre
La Celle-Guenand
Dangé-St-Romain
Le Grand-Pressigny
Clion
INDRE
VIENNE
Boussay
Preuilly-sur-Claise
Châtellerault
La Roche-Posay
Tournon-St-Martin
Loir
Demée
Loire
Masse
Beuvron
Indrois
Indre
Vienne
Creuse
Ozon
CHENONCEAUX ★★★ Highly recommended
Loches ★★ Recommended
Montpoupon ★ Interesting
Boussay Worth seeing
Driving tour with departure town
N

Amboise★★

The town of Amboise, on the south bank of the Loire below the remains of its castle, appears at its most attractive when seen from the bridge or the north bank of the river. The rock spur dominating the town, on which the château stands, has been fortified since the Gallo-Roman period. From the terrace overlooking the river, there is a fine overall view of the Loire Valley and of the blue-slate roofs of the town.

- **Population:** 12 691
- **Michelin Map:** 317: O-4
- **Info**: quai du Général-de-Gaulle, 37402 Amboise. 02 47 57 09 28. www.amboise-valdeloire.com.
- **Location:** On the south bank of the Loire, 10km/6mi from Chenonceau, and 26km/16mi W of Tours.
- **Parking:** There are a number of pay car parks overlooking the Loire on the quai Général de Gaulle, and parking in pl. St Denis.
- **Don't Miss:** The views of Amboise and the Loire from the terrace and towers of the château.
- **Timing:** Allow half a day for the château and the town.
- **Kids:** The *Son et Lumière* shows in the château, Parc des Mini-Châteaux, the models of Leonardo da Vinci's inventions at Le Clos Lucé, the Aquarium du Val de Loire 8km/5mi W of Amboise.

A BIT OF HISTORY

Charles VIII's taste for luxury – The golden age of Amboise was the 15C, when the château was enlarged and embellished by Louis XI and Charles VIII, who spent his childhood in the old castle. Work began in 1492 and for the five following years two ranges of buildings were added to the older structure. Hundreds of workmen laboured continuously, often by candlelight, to meet the King's demands.

In the meantime, the King visited Italy, where he was dazzled by the high artistic standards and extravagant lifestyle. He returned to France laden with furniture, works of art and fabrics. He recruited scholars, architects, sculptors, decorators, gardeners, tailors and even a poultry breeder who had invented the incubator. Thus the year 1496 marked the beginning of Italian influence over French art, although there is little to attest to these changes at Amboise, since the new building was by then well advanced.

Château d'Amboise seen from across the River Loire

A. Cassaigne/MICHELIN

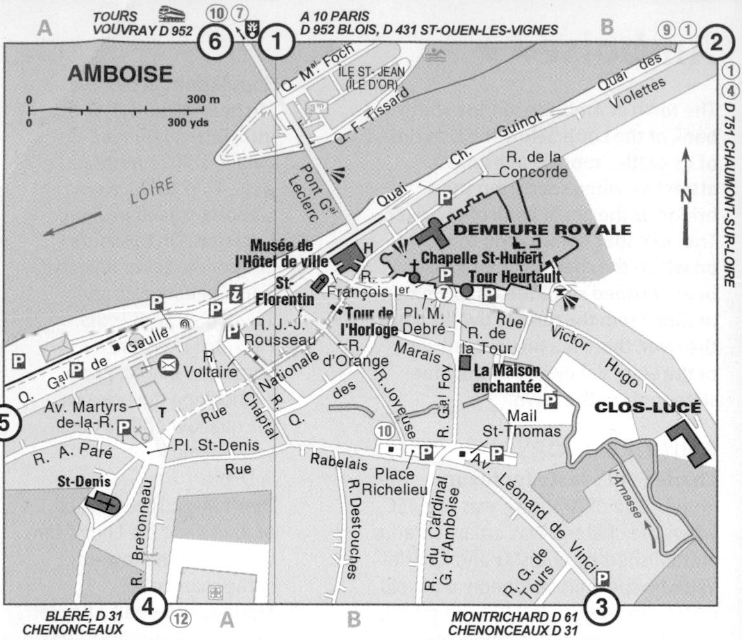

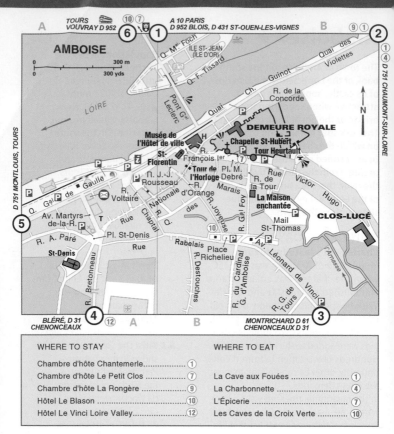

WHERE TO STAY		WHERE TO EAT	
Chambre d'hôte Chantemerle	1		
Chambre d'hôte Le Petit Clos	7	La Cave aux Fouées	1
Chambre d'hôte La Rongère	9	La Charbonnette	4
Hôtel Le Blason	10	L'Épicerie	7
Hôtel Le Vinci Loire Valley	12	Les Caves de la Croix Verte	10

Charles VIII was impressed by Italian gardens. On his return he instructed Pacello to design an ornamental garden on the terrace at Amboise.

Among the architects whom he employed were Fra Giocondo and Il Boccadoro; the latter, a leading figure in the introduction of Renaissance ideas into France, had worked at Blois and Chambord and on the Hôtel de Ville in Paris.

The Destruction of the Château – Together with Blois, Amboise passed to Gaston d'Orléans, Louis XIII's brother and a conspirator (*see Blois*). During one of his many rebellions, the château was captured by Royalist troops and the outer fortifications razed in 1631. It reverted to the crown and was used as a prison where Fouquet, his financial adviser, and the Duke of Lauzun were imprisoned by Louis XIV.

Later Napoleon granted the château to Roger Ducos, a former member of the Directory. As there were no subsidies for its upkeep, he had a large part of it demolished.

VISIT

Château★★

Open Jul–Aug 9am–7pm; Apr–Jun 9am–6.30pm; mid–end Mar and Sept–Oct 9am–6pm; early–mid-Nov 9am–5.30pm; mid-Nov–Jan 9am–noon, 2–4.45pm; early Feb–mid-Mar 9am–noon, 1.30–5.30pm. Closed 1 Jan, 25 Dec. 9€. 08 20 20 50 50. www.chateau-amboise.com.

Terrace

The château is entered via a ramp which opens onto the terrace overlooking the river. From here there is a magnificent **view**★★ of the Loire and of the town's pointed roofs and walls. The silhouette

The Amboise Conspiracy (1560)

This conspiracy was one of the bloodier episodes in the château's history. During the turbulent years leading up to the Wars of Religion, a Protestant aristocrat known as **La Renaudie** gathered a body of reformists around him in Brittany. These were dispatched to Blois in small groups to request of the young king, François II, the freedom to practise their religion. While they were there, the intention was that they should also try to lay hands on the Guises, the deadly enemies of the Huguenots.

The plot was uncovered and the court promptly withdrew from Blois, which was indefensible, to Amboise where the King signed an edict of pacification in an attempt to calm things down. The conspirators persisted, however, and on 17 March they were arrested and killed as fast as they arrived. La Renaudie also perished. The conspiracy was harshly suppressed; some of the conspirators were hanged from the balcony of the château, some from the battlements, others were thrown into the Loire in sacks, whereas the noblemen were beheaded and quartered. In 1563 there was a truce followed by an Act of Toleration, signed at Amboise, which brought an end to the first War of Religion. The country settled down to four years of peace.

of the 15C **Tour de l'Horloge** can be seen rising above the rooftops not far from the old ramparts, and to the west that of the **church of St-Denis**.

In the time of Charles VIII festivals were held in this enclosed courtyard: tapestries adorned the walls and a sky-blue awning decorated with sun, moon and stars, gave protection from the weather.

Chapelle St-Hubert

Curiously set astride the fortified town walls, this jewel of Flamboyant Gothic architecture dating from 1491 is all that remains of the buildings which once lined the ramparts. The transept houses the tomb thought to contain the body of the great artist Leonardo da Vinci, who died at Amboise.

Royal Apartments

The Royal Apartments are the only part of the château to have escaped demolition. The Gothic wing, overlooking the ramparts above the Loire, was built by Charles VIII.

The **Salle des Gardes nobles**, or guardroom, is roofed with vaulting supported on a single column, forming a Gothic palm-tree of ribs.

A spiral staircase leads up to the **Salle des Tambourineurs** (named after the drummers who accompanied the King on royal visits), where Charles VIII withdrew from the public gaze. The room features some interesting pieces of furniture (Cardinal Georges d'Amboise's pulpit) and a beautiful Brussels tapestry (16C) on the wall, **Homage to Alexander the Great**. Leading on from the Salle des Tambourineurs is the **Salle du Conseil**, also known as the Salle des États (Hall of State). This features a double stone vault supported by a line of columns down the centre of the room, liberally adorned with motifs of

Salle du Conseil

Son et Lumière

Entitled "At the Court of King François", this *son et lumière*, entirely written, staged and acted out by local volunteers, features around 400 jugglers, horsemen, fire-eaters and extras, assisted by some highly sophisticated technology (fireworks, fountains, huge images projected onto the surroundings). The show evokes the building of the château, the arrival of Louise of Savoy, the childhood and adolescence of François I, the Italian campaign, as well as daily life and festivities at Amboise to honour the King and his court.
Performances Wed and Sat (except on 14 Jul) from late Jun to 31 Aug (1hr 30min). The show starts at 10.30pm Jun-Jul and 10pm in Aug. 6€-16€ (children 7€). ☎02 47 57 14 47. www.renaissance-amboise.com.

the Kingdom of France and the Duchy of Brittany, the fleur-de-lis and ermine. The second wing was built at the beginning of the 16C and furnished in early French Renaissance style: wine-waiter's sideboard, a Gothic piece with a distinctive linen-fold motif, carved extendable tables and chests in walnut.
In **Henri II's bedchamber** *trompe-l'œil* decoration is echoed in the furniture and wall hangings.

Tour des Minimes or Tour Cavalière
This round tower adjoining the Logis Royal is famous for its wide ramp which horsemen could ride up, ensuring easy access for the provisioning of supplies from the outbuildings in the gardens. The ramp spirals round an empty core which provides air and light.
From the top there is a sweeping **view**★★ of the Loire Valley, the Gothic wing of the château and, to the left, the balcony from which several of the conspirators of 1560 were hanged.

Gardens
These pleasant gardens, redesigned in the 19C under Louis-Philippe, lie within the rampart walls where parts of the château once stood.

Le Clos-Lucé★ (Leonardo da Vinci's House)

Open Jul–Aug 9am–8pm; Feb–Jun and Sept–Oct 9am–7pm; Nov–Dec 9am–6pm; Jan 10am–6pm. Closed 1 Jan, 25 Dec. 12€. ☎02 47 57 00 73. www.vinci-closluce.com.
The manor house of Le Clos-Lucé was acquired by Charles VIII in 1490. François I also resided here. In 1516, François invited **Leonardo da Vinci** to Amboise and lodged him at Le Clos-Lucé where the great artist and scholar organised the court festivities and lived until his death on 2 May 1519 at the age of 67.
The wooden gallery in the courtyard gives a good view of the manor's main façade. On the first floor is Da Vinci's stu-

Bedroom of Leonardo de Vinci, Le Clos-Lucé

dio, and the bedroom where he died. This is where he is believed to have worked on his project for the draining of the Sologne and his design for a palace at **Romorantin** for Louise of Savoy. The basement houses the museum of Leonardo's **fabulous machines**, a collection of models based on the designs of this polymath, who was painter, sculptor, musician, poet, architect, engineer and scholar all in one, and whose ideas were four centuries ahead of his time.

> "The Wars of Religion have left here the ineffaceable stain which they left wherever they passed. An imaginative visitor at Amboise today may fancy that the traces of blood are mixed with the red rust on the crossed iron bars of the grim-looking balcony, to which the heads of the Huguenots executed on the discovery of the conspiracy of La Renaudie are rumoured to have been suspended. There was room on the stout balustrade – an admirable piece of work – for a ghastly array."
>
> **Henry James**
>
> *A Little Tour in France*

ADDITIONAL SIGHTS

Musée de l'Hôtel de Ville

Entrance on r. François-1er.
Open mid-Jun–mid-Sept Sun–Fri 10am–12.30pm, 2–6pm. 02 47 23 47 42. www.ville-amboise.fr.

The former town hall was built early in the 16C for Pierre Morin, treasurer to the King of France, and houses a museum containing examples of the royal signature, a 14C carving of the Virgin Mary, Aubusson tapestries, portraits of the Duke of Choiseul and six rare 18C gouaches of the Château de Chanteloup, depicting it at the height of its splendour.

Tour de l'Horloge

The clock tower, also known as the Amboise belfry, was built in the 15C at the expense of the inhabitants on the site of a town gateway called L'Amasse. It spans a busy pedestrian street.

EXCURSIONS

Parc des Mini-Châteaux

S of town, along the Chenonceaux road (D 81). Open mid-Jul–mid-Aug 10am–8pm; Jun–mid-Jul and rest of Aug 10am–7pm; Apr–May 10.30am–7pm; Sept–mid-Nov 10.30am–6pm (last admission 1hr before closing) 13.50€, 21€ combination ticket with aquarium (children 4–14 years 9.50€, 16€). 08 25 08 25 22. www.mini-chateaux.com.

This 2ha/5-acre park is home to 60 or so models (scale 1:25) of great châteaux and smaller manor houses of the Loire Valley, displayed in a setting commensurate with their size (bonsai trees, miniature TGV railway and boats on the river, etc.). By night, fibre-optical illuminations lend a fairytale atmosphere to the scene.

Pagode de Chanteloup★

3km/1.8mi S on D 31 towards Bléré.
Open Jul–Aug 9.30am–7.30pm; Jun 10am–7pm; May and Sept 10am–7pm; 2nd week of Feb and Mar weekends and school holidays 2–7pm; Apr 10am–6.30pm; Oct–mid-Nov school holidays 10.30am–noon 2–5pm, weekends and bank holidays 10.30am–5pm. Last admission 1hr before closing. 8.30€ (children 7–15 years 6.30€). 02 47 57 20 97. www.pagode-chanteloup.com.

At the edge of the Forest of Amboise, the pagoda is all that remains of the replica of Versailles that was built here by the **Duke of Choiseul**, minister of Louis XV. When the Duke was exiled to his estates by the King's mistress, Mme du Barry, Choiseul transformed Chanteloup into a haven of intellectual and artistic life and ordered the construction of the pagoda (1775–78) from architect Louis-Denis Le Camus. This folly was in keeping with the decorative fashion of the age for all things Chinese.

The **setting★** of the pagoda with its wide half-moon lake *(boats for hire)*, and the paths which fan out across the park give an idea of the grandeur of the sumptuous country residence built by

Château de Valmer

the exiled Duke of Choiseul. From the top of the pagoda *(149 steps)*, there are fine **views** of the Loire Valley, the Forest of Amboise and as far as Tours.

Aquarium du Val de Loire★

8km/5mi W on D 751. After Lussault-sur-Loire, take the D 283 and follow the signs. Open 31 Jul–22 Aug 10am–8pm; Jun–Jul and last Sat Aug 10am–7pm; Apr–May 10.30am–7pm; rest of year 10.30am–6pm (last admission 1hr before closing) Closed last 3 weeks Jan and last 2 weeks Nov. 13€, 22€ combination ticket with Mini-Châteaux (children 2–14 years 9€, 17€). 02 47 23 44 57. www.aquariumduvaldeloire.com.

The aquarium keeps 70 species of mostly European freshwater fish in open-air ponds with reconstituted natural environments. The main advantage of this approach is to allow the fish to develop at the natural rhythm of the seasons.

Négron

3.5km/2.2mi. Cross the river at Pont du Général Leclerc and turn left, following the D 952.

Standing below N 152 this village has a charming square overlooked by the church and a Gothic house with a Renaissance front.

Grounds of Château de Valmer

12km/7.5mi NW of Amboise via the D 751. Open May Sat–Sun and public holidays 10am–12.30pm, 2–7pm; Jun Tue–Sun 10am–12.30pm, 2–7pm; Jul–Aug Tue–Sun 10am–7pm; Sept–mid-Oct Tue–Sun 10am–12.30pm, 2–6pm. 8€. 02 47 52 93 12. www.chateaudevalmer.com. Wine tastings year round.

The park and **gardens★** of Valmer Castle occupy a remarkable position on a hillside overlooking the River Brenne. The castle was destroyed by fire in 1948. But the beautiful Italian-style terraced gardens with statues and fountains, the vast kitchen garden with its many varieties of forgotten vegetables and the park enclosed by a wall have remained as they were in the 17C. An unusual chapel hewn into the cliffside has retained two 16C stained-glass windows.

The estate produces fine Vouvray AOC and Touraine rosé wine and organises tastings all year round upon appointment. The moat provides welcome shade if visiting in summer and is planted with some superb hydrangeas. To get down, take the 15C spiral staircase hidden by the large clipped yew tree on the terrace in the Italian garden.

ADDRESSES

STAY

Chambre d'hôte le Petit Clos – *7 r. Balzac. 02 47 57 43 52. Closed 15 Oct–15 Mar except by reservation. 3 rms.* . On the northern bank of the Loire, this B&B provides three rooms with a separate entrance.

Chambre d'hôte Chantemerle – *1 imp. du Colombier. 02 47 57 06 33. www.chante-merle.com. Closed Dec–Feb except Christmas and Feb holidays. 5 rms.* . Recently built, this house, at the top of the town, has plain but comfortable rooms. Kitchenette available for guests.

Hôtel le Blason – *11 pl. Richelieu. 02 47 23 22 41. www.leblason.fr. Closed 15 Jan–1 Feb - 25 rms. 6.50€. Restaurant* . A 15C building near the town centre which has retained its original walls. The hotel offers rooms with exposed beams, some of which are attic rooms (shower only). The breakfast is of a high standard.

Chambred d'hôte La Rongère – *17 r. de la Résistance ,37530 Chargé. 02 47 57 21 71. www.amboise-larongere.com.* P *4 rms.* . The spacious and bright rooms occupy the outbuildings of this 18C house which tastefully combines different decorative styles. Calm grounds, heated pool and sauna. Bikes available for hire.

Hôtel Le Vinci Loire Valley – *12 av. E. Gounin, 1km/0.6mi S. 02 47 57 10 90. www.vinciloirevalley.com. 26 rms. 11€.* In the suburbs, this hotel is in a pleasant, contemporary syle. Comfortable, well-equipped rooms.

EAT

La Cave aux Fouées – *476 quai des Violettes. 02 47 30 56 80. www.lacave auxfouees.com.* An original place in a huge troglodytic cave. You can sample *rillettes* and other regional specialities, accompanied by *fouées*, flat bread rolls cooked in a wood-fired oven. On Saturday there is a DJ and live music.

Les Caves de la Croix Verte – *20 rte. d'Amboise. 37530 Pocé-sur-Cisse. 3.5km/2.2mi NE. 02 47 57 39 98. Closed Sun eve, Mon.* Also in a troglodytic cave, this place serves good meat dishes, *fois gras* and smoked salmon.

La Charbonnette – *11 pl. de l'Église. 41150 Onzain. 21km/13mi NE. 02 54 20 79 51. Closed Sun and Thu eves Nov–Apr.* Convivial atmosphere in two dining rooms. Local produce used.

L'Épicerie – *46 pl. Michel-Debré. 02 47 57 08 94. Closed 27 Oct–17 Dec, Mon and Tue.* Well-placed restaurant near the castle with a good reputation for the standard of cooking.

TAKING A BREAK

Gerard – *18 r. National. 02 47 57 21 07. Open Tue–Sun 7.30am–7.30pm. Closed Mon and 2 weeks Jun, 2 weeks Nov.* After visiting the castle, take a break in this welcoming pâtisserie and sample one of their numerous varieties of tea and chocolates. Speciality cakes include the *yoyo* – two meringues sandwiched with cream – and the *Soleillon*: almond, apple and honey shortbread.

LEISURE ACTIVITIES

Boat trips on the Loire – Ambacia – *quai Charles Guinot . www.croisieres delaloire.com. Tue–Sun Jul–Aug 11am, 2pm, 3pm, 4pm, 5pm; May–Jun, 11am bookings only, 3pm, 4pm; Oct–Nov and Mar–Apr bookings only. Closed Dec–Feb – 8.50€ (children 4–12 years 5.50€) . Pick up tickets 15min before departure.* Board the Toue Ambacia for river cruise with commentary (50min).

CALENDAR

Festivals – Brass-bands festival, mid-Jun; "Les Courants" contemporary music festival on l'île d'Or, late Jun-early Jul; classical music festival at Église St-Denis Jul-Aug; Fête de la Saint-Hubert 1st Sun Nov at the Château; European Festival of Renaissance Music at Le Clos-Lucé the last weekend in Sept.

Exhibition – "L'univers de la creation" at Le Clos-Lucé first 2 weeks in May.

Market – Jul–Aug: crafts, regional produce, open-air shows.

Wine – Weekends from Easter to 15 August in the Château tunnel. Fête du touraine primeur festival 3rd Fri in Nov.

Château-Renault

Château-Renault was founded in 1066 by Renault, son of Geoffroi de Château-Gontier, on a tongue of land between the River Brenne and the River Gault at the point where they meet. The main street runs in a large curve down to the river bank. The shaded terraces laid out beneath the castle keep offer fine views of the two rivers and their valleys.

- **Population:** 5 245
- **Michelin Map:** 317: O-3
- **Info:** 32 pl. Jean-Jaurès BP 60, 37110. 02 47 56 22 22.
- **Location:** Between Tours (28km/17mi to the S) and Vendôme (25km/15.5mi to the N).
- **Parking:** There are parking areas along the river Gault to the S and W of the château.
- **Don't Miss:** The view of the town from the terraces.
- **Timing:** Allow 2hrs for the town and its surroundings.

VISIT

Musée du Cuir et de la Tannerie

Open mid-May–Sept Tue–Sun 2–6pm (last admission 30min before closing). Closed 14 Jul. 3.80€. 02 47 56 03 59.

Housed in an old tannery, this Leather and Tanning Museum displays the various stages of traditional manufacture with, among other things, a collection of old currying machinery.

Château

A 14C gate, surmounted by a hoarding (to enable the defenders to protect the entrance) leads onto the terraces shaded by lime trees, from where there is an attractive **view★** over the town.

The top of the 12C keep *(donjon)* has been demolished. The town hall occupies the 17C château. This belonged to the owners of the château in Châteaudun and then to two illustrious sailors: the Marquis de Château-Renault under Louis XIV and, under Louis XVI, the Count of Estaing who died by the guillotine in 1793.

EXCURSION

St-Laurent-en-Gâtines

9km/5.6mi W.

At the roadside stands a massive brick and stone edifice. Known for many years as **La Grand' Maison** (Great House), it was once the residence of the abbots of Marmoutier, who owned the land of St-Laurent-en-Gâtines. The building was constructed in the 15C and converted into a church in the 19C; a spire was added to the polygonal tower which housed the stairs and two large Flamboyant windows were inserted on one side.

ADDRESSES

STAY / EAT

Chambre d'hôte La Maréchalerie – *Hameau le Sentier, 37110 Monthodon. 7km/4.3mi W of Château-Renault by D 54. 02 47 29 61 66. www.lamarechalerie.fr. . 5 rms, 1 suite. . Evening meal.* This old blacksmith's workshop is full of character with its half-timbering and exposed beams. The five rooms each have different furnishings, but are of equal comfort with private bathrooms. Meal at weekends only. Good value for money.

Soft Hôtel – *6 r. du Petit-Versailles. 02 47 29 50 41. www.soft-hotel.com . 15 rms. 6€. Restaurant.* Set in a green park with swimming pool, this hotel is reasonably priced with modern, comfortable rooms. Pretty dining room and separate seating area.

Château de Chaumont-sur-Loire★★

The Château de Chaumont is as well sited as Amboise on the south bank of the Loire, overlooking the town and the river. The feudal austerity of the structure is softened by its Renaissance influence, its elegant stair tower and its sumptuous Council Room.

- **Michelin Map:** 318: E-7
- **Info:** r. du Mar.-Leclerc, 41150 Chaumont-sur-Loire. ℘02 54 20 91 73. www.chaumontsurloire.info.
- **Location:** 20km/12mi N of Amboise and 17km/10mi S of Blois.
- **Parking:** By the entrance for disabled visitors. From the traffic lights in Chaumont follow signs for Montrichard, and turn right at the first crossroads.
- **Timing:** Allow 1–2hrs to visit the château.

A BIT OF HISTORY

The original fortress of Chaumont was demolished twice; it was rebuilt between 1445 and 1510 by Pierre d'Amboise, Charles I d'Amboise, the eldest of Pierre's 17 children, and Charles II, his grandson.

In 1560 Catherine de' Medici, the widow of Henri II, acquired the castle purely as a means of exacting revenge against Diane de Poitiers, the mistress of the late King. The Queen forced her rival to give up her favourite residence at Chenonceau in exchange for Chaumont. Catherine de' Medici's stay at Chaumont and the existence there of a room connected by a staircase with the top of a tower have given rise to plenty of speculation.

The room has been said to be the study of the Queen's astrologer, and the tower the observatory from which Catherine consulted the stars.

Since 1938 Chaumont has belonged to the French State.

VISIT

Park

Open mid-May–mid-Oct 9am until dusk; rest of year 10am–5pm. Closed 1 Jan, 1 and 11 Nov, 25 Dec. No charge. ℘02 54 51 26 26.

A 10min walk uphill will bring you to the castle. This pleasant stroll is an opportunity to admire the fine landscaped gardens designed by Henri Duchêne at the end of the 19C. The paths wind their way through cedars, lime trees and redwoods. The **view**★ from the terrace is remarkable.

The Buildings★★★

The outer west façade, which is the oldest, has an austere and military appearance. The two other façades, despite their feudal aspect, reflect the influence of the Renaissance.

At ground-floor level there is a frieze bearing the interlaced C's of Charles de Chaumont-Amboise, alternating with the rebus of the castle: a volcano or *chaud mont* (Chaumont).

Apartments

Open mid-May–mid-Sept 9.30am–6.30pm; Apr–early May and rest ofSept 10.30am–5.30pm; Oct–Mar 10am–5pm, (last admission 30min before closing). Closed 1 Jan, 1 May, 1 and 11 Nov, 25 Dec. 7.50€. ℘02 54 51 26 26. www.monum.fr.

Note the room of the two rivals, Catherine de' Medici and Diane de Poitiers, and also Ruggieri's study and the Council Room, which is paved with 17C Spanish majolica tiles bought in Palermo, Sicily, by the Prince of Broglie. These apartments contain fine 16C and 17C tapestries, good furniture and a collection of the terracotta medallions made by Nini, an 18C Italian artist who set up his workshop in the stables.

The size and luxurious fittings of the **stables** give an idea of the part played by horses in the lives of princely families.

Château de Chaumont-sur-Loire

The International Garden Festival

Every year, 30 landscape gardeners create individual plant displays in 30 separate plots, many influcenced by Pop Art. Visitors enter a curious and fascinating plant kingdom, which is neither a landscape garden nor a botanical park, but rather a unique site that pays tribute to the beauty of nature, where the creative genius of gardeners can be given free rein. This annual festival aims to introduce new creations and unusual combinations of plants and flowers.

Built in 1877 by the Prince de Broglie and fitted with electric lighting in 1906, the stables include stalls for the horses and ponies, boxes for the thoroughbreds, a kitchen, a remarkable harness room, horse-drawn carriages and a second courtyard known as the guests' court-yard, in which there is a small riding centre.

Conservatoire international des Parcs et Jardins du Paysage

Guided tour only (1hr15min) mid-Jun–mid-Oct, 9.30am until dusk. 9€ (children 12–18 years 6.50€, 6–12 years 3.50€). ℘02 54 20 99 22. www.eurabbey.com/garden.

The château farmhouse houses a centre offering thematic workshops on botany and horticulture. It also runs university courses in gardening and landscaping. An important **International Garden Festival** is held here.

ADDRESSES

EAT

La Chancelière – *Near the castle. 41150 Chaumont-sur-Loire. ℘02 54 20 96 95. Closed 14 Jan–13 Feb, 10 Nov–5 Dec, Wed and Thu.* This popular restaurant with a white façade is near the castle and beside the Loire. Two rustic-style dining rooms serve regional specialities.

Montrichard★

From the river bank and bridge over the Cher there is a good view of this town clustered around the church below the crumbling keep. The north bank above the town is pitted with quarries that have now been transformed into dwellings, caves for growing mushrooms and cellars for storing renowned sparkling wines. In many ways Monrichard is just a laid-back market town, but one that also happens to have a full complement of medieval and Renaissance buildings, plus a hilltop fortress.

- **Population:** 3 423
- **Michelin Map**318: E-7
- **Info:** 1 r. du Pont, 41400 Montrichard. ℘02 54 32 05 10.
- **Location:** 35km/29mi S of Blois, 45km/28mi E of Tours, and 32km/20mi N of Loches.
- **Don't Miss:** The Caves Monmousseau.
- **TImlng:** Give yourself 1–2hrs to explore fully.
- **Kids:** Bouré, and the reconstructed village.

WALKING TOUR

Donjon★

Open Jul–Aug 10am–6pm; Apr–Jun and Sept 10am–noon, 2–6pm. 5€. End Jul–mid-Aug, live visits with people in costume, 4.30pm: 8€ (children 7–12 years 5€). ℘02 54 32 05 10.

The square keep, which stands on the edge of the plateau above the River Cher, is enclosed by the remains of its curtain wall and by a complex system of ramparts that protected the entrance. It was built c. 1010 by Fulk Nerra, reinforced with a second wall in 1109 and then with a third in 1250. Despite having been reduced in height by 4m/13ft on the orders of Henri IV in 1589 for having fallen into the hands of the Catholic League at one stage, the keep still evokes its distant past. The **museums** retrace the archaeological history of the town and the surrounding area.

Église Ste-Croix

The church, which was originally the castle chapel, stands below the keep at the top of the flight of steps known as Grands Degrés Ste-Croix. The façade is decorated with elegant Romanesque arches; the arches of the porch are ornamented with a twisted torus. The elegant doorway is also Romanesque. **Jeanne de France**, the daughter of Louis XI, and her young cousin, the Duke of Orléans, were married in this chapel in 1476.

Old houses

Hôtel d'Effiat in rue Porte-au-Roi, which was built in the late 15C–early 16C, has Gothic decor with a few Renaissance elements. In the 16C it was the residence of Jacques de Beaune-Semblançay, Treasurer to Anne of Brittany and then to Louise of Savoy. The mansion has retained the name of its last owner, the Marquis d'Effiat, who at his death (1719) presented it to the town to be converted into an old people's home.

On the corner of rue du Pont stands the **Maison de l'Ave Maria** (16C) which has three gables and finely carved beams. Opposite are the Petits Degrés Ste-Croix which lead to troglodyte dwellings.

Montrichard

©Graham Salter/age fotostock

Further on, at the corner of rue du Prêche, stands the 11C stone façade of the **Maison du Prêche** (Sermon House).

Caves Monmousseau

Guided tours only (45min) Apr–mid-Nov 10–6pm; rest of year Mon–Fri 10am–noon, 2–5pm. Closed 23 Dec–5 Jan. 2.75€. 02 54 32 35 15. www.monmousseau.com.

These cellars *(15km/9mi of underground galleries)* are particularly interesting as they present age-old traditional methods alongside modern, more sophisticated techniques, known as the **Dom Pérignon method**.

Église de Nanteuil

On the road to Amboise (D 115).

This church is a tall Gothic building with a Flamboyant doorway; the apses are Romanesque decorated with carved capitals. The high, narrow nave features Angevin vaulting.

Above the entrance porch is a chapel built by Louis XI, which can be entered up internal or external flights of steps. There is a long-standing tradition of a pilgrimage to the Virgin Mary of Nanteuil on Whit Monday.

EXCURSIONS

Bourré

3km/2mi E.

The practice of digging underground galleries appears to have been widespread here since the days of Roman Antiquity and the local stone, tufa (*tuffeau*, also called *pierre de Bourré*) has often been used in the construction of châteaux.

However, these quarries were gradually abandoned and subsequently used as wine cellars or mushroom beds. Among the latter, the most fascinating is undoubtedly the **Caves champignonnières des Roches** *(guided tours (1hr) Easter–mid-Nov 10–11am, 3–5pm; 6€; 02 54 32 95 30)*.

Here you discover the strange and silent kingdom of mushrooms, lit by the glow of torchlights, where the oyster mushrooms, button mushroom, shiitake and pied-bleu varieties thrive in darkness.

La Ville souterraine

Open same hours as for the Caves champignonnières des Roches.

This is the lively reconstruction of a village square with its church, town hall and school: a dog is pushing a door open, a housewife is looking out of her window, a pair of clogs are waiting on the window sill.

La Magnanerie

4 chemin de la Croix-Bardin. Guided tours only Easter–end Aug 11am, 3pm, 4pm and 5pm (closed Tue); Sept 3pm, 4pm, 5pm (closed Tue–Wed), Oct–early Nov Fri and weekends 4pm. 7€ (children 4€). 02 54 32 63 91.

This troglodyte site gets its name from its role as a sikworm farm. Also features a display of a typical troglodyte dwelling and explains how the tufa stone was quarried. The terrace commands fine views of the Cher Valley.

Thésée

10km/6mi E along D 176.

West of the village stand the remains of the Gallo-Roman settlement of Tasciaca beside the Roman road from Bourges to Tours. During the 1C–3C it prospered from the making and selling of ceramic ware. Known as Les Maselles, the settlement extended over the area of modern Thésée and Pouillé.

Musée archéologique

Open Jul–Aug Wed–Mon 2–6pm; Easter–Jun Sat–Sun and public holidays 2-6pm. 3.50€. 02 54 71 00 88.

Housed in the town hall (an 18C winegrower's property in the middle of a splendid park), the museum's archaeological collection consists of objects excavated from the sanctuary *(fanum)* and from the numerous potteries unearthed on either side of the river.

Château du Gué-Péan

13km/8mi E along D 176 then D 21. 02 54 71 37 10. www.monthousurcher.fr. Open May-Sept 10am-12.30pm, 2-6.30pm; rest of year by appointment only. 6.50€.

The château is isolated in a quiet wooded valley; a picnic area has been set up in the grounds. It was built as a country house in the 16C and 17C, but the plan is that of a feudal castle: three ranges of buildings round a closed courtyard with a huge round tower at each corner, surrounded by a dry moat and reached by a stone bridge.

Access to the sentry walk.

Château de Montpoupon

12km/7.4mi S along D 764. Open Apr–Sept 10am–noon, 2–6pm; Oct–Dec, Feb–Mar Sat–Sun and public holidays 10am–noon, 2–6pm. Closed 25 Dec. 7€. 02 47 94 21 15. www.montpoupon.com.

Only the towers remain of the original 13C fortress on this site. The main building, which has mullioned windows and Gothic-style gables, was built in the 15C, whereas the **fortified gatehouse** is early 16C. Seen from the road, the whole complex conveys unmistakable elegance. The **outbuildings**★, house the hunt museum which features a display of clothing, art and artefacts illustrating the region's centuries-old tradition of hunting with hounds.

Pontlevoy

Pontlevoy is a small town situated in the agricultural region to the north of Montrichard, boasting a number of charming old houses with stone dressings. Some 30 panels, decorated with advertisements for Poulain chocolate, illustrate life in Pontlevoy at the turn of the 20C and the early days of motor cars.

Abbey★

02 54 32 99 39. www.eurabbey.com.

The main interest of the **old abbey** lies in its elegant 18C buildings (including two wings of the cloisters) and the 14C–15C Gothic chapel.

The abbey was founded in 1034 when, legend has it, Gelduin de Chaumont established a Benedictine community here as a token of gratitude for his surviving a shipwreck. In the 17C, when the reform of monastic life became essential, the abbey was entrusted to the Benedictines of St-Maur and the Abbot Pierre de Bérule, who opened an educational establishment in 1644 which made Pontlevoy famous until the 19C. The college was made into an École Royale Militaire in 1776 for training scholarship students chosen by the King from among the lower nobility.

Conventual buildings

These 18C conventual buildings include the refectory, the remarkable staircase leading to the upper floor, and the majestic façade giving onto the gardens, decorated with embla.

ADDRESSES

STAY

Chambre d'hôte Mme Galloux La Ferme des Bords – *rte. de Chaumont-sur-Loire, 8 Les Bordes, 41400 Pontlevoy. 02 54 32 51 08. www.chambredhote-41.fr. Closed 15 Nov–end Feb. . 6 rms.* . Peace and relaxation guaranteed on this working cereal farm close to the most famous châteaux of the Loire Valley. Six rooms (including 1 family room and 1 suite) occupy a separate building and are simply yet comfortably furnished.

Hotel Bellevue – *24 quai de la République. 02 54 32 06 17. 35 rms. 11€.* Most rooms offer a panoramic view of the Cher. The restaurant has bay windows facing out on the valley, and serves traditional cuisine.

LEISURE ACTIVITIES

Hot-air Ballooning – France Montgolfières – *24 r. Nationale, 41400 Montrichard. 02 54 32 20 48. www.france-montgolfière.com.* Dawn and dusk flights taking off from Chenonceau, Amboise and Loches. Snacks and refreshments included.

Distillerie Giradot – *62 rte. de Tours, 41400 Chissay-en-Touraine. 02 54 32 32 05. www.distillerie-girardot.fr. Shop: Mon–Sat 9am–noon, 2–7pm, Sun 10am–noon, 3–7pm - guided tours from Easter–late Sept 3–6pm (time of last tour).* A family-run distillery dating from the early 20C producing liqueurs and brandies that can be tasted. In fine weather the tour includes the tufa cellars and an explanation of distilling techniques.

Château de Chenonceau★★★

The beautiful Château de Chenonceau (the town of Chenonceaux is written with an "x", but not the château) stretches across the River Cher in a harmonious natural setting of water, greenery, gardens and trees. To this perfection is added the elegance of the château's architecture, interior décor and magnificent furniture. A superb avenue of plane trees leads to the château. Tourists with a fanciful imagination can try to imagine the entry of Charles IX, among mermaids, nymphs and satyrs.

- **Michelin Map:** 317: P-5.
- **Info:** ✆0 820 20 90 90. www.chenonceau.com.
- **Location:** 14km/8.7mi S of Amboise and 7km/4.3mi E of Bléré. By rail: several trains serve Chenonceaux: Tours-Vierzon line. The station is 200m/219yd from the entrance to the château. The return trip from Tours is possible in a day.
- **Don't Miss:** The night-time illuminations. View of the château from the grounds at any time of day.
- **Timing:** Allow at least 2hrs to tour the château and another hour to enjoy the gardens. The driving tour takes close to 2hrs.

A BIT OF HISTORY

A château shaped by women – The first château was built between 1513 and 1521 by **Thomas Bohier**, Treasury Superintendent under François I. Bohier's acquisition of Chenonceau and the château's frequent change of ownership thereafter make up an eventful tale. For 400 years the main protagonists, both happy and sad, were women, be they royal wives, mistresses or queens.

Katherine Briçonnet, the soul of an architect – In 1512, Chenonceau was put up for sale, whereupon Bohier bought it for 12 400 livres. He immediately demolished all the old buildings except for the keep. As he was kept busy by his duties and often had to be with the army near Milan, he could not supervise the building of his new residence. His wife Katherine took charge and was the creative spirit behind the project.

The new building was completed in 1521, but Bohier and his wife had little time in which to enjoy it as they died in 1524 and 1526 respectively.

Diane de Poitiers, the everlasting beauty – When Henri II came to the throne in 1547 he gave Chenonceau to Diane de Poitiers. She was 20 years older than he was, but was still radiantly attractive. Diane was the widow of Louis de Brézé, for whom she had a splendid tomb built in Rouen Cathedral, and in honour of whom she always wore black and white, the colours of mourning. Her influence over Henri II was such that, in addition to all the other favours she received, she made him wear mourning too, to the despair of the rejected and humiliated Queen. Diane was an able manager and set out to exploit her estate and her position; she took an interest in agriculture, in the sale of wine, in her income from taxes and in anything else that brought in money. Diane was a woman of good taste; she created a beautiful garden and had a bridge built linking the château with the south bank of the Cher.

When Henri II was killed in a tournament in 1559, Diane found herself face to face with Catherine de' Medici, who was now regent. While her husband was alive the Queen had been patient and dissembling and had accepted the situation, but now she wanted vengeance. Knowing that Diane was very attached to Chenonceau, she forced her to give up the property in exchange for Chaumont.

Château de Chenonceau

© Marco Gabbin/Fotolia.com

After a brief attempt at resistance, Diane gave in, left the banks of the Cher and retired to Anet Château where she died seven years later.

Catherine de' Medici, the lady of leisure – Catherine de' Medici satisfied her love of the arts and her thirst for magnificence on a grand scale at Chenonceau. She had a park laid out, built a graceful two-storey gallery on the bridge and added extensive outbuildings. She held one magnificent feast after another, greatly impressing her contemporaries. She put on a huge party for the arrival of François II and Mary Stuart, and an even more sumptuous one for Charles IX. No expense was spared at these festivities, which included banquets, dances, fancy dress balls, fireworks and even a naval battle on the Cher.

Louise de Lorraine, the inconsolable widow – Catherine bequeathed Chenonceau to her daughter-in-law, Louise de Lorraine, wife of Henri III. After the King's assassination by Jacques Clément, Louise retired to the château and according to royal custom put on white mourning which she continued to wear until the end of her life, earning herself the nickname White Queen or White Lady.

From Louise de Lorraine, Chenonceau passed on to her niece, Françoise de Lorraine, wife of César de Vendôme, the son of Henri IV and Gabrielle d'Estrées who had stayed at the château in 1598.

Madame Dupin, the literary spirit – In 1733 it became the property of Dupin, the farmer-general who was the tax collector. Madame Dupin held a salon which was attended by all the famous names of the time. **Jean-Jacques Rousseau** was her son's tutor and it was for the benefit of this boy that he wrote his treatise on education, *Émile*. In his *Confessions* the philosopher writes warmly of those happy days, "We had a good time in that beautiful place, we ate well, I became as fat as a monk".
Madame Dupin grew into old age encircled by the affection of the villagers, with the result that the château survived the Revolution unscathed. At her request she was buried in the park.

VISIT

Open Jul–Aug and Easter weekend 9am–8pm; Jun and Sept 9am–7.30pm; mid-Mar–May 9am–7pm; Oct 9am–6.30pm; Nov–Dec and Jan–early Feb 9am–5pm (end Oct–4 Nov 9am–6pm); last admission to château 30min before closure. 10€. 0 820 20 90 90. www.chenonceau.com.

Approach

As you walk towards the castle and pass between two sphinxes, the outbuildings erected after the plans of Philibert Delorme can be seen on the right. After crossing a bridge the path reaches a terrace surrounded by a moat. To the left is Diane de Poitiers' Italian garden; to the right, that of Catherine de' Medici, bounded by the great trees in the park. On the terrace stands the keep of the former 15C Château des Marques.

Château

The château consists of a rectangular mansion with turrets at the corners. It stands on two piers from the old mill, which rest on the bed of the Cher. Catherine de' Medici's two-storeyed gallery stretches across the bridge over the river. This building has a classical simplicity contrasting with the ornate appearance given to the older section which now looks like an annexe.

Ground floor

The four main rooms lead off the hall which features ribbed vaults with keystones aligned along a zigzag axis. The old guard-room *(left)* is paved with majolica tiles and adorned with 16C Flemish tapestries; in the chapel is a 16C marble low-relief sculpture of a Virgin and Child; the fireplace in Diane de Poitiers' bedroom was designed by Jean Goujon; note the touching Virgin and Child believed to be the work of Murillo. Pictures by Jordaens and Tintoretto and a 16C Brussels tapestry hang in Catherine de' Medici's **Green Cabinet**★★. The 16C ceiling is lined with fine layers of pewter decorated in green. The small adjacent room overlooking the River Cher was Catherine de' Medici's library; it has retained its splendid coffered ceiling in carved oak, dating from 1525. The **Great Gallery**★ overlooking the Cher is 60m/197ft long and has black and white chequered paving. During the First World War the gallery was converted into a military hospital and from 1940 to 1942 the demarcation line ran right through the middle. At the end of the gallery, a drawbridge, raised every evening, leads to the wooded area on the south bank of the Cher and to Madame Dupin's grave. Note the remarkable Renaissance fireplace in **François I's Bedchamber**★★, which contains paintings by Van Loo *(Three Graces)* and Il Primaticcio *(Diane de Poitiers as the Huntress Diana)*, and a handsome 15C Italian piece of furniture inlaid in ivory and mother-of-pearl.

First floor

This is reached by a straight staircase, which at the time it was built was an innovation in France. From the vestibule, with its Oudenaarde tapestries depicting hunting scenes, walk through to Gabrielle d'Estrées' Bedchamber, then the Royal or **Five Queens' Bedchamber**★, then Catherine de' Medici's Bedchamber and finally to that of César de Vendôme.

Second floor

The bedchamber of Louise de Lorraine, has an impressive funeral décor. The furniture is covered with black velvet, the curtains are made of black damask and the ceiling is decorated with crowns of thorns and cable motifs painted in white over a black background.

Kitchens★

Set up in two hollow piers of the château, resting on the very bed of the river, the kitchen quarters comprises several rooms: the butlery, the pantry, a larder for storing meat, the actual kitchen where royal meals were prepared and the refectory for staff members. From the bridge giving access to the kitchens, take a look at the mini-harbour through which supplies were delivered to the castle and which Diane de Poitiers is said to have used as a swimming pool.

Musée de Cires

Open same as the château.
Combined ticket for château, gardens and museum 11€ (children 7–18 years 9€). 02 47 23 90 07. www.chenonceau.com.

The Waxworks Museum is housed in the Dômes building, so called because of the shape of its roof. There are 15 scenes evoking life in the château and the personalities associated with it.

Gardens★★

These magnificent gardens stretch along the banks of the Cher, offering picturesque views of the château. There are picnic areas along the moat.

Garden of Diane de Poitiers – The layout includes intersecting straight and diagonal paths, eight triangular lawns and a décor of grey-leaved cotton lavender. The design has remained unchanged since the garden was first planted. Diane de Poitiers decided to create this magnificent garden in 1551. The ground level was raised and a walled terrace built to protect against flooding from the Cher.

In the centre rises a fountain wich sends a jet of water 6m/20ft into the air. Flowers (roses, lilies, violets) and vegetables (onions, leeks, cabbages and artichokes – new to France in the 16C), fruit trees and strawberries are used to create geometric designs. Today, in spring and autumn, the flower beds are planted with over 30 000 blooms.

Garden of Catherine de' Medici – Covering 5 500 sq m/6 580sq yds, five lawns bordered with lavender and rose trees encircle a round pond. Box shrubs clipped into spheres line the paths. Twice a year, the flower beds are relaid with 10 000 new plants. At Chenonceau, Catherine d' Medici staged sumptuous royal festivities and dedicated much of her time to improving the gardens.

Green Garden – laid out in front of the orangery by Bernard Palissy for Catherine d' Medici, the rolling lawn is bordered by tall trees.

Maze – 1ha/2.4acres of clipped yew hedges 1.3m/4ft tall delineate the circular maze which recalls those of the era of Catherine d' Medici. There are five entrances but only two paths to the central gazebo.

Kitchen garden – Set behind the 16C farm the kitchen garden also produces flowers (meticulously labelled) which make up the 150 bouquets that decorate the château every week.

DRIVING TOUR

Cher Valley

Round trip of 60km/37mi.
Allow 1hr45min.

Leave Chenonceaux eastwards (towards Montrichard), cross the Cher and take N 76 W towards Tours.

Bléré

At the entrance to Bléré stands an elegant monument with particularly fine Italian-style sculpted decoration; this is the funerary chapel (1526) of Guillaume de Salgne, Treasurer of the Royal Artillery under François I.

Beyond Bléré, continue along N 76 to Azay-sur-Cher.

Château de Leugny

Open Jul–Aug Tue–Sun 10am–noon, 2–6pm. 2.50€. 02 47 50 41 10.

This elegant château on the Cher was built by André Portier, a pupil of Gabriel, for his own use. It is furnished in the Louis XVI style.

Rejoin N 76 towards Tours.

Véretz

This little town tucked between the Cher and the hillside makes a charming picture from the north bank of the river: the houses and church lead the eye west to the tree-lined paths and terraces of the château.

Among those who once strolled in the château grounds were the Abbé de Rancé (1626–1700), who reformed the Trappist Order, the Abbé d'Effiat and Madame de Sévigné, the Princesse de Conti and the Abbé de Grécourt who wrote light verse; Voltaire stayed at the Château de Véretz in his youth. In the village square stands a monument to **Paul-Louis Courier** (1772–1825), an officer under the Empire who bought the Chavonnière estate with its large house on the Véretz plateau in 1816 and settled there with his young wife. From his country retreat he began to harass the government with wittily caustic

Château de la Bourdaisière

A. Cassaigne/MICHELIN

pamphlets, such as "A petty village tyrant under the Restoration".
Despite his talent his quarrelsome temperament made him unpopular, and on 10 April 1825 he was assassinated in Larçay Forest under mysterious circumstances.

Take D 85 N across the River Cher to Montlouis.

Montlouis-sur-Loire

Montlouis is built in terraces up a hillside of tufa which is riddled with caves. Its vineyards on the south-facing plateau between the Loire and the Cher produce a heady, fruity white wine made from the famous Pinot de la Loire grape.

Maison de la Loire

quai A.-Baillet. Open Tue–Sun 2–6pm. Closed public holidays. 3€. 02 47 50 97 52. http://maisonloire.free.fr. Exhibitions on the fauna and flora of the Loire region are displayed here.

Drive out of Montlouis towards Amboise then turn right to La Bourdaisière.

Château de la Bourdaisière

Guided tours (45min) May–Sept 10am–7pm; Apr, Oct–mid-Nov 10am–noon, 2–6pm. 6.50€. 02 47 45 16 31. www.chateaulabourdaisiere.com. Part of the château, the outbuildings, the gardens and the **kitchen garden**★ (specialising in tomato growing with more than 400 varieties) can be visited.

Return to Chenonceaux on D 40.

ADDRESSES

STAY

Chambre d'hôte La Marmittière – *22 Vallée de Mesvres, 37150 Civray-de Touraine. 4km/2.5mi W of Chenonceaux. 02 47 23 51 04. Closed mid-Nov-mid-Mar. 3rms. . Restaurant .* A delightful B&B owned by a wine producer; décor features stone.

Chambre d'hôte Prieuré de la Chaise – *8 r. du Prieuré, lieu-dit la Chaise, 41400 St-Georges-sur-Cher. 2km/1mi S of St Georges-sur-Cher. 02 54 32 59 77. www.prieuredelachaise.com. . 5 rms.* . It is impossible to resist the charm of this 16C priory, set amidst vines.

La Roseraie – *7 r. Bretonneau - 37150 Chenonceaux. 02 47 23 90 09. www.charmingroseraie.com. Closed 13 Nov–Feb. . 17 rms. 10€. Restaurant .* Typical regional building near the castle with spacious rooms. Meals served on the terrace in summer.

EAT

L'Orangerie – *Château de Chenonceaux. 02 47 23 91 97. Closed mid-Nov–mid-Mar.* Set in the heart of the château, the restaurant serves traditional cuisine.

SON ET LUMIÈRE

Nighttime at Chenonceau – *37150 Chenonceaux. 02 47 23 90 07. www. chenonceau.com. Sat–Sun in Jun and every night Jul–Aug 9.30–11pm. 5€.* Dazzling nighttime illuminations by designer Pierre Bideau in the gardens and grounds of Chenonceau accompanied by the music of Corelli.

St-Aignan★

St-Aignan stands on the south bank of the Cher at the heart of a region of woods and vineyards. Coteaux du Cher is the wine produced in Seigy and Couffy. Both the church and the Renaissance château are interesting and the nearby zoo boasts some rare white lions.

- **Population:** 3 542
- **Michelin Map:** 318: F-8
- **Info:** 60 r. Constant-Ragot, 41110 St-Aignan-sur-Cher. 02 54 75 22 85.
- **Location:** 17km/10.5mi E of Montrichard and 40km/25mi W of Romorantin.
- **Don't Miss:** There is a picturesque view of this little town from the bridge or from the north bank on the road (D 675) N of Noyers-sur-Cher.
- **Timing:** Allow 1hr to have a look around the town.
- **Kids:** Zoo-parc de Beauval.

SIGHTS

Château

From the château courtyard there is a pleasant view of the roofs of the town, a few made of slate but most of them are tiled. The château consists of two buildings at right angles, mostly built in the 16C and backing on to the remains of the medieval fortifications on the east side of the courtyard. The elegant Renaissance dwelling has pilasters flanking the windows, carved dormer gables and a handsome stair in an octagonal turret terminating in a lantern. The terrace overlooks the turbulent Cher passing under the bridge.

Maison de la Prévôté

r. Constant-Ragot. Open May–Sept Tue–Fri 11am–12.30pm, 3–6pm, Sat–Sun and public holidays 10am-noon, 3–6pm. No charge. 02 54 71 22 18.

The 15C building is used for hosting temporary exhibitions. Rue Constant-Ragot contains two Gothic houses and provides the best view of the chevet of the church. A stroll in the narrow streets and neighbouring square will reveal some 15C carved stone or half-timbered houses.

ADDITIONAL SIGHT

Église St-Aignan★

The collegiate church is a Romanesque building dating from the 11C and 12C with an impressive tower over the transept. A spacious tower-porch with delicately carved capitals leads into the high, radiant nave; the capitals are finely carved into acanthus leaves and fantastic animals; the chancel and ambulatory have historiated capitals showing the Flight into Egypt *(north ambulatory)*, the Sacrifice of Isaac and King David (south side).

Lower Church★★

Entrance in north transept.

Formerly known as the Church of St John or Church of the Grottoes, it was probably the early Romanesque church which was used as a stable or store during the Revolution. It is similar in plan to the chancel and decorated with **frescoes** (12C–15C): St John the Evangelist (15C) in the central chapel of the ambulatory; the Legend of St Giles in the south chapel. A great Christ in Majesty in a double mandorla (1200) fills the oven vaulting of the chancel and spreads his blessing through the mediation of St Peter and St James to the Sick who are prostrate; the vault over the transept crossing shows the figure of Christ in Judgement resting on a rainbow.

EXCURSIONS

Chapelle St-Lazare

2km/1mi NE on the north bank of the River Cher.

The chapel of St-Lazare, standing near the road, was once part of a leper house; note the gabled belfry.

Zoo-parc de Beauval★★

4km/2.5mi S along D 675.

Open mid-Mar–Oct 9am to dusk; Nov–mid-Mar 10am to dusk. 19€ (children 3–10 years 13€). 02 54 75 50 00. www.zoobeauval.com.

The road downhill to Beauval zoological park offers a fine view of the local vineyards. A haven for both animals and flowers, this 12ha/30-acre park, built on undulating woodland, has been conceived as an old-fashioned rose garden (2 000 rose bushes) and an Amazonian forest.

A visit to the zoo begins with its feathered residents. A 2 000m2/2 390sq yd **aviary under glass** is home to several hundred exotic birds (including some tiny humming birds) free to flutter about in the lush environment of an equatorial forest complete with waterfalls and streams. Outside, there are about 2 000 more birds to be seen, including over 400 parrots, some very rare.

The next port of call is the section of the zoo given over to mammals. The zoo is home to several species of big cat, including some rare white tigers with blue eyes, white lions, black panthers, pumas and hyenas. Numerous species of monkey and lemur are resident here as part of the European programme for the preservation of endangered species. Children will be fascinated by the intense, penetrating gaze and comical expression of small monkeys from the Congolese basin or the Guinean heights, whereas the acrobatics of the athletic orang-utans and various gibbons who inhabit the magnificent huge **tropical hothouse**★ never fail to delight.

The hothouse also contains a vivarium (with around 100 snakes) and an aqua-terrarium in which turtles and crocodiles are raised. Since 1997, a new hothouse creating an equatorial environment enables you to closely observe gorillas and their fascinating behaviour and, for the very first time in France, a group of manatees.

Several times a day from March to mid-October, there is an opportunity to watch the underwater antics of a group of sea-lions. There are also flight demonstrations with birds of prey, some of which have a wingspan of nearly 3m/10ft.

You can leave the zoo and go into the village for lunch by getting a 'Pass Out' stamp ('tampon de sortie') on the back of your hand, and then come back.

ADDRESSES

STAY

Chambre d'hôte Le Sousmont – *66 r. Maurice-Berteaux. 02 54 75 24 35.* P. *4 rms.* This 19C house is set in delightful grounds with views of the château de St-Aignan. Pleasant rooms (non-smoking) including one in a chalet in the garden. Reading lounge and attractive breakfast room.

Parc de Beauval – *4 km/2.5mi on D 675. 02 54 75 60 00. www.lesjardinsdebeauval.com. Closed Jan.* P. *92 rms. 12€. Restaurant ().* Indonesian style villas set in a tropical garden. Comfort and relaxation in a décor recalling Java and Bali: teak furniture and pictures of Ubud. Restaurant, heated pool, outdoor bar.

Hostellerie Le Clos du Cher – *2 r. Paul-Boncour, 41110 Noyers. sur-Cher Nord. 1km/0.6mi on D 675. 02 54 75 00 03. www.closducher.com. Closed 26 Oct–8 Nov, 21 Dec–3 Jan.* P. *10 rms. 10€. Restaurant().* Set in woodland grounds, this 19C manor features classical style rooms and proposes theme weekends (wine tastings, St Valentine's day, etc.). Family atmosphere and traditional cuisine in the brightly decorated restaurant.

EAT

Chez Constant – *17 pl. de la Paix 02 54 75 10 75 Closed Tue (except Jul–Aug) and Mon.* Historic town centre restaurant with a listed 16C façade. Dining room with open beams. Terrace under shady lime trees. Traditional cuisine.

Montrésor★

With its Renaissance château and Gothic church, this interesting village is reflected in the River Indrois. The town's old market is a timber-framed construction. A handsome 16C house with a watchtower in the main street now serves as the town hall. Montrésor has been named one of *Les plus beaux villages de France* (the most beautiful French villages), an association which includes 140 outstanding villages selected for their beautiful settings, fine buildings and lovely surroundings.

- **Population:** 379
- **Michelin Map:** 317: Q-6
- **Info:** Office du tourisme Val d'Indrois-Montrésor, 43 Grande-Rue, 37460 Montrésor. ☎ 02 47 92 70 71. www.tourisme-valdindrois-montresor.com.
- **Location:** 25km/15.5mi E of Loches and 23km/14mi S of Montrichard.
- **Timing:** Allow 1hr to explore the château; up to half a day for the valley.
- **Kids:** Sporting activities at the Lac de Chemillé.

VISIT

Château★

Open Apr–mid-Nov 10am–6pm (Jun–Sept 7pm); mid-Nov–Mar Sat–Sun 2–6pm. 7€. ☎ 02 47 92 60 04.

The curtain wall with its ruined towers belongs to the fortress built by Fulk Nerra in the 11C; within it at the centre of a charming, romantic park stands the residence built in the early 16C by **Imbert de Bastarnay**, Lord of Montrésor from 1493, adviser to several kings of France and grandfather to Diane de Poitiers. This building has mullioned windows on the south front facing the river, gabled dormers and two machicolated towers. In 1849 the château was restored by **Count Xavier Branicki**, a Polish émigré who accompanied Prince Napoleon to Constantinople during the Crimean War and tried to raise a Polish regiment.

Church

The church was built between 1519 and 1541 in the Gothic style – only the doorway is Renaissance and was originally a collegiate foundation set up by Imbert de Bastarnay.

EXCURSIONS

La Corroirie

5 km/3mi on D 760 towards Loches. Guided tours all year upon appointment. Open Easter–1 Nov 10am–7pm. 3€ (children free). ☎ 06 80 43 38 75. www.corroirie.com.

In the valley hollow, on the right behind a screen of trees, you can see the outline of some of the remains of the Abbaye du Liget, fortified in the 15C. To the west, the main gate and square tower with its drawbridge and machicolations can clearly be made out.

Château de Montrésor by the Indrois

A. Cassaigne/MICHELIN

The treasure of Montrésor

There are many theories as to origins of the name of Montrésor. The most endearing is that of a knight and his equerry who saw a lizard covered in gold dust scuttling over the rocks. Intrigued, they began searching the hillside and discovered a magnificent treasure trove. However, the true story is more mundane: one of the early lords of the manor was treasurer to the cathedral chapter in Tours and the place was named, quite naturally, *mons thesauri*, or Treasurer's Mount which, in time, became Montrésor.

Chartreuse du Liget

Guided visit (20min) 9am–noon, 2–6pm. 0.50€. 02 47 92 60 02.

Alongside the road, on the eastern edge of Loches Forest, stands the great wall of the **charter house**. The elegant 18C **gateway★** is flanked by numerous outbuildings indicating the size and wealth of the abbey before the Revolution. The abbey was founded in the 12C by Henry II of England in expiation, it is said, for the murder of Thomas Becket, Archbishop of Canterbury.

Walk down the central path.

In front of the house are the ruins of the 12C church, behind which still stands one side of the great cloisters built in 1787. In the cell walls are hatches through which monks received their meals.

Chapelle St-Jean-du-Liget

Return to the Loches road and 1km/0.5mi E turn left. Call in advance. 02 47 92 60 02.

Standing alone in the middle of a field is an unusual round 12C building where the first monks of the charter house probably lived.

DRIVING TOUR

VALLÉE DE L'INDROIS★

From Nouans-les-Fontaines to Azay-sur-Indre

33km/20mi along D 760 and D 10. Allow 2hrs.

The River Indrois winds its picturesque way westwards across the Montrésor marshland to join the Indre. Its course is lined by willows, alders and poplars and lush green meadows. The sunny slopes are planted with fruit trees, in orchards or espaliers, and a few vines.

Nouans-les-Fontaines

The 13C church in this village harbours a masterpiece of Primitive art: the **Deposition★★**, or *Pietà of Nouans*, by Jean Fouquet. This vast painting on wood is one of the finest late-15C French masterpieces.

Coulangé

At the entrance of this pleasant hamlet stands the bell-tower of the old parish church (12C). On the opposite river bank are the remains of the fortifications of the Benedictine abbey of Villeloin. Farther on, the road (D 10) offers scenic views of the lake at Chemillé-sur-Indrois and the countryside east of Genillé (swimming, fishing, pedalos).

Genillé

The houses climb up from the river to the late-15C château with its corner towers and dovecote. The church presents a striking belfry with a stone spire and, inside, a 16C Gothic chancel.

St-Quentin-sur-Indrois

The town occupies one of the best sites in the valley. East of the village the road (D 10) offers a fine view south of Loches Forest before joining the valley of the River Indre at Azay-sur-Indre.

Azay-sur-Indre

See LOCHES: Excursions

Loches★★

Loches is a small town on the south bank of the Indre; the old town, huddled on the slopes of a bluff above the river, still resembles a medieval fortified town, with two of its original three defensive walls remarkably well preserved.
Loches was the birthplace of the Romantic poet, Alfred de Vigny (1797–1863), whose mother's family had been closely involved with the town's history since the Renaissance. The poet left the town when he was only an infant.

- **Population:** 6 375
- **Michelin Map:** 317: O-6
- **Info**: pl. de la Marne, 37600 Loches. ℘02 47 91 82 82. www.loches-tourainecotesud.com.
- **Location:** A vast forest upon undulating terrain surrounds Loches.
- **Timing:** Spend the morning in medieval Loches before considering one of the excursions or a driving tour through the Indre Valley.

WALKING TOUR

MEDIEVAL TOWN★★

Allow 3hrs. *Park in the Mail Droulin.*
Loches remains largely as it was in the 15C and at the time of the Renaissance, except for the shops and the numerous stalls which liven up the lower part of the town on market days.

Porte Royale★

The Royal Gate (11C) had powerful defences; it was flanked by two towers in the 13C.

Go through the gateway; turn left onto r. Lansyer to reach the museum.

Maison Lansyer

Open Jul–Aug 10am–12.30pm, 1.30–6pm; Feb–May, Sept–Oct and mid-end Dec 10.30am–12.30pm, 2.30–5pm. Closed 1 Jan, 25 Dec. 3€. ℘02 47 59 05 45. www.loches-tourainecotesud.com. No 1. The family home of the artist **Emmanuel Lansyer** (1835–93), a pupil of Gustave Courbet and a friend of the poet José-Maria de Heredia, Lansyer was influenced by the landscape painters of the Barbizon School.

Église St-Ours★

In 1802 the old collegiate church of Notre-Dame became the parish church dedicated to St Ours, a local apostle in the 5C.
The **alabaster recumbent figure of Agnès Sorel**★ is of special interest. During the Revolution, soldiers took the favourite of Charles VII for a saint, chopped up her statue, desecrated her grave and scattered her remains. The monument was restored in Paris under

Loches

WHERE TO STAY

Chambre d'hôte Fleurs des Ées 1

Chambre d'hôte La Bihourderie 4

Chambre d'hôte Le Clos du Petit Marray 7

Hôtel Le George Sand 10

Luccotel 13

WHERE TO EAT

L'Entracte 1

L'Estaminet 4

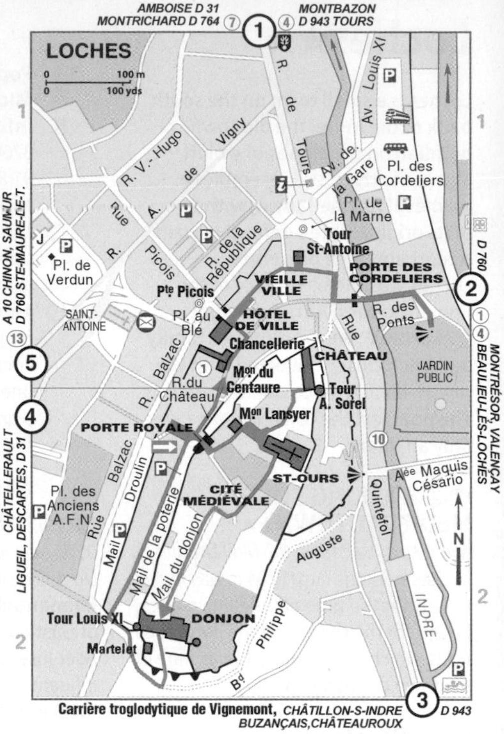

the Empire and was moved to the château in 1970. It was only returned to the church in 2005 following scientific research which determined that Agnès died from mercury poisoning, although whether murder or self-medication remains a mystery. An exhibition in the château explains the forensic work in some detail.

As you come out of the church, the castle is on your right.

CHÂTEAU★★

Open Apr–Sept 9am–7pm; Oct–Mar 9.30am–5pm. Closed 1 Jan, 25 Dec. Château and dungeon 7€. 02 47 59 01 32. www.chateau-loches.fr.

The tour starts from the **Tour Agnès Sorel**, a tower dating from the 13C traditionally referred to as the Beautiful Agnès Tower.

Royal Apartments

From the terrace, which commands a fine view of Loches and the Indre Valley, it is clear that the château was built at two different periods. The Vieux Logis (14C), the older, taller building, is heavily fortified with four turrets linked by a sentry walk at the base of the roof. It was enlarged under Charles VIII and Louis XII by the addition of the more recent Nouveau Logis, in the Flamboyant Gothic style.

Another room contains an interesting **triptych**★ from the 15C School of Jean Fouquet, which originally came from the church of St-Antoine, with panels evoking the Crucifixion, the Carrying of the Cross and the Deposition.

The tour ends with Anne of Brittany's **oratory**, a tiny room decorated with finely worked motifs of the ermine of Brittany and the girdle of St Francis.

Make for the keep through the streets of the medieval town.

Donjon★★

Open Apr–Sept 9am–7pm; Oct–Mar 9.30am–5pm. Closed 1 Jan, 25 Dec. Château and dungeon 7€. 02 47 59 01 32. www.chateau-loches.fr.

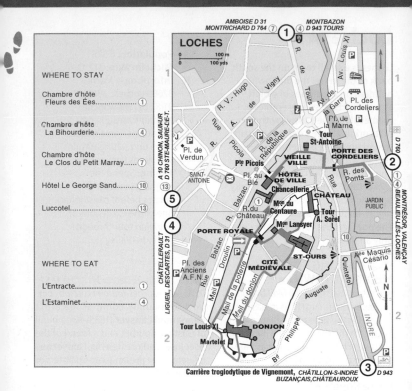

A Thousand-year-old Fortress

Loches is built on a natural strong point, which has been occupied since at least the 6C when Gregory of Tours made reference to a fortress commanding a monastery and a small town. From the 10C to the 13C Loches was under the sway of the counts of Anjou, who altered the fortress by building a residential palace and a moated keep at the tip of the promontory. Henry II of England reinforced the defences. On his death in 1189 his son Richard the Lionheart took possession of the land before leaving on crusade with Philippe Auguste.

In the Holy Land Philippe Auguste, an artful schemer, abandoned Richard and hurried back to France (1191) where he plotted with John Lackland, Richard's brother, who agreed to give up the fortress (1193). When Richard was finally ransomed – he had been held captive in Austria – he hastened to Loches and seized the castle in less than three hours (1194), an exploit which was celebrated in all the chronicles of the day. When Richard died, Philippe Auguste recaptured the castle by way of revenge but much less impressively: the siege lasted a whole year (1205). Loches was given to Dreu V de Mello, son of the victorious besiegers' leader, and repurchased by Louis IX In 1249.

Loches took on the role of royal residence for a succession of monarchs. In 1429, after her victory at Orléans, Joan of Arc rejoined Charles VII at Loches and insisted that he should set out for Reims.

This keep was built in the 11C by Fulk Nerra to defend the fortified town from the south. It is a solid square construction which, together with the Ronde and Martelet towers, forms an imposing defensive system.

Tour ronde

Like the Martelet it was built in the 15C to complete the fortifications. To the left, in the entrance pavilion, Philippe de Commines' cell presents an iron collar weighing 16kg/35lb and the reconstitution of one of Louis XI's famous cages.

Martelet

The most impressive dungeons, occupying several floors below ground, are to be found in this building. The first was that of **Ludovico Sforza**, Duke of Milan, nicknamed the Moor, who was taken prisoner by Louis XII.

For four years he paid for his treachery. On the day of his release the sunlight was so bright and the excitement of freedom so great that he fell down dead. Ludovico, who was Leonardo da Vinci's patron, covered the walls of his prison with paintings and inscriptions.

As you come out of the Martelet, walk back to the Porte Royale and turn right onto rue du Château for a stroll through the old town which developed at the foot of the fortress.

OLD TOWN★

Located inside the second perimeter wall, the old town is criss-crossed with narrow streets lined with old houses built of tufa. A leisurely walk will take you past the **chancellerie**, dating from the Henry II period (mid-16C), embellished with fluted columns, pilasters and wrought-iron balconies; nearby is the **Maison du Centaure**, which owes its name to the low-relief sculpture on the façade, which depicts the centaur Nessus abducting Deianira; proceed to the 15C **Porte Picois**, also with machicolations. This tower stands next to the **hôtel de ville**★, an elegant Renaissance building with flower-decked balconies. From there, head for the 16C **Tour St-Antoine**, one of the rare belfries to be found in central France and continue to the late-15C **Porte des Cordeliers**★; this and the Porte Picois are the only two remaining gates of the town's original four.

Walk across the bridge to the public garden which offers a fine view of the medieval town.

EXCURSIONS

Carrière troglodytique de Vignemont★

55 ter r. des Roches, S towards Châteauroux (warm clothing recommended). Parking available at the municipal pool. Open Jul–Aug 10am–7pm; Apr–Jun, Sept–Oct 10am–noon, 2–6pm; rest of year by reservation. Possibly closed in Jan. 8€. 02 47 91 54 54.

The tour of the quarry explains all there is to know about the extraction and use of the famous white limestone which brightens up castles and villages of the Loire valley.

Beaulieu-lès-Loches

1km/0.6mi E along the east bank of the River Indre.

This old village contains the ruins of a famous abbey founded in 1004 by Fulk Nerra, who was buried there.

Bridoré

14km/8.7mi SE via N 143 and D 241. Open Jun–Sept 1–7pm. 5€. 02 47 94 72 63. www.chateau-bridore.com.

The **castle**, which belonged to Marshal Boucicaut in the 14C, was altered in the 15C by Imbert de Bastarnay, Secretary to Louis XI. It is an imposing, well-preserved complex, bordered by towers, *caponnières* and a deep dry moat.

DRIVING TOUR

Vallée de l'Indre★

27km/16.7mi NW via N 143 and D 17. Allow 1hr.

From Chambourg-sur-Indre to Esvres the road (D 17) follows a pretty route beside the Indre which meanders lazily past a windmill here or a boat there moored in the reeds.

Azay-sur-Indre

Azay stands in a pleasant setting at the confluence of the Indre and the Indrois. Adjoining it is the park of the château that once belonged to La Fayette.

Reignac-sur-Indre

Visible from the bridge spanning the Indre (on the road to Cigogné) is Reignac windmill, standing on a small lake set in lush, verdant surroundings.

Take D 58 towards N 143 until you reach the locality named Le Café Brûlé.

Cormery

Cormery, which is famous for its macaroons, sits prettily beside the Indre with inns on either bank. Near the bridge, half-hidden under the weeping willows is an old mill; downstream the river feeds the old washing place. The Benedictine **abbey**, founded in 791, was suppressed 1 000 years later during the Revolution. The scale of the abbey in its heyday can be measured from the model which shows the edifice as it was in the 14C and 15C and the different ruins that remain in the village. The rue de l'Abbaye passes under a tall ruined tower, **tour St-Paul,** an 11C belfry which marked the entrance to the church. The nearby prior's lodge, **logis du prieur** (15C), is reached by a graceful curved staircase. The small street to the left leads to the ruins of the cloister and the arches of the **refectory** (13C).

Église N.-D.-du-Fougeray

Overlooking the valley, this Romaneque curch (12C) features a majestic triple apse supported by buttress columns.

Cross the Indre and follow N 143 towards Tours for 1km/0.6mi then bear left onto D 17 to Esvres. addresses

ADDRESSES

STAY

Chambre d'hôte Fleurs des Ées – *13 chemin du Clos-Garnier, 37600 Ferrière -sur-Beaulieu. 4km/2.5mi E of Loches. 02 47 92 79 60. www.joligite.com. 5 rms.* Close to the medieval city this restored farmhouse is ideal for a family.

Hotel le George Sand – *39 r. Quintefol 02 47 59 39 74. www.hotelrestaurant-georgesand.com. 19 rms. Evening meal.* A 15C building, with a pleasant restaurant and a terrace overlooking the river.

Luccotel – *12 r. des Lézards. 02 47 91 30 30. 69 rms. Evening meal.* Functional hotel with copious buffet breakfasts and meals at reasonable prices.

Chambre d'hôte La Bihourderie – *37310 Azay-sur-Indre. 11km/7mi N of Loches. 02 47 92 58 58. 4 rms. Evening meal.* In spite of its proximity to a main road, this B&B is very quiet. Regional cuisine is based on seasonal produce.

Chambre d'hôte Le Clos du Petit Marray – *37310 Chambourg-sur-Indre. 5km/3mi N of Loches on N 143 towards Tours. 02 47 92 50 67. 4 rms. Evening meal.* An imposing country property set in a large garden, with a small lake. The rooms are spacious and attractively decorated.

EAT

L'Estaminet –*14 r. de l'Abbaye, 37600 Beaulieu-lès-Loches. 02 47 59 35 47.* Set in a shaded nook close by the abbey, serves traditional cuisine.

L'Entracte – *4 r. du Château. 02 47 94 05 70.* Set in a picturesque street close to the château. Good-size portions of tasty dishes.

SON ET LUMIÈRE

Féerie nocturne (Nighttime extravaganza); performance Wed, Fri and Sat from the second Fri in July until the end of August.

Ste-Maure-de-Touraine

- **Population:** 3 995
- **Michelin Map:** 317: M-6
- **Info:** r. du Château, 37800 Ste-Maure-de-Touraine. 02 47 65 66 20.
- **Location:** On the N 10 between Tours and Chatellerault to the S.

This small town occupies a sunny site on a knoll commanding the Manse Valley. The settlement, which is Roman in origin, developed in the 6C round the tombs of St Britta and St Maurus, and then round the keep built by Fulk Nerra. The Rohan-Montbazon family were the overlords from 1492 to the Revolution. The town is known for its busy poultry markets and its local goats' milk cheeses.

CHURCH

The church is 11C, but its original appearance was altered when it was restored in 1866. A chapel to the right of the chancel has a 16C white-marble statue of the Virgin Mary by the Italian School.

DRIVING TOUR

Plateau de Ste-Maure

The plateau is dissected by the green valleys of two rivers – the Manse and the Esves – and bordered by three others – the Indre, the Vienne and the Creuse. It is composed of limestone which is easily eroded by running water.

Leave Ste-Maure on D 59 going SE.

Maison du souvenir à Maillé

On the right when coming into the village. Open 10.30am-1pm, 2-6pm; Sun-Mon 2-6pm. Closed Tue, 1 Jan and 25 Dec. 5.40€ (children 12–18 years 2.70€). 02 47 65 24 89. www.maille.fr.

On 25 August 1944, just as Paris was enjoying its first taste of liberation, 124 residents of Maillé, mostly women, children and old people, were massacred by the German army. The village was pillaged and put to the torch. The Maison du souvenir, which is also a research centre, displays objects, photographs, documents and films from the period in a moving and sombre tribute to the children of the martyred village.

Follow D 91 via Draché to Sepmes, then D 59 on the right.

At **Bourman**, the Romanesque church has a beautiful apse and tower over the side chapel.

Ligueil is a small town built of white stone; there are a few old houses. The decorated wooden washing place is on the edge of the town on the road to Loches (D 31).

Esves-le-Moutier

The village, which lies on the south bank of the Esves, takes its name from a priory which was surrounded by a fortified wall.

Château de Grillemont

The huge white château stands half way up a slope overlooking an attractive **valley**★ of meadows round a lake; the slopes are capped by oak and pine woods. The huge round towers of the castle with their pepper-pot roofs were built in the reign of Charles VII for Lescoet, the governor of Loches Castle; in 1765 the 15C curtain wall was replaced by magnificent Classical buildings.

Drive to Bossée and follow D 101.

Ste-Catherine-de-Fierbois

The spirit of Joan of Arc hovers over this village which lies grouped round its church, east of the main road (N 10). On 23 April 1429, following directions given by Joan of Arc, a sword marked with five crosses was found on this site. It was supposed to have been placed there by **Charles Martel** after his victory over the Saracens at Poitiers in 732.

N 10 leads back to Ste-Maure.

Descartes

It was in Descartes, which used to be called La Haye, that René Descartes (1590–1650), the famous French philosopher, physicist and mathematician, was baptised, although the family home was in the neighbouring town of Châtellerault. Descartes' work gave birth to an intellectual revolution, one of whose first fruits was analytical geometry.

- **Population:** 4 019
- **Michelin Map:** 317: N-7
- **Info:** Pl. Blaise-Pascal, 37160 Descartes. 02 47 92 42 20.
- **Location:** 58km/36mi S of Tours, and 50km/31mi E of Chinon.
- **Timing:** Allow 1hr to explore the village.

A BIT OF HISTORY

A Remarkable Individual – At the age of eight Descartes was sent to the Jesuit College of Henri IV in La Flèche, where he received a semi-military education, before joining the army under the Prince of Nassau. While pursuing his military career, he travelled widely throughout Europe, devoting most of his time to study, and the pursuit of his life's mission as it was revealed to him on 10 November 1619. In 1629 he returned to Holland, where he stayed for 20 years, studying at various universities and writing and publishing some of his most famous works.

Cartesian Thought – Descartes' *Discourse on Method* (1637) was published four years after Galileo's condemnation by the Inquisition. This seminal work met with quite a different reception and was destined to confound the sceptics;

it marked the beginning of modern thought and scientific rationalism.
In it, Descartes broke with scholasticism and founded a way of thinking based entirely on reasoned methodology and the systematic application of doubt. His method included the questioning of one's own existence, which he resolved in the following way, "I who doubt, I who am deceived, at least while I doubt, I must exist, and as doubting is thinking, it is indubitable that while I think, I am."

VISIT

Musée Descartes

29 r. Descartes. Open mid-Mar–mid-Nov Wed–Mon 2–6pm. 4.60€. 02 47 59 79 19. www.ville-descartes.fr.
This museum is housed in Descartes' childhood home. Documents illustrating his life and works are on display.

EXCURSIONS

Château du Châtelier

10km/6mi E along D 100.
Standing on a rocky outcrop, this austere castle has preserved some of its medieval fortifications and, to the east of its rampart, an imposing round keep with large window openings.

Ferrière-Larçon

16km/10mi E along D 100.
Emerging from among the tiled roofs along the valley, the **church** is architecturally interesting with its narrow Romanesque nave (12C) and tall, open Gothic chancel (13C). Rising above in the centre is a fine Romanesque bell-tower sourrounded by four smaller corner bell turrets.

Le Grand-Pressigny

Le Grand-Pressigny stands in an attractive location facing the confluence of the River Claise and River Aigronne. It was once protected by its hilltop castle. The site is well known in the field of prehistory on account of its many flint workshops where large numbers of blades were made at the end of the Neolithic Era.

- **Population:** 1 084
- **Michelin Map:** 317: N-7
- **Info:** Place Savoie-Villars, 37350 Le Grand-Pressigny. 02 47 94 96 82.
- **Location:** 70km/44mi S of Tours.
- **Don't Miss:** The terraces offer superb views of the valley below.
- **Timing:** Allow 1–2hrs to explore the area.

CHÂTEAU★

Call for opening times. 02 47 94 90 20.
The castle which provides a setting for the Prehistory Museum has retained characteristics of the medieval fortress of Guillaume de Pressigny: ramparts flanked by towers, fortified gateway, keep and late-12C underground gallery. Amid the carefully tended gardens stands the 16C seigneurial home; the elegant Renaissance gallery opens through a pretty portico onto the Court of Honour, laid out as French gardens.
The **Musée départemental de Préhistoire** traces the different stages of prehistoric evolution made in major sites in the Touraine. There are special facilities for the blind.
The 16C coach house, containing a section on palaeontology, displays fossils from the Touraine, in particular those found in deposits from the Faluns Sea to the north and south of the Loire.

EXCURSION

La Celle-Guenand

8.5km/5.3mi NE along D 13.

La Celle-Guenand has a harmoniously proportioned church with a sober Romanesque façade. The covings in the façade's central doorway have been finely carved with masks and imaginary figures.

ADDRESSES

STAY

Chambre d'hôte chez Laudrice – *2 rte. de Barrou. 02 47 91 03 02. or 06 74 36 15 71. www.leschambresdelaudrice.com. 3 rms. . Meals 20€.* The old station café has been converted into this unfussy yet welcoming chambre d'hôte. All 3 rooms have spa showers. Home-cooked meals using fresh local produce are available, but book ahead.

Preuilly-sur-Claise

Preuilly, which has retained numerous interesting old houses and the former abbey church beneath the ruins of its fortress, rises in terraces on the north bank of the Claise amid woodland, green meadows and vineyards.
The town was once considered to be the leading barony of the Touraine region, held by such illustrious families as those of Amboise, La Rochefoucauld, César de Vendôme, Gallifet and Breteuil. Five churches and a collegiate church were barely enough to accommodate the town's worshippers in its heyday.

- **Population:** 1 120
- **Michelin Map:** 317: O-7
- **Info:** Grande-Rue, 37290. 02 47 94 59 43. www.tourainedusud.com
- **Location:** To the SE of Descartes (24km/15mi) and 35km/22mi S of Loches.
- **Timing:** Allow 30min to visit the church.

ÉGLISE ST-PIERRE

This old Benedictine abbey church (c. 1000) is a Romanesque building in which traces of the architectural styles of the Poitou and Touraine regions are evident. Architect Phidias Vestier carried out some excellent repair work in 1846, but the church was subsequently subjected to shoddy restoration in 1873, the year when the tower was built.
Near the church, there are several 17C mansions, one of which has been turned into a hospice (previously Hôtel de la Rallière).

EXCURSION

Boussay

5.3km/3.3mi along D 725.

The château here combines such diverse elements as 15C machicolated towers, a wing in the Baroque style of Mansart, the architect who designed much of the château at Versailles, and an 18C façade. It stands in fine gardens in the French style.

ADDRESSES

STAY

Auberge St-Nicolas – *4 Grande-Rue. 02 47 94 50 80. aubergestnicolas@free.fr. Closed 9 Sept–8 Oct, Sun eve and Mon. 6 rms. 7€.* This modest town centre inn has bright Provençal décor. Huge exposed beams in the dining room. Rooms are simply furnished and spotlessly clean.

The western region of Touraine encapsulates the richness and variety of the Loire Valley. It is home to the largest city, Tours, and some of the most stunning châteaux at Villandry, Azay-le-Rideau and Chinon. Its fertile green valleys have rightly earned it the title of the "Garden of France" and its important role in the country's history and culture is dominated by the presence of such towering figures as Joan of Arc and Honoré de Balzac. It is worth spending a few days in the region to take in all the magnificent attractions it has to offer.

Garden of France

You may choose to follow in the footsteps of Henry James during his Little Tour in France and use Tours as a base for excursions in the region, but the town itself, standing astride the Loire and boasting a mixture of classical art and artisan crafts, is a lovely place to spend a couple of days. Home to 30 street markets, from the Tuesday produce market to the annual Foire à l'ail et au basilic (garlic and basil fair), the town is a gastronomic destination in its own right. The historic district around Place Plumereau, the Cathédrale St-Gatien and the Fine Arts museum has been magnificently restored: visitors can enjoy a stroll along winding streets, past half-timbered houses and shops before resting outside a café to soak up the atmosphere and take in the view. The rich soils of the surrounding countryside have been cultivated for millennia and the region offers a vast array of fresh fruit and vegetables throughout the seasons. The history of the French monarchy in the Loire Valley is best witnessed at nearby Langeais, the favourite château of Louis XI, and the now ruined fortress of Chinon, a Plantagenet stronghold and scene of the famous meeting between Joan of Arc and Charles VII during France's struggle against England in the Hundred Years War.

Highlights

1. Walking around the old quarter of **Tours** (p192)
2. The **Villandry** gardens (p202)
3. Richly furnished apartments of **Château de Langeais** (p204)
4. Charming, romantic **Azay-le-Rideau** (p209)
5. **Chinon**, both the town and the impressive château (p214)

Renaissance treasures

With Villandry and Azay-le-Rideau, the region boasts two of the most beautiful châteaux of the Loire Valley. Villandry is famous throughout the world for

Château de Langeais

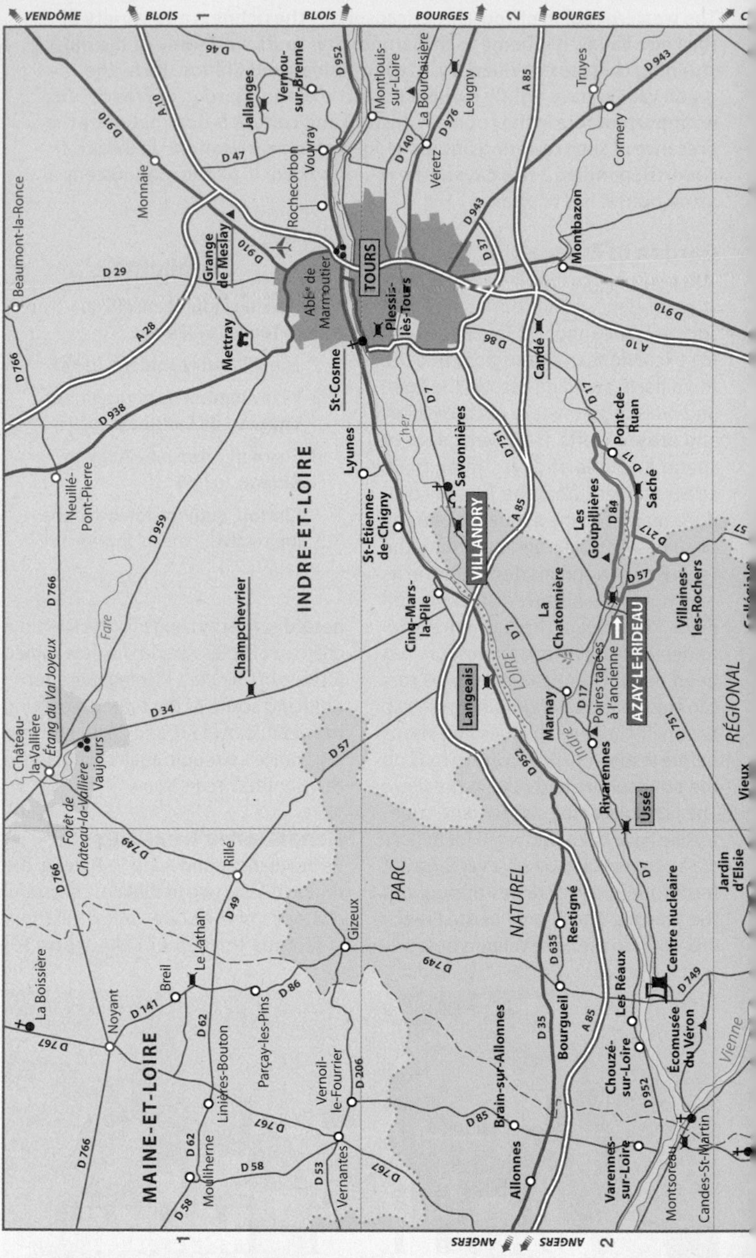

its spectacular gardens, the result of a lifetime's work by Joachim Carvallo, a Spaniard who set about restoring them to their original Renaissance splendour after buying the run-down estate in the early 20C. Many connoisseurs admire Azay-le-Rideau as the perfect embodiment of French Renaissance architecture. Built by a rich financier, it suffered a similar fate to that of Chenonceau

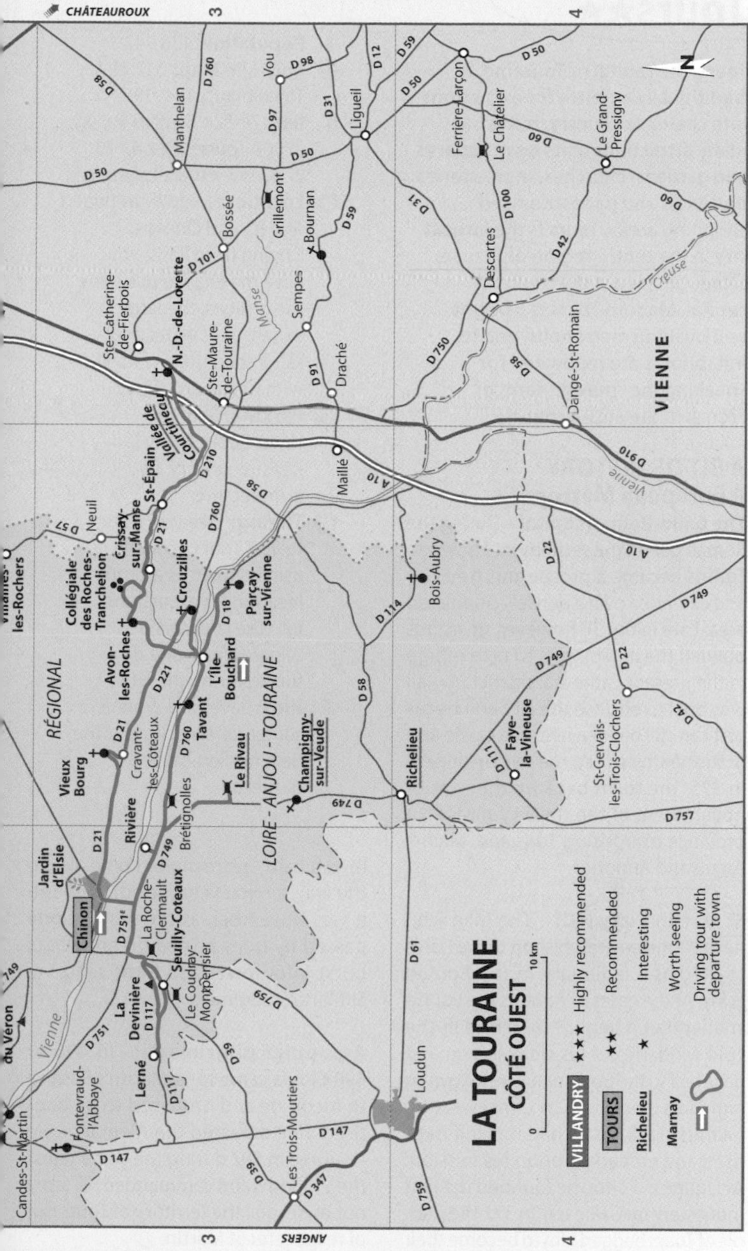

as its splendours attracted the jealous gaze of the King – François I in the case of Azay-le-Rideau – who took the first opportunity to confiscate it for his own pleasure. After some intensive château visiting and sightseeing, explore Vouvray and Bourgueil where some of the region's finest wines are made.

…ours★★

Tours, the capital of Touraine, is traditionally a centre for excursions into châteaux country, but it has many attractions of its own: squares and gardens, churches, monasteries, museums and pedestrianised shopping areas. Tours is the largest city in the centre region of France, although it is not the regional capital. Modern Tours is a bright and bustling metropolis, and its inhabitants are renowned for speaking the "purest" form of French in the entire country.

- **Population:** 136 942
- **Michelin Map:** 317: N-4 Town plan, p194–195
- **Info:** 78-82 r. Bernard-Palissy, 37000 Tours. ℘02 47 70 37 37. www.tours-tourisme.fr.
- **Location:** Midway between Angers and Orléans. Driving from Paris, you have the chance to survey the bridges, the large expanses of water and sand, then the city itself, with its slate rooftops.
- **Parking:** Near the Hôtel Gouin, pl. de la Résistance or pl. de la Préfecture.
- **Timing:** Take two days to visit Tours, more if you use the town as a central location for excursions into the countryside. Allow at least one day for exploring the city
- **Kids:** Caves at Savonnières, *son-et-lumière* show at the Beaune-Semblançay gardens.

A BIT OF HISTORY

A European Metropolis

The Gallo-Roman capital – During the Roman period the settlement known as Turons became a prosperous free city and extended over a densely populated area. Late in the 3C however, invasions obliged the inhabitants to take refuge in the present cathedral district. A wall was built to enclose the city and traces of it can still be seen near the castle and in the nearby street, rue des Ursulines. In 375, the town became the seat of government of the third Lyonnaise, a province comprising Touraine, Maine, Anjou and Armorica.

St Martin's city (4C) – The man who became the greatest bishop of the Gauls started as a legionary in the Roman army. At the gates of Amiens the young soldier met a beggar shivering in the cold wind. He cut his cloak in two and gave half to the poor man. The following night in a dream he saw Christ wearing half his cloak, so he had himself baptised and embarked upon his mission. At Ligugé in Poitou he founded the first monastery on Gallic soil. In 372 the people of Tours begged him to become their bishop. The monastery of Marmoutier was built at the gates of Tours.

St Martin died in Candes in 397. The monks of Ligugé and Marmoutier quarrelled over his body; while the men of Poitou slept, the men of Tours transferred the saint's body to a boat and rowed hard upstream for home. Along the way, a miracle occurred: although it was November, as the saint's body passed by trees turned green, plants burst into flower and birds sang – a St Martin's summer.

A popular pilgrimage – In 496 or 498 **Clovis** came to St-Martin's Basilica to meditate and promised to be baptised if he defeated the Alemanni. He returned in 507 during the war against the Visigoths and commanded his army not to despoil the territory of Tours out of respect for St Martin.

After his victory at Vouillé, near Poitiers, he did not forget to visit the basilica on which he bestowed many presents in thanksgiving. These visits by Clovis were the beginning of the special protection which the Merovingians granted to the sanctuary.

Gregory of Tours

In 563 a young deacon in poor health, who was heir to a noble Gallo-Roman family in the Arverne (later Auvergne), visited St Martin's tomb. His name was Gregory. He was cured and settled in Tours. Owing to his piety and probity, coupled with the renown of several of his relatives (he was the great-nephew of St Nizier of Lyon) he was elected bishop in 573. Gregory of Tours produced many written works, especially the *History of the Franks*, which has been the main source of information about the Merovingian period. He also wrote eight *Books of Miracles* and the *Lives of the Fathers*. Under his enlightened direction the town developed and an abbey grew up round St-Martin's Basilica. Gregory died in 594.

For many years pilgrims had been flocking to Tours for cure or counsel. Besides the ordinary pilgrims in search of the supernatural, kings, princes and powerful lords came seeking absolution for their many crimes and abuses. The sanctuary was also a place of asylum, an inviolable refuge for both the persecuted and the criminal. The popularity of the cult of St Martin brought the abbey great wealth; its estates, the result of many donations, extended as far as Berry and Bordelais.

From the early Capets to Louis XI – The Viking invasions reached Tours in 853: the cathedral, the abbeys and the churches were set on fire and destroyed. The relics of St Martin were removed and hidden in the Auvergne. In 903, after further attacks, the abbey was surrounded by a wall and a new town grew up to the west of the old city; it was called Châteauneuf or Martinopolis.

The Robertians, in charge of St-Martin's Abbey, held immense temporal power and the opportunity to pursue ecclesiastical careers; abbots, bishops and archbishops were appointed from among the 200 canons attached to the abbey.

The nickname **Capet**, by which King Hugh was known at the end of the 10C, comes from an allusion to the *cappa* (cloak) of St Martin, thus proving that the success of the new royal dynasty owed much to the famous monastery.

In 997 a huge fire destroyed Châteauneuf and St Martin's Abbey, which had to be completely rebuilt.

The rivalry in the 11C between the houses of Blois and Anjou, whose domains met in Touraine, ended with victory for the Angevins.

When Pope Alexander III held a great council in Tours in 1163, Touraine belonged to the Plantagenets, but in 1205 **Philippe Auguste** captured the town, which then remained French.

The 13C was a period of peace and prosperity; the **denier tournois**, the money minted in Tours, was adopted as the official currency in preference to the denier parisis.

In 1308 Tours played host to the États Généraux (French Parliament). Less welcome events soon followed; the arrival of the **Black Death** (1351) and the beginning of the Hundred Years War forced the citizens to build a new wall in 1356, enclosing Tours and Châteauneuf.

In 1429 Joan of Arc stayed in Tours while her armour was being made. Charles VII settled in Tours in 1444 and on 28 May he signed the Treaty of Tours with Henry VI of England.

Under **Louis XI** Tours was very much in favour; the city acted as the capital of the kingdom and a mayor was appointed in 1462. The King liked the region and lived at the Château de Plessis-lès-Tours (*see p199*).

Once again life became pleasant and the presence of the court attracted a number of artists of which the most famous was **Jean Fouquet** (born in Tours c. 1420).

The abbey once again enjoyed royal favour and recovered some of its former prestige. Louis XI died in 1483 at Plessis, whereupon the court moved to Amboise.

Silk weaving and the Wars of Religion – Louis XI had promoted the weaving of silk and cloth of gold in Lyon, but the project had not met with much enthusiasm, so the weavers and their looms were moved to Touraine.

In this world of craftsmen, intellectuals and artists, the **Reformation** found its first supporters and Tours, like Lyon and Nîmes, became one of the most active centres of the new religion. In 1562 the Calvinists caused great disorder, particularly in St-Martin's Abbey. The Roman Catholics were merciless in their revenge; ten years before Paris, Tours had its own St Bartholomew's Day Massacre, with 200-300 Huguenots being drowned in the Loire. In May 1589 Henri III and the Parliament retreated from Paris to Tours which once again resumed its role as royal capital.

In the latter half of the 18C, extensive town planning by royal decree opened up a wide road on a north-south axis along which Tours was to develop in the future.

Wars – Owing to its communications facilities, Tours was chosen in 1870 as the seat of the **Government for the National Defence**, but three months later, in the face of the Prussian advance, the government withdrew to Bordeaux. In June 1940 the same chain of events took place, but at greater speed. The town was bombed and burned for three days. In 1944 the bombings resumed. In all, between 1940 and 1944, 1 543 buildings were destroyed and 7 960 damaged; the town centre and the districts on the banks of the Loire were the most badly hit.

WALKING TOURS

1 THE OLD TOWN★★★

The vast restoration work begun about 1970 around place Plumereau, and the building of the Faculté des Lettres beside the Loire, have brought the old quarter to life; its narrow streets, often pedestrian precincts, have attracted shops and craftsmen, and the whole quarter near the university has become one of the liveliest parts of town.

Place Plumereau★

This picturesque and animated square, once the hat market, is lined with fine 15C timber-framed houses alternating with stone façades. Pavement cafés and restaurants overflow onto the square. On the corner of rue du Change and rue de la Monnaie there is a lovely house featuring two slate-roofed gables and posts decorated with sculptures. Continue to the corner of rue de la Rôtisserie where there is an old façade with wooden lattice-work. To the north of the square a vaulted passageway opens on to the attractive little **place St-Pierre-le-Puellier**, with its pleasant gardens.

Place Plumereau

Rue du Grand-Marché
This is one of the most interesting streets in old Tours, with a great number of half-timbered façades embellished with bricks or slates.

Rue Bretonneau
At no. 33 stands a 16C hôtel with pretty Renaissance carved foliage; the northern wing was added towards 1875.

Musée du Gemmail
Entrance at no. 7 r. du Mûrier. Open Easter–mid-Oct Tue–Sun 2–6.30pm. Closed 1 May. 5.50€. 02 47 61 01 19. www.gemmail.com.
The **Hôtel Raimbault** (1835), a Restoration building with columns, contains a collection of non-leaded stained-glass windows graced with the luminosity of ordinary stained glass and the brilliance of precious stones.

Rue Briçonnet★
This charming street is bordered by houses showing a rich variety of local styles, from the Romanesque façade to the 18C mansion. Off the narrow rue du Poirier, no. 35 has a Romanesque façade, no. 31 a late-13C Gothic façade; opposite, at no 32, stands a Renaissance house with lovely wooden statuettes. Not far away, an elegant staircase tower marks the entrance to place St-Pierre-le-Puellier. Further north, on the left, no. 23 has a Classical façade. No. 16 is the Maison de Tristan, a remarkable stone and brick construction with a late-15C pierced gable: it is used as the premises of a modern languages centre, the Centre d'Études de Langues Vivantes.

Rue Paul-Louis-Courier
In the inner courtyard, above the doorway of the 15C–16C Hôtel Binet (no. 10) is an elegant wooden gallery served by two spiral staircases.

Place de Châteauneuf
There is a fine view of the **Tour Charlemagne** and the remains of the **Ancienne basilique St-Martin**, built in the 11C and 13C over the tomb of the Bishop of Tours after the Vikings had destroyed the 5C sanctuary.
Opposite, the 14C ducal residence, **Logis des ducs de Touraine**, houses a centre for military servicemen, the Maison des Combattants, while the late-15C church of **St-Denis** has been converted into a music centre. Further along rue des Halles stands the **Tour de l'Horloge**, a clock tower marking the façade of the basilica which was crowned with a dome in the 19C.

Musée St-Martin
Open mid-Mar–mid-Nov Wed–Mon 9.30am–12.30pm, 2–5.30pm. Closed 1 May and 14 Jul. 2€. 02 47 64 48 87. www.musees-regioncentre.fr.
This museum in rue Rapin is housed in the 13C Chapel of St-Jean, once an outbuilding of St Martin's cloisters. Texts and engravings evoke crucial events in the life of the saint and his influence on the Christian world. The museum also displays remains from the basilicas built in succession over the saint's tomb. Among them are carved marble items from the one built in about 470 as well as murals and mosaics from the 11C Romanesque basilica.

Nouvelle Basilique St-Martin
r. Descartes. 02 47 05 63 87.
Built between 1886 and 1924 in the Neo-Byzatine style, the new basilica is the work of local architect Victor Laloux (1850–1937). The crypt holds the tomb of St Martin and is still a popular pilgrimage site, particularly on 11 November and the following Sunday.

Return to pl. Plumereau along r. du Change.

2 CATHEDRAL DISTRICT★★
This peaceful district has retained a few fine mansions and the Archbishop's Palace nestling round the cathedral.

Cathédrale St-Gatien★★
Work on the cathedral started in the mid-13C and was completed in the 16C. It demonstrates the complete evolution of the French Gothic style; the chevet

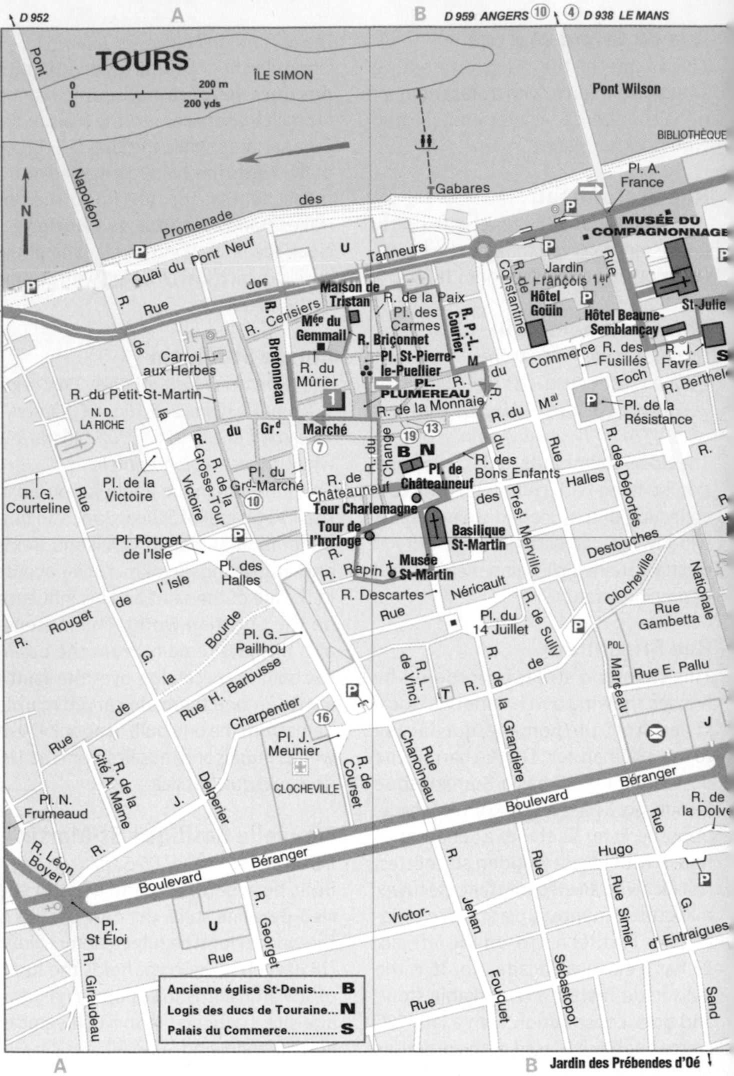

WHERE TO STAY

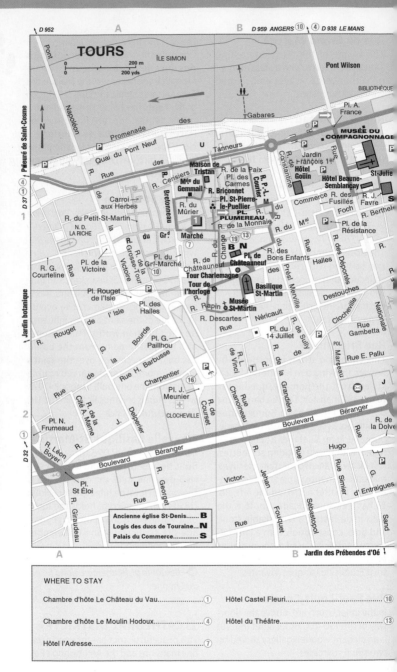

Chambre d'hôte Le Château du Vau.......................1
Chambre d'hôte Le Moulin Hodoux.......................4
Hôtel l'Adresse..7
Hôtel Castel Fleuri...10
Hôtel du Théâtre...13

typifies the early phase, the transept and nave the development of the style and the Flamboyant west front belongs to the final phase (*see Architecture in the Introduction*). The first traces of the Renaissance are visible in the tops of the towers.

Despite the mixture of styles the soaring **west front** is a harmonious entity. A slight asymmetry of detail ensures that the façade is not monotonous. The foundations of the towers are a Gallo-Roman

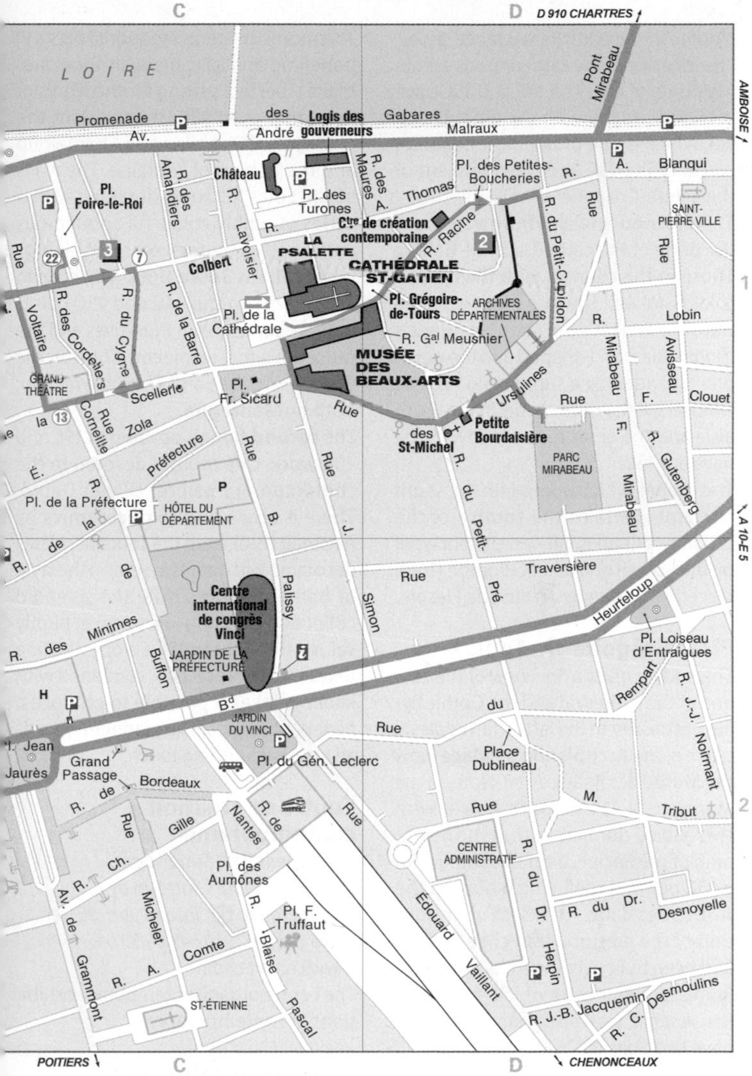

WHERE TO EAT

Auberge de Port Vallières	1	La Deuvalière	13
Bistrot de la Tranchée	4	La Trattoria des Halles	16
Cap Sud	7	Léonard de Vinci	19
L'Atelier Gourmand	10	Le Petit Patrimoine	22

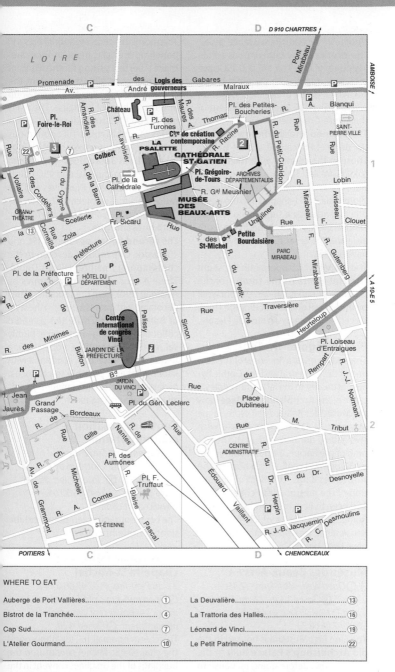

wall and solid buttresses indicate that the bases are Romanesque. The rich Flamboyant decoration was added to the west front in the 15C. The buttresses, which rise to the base of the belfries, were decorated at the same period with niches and crocketed pinnacles.

The upper section of the 15C north tower is surmounted by an elegant lantern dome in the early Renaissance style. The south belfry, built in the 16C on the Romanesque tower, is surmounted by a dome in the early Renaissance style. The **interior** of the cathedral has a striking purity of line. The 14C and 15C nave blends perfectly with the older **chancel**, which is one of the most beautiful works of the 13C and is reminiscent of the Sainte-Chapelle in Paris.

The **stained-glass windows**★★ are the pride of the cathedral of St-Gatien. Those in the chancel with their warm colours are 13C. The rose windows in the transept are 14C; the south window is slightly diamond-shaped and the north one is divided by a supporting rib. The windows in the third chapel in the south aisle and the great rose window in the nave are 15C.

The chapel, which opens into the south transept, contains the **tomb**★ of the children of Charles VIII – an elegant work by the School of Michel Colombe (16C), placed on a base by Jerome de Fiesole.

Place Grégoire-de-Tours★

This square gives a fine view of the east end of the cathedral and the Gothic flying buttresses; to the left is the medieval gable of the **Archbishop's Palace** (now the Musée des Beaux-Arts). Note, in rue Manceau, a 15C canon's house with two gabled dormers and, at the beginning of rue Racine, a tufa building with a 15C pointed roof, which housed the Justice des Bains – the seat of jurisdiction of the metropolitan chapter. This had been built over the ruins of a Gallo-Roman amphitheatre which, during the Renaissance, was mistakenly believed to have been baths.

Musée des Beaux-Arts★★

Open Wed–Mon 9am–12.45pm, 2–6pm. Closed 1 Jan, 1 May, 14 Jul, 1 and 11 Nov, 25 Dec. 4€. 02 47 05 68 73.

The Fine Arts Museum is housed in the old **Archbishop's Palace** built in the 17C and 18C. Before going in, pause to admire the imposing cedar of Lebanon, perfect in shape, which was planted in the main courtyard around 1804. From the formal garden there is a good **view** of the front of the museum and the cathedral.

The rooms are decorated with Louis XVI panelling and silks made in Tours and make a perfect setting for the works of art, some of which used to adorn the châteaux of Richelieu and Chanteloup and the abbeys of Touraine. The walls of the Louis XIII room are hung with a series of highly colourful anonymous paintings executed after engravings by **Abraham Bosse** (1602–76), born in Tours. Among the 14C and 15C paintings are some Italian Primitives and the museum's masterpieces, *Christ in the Garden of Olives* and *The Resurrection*, both by **Mantegna**.

The **second floor** is devoted to 19C and 20C work. One room is devoted to the contemporary painter Olivier Debré. There is also a display of **ceramics** by Avisseau (19C), from the Touraine: plates decorated with motifs in relief in the style of Bernard Palissy. Note the splendid collections of Langeais faïence, highly valued throughout 19C Europe: the fine texture of the local clay, combined with kaolin, makes it possible to produce a variety of shapes. The platinum glaze is an unusual finishing touch.

Centre de création contemporaine

Open Wed–Sun 2–6pm. Guided tours Sat–Sun by arrangement. Closed 1 Jan, 25 Dec. No charge. 02 47 66 50 00. www.ccc-art.com.

The centre organises temporary exhibitions of contemporary art.

Petite Bourdaisière et chapelle St-Michel

2 r. du Petit-Pré. 02 47 66 02 44. Open mid-Jun–mid-Sept 10am–noon, 3–6pm; rest of year upon appointment. Closed Wed.

This charming small 15C townhouse and the chapelle St-Michel constituted the buildings of the Ursulines convent in the 17C. A museum presents the life and work of Marie de l'Incarnation Guyart, an ursuline nun who worked as a missionary in Canada where she founded the first Ursulines convent in Quebec in 1639.

Turn right at the end of r. des Ursulines. From pl. François-Sicard you have fine views of the cathedral.

On the corner of rue du Petit-Cupidon and rue des Ursulines is an arched passage through buildings which leads into the garden of the Archives of the Indre-et-Loire *département*. This spot contains the best-preserved part of the Gallo-Roman walls and the ancient city of Caesarodunum with one of its defence towers, known as the Tour du Petit Cupidon, and, carved out of the wall, the southern postern which would have been the entrance to a Roman road.

3 ST-JULIEN DISTRICT★

The streets near the bridge over the Loire suffered considerable bomb damage in the Second World War, but behind the regular modern façades in rue Nationale some charming squares have survived.

Musée du Compagnonnage★★

Entrance through a porch, 8 r. Nationale, and over a footbridge. Open mid-Jun–mid-Sept 9am–12.30pm, 2–6pm; rest of year Wed–Mon 9am–noon, 2–6pm. Last admission 30min before closing. Closed 1 Jan, 1 May, 14 Jul, 1 and 11 Nov, 25 Dec. 5€. 02 47 21 62 20.

The Trade Guild Museum is housed in the Guest Room (11C) and the monks' dormitory (16C) above the chapter house of the abbey of St-Julien. It traces the history, customs and skills of trade guilds which provided training for their members and protected their interests. Both current and obsolete trades (weavers, ropemakers, woodturners, etc.) are represented through their tools, historical documents and the many masterpieces which the companions (derived from *com pani* and meaning someone with whom one shares one's bread) had to produce to receive their official title.

Église St-Julien

The 11C belfry-porch is set back from the street in front of the 13C church. The sombre Gothic interior is lit through stained-glass windows (1960) executed by Max Ingrand and Le Chevalier.

The **Celliers St-Julien** (12C) is a huge vaulted chamber which now houses a local Wine Museum, the **Musée des Vins de Touraine** (*see Additional Sights*).

Hôtel Goüin★

25 r. du Commerce. Call for information. 02 47 66 22 32. www.monuments-touraine.fr.

This mansion, a fine example of living accommodation during the Renaissance, is one of the most interesting of its kind in Tours. It was burnt out in June 1940, but the **south façade**★, with its finely sculpted Renaissance ornamental foliage, and the north façade, with its fine staircase tower, were spared.

It houses the museum of the Touraine Archaeological Society which has a very varied collection of exhibits from the prehistoric era through the Gallo-Roman, medieval and Renaissance periods to the 19C.

Displayed against a background of 18C panelling are the instruments from the physics study at Chenonceau Château designed by Dupin de Francueil and Jean-Jacques Rousseau as part of the education of Dupin's son. Exhibits include an Archimedes' screw, an inclined plane and a vacuum pump.

Beaune-Semblançay Garden★

Entrance through a porch, 28 r. Nationale.

The **Hôtel de Beaune-Semblançay** belonged to the unfortunate Minister of Finance who was hanged during the reign of François I.

In rue Jules-Favre stands the sober and elegant façade of the **Palais du Commerce** which was built in the 18C for the merchants of Tours.

Rue Colbert

Before Wilson Bridge was built, this street together with its extension, rue du Commerce, was the main axis of the city. The half-timbered house at no. 41 bears the sign *À la Pucelle armée* (The Armed Maiden); Joan of Arc's armour is believed to have been made by the craftsman living here in April 1429. Rue Colbert and rue de la Scellerie, which is reached via rue du Cygne, are home to several antique dealers.

Place Foire-le-Roi

This was the site of the free fairs established by François I; it was also the stage for the mystery plays which were performed when the kings visited Tours. The north side is lined by 15C gabled houses. The beautiful Renaissance mansion (no. 8) belonged to Philibert Babou de la Bourdaisière. On the west side, a side street leads into the narrow and winding passage du Cœur-Navré (Broken-Heart Passage) which leads onto rue Colbert.

ADDITIONAL SIGHTS

Jardins Historiques

Follow signs for „parcs et jardins de la ville de Tours" 1–3 r. des Minimes. 02 47 21 62 67 Open 7.45am–10pm (summer) and 7.45am–5.30pm (winter); until 7pm in Apr–May and Sept.

In the heart of the city, several public gardens are the ideal spot for a quiet stroll. **Jardin Botanique** (5.8ha/14acres) – *35 bd. Tonnellé . 02 47 21 62 68. No charge.*

On the western edge of the city, Tours' oldest garden comprises an arboretum, a water lily and lotus pond, a Mediterranean garden, a historical garden, a small zoo and play areas. The orangery and greenhouses *(tropical greenhouses open weekends 2–5pm)* separate the garden from the propagation houses.

Jardin des Prébendes d'Oé (5ha/12acres) – This garden was created by Eugène Bühler in 1874 and features some fine ornamental trees planted by species groups *(the garden is lit in summer until 10pm)*.

Close to the Vinci conference centre, **square de la Préfecture** (1ha/2.5 acres) presents a mixture of styles. From **square François-Sicard**, opposite the Fine Arts Museum, there are good views of Cathédrale St-Gatien. There are some interesting statues in the **parc Mirabeau** *(1ha/2.5acres; open daily from 7.45am)*.

La Psalette★

Open Jun–Sept Mon–Sat 9.30am–12.30pm, 2–6pm, Sun 2–6pm; Apr–May Mon–Sat 10am–12.30pm, 2–5.30pm, Sun 2–5.30pm; rest of year Wed–Sat 9.30am–-2.30pm, 2–5.30pm, Sun 2–5.30pm. Guided tours (30min) possible. Closed 1 Jan, 1 May, 25 Dec. 3€. 02 47 47 05 19.

This elegant Gothic-Renaissance building once housed the canons and choir, hence the name La Psalette – the place where psalms were sung.

The cloisters have three ranges: the west range (1460) supports the first-floor library whereas the north and east ranges (1508–24) are almost completely covered by terraces. A Renaissance spiral staircase leads to the scriptorium (1520) next to the library, a beautiful room with ogive vaulting and an exhibition of the 13C–14C frescoes from the church in Beaumont-Village.

Musée des Vins de Touraine

16 r. Nationale. 02 47 21 62 20. Open Wed–Mon 9am–noon, 2–6pm; last admission 30min before closure. Closed 1 Jan, 1 May, 14 Jul, 1 and 11 Nov, 25 Dec. 3.20€.

Housed in the huge 12C vaulted cellars of St-Julien Church, this museum illustrates the history of Touraine wines with displays of tools, stills and old wine presses.

Château

A tree-lined walk beside the Loire skirts the heterogeneous buildings of the castle, reminders of past ages. The **Tour de Guise**, with machicolations and a pepper-pot roof, was part of the 13C fortress; the tower owes its name to the young Duke of Guise who was imprisoned in the castle after the assassination of his father and then escaped.

On the quay stands the **Logis des Gouverneurs**, a 15C building with gable dormers. At its base and running towards the Tour de Guise is the Gallo-Roman wall, composed of courses of brick alternating with small stones, typical of the period. On the second floor, the **Atelier Histoire de Tours** (*open Wed and Sat 2–6pm; closed public holidays; no* *charge)* contains archaeological and historical documents as well as models and audiovisual presentations which explain the history of Tours and the development of its townscape. In conjunction with these permanent displays there are temporary exhibitions about living in Tours (*Vivre à Tours*) which highlight its history.

Centre International de congrès Vinci

No public access.

Designed by architect Jean Nouvel (1993). Standing beside the railway and coach stations, it is distinctive for its prominent glass bow. The three auditoriums seem to be suspended in space and can seat 350, 700 and 2 000 people each.

Musée des Équipages militaires et du Train★

Go S on r. Giraudeau. Enter at the corner of r. du Plat-d'Étain and r. Walvein. Open Mon–Fri Sept–Jul 2–5.30pm. Guided tours possible. No charge. 02 47 77 33 07.

In 1807 Napoleon created the service corps to remedy the problem of insufficient transport means: up to then, the army administration had resorted to using the services of civilian companies, whose efficiency left something to be desired. The museum has been set up in the **Pavillon de Condé** (the only vestiges of the abbey of Ste-Marie in Beaumont). Ten carefully laid out rooms retrace the history of the service corps.

Prieuré de St-Cosme★

3km/2mi W via quai du Pont-Neuf and av. Proudhon, then along the riverside embankment. Open daily May–Aug 10am–7pm; mid-Mar–Apr and Sept–mid-Oct 10am–6pm; rest of year Wed–Mon 10am–12.30pm, 2–5pm. Guided tours possible. Closed 1 Jan, 25 Dec. 4.50€. 02 47 37 32 70. www.monuments-touraine.fr.

A haven of peace set amid well-tended gardens, the priory is the perfect place for a leisurely stroll. The gardens boast more than 200 varieties of roses and irises. These form a charming backdrop to the former priory buildings.

The **Prior's Lodging**, where Ronsard lived and died, is a charming little 15C house; in Ronsard's time an outside staircase led to the first floor of the residence, which had only one large room on each level. This staircase was pulled down in the 17C.

Château de Plessis-lès-Tours

1km/0.6mi from the Prieuré de St-Cosme along av. du Prieuré.

This modest brick building *(closed to the public)* is only a small part of the château built by Louis XI in the 15C.

EXCURSIONS

Grange de Meslay★

10km/6mi NE via N 10 and road to the right. Open Apr–Oct Wed, Sat–Sun and public holidays 3–6.30pm. 4€. 02 47 29 19 29. www.meslay.com.

This former **fortified tithe farm** belonging to Marmoutier Abbey has a beautiful porch, the remains of a perimeter wall and a remarkable barn. The barn is a very good example of 13C secular architecture. The rounded main door is set in a pointed gable and the 15C timber roof is supported by four rows of oak heartwood pillars.

Montbazon

9km/5.6mi S along N 10.

This is one of the 20 fortresses built by Fulk Nerra; violent storms damaged it in 2001.

Dolmen de Mettray

10km/6.2mi NW along N 138 turning right onto D 76 to Mettray.

In a spinney in St-Antoine-du-Rocher to the north of Mettray on the right bank of the Choisille (*signposted*) stands the beautiful dolmen of the Fairy Grotto, one of the most skilfully constructed megalithic monuments in France.

Luynes

7km/4.3mi W along N 152 then right.

From the road running along the Loire embankment, there is a pretty view of this charming little town built in tiers up the hillside. Luynes still features numerous cellars hollowed out of the rock face, and a handsome timber-frame covered market hall, the **halles**, dating from the 15C, with a high roof of flat tiles.

Château★

Guided tours (45min) Apr–Sept. 9€. 02 47 55 67 55.

Only three families have lived in the castle since the 11C, the Maillés, the Lavals and the Luynes. The castle is now occupied by the 12th Duc de Luynes. The elegant residential block of the château, in brick and stone, was built during the reign of Louis XI, whereas the two wings date from the 17C. The interior houses sumptuous tapestries, paintings and antique furniture.

Vernou-sur-Brenne

15km/10mi NE of Tours.

Vernou's attractive old houses are surrounded by Vouvray vineyards against a hillside riddled with caves.

Vouvray

At the heart of the famous vineyard is the village of Vouvray, which is set on the south-facing slopes of the hills that overlook the north bank of the Loire upstream from Tours. There are one or two old cliffside dwellings in the village.

Vouvray boasts a statue of Gaudissart, the famous travelling salesman whom Balzac described in one of his novels. **Honoré de Balzac** was born in Tours and often came to visit friends in Vouvray.

Still or sparkling white **Vouvray wines** are some of the finest of Touraine. Many wine producers and merchants have cellars *(caves)* open to the public.

On approaching **Rochecorbon**, a small town at the foot of a bluff riddled with dwellings hewn in the rock, note the **lantern**, a watchtower on the top of the hill. Further on, at the end of a long wall *(right)* stands an imposing 13C doorway, part of the **Abbaye de Marmoutier**, which was founded by St Martin in 372 and fortified in the 13C and 14C.

Château de Jallanges

19.5km/12mi NE of Tours or 3.7km/2.3mi N of Vernou-sur-Brenne. Open Mar–Oct 10am–noon, 2–6pm. 7.50€. 02 47 52 06 66. www.chateaudejallanges.fr.

This grand brick-and-stone edifice comes into sight on a small ridge rising out of a sea of vineyards. It is Renaissance with a 17C chapel and a superb park. It is operated as a bed and breakfast/conference centre.

Château de Candé★

20km/12.4mi S of Tours, on N 10 and D 87 at Monts. Open Easter–end Sept Wed–Sun and public holidays 10am–6pm; Jan–Mar upon appointment. 4.50€ (children 12–18 years 3€); free guided tours. Picnic area. 02 47 34 03 70. www.chateau-cande.fr.

The **château** hosted the most talked-about wedding of the age between Wallis Simpson and the Duke of Windsor. Fifteen rooms are open to the public including the music room where the duke and duchess exchanged vows. In the library, admire the Skinner organ★★. Fern Bedaux's Art Deco bathroom features all mod cons including heated a towel rail and a system to fill and empty the bath in less than a minute.

Covering 200ha/494acres, the **grounds** are a rich reserve for local plants and wildlife. Around 60 deer wander freely and many species of birds nest in the superb trees which include sequoias, ginkgo bilobas, cedars and plane trees.

Savonnières: Grottes Pétrifiantes

To the W of town, on the road to Villandry. Phone for opening times and guided tour information. 5.90€ (children 4.40€). 02 47 50 00 09. www.grottes-savonnieres.com.

The caves were used as quarries in the 12C and then partially flooded with water. The continuing infiltration of water saturated with limestone is slowly creating stalactites, pools and curtains.

ADDRESSES

STAY

Chambre d'hôte le Moulin Hodoux – *Le Moulin Hodoux, 37230 Luynes, 14km/8.7mi W. 02 47 55 76 27. 4 rms.* Close to the Château de Luynes this former 18C water mill enjoys a favourable rural setting.

Hotel l'Adresse – *12 r. de la Rotisserie. 02 47 20 85 76. www.hotel-ladresse.com. 17 rms. 8€.* A place of 18C charm, but with modern décor and service. A quiet oasis in the Plumereau district.

Hotel Castel Fleuri – *10–12 r. Groison. 02 47 54 50 99. www.castel-fleuri-tours.com. 15 rms. P. Closed end Feb–1st wk Mar, 2 wks in Aug. 8€.* This hotel is in a quiet part of town that has a little bit of everything.

Hotel du Théâtre – *57 r. Scellerie. 02 47 05 31 29. www.hotel-du-theatre 37.com. 14 rms. 8.50€.* The small rooms are warm, cosy and well kept.

Chambre d'hôte le Château du Vau – *37510 Ballan-Miré, 10km/6mi SW. 02 47 67 84 04. www.chateau-du-vau.com. 5 rms.* A stony track leads to this 18C château in the middle of an immense park. Refined rooms.

EAT

L'Atelier Gourmand – *37 r. Etienne-Marcel. 02 47 38 59 87. www.latelier gourmand.fr. Closed 15 Dec–5 Jan, Sun, Sat and Mon lunches.* Classic cuisine served in a rustic dining room.

Bistrot de la Tranchée – *103 av. Tranchée. 02 47 41 09 08. Closed 5–26 Aug, Sun–Mon.* Dark wood panelling, bottles of wine, comfortable wall sofas and old-fashioned pizza ovens make up the décor of this pleasant bistro.

Auberge de Port Vallières – *37230 Fondettes. 02 47 42 24 04. www.tourainegourmand.com. Closed 3 wks in Aug, Mon, Tue and Sun eves, Wed.* On the flood banks of the Loire; regional cuisine.

Cap Sud – *88 r. Colbert. 02 47 05 24 81. www.capsudrestaurant.fr. Closed 12 Aug–7 Sept, 24 Dec–8 Jan, Sat–Sun.* A light and refined cuisine amid a simple and warm décor.

Léonard de Vinci – *19 r. de la Monnaie. 02 47 61 07 88. www.leonardde-vinci.info. Closed Sun eve, M… Reservation required in evenings.* A taste of Tuscany in the heart of the Touraine. This Italian restaurant's claim to fame is that it doesn't serve pizzas!

Le Petit Patrimoine – *58 r. Colbert. 02 47 66 05 81. Closed Sun lunch.* A hearty and simple cuisine based on fresh local produce.

La Trattoria des Halles – *31 pl. Paulhou. 02 47 64 26 64. Closed Aug, Sun and Mon.* Chic and relaxed atmosphere in this contemporary bistro.

La Deuvalière – *18 r. de la Monnaie. 02 47 64 01 57. Closed Sat lunch, Sun-Mon.* A tasteful blend of a 15C building and modern styles; contemporary takes on traditional cuisine.

SHOPPING

La Chocolatière – *6 r. de la Scellerie. 02 47 05 66 75. www.la-chocolatiere.com.* The pavé de Tours chocolate cake is the speciality at this luxury pâtisserie in a stylish setting of mirrors, wood panels and antiques.

La Livre Tournois – *6 r. Nationale. 02 47 66 99 99. Open 9am–12.30pm 2–7pm, closed Sun and public holidays.* Try the delicious *livre tournois*, a cake of bitter chocolate, coffee and orange, as well as the *muscadine*, stuffed prunes, nougat, barley sugar and other delights.

SPORT AND LEISURE

Golf du Touraine – *Château de la Touche. 37510 Ballan-Miré. 02 47 53 20 28. www.golfdetouraine.com.* 18-hole course.

Boat trips on the Loire – *56 quai de la Loire, 37210 Rochecorbon. 02 47 52 68 88. Call for times during season. www.naviloire.com. 9€ (children under 12 years 6€). Cruises last 50min. Loire cruises on board the* Saint-Martin-de-Tours. An activities programme helps kids discover the heritage, nature and crafts of the Loire Valley. During the boat trip find out how man has worked in harmony with nature, see a beaver's dam, a vine plant and silkworm cocoon.

y★★★

ndry was one of the last great Renaissance châteaux to be built on the Loire; it has unusual features for Touraine, like rectangular pavilions (instead of round towers) as well as the layout of the esplanade and its moat. Villandry's international fame is based not so much on its château as on its gardens, which are among the most fascinating in France.**

- **Michelin Map:** 317: M-4
- **Info:** Le Potager, 37510 Villandry. ✆02 47 50 12 66. www.chateauvillandry.com.
- **Location:** 32.6km/2mi NE of Chinon.
- **Kids:** Play area, maze.
- **Timing:** Allow 1hr to walk through the gardens before taking a 2hr guided tour of the château.

VISIT

Gardens★★★

Open daily from 9am (Jul–Aug until 7.30pm; Apr–Jun and Sept 7pm; Oct 6.30pm; Mar 6pm; Feb and end Oct–mid -Nov 5.30pm; Jan–Feb and mid-Nov–Dec 5pm). 6€. ✆02 47 50 02 09. www.chateauvillandry.com.

The best overall **view** of the gardens is from the terraces to the rear of the château or from the top of the keep.

The **Promenade dans les Bois** is an itinerary leading to the new belvedere and, from there, to the greenhouses, offering pretty views all along. The tour continues south to the water garden, the maze, the herb and kitchen gardens.

The gardens at Villandry are the most complete example in France of the formal Renaissance style adopted under the influence of the Italian gardeners brought to France by Charles VIII.

There are three terraces one above the other: the highest, the water garden, has a fine sheet of water acting as a reservoir; below it is the **flower garden**, consisting of geometric designs outlined in box, one representing allegories of Love, the other symbolising Music; further designs are based on the Maltese, Languedoc and Basque crosses.

At the lowest level is the fascinating **ornamental kitchen garden**, a multi-coloured chequerboard of vegetables and fruit trees arranged in nine squares and enclosed by clipped hedges of box and yew. Between this and the church a herb garden has been laid out; as was the case in the Middle Ages, it is devoted to aromatic herbs and medicinal plants.

Jardins et Château de Villandry

©HC-Villandry

Château★★

Open Jul–Aug 9am–6.30pm; Apr–Jun and Sept–Oct 9am–6pm; Mar 9am–5.30pm; Feb and early–mid-Nov 9am–5pm. Christmas holidays 9.30am–4.30pm. Guided tours (2hr, at set times) except in Feb, Dec and Sun from May–Sept. (château and gardens) 8€ (children 8-18 years 5€). 02 47 50 02 09. www.chateauvillandry.com.

Nothing remains of the early fortress except the keep, a square tower incorporated in the present structure which was built in the 16C by Jean Le Breton, Secretary of State to François I.

Joachim Carvallo, a Spaniard, furnished the château with an interesting collection of furniture and paintings. The grand staircase leads to the first floor where you will see a brightly coloured Empire-style bedroom; at the end of the corridor, Madame Carvallo's bedroom commands a fine view of the gardens.

Return to the staircase; the other wing houses the picture gallery which contains a great deal of Spanish religious painting; note, however, a striking work by Goya depicting a severed head, as well as two 16C Italian paintings on wood *(St Paul and St John)* in lively colours and a portrait of the Infanta by the Velasquez School.

At the end of the gallery is the room with the 13C **Mudéjar ceiling**★ from Toledo; the coffers are painted and gilded with typical Moorish motifs, an unexpected sight under northern skies.

Villandry's kitchen garden

The arrival of new vegetables from the Americas revolutionised kitchen gardens during the Renaissance. The garden at Villandry was recreated in the early 20C by Joachim Carvallo (1869–1936) using 16C documents. He combined geometric designs of the monastic tradition with the style of Italian monastic gardens. Nearby interesting gardens include La Bourdaisière with 400 varieties of tomato; Valmer, forgotten fruit and vegetables; Montriou has marrows, pumpkins and other cucurbitaceae; and the château du Rivau evokes the world of François Rabelais with Gargantua's kitchen garden.

ADDRESSES

STAY

Chambre d'hôte Le Prieuré des Granges – *15 r. des Fontaines, 37510 Savonnières. 2km/1mi E of Villandry on D 7. 02 47 50 09 67. Closed Dec–Feb. 6 rms.* A dream come true! You are made to feel truly at home, and each of the elegant rooms has its own entrance. Stroll in the park and admire the statues.

EAT

Domaine de la Giraudière – *37510 Villandry. 1km/0.5mi S of Villandry on D 121 towards Druye. 02 47 50 08 60. www.letapegourmande.com. Closed 12 Nov–15 Mar. Reservation required for weekends.* This property was formerly a convent, then the castle's home farm; today La Giraudière has become a famous place for gourmets. The magnificent farm is an appropriate setting for fine regional cooking. Shop selling local produce.

La Doulce Terrace – *02 47 50 02 10. The château's restaurant and tearoom (open 9am–7/8pm. Closed mid-Nov–mid-Feb.* Charming spot for traditional food with an original touch. Try the *coupe gourmande* aperitif (mini-savoury snacks and a glass of sparkling vouvray) and the *café gourmand* (selection of all deserts on the menu and a hot drink).

SHOPPING

La boutique du château et la boutique du jardinier – *Same opening hours as château.* The gift shops on site sell a selection of books, plants, tools and accessories for the house and garden.

Château de Langeais★★

The town's white houses nestle beneath the high walls of the château. Facing the château there is a lovely Renaissance house decorated with pilasters; the church's tower is also Renaissance.

- **Population:** 3 914
- **Michelin Map:** 317: L-5
- **Info:** Office de tourisme – pl. du 14-Juillet, 37130 Langeais. ℘02 47 96 58 22.
- **Location:** Situated along the Loire, between Tours (30km/19mi to the E) and Saumur (N 152) (43km/27mi to the W).
- **Timing:** Allow 1–2hrs to explore the château.

A BIT OF HISTORY

Louis XI's château – At the end of the 10C the Count of Anjou built a donjon, the ruins of which still stand in the gardens, which is thought be the oldest surviving castle keep in France.

The château itself was built by Louis XI from 1465 to 1469 as a stronghold on the road from Nantes, the route most likely to be taken by an invading Breton army. This threat vanished after the marriage of Charles VIII and Anne of Brittany was celebrated at Langeais itself in 1491.

VISIT

Open Jul–Aug 9am–7pm; Apr–Jun, Sept–mid-Nov 9.30am–6.30pm; mid-Nov–Jan 10am–5pm. Feb–Mar 9.30am–5.30pm. 8.20€. ℘02 47 96 72 60. www.chateau-de-langeais.com.

The château was built in one go, a rare event. It has not been altered since, also a rarity. It is one of the most interesting in the Loire Valley, owing to the patient efforts of Jacques Siegfried, the last owner, who refurnished it in the style of the 15C and who bequeathed it to the Institut de France. On the town side, it resembles a feudal fortress: high walls, round towers, a crenellated and machicolated sentry walk and a drawbridge spanning the moat.

Apartments★★★

These apartments exude an atmosphere much more alive than in many old castles. They also convey an accurate picture of aristocratic life in the 15C. The guard room, converted into a dining room, has a monumental chimneypiece, the hood of which represents a castle with battlements manned by small figures. On the first-floor, in the Crucifixion room, note an early four-poster bed and a 17C panel from Brussels. On the second floor, in Charles VIII's bedchamber, stands a curious 17C clock with only one hand as well as two 16C tapestries. The great hall has a chestnut timber roof in the form of a ship's hull; 15 wax figures re-create the scene of Charles VIII and Anne of Brittany.

Le donjon – Medieval scaffolding has been reconstructed to show siege techniques. It also gives great views of the château and the town.

Le Parc de l'an mil – This recently laid out tree-lined park is the perfect spot for a leisurely stroll. Kids will love the play areas and treehouse.

Some of the ruins of the chapelle Saint-Sauveur (11C) can still be seen. From the terrace there are fine **views** of the Loire, the bridge in Langeais and, further afield, the Forest of Chinon.

EXCURSIONS

Cinq-Mars-la-Pile

5km/3mi E on N 152.

The place name is derived from a brick-built monument in the shape of a slender tower that dominates the ridge east of the village. The structure is topped by four small pyramids.

Château

Open May–Oct Wed–Mon 11am–7pm; Apr–Jun and mid-Oct Sat–Sun 11am–6pm. 4€. ℘02 47 96 40 49.

Two 13C round towers on the hillside mark the site of the medieval castle where the Marquis of Cinq-Mars was born. He was the favourite of Louis XIII, but was convicted of conspiring against Richelieu and beheaded in Lyon in 1642 at the age of 22. The **park★** is particularly beautiful: here a garden, there a maze, elsewhere dense woodland.

St-Étienne-de-Chigny

7.5km/4.7mi NE on N 152; fork left onto D 76 and left again onto D 126 towards Vieux Bourg.

Set back from the village, which lies on the Loire embankment, is the Vieux Bourg nestling in the Bresme Valley, featuring old houses with steep gables.

Château de Champchevrier★

12km/7.4mi N on D 15 then D 34; turn right when leaving Cléré-les-Pins.

Located at the heart of a wooded area in which wolves roamed for many years. The château, surrounded by a late-17C moat, stands on the site of an old stronghold, which played a defensive role in the area for many centuries. The present building, dating from the 16C, was modified in the 17C and 18C, and has been occupied by the same family since 1728. The interior is enhanced by superb **Regency furniture**. The series of **tapestries★** was executed by the Manufacture Royale d'Amiens after cartoons by Simon Vouet. The wood panelling of the wide staircase and its polychrome coffers were taken from the **Château de Richelieu** (*see RICHELIEU*), demolished in 1805.

Three Weddings and a Funeral

In 1490, Anne de Bretagne, who was barely 14, was married by proxy to Maximilian of Austria. However, the marriage was annulled a year later so that Anne could marry the King of France, Charles VIII. Brittany was thus united with France and the wedding contract stipulated that if the King died, she should marry his successor ... which is exactly what she did six years later when Louis XII succeeded Charles VIII.

ADDRESSES

STAY

Chambre d'hôte La Meulière – *10 r. de la Gare, 37130 Cinq-Mars-la-Pile. 02 47 96 53 63. lameuliere.free.fr.* P. *3 rms.* This 19C house is quiet despite being close to the station. The colourful rooms are well sound-proofed and pleasantly furnished. Attractive breakfast room and garden.

Chambre d'hôte Anne de Bretagne – *27 r. Anne-de-Bretagne. 02 47 96 08 52. www.chambresdhotes-langeais.fr.* P. *4 rms.* Charming 19C house in the heart of the village. 4 comfortable rooms with a quiet garden to the rear. China and silverware for a stylish breakfast.

Domaine du Château de Hommes – *rte. de Gizeux, 37340 Hommes. 02 47 24 95 13. www.le-vieux-chateau-de-hommes.com.* P. *5 rms.* Small 15C château set in the countryside. There are 4 pleasantly furnished rooms in the old barn and the 5th, in the tower, is perfect for a romantic getaway. Attractive 175ha/432-acre park, spa, jacuzzi, heated pool, hiking and fishing. Bikes available.

EAT

Le Pont Levis – *pl. Pierre-de-Brosse (below the château). 02 47 96 82 23. Closed 20 Dec–5 Jan, 28 Jun–4 Jul, autumn school holidays, Mon (except public holidays) and dinner in low season. Open Tue, Wed and Sat eve 15 Jun–15 Sept.* This restaurant enjoys a great location by the château beside a river with lilypads. Exposed beams and stonework. Traditional brasserie-style meals.

Bourgueil

Bourgueil enjoys a fortunate location in a fertile region between the Loire and the Authion at the eastern end of the Anjou Valley, where vines and woodland abound. French poet Pierre de Ronsard (1524–85) was a frequent visitor, and it was here that he met the Marie mentioned in his romantic ballads. Nowadays the little town's renown derives from the full-bodied red wines yielded by the ancient Breton vines found only in that area.

- **Population:** 3 923
- **Michelin Map:** 317: J-5.
- **Info:** pl. de l'Église, 37140 Bourgueil. ℘02 47 97 91 39.
- **Location:** A crossroads on the D 35 and D 10 between Langeais (22km/14mi to the E) and Saumur (30km/19mi to the W).
- **Timing:** 1hr for the abbey.

SIGHTS

Church

Open Mon–Sat 9am–5pm.

The large Gothic chancel of this parish church is roofed with ribbed vaulting. Its width contrasts with the narrow and simple 11C Romanesque nave.

Market

Backing on to the old town hall, sits the elegant covered marketplace *(halles)* with stone arcades.

Abbey St-Pierre

E of town on the road to Restigné.

Guided tours (1hr) Jul–Aug Wed–Mon 2–6pm; Apr–Jun Sat–Sun and public holidays 2–6pm. 5.30€. ℘02 47 97 72 04.

The abbey was founded at the end of the 10C by the Benedictines and was one of the richest in Anjou. Its vineyards stretched over the entire hillside and its woods reached down to the Loire. In the 13C and 14C it was fortified and surrounded by a moat. The elegant building by the roadside containing the **cellar** and **granary** dates from the same period. Another (18C) building has a monumental **staircase★**.

EXCURSIONS

Moulin bleu

2km/1mi N.

The Blue Windmill has a wooden cabin is perched on top of a cone made of ashlar-work supported by a vaulted substructure, so that the top can pivot to bring the sails into the wind. The tannin obtained from grinding the bark of the chestnut tree was used in the tanneries in Bourgueil.

Restigné

5km/3mi E.

The wine-growing village lies just off the main road clustered round the church. The façade is decorated with a diaper pattern and the lintel of the south doorway is carved with fantastic beasts and Daniel in the lion's den. The Romanesque nave is roofed with early-16C timberwork; the beams are decorated with the heads of monsters.

Les Réaux

4km/2.5mi S.

This charming **château** *(closed to the public)*, dates from the late 15C. The château is surrounded by a moat and the entrance pavilion is flanked by two machicolated towers; the defensive features have been subordinated to the decorative ones: chequerwork in brick and stone; gracefully carved ornamentation in the shell-shaped dormer windows; the salamander above the entrance; and soldiers for weather vanes.

Chouzé-sur-Loire

7km/4.3mi SW.

The attractive village on the north bank of the Loire was once a busy port; the deserted dockside where the mooring rings are rusting and the **Musée des Mariniers** (Nautical Museum) *(open mid-Jun–mid-Sept Fri–Sun and public holidays 2–6pm; 3€; ℘02 47 95 10 10)* recall the past.

Varennes-sur-Loire

15km/9mi SW.

From the old river port on the Loire there is a very attractive view of Montsoreau Château. The towpath makes a pleasant place for a walk.

Brain-sur-Allonnes

10km/6mi W.

Excavations in a 14C house have uncovered the medieval site of the **Cave peinte** (painted cellar *open Apr–Sept Tue–Sun 2–6pm; closed public holidays; 5€; 02 41 52 87 40*). Some beautiful faïence tiles are displayed in the adjoining **museum** (*open Apr–Sept Tue–Sat 10am–noon, 2–6pm, Sun 10am–noon; closed public holidays; 5€; 02 41 52 87 40*).

Parc Ma… Bois Sa…

Châte… Allonne… 10am–… 2–7pm… (children under 15 free… hire 12€ (1hr) for 4 pers. 06 18 0… 85 36. www.parcmaupassant.com.

A 22ha/54-acre park with rose garden (11 000 roses), kitchen garden, ponds, statues, tulip and peony collections (2 000 peonies).

The **Bosquets du Parc** are theme gardens divided into 16 sections including the Mediterranean garden, the 4 seasons, Japanese garden, square garden, the spherical maze and the garden of the forbidden fruit. In the dovecote note the 15C chimney piece.

DISCOVERING W…

Château d'Ussé★★

The château stands with its back to a cliff on the edge of Chinon Forest, its terraced gardens overlooking the Indre. Its impressive bulk and fortified towers contrast sharply with the white stone and myriad roofs, turrets, dormers and chimneys rising against a green background. Tradition has it that when Charles Perrault, the famous French writer of fairy tales, was looking for a setting for *Sleeping Beauty*, he chose Ussé as his model.

- **Michelin Map:** 317: K-5
- **Info:** Office du Tourisme du Pays d'Azay-le-Rideau, 4 r. du Château, 37190 Azay-le-Rideau. 02 47 45 44 40. www.otpaysazaylerideau.fr.
- **Location:** 41km/25mi SW of Tours and 14km/8.7mi NE of Chinon on the left bank of the Indre.
- **Don't Miss:** Every year, Ussé hosts an exhibition of historic costumes (mannequins, fashion accessories).
- **Timing:** Allow 2hrs to explore the château and grounds.

A BIT OF HISTORY

From the Bueils to the Blacas – Ussé is a very old fortress; in the 15C it became the property of a great family from Touraine, the Bueils, who had distinguished themselves in the Hundred Years War (1337–1453). In 1485, Antoine de Bueil, sold Ussé to the Espinays, a Breton family who had been chamberlains and cup-bearers to the Duke of Brittany and to Louis XI and Charles VIII.

The château frequently changed hands. Among its owners was Vauban's son-in-law, Louis Bernin de Valentinay; the great engineer paid frequent visits to Ussé. Voltaire and Châteaubriand were guests at the château. The estate has belonged to the Blacas family since the late 19C.

VISIT

Open Jul–Aug 9.30am–7pm; Apr–Jun 10am–7pm; mid-Feb–Mar and Sept–mid-Nov 10am–6pm. 12€. 02 47 95 54 05. www.chateaudusse.fr.

Dried Pears, a Speciality of Rivarennes

…e recipe is virtually identical to that used for making dried apples: the pears are peeled whole, then left to dry in a bread oven for four days. During this process, they lose 70 percent of their weight. They are then beaten flat with a spatula in order to remove the remaining air, and kept dried or preserved in glass jars. These dried pears provide a perfect accompaniment to game or meat dishes served with gravy, in which case they are simply made to swell by soaking in a good Chinon wine.

Exterior

On the walk up towards the château, a lovely kaleidoscope of roofs and turrets can be glimpsed through the leaves of the stately cedars of Lebanon, said to have been planted by the great French author Chateaubriand.

The outside walls (15C) have a military appearance whereas the buildings overlooking the courtyard are more welcoming and some even carry an elegant Renaissance touch.

Chapel★

Standing on its own in the park, the chapel was built from 1520 to 1538 in the pure Renaissance style. The initials C and L, to be found in other parts of the domain, are used as a decorative motif; they refer to the first names of Charles d'Espinay, who built the chapel, and his wife Lucrèce de Pons. The lofty, luminous interior contains fine 16C stalls decorated with carved figures.

Interior

Salle des Gardes

In a corner of the building, the guard room boasts a 17C *trompe-l'œil* ceiling and a collection of Oriental weapons.

Ancienne chapelle

The old chapel, which has been converted into a salon, has a fine set of furniture, including a Mazarin desk fashioned from lemon-tree wood and three vivid 400-year-old Brussels tapestries.

Grande Galerie

Linking the east and west wings of the château, the Great Gallery is hung with **Flemish tapestries**★ depicting lively, realistic country scenes inspired by the work of Teniers. Beyond the room

Château d'Ussé

Ph. Gajic/MICHELIN

devoted to hunting trophies, the wide 17C staircase (fine wrought-iron banister) leads to the rooms on the first floor: the library and the King's apartment. In the antechamber there is a splendid 16C Italian cabinet with 49 drawers (admire the ebony marquetry inside, inlaid with ivory and mother-of-pearl).

Chambre du Roi

As in all large stately residences, one of the bedrooms was set aside for the king in the event of his paying a visit to the château. This particular room was in fact never occupied by the sovereign.

Salle de Jeux★

The top of the *donjon* (keep) houses an extremely interesting recreation room with china dinner services, toy trains and miniature furniture items from dolls' houses.

Wall Walk

Dotted alc display cal Sleeping childhood

EXCURSION

Rivarennes

5km/3mi from Rigny-Ussé.

Lying on the banks of the River Indre, Rivarennes once boasted some 60 ovens producing the famous dried pears.

La Poire Tapée à l'Ancienne

Open daily 10am–noon, 2–6pm.
02 47 95 49 19.
www.poirestapees.com.

This troglodytic cave contains an old oven where pears are still dried today. Its owners will tell you the story of this regional speciality and explain how it is made.

Azay-le-Rideau★★★

A luxuriant setting on the banks of the Indre provides the backdrop to the Château d'Azay-le-Rideau, one of the gems of the Renaissance. Similar to Chenonceau, but less grandiose, its lines and dimensions suit the site so perfectly that it conveys an unforgettable impression of elegance. It is named after one of its lords, Ridel or Rideau d'Azay, who was knighted by Philippe Auguste and built a strong castle. The most tragic incident in its history was a massacre which occurred in 1418. When Charles VII was Dauphin he was insulted by the Burgundian guard as he passed through Azay. Instant reprisals followed. The town was seized and burnt and the captain and his 350 soldiers were executed. Azay was called Azay-le-Brûlé (Azay the Burnt) until the 18C.

- **Population:** 3 100
- **Michelin Map:** 317: L-5
- **Info:** 4 r. du Château, 37190 Azay-Le-Rideau. 02 47 45 44 40.
- **Location:** Almost midway between Tours and Chinon, via the D 751.
- **Parking:** On-site parking, as well as pay car parks in the town centre.
- **Don't Miss:** A walk around the lake to get the best view of the château.
- **Timing:** You should spend around 1hr exploring the château and its grounds, but up to half a day to make the most of the town.
- **Kids:** Musée Maurice-Dufresne, and the toy collection at Jouets d'autrefois, rêves d'aujourd'hui.

Son et Lumière

Visitor-spectators are free to walk round this *son et lumière* display in the park and château at their own pace. The illuminated façades, the music seeming to drift out of the surrounding woodland and the play of lights upon the water combine to create a fairytale atmosphere and summon up the spirit of that powerful surge of creativity seen here during the Renaissance. *Allow 1hr for the walk. Gates open Jul at 9.45pm; Aug 9pm. Closes at 12.30am; last tickets sold at 11.45pm. 9€. 02 47 45 42 04 or 02 47 45 44 40. www.monuments-nationaux.fr.*

VISIT

Château★★★

Open Jul and Aug 9.30am–7pm; Apr–Jun and Sept 9.30–6pm; Oct–Mar 10am–12.30pm, 2–5.30pm. Last admission 45min before closing. Guided tours or audio-guide +4€. Closed 1 Jan, 1 May, 25 Dec. 7.50€; no charge 1 Sun of month (Nov–Mar). 02 47 45 42 04. www.monum.fr.

A BIT OF HISTORY

A financier's creation (16C) – When it rose from its ruins Azay became the property of **Gilles Berthelot**, one of the great financiers of the time. He had the present delightful mansion built between 1518 and 1527. His wife, **Philippa Lesbahy**, directed the work, as Katherine Briçonnet had directed that of Chenonceau. François I confiscated Azay and gave it to one of his companions in arms from the Italian campaigns, **Antoine Raffin**.

In 1870, when Prince Frederick-Charles of Prussia was staying in the château, one of the chandeliers crashed down on to the table. The Prince thought that his life was being threatened and Azay barely escaped further retribution. In 1905 the château was bought by the French State for 200 000 francs.

Though Gothic in outline, Azay is forward-looking in its bright appearance and the handsome design of its façades.

The medieval defences are purely symbolic and testify only to the high rank of the owners. Partly built over the Indre, Azay-le-Rideau consists of two main wings set at right angles. The reflections in the water add to the quality of the site and, together with the rows of houses and gardens along the River Indre, make

Château d'Azay-le-Rideau

©Jose I. Soto/Dreamstime.com

excellent subjects for photographs. The château's most striking feature is the **grand staircase** with its three storeys of twin bays forming loggias opening onto the courtyard and its elaborately decorated pediment.

The interior is lavishly decorated and furnished with some pieces of outstanding beauty: late-15C oak canopy throne, fine brocade bed dating from the late 17C, credence tables, cabinets, etc. A splendid collection of 16C and 17C **tapestries**★ are exhibited on the walls: *verdures* (landscapes dominated by flower and plant motifs) from Antwerp and Tournai; lovely compositions woven in Oudenaarde (scenes from the Old Testament) and Brussels (Story of Psyche series); the fine Tenture de Renaud et Armide, executed in the Parisian workshops of the Faubourg St-Marcel after cartoons by Simon Vouet; and superb 17C hunting scenes which have retained their beautiful colours.

Summer treat: An actor leads children aged 6–13 on a tour of the castle to find the key to a puzzle.

ADDITIONAL SIGHT

Jouets d'autrefois, rêves d'aujourd'hui

31 r. Nationale. Open Jul–mid-Sept Wed–Mon 3–6pm; rest of year 9am–7pm by request. Guided tours possible (30 min) 5.50€ (up to 2 children under 12, free) 02 47 45 97 65. www.jouetsdautrefois.com.

Interesting collection of model trains (JEP), lead soldiers and Meccano (for amateur engineers!).

EXCURSION

Jardins et Château de la Chatonnière

3km/1.8mi NW of Azay-le-Rideau on D 57 towards Langeais then follow signs on the left. La Chatonnière, 37190 Azay-le-Rideau. com. Open early Mar–mid-Nov 10am–7pm; high season 7€ (children under 12 years 3€), low season 6€ (children under 12 years 2€). 02 47 45 40 29 and 02 47 45 44 40. www.lachatonniere.fr.

Surrounding a small Renaissance château, 12 superb terraced gardens designed by Béatrice de Andia and laid out by Ahmed Azéroual (from Villandry). Each space is inspired by a different theme reflected in the garden names: gardens of elegance, intelligence, romance, plenty, perfumes, exuberance and, quite simply, the senses.

From the formal French garden with its pergolas, to the medicinal plants, poppies, wildflowers, vegetables and colourful perennials, hundreds of varieties adorn this delightful 12ha/30-acre park.

Vallée troglodytique des Goupillières

3km/1.8mi via ID 84, rte. d'Artannes. Open Apr–mid-Nov 10am–7pm; winter half-term school holidays 2–6pm; weekends in Mar 2–9pm. Guided tours available. 6€ (children 5–12 years 4.50€) evening visits Jul–Aug (9.30–11pm 4€ (children 5–12 years 3€). 02 47 45 46 89. www.troglodytedesgoupillieres.fr.

A remarkable series of troglodyte farms shows what country life used to be like in this valley. Explore the stables, wells, bread ovens, grain stores and medieval refuge and then get close to the farm animals including black pigs, poultry, goats, donkeys, horses, etc.

Marnay

6km/3.7mi NW on D 57, then D 120.

Musée Maurice-Dufresne★

Open Apr–Sept 9.15am–7pm; Feb–Mar and Oct–Nov 10am–6pm. 10€ (children 6–15 years 5€). 02 47 45 36 18. www.musee-dufresne.com.

Set up in a former paper mill, this museum is devoted to locomotion. The exhibits were painstakingly gathered over 30 years, restored and painted in their original bold colours. They take the visitor on an unexpected and unusual tour through the ages: American, German and French military vehicles from the First and Second World Wars, converted into farming machinery; gypsy caravans from the turn of the 20C; the first French machine used for making draught beer; a Blériot monoplane, identical to the one that crossed the

Mobiles and Stabiles

Having studied mechanical engineering, **Alexander Calder** turned to art, enrolling in a course in New York. He was a skilled draughtsman, able to capture a subject in a few swift strokes. Before long he had moved into making wire sculptures, initially of figurative, and later abstract, subjects. From the early 1930s he began producing abstract constructions which moved either by means of a motor or when touched. In 1932 Marcel Duchamp, a fellow member of the Abstraction-Création group in Paris in which Calder became involved at this time, coined the name "mobiles" for these, whereupon Arp came up with "stabiles" for Calder's non-moving sculptures.

Calder is best known for the mobiles he made of tin shapes, which were usually suspended or balanced in such a way as to move in response to draughts of air or even their own weight. Calder referred to them as his four-dimensional drawings and made no secret of the fact that his abstract geometrical creations were influenced in part by Mondrian. Calder's reputation rests to no small degree on the fact that he was one of the first artists to include movement in sculptural art. Although he might be regarded as a precursor of Kinetic art, Calder was far more concerned with exploring free movement, rather than the more controlled motion produced by Kinetic artists. Most of Calder's works are on show in the United States (such as the enormous motorised mobile *Red, Black and Blue* hanging at Dallas airport), but others are displayed at the Tate Modern Art Galley in London and the Pompidou Centre in Paris.

Channel in July 1909. Each presentation portrays the history of mankind: a small Bauche tractor found in an attic, entirely dismantled to avoid being requisitioned; a Hanomag mine extractor-excavator which helped to erect the Wall of the Atlantic; or one of the several hundred Fordson tanks that landed in Arromanches on 6 June 1944.

Basket weaver, Société coopérative agricole Vannerie de Villaines

S. Sauvignier/MICHELIN

DRIVING TOUR

Vallée de l'Indre

26km/16mi round tour E of Azay-le-Rideau – about 2hrs.

Leave Azay going S by the bridge over the Indre which gives an attractive view of the château through the trees of the park. Bear left immediately onto D 17 and then right onto D 57.

Villaines-les-Rochers

Wickerwork has always been the mainstay of the village. The black and yellow water-willow and green rushes are cut in winter and steeped in water until May when they are stripped and woven. This craft was traditionally handed down from father to son who worked in troglodyte workshops (several such dwellings can be seen).

The **Société coopérative agricole Vannerie de Villaines** (*♿, open Jul–Aug daily 9am–7pm; rest of year Mon–Sat 9am–noon, 2–7pm, Sun and public holidays 10am–noon, 2–7pm; closed 1 Jan, 25 Dec; no charge; 02 47 45*

43 03; www.vannerie.com), which was founded in 1849 by the parish priest, numbers about 80 families; several basketwork workshops have been set up where young craftsmen are trained. The workshops can be visited and the craftsmen's work is on sale.

Rejoin D 17 via D 217, which runs beside the River Villaine.

Saché

Saché won a degree of renown through its association with novelist **Honoré de Balzac** who stayed there on several occasions. A more recent famous resident was the American sculptor, **Alexander Calder** (1898–1976), who created mobiles and stabiles in abstract forms; one of his mobiles is displayed in the main square of Saché, which bears his name.

Château de Saché

Open Jul–Aug 10am–7pm; Apr–Jun and Sept 10am–6pm; Oct–Mar Wed–Mon 10am–12.30pm, 2–5pm. Guided tours (1hr). Closed 1 Jan, 25 Dec. 4.50€. 02 47 26 86 50. www.musee-balzac.fr.

The 16C and 18C château is set in a pleasant park. In the last century it belonged to M de Margonne, a friend of **Balzac**. The writer loved to escape to Saché from the bustle of Paris (he came here every year from 1828 to 1838).

In the tranquil setting of the château he wrote easily, and one of his novels, *Le Lys dans la Vallée*, is set in the Indre Valley between Saché and Pont-de-Ruan. He found plenty of material locally for characters and places which appeared in his *Scènes de la Vie de Province*. The room where Balzac worked remains as it was in his lifetime.

Pont-de-Ruan

Do not miss the beautiful scene as the road crosses the Indre of the two windmills, each on an island, set among trees. The site is described at length by Balzac in *Le Lys dans la Vallée*.

Return to Azay on D 84.

ADDRESSES

STAY

Chambre d'hôte La Petite Loge – *15 rte. de Tours, 37190 Azay-le-Rideau. 02 47 45 26 05. http://lapetiteloge.free.fr. Closed Dec–Feb. . 5 rms. .* Despite being near the road, this B&B just outside Azay is a quiet place to stay. The simple rooms have a separate entrance, and a fully equipped kitchen is available for the guests to use. In summer you can enjoy the garden and barbecue.

Hôtel des Château – *2 rte. Villandry, 37190 Azay-le-Rideau. 02 47 45 94 59. www.hoteldeschateaux.com. 27 rms. 7.50€. Restaurant .* This prestigious château stands out among touring itineraries. Take the time to refresh yourself in one of the small but attractive rooms. In the modest but agreeable dining room, you'll find casseroles and other dishes typical of brasserie cuisine.

EAT

La Ridelloise – *34-36 r. Nationale, 37190 Azay-le-Rideau. 02 47 45 46 53. Closed mid-Nov–Mar*. This two-roomed restaurant in the centre of town focuses on traditional, simple cooking.

L'Aigle d'Or – *10 av. Adélaïde-Riché, 37190 Azay-le-Rideau. 02 47 45 24 58. Closed 1–7 Sept, 17–30 Nov, Feb, Mon eve Nov–Mar, Tue eve except in Jul-Aug, Sun eve, Wed.* Don't hesitate to open the door of this pretty stone house, sitting a few yards from the château. The dining room, done in pastel tones, is elegant. Tasty, traditional cuisine.

Auberge du XIIe Siècle – *37190 Saché. 6.5km/4mi E of Azay-le Rideau on D 17. 02 47 26 88 77. Closed 6–28 Jan, 10–18 Jun, 1–9 Sept, Sun eve, Mon lunch, Tue. Reservation required on Sun.* This old half-timbered inn in the village centre is famous for its cuisine. The exposed beams and stone walls, together with the fireplace, give a warm atmosphere to the two dining rooms.

Chinon★★

Chinon lies at the heart of a well-known wine region, surrounded by the fertile Véron and beautiful Chinon Forest. The road approaching Chinon from the south gives the best view★★ of the spectacular setting of the town and castle. The well-preserved old houses of this medieval town are strung along the banks of the Vienne beneath the crumbling walls of its gigantic ruined fortress.
An annual medieval market plunges visitors into the lively atmosphere of the late Middle Ages.

- **Population:** 8 169
- **Michelin Map:** 317: k 5-6
- **Info:** pl. Hosheim, BP 141, 37501 Chinon. ℘02 47 93 17 85. www.chinon.com.
- **Location:** Chinon is 22km/13.6mi NW of Richelieu and 10km/6mi SW of Château d'Ussé.
- **Parking:** It isn't easy to get around town by car in the summer months, so leave your car at your hotel or in the riverside parking area and use the little **tourist train** that leaves from the Hôtel de Ville. There are two parking areas near the entrance to the château. Park along quai Danton to absorb the sweeping panorama and take a few photographs.
- **Timing:** Allow 45min for the Old Chinon walking tour, 1hr for the castle, 1hr for the museums and 1 day for the driving tours.
- **Kids:** The River Museum.

A BIT OF HISTORY

François Rabelais – (1494–1553) was born near Chinon at La Devinière and grew up in Chinon in his parents house in rue de la Lamproie. He was the author of the spirited adventures of Pantagruel and his father Gargantua. Written in the manner of a burlesque farce, his books were intended for the budding bourgeoisie: they denounced priggishness and ignorance and praised a moral society based on free, honest citizenship.

From the Plantagenets to the Valois – Chinon was originally a Gallo-Roman camp and then a fortress belonging to the counts of Blois. In the 11C it passed to their enemies, the counts of Anjou, one of whom, **Henry Plantagenet**, built the major part of the present castle. In 1154 he became King of England but Chinon remained one of his favourite residences; he died there on 6 July 1189. **John Lackland**, the youngest son of Henry II, inherited the Plantagenet kingdom on the death of his elder brother Richard the Lionheart, who was killed at Châlus in 1199. His deceitful character and underhand plotting earned him many enemies. First he quarrelled with his nephew, Arthur of Brittany, who sought refuge at the French court. Then he abducted Isabelle d'Angoulême, the fiancée of the Count of La Marche, and married her at Chinon on 30 August 1200. Discontented with the behaviour of their overlord, the knights of Poitou appealed to the royal court in Paris. John refused to attend the hearing, at which

PRACTICAL INFORMATION

TOURS OF THE TOWN

(90min) Information at the tourist office or online at www.vpah.culture.fr.

FESTIVALS IN CHINON

There are several fairs and other events organised in Chinon, don't miss them if you're in town! In April visit the Salon des Vins (wine fair); in late June and on 15 August, there are horse races. In July the town is the venue of a Festival of Musical Comedy. An old-fashioned market is held on the 3rd Saturday in August.

©Sylvaine Poitau/Apa Publications

he was condemned to forfeit his French fiefs. One by one, Philippe Auguste recaptured all the English strongholds in France; in 1205 Chinon passed to the French crown. After the truce of October 1206 John was forced to give up.

The Court of the King of Bourges (early 15C) – With the accession of **Charles VII** Chinon moved into the limelight. France was in a terrible predicament. Henry VI, King of England, was also King of Paris; Charles VII was only King of Bourges when he set up his little court at Chinon in 1427. The following year he called a meeting of the States-General of the central and southern provinces which had remained faithful to him. They voted 400 000 livres for organising the defence of Orléans besieged by the English (*see ORLÉANS*). Then, in 1429, Joan of Arc appeared on the scene.

WALKING TOUR

OLD CHINON★★

Formerly surrounded by high walls that earned it the name Ville-Fort (Fortified Town), the old city (Le Vieux Chinon) with its pointed roofs and winding streets lies tucked between the banks of the River Vienne and the castle bluff. Numerous medieval houses show off picturesque details: half-timbered houses with carved corbels, stone gables with corner turrets, mullioned windows and sculpted doorways. One of the many pleasant activities Chinon has to offer is a walk along the banks of the Vienne, particularly near the English-style landscape garden, the **Jardin anglais**, where flourishing palm trees are a testimony to the mild climate of the Loire Valley.

Start from r. Haute-St-Maurice. The 12–18C Église St-Maurice stands on the main thoroughfare of the old town.

Palais du Bailliage

73 r. Haute-St-Maurice.

Walk round onto rue Jacques-Cœur to admire the southern façade of this building which houses the Bailiff's Court and the Hôtellerie Gargantua.

Grand Carroi★★

Despite its small size, which hardly merited such a grand name (*carroi* means crossroads), this was the centre of town in the Middle Ages, where rue Haute-St-Maurice intersected rue du Grand-Carroi.

The broad stone doorway of no. 48, the 17C **Hôtel du Gouvernement** (Government House), opens into an attractive courtyard lined with elegant arcades; another half-timbered house, no. 45, is decorated with statues serving as columns; no. 44, the **Hôtel des États-Généraux** (States-General House), is a handsome 15C–16C brick building, which houses the Museum of Old Chinon; no. 38, called the **Maison rouge** (Red House – 14C), is half-timbered with brick and an overhanging storey.

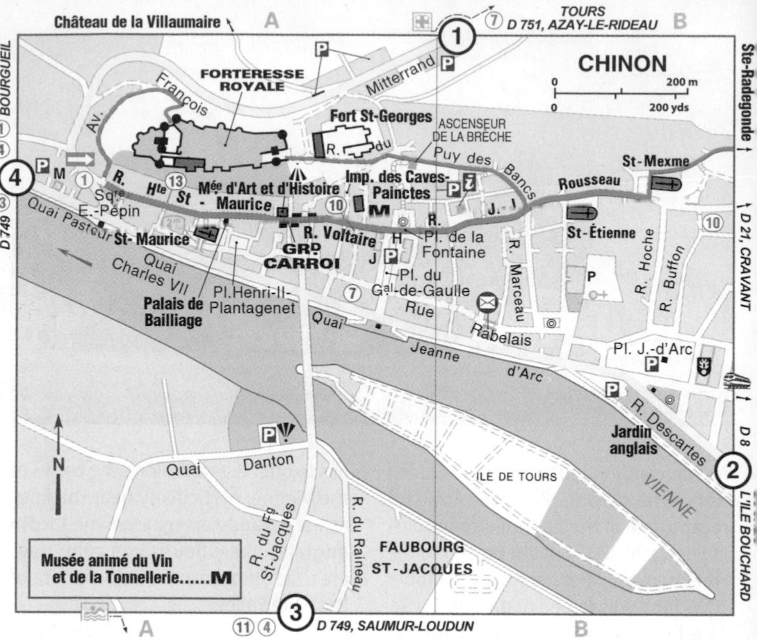

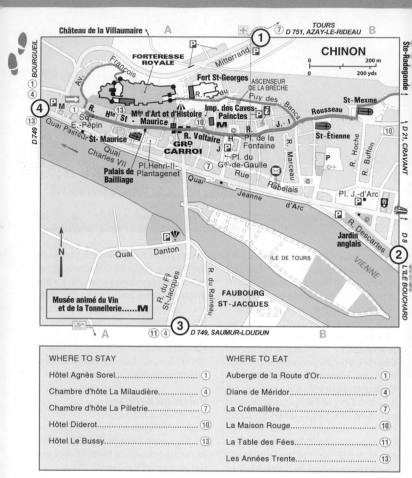

WHERE TO STAY		WHERE TO EAT	
Hôtel Agnès Sorel	1	Auberge de la Route d'Or	1
Chambre d'hôte La Milaudière	4	Diane de Méridor	4
Chambre d'hôte La Pilletrie	7	La Crémaillère	7
Hôtel Diderot	10	La Maison Rouge	10
Hôtel Le Bussy	13	La Table des Fées	11
		Les Années Trente	13

Musée d'Art et d'Histoire

44 r. Haute-St-Maurice. Open daily May–Sept 2–6pm. 2€ (children no charge). 02 47 93 18 12. www.chinon-histoire.org.

The museum, devoted to the history of the town, is housed in the Hôtel des États-Généraux, where Richard the Lionheart is said to have died in 1199 after being wounded at the siege of Châlus in the Limousin, and where the French Parliament met in 1428 at the behest of Charles VII to provide money to continue waging war against the English.

Hôtel Torterue de Langardière

The classical façade of this 18C mansion is enhanced by handsome wrought-iron balconies.

Further on, rue Jeanne-d'Arc starts its steep climb up to the castle; a plaque marks the **well** where, according to tradition, Joan of Arc is said to have placed her foot on dismounting from her horse.

Impasse des Caves-Painctes

This narrow alley leading up the hillside will take you to the **Caves Paininctes** (Painted Cellars), where Pantagruel drained many a glass of cool wine according to his creator Rabelais, who was known to patronise the establishment on frequent occasions. The paintings have since disappeared but these old quarries have always been dedicated to the Sacred Bottle; the annual ceremony of the **Bons Entonneurs Rabelaisiens** (Wine-Growers' Brotherhood) is held here (Contact: *Secrétariat de la Confrérie, imp. des Caves-Paintes, 37500 Chinon; 02 47 93 30 44*).

Musée Animé du Vin et de la Tonellerie

12 r. Voltaire. Open daily Apr–Sept 10am–10pm 4.50€ (children 3.50€). Visit concludes with a tasting session of Chinon wine. 02 47 93 25 63.

The museum features life-sized animated models of Rabelais and his fellow revellers who explain all about working in the vineyards, wine-making and how barrels are made.

Rue Jean-Jacques-Rousseau

Several striking medieval houses can be seen, especially nos. 71 and 73 at the crossroads with rue du Puy-des-Bancs.

Église St-Étienne

A finely sculpted Flamboyant Gothic doorway bears the arms of Philippe de Commynes (1480) governor of Chinon.

Collégiale St-Mexeme

Only the nave and narthex remain of this 10C–11C church.

Chapelle Ste-Radegonde

Access on foot up the steep path northeast of the church of St-Mexme. Guided tours (1hr) Jul–Aug 10am–6pm; rest of year by request. 3€. 02 47 93 18 12. www.chinon-histoire.org.

In the 6C a pious hermit had his cell built in the cave. Radegund, the wife of King Clotair I, came to consult the hermit about her intention to leave the court and found the convent of the Holy Cross (Ste-Croix) in Poitiers.

Also of interest to visitors are the cave dwelling adjoining the chapel and the **Musée des Arts et Traditions populaires.**

CHÂTEAU★★

Open Apr–Sept 9am–7pm; Oct–Mar 9.30am–5pm. Closed 1 Jan, 25 Dec. 3€. 02 47 93 13 45. www.fortresse-chinon.fr. Renovations being carried out; some areas closed to the public.

It is best to approach the château by route de Tours (D 751) which skirts the massive walls on the north side. Built on a spur overlooking the Vienne, this vast fortress dates mostly from the reign of Henry II (12C). Abandoned by the court after the 15C and bought in the 17C by Cardinal de Richelieu, the castle was dismantled little by little until Prosper Mérimée undertook to preserve it.

Château du Milieu – The entrance to the Middle Castle is across the moat and through the 14C Tour de l'Horloge (Clock Tower) which is unusually shallow. A bell, the Marie Javelle, dated 1399, sounds the hour from the lantern at the top of the tower.

Fort du Coudray – West of the gardens another bridge crosses the moat to the Fort du Coudray on the point of the rock spur. The keep *(right)* was built early in the 13C; the Templars were imprisoned here by Philip the Fair in 1308 and it was they who carved the graffiti on the north wall of the present entrance.

Royal Apartments – Joan of Arc was received in the great hall on the first floor, of which only the fireplace remains. The guard room on the ground floor displays a large model of the castle as it was in the 15C.

ADDITIONAL SIGHTS

Maison de la Rivière

12 quai Pasteur. Open Jul–Aug Tue–Sun; call for opening hours. 3€. 02 47 95 93 15. www.cpie-val-de-loire.org.

This riverside museum illustrates inland water transport in the Loire Valley.

EXCURSIONS

Le Jardin d'Elsie

1–5 rte. de Huismes. Guided tours upon request. 6€. 02 47 98 07 58. www.elsiederaedt.com.

On the northwestern edge of the town, the garden features almost 1 000 plants, bushes and trees in the grounds of a 19C house. The main atraction is the rose garden (over 300 varieties), at their best between mid-May and early summer.

Joan of Arc at Chinon

Escorted by six men-at-arms, Joan travelled from Lorraine to Chinon, arriving on 6 March 1429, without encountering any of the armed bands which were ravaging the country. The people took this as a clear sign of divine protection. Waiting to be received by Charles VII, Joan spent two days at an inn in the lower town, fasting and praying. When the 18-year-old peasant girl was finally admitted to the palace, an attempt was made to put her out of countenance. The great hall was lit by 50 torches and 300 courtiers in rich apparel were assembled there. The King was hiding among the crowd while a courtier wore his robes. Joan ventured forward, immediately recognised the real King and went straight up to him. "Gentle Dauphin", she said – for Charles, not having been crowned, was only the Dauphin to her – "my name is Jehanne la Pucelle (Joan the Maid). The King of Heaven sends word by me that you will be anointed and crowned in the city of Reims, and you will be the Lieutenant of the King of Heaven, who is the King of France." Charles was consumed with doubts about his birthright as a result of the scandalous behaviour of his mother, Isabella of Bavaria. When Joan said to him, "I tell you in the name of Our Lord Christ that you are the heir of France and the true son of the King", he was reassured and almost believed in the courageous girl's mission.

His advisers were more stubborn, however. Joan was made to appear before the court at Poitiers. A tribunal of doctors and midwives was set up to decide whether she was inspired by God or the devil. The simplicity and swiftness of her responses, her piety and her confidence in her heavenly mission convinced even the most sceptical and she was declared to be truly a "Messenger of God". She returned to Chinon, where she was given troops and equipment. She left on 20 April 1429 to fulfill her miraculous and tragic destiny.

Centre Nucléaire de Production d'Électricité de Chinon

12km/7.4mi NW towards Borgueil. Information centre and museum: by appointment. Open Tue 9am–noon, Thu 2–5pm, no charge. 02 47 98 77 77 (proof of identity must be shown).

France's first nuclear power station, EDF1, was opened at Avoine in 1963. The site's current four 900MW generators provide 40 percent of the power used in the Loire Valley, Brittany and Centre region.

Écomusée de Véron

10km/6.2mi NW towards Candes-St-Martin. 80 rte. de Candes, 37420 Savigny-en-Véron. Open daily Jun–Sept 10am–12.30pm 2–6pm, rest of year daily except Tue 10am–12.30pm 2–6pm, weekends 2–6pm. Closed mid-Nov–mid-Feb, 1 May, 1 Nov, 11 Nov. 3.50€ (children 6–18 years 2.20€). 02 47 58 09 05. www.cc-veron/ecomusee.

The presqu'île du Véron lies at the confluence of the Loire and Vienne rivers. The ecomuseum presents the different aspects of 19C rural life: working among the vineyards and the tools and implements winegrowers used, a collection of headdresses, raising cattle and goats, beekeeping, the influence of river flooding on local life, etc. The visit concludes with an encounter with farm animals.

DRIVING TOURS

1 RABELAIS COUNTRY★

25km/15.5mi round-trip.

Leave by ③ on the town map. The road runs through a tunnel of tall plane trees to St-Lazare; turn right onto D 751, an old Roman road; after 3km/2mi turn left onto D 759; then right onto D 224 and continue along D 117.

Musée Rabelais – La Devinière

Open Jul–Aug 10am–7pm; Apr–Jun and Sept Wed–Mon 10am–12.30pm, 2–6pm (rest of year 5pm). Closed

Chinon, a great wine at the heart of the Val de Loire

The area entitled to carry the Chinon appellation covers 2 000ha/5 000sq yd embracing 19 winemaking localities. Red Chinon is made with a single grape variety, Cabernet-Franc. Graced with a subtle bouquet of violets and wild strawberries, Chinon is definitely a wine for laying down, sometimes for many years. But, depending on the *terroir*, some bottles may be drunk young, as early as Easter. Generally speaking, Chinon is a perfect accompaniment to red meat, poultry and game and can round off a meal nicely when served with a mild cheese. The serving temperature should be between 14°C/57.2°F and 16°C/60.8°F for reds and between 8°C/46.4°F and 12°C/53.6°F for rosés and whites, of which there are far fewer varieties. *For further information, apply to the Syndicat des Vins de Chinon, impasse des Caves-Painctes, ℘02 47 93 30 44.*

1 Jan, 25 Dec. 4.50€. ℘02 47 95 91 18. www.musee-rabelais.fr.
This farmhouse was the birthplace of **François Rabelais** (1494–1553), son of a Chinon lawyer, who became a monk after a studious childhood, fell in love with Ancient Greek and studied the humanists. He transferred to the secular clergy, studied medicine at Montpellier and became a famous doctor.
With the publication of *Pantagruel* in 1532, Rabelais, the distinguished Hellenist, revealed the humorous side of his character by choosing burlesque farce and every kind of comedy to express his philosophy. At La Devinière visitors can see Rabelais' room and a small museum illustrating his life and work.

Rejoin D 117 and turn right.

On the opposite side of the valley stands the beautiful **Château du Coudray-Montpensier** (15C) with its numerous roofs, restored in the 1930s. Next comes **Seuilly-Côteaux**, a long straggling street of troglodyte houses. It was in the abbey at Seuilly that Rabelais was educated.

Lerné

In Rabelais' book this was the village from which the bakers *(fouaciers)* of a special sort of bread set out to sell their goods *(fouaces)* in Chinon market.

Return to Chinon along D 224 through Seuilly-Bourg.

2 VALLÉE DE LA VIENNE★

60km/38mi round-trip – about 3hrs.

Leave Chinon to the E on r. Diderot and D 21 (see map).

The road follows the chalky hillside through the well-known vineyards of Cravant-les-Coteaux.

Vieux Bourg de Cravant

1km/0.5mi N of Cravant-les-Coteaux.
No longer used, the **church** in this old town boasts a nave that is a rare example of the Carolingian style (early 10C), built of characteristically small stones (*open mid-Feb–mid-Nov 9am–7pm; rest of year Sat–Sun and public holidays 9am–7pm; 3€; ℘06 07 04 43 34).*

Follow D 21 to Panzoult and then take D 221 to Crouzilles.

Crouzilles

Built in the 12C the **church**, was covered with Angevin vaulting in the 13C.

Take D 760 W to L'Île-Bouchard.

L'Île-Bouchard *see L'ÎLE-BOUCHARD*

Take D 18 E to Parçay-sur-Vienne.

Parçay-sur-Vienne

This 12C **church** has a fine Romanesque doorway flanked by blind arcades. It is decorated with carved archivolts representing bearded faces (33 in total), foliated scrolls and palmettes, and the ensemble is surmounted by a motif resembling fish scales.

Return to L'Île-Bouchard and take D 760 W on the Vienne's south bank.

Tavant

The Romanesque **church** (*guided tours (45min) Apr–Sept Wed–Sun 10am–12.30pm, 1.30–6pm, Mar and Oct–Nov Mon–Fri 10am–12.30pm, 1.30–6pm; 02 47 58 58 01)* here is of special interest because of the 12C **frescoes**★ which adorn the vaulting, apse and crypt. About 3km/2mi further on, beyond Sazilly, the road (D 760) passes the **Château de Brétignolles** *(left)*, a Louis XII-style building with turrets.

Turn left onto D 749.

Rivière

The church of Notre-Dame (11C–12C), close to the banks of the Vienne, is the oldest church dedicated to the Virgin Mary in Touraine. An early pilgrimage site was established in the 3C. Famous pilgrims incude Saint Martin and Joan of Arc who stopped here on her way to Chinon. Under the triple arcaded porch note the Romanesque frieze on the right showing the resurrection of Lazarus. Inside, the Neo-Gothic friezes are 19C. The layout is unusual: two side staircases lead to the raised chancel and a semi-interred crypt with three small chapels housing the statue of Notre-Dame de Rivière and 16C tomb effigies of the lords of Basché.

Château et jardins du Rivau★

Open Jun–Sept daily 10am–7pm; Easter–May and Oct–early Nov Wed–Mon 10am–12.30pm, 2-7pm. 8€ 02 47 95 77 47. www.chateaudurivau.com. Erected in the 13C and fortified in the 15C, the Château du Rivau is a fine building of great distinction. Joan of Arc found horses for her soldiers here on her way to the siege of Orléans. The château is circled by a dry moat and defended by a drawbridge.

Return to Chinon along D 749.

ADDRESSES

STAY

Chambre d'hôte la Milaudière – *5 r. St Martin, 37500 Ligré. 8km/5mi SW. 02 47 98 37 53. www.milaudiere.com. 7 rms.* Tastefully decorated rooms in a former farm.

Chambre d'hôte La Pilleterie – *37420 Huismes. 6km/3.7mi N of Chinon on D 16. 02 47 95 58 07. www.lapilleterie.com. 4 rms.* This property in the heart of the country is a delight if you want peace and quiet. Pleasant, rustic-style rooms.

Hôtel Agnès Sorel – *4 quai Pasteur. 02 47 93 04 37. www.agnes-sorel.com. 10 rms. 9€.* Not far from the town centre, this hotel on the banks of the Vienne is almost like home.

Hote le Bussy – *4 r. Jehanne-d'Arc, 49730 Montsoreau. 02 41 38 11 11. www.hotel-lebussy.fr. 12 rms.* Furnished in the style of Louis-Philippe, evoking memories of Bussy d'Amboise.

Hotel Diderot – *4 r. Buffon. 02 47 93 18 87. www.hoteldiderot.com. 26 rms.* You will be pleased with this 18C building, and its simple rooms furnished with antiques.

EAT

Auberge de la Route d'Or – *2 pl. de l'Eglise, 37500 Candes-St-Martin. 16km/10mi NW. 02 47 95 81 10. Closed Nov–Feb, Tue eve (except Jul–Aug).* This little auberge is located within 17C walls, and serves cuisine inspired by local produce.

La Crémaillère – *22 r. du Commerce. 02 47 98 47 15. Closed Wed.* This long, narrow restaurant is original: the wooden dining room is divided into compartments, with friezes of pine trees and painted walls reminiscent of Savoie.

La Maison Rouge – *38 r. Voltaire. 02 47 98 43 65. Closed 5 weeks in winter.* This half-timbered restaurant in the medieval quarter is the place to indulge in generous helpings of regional specialities.

⊜⊜ **La Table des Fées** – *Château du Rivau. ☎ 02 47 95 77 47. www.chateaudurivau.com/gastronomie.html. Open Jun-Sept.* Local specialities using fresh garden produce.

⊜⊜⊜ **Les Années Trente** – *78 r. Voltaire. ☎02 47 93 37 18. Closed 2 weeks in Mar, 1 week in Jun, 2 weeks in Oct, Tue and Thu lunches, Wed. Reservations required.* This restaurant is located in a 14C building between the Musée du Vieux Chinon and the Musée du Vin et de la Tonnellerie. Friendly atmosphere and reasonable prices.

⊜⊜⊜ **Diane de Méridor** – *12 quai Philippe-de-Commines, 49730 Montsoreau. ☎02 41 51 71 76. Closed Tue–Wed except Jul–Aug.* A place for gourmands, serving a cuisine half traditional, half regional in a warming rustic setting.

Richelieu★

Lying on the southern limits of Touraine, bordering on Poitou, Richelieu is a quiet town that comes to life on market days. It is a rare example of Classical town planning, the project of one man: the statesman and churchman Cardinal de Richelieu, who was eager to lodge his court near his château, then under construction. The building of the town itself started in 1631 at a time when Versailles was still only an idea.

- **Population:** 1 993
- **Michelin Map:** 317: K-6
- **Info:** Pl. Louis-XIII, 37120. ☎02 47 58 13 62. www.cc-pays-de-richelieu.fr.
- **Location:** 20km/12.4mi S of Chinon.
- **Kids:** Bikes for hire in the park.
- **Timing:** Allow 2hrs for the town and 1hr for the château grounds.

A BIT OF HISTORY

Cardinal de Richelieu

In 1621, when **Armand du Plessis** (1585–1642) bought the property of Richelieu, it consisted of a village and manor on the banks of the Mable. Ten years later the estate was raised to the status of a duchy. On becoming Cardinal and First Minister of France, Richelieu commissioned Jacques Le Mercier, the architect of the Sorbonne and the Palais-Royal in Paris, to prepare plans for a château and a walled town. The project was considered to be a marvel of urban planning.

Determined not to have his creation outstripped in grandeur, Richelieu created a small principality around his masterpiece and jealously razed in whole or in part many other châteaux in the vicinity. An enormous park was once the setting for a marvellous palace filled with great works of art. Two vast courtyards surrounded by outbuildings stood in front of the château, which was protected by moats, bastions and watchtowers. The gardens were dotted with copies of Antique statues and artificial grottoes which concealed the then-popular water tricks (fountains or jets which would spring up unexpectedly, soaking unwary visitors). It was in these gardens that the first poplar trees from Italy were planted. After the Revolution the descendants of Richelieu ceded the château to a certain Boutron who demolished it for the sale of the building materials.

SIGHTS

The Town★

The walled town, which Richelieu planned at the gates of his château, was in itself a fine example of the Louis XIII style designed by Jacques Le Mercier. The town embodies the sense of order, balance and symmetry which characterised the 17C, or Grand Siècle, in France. The rectangular ground plan was surrounded by ramparts and a moat. The impressive entrance gates are flanked by rusticated and pedimented gatehouses surmounted by high French roofs.

Grande-Rue

The main street crosses Richelieu from north to south. In addition to the gateways note the Louis XIII-style *hôtels* with the decorative elements in white tufa stone, especially no. 17, Hôtel du Sénéchal, which has retained its elegant courtyard with busts of Roman emperors.

Place du Marché

In the southern square, opposite the church, stands the 17C covered market, its slate roof supported by a fine chestnut timber frame.

Hôtel de Ville

Open Jul–Aug Wed–Mon 10am–noon, 2–6pm; rest of the year Wed–Mon, Sat–Sun and public holidays 10am–noon, 2–4pm. 2€. 02 47 58 10 13.

This former law court houses a **museum**, which contains documents and works of art pertaining to both the Richelieu family and the château.

Parc du château

Open Apr–Oct 10am–7pm; Nov–Mar 10am–6pm. Closed 1 Jan, 25 Dec. 02 47 58 10 09. www.parc-richelieu.fr.

A magnificent statue of Richelieu by Ramey stands at the southern end of the main street in front of the park, which is criss-crossed by straight avenues of chestnut and plane trees.

Of the many splendid buildings once to be found here, there remains a domed pavilion (part of the outbuildings), which houses a small **museum** containing historical documents on Richelieu.

Steam train of Touraine

A genuine steam train dating from the turn of the 20C runs between Richelieu and Ligré via Champigny-sur-Veude. The museum at Richelieu station displays ancient machinery: early-20C locomotives, saloon-carriages (1900) belonging to the company PLM, an American diesel engine (a relic of the Marshall Plan).

EXCURSIONS

Champigny-sur-Veude★

6km/3.7mi N along D 749.

Champigny lies in the green valley of the Veude. The collegiate chapel is a remarkable instance of Renaissance art at its height; it was part of a château built from 1508 to 1543 by Louis I and Louis II de Bourbon-Montpensier.

Sainte-Chapelle★

Open May–Sept 2.30–6.30pm. 4€. 02 47 95 71 46.

The Sainte-Chapelle, which owed its name to the portion of the True Cross which was kept there, was saved by the intervention of Pope Urban VIII.

Installed in the middle of the 16C, the eleven **stained-glass windows**★★ are the chapel's most precious jewel, forming a remarkable example of Renaissance glasswork. They comprise 34 portraits of the Bourbon-Montpensier House; above are scenes from the Passion. The vivid yet subtle combination of colours throughout the whole work deserve special mention, particularly the purplish blues with their bronze highlights which are truly outstanding.

Faye-la-Vineuse

7km/4.3mi S along D 749 and D 757.

Faye-la-Vineuse stands on a rise once covered in vineyards overlooking the valley formed by a tributary of the Veude. During the Middle Ages it was a prosperous walled city of five parishes and 11 000 inhabitants.

Abbaye de Bois-Aubry

16km/10mi E on D 757 then D 58 and D 114. Open 10am–6pm (Sun and public holidays 11.30am–6pm). 3€. 02 47 58 34 48.

The 12C Benedictine abbey is heralded by its great stone spire. The best-preserved feature of the ruins (*currently under restoration*) is the 15C bell-tower.

L'Île-Bouchard

The ancient settlement of L'Île-Bouchard, once a port on the River Vienne, derives its name from the midstream island where in the 9C the first known lord, Bouchard I, is said to have built a fortress that was destroyed in the 17C.

- **Population:** 1 740
- **Michelin Map:** 317: L-6
- **Info:** 16 pl. Bouchard, 37220 L'Île-Bouchard. 02 47 58 67 75.
- **Location:** Midway between Chinon (15km/9mi to the W) and Ste-Maure-de-Touraine.
- **Timing:** Allow 1hr to explore the town and 2hrs for the driving tour.

PRIEURÉ ST-LÉONARD

The priory church stood on the lower slopes of the valley. There are few vestiges of the original edifice: the 11C Romanesque apse in white tufa, an ambulatory and radiating chapels.

DRIVING TOUR

Vallée de la Manse★

27km/16.7mi. About 2hrs.

The **River Manse** flows west through quiet picturesque countryside away from the main roads to join the Vienne at L'Île-Bouchard.

Leave L'Île-Bouchard to the N along the D 757.

Avon-les-Roches

The 12C–13C **church** has a stone spire over the right transept. The arches of the porch and the door are decorated with archivolts and delicately carved capitals; an inscription in the porch *(left)* tells of the death of Charles the Bold.

Take the road E towards Crissay; after 1km/0.6mi turn left.

Collégiale des Roches-Tranchelion

The ruins of this Gothic collegiate church (1527) can be seen from some way off. Car drivers can take the steep earth track which leads up to the church. These ruins perched on a hill overlooking the surrounding countryside bear witness to past greatness. Little remains of the church vaulting, but the elegant façade is still standing, decorated with delicate carving; note the seated figure above the great window under the triumphal arch, and the Renaissance decoration of pilasters and medallions representing the local feudal lords.

Crissay-sur-Manse

The ruins of the partly troglodytic 15C castle *(left)*, the stone spire of the village church *(right)* and the several 15C houses with square turrets make up a charming scene.

St-Épain

The village **church** (12C, 13C and 15C) is capped by a 13C square tower. Adjoining it is a **fortified gate**, all that remains of the 15C curtain wall. On the other side of the main street stands a house with a watch turret where the road bends southeast to Ste-Maure. This road leads up the lush Manse Valley.

After passing under the railway, bear left.

Vallée de Courtineau★

This small scenic road winds between the stream hidden amid the trees and the cliff dotted with dwellings hewn out of the rock. The Chapelle **Notre-Dame-de-Lorette**, a small 15C oratory, has been carved into the cliff face beside a small dwelling of the same period.

THE SAUMUR AND BAUGE REGIONS

This region is renowned for its many vineyards which produce some of France's finest wines including the Chinon, Borgueil, Côteaux du Layon and Saumur *appellations.* Most of the Saumurois and Baugeois is taken up by the Loire-Anjou-Touraine Regional Nature Park, one of 46 such entities in France which have been set up to coordinate economic, environmental and social initiatives to improve the quality of life within the parks' boundaries.

Highlights

1. A day in elegant **Saumur** (p226)
2. **Fontevraud l'Abbaye**: the largest group of monastic buildings in France (p237)
3. Incredible underground tunnels at **Château de Brézé** (p240)
4. Contemporary art in a Renaissance setting: **Château d'Oiron** (p243)
5. **Château de Brissac**'s magnificent guilded theatre (p245)

The Art of Horsemanship

Alongside its imposing château, Saumur is best known for the Cadre Noir equestrian academy, now part of the National Riding School. It is a unique establishment, recognised as one of the world's finest practitioners of classical equitation, and gives regular performances throughout the year. Fontevraud l'Abbaye, 15km/9mi southeast of Saumur, founded in the 12C, was one of France's most important monastic communities richly endowed by royal and aristocratic benefactors down the ages. In addition to the superbly restored buildings, the abbey's main attractions are the tomb effigies of Plantagenet monarchs Henry II, his wife Eleanor of Aquitaine and their son Richard I. It is now used as a major cultural centre for exhibitions, concerts and conferences.

Cadre Noir of Saumur

©Alain Laurioux - IFCE

Château life

The Château de Brézé and Château d'Oiron are two of the lesser known Renaissance châteaux of the Loire but both are architectural gems. And the Château de Brissac, one of the tallest in France, combines elements of the original medieval fortress with the more ornate Renaissance structure. It has been in the same family since the early 16C and every year hosts the Festival de la Vallée de la Loire. The estate also includes a 28ha/70-acre vineyard which produces red and rosé AOC Anjou wines. Overnight guests are welcome as the château has *chambre d'hôte* accommodation with dinner. A truly splendid way to experience life in one of the Loire Valley's most prestigious monuments!

Twisted spires

The Bauge region is known for its prevalence of curious church spires. Their origin is a highly controversial subject: according to water diviners, the spires follow the path of underground water running beneath the churches: according to poets, they are like windmills facing the wind; sailors think they were built by inexperienced shipwrights; whereas joiners believe that the timber used for building them was still green and became warped with time.

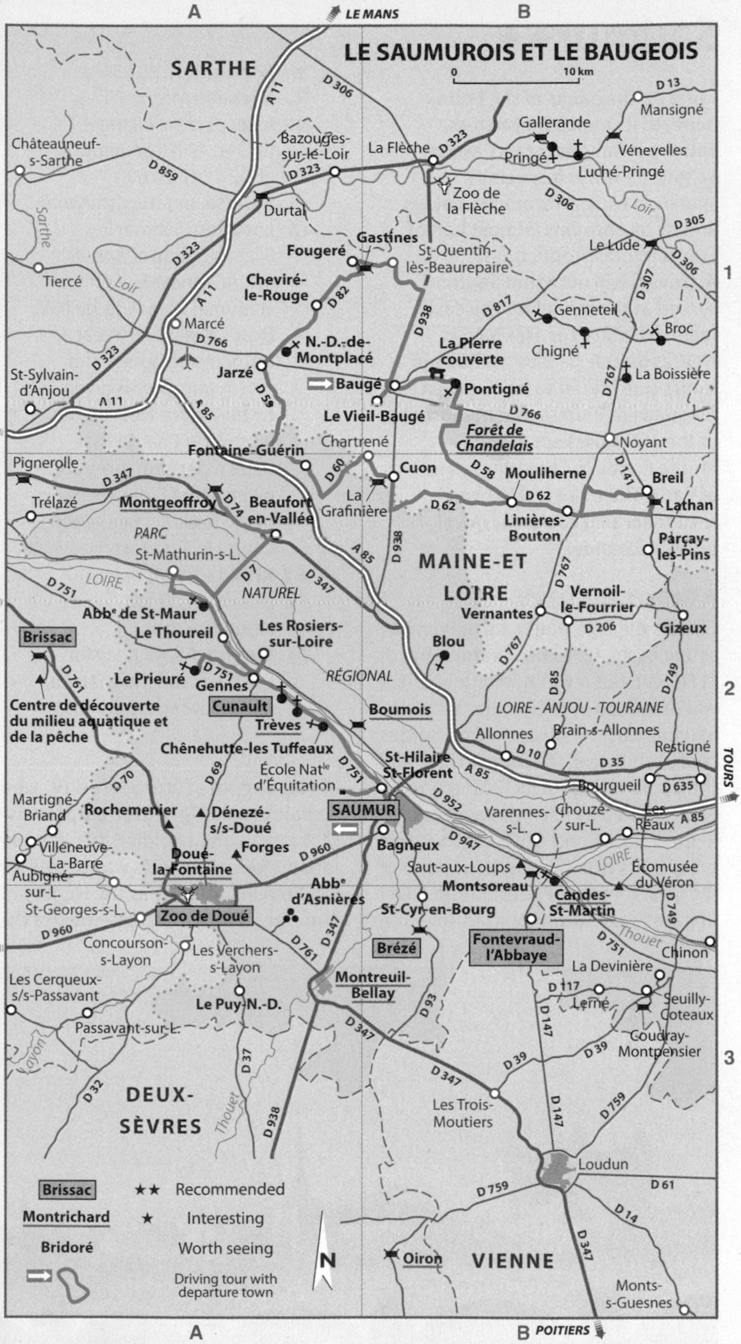
LE SAUMUROIS ET LE BAUGEOIS
0
10 km
LE MANS
A
B
SARTHE
MAINE-ET
LOIRE
DEUX-
SÈVRES
VIENNE
Châteauneuf-
s-Sarthe
Bazouges-
sur-le-Loir
La Flèche
Gallerande
Mansigné
Pringé
Vénevelles
Luché-Pringé
Zoo de
la Flèche
Durtal
Le Lude
Gastines
Fougeré
St-Quentin-
lès-Beaurepaire
Tiercé
Chevirè-
le-Rouge
Genneteil
Broc
Marcé
N.-D.-de-
Montplacé
La Pierre
couverte
Chigné
La Boissière
St-Sylvain-
d'Anjou
Jarzé
Baugé
Pontigné
Le Vieil-Baugé
Forêt de
Chandelais
Noyant
Fontaine-Guérin
Chartrené
Pignerolle
Cuon
Mouliherne
Breil
Trélazé
Montgeoffroy
Beaufort-
en-Vallée
La
Grafinière
Lathan
Linières-
Bouton
Parçay-
les-Pins
PARC
St-Mathurin-s-L.
NATUREL
RÉGIONAL
LOIRE - ANJOU - TOURAINE
LOIRE
Vernantes
Vernoil-
le-Fourrier
Gizeux
Abbe de St-Maur
Le Thoureil
Les Rosiers-
sur-Loire
Brissac
Blou
Le Prieuré
Gennes
Cunault
Centre de découverte
du milieu aquatique et
de la pêche
Trèves
Boumois
Allonnes
Brain-s-Allonnes
Chênehutte-les Tuffeaux
Restigné
St-Hilaire
St-Florent
École Natle
d'Équitation
Bourgueil
Martigné-
Briand
Rochemenier
Dénezé-
s/s-Doué
SAUMUR
Varennes-
s-L.
Chouzé-
sur-L.
Les
Réaux
Villeneuve-
La-Barre
Forges
Bagneux
Aubigné-
sur-L.
Doué-
la-Fontaine
Saut-aux-Loups
Écomusée
du Véron
Montsoreau
Abbe
d'Asnières
Candes-
St-Martin
St-Georges-s-L.
Zoo de Doué
St-Cyr-en-Bourg
Chinon
Concourson-
s-Layon
Les Verchers-
s-Layon
Brézé
Fontevraud-
l'Abbaye
La Devinière
Les Cerqueux-
s/s-Passavant
Montreuil-
Bellay
Lerné
Seuilly-
Coteaux
Le Puy-N.-D.
Passavant-sur-L.
Coudray-
Montpensier
Les Trois-
Moutiers
Loudun
Oiron
Monts-
s-Guesnes
ANGERS
CHOLET
TOURS
POITIERS
1
2
3
Brissac ★★ Recommended
Montrichard ★ Interesting
Bridoré Worth seeing
Driving tour with
departure town
N

Saumur★★

Lying on the banks of the Loire, beneath its imposing fortress, Saumur is famous for its Cavalry School, its wines (especially sparkling wines), its medal makers and its mushrooms (almost half of France's total production).
Art lovers will note that Saumur served as the model for the castle featured in the *Les Très Riches Heures du Duc de Berry*, a Book of Hours considered to be the most magnificent illuminated manuscript of the 15C, now kept at the Musée Condé in Chantilly, north of Paris. The town is also the setting for Balzac's great novel *Eugénie Grandet*.

- **Population:** 28 654
- **Michelin Map:** 317: I-5.
- **Info:** pl. de la Bilange, BP 241, 49418 Saumur. ✆02 41 40 20 60. www.saumur-tourisme.com.
- **Location:** Saumur lies 65km/40mi SE of Angers, 32km/20min NE of Chinon, 1hr40min from Paris by TGV.
- **Don't Miss:** Every year a tattoo using horses and motor transport is given by the **Cadre Noir** on the vast pl. du Chardonnet Repeat performances are given in the Riding School of the National Equitation Centre in Terrefort.
- **Kids:** Le trésor des Ducs d'Anjou *son-et-lumière* show.
- **Timing:** Allow 1 day for the town and the château, half a day for excursions.

A BIT OF HISTORY

Charles the Bald built a fortified monastery in the 9C to house the relics of St Florent, but it was not long before it was destroyed by the Vikings. In the 11C Saumur was the subject of numerous conflicts between the Count of Blois and the Count of Anjou. In 1203, the town was captured by Philippe Auguste.
In the late 16C and early 17C the town enjoyed its true heyday. It was one of the great centres of Protestantism. Henri III gave it as a stronghold to the King of Navarre, the future Henri IV, who appointed as Governor **Duplessis-Mornay**, a great soldier, scholar and fervent Reformer, who was known by the Roman Catholics as the Huguenot Pope. In 1611 a general assembly of the

Pont Cessart over the Loire, Château de Saumur on the left

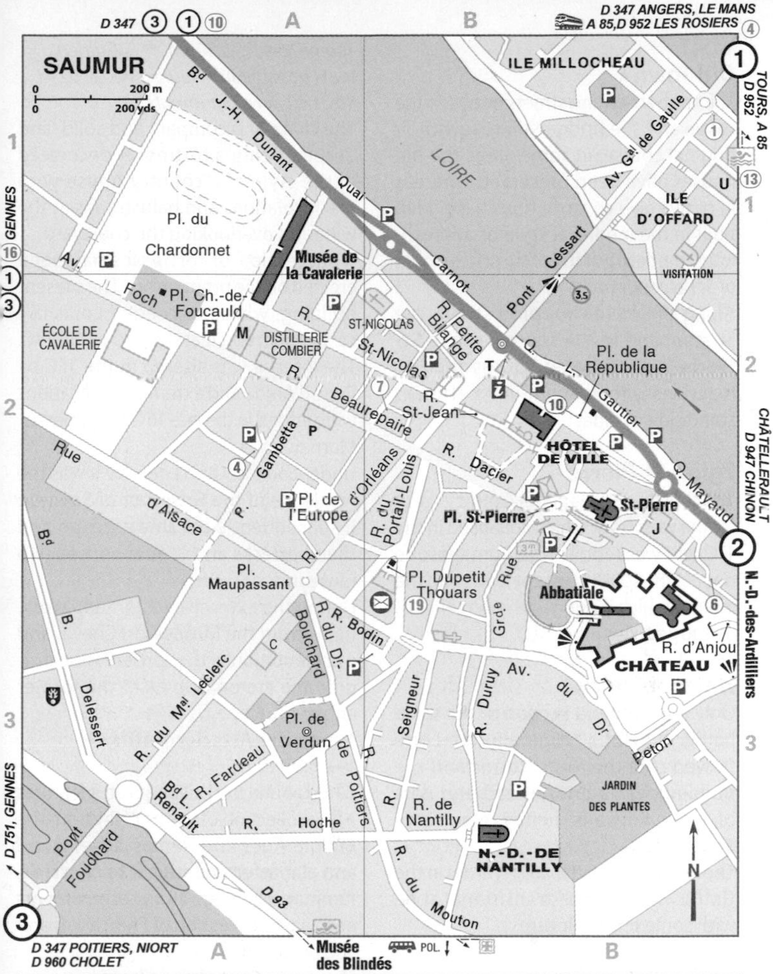

WHERE TO STAY		WHERE TO EAT
	Hôtel Les Terrasses de Saumur.................. (10)	
Hôtel Adagio.................. (1)	Camping L'Île d'Offard.... (13)	Le Gambetta.................. (4)
Hôtel Alcyon.................. (4)	Village hôtelier Le Bois de Terrefort................ (16)	Les Ménestrels.............. (6)
Hôtel Kyriad.................. (7)	Hôtel Le Volney.............. (19)	Le Tire-Bouchon............ (10)

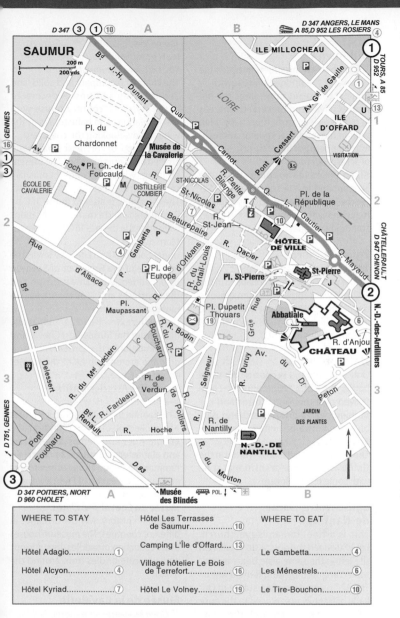

Protestant churches was held there to consolidate their organisation following the death of Henri IV and the departure of Sully. Louis XIII grew alarmed at the Protestant danger and ordered the town walls to be demolished in 1623. The Revocation of the Edict of Nantes in 1685 dealt Saumur a fatal blow; many of the inhabitants emigrated and the Protestant church was demolished.

École d'application de l'arme blindée et de la cavalerie (EAABC) – It is interesting to note the mementoes of officers who served in the cavalry of the African Army between 1830 and 1962: Bugeaud, Gallifet, Charles de Foucault, who was an officer before he became a recluse, Lyautey, Henry de Bournazel and Leclerc de Hauteclocque.

VISIT

Old Town★

The narrow twisting streets between the castle and the bridge still follow their original course; in some areas the old houses have been preserved whereas in others new constructions have been built in the medieval style or are resolutely modern but full of surprises *(south of St Peter's Church)*.

Along the main shopping street, rue St-Jean, and in the square, **place St-Pierre**, half-timbered houses and 18C mansions with wrought-iron balconies stand side by side.

Église St-Pierre

The church is Plantagenet Gothic except for the west front which collapsed in the 17C and was rebuilt. The Romanesque door in the south transept leads into the interior which is hung with two series of 16C **tapestries**★.

Hôtel de Ville★

Only the left-hand section of the town hall is old (16C). Originally the Loire flowed past the foundations and the building was a bridgehead and part of the town walls, hence its military appearance.

The façade facing the courtyard is in the Gothic Renaissance transitional style with some fine sculpture.

Église Notre-Dame-de-Nantilly★

This is a fine Romanesque church. Louis XI added the right aisle. A pillar on the left in the same aisle bears an epitaph composed by King René d'Anjou. The 12C painted wooden statue of Our Lady of Nantilly was placed in the apse on the right of the chancel. The organ case dates from 1690. There are fine **tapestries**★★ dating from the 15C and 16C except for eight in the nave which were made at Aubusson in the 17C.

SIGHTS

Château★★

Interior closed for maintenance. ***Exterior:*** *open Jul–Aug Tue–Sun 10am–6pm; Apr–Jun and Sept 10am–1pm, 2–5.30pm. Guided tours possible Jul–Aug. 3€. 02 41 40 24 40. www.saumur.fr.*

The château is compact and solid, and despite being a fortress is decorated in the style of a country house with machicolations and balustrades at the windows overlooking the courtyard.

A succession of fortresses has been erected on the promontory. The present building, which succeeded Louis IX's castle, was rebuilt at the end of the 14C. The interior was altered in the 15C by René d'Anjou and external fortifications were added in the late 16C by Duplessis-Mornay.

Under Louis XIV and Louis XV it was the residence of the Governor of Saumur; it subsequently became a prison and then barracks and it now houses two museums.

During the extensive restoration work, items from the Muséee du Cheval and a presentation of the conservation programme are on display in the former abbey church.

Musée des Arts décoratifs★★

Closed.

Based aound the Lair bequest, it features a fine collection of works of art from the Middle Ages and Renaissance: wood and alabaster sculptures, **tapestries**, furniture, paintings, liturgical ornaments and a large collection of French 17C and 18C porcelain.

Musée du Cheval *Closed.*

Equestrian history over the centuries in different countries. The museum houses a rare collection of saddles, bits, stirrups and exquisite bridles from around the world.

Musée de la Cavalerie

Open Mon–Thu 9am–noon, 2–5pm, Sat, Sun 2–6pm. 02 41 83 69 23.

In 1763 the Carabiniers Regiment, a crack corps recruited from the best horsemen in the army, was sent to Saumur. The present central building was constructed between 1767 and 1770 as their barracks.

This museum's rich display of souvenirs, created in 1936 from Barbet de Vaux collections, traces the heroic deeds of the

French Cavalry and the Armoured Corps since the 18C.

Musée des Blindés★★

Via bd. Louis-Renault; follow the signposts. Open daily Jul–Aug 9.30am–6.30pm; May, Jun and Sept 10am–6pm; Jan–Apr and Oct–Dec 10am–5pm (Sat–Sun and public holidays 11am –6pm; Easter 10am–6pm). Closed 1 Jan, 25 Dec. 6€. 02 41 83 69 95. www.musee-des-blindes.asso.fr.

This museum and information centre on tanks houses over 100 vehicles (tanks, armoured vehicles, artillery equipment), many of which are still in working order, coming from a dozen or more countries. The most prestigious or rare exhibits are the **St-Chamond** and the **Schneider** (the first French tanks), the Renault FT 17 (French tank used in the very last stages of the First World War), the Somua S 35, the B1bis (issued to the 2nd Armoured Division under General de Gaulle in 1940) and German tanks dating from the French Campaign until the fall of Berlin (Panzers III and IV, Panther, Tiger), the Comet A 34 (the British tank used in the Normandy landing), the Churchill A 22, the Sherman M 4 and AMX 13 and 30.

Église Notre-Dame-des-Ardilliers★

On the eastern edge of the city, quai L.-Mayaud, D 947.

This beautiful 17C church building is one of the most popular places of pilgrimage in France.

Devotion to Our Lady of Ardilliers began to develop in the reign of François I thanks to a miraculous statue a farm labourer was supposed to have discovered on this spot in the previous century, but it was to reach its height in the 17C when pilgrims exceeded 10 000 a year.

EXCURSIONS

Bagneux

S of Saumur.

Bagneux, which lies at the heart of the oldest inhabited region of Anjou, is an old village on the banks of the Thouet. The engines displayed in the **Musée du Moteur** *(18 r. Alphonse-Çailleau; second street on the left after Fouchard bridge; open Tue–Sun 2–6pm; Sun and public holidays 2–6pm, rest of year call for opening hours; closed mid-Dec–end Jan; 5€; 02 41 50 26 10, www.musee-dumoteur.fr)* have been collected by mechanics enthusiasts, most of whom attended the Saumur Industrial School and wish to preserve and restore old and contemporary engines.

Return to r. du Pont-Fouchard for a short distance. Beyond the town hall, bear left onto r. du Dolmen.

Le Grand Dolmen

Open Jul–Aug 9am–7pm; Sept–Oct and Apr–Jun Thu–Tue 9am–7pm. Guided tours (30min) possible. 3.50€. 02 41 50 23 02. www.saumur-dolmen.com.

The Great Dolmen, situated in the centre of the village, is one of the most remarkable in Europe. It consists of 16 standing stones forming a passage and supporting a roof composed of four capstones.

St-Cyr-en-Bourg

8km/5mi S on D 93.

A visit to the **Cave des vignerons de Saumur** *(guided tours (1hr); open May–Sept 9.30am–12.30pm, 2–6.30pm; Oct–Apr by appointment; closed 1 and 11 Nov, 25 Dec; 2.50€; 02 41 53 06 18; www.cavedesaumur.com)* is a good way of learning more about the whole winemaking process, from the grape to the finished product, in a series of underground galleries.

Château de Montsoreau

13km/8mi E on the D 947. Open May–Sept daily 10am–7pm; Apr and Oct–early Nov daily 2–6pm; Mar Sat–Sun 2–6pm; rest of year group tours only, by request. 8.30€. 02 41 67 12 60. www.chateau-montsoreau.com.

Montsoreau is famed for its château which overlooks the confluence of the Loire and the Vienne. The château was rebuilt in the 15C by a member of the Chambes family. The river front, which was once at the water's edge, is an

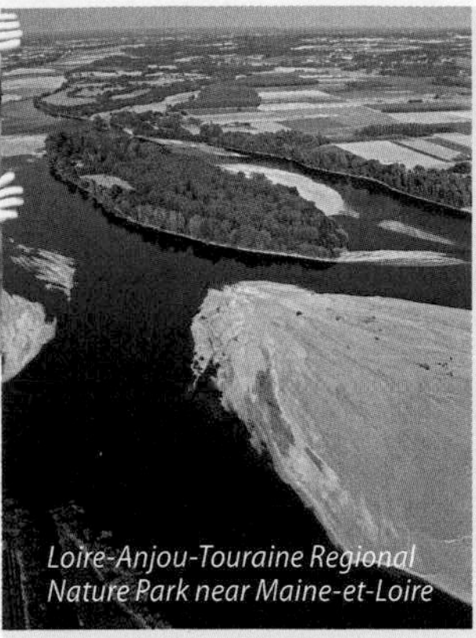

Loire-Anjou-Touraine Regional Nature Park near Maine-et-Loire

©Louis-Marie Preau/hemis.fr

Parc Naturel Régional Loire-Anjou-Touraine

Maison du Parc, 7 r. Jehanne-d'Arc, 49730 Montsoreau. ☎02 41 53 66 00. www.parc-loire-anjou-touraine.fr.

Parcs naturels régionaux are zones set aside for both protection and development. Unlike nature reserves or national parks, these zones are inhabited, and measures are taken to stimulate environmentally friendly economic activities that respect the traditions and customs of the region.

The parks are run by a committee comprising local politicians, landowners and community groups. Stakeholders draw up a charter and ensure that its provisions and aims are correctly applied and respected. The Loire-Anjou-Touraine Regional Nature Park was set up in 1996 and covers 136 towns and villages across the departments of Indre-et-Loire (Centre region) and Maine-et-Loire (Pays-de-la-Loire region), and spreads over 235 000 ha/580 000 acres. The park straddles the Loire and its Indre, Vienne and Thouet affluents while the landscape encompasses valleys, farmland and hedgerows, woodland and open heaths.

Planning your visit

The Information Centre, which doubles up as the Montsoreau tourist office, has been built to high environmental quality standards and is specially designed to welcome visitors with access requirements, and has interactive displays, films and booklets available.

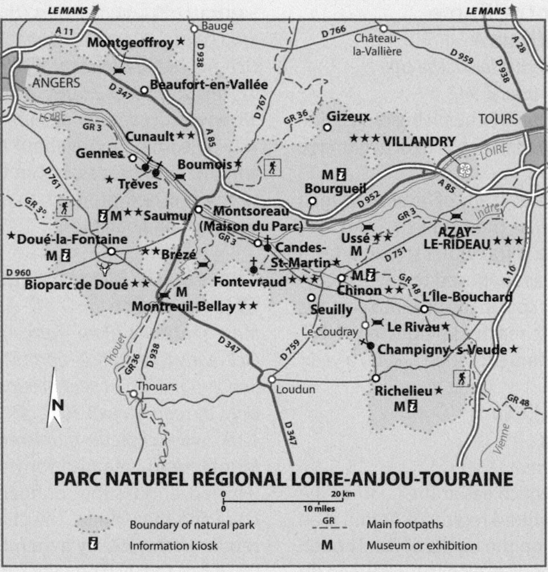

impressive example of military architecture. The façade giving onto the courtyard features far more gentle contours and presents two staircase turrets.

From the bridge over the Loire west of Montsoreau there is a fine view upstream of Montsoreau and Candes and downstream of Saumur Château which is just visible. The road (D 947) is bordered by troglodyte dwellings and white Renaissance houses.

Champignonnière du Saut-aux-Loups

At Saut-aux-Loups, just beyond Montsoreau on the Maumenière hillside, galleries (*guided tours (1hr) Jul–Aug 10am–6.30pm; Mar–Jun and Sept–mid -Nov 10am–noon, 2.15–6pm; 5.90€ (children 6–14 years 4.50€); 02 41 51 70 30. www.troglosautauxloups.com)* a display of the different stages of mushroom cultivation and an exhibition of some of the rarer varieties such as Japanese shitake which is increasingly popular in France's restaurants and health shops. If in season, try the delicious *galipettes*, harvested at full maturity and baked in a bread oven. The terrace offers fine **views** of the Loire.

Troglo des pommes tapées

Val-Hulin in the **Turquant** district, features the art of drying apples *(pommes tapées)* in an enormous cave decorated with ancient farming implements.

Candes-St-Martin★

14km/8.7m E on the D 947.

The village of Candes stands on the south bank of the Vienne at its confluence with the Loire; the church was built on the spot where St Martin died in 397 and it was from here that his body was taken on its miraculous journey up the Loire to Tours (*see TOURS*).

Collégiale★ The church was built in the 12C and 13C and fortified in the 15C. The roadside façade stands out for its mixture of military architecture and richly decorative features. Inside, the vaulted roof is supported by finely tapering pillars which create an impression of lightness. Outside, the path to the right of the church leads to the top of a hill (*15min walk round trip*) with fine views of the river. There is a pleasant walk from rue St-Martin, below the church, to rue du Bas (riverbank and paved path).

Château de Boumois

7km/4.3mi NW, on the north bank of the Loire. Guided tours (45min). Open Jul–Aug Wed–Mon 10am–noon, 2-6pm. 6€. 02 41 38 43 16.

Boumois was the birthplace in 1760 of **Aristide Dupetit-Thouars**. This highly experienced naval officer took part in the French expedition to Egypt. In the course of the Battle of the Nile, Dupetit-Thouars preferred to die a hero's death on the quarterdeck of his ship, the *Tonnant*, rather than haul down his flag.

The apparently feudal exterior of the 16C château conceals an elegant residence in the Flamboyant and Renaissance styles. The driveway leads to the main entrance; on the left stands a 17C dovecote still with its rotating ladder and nesting places for 1 800 birds.

The house itself, which is late 15C, is flanked by two huge machicolated towers. The entrance to the stair turret in the inner courtyard is closed by a door with detailed Renaissance motifs and the original and wrought-iron lock.

The Great Hall contains a marble effigy of Marguerite de Valois, a full-length portrait of Elizabeth I of England and an Indian screen from Coromandel. In the beautiful Flamboyant chapel is a Virgin and Child by Salviati and a 15C Burgundian sculpture of the Holy Family.

Blou

16km/10mi N of Saumur via D 347.

The Romanesque **church** (*open Easter–Oct 8am–7pm; rest of year key available at the café opposite the church Mon–Sat)* with its massive buttresses has curious 11C diapering on its north transept.

Vernantes

20km/12mi N of Saumur on D 347.

A 12C tower marks the site of the **church**, of which only the chancel is still standing. The nave, destroyed by lightning in the 19C, has been replaced by a simple porch. A new church has been built on the other side of the square.

Vernoil

23km/14mi N of Saumur via D 347

The **church** has a massive bell-tower. Enter the priory yard (*right*) to see the solid octagonal turret and mullioned windows of the old prior's lodging.

Gizeux

33km/20mi NE of Saumur via D 347

East of the village of Gizeux, along a tree-lined avenue, stands an imposing château of the Angers area, which was the fief of the Du Bellay, princes of Yvetot, from 1330 to 1661 and which has been occupied by the same family since 1786.

Château

Guided tours (45min).

Open May–Sept 10am–6pm (Sun and public holidays 2–6pm); Apr and Oct 2–5pm. 7.50€. Closed Nov–Mar. 02 47 96 50 92. www.chateaudegizeux.com.

The central building, flanked by two perpendicular wings, was erected on the site of the old fortress in 1560. All that remains of the former building is the machicolated tower in the front of the Court of Honour.

The interior boasts a fine set of Louis XV furniture. **Salle François-Ier** is decorated with paintings on wood executed by Italian artists.

The **Galerie des Châteaux**★ features 17C frescoes depicting royal châteaux (Chambord, Vincennes, Fontainebleau, Versailles).

Parçay-les-Pins

6km/3.7mi N along D 15 and D 86.

Open mid-Jun–mid-Sept Tue–Sun 11am–1pm, 2.30–6pm; Apr–mid-Jun and mid-Sept–Oct Sat–Sun and public holidays 2.30–6pm. 4€.

The **Musée Jules-Desbois** houses sculpture by Rodin's friend, a group of sensual works (*Leda and the Swan*) displayed to full advantage in this former farmhouse.

DRIVING TOUR

From Saumur to Angers

48km/30mi. About 3hr 30min.

La Loire Angevine★

Leave Saumur along D 751.

St-Hilaire-St-Florent

2km/1mi NW.

The village consists of one long street straggling at the foot of the hill beside the River Thouet. It is in fact a suburb of Saumur, which is given over mainly to the production of a famous sparkling white wine made by the Champagne method.

Caves Bouvet-Ladubay

Guided tours (1hr) Jun–Sept Mon–Fri 8.30am–7pm (Sat from 9am, Sun from 9.30am); Oct–May 8.30am–12.30pm, 2–6pm (Sun and public holidays 10.30am–12.30pm, 2.30–6pm). Closed 1 Jan, 25 Dec. 1€. 02 41 83 83 83. www.bouvet-ladubay.fr.

From its premises in galleries hollowed out of the tufa rock, this leading producer of Saumur Brut unveils the stages involved in the production of its wines, from the initial fermentation to the sophisticated design of its bottles. There is an outstanding collection of labels.

Galerie d'Art Contemporain Bouvet-Ladubay

Open Jul–Aug 10am–noon, 2–6pm (Sat–Sun and public holidays 2–6pm); Apr–Jun and Sept 10am–noon, 2–5pm (Sat–Sun and public holidays 3–6pm). Closed 25 Dec. No charge. 02 41 83 83 82. www.bouvet-ladubay.fr.

This contemporary art gallery consists of nine rooms exhibiting works by contemporary artists.

There is also a section on journalism. A delightful little theatre founded in the late 19C to entertain staff has been reopened.

École nationale d'équitation★

Guided tours (1hr, tours begin every 30min) Apr–early Oct Tue–Fri 9.30am–11.30am, 2–4pm, Mon 2–6pm, Sat 9.30–11am. 7.50€. Closed public holidays. 02 41 53 50 60.

The riding school, opened in 1972, is a modern establishment consisting of several units, each comprising a granary where foodstuffs are stored, a large dressage arena that can seat 1 200 spectators and stabling for 400 horses with harness rooms and showers. One of the vocations of the school, which comes under the auspices of the French Ministry for Youth and Sport, is to maintain the level of French horsemanship and further its renown. The **Cadre Noir** (Black Squad) has been based here since 1984. A fundamental part of the school, it is involved in all its projects and gives its traditional repeat performances of *Manège* (dressage) and *Sauteurs en liberté* (jumps) in France and all over the world.

Musée du Champignon

Open Apr–Sept 10am–7pm; mid-Feb–Mar and Oct–mid-Nov 10am–12.30pm, 2–6pm. 7.30€ (children 5.50€). 02 41 50 31 55. www.musee-du-champignon.com.

Large areas of the old tufa quarries that pit the hillsides around Saumur are used for the cultivation of mushrooms which need humidity and a constant temperature. Mushrooms have been grown in the quarries since the time of Napoleon I, but production has escalated to industrial scale yielding some 200 000t.

The museum is a thriving mushroom bed which explains the various options open to growers; the oldest method of growing in mushroom beds is gradually being replaced by more modern techniques using wooden crates, plastic bags, bales of straw and tree trunks.

Parc miniature Pierre et Lumière

On the way out of St-Hilaire-St-Florent. Open Apr–Sept 10am–7pm; Feb–Mar and Oct–mid-Nov 10am–12.30pm, 2–6pm; Christmas holidays 2–6pm. 7.30€ (children 4.60€). 02 41 50 70 04. www.pierre-et-lumiere.com.

This former underground quarry houses remarkable sculptures by Pierre Cormant. A fascinating educational tour.

Chênehutte-les-Tuffeaux

The village **church** stands beside the road on the north side of the village. It is an attractive Romanesque building with a handsome doorway in the same style; the arch stones are carved.

Trèves-Cunault★

A 15C crenellated keep is all that remains of the old castle. Tucked in beside it is the little **church**★ of Trèves, once the castle chapel. It has a beautiful interior with great arches supporting the broad Romanesque nave; the chancel arch frames the rood beam on which there is a Crucifix.

Église de Cunault★★

Cunault Abbey was founded in 847 by monks from Noirmoutier; in 862 they had to take refuge further away in Tournus in Burgundy where they deposited the relics of St Philibert. Cunault therefore became a rich Benedictine priory dependent on Tournus Abbey. The monastic church is a Romanesque structure dating from the 11C to the 13C. Cunault Church was built in the regular Benedictine style to provide for the liturgical ceremonies (seven per day) and for

Église de Cunault

the crowds that attended the pilgrimage on 8 September.

Gennes

Among the wooded hills hereabouts are numerous megaliths including the **Madeleine dolmen** south of the Doué road. Discoveries including an aqueduct, baths, an amphitheatre and the figure of a nymph point to the former existence of a Gallo-Roman shrine dedicated to a water cult.

Amphithéâtre

Open Jul and Aug daily except Sat 10am–6.30pm; Apr–Jun and Sept Sun and public holidays 3–6.30pm. Guided tours (45min) possible. Closed 1 Jan, 25 Dec. 3.50€. 02 41 51 55 04.

Discovered as long ago as 1837 and still being excavated, this is assumed to have been the structure serving as the local amphitheatre between the 1C and 3C. It is set into a terraced slope cut into on the northeast by a podium and has an elliptical arena. On the north side is the boundary wall built of sandstone, tufa and brick paralleled by a paved drainage corridor.

Église St-Eusèbe

This church, overlooking the Loire, has kept only its transept, its tower from the 12C and, on the north side, a small 11C doorway. From the tower there is a vast **panorama** over Gennes and the Loire Valley from the Avoine nuclear power station to Longue and Beaufort.

6.5km/4mi W of Gennes on D 751, turn left beyond Le Sale-Village.

Le Prieuré

The hamlet clusters around this priory whose church (12C and 13C) has a square Romanesque tower and a painted wooden altar (17C).

Les Rosiers-sur-Loire

1km/0.6mi N of Gennes.

Linked to Gennes by a suspension bridge, this village has a church whose Renaissance tower was built by the Angers architect Jean de l'Espine; the staircase turret flanking it is pierced by pilastered windows.

Cross back over the bridge; turn right immediately onto D 132 along the south bank.

Le Thoureil

This quiet, spruce village was formerly an active river port for the handling of apples. Inside the church, on either side of the chancel there are two beautiful wooden reliquary shrines dating from the late 16C, which originally belonged to the abbey of St-Maur-de-Glanfeuil (*see below*); they are adorned with statuettes of Benedictine monks and saints who were popular locally.

Abbaye de St-Maur-de-Glanfeuil

This ruined Benedictine abbey is believed to be named after St Maurus, a hermit who came from Angers and founded a monastery in the 6C on the site of the Roman villa of Glanfeuil on the Loire. The abbey houses an international ecumenical centre and is home to a religious community of Augustinians (*closed to the public*).

Cross the river via D 55. In St-Mathurin, turn right onto D 952 and left onto D 7.

Beaufort-en-Vallée

Beaufort nestles amid the rich plains of the Anjou Valley. In the 18C–19C it was one of the largest manufacturers of sailcloth in France. The town is dominated by the ruins of the château, built in the 14C by Guillaume Roger, Count of Beaufort and father of Pope Gregory XI. The Tour Jeanne de Laval was rebuilt in the 15C by King René. From the top of the bluff on which the ruins stand there is a fine view of the surrounding country. **Musée Josep-Denais** *5 pl. Notre-Dame. 02 41 82 68 11. www.damm49.fr.* An unusual collection of disparate objects and artefacts make up this 19C cabinet of curiosities.

Follow N 147, then turn right onto the D 74.

Château de Montgeoffroy★
Open mid-Jun–mid-Sept 9.30am–6.30pm; mid-Mar–mid -Jun and mid-Sept–mid-Nov 9.30am–12.30pm, 2.30–6.30pm. 9€. 02 41 80 60 02. www.tourisme-beaufortenanjou.com.
This elegant château, overlooking the Authion Valley, has a harmonious Louis XV façade. The two round towers attached to the wings, the curvilinear moat defining the courtyard and the chapel to the right are the only remains of the original 16C building.
The Montgeoffroy estate came into the possession of Erasme de Contades in 1676; the buildings owe their appearance to his grandson, the famous Marshal who commanded the German army in the Seven Years War and who was Governor of Alsace for 25 years.
The **château** has remained in the family, and has consequently kept its original furnishings and decor, which combine to create an effect of great charm.
In the **stables** is a collection of horse-drawn vehicles. The magnificent **Harness Room** fitted out in Norway spruce contains a collection of saddles, stirrups, bridles, whips and riding crops.

N 147 leads to Angers.

ADDRESSES

STAY

Camping l'Ile d'Offard – *02 41 40 30 00. www.cvtloisirs.com. Open Mar–Nov.* Occupying a great part of the island, with 260 places.

Hotel Alcyon – *2 bis r. de Rouen. 02 41 67 51 25. www.alcyon-saumur.com. 16 rms. 7€.* Close to the centre, newly renovated. Hotel shuttle bus.

Hotel Volney – *1 r. Volney. 02 41 51 25 41. www.levolney.com. Closed 15 Dec–2 Jan. 14 rms. 7€.* A central location, modest but stylish rooms, a nice reception and regular room service: here is a small, pleasant hotel perfect for discovering "the pearl of Anjou" without breaking the bank.

Chambre d'hôte La Butte de l'Épine – *37340 Continvoir. 2km/1mi E of Gizeux on D 15. 02 47 96 62 25. Closed 24 Dec–5 Jan. 3 rms.* This 16C–17C property has been charmingly restored. The main room has old furniture and a huge fireplace, the bedrooms are really exquisite and romantic, and the park is full of flowers.

Hotel Kyriad – *23 r. Daillé. 02 41 51 05 78. www.central-kyriad.com. 29 rms. 8€.* A central location, but in an area of calm; agreeable on all levels.

Hotel les Terrasses de Saumur – *chemin de l'Alat, 49400 St-Hilaire-St-Florent. 02 41 67 28 48. Closed 21 Dec–19 Jan. 22 rms. 12€.* Overlooks the château, and offers tasteful rooms, and a swimming pool.

Village hôtelier Le Bois de Terrefort – *av. de l'Éducation-Nationale-d'Équitation, 49400 St-Hilaire-St-Florent. 2km/1.5mi W of Saumar on D 751. 02 41 50 94 41. www.village hotelier.com. 14 rms. 7€.* A hotel-village near the national riding school, not far from Saumur. The peaceful country setting and reasonable prices make it an ideal place to stay for those on a tight budget.

Hotel Adagio – *94 av. du Gén-de-Gaulle. 02 41 67 45 30. www.hotel adagio.com. Closed 23 Dec–2 Jan. 36 rms. 12€.* A fine hotel located on the Ile de la Loire, facing the château. Rooms have been renovated.

EAT

Le Tire-Bouchon – *10 pl. de la République. 02 41 67 35 05. www. tirebouchon.net. Closed Sun eve in Jan–Feb, Tue. Reservation recommended.* Delicious food in generous portions, a relaxed atmosphere with pleasant décor explains the success of this small restaurant ideally situated on the wharf.

Le Gambetta – *12 r. Gambetta. 02 41 67 66 66. www.restaurant legambetta.com. Closed Sun and Mon, Feb holidays.* Simple, delicious food at good prices.

Mercure bord de Loire – *r. du Vieux Pont. ℘02 41 67 22 42.* Located on the Ile d'Offard and with a great view of the river.

Les Ménestrels – *11 r. Raspail - ℘02 41 67 71 10. Closed 21-28 Dec, Mon (except Apr-Oct), and Sun.* Delicious modern cuisine and excellent range of wines. Moroccan influences.

NIGHTLIFE

Blues Rock Magazine – *7 r. de la Petite-Bilange. ℘02 41 50 41 69. Closed Mon.* A private dance club which is the cool place to be seen in Saumur.

L'Absynthe – *27 r. Molière. ℘02 41 51 23 37. Closed Sun–Mon.* This atmospheric bar with a Canadian influence is probably the liveliest in the staid city of Saumur, and is popular with the younger crowd.

Place St-Pierre – Several of the 18C half-timbered buildings of St Pierre house cafés with shady terraces in this lovely square.

SHOPPING

Sébastien Giradeau – *51–53 r. St-Nicolas. ℘02 41 51 30 33. www.le-pied-de-cochon.fr. Closed 3 weeks in Feb and 2 weeks in Aug and afternnons on public holidays.* Ideally located for stocking up on regional products: pig's trotters (award winning speciality), *foie gras, boudin noir* (European champion for *boudin blanc* with truffles), and fine wine as well.

La Duchesse Anne – *22 r. Franklin-Roosevelt. ℘02 41 51 07 50. www.laduchesseanne.fr. Open daily 9am–7.15pm, Sat 8.30am–7.30pm, Sun and public holidays 8am–1pm.* The creations of this master chocolatier are often inspired by the history of Saumur.

LEISURE ACTIVITIES

Au Bureau – *19 pl. Bilange. ℘02 41 67 39 71.* Terrace seating 120, attentive waiters, brass beer pumps, immaculate wood panelling and plush carpets.

Maison du Vin de Saumur – *quai Lucien-Gautier. ℘02 41 38 45 83, www.vinsvaldelaoire.fr. Closed Mon.* Located next to the tourist office, this is a good place to learn about the wines of Saumur.

Distillerie Combier – *48 r. Beaurepaire. ℘02 41 40 23 00. www.combier.fr. Phone for opening times. 4€ guided tour and tasting session (children under 18 no charge).* The oldest distillery in the Loire Valley; taste the liqueur of your choice and take home a bottle of absinthe, guignolet, pastis d'antan or fruit brandy.

La Cave de Saumur – *14 rte. de Saumoussay. 49260 St-Cyr-en-Bourg. ℘02 41 53 06 18. www.cavedesaumur.com. Phone for opening times. 2.50€ guided tour of the cellars (children under 14 years 2€).* This cooperative brings together 300 winegrowers making it the ideal halt for discovering the wines of Saumur: wine storehouses and cellars (10km/6mi of galleries in the old tufa quarries) and a tasting session. Wines on sale all bear the AOC label and Les Pouches (white), La Mouraude (red) and Les Poyeux (saumur-champigny) are highly recommended.

CALENDAR

Easter – International equestrian vaulting competition.

Apr–Oct – Series of equestrian exhibitions, gala evening performances and guided tours of the Cadre Noir and National Riding School.

May – Journées nationales du livre. et du vin literature and wine festival; international 3-day event competition.

June – International military music festival; international carriage driving competition.

July – Carrousel de Saumur; Loire en fête, the military and equestrian tattoo.

July-August – Les Estivales du comité des fêtes summer fair.

August – La Grande Tablée du saumur-champigny, a huge outdoor feast for thousands of diners.

September – Grande Semaine de Saumur (major equestrian show with carriage driving, dressage, shows). Grape harvesting at the château and organic market (last Sun of month).

November – Salon international de Saumur "Ar(t) Cheval", annual gathering of contemporary art on the theme of horses.

Fontevraud-l'Abbaye★★

Fontevraud Abbey stands on the borders of Anjou, Touraine and Poitou. Despite the ravages of history, it remains the largest group of monastic buildings in France, having retained many features typical of Anjou architecture.

- **Population:** 1 497
- **Michelin Map:** 317: J-5
- **Info:** pl. St-Michel, 49590 Fontevraud-l'Abbaye. ☎02 41 51 79 45.
- **Location:** Between Saumur (15km/9mi to the NW) and Chinon (18km/11mi to the E).
- **Timing:** Allow 2hrs to explore at leisure.

A BIT OF HISTORY

An aristocratic Order – The success of the new Order was immediate and soon took on an aristocratic character. The **Plantagenets** showered it with wealth. The tomb effigies of Henry II, his wife Eleanor of Aquitaine and their son Richard the Lionheart lie in the nave.

The abbey became a refuge for repudiated queens and daughters of royal or highly placed families who, voluntarily or under compulsion, retired from the secular world. There were 36 abbesses, half of whom were of royal blood including five from the House of Bourbon, between 1115 and 1789.

Violation of the abbey – The Huguenots desecrated the abbey in 1561; in 1792 the Order was suppressed by the Revolutionaries who completely destroyed the monks' priory. In 1804 Napoleon converted the remaining buildings into a prison which closed only in 1963.

Touring Tip

Every evening in August, the abbey organises Les Rencontres Imaginaires, an open-air *son et lumière* performance involving artists as well as professional and amateur actors.

Cultural vocation – In 1975 the abbey embarked on a new vocation as a venue for cultural events, the **Centre culturel de l'Ouest**.

VILLAGE

Église St-Michel★

Although the church was enlarged and remodelled in the 13C and 15C, an inner arcade remains from the original Romanesque building.

Abbey church of Fontevraud

A. Cassaigne/MICHELIN

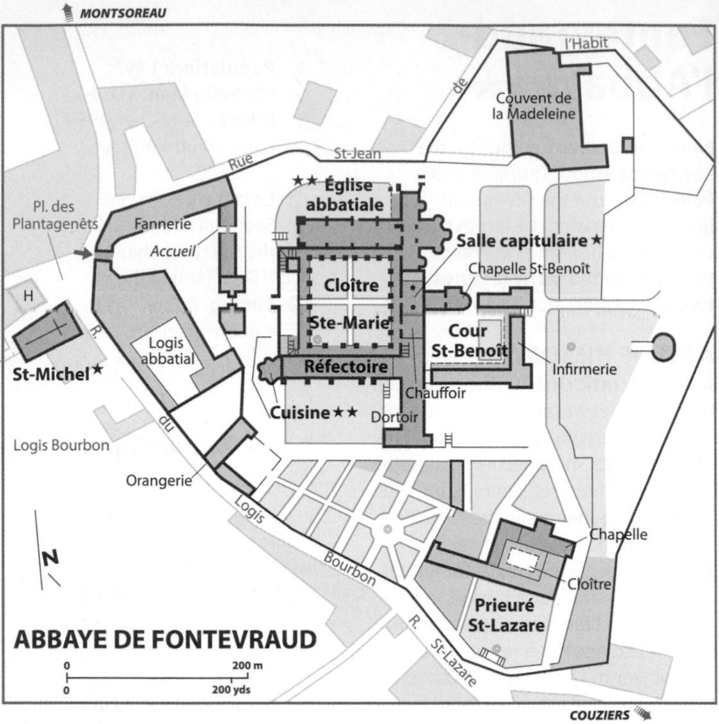

ABBEY★★

Open Jun–Sept 9am–6.30pm; Oct, Apr and May 10am–6pm; Nov–Mar 10am-5.30pm. Last admission 30 min before closing. Closed 1 Jan, 1 and 11 Nov, 25 Dec. 6.50-7.90€. 02 41 51 71 41. www.abbaye-fontevraud.com.

Fontevraud Abbey kitchen

S. Sauvignier/MICHELN

Among the buildings around the entrance court, most of which date from the 19C are, on the left, the vast 18C stables (*fannerie*) and, on the right, the 17C and 18C abbess' house.

Abbey Church★★

This now-restored 12C abbey church was divided into storeys at the time when it served as a prison.

The vast nave is roofed by a series of domes, characteristic of churches in the southwest of France. Fontevraud is the northernmost example of these domed churches, explained by the important links between Anjou and Aquitaine during the Plantagenet reign.

The building houses 13C **polychrome recumbent figures of the Plantagenets**★, representing Henry II, Count of Anjou and King of England, his wife Eleanor of Aquitaine, who died at Fontevraud in 1204, their son Richard the Lionheart and lastly Isabella of Angoulême, second wife of their son, King John of England.

Foundation of the Abbey (1101)

The monastic order at Fontevraud was founded by **Robert d'Arbrissel** (c. 1045–1117) who had been a hermit in Mayenne Forest before being appointed by Urban II to preach in the west of France. He soon gained a large group of disciples of both sexes and chose this place to found a double community.

From the beginning the abbey was unique among religious houses in that it had five separate buildings accommodating priests and lay brothers (St-Jean-de-l'Habit), contemplative nuns (Ste-Marie), lepers (St-Lazare), invalids (St Benoît) and lay sisters (Ste Marie Madeleine). Each body led its own life, with its own church and cloister, chapter house, refectory, kitchen and dormitory. Robert d'Arbrissel had ordained that the whole community be directed by an abbess chosen from among widows; she was later designated as Head and General of the Order and this female supremacy was to be maintained right up to the French Revolution.

Cloître Ste-Marie

The cloisters in the nuns' convent have Renaissance vaulting except on the south side, which is Gothic inspired.

A richly carved doorway in the east gallery, paved with the Bourbon coat of arms, opens into the **chapter house**★ which has 16C murals representing some of the abbesses.

Refectory

This large hall with its Romanesque walls is roofed with Gothic vaulting which replaced a timber ceiling in 1515.

Kitchen★★

This is the only Romanesque **kitchen** in France to have survived the centuries. In many respects it resembles the abbot's kitchen at Glastonbury.

This most intriguing building is roofed with overlapping lozenge-shaped stones and topped by numerous chimneys, added in 1904 during restoration by the architect Magne. Originally, the building was free-standing, built on an octagonal plan and capped by an octagonal hood.

Prieuré St-Lazare

This priory houses a hostelry but it also provides access to the chapel and its splendid 18C **spiral staircase**; in summer the small cloisters are used as a restaurant.

ADDRESSES

STAY

Chambre d'hôte Domaine de Mestré – *1km/0.6mi N of Fontevraud on D 947, towards Montsoreau. ℘02 41 51 72 32. www.dauge-fontevraud.com. Closed 24 Dec–1 Mar (open Sat–Sun in Mar). 12 rms. 9€. Evening meal.* Spend a night or two at the old royal abbey farm on your way through the Loire Valley. Lovely park planted with centuries-old cedar and lime trees.

Hôtellerie Prieuré St-Lazare – *R. St-Jean-de-l'Habit. ℘02 41 51 73 16. www.hotelfp-fontevraud.com. Closed Nov–Mar.* A haven of peace in the heart of the abbey gardens, the old priory of St-Lazare encourages spiritual repose; guests stay in the old monastic cells.

Recumbent figures of Henry II and Eleanor of Aquitaine

A. Cassaigne/MICHELIN

Château de Brézé★★

The castle's imposing outline towers above one of the oldest vineyards of the Loire Valley. Apart from that, little seems to distinguish this château from its neighbours. But closer examination reveals intriguing openings in the moat, the only outward signs of underground galleries and the most extensive underground fortress discovered to date.

- **Michelin Map:** 317: I-5
- **Info:** ✆02 41 51 60 15. www.chateaudebreze.com.
- **Location:** 10km/6mi S of Saumur.
- **Don't Miss:** The underground rooms.
- **Timing:** To make the most of your visit allow 2–4hrs.
- **Kids:** The caves

A BIT OF HISTORY

The lords of Brézé built the original fortress in the 11C. Their descendants erected the Renaissance living quarters. The Grand Condé, a leader of the uprising known as the "Fronde", which took place at the beginning of Louis XIV's reign, found refuge inside the castle with his whole army. In 1682, he exchanged the property against the Galissonnière estate belonging to the Dreux, who subsequently took the name of Dreux-Brézé. Their descendants still live in the château.

VISIT

Open Apr–Sept 10am–6.30pm; Oct–Dec and Feb–Mar Tue–Sun 2–6pm, Sat–Sun 10am–6pm. Closed Jan, 24 and 25 Dec. 14€ (château and subterranean passages).

Château★

Beyond the moat stands the elegant Renaissance edifice remodelled in 1824 by Hodé. Surrounding the courtyard are the main building, the gallery and the gatehouse flanked by two large round towers; a terrace makes up the fourth side. From the rooftop, the panoramic view reveals the different stages of construction of the castle.

Ensemble troglodytique★★

A discreet door opening onto the main courtyard gives access to a gallery dug in the 15C that leads to a vast underground network steeped in mystery. Its complexity is due to the various uses to which it was put through the centuries: stone quarry for the construction of the castle, cellars for storing the wine production, etc.

Château de Brézé

S. Sauvignier/MICHELIN

Roche de Brézé★
Located beneath the castle, these underground living quarters were mentioned in the 9C. The area was originally accessed through a well-guarded narrow corridor with a bend in it.
A corridor leads from this area to the underground watch-path with loopholes opening into the moat. The path ends in the moat via a drawbridge spanning a pit.

Underground bakery★
Reached by a staircase hewn out of the rock, the bakery has an imposing fireplace and an impressive baking oven. Opposite, the quarters allotted to the baker's boy amount to a recess resembling a mezzanine dug in the rockface. The heat from the ovens made the bread dough stored in the room above rise more quickly and enabled silk-worm breeding to take place in the adjacent room.

Winepress and cellars
The vast winepress cellar was used in the making of the famous Brézé white wines. The harvest fell directly into the wine press from a well dug into the rock, which opened in the middle of the vineyards. The grape juice then flowed directly into the vats, along channels running at ground level.
The 20ha/48-acre **Parc** is perfect for a quiet stroll. Built in 1550 by the entrance to the château, the **Dovecote★** can accommodate up to 3 700 birds.

Montreuil-Bellay★

Occupying a charming site★ beside the Thouet on the border of the Poitou and Anjou regions, the little town of Montreuil-Bellay has retained its authentic medieval character.

- **Population:** 4 060
- **Michelin Map:** 317: I-6
- **Info:** pl. du Concorde, 49260 Montreuil-Bellay. 02 41 52 32 39. www.ville-montreuil-bellay.fr.
- **Location:** 15km/9mi Sof Saumur (N 147) and 10km/6mi SE of Doué-la-Fontaine.
- **Don't Miss:** The medieval kitchen in the château.
- **Timing:** Allow 2hrs.

CHÂTEAU★★

Guided tours (1hr) Jul–Aug 10am–6.30pm; Apr–Jun and Sept–Oct Wed–Mon 10am–noon, 2–6pm. 8€, gardens only €4. 02 41 52 33 06. www.chateau-de-montreuil-bellay.fr.

In front of the castle stretches the picturesque place des Ormeaux (*parking space*). Imposing walls, pleasant gardens and remarkable furnishings are the main features of Montreuil Château.
Beyond the barbican, inside the fortified gateway, stands the graceful residence built by the Harcourt family in the 15C.
The **medieval kitchen** with its central fireplace was slightly altered in the 15C and is still in perfect condition, with a set of copper pans and a kitchen range with seven fire boxes fuelled by charcoal.
The 15C **canons' lodge** has four staircase turrets with conical roofs serving four separate sets of rooms, each consisting of living rooms over a storeroom (one was converted into a steam room).
The **château neuf** was built in the 15C. It features a beautiful staircase turret decorated with mullioned windows protected by delicately carved mock balustrades.
The little **oratory** decorated with frescoes is late 15C. Visitors see the bedchamber of the **Duchess of Longueville**, Prince Condé's sister, who

Recalcitrant Vassals

In 1025, **Fulk Nerra**, Count of Anjou, gave this stronghold to his vassal Berlay (distorted into Bellay), who made it into a powerful fortress. A century later, safe behind their stout walls, his successors plotted against their overlord. In 1151, one of them, Giraud, held out for a year before he capitulated to Geoffrey Plantagenet, who razed the keep he had just taken with the aid of an early incendiary bomb. When the Plantagenets acceded to the throne of England and thus became the main enemy of the King of France, the Berlays (who later became the Du Bellays) pledged allegiance to their immediate overlord; Philippe Auguste thereupon besieged their castle and demolished it.

was one of the main instigators behind the Fronde uprising and was exiled by Louis XIV to Montreuil where she lived in luxurious style. In the Grand Salon there is a Brussels tapestry and a German marquetry cupboard; in the small music salon there is a superb bureau by Boulle (1642–1732), inlaid with copper and tortoiseshell.

In the vaulted **cellar** the brotherhood of the Sacavins holds its meetings; it was founded in 1904 by the then owner of the castle, Georges de Grandmaison, to advertise Anjou wine. The winepress, into which the grapes were poured directly from the courtyard through a trapdoor, was still in use at the beginning of the last century.

THE TOWN

As you come out of the château, turn right onto r. du Marché, then follow r. du Tertre.

Les Nobis

Deep in the vegetation beside the Thouet are the ruins of the church of St-Pierre which was burnt down by the Huguenots in the 16C. Nearby are two wings of some 17C cloisters.

Walk up the St-Pierre steps and turn right.

Maison Dovalle

69 r. Dovalle.

The façade of this 16C house was altered in the 18C. The building is named after the Romantic poet **Charles Dovalle** (1807–29) whose collected works, *Le Sylphe*, were published posthumously.

Continue along rue Dovalle to reach *(on the left)* long stretches of the medieval wall; a path then leads to the **Porte St-Jean**, a 15C gate flanked by two large rusticated towers. Proceed along rue Nationale, the town's high street; at the other end stands the Porte Nouvelle.

EXCURSIONS

Ancienne abbaye d'Asnières

7.5km/5mi NW along D 761 then right to Cizay. Guided tours (30min) by request Jul–Aug Wed–Mon 2–6.30pm. 2.50€. 02 41 67 04 70.

On the northern edge of Cizay Forest are the evocative ruins of what was once an important monastery founded in the 12C.

Le Puy-Notre-Dame

7km/4.3mi W along D 77.

The **collegiate church**★, built in the 13C, is a remarkable example of Angevin architecture.

The tall, narrow nave and aisles lend majesty to the interior. The carved stalls beyond the high altar are 16C.

Nature lovers: stay within the authorised areas in parks and gardens. Do not collect plant species.

Château d'Oiron★

The magnificent Renaissance Château d'Oiron is set in the heart of a forest of cedar trees. Since 1993, it has successfully achieved a surprising marriage of old and modern art. This unexpected encounter between past and present brings to life the many changing artistic trends over the centuries. It is a daring exchange but one of wonder and curiosity.

- **Population:** 945
- **Michelin Map:** 322: F-3
- **Info:** 05 49 96 51 25. www.oiron.fr.
- **Location:** 45km/28mi S of Saumur, between Thouars and Loudun, Oiron is a small village set in the country.
- **Kids:** Special children's art workshops (upon appointment).
- **Timing:** Allow at least 2hrs.

CHÂTEAU★★

Open Jun–Sept 10.30am–6pm; rest of year 10.30am–5pm (last admission 1hr before closing). Closed 1 Jan, 1 May, 1 Nov, 11 Nov, 25 Dec. 7€ (under 26 years no charge) no charge 1st Sun in month (Nov–May). 05 49 96 51 25. www.oiron.fr.

Exterior

Preceded by two 17C pavilions, the château comprises a central block (17C) with a steep Mansard roof, flanked by two square pavilions crowned by a balustrade. The courtyard is delineated by two wings (16C and 17C). On the left, the upper section of the **galerie à arcades** features sculpted marble medallions of Roman emperors.

Interior

From the period of the Gouffier family, Oiron has retained its **cabinet des Muses** *(king's pavilion)*, adorned with a Diana the huntress and her nymphs, and its majestic **galerie peinte**★★ *(Renaissance wing)*, whose walls feature remarkable scenes inspired by incidents from the Trojan War and the *The Aeneid*. The Louis XIII ceiling commissioned by Louis Gouffier comprises 1 670 painted panels of animals, birds and weaponry. The main body of the château, the **corps central,** was altered by La Feuillade, who married Charlotte Gouffier in 1667, and features a fine Renaissance staircase, inspired by the one at Azay-le-Rideau.

The encounter with modern art begins with the **chambre du Coquatrix** (1993), by Joan Fontcuberta, portraying a discovery of this imaginary animal in the cellars of the château. The **cabinet de curiosités de Claude Gouffier** (1995), by Guillaume Bijl, evokes the passion of the château's first owner for nature's most fantastic creations, echoed by Thomas Grünfeld (1992) whose **cabinet des Monstres** is a hotch-potch of weird creatures put together from various parts of stuffed animals.
in the **couloir des Illusions**, Félice Varini projects absract lines onto the walls as part of a clever game of optical effects while the **galerie des Chevaux** presents charcoal sketches by Georg Ettl on the remains of the original plasterwork to evoke the portraits of Henri II's finest horses that used to hang here.

La collégiale★

The Renaissance façade comprises twin doors and a large arch surmounted by a pediment bearing the Gouffier coat of arms. In the transept, note the tombs of the Gouffier family, the work of Tuscan sculptors who brought their skills to Tours. In the left transept arm is the tomb effigy of Philippine de Montmorency, second wife Guillaume Gouffier, who died in 1516; nearby is the mausoleum of her son, Admiral Bonnivet, killed at the battle of Pavia in 1525.

Doué-la-Fontaine★

Doué and its outskirts are built on a chalk plateau riddled with caves. The town's flower show, **Journées de la rose**, takes place each year in mid-July in the arena and at a large park, where late-18C stables belonging to Baron Foullon have been converted into an open-air museum of old-fashioned shops.

THE TOWN
Old Houses

Alongside its troglodyte dwellings (*rue des Perrières and rue d'Anjou*) Doué has kept some of its **old houses** with towers and outside stairs. On the Saumur road is a **fine windmill,** the only one remaining out of the hundreds that once stood on the hills in the region.

Arènes (*r. des Arènes;* ◷ *unaccompanied visit outside;* ⌁ *guided tours available (40min) Jul–Aug;* ℘*02 41 59 20 49; www.ot-douelafontaine.fr*). These disused open-air quarries were converted into arenas in the 15C. They are now used for live performances and flower shows. The vast underground areas were inhabited for many years and used as a prison during the Revolution.

♟ Musée aux Anciens Commerces
Ecuries Foullon, towards St-Georges-sur-Layon; ♿ ◷*phone for opening times;* ◉ *6.50€;* ℘*02 41 52 91 58).* Set in the stables (the only remaining parts of the château) of Baron Foullon, two reconstituted streets with 20 shops from bygone days tell the story of shopkeeping from 1850–1950 including an apothecary's, milliner's and hardware shop which are all recreated in painstaking detail.

♟ Zoo de Doué★★
◷*Phone for opening times.* ◉*15€ (children 3–10 years 10€).* ℘*02 41 59 18 58. www.zoodoue.fr.*

The zoo is on the western edge of Doué, in a troglodyte **setting**★. The old quarries make an unusual habitat for the animals that live here, more or less at liberty.

▶ **Population:** 7 442
♿ **Michelin Map:** 317: H-5 Local map see Vallée du Layon.
🗎 **Info:** 30 pl. des Fontaines, 49700 Doué-La-Fontaine. ℘02 41 59 20 49. www.ville-douelafontaine.fr.
▶ **Location:** 20km/12.4mi SW of Saumur.
◷ **Timing:** Doué is a fascinating place; allow half a day.
♟ **Kids:** Zoo de Doué.

EXCURSIONS
Les Chemins de la rose★
Parc de Courcilpleu, D 960, rte. de Cholet. ℘ *02 41 59 95 95. www.cheminsde larose.com.* ♿⌁ ◷*Open mid-May– mid-Aug 9.30am–7pm; mid-Aug–mid-Sept and last 2 weekends of Sept 10am– 6.30pm.* ◉ *6.50€ (children 5–15 years 4€). The gardeners are happy to answer visitors' questions.*

This 4ha/10acre garden is planted with over 1 300 varieties of old and modern roses from all over the world including the Damascus rose (brought back from the Crusades in the 13C) and the York and Lancaster rose of England.

♟ Village troglodytique Rochemenier
◷*Phone for opening times.* ◉*5€ (children 2.50€).* ℘*02 41 59 18 15. www.troglodyte.info.*

The underground village of Rochemenier was dug out of the marly deposit, and extends over a wide area.

♟ Maisons troglodytes de Forges
▶ *3.5km/2mi N on D 214.* ◷*Open Jun– Sept 9.30am–7pm; Mar–May and Oct 9.30am–12,30pm, 2–6.30pm).* ◉*5€ (children 8–17 years 3€).* ℘*02 41 59 00 32.* Excavations in 1979 revealed this fine example of a type of rural architecture that was formerly unappreciated. Nearby is the Caverne sculpté de Dénézé-sous-Doué (℘*02 41 59 15 40*).

Château de Brissac★★

The château is set in a fine park shaded by magnificent cedar trees★. The building is unusual both because it is exceptionally tall (48m/157ft), and because it comprises two juxtaposed buildings, one of which was intended to replace the other, rather than stand next to it. Built c. 1455 by Pierre de Brézé, Minister to Charles VII and then to Louis XI, the château was bought by René de Cossé in 1502 and has remained in the family ever since. René's grandson, Charles de Cossé, Count of Brissac, was one of the leaders of the League, the Catholic party which supported the Guises (*see BLOIS*) in the 16C. In 1594, as Governor of Paris, he handed the keys of the city to Henri IV who had arrived newly converted to Roman Catholicism at the city gates. In gratitude the King raised him to the status of duke. The new duke began to rebuild his house but work was brought to a halt by his death in 1621 and the château has been left unaltered ever since.

- **Michelin Map:** 317: G-4
- **Info:** 8 pl. de la République, 49320 Brissac-Quincé. 02 41 91 21 50. www.ot-brissac-loire-aubance.fr.
- **Location:** 15km/9mi S of Angers, in the direction of Doué-la-Fontaine.
- **Don't Miss:** The luxuriously gilded theatre.
- **Timing:** Allow 1hr 30min.
- **Kids:** The discovery tour and special events at Christmas and Easter.

Château de Brissac
©Château de Brissac

VISIT

Guided tours (45min) Jul–Aug daily 10am–6.30pm; Apr–Jun and Sept–Oct Tue–Sun 10.15am–12.15pm, 2–6pm; Nov–Mar school holidays only, call for hours. 8.50€. 02 41 91 22 21. www.brissac.fr.

The main façade is flanked by two towers with conical roofs, ringed by elegantly sculpted machicolations. Inside, the **ceilings** are still adorned with their original 17C paintings; the walls are hung with superb **tapestries**. The **Louis XIII staircase** leads to the guard-room on the first floor, as well as to the bedchamber where Louis XIII and his mother, Marie de' Medici, were at least temporarily reconciled after the Battle of Les Ponts-de-Cé in 1620.

The vineyards yield 1 500 bottles of Anjou-Village wine every year.

EXCURSION

Centre de découverte du milieu aquatique et de la pêche

Take D 748 S of Brissac-Quincé and follow the signposted route. Open Jul–Aug Mon–Fri 2–6pm. 5.60€. 02 41 91 24 25.

This fish-breeding centre, located on a lovely site on the banks of the **Étang de Montayer**, enlightens visitors on the river and local efforts to protect its ecosystem. Besides viewing fish typical of the Loire Basin, visitors can watch the various stages involved in the breeding of pike, from the hatching of eggs to the growing of young fry in basins.

A botanical trail reveals the flora characteristic of shores and wetlands. A pretty footpath around the lake-shore is an agreeable way to round off the visit.

Baugé

Baugé, a peaceful town with noble dwellings, is the capital and market town of the surrounding region, a countryside of heaths, forests and vast clearings. There is a good view of the town's ruined walls from rue Foulques-Nerra to the west.

- **Population:** 3 561
- **Michelin Map:** 317: I-3
- **Info:** pl. de l'Europe, 49150 Baugé. ✆02 41 89 18 07. www.tourisme-bauge.fr.st.
- **Location:** Located at the crossroads of the roads to Angers, Saumur, Tours and others, Baugé sits on the right bank of the Couasnon River and borders the lovely Chandelais forest.
- **Parking:** Available at pl. de l'Europe, near the château.
- **Don't Miss:** The finely crafted cross of Anjou, set with precious stones.
- **Timing**: Allow 1hr to see the château and the quiet streets of the town.

A BIT OF HISTORY

Founded in 1000 by **Fulk Nerra**, Baugé became one of the favourite residences of Yolanda of Aragon, Queen of Sicily, and her son, King René, in the 15C. Yolanda, who was a faithful supporter of Charles VII and Joan of Arc, repulsed the English from Anjou at the battle of Le Vieil-Baugé (1421) in which Sir Guérin de Fontaines distinguished himself at the head of the Angevins and Scottish mercenaries.

CHÂTEAU

Visit by guided tours only (2hrs). Phone for opening hours. 7€. ✆02 41 84 00 74. www.chateaubauge.com.

This 15C building now serves as a tourist office and museum (collections of weapons, porcelain and old coins). In 1455 King René himself supervised the building of the turrets, dormer windows and the oratory as well as the bartizan on the rear façade, where the master masons are portrayed. An ogee-arched doorway gives access to the **spiral staircase** which terminates with a magnificent palm tree vault, decorated with the Anjou-Sicily coat of arms and other emblems: angels, tau crosses (T-shaped), symbols of the cross of Christ and stars which, in the Apocalypse, represent the souls of the blessed in eternity.

Chapelle des Filles-du-Cœur-de-Marie

Visit by guided tours only Wed-Mon 2.30–4.30pm. Closed according to the needs of the community. ✆02 41 89 12 20.

Formerly part of an 18C hospice, the chapel now houses a particularly valuable piece of treasure, the **Cross of Anjou★★**. With two transoms (the upper one carried the inscription), it is also known as the Cross of Jerusalem, and was venerated as a piece of the Cross of Christ by the dukes of Anjou, in particular by King René.

At the end of the 15C after the Battle of Nancy in which René II, Duke of Lorraine, a descendant of the dukes of Anjou, defeated Charles the Bold, the Lorraine troops adopted the Cross of Anjou as their own symbol in order to recognize one another in battle. It became known henceforward as the Cross of Lorraine. It is supposed to be made from a piece of the True Cross, brought back from the Holy Land after the crusade in 1241; it is a marvel of the goldsmith's craft, set with precious stones and fine pearls and was created at the end of the 14C for Louis, first Duke of Anjou, by his brother Charles V's Parisian goldsmith.

Hôtel-Dieu

r. Anne-de-Melun. Phone for opening times. Guided tours every hour (last visit 5.30pm). 6€ (children 11–16 years 2.50€), combined ticket with château and museum available. ✆02 41 84 00 74.

Part of the vast hospital building is open to the public. The Hôtel-Dieu was founded in 1639 by Marthe de la Beausse, helped by Princess Anne de Melun and the Hospitaller Sisters from La Flèche. Don't miss the **apothecary★** which is unchanged since it was set up in 1675. Carefully stored away among the Louis XIII walnut and oak surrounds are over 600 painted boxes, Nevers earthen ware pots and 16C Italian-Moorish jars containing crayfish eyes, stag horns, powdered beetle and other medicines. Before reaching the Baroque chapel, cross through the main infirmary dor mitory to see the "Care for the body; care for the soul" exhibition. Other quiet streets of old Baugé are lined with noble mansions (*hôtels*) with high doorways: rue de l'Église, rue de la Girouardière and place de la Croix-Orée.

DRIVING TOUR

Baugeois Region

82km/51mi – about 3hrs. Leave Baugé on D 141 E along the Couasnon Valley.

Dolmen de la Pierre couverte

Leave the car at the side of the road 3.5km/2mi from Baugé. Some steps on the left lead to the dolmen standing in a forest clearing.

Return to the car and take D 141 towards Pontigné.

Pontigné

The **church** (St Denis) is crowned by an unusual twisting spiral bell-tower. Inside, Angevin vaulting covers the nave whereas the capitals of the transept present monstrous heads and water-lily leaf motifs and the charming central apse is supported by a complex network of radiating tori.

Take the road behind the church; turn right onto D 766 which offers a fine view of the orchards in the valley. Bear left and then turn right towards Bocé.

Forêt de Chandelais★

This is a magnificent state-owned forest, covering 800ha/2 000 acres. The splendid fully grown oak and beech trees are replanted every 210 years.

Follow the forest road to the central crossroads before turning right towards Bocé. Turn left on reaching D 58.

Mouliherne

Mouliherne stands on a rock on the north bank of the Riverolle, at the heart of the Baugé region. The quiet, peaceful atmosphere of the area makes it ideal for bicycle rides.

The **church** is all that remains of a fortress belonging to the counts of Anjou; built on a mound, it has a beautiful square 13C bell-tower with splayed windows and a twisting spire typical of the Baugé region.

Linières-Bouton

5km/3mi E on D 62.

This is a quiet village just off the main road. The church has a beautiful **chancel** built in the Plantagenet style.

Turn left onto D 767 then follow a road to the right which leads to Breil.

Breil

The path to Breil through Baugeois Woods makes a pleasant walk.

The semicircular apse and the tall stone spire of the **church** are characteristically Romanesque exterior features; note the Plantagenet vaulting in the chancel.

Parc et château de Lathan

Open Easter–Oct Wed–Mon 10am–6pm. 3€. 02 41 82 31 00.

Opposite the church stands a double formal park dating from the 17C. It features charming arbours, a long sweep of green lawn adorned with clipped yews and a double avenue of lime trees. There is a delightful view along the ornamental canal to an elegant 18C gazebo.

Follow D 62 until you reach D 938 then turn right.

Cuon
Behind the church with the curious conical spire is a charming 15C manor house. Opposite the church an old inn still bears the inscription *"Au Soleil d'Or"* (The Golden Sun) where travellers on foot or on horseback could find lodging.

From Cuon; road to Chartrené.

The wooded park on the left marks the site of the Château de la Grafinière.

Beyond Chartrené turn left onto D 60. After 4.5km/3mi follow D 211 to the right, crossing heaths and woodlands, to reach Fontaine-Guérin.

Fontaine-Guérin
The belfry of the heavily restored Romanesque **church** is crowned by a twisting spire. The road D 211 towards St-Georges-du-Bois leads to an artificial lake with facilities for swimming, sailboarding and picnicking.

From St-Georges-du-Bois, follow D 59 to Jarzé.

Jarzé-en-Baugeois
The countryside around Jarzé is divided between pasture, crops and woodland. The castle was built in 1500, burnt down in 1794 and restored in the 19C.
The **church** was first a collegiate church built in the Flamboyant Gothic style on the foundations of an 11C building. The seigneurial chapel is covered with lierne and tierceron vaulting. The 16C stalls in the chancel are decorated with amusing carvings.

2.5km/1.2mi on D 82 towards La Flèche; take the first turn on the right.

Chapelle Notre-Dame-de-Montplacé
Guided tours Jul–Aug Sun pm. Call in advance. 02 41 95 40 03.
The chapel, standing in splendid isolation on its bluff, can be seen from some way off. The neighbouring farm buildings add a touch of simplicity to its elegant appearance.

Follow D 82, road to La Flèche.

Cheviré-le-Rouge
Set the middle of the village, the **Église St-Médard** is of note for its 11C spire. The chancel vaulting (12C) is a remarkable example of the Plantagenet style. Changing exhibition in the transept.

Continue along D 82 towards La Flèche.

Jardins du château de Gastine
The gardens designed by Louis Benech give a majestic backdrop to the château (16C–18C) with a box terrace planted with yews, roses, lavender and Japanese anemones. Other features include ponds and fountains, clipped hornbeam hedges, and beds of dwarf bamboo.

Go back along D 82 to drive into Fougeré.

Fougeré
Fougeré takes its name from the French word for fern, *fougère*, but is better known for its twisted spire. The **Église St-Étienne** (11C) features one of the most beautiful chevets in the region and the 13C chancel is pure Plantagenet style. The nave vaulting (16C) was repainted by Grandin de Tours in 1871. Note the engouled beams with monsters' heads and, outside, (place de la Mairie), the graffiti (11C–12C).

Leave Fougeré on D 138 and drive to St-Quentin-lès-Beaurepaire. Turn right towards Vaulandry. At the junction with D 938, turn right towards Baugé. From Baugé, follow signs for Le Vieil-Baugé

Le Vieil-Baugé
The old village crowns a hilltop overlooking the Couasnon Valley.
Notice the slender twisted spire of **Église St-Symphorien** which leans as a result of the distortion of the internal wooden framework. The nave is partially 11C and the handsome **chancel★** is 13C with Angevin vaulting.

ANJOU AND THE MAUGES COUNTRY

The delightful pace of life enjoyed in the region is perfectly encapsulated in the expression *Douceur Angevine*, the gentler side of living, with its beautiful countryside, historic and vibrant towns, rich cultural and artistic activities, clement weather, outstanding food and wine, and limitless opportunities for leisure pursuits. The ancient province of Anjou is the birthplace of the Plantagenet dynasty whose princes, at different times, reigned in England, Hungary, Naples, Provence and Jerusalem. And the region is still important today as a major hub of economic and industrial activities, services and education with 33 000 students enrolled at the University of Angers.

Tapestry Masterpiece

If you see only one thing in Angers then it has to be the Tapestry of the Apocalypse, a wondrous medieval work of art of unrivalled finesse that puts the Bayeux Tapestry into the shade in terms of its sheer scale and breathtaking beauty. Around the historical district of the castle, the town is a bustling modern business centre. Outside Angers, the region boasts some of the Loire's more striking noble residences with the Châteaux de Plessis-Macé, rebuilt in the 15C after the ravages of the Hundred Years War on the ruins of the original 11C fortress, and the Châteaux de Serrant, a superb moated Renaissance and 17C edifice which is renowned for its magnificent library containing more than 12 000 books.

Anjou's famous *art de vivre* is best appreciated in the countryside on a driving tour through the Vallée du Layon, a landscape of vineyards, orchards and windmills, and in the excellent Côteaux-du-Layon sweet white wines. Les Mauges, the southernmost part of Anjou, and the town of Cholet tell a dark chapter in the history of France and the terrible events of the Vendée War during the Revolution. Some remarkable stained-glass windows in the region's churches evoke the many massacres that were perpetrated as Revolutionary troops (Blues) fought Royalist insurgents (Whites). On a lighter note, the region counts the largest concentration of troglodyte dwellings in Europe as hundreds of homes have been carved out in disused tufa quarries.

Highlights

1. **Angers**, city of tapestry (p252)
2. Anjou theatre festival at **Château du Plessis-Macé** (p266)
3. The library at **Château de Serrant** (p268)
4. Driving through the vineyards of the **Vallée du Layon** (p268)
5. Musée du Textile, **Cholet** (p270)

Tapestry of the Apocalypse, Château d'Angers

O. Forir/MICHELIN

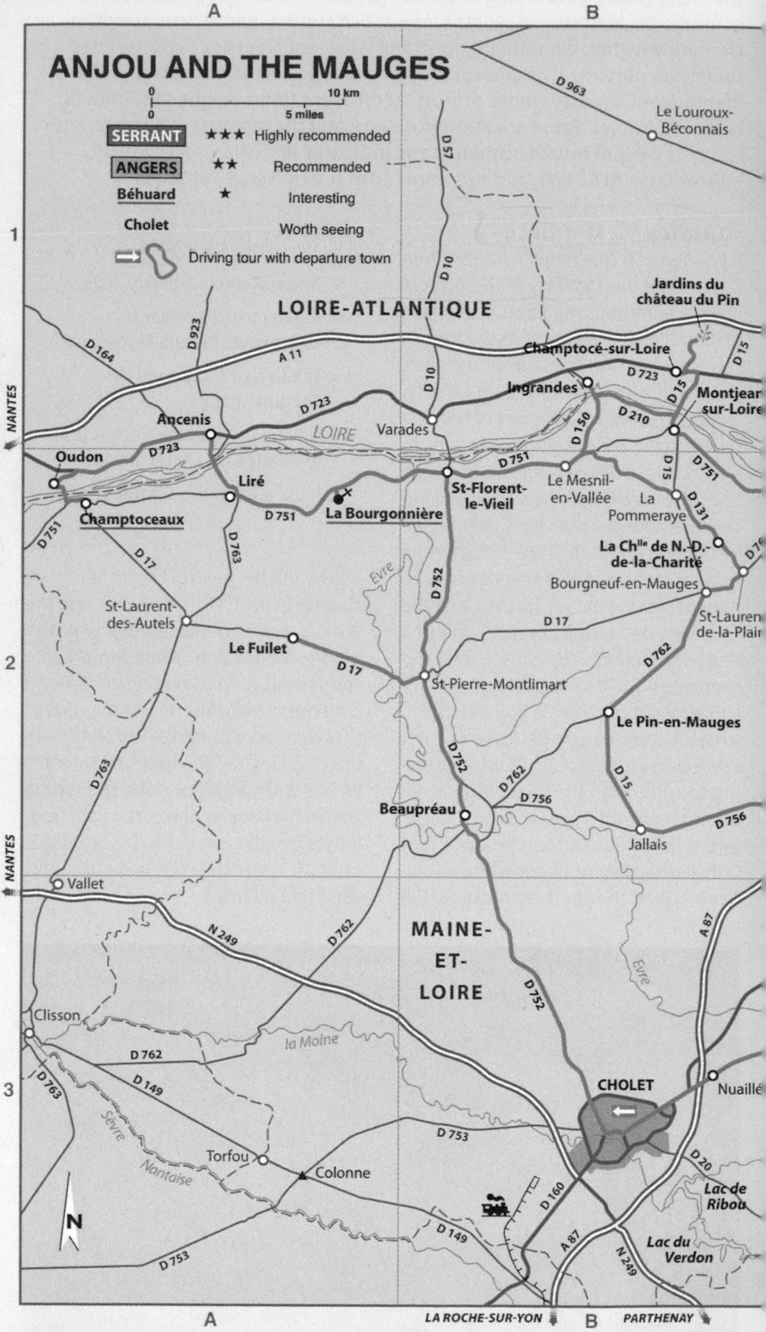
ANJOU AND THE MAUGES
0 10 km
0 5 miles
SERRANT ★★★ Highly recommended
ANGERS ★★ Recommended
Béhuard ★ Interesting
Cholet Worth seeing
Driving tour with departure town
LOIRE-ATLANTIQUE
MAINE-ET-LOIRE
Le Louroux-Béconnais
Jardins du château du Pin
Champtocé-sur-Loire
Ingrandes
Montjean-sur-Loire
Ancenis
Varades
LOIRE
Oudon
Liré
La Bourgonnière
St-Florent-le-Vieil
Le Mesnil-en-Vallée
La Pommeraye
Champtoceaux
La Chlle de N.-D.-de-la-Charité
Bourgneuf-en-Mauges
St-Laurent-des-Autels
Le Fuilet
St-Pierre-Montlimart
Le Pin-en-Mauges
Beaupréau
Jallais
Vallet
Clisson
la Moine
Torfou
Colonne
Sèvre Nantaise
CHOLET
Nuaillé
Lac de Ribou
Lac du Verdon
NANTES
NANTES
LA ROCHE-SUR-YON
PARTHENAY
Evre
N

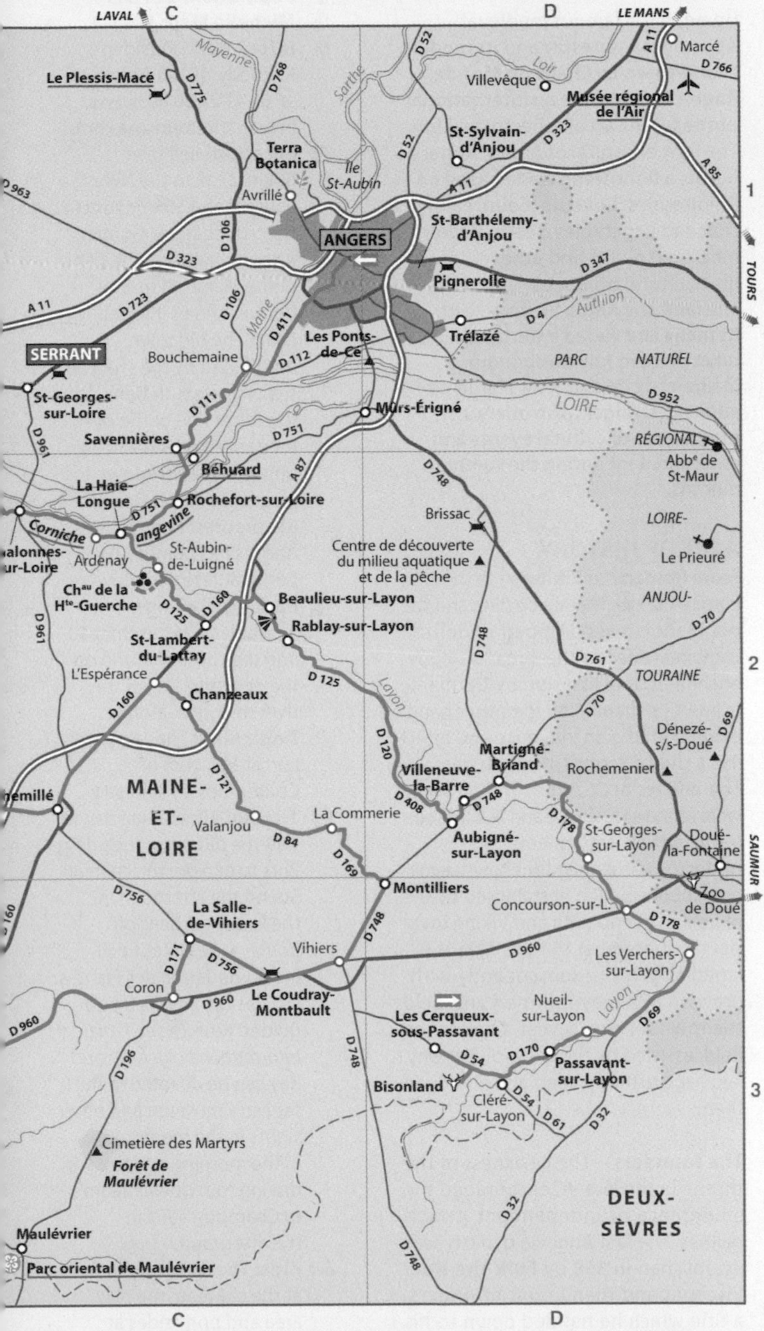

LAVAL
C
D
LE MANS
Le Plessis-Macé
Mayenne
D 775
D 768
Sarthe
D 52
Loir
Villevêque
Marcé
D 766
A 11
Musée régional de l'Air
Terra Botanica
Île St-Aubin
St-Sylvain-d'Anjou
D 323
A 85
D 963
Avrillé
A 11
St-Barthélemy-d'Anjou
ANGERS
D 106
D 323
D 347
TOURS
Pignerolle
A 11
D 723
Maine
D 411
Authion
D 4
Les Ponts-de-Cé
Trélazé
SERRANT
Bouchemaine
D 112
PARC
NATUREL
St-Georges-sur-Loire
D 111
Mûrs-Érigné
LOIRE
D 952
D 961
Savennières
D 751
RÉGIONAL
Abbe de St-Maur
Béhuard
A 87
D 748
La Haie-Longue
Rochefort-sur-Loire
D 751
angevine
Brissac
LOIRE-
Corniche
Chalonnes-sur-Loire
Ardenay
St-Aubin-de-Luigné
Centre de découverte du milieu aquatique et de la pêche
Le Prieuré
Chau de la Hte-Guerche
D 160
D 125
Beaulieu-sur-Layon
ANJOU-
Rablay-sur-Layon
D 961
St-Lambert-du-Lattay
D 748
D 70
D 125
D 761
TOURAINE
L'Espérance
Layon
D 160
Chanzeaux
D 70
D 69
D 120
Dénezé-s/s-Doué
Martigné-Briand
Rochemenier
MAINE-ET-LOIRE
D 121
Villeneuve-la-Barre
Chemillé
D 748
D 408
D 178
St-Georges-sur-Layon
Valanjou
La Commerie
Aubigné-sur-Layon
Doué-la-Fontaine
D 84
SAUMUR
D 169
Montilliers
D 756
Zoo de Doué
La Salle-de-Vihiers
Concourson-sur-L.
D 178
D 160
D 748
D 171
D 756
Vihiers
D 960
Les Verchers-sur-Layon
Coron
Le Coudray-Montbault
D 960
D 960
Nueil-sur-Layon
Layon
Les Cerqueux-sous-Passavant
D 69
D 196
D 748
D 54
D 170
Passavant-sur-Layon
Bisonland
Cléré-sur-Layon
D 54
D 61
D 32
Cimetière des Martyrs
Forêt de Maulévrier
DEUX-SÈVRES
D 32
Maulévrier
D 748
Parc oriental de Maulévrier
C
D
1
2
3

Angers★★

Home to the famous medieval Apocalypse tapestry and its modern counterpart, Le Chant du Monde, Angers has become an international centre for the art of tapestry making. The former capital of Anjou, Angers boasts a flourishing trade based on Anjou wines, liqueurs (Cointreau), fruit and vegetables, seeds, flowers, medicinal plants and other horticultural products.
The fantastic Anjou Festival, with its many and varied entertainments takes place in July throughout Maine-et-Loire and draws large audiences. Angers also offers a programme of cultural events and entertainment during the summer months.

- **Population:** 226 843
- **Michelin Map:** 317: F-4
- **Info:** 7 pl. du Président Kennedy, 49100 Angers. ☎02 41 23 50 00. www.angersloiretourisme.com.
- **Location:** Just over 60km/37mi to the NW of Saumur and 50km/31mi to the S of Château-Gontier, Angers stands on the banks of the Maine, 8km/5mi before it flows into the Loire. The old town, dominated by the château, sits on the south bank. On the other side of the river, modern Angers is a lively university town known for its quality of life. One of the prettiest French cities, Angers has numerous parks, ablaze with flowers.
- **Parking:** Parking is available near the château and the cathedral, and on the opposite side of the river near quai Monge.
- **Don't Miss:** The Jean-Lurçat Museum of Contemporary Tapestry.
- **Timing:** Allow a half day to visit the old town, including 2hrs to explore the château. Spend the afternoon in the lovely gardens off Boulevard du Mal. Foch, including Jardin des Plantes. Or, you can always take a guided tour (see *Practical Information box*). A second day can be devoted to the tapestry museum and other sights in the modern city in the morning and the 4hr driving tour downstream to Champtoceaux in the afternoon.
- **Kids:** The discovery tour at the château, the play area and pony rides at the Jardin du Mail.

A BIT OF HISTORY

From Romans to Vikings – In the Late Empire the city fell into decline and the population level dropped under the combined effect of the threat of impoverishment, and invasion by Germanic tribes. Christianity, on the other hand, continued to gain influence and in AD 453 a church council met in Angers. The abbeys of St-Aubin and St-Serge were founded in the 6C and 7C and soon attracted new settlements.
Under the Carolingians the town recovered, but was soon destabilised by the revolts of the nobility and Viking invasions. In December 854 the Vikings pillaged Angers but subsequently withdrew. In 872 they returned and held the town for over a year. Charles the Bald, assisted by the Duke of Brittany, laid siege to the invaders and dislodged them.

The founders – The weakness of the throne in the late 9C encouraged the emergence of independent principalities. The first Angevin dynasty was established in 898 by **Fulk the Red**, Viscount and then Count of Angers, a title which he handed down to his descendants.

Fulk II the Good extended his territory into Maine showing scant regard for the King of France, delicate Louis IV of Outre-Mer, whom he openly despised.

Fulk Nerra and his successors – The rise of the Angevin dynasty to the height of its power in the 11C and 12C was due to its members' exceptional political skill, uninhibited by any scruples, remarkable ability in warfare and keen eye for alliances through marriage.

Fulk III Nerra's son Geoffrey II (1040–60) continued his father's work consolidating the conquest of Maine and Touraine. The succession was divided between his two nephews who lost no time in quarrelling. **Fulk IV the Morose** finally gained the upper hand over Geoffrey III, at the cost of the Saintonge, Maine and Gâtinais, which he was too lazy to try to recover. In 1092 his second wife, the young and beautiful Bertrade de Monfort, was seduced, abducted and married by King Philip I.

For this scandalous behaviour the King was excommunicated (*see BEAUGENCY*). The family's fortunes were salvaged by Geoffrey IV Martel, killed in 1106, and most of all by **Fulk V the Younger** (1109–31), who took advantage of Anglo-French rivalry and made judicious marriage alliances. He recovered Maine through his own marriage in 1109; later on, with the family's approval, he married his two daughters to the Kings of France and England. His greatest success was the marriage in 1128 of his son Geoffrey to Mathilda of England, heir to Henry I and widow of the German Emperor Henry V. His ultimate achievement concerned himself: in 1129, by then a widower, he married Melisand, daughter of Baldwin II and heir to the kingdom of Jerusalem.

Geoffrey V (1131–51), known as Plantagenet because he wore a sprig of broom *(genêt)* in his hair, ruled with a rod of iron over Greater Anjou (Anjou, Touraine and Maine) and tried to exercise his wife's rights over Normandy (annexed in 1144), and England, where Stephen of Blois had been King since 1135.

PRACTICAL INFORMATION

TOURS Discover Angers' art and history *(2hrs)*. For information and reservations, contact the tourist office.

Plantagenets and Capets – In 1152 **Henry Plantagenet**, son of Geoffrey and Mathilda, married Eleanor of Aquitaine whom Louis VII had recently divorced. He already held Anjou, Maine, Touraine and Normandy; by his marriage he acquired Poitou, Périgord, the Limoges and Angoulême regions, Saintonge, Gascony and suzerainty of the Auvergne and the County of Toulouse. In 1153 he forced Stephen of Blois to recognise him as his heir and the following year succeeded him on the throne of England. He was then more powerful than his Capet rival. Henry II of England spent most of his time in France, often at Angers.

Successive Anjou dynasties (13C–15C) – During the regency of Blanche of Castille, Anjou was again lost as a result of the barons' revolt when Pierre de Dreux surrendered the province to Henry III. Taking advantage of a truce in 1231 Blanche and her son Louis began to build the fortress of Angers.

Anjou returned to the Capet sphere of influence and in 1246 St Louis gave it, together with Maine, to his younger brother Charles as an apanage. In 1258 it was confirmed as a French possession by the Treaty of Paris. In 1360 Anjou was raised to a duchy by John the Good for his son Louis. From the 13C to the 15C Anjou was governed by the direct line of Capet princes and then by the Valois. The beginning and end of this period were marked by two outstanding personalities, Charles I and King René.

Charles of Anjou – Charles was an unusual character: deeply religious and wildly ambitious. At the request of the Pope, he conquered Sicily and the Kingdom of Naples and established his influence over the Italian peninsula. Intoxicated with success, he dreamt of adding the Holy Land, Egypt and Constantinople

Fulk the Terrible

Fulk III Nerra (987–1040) was the most formidable of a line of feudal masters. Hot-blooded and aggressive, he was always waging war to extend his territory; he obtained Saintonge, annexed Les Mauges, extended his boundaries to Blois and Châteaudun, captured Langeais and Tours (he was expelled from the latter by Robert the Pious), intervened in the Vendômois, took Saumur, etc. Ambitious, predatory, covetous, brutal and criminally violent, Fulk Nerra (the Black – owing to his very dark complexion) was typical of the great feudal lord in the year 1000. Every so often he would have sudden fits of Christian humility and penitence when he would shower gifts on churches and abbeys or take up the pilgrim's staff and depart for Jerusalem. He also built many fortresses along the Loire.

to his conquests, but the Sicilian Vespers awoke him rudely to reality: on Easter Monday 1282 the Sicilians revolted and massacred 6 000 Frenchmen, half of whom were Angevins.

Good King René – The last of the dukes was Good King René – titular monarch of Sicily. He had one of the most cultivated minds of his day, having mastered Latin, Greek, Italian, Hebrew and Catalan. He also painted and wrote poetry, played and composed music and was knowledgeable about mathematics, geology and law. He was an easygoing, informal ruler who liked to talk to his subjects; he organised popular festivities and revived the old games of the age of chivalry. He loved flower gardens and introduced the carnation and the Provins rose.

At the age of 12 he married Isabelle de Lorraine and was devoted to her for 33 years until her death, shortly after which, at the age of 47, he married Jeanne de Laval, who was only 21.

Towards the end of his life René accepted the annexation of Anjou by Louis XI philosophically. As he was also Count of Provence he left Angers and ended his days in Aix-en-Provence at the age of 72 (1480).

Henri IV to the present – The Wars of Religion took on a bitter twist at Angers, where there was a strongly entrenched Calvinist church; a dispute on 14 October 1560 brought death to numerous townspeople. Thereafter, confrontations grew more frequent and in 1572 the town had its own St Barthlomew's Day Massacre.

It was at the Château d'Angers in 1598 that Henri IV finally brought the fomenting discontent of the Catholic League to an end by promising his son **César** *(see VENDÔME)* to Françoise de Lorraine, daughter of the Duc de Mercœur, the leader of the Catholic party. The promise of marriage was signed on 5 April, when the future bride and groom were six and three years old. A week later the Edict of Nantes came into force; the Protestants had obtained freedom of worship.

In 1652, although held by the forces of the Fronde, Angers had to submit to Mazarin; in 1657 the town lost its right to elect local magistrates. After his arrest in Nantes, Louis XIV's Finance Minister, **Fouquet**, spent three weeks in the château in the governor's apartments, guarded by d'Artagnan. By then the town numbered 25 000 inhabitants and was only slightly industrialised.

At the outbreak of the Revolution in 1789, Angers declared enthusiastically for the reformers. The cathedral was sacked and turned into a Temple of Reason.

In 1793 the defection of the Girondin administration allowed the Royalist Vendée party to capture the town between 20 June and 4 July. The Republicans lost no time in retaking it and the Terror claimed many victims.

In the early 19C Angers dozed until awakened by the arrival of the railway line from Paris to Nantes: the station was opened in 1849 by Louis Napoleon. Modern development had begun and, apart from a lull early in the 20C, it has continued to expand in recent decades.

VISIT

Château★★★

Open May–Aug 9.30am–6.30pm; rest of year 10am–5.30pm; last admission 45min before closing. Closed 1 Jan, 1 May, 1 and 11 Nov, 25 Dec. 7.50€. 02 41 86 48 77. www.monum.fr.

The **fortress**, which incorporates the former Plantagenet fief, was built by St Louis between 1228 and 1238 and is a fine specimen of feudal architecture in dark schist alternating with courses of white stone. The castle moats are now laid out as splendid gardens.

The towers were originally one or two storeys taller and crowned with pepper-pot roofs and machicolations. They were reduced to the level of the curtain walls under Henri III during the Wars of Religion. The original order had been to demolish the fortress entirely, but the governor simply removed the tops of the towers and laid down terraces.

From the top of the highest tower, **Tour du Moulin**, on the north corner, there are **views**★ over the town, the cathedral towers and St-Aubin, the banks of the Maine and the gardens laid out at the foot of the castle, and, in the castle precincts, the series of towers on the curtain wall, the sophisticated design of the gardens, the chapel and the **Logis royal** (Royal Apartments), residence of the dukes of Anjou in the 15C.

Follow the **rampart walk** along the east side where a charming medieval garden is laid out w[…] and hollyhocks gr[…] near a vine like th[…] loved to plant.

Apocalypse Tapestry★★★

Open same hours as the château.

Housed in a gallery especially designed to ensure maximum preservation conditions, this legendary tapestry is the oldest, apart from the Bayeux Tapestry, to survive until the present. It was commissioned for Duke Louis I of Anjou and probably made in Paris at the workshops of Robert Poinçon between 1373 and 1383, after cartoons by Hennequin of Bruges, based on an illuminated manuscript belonging to King Charles V. It was subsequently hung in the courtyard of the bishop's palace in Arles to celebrate the marriage of Louis II of Anjou to Yolande of Aragon in 1400.

Donated to Angers Cathedral by Good King René (d. 1480), it was often displayed during religious festivities up to the late 18C, when it fell into oblivion. However, Joubert, one of the cathedral canons, had it restored between 1843 and 1870.

Originally 133m/436ft long and 6m/20ft high, it consisted of six sections of equal size, each featuring a main character seated under a canopy, eyes turned towards two rows of seven pictures, whose alternating red and blue backgrounds form a chequered design.

Château d'Angers

© Liane Matrisch/Dreamstime.com

ANGERS

WHERE TO STAY

- Chambre d'hôte du Domaine des Chesnaies......... ①
- Chambre d'hôte La Béchalière......................... ④
- Chambre d'hôte La Rousselière....................... ⑦
- Chambre d'hôte Le Grand Talon...................... ⑩
- Château de Noirieux.................. ⑪
- Gîte de charme La Pointerolle.... ⑫
- Grand Hôtel de la Gare.............. ⑬
- Hôtel d'Anjou Best Western....... ⑭
- Hôtel de France........................ ⑮
- Hôtel Cavier.............................. ⑯
- Hôtel de Champagne................. ⑰
- Hôtel Le Continental.................. ⑲
- Hôtel Le Progrès........................ ㉒
- Hôtel Mail.................................. ㉕

WHERE TO EAT

- Chez Rémi.................................. ①
- Le Crèmet d'Anjou...................... ②
- L'Hoirie...................................... ④
- Le Favre d'Anne......................... ⑤
- La Ferme.................................... ⑦
- Le Grand Jardin.......................... ⑧
- Le Napoli.................................... ⑨
- Le Petit Comptoir....................... ⑩
- Le Relais..................................... ⑬
- Le Théâtre.................................. ⑯
- La Villa Toussaint....................... ⑱
- Ma Campagne.............................. ⑳
- Provence Caffé........................... ㉒
- Une Île.. ㉔

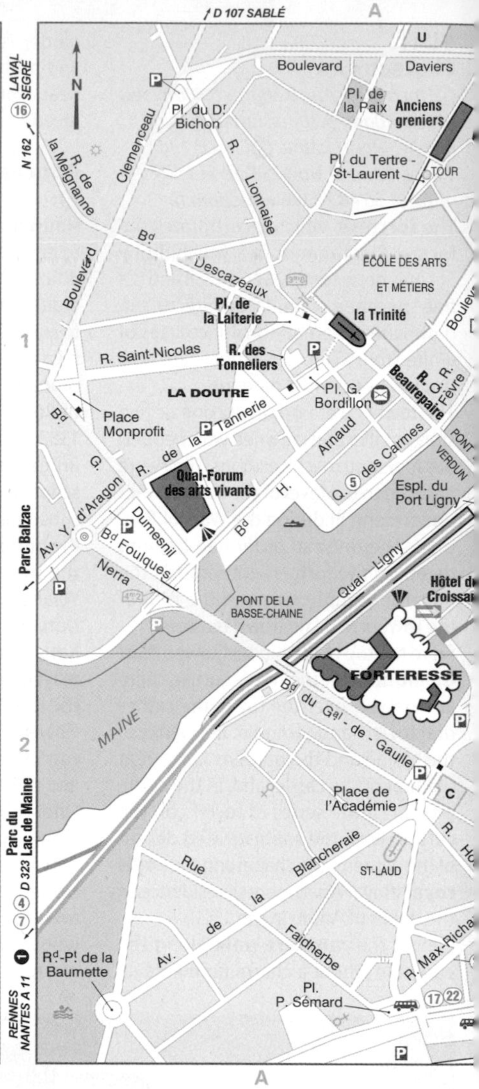

Chapel and Royal Apartments

These 15C buildings, which house the chapel and Royal Apartments, stand inside the rampart wall. In the vast and well-lit chapel, note the finely sculpted Gothic leaves of the door, the small separate ducal chapel with its fireplace and, on a keystone, a representation of the Anjou cross (*see BAUGÉ*). The adjoining staircase, the work of King René, leads to the upper floor of the apartments.

Passion and Mille-fleurs tapestries★★

The Royal Apartments house a beautiful collection of 15C and 16C tapestries including the four hangings of the late-15C **Passion tapestry**, which are wonderfully rich in colour, and several mille-fleurs tapestries. Among these is the tapestry entitled **Angels Carrying the Instruments of the Passion**, which is unusual in that it has a religious theme, the admirable 16C **Lady at the Organ** and a fragment showing **Penthesilea**,

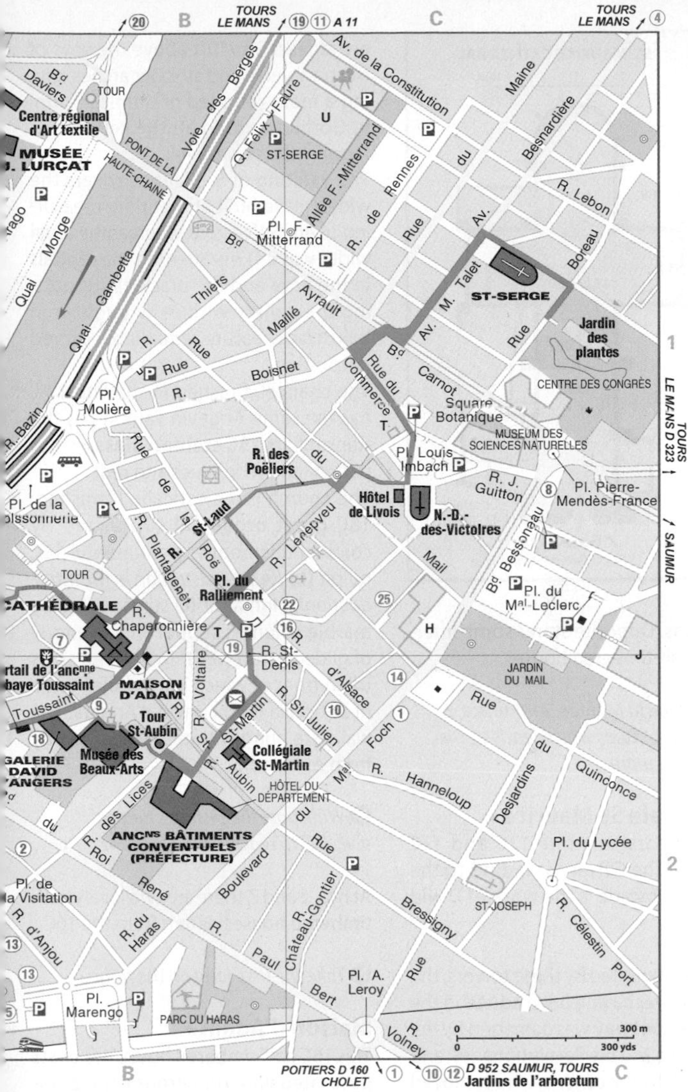

the Queen of the Amazons, from a hanging of the Nine Heroines, women with chivalrous virtues.

WALKING TOUR

OLD TOWN★

Allow a half day.

Walking through the streets of the old town is like visiting an open-air museum. If the weather is nice, you can enjoy a pleasant break for a picnic lunch in the Jardin des Plantes.

Start from the château entrance and take the narrow r. St-Aignan.

Hôtel du Croissant

This 15C mansion, with mullion windows and ogee arches, housed the registrar of the Order of the Crescent (Ordre du Croissant), a military and religious chivalrous order founded by King René. The blazon on the façade bears the coat of arms of St Maurice, patron of the order, a 4C Christian legionary put to death because he refused to kill his fellow

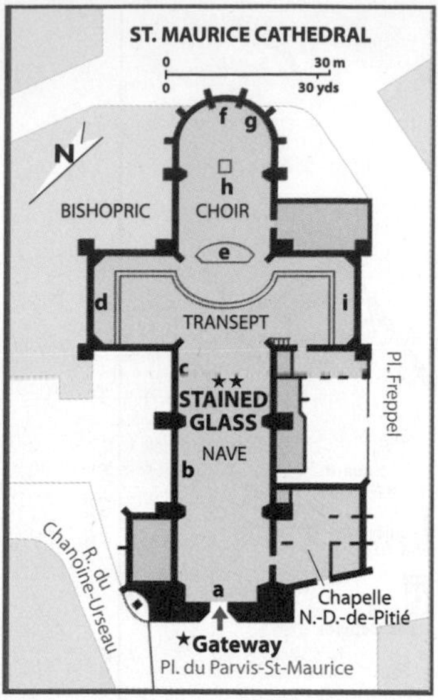

Christians. Opposite stand some interesting half-timbered houses.

Continue to Montée St-Maurice, a long flight of steps which leads to the cathedral square.

Cathédrale St-Maurice★

The cathedral is a fine 12C and 13C building. The Calvary standing to the left of the façade is the work of David d'Angers.

Façade

This is surmounted by three towers, the central tower having been added in the 16C. The **doorway** was damaged by the Protestants and the Revolutionaries, and in the 18C by the canons, who removed the central pier and the lintel to make way for processions.

Above at the third-storey level are eight niches containing roughly carved, bearded figures in 16C military uniforms: St Maurice and his companions.

Interior

The single nave is roofed with one of the earliest examples of Gothic vaulting, which originated in Anjou in the mid-12C. This transitional style, known as Angevin or Plantagenet vaulting, has the characteristic feature that the keystones of the diagonal (ogive) arches are at least 3m/10ft above the keys of the transverse and stringer arches, giving a more rounded or domical form. In Gothic vaulting all the keys are at roughly the same level.

The vaulting of St-Maurice covers the widest nave built at that time measuring 16.4m/54ft across, whereas the usual width was 9–12m/30–40ft; the capitals in the nave and the brackets supporting the gallery with its wrought-iron balustrade feature remarkable carved decoration.

The chancel, finished in the late 12C, has the same Angevin vaulting as the transept. Its **13C stained glass**★★ has particularly vivid blues and reds.

The church is majestically furnished: 18C great organ **(a)** supported by colossal telamones, monumental 19C pulpit **(b)** (*see illustration in the Introduction*), high altar **(c)** surmounted by marble columns supporting a canopy of gilded wood (18C), 18C carved stalls **(d)** in front of which is a marble statue of St Cecilia **(e)** by David d'Angers. The walls are hung with tapestries, mostly from Aubusson.

Walk past the Bishop's Palace (Évêché) to reach r. de l'Oisellerie.

At nos. 5 and 7, there are two lovely half-timbered houses dating from the 16C.

Take the first road on the right.

Maison d'Adam★

This 16C half-timbered house has posts decorated with numerous carved figures. It owes its name to the apple tree which appears to hold up the corner turret and which was flanked by statues of Adam and Eve until the Revolution.

Continue along r. Toussaint.

No. 37 has a Classical doorway, once the entrance to the **abbey of Toussaint** (All Saints); it leads to an elegant courtyard flanked by a turret on a squinch.

Walk back and follow r. du Musée.

Galerie David-d'Angers★

33 bis r. Toussaint. Phone for opening times. 4€. 02 41 05 38 00. Guided tours (90min) by request. 02 41 05 38 38. www.musees-angers.fr.

The gallery in this restored 13C abbey church houses the vast majority of plaster casts donated by the sculptor **David d'Angers** (1788–1856) to his native town.

The well-displayed collection comprises monumental statues (King René, Gutenberg, Jean Bart, Larrey), funerary monuments (e.g. of General Bonchamps whose tomb is in the church of **St-Florent-le-Vieil**), busts of famous authors and medallions in bronze depicting contemporary figures.

Musée des Beaux-Arts★★ (Logis Barrault)

Phone for opening times. 4€. 02 41 05 38 00. www.musees-angers.fr.

This beautiful late-15C residence housing a **Fine Arts Museum** was built by Olivier Barrault, the King's Secretary, Treasurer to the Brittany States and Mayor of Angers. In the 17C it was taken over by the seminary, whose pupils included **Talleyrand** (*see VALENÇAY*), the future Bishop of Autun.

On the first floor are collections belonging to the Archaeological Museum, evoking the history of Anjou from the 12C to the 14C, including the 16C terracotta **Virgin of Tremblay**.

The second floor is devoted to paintings: lovely Primitive works, two remarkable small portraits of Charles IX as a young man and Catherine de' Medici after Clouet; 17C paintings and, above all, works of the 18C and 19C French School. There are also canvases by the local painters Lenepveu and Bodinier, and pastels *(separate room)* by Alexis Axilette, who was born in Durtal.

Tour St-Aubin

This is the belfry (12C) of the former St-Aubin monastery, a wealthy Benedictine abbey founded in the 6C. The tower takes its name from St Aubin, Bishop of Angers (538–50), who was buried here.

Monastery buildings★

pl. Michel-Debré. Open Mon–Fri 9am–5.30pm. No charge. 02 41 81 49 49. www.cg49.fr.

The abbey buildings, extensively restored in the 17C and 18C, presently house local government offices. On the left side of the courtyard is a glazed-in **Romanesque arcade**★★, part of the cloisters, with sculptures of remarkably refined craftsmanship. The door with sculpted arch mouldings led to the chapter house; the arcades support a gallery from which those monks who had no voice in the chapter could listen to the proceedings.

Take r. St-Martin.

Collégiale St-Martin

23 r. St-Martin. Open daily Jun–Sept 10am–7pm; Oct–May daily except Mon 1–6pm. Closed 1 Jan, 1 and 8 May, 1 and 11 Nov, 25 Dec. 3€ (children under 18 years no charge). Citypass audioguide in 5 languages included in the ticket price. 02 41 81 16 00. www.collegiale-saint-martin.fr.

The first church was built on this site in the 5C, outside the city walls. The nave is one of the few remaining examples in France of Carolingian architecture on a large scale. Vaulting was added to the transept crossing by Fulk Nerra (11C) and the Angevine Gothic chancel was added in the 12C, doubling the length of the church. Forty religious artefacts illustrate terracotta techniques of the Angevine and Le Mans schools (17C). There is a permanent exhibition which tells the history of the collegiate church.

Take r. St-Denis to reach pl. du Ralliement.

Place du Ralliement

This lively square is the centre of town. Its shops are dominated by the monumental façade of the theatre, embellished with columns and statues.

Hôtel Pincé★

32 bis r. Lenepveu. 02 41 05 38 00. www.musees.angers.fr.

This elegant Renaissance mansion, built for a mayor of Angers and bequeathed to the town in 1861, houses the **musée Turpin de Crissé** (1772–1859). A painter born in Angers and chamberlin to Empress Joséphine, he donated to the town a magnificent collection of exotic artefacts which are on display including Greek and Etruscan vases, ceramics, and Japanese masks and prints.

In r. Lenepveu, take the first left, r. de l'Espine.

St-Laud district

The small rue St-Laud is the axis of a pleasant pedestrian and shopping district, where a number of very old façades can be admired: particularly fine examples include no. 21 rue St-Laud (15C) and no. 9 rue des Poëliers (16C).

Turn right into r. J.-Guitton to the Muséum des sciences naturelles or walk diagonally across pl. Louis-Imbach into r. St-Étienne and r. du Commerce. Cross bd. Carnot.

Muséum des Sciences Naturelles

43 r. Jules-Guitton. Phone for opening times. 4€ (children under18 years no charge). 02 41 05 48 50. www.angers.fr/museum.

Two charming historic buildings in the town centre house this treasure trove of a museum which includes some 700 stuffed animals, 50 000 fossils, 200 000 shells and 2 500 birds.

Take r. St-Étienne and r. du Commerce, then cross bd. Carnot to reach the church of St-Serge.

Église St-Serge★

Until 1802 this was the church of the Benedictine abbey of the same name founded in the 7C. The 13C **chancel**★★ is remarkably wide, elegant and well lit, a perfect example of the Angevin style, with its lierne vaulting descending in feathered clusters onto slender columns. In contrast, the 15C nave seems narrower because of its massive pillars. The high windows at the end are filled with graceful 15C stained glass.

GARDENS★

Jardin des Plantes

Located behind the Centre des Congrès and opposite the old conventual buildings (18C) of St-Serge abbey church, this botanical garden is home to some beautiful, rare species of tree (such as the *Davidia*, or handkerchief tree). There is a pool in the lower part of the garden. Parrots can be heard squawking in the aviary.

Jardin du Mail

bd. de la Résistance-et-de-la-Déportation, opposite the hôtel de ville.

A Neoclassical garden centred on a large fountain and pond. There is a large play area with a roundabout and pony rides for children. The garden is at its best when in full bloom in summer.

Parc de l'Arboretum, le jardin des collections★

7 r. du Château-d'Orgement. Open 8am–dusk. Jardins de l'Arboretum daily except Wed 2–8pm (winter 5.30pm). 02 41 22 53 00.

Southwest of the town centre, this innovative garden is sheltered by the great trees of the Gaston-Allard arboretum (7ha/17 acre Ñ s of oaks, conifers and shrubs). A superb drive lined with different varities of oak leads to the house of the botanist and the park's founder, Gaston Allard (1838–1918). The garden of the senses combines perfume, touch and sight with a range of unusual flowers and fruits including the rare paper mulberry which gives orange fruit in summer. An oculus in the wall allows visitors to peep into the superb **National Hydrangea Collection** *(visits by appointment).*

Parc de Balzac★

Cross the Maine on pont de la Basse-Chaîne and park in the Yolande-d'Aragon car park or Farcy-Balzac car park. Open 8am–8pm (5.30pm winter). No charge. 02 41 22 53 26.

This 50ha/123acre park links the nearby town centre with the Parc de la Maine leisure complex. Along the banks of the Maine, the **floodplains** are typical of the marshlands that lie between here and the Atlantic coast with hedgerows, poplar trees, donkeys and cattle herds. The plains are criss-crossed by raised paths. Slightly set back but still prone to flooding, the **theme areas★** show off more of the gardener's art with flower-rich fields, seedbeds and bird-filled trees. Deeper in the park, the 120 **family allotments ★**, with their pink and blue huts produce fruit and vegetables and are separated by great climbing roses. Conclude your visit with the fascinating **chênaie**, an avenue of 1 100 hybrid oaks and trees from America, China and the rest of the world, whose variety can be seen in the shape of the leaves and the acorns.

Parc St-Nicolas

Les Combes entrance, bd. Lavoisier.
No charge.

Four semi-natural parks form a sort of necklace of greenery along the St-Nicolas pond. They alternate carefully tended walks on the banks with more untamed vegetation on the steeper slopes in the former slate quarries. This unusual park covers 112ha/277 acres in the centre of the town. It also features an animal park which is popular with children.

Parc de la Maine

Access via the riverside road, follow signs for Nantes.

200ha/490 acres of woods and lawns surround the Lac de Maine. The leisure complex (swimming, windsurfing, canoeing, bikes, hiking, tennis, golf driving range, etc.) is a popular attraction with locals at weekends.

NORTH BANK OF THE RIVER MAINE

Musée Jean-Lurçat et de la Tapisserie contemporaine★★

Phone for opening times. 4€.
02 41 05 38 00. www.musees-angers.fr.

This Museum of Contemporary Tapestry is housed in the **Ancien hôpital St-Jean★**, a hospital founded in 1174 by Étienne de Marçay, Seneschal to the Plantagenet King Henry I, which provided treatment and care for the sick until 1854.

The vast hospital ward features Angevin vaulting resting on slender columns; to the right of the entrance is the 17C **dispensary★** with glazed earthenware jars and trivets on wooden shelves. In the central recess stands a splendid pewter vessel (1720) which once contained treacle, an antidote to snake bites. The room is hung with Lurçat's series of tapestries called the **Chant du Monde★★** (Song of the World). **Jean Lurçat** (1892–1966), who was largely responsible for reviving the art of tapestry, had discovered the **Apocalypse Tapestry** *(see p255)* in 1938 and had been profoundly impressed by it, declaring it to be one of the masterpieces of Western art. Nineteen years later he began work on the tapestry series displayed here, his masterpiece. It is coarsely woven and characterised by an almost total lack of perspective and deliberate restriction of the range of colours.

A short distance away, at no 3 boulevard Daviers, the **Centre régional d'Art textile**, which consists of a group of workshops for about 20 warp-weavers, organises tours and courses in the art of tapestry. The weavers here produce remarkable creations, displayed at national and international exhibitions, which can be then bought or hired.

La Doutre★

This district has preserved some fine half-timbered houses: on the pretty **place de la Laiterie**, in rue Beaurepaire which runs from the square to the bridge (particularly at no. 67, the house dated 1582 of apothecary Simon Poisson, adorned with statues), and along rue des Tonneliers. Note also the **Église de La Trinité** (12C), with its 16C belltower, and the **Abbaye du Ronceray,** founded in the 11C with its present buildings dating from the 17C. At no. 23 boulevard Descazeaux, don't miss the **hôtel des Pénitentes**, an elegant mansion with towers and Renaissance dormer windows. Used successively as a refuge, prison and hospice, it owes its name to the community of women who lived here in the 17C and 18C.

Le Quai

The town's new cultural centre comprises three creative structures: the **NTA** (Nouveau Théâtre d'Angers), which stages drama, the **CNDC** (Centre national de danse contemporaine), a school of modern dance, and **Open-Arts** which focuses on the circus, visual and street art in addition to music.

The ground floor forum hosts temporary exhibitions. The roof terrace gives superb **views** of the castle, town and river Maine *(free lift to roof: Sun–Thu 11.30am–10.30pm; Fri–Sat 11.30am–midnight).*

ADDITIONAL SIGHT

Musée du Génie

106 r. Eblé. Phone for opening times. 4€ (children under 12 years 2.50€; family ticket 10€). 02 41 24 82 85. www.musee-du-genie-angers.fr.

The collections present the expertise of firemen from Antiquity to the present day. Engravings, maps, paintings, models, uniforms and arms tell the firefighting story along with films and interactive displays. An unusual way of finding out more about the history of France.

EXCURSIONS

Musée régional de l'Air★

Aéroport d'Angers-Marcé, 18km/11mi via the Paris motorway.

Phone for opening times.

5€ (children 2€) 02 41 33 04 10. www.musee-aviation-angers.com.

This aircraft museum illustrates the early days of flying with a display of old aeroplanes such as René Garnier's biplane, the Cri-cri air car (smallest twin-engine plane in the world) and the starck (the ancestor of microlights). **Flights** aboard light aircraft are organised by the Aéro-club d'Angers-Marcé.

St-Barthélemy-d'Anjou

Take the Le Mans road, E on the town plan; then turn right onto bd. de la Romanerie.

Musée Cointreau

Visits by arrangement only.

Closed Jan, 25 Dec. 6.20€/9.80€. 02 41 31 50 50. www.cointreau.fr.

The distillery was founded in 1849 by the Cointreau brothers who invented the orange-flavoured liqueur. Various attempts to fake it are on display here, as is the firm's own publicity material.

Château de Pignerolle★

8km/5mi E on D 61 (just past St-Barthélemy-d'Anjou).

This château is a replica of the Petit Trianon in Versailles. It was built in the 18C for Marcel Avril, the King's equerry and master of the Riding Academy of Angers. During WW II the castle served successively as the seat of the Polish government in exile, the headquarters of the German admiral Doenitz, and, after the Liberation of France, the quarters for American units under General Patton.

The château now houses the **Musée Européen de la Communication**★★ (European Museum of Communication) *(phone for opening times; 5.50€; 02 41 93 38 38; www.musee-communication.com).*

The rich collection of scientific apparatus displayed in an instructive and lively manner traces the fascinating history of communication, the major steps in its development and the various modes of expression employed from Sat Nav to the satellite.

The ground floor is dedicated to Leonardo da Vinci. On the first floor is a retrospective from wireless to radio. The second floor displays include a reconstruction of Armstrong's landing on the moon.

St-Sylvain-d'Anjou

9km/5.6mi NE on the Le Mans road.

Archaeologists and master carpenters have worked closely together to reconstruct as faithfully as possible a medieval **motte-and-bailey**. At the end of the 10C and during the 11C and 12C, these wooden strongholds built on a steep man-made earthen mound (*motte*) with a lower courtyard (the bailey or ward), were a common defensive feature.

Les Ponts-de-Cé

7km/4.3mi S on N 160.

This is a straggling town about 3km/2mi long; its main street spans a canal and several arms of the Loire, affording some fine views from its four bridges. The history of this small town includes many bloody episodes in French history. Under Charles IX 800 camp-followers were thrown into the Loire; when the château was taken from the Huguenots in 1562, any surviving defenders were treated to a similar fate.

Trélazé

7km/4.3mi E on the road to Saumur.

Trélazé is famous for its slate which has been quarried since the 12C. When the Loire was still a commercial highway, the blue-grey slates were transported upstream by boat to provide roofs for all the châteaux, manor houses and more modest residences which lined the banks of the river.

A slate museum, the **Musée de l'Ardoise** (*phone for opening times; €5.50; 02 41 69 04 71*) has been set up near a disused quarry.

L'île St-Aubin

Drive N towards the Hospital then follow the signs. In spring and autumn access only by boat, bike or on foot.

On the edge of Angers, the île Saint-Aubin is a world away from the bustle of the city centre. The boat crossing and stop at the traditional *guinguette* outdoor café are worth the trip alone. Covering 600ha/1 480 acres, the island is a protected natural site. A signposted trail explains local flora and fauna. Special events are staged during the summer.

Terra Botanica

rte. de Cantenay-Epinard. Phone for opening times. €17.50 (family ticket 50€). www.terrabotanica.fr.

Terra Botanica is a botanical theme park. It provides a fun way of learning about nature and plant life: gardens, water areas and hothouses with 40 rides and attractions.

La Roche de Mûrs

10km/6mi from Angers on D 160, then towards Nantes, and r. de la Roche-de-Mûrs.

This promontory overlooks the Louet and offers magnificent **views★** of the Loire Valley. This site is steeped in history as it commemorates the loss of a Republican battalion during the Revolution. In July 1793, following a season of relentless conflicts during the Vendée War, 12 000 rebels pushed the soldiers into the void and to their destruction. A monument to those who "died for the Republic" was erected to mark the centenary of the French Revolution.

A 6km/3.7mi walk (allow 2hrs) takes you along the Louet to the village of Mûrs-Érigné *(follow green signs; 02 41 05 50 00; a booklet of local walks is available from tourist offices and local bookshops; €8).*

DRIVING TOUR

LA LOIRE MAUGEOISE★

Leave Angers by bd. du Bon-Pasteur then D 111, dir. Bouchemaine.

Beyond the riverside settlement of La Pointe the road leaves the Loire to wind through vineyards to Épiré, before dropping into the valley of a stream which joins the Loire at Savennières.

Béhuard★

Béhuard Island has formed around a rock on which a little church stands. A short path leads down to the Loire and a sandy beach. In the pagan era there was a shrine on the island dedicated to a marine goddess, which was replaced in the 5C by a small oratory where prayers were said for sailors in peril

Rochefort-sur-Loire

Rochefort lies in a rural setting on the Louet. The neighbouring slopes produce the famous **Quarts de Chaume**, a distinctive and heady white wine. Several old houses, with turrets or bartizans stand on the square beneath D 751.

Corniche Angevine★
From Rochefort to Chalonnes the road (D 751) along the south bank of the Loire twists and turns through many tight bends cut into the cliff face.

La Haie-Longue
In a bend in the road at the entrance to La Haie-Longue is a chapel dedicated to **Our Lady of Loretto**, the patron saint of aviators. Legend has it that her house was carried by the breeze from Nazareth to the Dalmatian coast and thence to Loretto on the Italian coast where it is venerated as a holy house.

Montjean-sur-Loire
The narrow streets of Montjean are confined on a rocky promontory overlooking the Loire. From the terrace near the church there is a broad view of the Loire Valley and of villages with slate roofs.

From Montjean to St-Florent take D 210.

The **road★** along the river embankment provides views over the Loire and of the slopes rising to the south of the Thau, once a tributary of the Loire *(left)*.

Ingrandes
In the 17C and 18C Ingrandes was a major port. Its position just south of the Breton border made it an important centre for smuggling salt. Anjou was subject to the salt tax, unpopular since salt was the only means of preserving food.

6km/3.7mi E of Ingrandes on N 23.

Champtocé-sur-Loire
On the northeast side of the town stand the ruins of the castle of Gilles de Rais (1404–40), a powerful lord, a Maréchal de France by the age of 25 and the faithful companion of Joan of Arc whom he attempted to rescue from prison in Rouen.

St-Florent-le-Vieil
From the bridge over the Loire there is a good view of the town and its hilltop church. The **Musée d'Histoire locale et des Guerres de Vendée** *(phone for opening times and tour details; 3€; 02 41 72 62 32)* housed in the 17C Sacré-Cœur Chapel, contains documents, costumes (old-fashioned types of traditional headgear), uniforms and weapons mostly relating to the Vendée War and its leaders

West of St-Florent-le-Vieil the road (D 751) winds through gentle hills.

Chapelle de la Bourgonnière★
Visit by arrangement only. 02 40 98 10 18.
Towers, turrets and buttresses adorn the edifice which is decorated with shells, the initials LC and T-shaped crosses: all symbols of the Antonians, properly known as the Hospital Brothers of St Anthony.

Liré
The village of Liré in the Loire Valley owes its fame to **Joachim du Bellay**, the poet, who was born not far from here. The **Musée Joachim-du-Bellay** *(phone for opening times; 4.50€; 02 40 09 04 13; www.museedubellay.com)* occupies a 16C house (restored) in the middle of the town. Mementoes of the poet are displayed on the first floor; the ground floor is devoted to local customs.

Ancenis
The town fortifications and the castle ramparts, now in ruins, once commanded the valley so that Ancenis became known as the key to Brittany.
The dominant feature of **Oudon** is the medieval keep, built between 1392 and 1415. From the top of the **tower** *(phone for opening times; 02 40 83 60 00; www.champtoceaux.fr)*, there is a beautiful view of the valley.
Champtoceaux★ is perched on a memorable **site★** overlooking the Loire Valley. Behind the church, the **promenade de Champalud★★** has good views.

ADDRESSES

STAY

Chambre d'hôte la Béchalière – *49480 St Sylvain-d'Anjou. 5km/3mi NE. 02 41 76 72 22. 5 rms.* A convivial B&B amid verdant loveliness.

Chambre d'hôte du Domaine des Chesnaies – *La Noue, 49190 Denée. 02 41 78 79 80. www.domainedeschesnaies.com. 4 rms.* Spacious and opening onto a 19C-style garden.

Chambre d'hôte Le Grand Talon – *3 rte. des Chapelles. 49800 Andard. 11km/6.8mi E. 02 41 80 42 85. 3 rms.* This elegant 18C house, decked out with leafy vines, is a haven of peace.

Grand Hotel de la Gare – *26 r. Denis-Papin. 02 41 88 40 69. www.hotel-angers.fr. 52 rms. 8€.* A traditional, welcoming hotel overlooking the jet d'eau.

Hôtel Cavier – *La Croix-Cadeau, 49240 Avrillé. 8km/5mi NW of Angers on N 162. 02 41 42 30 45. www.lacroixcadeau.fr. P. 43 rms. 10€.* Modern bedrooms in the recent wing of an 18C windmill, which houses the restaurant.

Hôtel de Champagne – *34 av. Denis-Papin, 49100 Angers. 02 41 25 78 78. www.hoteldechampagne.com. 29 rms. 8€.* Renovated rooms are tastefully decorated. Near city centre.

Gîte de Charme La Pointerolle – *chemin des Landes, 49800 Trélazé. 02 41 57 15 54 or 06 47 03 38 20. http://gitelapointerolle.monsite.orange.fr. P.* Near the Château de Pignerolle, this charming gîte sleeps 2 people in a haven of vegetation. Attractive pond in the garden. Bikes available.

Hotel le Continental – *14 r. Louis-de-Romain. 02 41 86 94 94. www.hotellecontinental.com. 25 rms. 13€.* A central location, with traditional furnishings.

Hotel de France – *8 pl. de la Gare. 02 41 88 49 42. 55 rms. 13€.* A popular hotel, with a fine restuarant and good selection of wines. Cosy rooms.

Hôtel Mail – *8 r. des Ursules. 02 41 25 05 25. www.hotel-du-mail.com. P. 28 rms. €15.* The thick walls of this former convent keep out the noise from the nearby town centre.

Hotel le Progrès – *26 r. Denis-Papin. 02 41 88 10 14. www.hotelleprogres.com. Closed 7–15 Aug, 24 Dec–1 Jan - 41 rms. 8.50€.* Near the train station, this is a friendly place with modern rooms. Enjoy coffee in the breakfast room, with its décor inspired by the bright colours of Provence.

Chambre d'hôte la Rousselière – *49170 La Possonnière. 18km/11mi SE. 02 41 39 13 21. 5 rms. Closed 20 Nov–15 Dec.* Refined rooms with antique furnishings, set in a large park with a swimming pool.

Best Western – *1 bd. Maréchal-Foch. 02 41 21 12 11. www.hoteldanjou.fr. 53 rms. 13.50€.* 3-star hotel with plenty of character set in the heart of the city in a historic townhouse.

Château de Noirieux – *Relais et châteaux. 26 rte. du Moulin 49125 Briollay. 17km/10.5mi NE of Angers. 02 41 42 50 05. www.chateaudenoirieux.com. Closed 14 Feb–25 Mar, 14 Nov–1 Dec and Sun–Mon Oct-May. 22€.* Elegant château overlooking the Loir, set in grounds that are ideal for a stroll. Superbly decorated rooms and sophisticated cuisine.

EAT

Le Théâtre – *2 pl. du Ralliement - 02 41 24 15 15.* Easy to find opposite the theatre; excellent and fresh cuisine.

Le Napoli – *5 r. Toussaint. 02 41 87 68 09. Closed Sun and Mon.* Often consdered the best pizza restaurant in Angers. Reservations recommended.

Chez Rémi – *7 bis bd. Foch. 02 41 24 95 44. Closed Sat lunch, Sun and Mon lunch.* Inventive cuisine using fresh local market produce. Good value; reservations recommended.

Ma Campagne – *14 prom. de Reculée. 02 41 48 38 06. Closed Sun eve, Mon, and Tue eve.* Rustic décor and views of the river Maine at this good value place.

La Ferme – *2 pl. Freppel. 02 41 87 09 90. www.la-ferme.fr. Closed 20 Jul–12 Aug, Sun eve, Wed. Reservations required.*

Traditional local cooking in a simple setting near the cathedral.

⊜⊜**L'Hoirie** – *r. Henri-Faris, 49070 Beaucouzé. ℘02 41 72 06 09. Closed Sun eve, Mon.* Serves appetising, modern cuisine in a quiet room.

⊜⊜**Le Grand Jardin** – *1 pl. Mendès-France. ℘02 41 60 34 81.* The restaurant of the hôtel Mercure opens onto the Jardin des plantes.

⊜**La Villa Toussaint** – *43 r. Toussaint. ℘02 41 88 15 64. Closed Sun.* World cuisine in a trendy, zen atmosphere.

⊜⊜**Provence Caffé** – *9 pl. du Ralliement. ℘02 41 87 44 15. Closed 3 Jan, 1–24 Aug, 19 Dec, Sun–Mon. Reservations required.* Carefully prepared cuisine at moderate prices.

⊜⊜**Le Relais** – *9 r. de la Gare. ℘02 41 88 42 51. Closed 22 Aug–13 Sept, 24 Dec–4 Jan, Sun–Mon and public holidays.* The woodwork and the murals in this tavern recall the vineyard and grape harvest.

⊜⊜⊜**Le Favre d'Anne** – *18 quai des Carmes. ℘02 41 36 12 12. Closed 29 Jul-13 Aug, Sun–Mon.* Creative and modern cuisine, plus a view of the Château.

⊜⊜⊜**Le Petit Comptoir** – *40 r. David d'Angers. ℘02 41 88 81 57. 16-25 Jan, 30 Jul-21 Aug, Sun–Mon.* Relaxed atmosphere; inventive cuisine.

⊜⊜⊜**Une Île** – *9 r. Max-Richard. ℘02 41 19 14 48. Closed weekends.* Refined cuisine and an emphasis on regional wines.

Château du Plessis-Macé★

- **Michelin Map:** 317: E-3
- **Info:** 7 pl. du Prés-Kennedy, BP15157 49051 Angers. ℘02 41 23 50 00. www.angersloire tourisme.com.
- **Location:** 15km/9mi NW of Angers.
- **Timing:** Allow 1hr.

Set apart from the village and hidden amid greenery, this château is protected by a wide moat. Begun in the 11C by a certain Macé, the château became the property in the mid-15C of Louis de Beaumont, the Chamberlain and favourite of Louis XI, who had it rebuilt into a residence fit to accommodate his royal master. A theatre festival is held here each June and July.

VISIT

Guided tours (1hr) Jul–Aug 10.30am –7pm; Apr-Jun and Sept–early Nov Wed–Sun 1.30–6pm. ⊜5.50€. ℘02 41 32 67 93. www.chateauplessismace.fr.

From the outside, Le Plessis still has the appearance of a fortress with its tower-studded wall and rectangular keep, stripped of all fortifications except the battlements. Once you enter the great courtyard, you notice that the building is similar to a country residence: decorative elements in white-tufa stone enhance the dark grey of the schist; the imposing ruined keep towers over the west side of the enclosure. To the right are the outbuildings housing the stables and guard room. To the left are the chapel, an unusual staircase turret which gets larger as it goes up and the main residential wing surmounted by pointed gables. In the corner with the main wing is a charming **hanging gallery**★, from where the ladies would watch jousting tournaments and other entertainments. A second balcony, opposite, in the outbuildings, was reserved for the servants.

The tour includes the dining room, the large banqueting hall, several bedrooms, one of which was the King's, and the **chapel**, which still features rare 15C Gothic **panelling**★ forming two levels of galleries, the first reserved for the lord and his squires, the second for the servants.

Château de Serrant★★★

Although built over a period of three centuries, 16C to 18C, this sumptuous moated mansion has great unity of style and perfection of detail. Its massive domed towers and the contrast between the dark schist and the white tufa give it considerable character. Today, it is classed as a Monument historique

- **Michelin Map:** 317: E-4
- **Location:** The château is located off the N23 20km/10mi W of Angers, just before Saint-Georges-sur-Loire.
- **Don't Miss:** The furniture in the château is extremely elegant and very well preserved.
- **Timing:** Take the 1hr guided tour of the château before taking the excursion to the abbey at St-George.

VISIT

Château

Guided tours (1hr) Jul–Aug 9.45am–5.15pm; rest of year Tue–Sun 9.45am–noon, 2–5.15pm. 9.50€. 02 41 39 13 01. www.chateau-serrant.net.

The **Château de Serrant** was begun in 1546 by Charles de Brie supposedly after drawings by Philibert Delorme, the architect responsible for the construction of Fontainebleau.

The castle was bought by Hercule de Rohan, Duke of Montbazon, in 1596, and sold in 1636 to Guillaume Bautru whose granddaughter married the Marquis of Vaubrun, Lieutenant-General of the King's army. On the death of her husband, the Marchioness continued construction work until 1705. She commissioned Jules Hardouin-Mansart to build the beautiful chapel in memory of her husband, and Coysevox to design the mausoleum. During the 18C, the property was acquired by Antoine Walsh, a member of the Irish nobility who followed James II into exile in France and became a shipowner in Nantes.

Interior

In addition to the superb Renaissance staircase surmounted by coffered vaulting, the whole interior is very attractive. The **apartments**★★★ are magnificently furnished and this exceptional collection of furniture was added to the list of Historic Monuments. Sumptuous Flemish and Brussels tapestries hang in the reception rooms which contain rare pieces of furniture such as the unique ebony cabinet by Pierre Gole (17C) adorning the Grand Salon. Note

Library, Château de Serrant

also 17C, 18C and early-19C furniture by prestigious cabinet-makers (Saunier, JE de Saint-Georges) and Empire-style furniture by Jacob, upholstered with Beauvais tapestry, commissioned for Napoleon and Josephine's visit.

There are fine paintings representing the French and Italian schools, a bust of the Empress Marie-Louise by Canova, and two terracotta nymphs by Coysevox in the sumptuous **Grand Salon★★**.

The **library★★★** houses 12 000 volumes. Some of the books are marked with the Trémoille seal showing four T's symbolising the main estates owned by the family: Trémoille, Thouars, Talmont and Tarente. Opening onto the main courtyard, the chapel built by Jules Hardouin-Mansart contains the magnificent white-marble funeral monument of the Marquis de Vaubrun killed at the battle of Altenheim (1673).

EXCURSIONS

St-Georges-sur-Loire

2km/1mi by N 23.

St-Georges, on the north bank of the Loire, is situated not far from the famous vineyards, the **Coulée de Serrant** and the **Roche aux Moines**, where some of Anjou's finest white wines are produced.

The abbey (*open Jul-Aug Tue-Sun 11am-12.30pm, 2.30-6.30pm; rest of the year by request, enquire at town hall; 02 41 72 14 80)* was founded in 1158 by the Augustinian Order. The building (1684) contains a grand staircase with a wrought-iron banister and a chapter house with original wainscoting.

Jardins du Château du Pin

At Champtocé-sur-Loire, 8km/5mi W on D 723. Phone for opening times. €5 (children under 12 years no charge). 06 11 68 61 81. www.lesjardinsduchateaudupin.com and www.sci-le-pin.com.

The gardens around this 12C–15C château cover 14 different levels and 5ha/12 acres. Highlights include a collection of citrus, avocado, banana and oleander trees. Perennials, irises, lavender and yellow roses surround ponds. the 700-year old chestnut walk, kitchen garden and elegant 18C chapel with its working clock (16C) complete the bucolic scene.

Vallée du Layon

The Layon flows into the Loire downstream of Angers. The region is pretty with vineyards, fields of crops interspersed with fruit trees (walnut, peach, plum, etc.), hillsides crowned with windmills and wine-growing villages with graveyards in which dark green cypresses grow.

Michelin Map: 317: E-4–H-6

Info: Office du Tourisme Loire Layon, pl. de l'Hôtel-de-Ville, 49290 Chalonnes-sur-Loire. 02 41 78 26 21. www.loire-layon-tourisme.com.

Don't Miss: The delicious mellow white wines of the Layon vineyards produced by the chenin, a variety of grape often known as pineau. Bonnezeaux and Quarts de Chaume are well-known wines from this area.

DRIVING TOUR

The Vineyards

72km/45mi. About 3hr 30min.

Les Cerqueux-sous-Passavant

Guided tours (2hrs) Jul–Aug Mon–Fri 10am–7pm, Sat–Sun and public holidays 2–7pm. 5.50€. 02 41 59 58 02.

The grounds of a 19C Landes château are home to a farm of buffaloes and fallow deer.

Follow the road towards Cléré-sur-Layon (D 54). At the entrance to the village turn left to Passavant.

Passavant-sur-Layon

This pretty village on the edge of a lake is enhanced by the ruins of its castle.

Take D 170 to Nueil-sur-Layon; go right after the church onto D 77; after the bridge over the Layon bear left onto D 69 towards Doué-la-Fontaine.

The landscape at this point is typical of the Poitou: hedgerows, sunken roads and farmsteads roofed with tiles. Vineyards are grouped on the exposed slopes. Note at Nueil the slate roofs, more typical of northern France.

Beyond Les Verchers bear left onto D 178 towards Concourson. The road runs parallel with the Layon through fertile countryside. In St-Georges-sur-Layon go N towards Brigné, turning left onto D 83 to Martigné-Briand.

Martigné-Briand

This wine-growing village lies clustered round a château built in the early 16C.

Take D 748 SW towards Aubigné, turning right to Villeneuve-la-Barre.

Aubigné-sur-Layon

This delightful village still has several elegant old town houses. Near the 11C church stands an old fortified gateway where the remains of the portcullis and drawbridge can still be seen.

Leave Aubigné on D 408 to Faveraye-Mâchelles and turn right onto D 120. After crossing D 24 bear left onto D 125.

Rablay-sur-Layon

This pretty little wine-growing village occupies a well-sheltered site. In Grande-Rue there is a brick and half-timbered tithe house (15C) with an overhanging upper storey. A building dating from the 17C now houses artists' studios.

The road (D 54) crosses the Layon, then skirts a cirque with vine-clad slopes; from the plateau there is a broad view of the valley.

A disused railway line converted into a footpath follows the Layon, offering strolls in pastoral surroundings.

Beaulieu-sur-Layon

This wine-growing village amid the Layon vineyards has attractive mansard-roofed houses.

The main road drops into the valley, past the steep sides riddled with caves and quarries. At Pont-Barré there is an view of the narrow course of the Layon and a ruined medieval bridge, scene of a bloody struggle on 19 September 1793 (*see CHOLET*).

Drive to N 60 and follow it S.

St-Lambert-du-Lattay

Wine-growing and cooperage tools, illustrations, a collection of presses and commentaries embody the living memory of a people who have always been engaged in the cultivation of the grape at the **Musée de la Vigne et du Vin d'Anjou** (*phone for opening times; 5.10€; 02 41 78 42 75; www.mvvanjou.com*). The room entitled *L'Imaginaire du Vin* appeals to visitors' senses of sight, smell and taste in a display on wine which emphasises variety of bouquet and flavour.

Before entering St-Aubin turn left onto D 106 and soon after turn right.

Château de la Haute-Guerche

Open Jul and Aug 9am–noon, 2–6pm; rest of year by request. No charge. 02 41 78 41 48.

This castle was built in the reign of Charles VII and burned down in the Vendée Wars; all that can now be seen from the valley are its ruined towers.

Return to St-Aubin then drive onto Chaudefonds and continue to Ardenay to reach the Corniche Angevine (see ANGERS: La Loire Maugeoise).

Cholet

Cholet is a thriving industrial town, with a long-standing tradition as a textile centre. Surrounded by the pastures of Les Mauges, it is also an important cattle market. There is scarcely a building in Cholet that dates from before the Revolution since the town suffered sorely in the Vendée War *(see p271)*.

- **Population:** 56 761
- **Michelin Map:** 317: D-6
- **Info:** 14 av. Maudet, BP 636, 49306 Cholet. 02 41 49 80 00. www.ot-cholet.fr.
- **Location:** 70km/44mi from Angers (to the SW) and from Nantes (to the SE); 120km/74.5mi NW of Poitiers.
- **Parking:** Mainly on-street parking in the town centre.
- **Don't Miss:** The Textile Museum, and the Parc oriental de Maulévrier.
- **Timing:** Allow 1–2hrs to explore the town, but a whole day for the locality.
- **Kids:** The watersports at Lac de Ribou.

SIGHTS

Musée d'Art et d'Histoire★

27 av. de l'Abreuvoir. Open Wed–Sun and public holidays 10am–noon, 2–6pm. Closed 1 Jan, 1 May, 25 Dec. 3.40€. 02 41 49 29 00. www.ville-cholet.fr.

Housed in a building opposite the Hôtel de Ville, the Art and History Museum consists of two separate galleries.

The **History Gallery** evokes Cholet in 1793, as well as the Vendée wars (1793–96, 1815, 1832) and the sequence of events that ravaged the city.

The **Art Gallery** has a strong 18C collection with works by the local artist Pierre-Charles Trémolières (1703–39).

Musée du Textile

Open Wed-Sun 10am–noon, 2–6pm, Thu–Fri 2–6pm. Closed 1 Jan, 1 May, 25 Dec. 1.70€. 02 41 75 25 40. www.museedutextile.com.

This Textile Museum has been set up in an old bleaching house by the River Sauvageau, a remarkable piece of 19C industrial heritage.

The museum visit begins in an unusual modern building, modelled on Crystal Palace in London. This demonstration room houses four looms still in working order, the oldest dating from 1910.

Next comes the steam-engine room, in which the furnace and enormous machinery generated the energy for the entire factory.

Old houses

A pedestrian precinct has been created in the town centre, where place Rougé, rue du Devau and its continuation rue du Commerce have a number of old houses with rare 18C wrought-iron balconies.

EXCURSIONS

Lac de Ribou

3.5km/2mi SE

This vast reservoir encircled by hills provides facilities for a variety of **water sports** including windsurfing, rowing, sailing, etc. as well as fishing (*CISPA, Port de Ribou*). The gently sloping, grassy shores are suitable for other sports such as archery, golf and riding.

There is also a campsite.

Lac du Verdon

5km/3.1mi SE

This lake lies immediately downstream from the Lac de Ribou and covers an area of 280ha/692 acres. One end of the lake stretches into the hills. The lake has become a nature reserve for **migratory birds**, which flock here in thousands.

Maulévrier

13km/8mi SE along the D 20

The name Maulévrier is believed to date from the Merovingian period and means bad greyhound *(mauvais lévrier)*.

Fulk Nerra built the first castle here in 1036 and set up a barony which, under

The Vendée War (1793–96)

At the beginning of the peasant insurrection the town was captured by the Royalist Whites (15 March 1793), who then regrouped before marching victoriously on Saumur and Angers. On 17 October Cholet was captured by Kléber after a bloody battle in which 40 000 Whites faced 25 000 Blues; the victor described it as a "battle between lions and tigers"; the dead numbered 10 000. Between 60 000 and 80 000 Whites – panic-stricken men, women and children – crossed the Loire. In an episode that became a byword for brutality in French annals, the survivors were massacred in their thousands, shot down or drowned in the Loire. General Westermann wrote a chilling account of events to the Convention; "There is no more Vendée; it has died under our sword of liberty ... I have had the children crushed under horses' feet and the women massacred. I have not a single prisoner with which to reproach myself". On 10 March 1794, after vicious hand-to-hand fighting in the streets Jean-Nicolas Stofflet won Cholet back for the Whites, but a few days later the "infernal columns" under General Turreau put Cholet to fire and the sword. On 18 March Stofflet returned once more but was soon driven out by General Cordellier, leaving the town of Cholet in ruins.

Louis XIV, was passed on to Colbert's brother, whose descendants owned it until 1895.

The castle, which was partly destroyed during the Revolution, was rebuilt to its original plan in the 19C. At the end of the century, a manufacturer from Cholet called upon the architect **Alexandre Marcel** to restore it and lay out an oriental-style park in the grounds.

Today Maulévrier is well known for its greyhound races.

Parc oriental de Maulévrier★

Open Jul–Aug daily 10.30am–7.30pm; Mar–Jun and Sept–Oct Tue–Sun 2–6pm, Sun and public holidays 2–7pm; Nov Tue–Sun 2–6pm. 6€. 02 41 55 50 14. www.parc-oriental.com.

The terraces of Colbert Castle overlook the oriental park of 28ha/70 acres that was laid out by Alexandre Marcel between 1899 and 1910. Designed to resemble a Japanese garden, it was laid out around a peaceful lake to represent the changing seasons and the progression of living things.

A path with Japanese lanterns leads around the lake through exotic species of shrubs and trees (Japanese maples, magnolia stellata, cryptomerias, flowering cherries and aucubas) to a pagoda and garden with a spring. Beyond the shadowy lanes of conifers are a bonsai exhibition and a Raku earthenware workshop.

The best time of year to visit the park is from mid-April to mid-May and from mid-October to mid-November.

Forêt de Maulévrier

The **Cimetière des Martyrs** in the Maine-et-Loire is surrounded by a forest of tall oak trees. During the Vendée War, Stofflet used the inaccessibility of this cemetery to conceal his headquarters where the wounded were brought for treatment.

On 25 March 1794, however, the Blues penetrated the forest and massacred 1 200 of the Whites; two days later the latter took their revenge with a second massacre. The commemorative chapel standing alone in the forest is now a peaceful place.

Château du Coudray-Montbault

The moated 16C château with its two massive round towers of brick and stone and green lozenge decoration was built on the ruins of a 13C castle.

DRIVING TOUR

Les Mauges

The southern part of Anjou, on the borders of the Vendée and Poitou, which is known as Les Mauges, is a peaceful, somewhat secluded region. Les Mauges is a mixture of woodland and pasture used for cattle rearing, where the Durham-Mancelle breed is fattened before being sold in its thousands at the markets in Chemillé and Cholet.
The straight main roads, which were laid down during the Revolution and under the Empire for political reasons, are superimposed on a network of deep lanes well-suited to the ambushes, which played a prominent part in the Vendée War. The windmills still crowning the hillsides were often used by the Royalist Whites to send signals.

Drive NW out of Cholet along D 752.

Beaupréau
Beaupréau is a small town built on a steep slope on the north bank of the River Èvre. In 1793 it was the headquarters of the Whites; their leader, D'Elbée, owned a manor at St-Martin, on the east side of the town, which now houses the public library. The 15C **château** overlooking the River Evre (good view from the south bank) is now a clinic.

Continue along D 752 then turn left onto D 17.

Le Fuilet
Le Fuilet and the neighbouring hamlets – Les Challonges, Bellevue, Les Recoins and others – stand on an excellent clay soil which has given rise to numerous brickworks and potteries producing a variety of articles (ornamental, horticultural or artistic). The potteries are open to the public during working hours.

Retrace your steps and drive along D 17 to St-Laurent-de-la-Plaine.

St-Florent-le-Veil
The Angevine chapter in the Vendée insurrection began here during the Revolution. It was here that Royalist commander Jacques Cathelineau died on 14 July and the Marquis de Bonchamps, mortally wounded, freed 5 000 Republican prisoners held in the church.
Église abbatiale – This historic stained-glass windows in the chancel portray the insurrection of 12 March 1793, the death of Cathelineau, the prisoners on the field of martyrs, the farewell of Robin the curate and the peace of St-Florent.

Follow D 751 to Mesnil-en-Vallée. Around 1km/0.6mi after the village, turn right to Pommeraye, then take D 131. Before reaching St-Laurent-de-la-Plaine, stop by the chapel on the left.

Chapelle Notre-Dame-de-la-Charité. Two fine stained-glass windows illustrate Cathelineau's pilgrimage to the chapel, and the apparition of the Virgin

Alexandre Marcel (1860–1928)

The Parisian architect Alexandre Marcel restored many old buildings before gaining recognition for his thermal baths *(Grands Thermes)* in Châtelguyon, private mansions in Paris and Cholet, and a magnificent palace for the Maharajah of Kapurthala. His love of the Orient resulted in La Pagode *(now a cinema)* in rue Babylone in Paris and acclaimed buildings for several international exhibitions. He designed the Round the World Panorama *(Panorama du Tour du Monde)* hall for the French shipping company Messageries Maritimes, and the Cambodian Pavilion, in which he reproduced parts of the Temple of Angkor Wat for the Universal Exhibition in 1900.
Thanks to these constructions he was brought to the notice of King Leopold II of Belgium, who asked him to rebuild, in Laeken Park (Brussels), the Japanese Tower and Chinese Pavilion, which would have otherwise been demolished.

Cholet Handkerchiefs

Weaving is a long-established industry in Cholet, where hemp and flax have been cultivated and spun since the 11C. In the 16C the handkerchief was introduced into France from Italy. In the 17C, as the practice of bleaching cloth became ever more widespread, local manufacturers came up with a whiteness for which Cholet was to become famous, by spreading their cloth out to bleach in the sun on green meadows where the damp clay soil prevented it drying out too much. In the 18C Cholet cloth was part of the cargo of manufactured goods which the shipowners of Nantes and La Rochelle traded on the coasts of Africa in exchange for slaves who were then sold in the West Indies, from where the rum bought with the profits was imported into France, in the notorious trade triangle.

Despite the devastation wrought on the town during the revolutionary wars, Cholet was not destroyed; it re-established its crafts and tenaciously fostered its textile industry throughout the 19C. Cholet table and bed linen is now renowned for its high quality and as well known as the traditional red Cholet handkerchief, which is holding its own against stiff competition from abroad and from the disposable handkerchief industry. Many French department stores traditionally hold cut-price sales of table and bed linen in January – *le mois du blanc:* the "white sale" is an idea which originated in Cholet!

in an oak tree at this ancient place of worship. A cross marks the spot of the tree which was destroyed by the Revolutionary "Blues" on 29 August 1791. Half the population of St-Laurent-de-la-Plaine died in the prisons of Angers and on the Avrillé field of martyrs.

St-Laurent-de-la-Plaine

A museum of traditional crafts, the **Musée des métiers de tradition**★ (*♿ phone for opening times; 5.70€ (children 3.20€); 02 41 78 24 08*), is housed in a complex of several buildings, among them the 18C vicarage: one of the only two houses in the village to survive the ravages of the Republicans in 1794. About 70 trades are illustrated with implements collected from all over France. In addition to the traditional exhibition rooms (lace), a number of **workshops** have been reconstructed inside a magnificent timber-built barn.

Take D17 E to Bourgneuf-en-Mauges, then turn left on D 762.

Le Pin-en-Mauges

The statue of local hero , Jacques Cathelineau, dominates the centre of the village. Behind it, the Neo-Gothic church of St-Pavin (1893) houses a remarkable collection of 15 historic **stained-glass windows**★, the work of Jean Clamens (1896–99). The scenes show the entire story of the Vendée War, its generals, mainly Cathelineau, known as the "Saint of Anjou". In the north transept, his tomb (parts of his remains lie in St-Florent-le-Vieil) is the work of Choletais Biron, who portrays him sword in hand. The small **musée Cathelineau** is open upon appointment – *02 41 75 38 31 (Beaupréau tourist office).*

Leave the village S and take D 15 to Jallais, then D 756.

Chemillé

This town is an important centre for stock-rearing and for the production of medicinal plants (demonstration garden with some 300 species of plants in the grounds of the town hall). In place du Château there is a 13C doorway with honeycomb decoration

At the N end of the town, take D 160 towards Angers. After l'Espérance, turn right.

Chanzeaux

As you continue along the lush Vallée de l'Hyrôme, making a slight detour into the the Loir-Layon country, you will first note the elegant 16C château as you take the wide bend just before the village. The church, burnt down in 1794 and rebuilt in the 19C, backs onto a 13C bell-tower. On 9 April 1795, ten women and eighteen men, including a priest, took refuge in this tower and held out for five hours before it was put to the torch.

In the church at the foot of the tower, a stained-glass window by Jean Clamens portrays the tragic event. It was yet another in the series of massacres in Chanzeaux which saw over half its population (700 victims) killed during the Revolution. Several more modern stained-glass windows (1955) illustrate the main events of the Vendée War.

Leave by the S, follow D 121 to Valanjou, then D 84. After la Commerie, turn right and take D 169 to Montilliers.

Montilliers

The church (1900) was rebuilt around the 11C chancel and bell-tower. It features some superb stained-glass windows including the "massacre of the Moulin de la Reine" by Jean Clamens, in whch the "Blues" spared the lives of only two children.

Leave the village by the S on D 748, drive through Vihiers and take D 960 towards Cholet for about 3km/2mi. Turn right on D 756 towards Chemillé.

La Salle-de-Vihiers

You are now back in Les Mauges. The historic stained-glass windows can be seen in the south transept of the church of St-Martin (late 19C) . In 1794, thirty women and children from the village were gunned down by one of General Turreau's infamous roving firing squads, the *colonnes infernales*.

Head S on D 171 to Coron, then turn right on D 960 to Cholet.

ADDRESSES

STAY

Chambre d'hôte Parfum d'Ici et d'ailleurs – *La Foy Moreau, 49450 La Renaudière. ℘02 41 30 85 20 - www.lafoymoreau.com. 4 rms.* This reconverted farmhouse has kept its authentic agricultural feel in a floral setting. The rooms are decorated in a variety of styles from rustic to Spanish by way of the Far East. Home-raised meat served for the *table d'hôte* dinners.

Chambre d'hôte Le Clos du Marais – *6 chemin du Marais, 49120 Chemillé. ℘02 41 30 08 04 or 06 62 00 12 77. www.closdumarais.com. Closed Oct.* Behind the walls of this large house on the hills of Chemillé lies a superb interior with generous volumes and a rich décor. The 5 rooms occupy the mezzanine floor and are all named after medicinal plants. Outdoors, the grounds with the pond and water garden complete the idyllic setting.

EAT

Au Passé Simple – *181 r.Nationale. ℘02 41 75 90 06. Closed 17 Aug–6 Sept, Sun eve, Tue lunch, Mon.* A small, unpretentious restaurant with a friendly atmosphere in its country-style dining room.

L'Ourdissoir – *40 r. St-Bonaventure. ℘02 41 58 55 18. Closed 19 Feb–1 Mar, 18 Jul–10 Aug, Sun eve, Wed.* This restaurant in the heart of Cholet has two rustic dining rooms, one of which was formerly a weaving workshop.

LEISURE ACTIVITIES

C.I.S.P.A. – *Port de Ribou. ℘02 41 49 80 60. www.cholet-sports-loisirs.com.Closed Sat–Sun.* Situated on the outskirts of town, the Centre d'Initiation aux Sports de Plein-Air occupies a site in a green valley next to an artificial lake. All equipment can be hired on the spot for water sports such as sailing, wind-surfing, canoeing and kayaking, or for other activities such as tennis, archery, golf, climbing and mountain biking.

LAVAL AND THE MAYENNE VALLEY

Sandwiched between Normandy and the Loire Valley, the sleepy rural *département* of Mayenne has a seductive low-key charm. Its classic *bocage* landscapes hold much to discover among the undulating fields and hedgerows, including châteaux dating from the 11C, richly frescoed Romanesque churches and the charming ancient towns of Laval and Château-Gontier straddling the River Mayenne as it winds its way south to join the Loire at Angers. To see country life in full swing, visit Château-Gontier when the Thursday cattle market comes to town.

Working Rural Idyll

Green fields provide pasture for dairy cows – some say there are more cattle than people in these parts. Laval might be an unshowy sort of provincial town but the quaysides make for pleasant strolling, punctuated by a café pause by the Mayenne to take in the imposing 11C château looming above. Don't miss its excellent museum that pays tribute to a local lad made good, the painter Henri Rousseau.

Detour off to the east, and you are into the region known as the Alpes Mancelles – scarcely Alpine, but it is at least verdant and hilly, with pretty villages, orchards and fields of grazing sheep forming a backdrop to a foray underground into the Grottes de Saulges.

Back on the banks of the Mayenne, the delightful old town of Château-Gontier is dominated by the bell-tower of the Romanesque church of St-Jean-Baptiste.

Château-hounds should take in a trip to Segré, with its bustling quaysides and old stone bridge on the Oudon, where the Château de la Lorie has a richly-decorated interior. Also on the Oudon, the white stone château at medieval Craon is worth visiting too. The stand-out star of the region, however, is to be found at Le Plessis-Bourré, where the magnificent moated 15C château is the stuff of fantasy, offering a unique insight into the life of a Renaissance Lord of the manor. No surprise then, that its fairytale turrets and fully-working drawbridge have been the setting for numerous films.

Highlights

1. Old **Laval** and its Château (p277)
2. Impressive cave paintings at the **Grottes de Saulges** (p279)
3. **Château-Gontier** old town (p280)
4. **Château de Plessis-Bourré**, and its fully working drawbridge (p284)
5. Segré and the sumptious **Château de la Lorie** (p286)

Laval by the Mayenne

© Kevin O'Hara/age fotostock

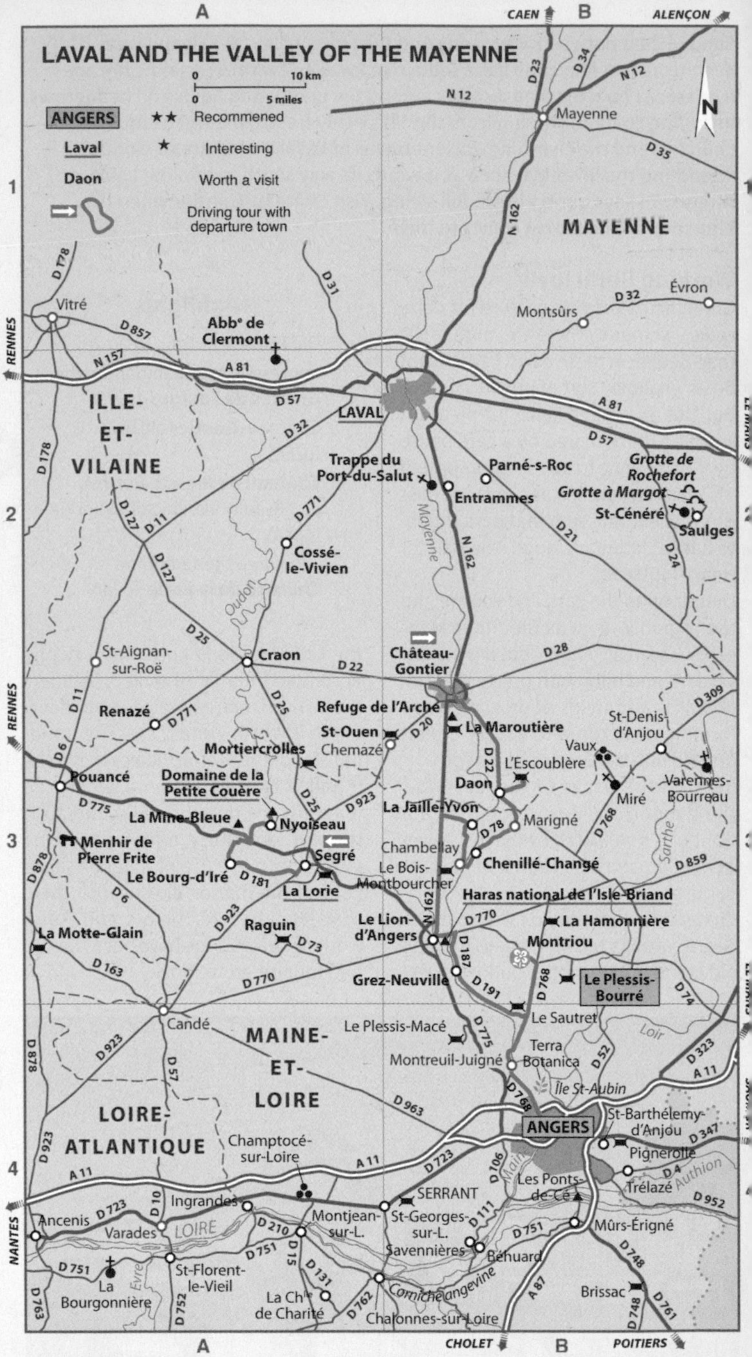
LAVAL AND THE VALLEY OF THE MAYENNE
0 10 km
0 5 miles
ANGERS ★★ Recommened
Laval ★ Interesting
Daon Worth a visit
Driving tour with departure town
A
B
1
2
3
4
CAEN
ALENÇON
RENNES
NANTES
CHOLET
POITIERS
N
MAYENNE
ILLE-ET-VILAINE
MAINE-ET-LOIRE
LOIRE-ATLANTIQUE
Mayenne
Vitré
Abbᵉ de Clermont
LAVAL
Montsûrs
Évron
Trappe du Port-du-Salut
Entrammes
Parné-s-Roc
Grotte de Rochefort
Grotte à Margot
St-Céneré
Saulges
Cossé-le-Vivien
Craon
St-Aignan-sur-Roë
Château-Gontier
Renazé
Refuge de l'Arche
St-Ouen
Chemazé
La Maroutière
St-Denis-d'Anjou
Vaux
Mortiercrolles
L'Escoublère
Pouancé
Domaine de la Petite Couère
Daon
Miré
Varennes-Bourreau
La Mine-Bleue
Nyoiseau
La Jaille-Yvon
Marigné
Menhir de Pierre Frite
Segré
Chambellay
Chenillé-Changé
Le Bourg-d'Iré
Le Bois-Montbourcher
La Lorie
Haras national de l'Isle-Briand
La Motte-Glain
Raguin
Le Lion-d'Angers
La Hamonnière
Montriou
Grez-Neuville
Le Plessis-Bourré
Candé
Le Plessis-Macé
Le Sautret
Montreuil-Juigné
Terra Botanica
Île St-Aubin
ANGERS
St-Barthélemy-d'Anjou
Pignerolle
Champtocé-sur-Loire
Les Ponts-de-Cé
Trélazé
Ingrandes
SERRANT
Ancenis
Varades
Montjean-sur-L.
St-Georges-sur-L.
Savennières
Mûrs-Érigné
Béhuard
La Bourgonnière
St-Florent-le-Vieil
La Chᵖᵉ de Charité
Corniche angevine
Chalonnes-sur-Loire
Brissac
Mayenne
Oudon
Sarthe
Loir
Maine
Authion
LOIRE
Èvre
N 12
D 23
D 34
D 35
N 162
D 31
D 32
D 178
D 857
N 157
A 81
D 57
D 771
D 127
D 11
D 21
D 24
D 25
D 22
D 28
D 309
D 20
D 6
D 775
D 923
D 78
D 768
D 859
D 878
D 181
D 770
D 187
D 73
D 163
D 191
D 74
D 52
D 323
A 11
D 963
D 347
D 723
D 106
D 4
D 952
D 10
D 210
D 111
D 751
D 15
D 131
D 762
A 87
D 748
D 761
D 763
D 752

Laval★

Laval has neither jungles nor tigers, but the artist Henri "Douanier" Rousseau is still the star of the Museum of Naïve Art in the old château. His work is an inspiration to travel, one which the famous navigator Alain Gerbault would not deny. The timbered houses of his charming native town lead down to the quaysides of the Mayenne: just the spot for a boat trip.

- **Population:** 51 233
- **Michelin Map:** 310-E6
- **Info:** ℘02 43 49 46 46. www.laval-tourism.com.
- **Location:** 32km/20mi S of Mayenne on N 162. Le Mans lies 86km/54mi to the W on D 57.
- **Kids:** Learn all about milk at Lactopole.
- **Timing:** Allow around 1hr to explore the old town on foot.

OLD TOWN★

The core of the medieval town climbs above the right bank of the Mayenne and huddles against the château. The modern town sprawls north of the walls and along the opposite bank.

Place de La Trémoille

The square is named after Prince Antoine-Phillipe de Talmont, Duke of La Trémoille. Its highlight is the Renaissance façade of the **Nouveau Château**, the seat of the Counts of Laval since the 16th century. It now houses the palais de justice (law courts).

Vieux Château★

pl. de la Trémoille. Phone for opening times. ℘ 02 43 53 39 89. www.mairie-laval.fr.

Climb the ramparts for a superb **view★** of the roofscape of the old town, and spot the statue of **Béatrix de Gavre**, a Baroness of Laval who helped develop the town's weaving trade in the 14C, the golden age for linen weaving throughout the region.

Nowadays, the mills produce cotton and synthetic textiles. Although its crypt and keep date back to the 12C and 13C, the château was built mainly between the 13C and 15C, and its rooms are hung with paintings by French and foreign artists.

Amazingly, the **keep** still has its original roofing, as well as the **hourd★★**, a wooden gallery jutting from the wall to help defend the bridge and base of the ramparts, which are 2m/6.5ft thick to support its weight.

Musée d'Art naïf★

The studio of **Henri Rousseau** (1844–1910) nicknamed the "Douanier" or customs officer, is recreated here using memorabilia and a couple of his works. A native of Laval, the naïve artist used to measure up his subjects like a tailor before painting them – the writer **Alfred Jarry** who also hailed from Laval, featured in one of his works.

The quayside★

The best views of Laval are to be had from the quaysides of the Mayenne. Seen from the humpacked Pont Vieux bridge, the old town is a knot of slate roofs and skinny streets of timbered houses beneath the castle keep.

Jardin de la Perrine★

The terraced gardens offer lovely rose beds, lawns, flowery parterres, water features and mature trees such as cedars of Lebanon, as well as fine views of the Mayenne, lower town and castle keep. The Espace Alain Gerbault celebrates the life of the little-known lavallois navigator who crossed the Atlantic in 1923 in a single-masted cutter and lived out his life in Polynesia.

ADDITIONAL SIGHTS

Église Notre-Dame-des-Cordeliers★

Open daily except Sun 8am–9pm.

Built between 1397 and 1407 for a Franciscan brotherhood, this church – the former convent chapel – houses a remarkable collection of seven altarpieces in limestone and marble by the lavallois architect Pierre Corbineau. The Corbineau family made Laval into a renowned centre for the production of Baroqur altarpieces in the 17C.

Lactopole André-Besnier★★

r. Adolphe-Beck (towards Tours). 02 43 59 51 90. www.lactopole.com.

A fascinating modern interpretation covering all you could ever want to know about milk, dairy products and the people who have produced them, from the artisan producers of the 1950s all the way to the modern industrial methods of the Lactalis group.

EXCURSIONS

Abbaye de Clermont

Open 9am until dusk. 4€ (children 10–16 years 2€) 16km/10mi W on D57, then right onto D 115 at la Chapelle-du-Chene.

The ruined abbey sits in a rustic site. Inside the church, vast window bays illuminate the wide transept and show the scale of the original edifice. The layout of the six windows of the chancel and the rectangular chapels in the transept conform to Cistercian style. Note also the fine vaulted spaces of the cellar and refectory.

Entrammes

13km/8mi S of Laval on N 162.

Taken from the Latin *inter amnes* meaning 'between rivers' this small town does indeed sit at a ford on the confluence of several waterways. During restoration work on the church, remnants of a thermal bath came to light, confirming the importance of the Mayenne region during the Gallo-Roman era.

Trappe du Port-du-Salut

13km/8mi S of Laval on N 162.

Monks made the famous Port-Salut cheese on this site until 1959. Nowadays the monastic community makes a living from a small dam visible across the Mayenne, producing electricity which is sold to EDF. Visit also the abbey church and chapel.

Parné-sur-Roc

14km/8.5mi S of Laval on N 162, then D 21.

This little village perched on a rocky outcrop boasts an 11C church which is home to interesting 15C and 16C murals. On the left, the silhouette of a resurrected Christ is depicted against a backdrop of red stars and a Virgin of Seven Sorrows; on the right are Saints Cosmas and Damian, twin brothers, physicians and early-Christian martyrs who were popular figures in the middle ages.

ADDRESSES

STAY

Marin'Hôtel – *102 av. R Buron 02 43 53 09 68. www.marin-hotel.fr.* 7€ The badges on the walls speak of an ancient building, but the rooms within are modern and practical. For a quiet time, go for one at the rear of the hotel.

Chambre d'hôte Le Bas du Gast – *6 r. de la Halle-aux-Toiles. 02 43 49 22 79. www.chateaulebas dugast.fr.* 11€ Built in the heart of old Laval in the 17C and 18C, this château sits in a garden with 80 topiary bushes. Inside, breathe in the smell of beeswax that perfumes the oak parquet floors and period furniture. Its spacious rooms are decorated with care.

EAT

La Table Ronde – *pl. de la Mairie. 53810 Changé. 02 43 53 43 33.* The establishment sits opposite the château. On the first floor is the gastronomic restaurant with its immaculately laid Louis XVI-style tables and chairs. On the ground floor is the bistro.

Saulges

Surrounded by the *bocage* landscapes of the mayennais, this enchanting town will delight lovers of both nature and history with its bright landscapes dominating the Erve Valley, the church built over a Merovingian cemetery, the mysterious legends of its 20 prehistoric caves, and a well whose waters have magical properties.

- **Population:** 341
- **Michelin Map:** 310 G-7
- **Info:** 02 43 90 49 81. www.tourisme.lescoevrons.com.
- **Location:** 40km/24.5mi SE of Laval.
- **Kids:** Outdoor action – rock climbing and exploring caves.
- **Timing:** Allow half a day for the caves and Saulges.

THE TOWN

Église St-Pierre

Opposite the parish church on the village square. In the 16C **chapelle St-Sérénède** the relics of the eponymous saint who spread the gospel throughout the region in the 7C are venerated.

The fresco on the right-hand wall of the chapel depicts, on the left, Saint Cénéré, then over on the right, Saint Anne learning to read with the Virgin Mary.

Descend a few steps into the little **chapelle St-Pierre,** a rare vestige of the Merovingian era built by Saint Cénéré in the mid-7C.

Oratoire St-Cénéré

1km/0.6mi W. Leaving Saulges in the direction of Vaiges, go left along a gently sloping lane as far as the car park.

A footbridge straddling the river leads to the hermitage which occupies a pleasantly tree-shaded spot at the foot of the rocks. Every year pilgrims flock here to pray to the saint and drink from the miraculous spring that he is said to have caused to gush forth.

Off to the side, the River Erve broadens to form a little lake that is a popular spot with anglers.

Grottes de Saulges

Phone for opening times. 1 cave €5.70 (children 3.90€), 2 caves €8.70 (children 5.70€). 02 43 90 51 30. www.grottes-de-saulges.com.

The entrance to the caves lies in a pretty spot north of the village; inside are interesting rock formations and excavations have unearthed a wealth of bone fragments and flint tools that attest to human occupation during the paleolithic era.

The first prehistoric decorations were discovered here in 2005. The **Grotte à Margot** has narrow passageways and decorations, while the **Grotte de Rochefort** contains a small underground lake.

ADDRESSES

STAY

Hôtel Ermitage – *r. des Deux-Églises. 02 43 64 66 00. www.hotel-ermitage. 10€.* Adjoining the Église St-Pierre, this hotel has all you need to stay fit. Enjoy a spot of leisure in the pool or gym, then relax in the flowery garden. Go for the spacious rooms in the modern wing.

LEISURE ACTIVITIES

Ateliers préhistoriques – *www.grottes-de-saulges.com. May–Jun and Sept–Oct. 5€.* Workshops cover prehistoric jewellery and make-up and stone-age cave art. Introductory classes in rock climbing (min. age 6) and caving (min. age 16).

Site d'escalade (rock climbing) – *www.escaladeenmayenne.fr.*

Château-Gontier

- **Population:** 11 025
- **Michelin Map:** 310: E-8
- **Info:** Office de Tourisme, pl. Andre-Counord. ☎02 43 70 42 74. www.sudmayenne.com
- **Location:** Château-Gontier is divided into the upper town on the west bank of the river, and the suburb around St-Julien Hospital on the east bank. The quays recall days when Château-Gontier was a port on the canalised Mayenne (*for boat trips on the Mayenne, see Touring Tip*).
- **Don't Miss:** The town has always been a great centre for fairs and markets, and every Thursday morning hosts a market for sheep and calves, one of the most important of its kind in Europe (*see Addresses*).
- **Timing:** Itineraries for walking, cycling or riding are available from the tourist office.

On the border between Brittany and the Maine region, Château-Gontier is a striking old town, the capital of the Mayenne country and founded in the 11C. Sitting at the edge of the Mayenne River, the town offers an excellent base from which to follow the river until Angers. The town was a centre of Royalist resistance to the French Revolution.

A BIT OF HISTORY

It was **Fulk Nerra**, Count of Anjou, who constructed a castle on the rocky spur overlooking the river and put it in the keeping of one Gontier, an officer in his army. The surrounding area belonged to the Benedictines of the abbey of St-Aubin at Angers, and it was they who built the 11C priory of St-Jean-Baptiste by the castle.

The Royalist leader and friend of Cadoudal (leader of the Royalist rebels known as the *Chouans*), **Pierre-Mathurin Mercier**, was born the son of an innkeeper in rue Trouvée.

WALKING TOUR

Allow 2hrs.

UPPER TOWN

Start from pl. St-Jean.

Jardin du Bout du Monde

These pretty gardens laid out in the grounds of the old priory are a pleasant place for a stroll and afford glimpses of the river and the far bank.

Viewpoint

From under the elm trees on the terrace built on the old ramparts there is a fine view of the far bank of the river.

Église St-Jean-Baptiste★

Open daily 8am–7pm. Guided tours by appointment. ☎02 43 70 42 74.

The church is built in flint and red sandstone. The **interior**★ reflects a remarkably forceful yet pure Romanesque style. The nave has modern stained glass and irregularly spaced columns supporting impressive arcades, whereas the crossing is roofed by an unusual dome. Although there are remains of 13C and 14C frescoes in the nave, those in the transepts date from the 12C.

The walk down to pl. St-Just gives a glimpse of the steep rise known as montée du Vieux-Collège. Walk along montée St-Just to Grande-Rue.

At the corner of Grande-Rue and rue de la Harelle there is a fine 15C timber-framed house and, opposite, the old salt store built in tufa and with a turret dating from the 16C.

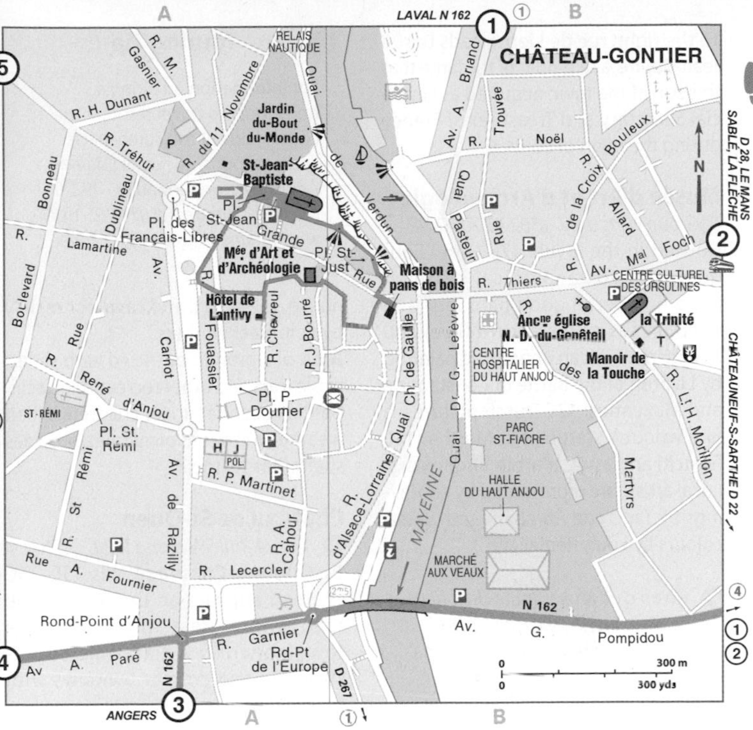

WHERE TO STAY		WHERE TO EAT	
Chambre d'hôte du Logis Villeprouvée	①	Aquarelle	①
Chambre d'hôte Le Chêne Vert	④	L'Amphitryon	④

Go up Grande-Rue and turn left onto r. de Thionville, then right onto r. d'Enfer.

This cobbled street is bordered on the left by the foundation structure of the church of St-Jean-l'Évangéliste.

Château-Gontier

To the right, rue de Lierru leads to rue Jean-Bourré, a reminder of the fame that this son of the town acquired as Financial Secretary and Treasurer of France during the reign of Louis XI.

Musée d'Art et d'Archéologie

Group visits only. 02 43 70 42 74.
Housed in the lovely 17C Hôtel Fouquet, the archaeological museum has a number of good paintings and sculptures as well as Ancient Greek and Roman remains: an unfinished painting by Le Brun of the Battle of Constantine and Maxentius; 17C Dutch pictures; a fine wooden statue of St Martha (15C French) and a 14C marble Virgin Mary. Local artists are represented by engravings by Tancrède Abraham and watercolours by Louis Rénier (19C).

Go up r. du Musée (note the building on the corner with r. Bruchemotte that has an elegant turret) and onto r. Chevreul.

Hôtel de Lantivy

This town house (no. 26) has a particularly interesting 16C façade.

Take r. René-Homo to the left, then on the right r. Fouassier and r. de l'Allemandier to pl. St-Jean.

LE FAUBOURG

This large quarter on the east bank of the river offers fine views of the upper town from the Pierre-de-Coubertin quayside.

EXCURSIONS

Refuge de l'Arche

On the outskirts of town along D 267. Open May–Aug 9.30am–7pm; Mar–Apr and Sept–Oct 10am–6pm; Nov–Feb 1.30–6pm. Closed 1 Jan, 25 Dec. 7€ (children 5€). 02 43 07 24 38.www.refuge-arche.org.
Halfway between a zoo and a veterinary clinic, this 10ha/25-acre sanctuary is committed to the shelter, care and protection of sick, wounded or abandoned animals (not including domestic pets such as cats or dogs). It has around 800 house guests, fed and cared for mainly by volunteer workers.
A playground outfitted with slides, cable-cars and other recreational facilities has been set up for children. In bad weather, a covered picnic area provides shelter for visitors.

> **Touring Tip**
>
> For information on hiring a houseboat to travel through the countryside at a leisurely pace, contact Tourisme fluvial *(Maine-Anjou Rivières - Le Moulin - 49220 Chenillé-Changé - 02 41 95 10 83 - www.maine-anjou-rivieres.com).*

Château de St-Ouen

7km/4.3mi SW along D 20.
Just before **Chemazé** this 15C–16C château appears on the right of the road with a great square staircase tower bearing a tiara-like superstructure and dormer windows with sculpted gables.

DRIVING TOUR

Vallée de La Mayenne★

71km/44mi. Allow one day.

The quiet Mayenne follows a picturesque and winding course between steep wooded banks as it flows south to join the Loire. The river was made navigable in the 19C when 39 locks were built between Laval (*see Green Guide Normandy*) and Angers and it is now ideal for pleasure craft.
The valley is too steep for any houses to be built beside the river so it has been preserved in its natural state. The route described below passes through the villages of low red-stone houses with slate roofs which crown the top of the slopes. There are good views of the river, some from a bridge and some from the by-roads which lead down to a picturesque site on the river bank to a mill or an isolated château.

Daon
The village and its 16C manor house are superbly sited on a slope above the Mayenne. Daon was the birthplace of Abbé Bernier who negotiated the peace between the Chouans and the Republicans.

In Daon take D 213 E, turn left then left again.

A long avenue of lime and plane trees leads straight to the attractive 16C moated **Manoir de l'Escoublère**.

Beyond Daon, turn right off D 22 onto D 190 to Marigné.

Chenillé-Changé
This attractive village in the Segréen region boasts a fortified **watermill** (*open May–Sept Mon–Sat 10am–noon, 2.30–6.30pm, Sun and public holidays 3–6pm, Mar–Apr and Oct Mon–Sat 2.30–6pm; 3.20€; 02 41 95 10 83; www.chenille-change.com*), dating from the turn of the 19C. The white streaks of flour on the schist walls are evidence of its use even today. The old houses and a river boat centre with small barges moored along the shady banks of the Mayenne, all add to the peace and beauty of the scene. Take the road across the river to Chambellay and turn right onto D 187.

La Jaille-Yvon
The village is perched on the cliff above the river. From the east end of the church there is an extensive view of the fields and meadows in the valley.

Take D 189 W and turn left onto N 162 going S.

Shortly after the turning to Chambellay the imposing 15C–17C buildings of the **Château du Bois-Montbourcher** come into sight *(left)*, surrounded by lawns and woods on the edge of a vast lake.

Le Lion-d'Angers
The town occupies a picturesque site on the west bank of the River Oudon just north of the confluence with the Mayenne. It is a horse breeding centre, particularly of half-breeds; the horse racing and competitions held here are famous throughout Anjou.

Haras national du Lion d'Angers★
1km/0.6mi E of Le Lion-d'Angers. Open mid Apr–Sept. Guided tours (1hr) 10.30am, 2.30pm, 4pm. 6€ (children 8–16 years 3€). 02 41 18 05 05. www.lelion-hn.com.
In 1974 the premises of the national stud farm, which were too cramped in Angers city centre, were transferred to the **Isle-Briand estate**, where now some 55 horses are stabled in an ultra-modern facility.
The tour of the farm includes the barns, the harness room, the forge (with oak flooring, more comfortable for the horses' hooves) and the riding school.

Grez-Neuville
This picturesque village in the heart of the Maine basin slopes gently to the banks of the Mayenne, its slate-roofed bell-tower reflected in the water. Grez-Neuville is the departure point for **river cruises** along the Mayenne and Oudon.
The road down the east bank (D 191) sometimes overhangs the river; it passes *(left)* **Château du Sautret**, an impressive building with a dry moat.

In Feneu take D 768 S across the river to Montreuil-Juigné then follow N 162 to Angers.

Parc et Jardin du Château de Montriou
Open Jun–Oct, 2pm–7pm. Closed Mon. 5€ (children under 12 years free). 02 41 93 30 11. www.chateau-de-montriou.com.
Montriou is known for its amazing collection of cucurbitaceae – that's to say marrows, courgettes, pumpkins, gourds and colocynths – which hang like spectacular vegetable stalactites from the pergolas.
Don't miss the giant sequoia (the biggest tree in the department of Maine-et-Loire with a girth of 9.4m/31ft) the

kitchen garden, the lovely view of the 15C and 19C château and the pretty 15C chapel.

Rejoin the D 786 and head towards Feneu.In Feneu take D 768 S across the river to Montreuil-Juigné then follow N 162 to Angers.

ADDRESSES

STAY

Chambre d'hôte du Logis Villeprouvée – *rte .du Bignon-du-Maine, 53170 Ruillé-Froid-Fonds. ℘02 43 07 71 62. 4 rms.* This ancient priory has been turned into a B&B.

Chambre d'hôte le Chêne Vert – *rte. de Nantes. ℘02 43 07 90 48. www.chenevert-chateaugontier.com. Closed Sun eve, Mon–Tue.* Opposite the church, serving traditional cuisine.

EAT

L'Amphitryon – *2 rte. Daon, 53200 Coudray. 7km /4mi SE by D 22. ℘02 43 70 46 46. Closed Sun eve, Mon–Tue.* Opposite the church, serving traditional cuisine. Pleasant contemporary rooms

Aquarelle – *2 r. Félix-Marchand, 53200 St Fort. ℘02 43 70 15 44. www restaurant-laquarelle.com. Closed Sun eve, Tue eve, Wed.* Welcoming house with superb cuisine and glorious views of the Mayenne.

CALENDAR

Horse show – On the 3rd weekend in Oct, the annual "Mondial du Lion", horse show takes place. This international riding competition brings together many amateur riders to compete on a complex and inventive course designed to test the talents of both horse and rider in jumping, agility, speed and precision. Riders from around twenty nations take part. *www.mondialdulion.com.*

Château du Plessis-Bourré★★

Le Plessis-Bourré stands at the far end of a vista of meadowland dotted with copses. This white building beneath blue-grey slate roofs gives a very strong idea of what seigneurial life in the 15C would have been like.

- **Michelin Map:** 317: F-3
- **Info:** 7 pl. du Président-Kennedy, BP15157, 49051 Angers. ℘02 41 23 50 00. www.angersloire tourisme.com.
- **Location:** 17km/10.5mi NE of Angers.
- **Timing:** Allow 1hr 30min for the château and surrounds.

A BIT OF HISTORY

Born in Château-Gontier, **Jean Bourré** (1424–1506) first entered royal service under Dauphin Louis, the son of Charles VII, whom he served faithfully. When Louis XI assumed the crown in 1461, Bourré was given the post of Financial Secretary and Treasurer of France. In addition to building several châteaux he bought the estate of Plessis-le-Vent. In 1468 work began on the new château, inspired by the château at Langeais which he had supervised during its construction. Le Plessis, built in a single go, boasts magnificent unity of style.

VISIT

Open Jul–Aug daily 10am–6pm; Apr–Jun and Sept Fri–Tue 10am–noon, 2–6pm, Thu 2–6pm; Feb–Mar and Oct–Nov Thu–Tue 2–6pm. Guided tours (1hr) 9€. ℘02 41 32 06 72. www.plessis-bourre.com.

On the outside, Le Plessis, enclosed by a wide moat spanned by a long bridge enhanced by many arches, is plainly a fortress protected by a gatehouse with a double drawbridge and four flanking towers.

Château du Plessis-Bourré

The largest of these is battlemented and served as a keep. A 3m/10ft-wide platform at the base of the wall provided for artillery crossfire. To the left of the gatehouse the chapel's slender spire rises above the roof. Inside of the entrance archway, Le Plessis has been converted into a country mansion with a spacious courtyard, low wings, an arcaded gallery, turret staircases and high dormer windows.

On the ground floor you see the splendid, richly furnished and decorated **State Apartments**. The wing built at right angles houses the Parliament Hall, a vast dining hall with a superb monumental fireplace. A spiral staircase leads to the splendid guard-room, which has a coffered wooden **ceiling**★★★.

There are also humorous scenes with a moral message, depicting for example the unskilled barber at work on a client, the presumptuous man trying to wring the neck of an eel, and a woman sewing up a chicken's crop.

The crude realism of some of the scenes, accompanied by lines of verse, and their outstandingly fresh and graphic quality make them all the more striking and evocative. The castle grounds have been laid out as a park and are a pleasant place for a walk.

EXCURSION

Manoir de la Hamonnière

9km/5.6mi N via Écuillé. Guided tours (30min) by appointment. 1€. 02 41 42 01 38.

The architecture of this manor house, which was built between 1420 and 1575, shows the evolution of the Renaissance style. The buildings laid out around the courtyard consist of a plain residential block *(right)* with a stair turret, a Henri III section *(left)* with a window bay framed by pilasters and capitals following the Classical progression of the orders, and at a right angle, a low wing with two twisted columns supporting a dormer window.

To the rear stands the keep, probably the last addition made in the 16C, with a staircase turret and round-arched windows, contrasting with the other architectural features.

ADDRESSES

EAT

La Table d'Anjou – *16 r. d'Anjou, 49125 Tiercé. 02 41 42 14 42. www.destination-anjou.com/tabledanjou.* Welcoming village restaurant with modern rustic-chic dining rooms.

Segré

The schist houses of Segré cascade down the slope to the river which is bordered by quays and spanned by attractive bridges. The town is the capital of the Segréen, a region of woods and meadows devoted to mixed farming and known for its high-grade iron ore.

- **Population:** 7 081
- **Michelin Map:** 317: D-2
- **Info:** 5 r. David-d'Angers. 02 41 92 86 83.
- **Location:** Between Laval and Angers.
- **Don't miss:** The sumptuous Château de la Lorie.

CHÂTEAU DE LA LORIE★

E along D 863. Open Wed–Mon 10am–noon, 3–6pm. Guided tours available. 7€. 02 41 92 10 04. www.chateaudelalorie.fr

La Lorie is an imposing 18C château approached up a long avenue of trees. A dry moat surrounds a square courtyard bordered on three sides by ranges of buildings with white-tufa tiles; the château's imposing dimensions are due to the addition of the two wings and the symmetrical outbuildings (late 18C). Highlights inside are the Great Gallery decorated with beautiful Chinese vases, the late-18C Marble Salon, the adjoining chapel and 18C woodwork in the Dining Hall. The Great Salon is lavishly decorated with Sablé marble and was designed by Jean-Sébastien Leysner in 1779.

EXCURSIONS

Château de Raguin

8.5km/5mi S on D 923 then left on D 183 at St Gemmes-d'Andigné.

Around 1600 Guy du Bellay, son of Pierre du Bellay, built this glorious Renaissance pile on the site of the old 15C château. A brigadier of the King's armies, Pierre du Bellay had a taste for splendour, and for his son Antoine's marriage in 1648 he had the walls and ceilings of the first-floor salon and the "Lovers' Bedroom" panelled and painted.

La Mine Bleue

12km/7.5mi W on D775 towards Rennes, turn off to Bel-Air and follow D 219 to la Gâtelière. 02 41 94 39 69. www.laminebleue.com.

For 30 years, slate – the "black gold" of Anjou – was mined in the region. After the mine closed it was intelligently reinterpreted as a tourist site. After a 130m/425ft descent underground the former miners' train takes you to the galleries at the heart of the mine, where the guide brings to life the miners' daily toils *(in French)*.

DRIVING TOUR

Cher Valley

21km/13mi. Allow 45min.

Leave Segré to the S on D 923 towards Candé. After the level crossing turn right onto D 181.

Le Bourg-d'Iré

8km/5mi W on D 181, then after the Verzée Valley, right on D 29. After Noyant-la Gravoyère continue to Nyoiseau on D 775 towards Segré then take first left.

The route follows a small valley dotted with ponds, notably those at St-Blaise and la Corbinière, where there is a leisure park.

Nyoiseau

This village (meaning "little nest") perched on the heights of the Oudon Valley is home to a ruined benedictine nun's convent, now a farm and town hall. North of Nyoiseau is **Domaine de la Petite Couère★** *(02 41 61 06 31 or 02 41 92 22 51; www.lapetitecouere.fr)* a vast 82ha/200-acre leisure park with outdoor activities for all the family, including a tractor museum, a reconstructed early 20C village, and walking trails.

Pouancé

Sitting within its protective ring of lakes, Pouancé hugs the border between Anjou and Brittany. In the Middle Ages the town played an important economic role owing to its iron foundries that were supplied with ore from the Segré Basin.

- **Population:** 3 192
- **Michelin Map:** 317: B-2
- **Info:** 2 bis r. Porte-Angevine, 49420 Pouancé. 02 41 92 45 86.
- **Location:** SW of Château-Gontier (40km/25mi) and 23km/14mi W of Segré.
- **Timing:** Allow 1hr for the castle tour.

CHÂTEAU

Guided tours (1hr) available mid-Jun–Aug Wed–Fri and Mon 10am–noon, 2–6.30pm, Tue 2–6.30pm, weekend 2–7.30pm. 2.10€. 02 41 92 41 08. www.ville-pouance.fr.

The N 171 skirts the town, passing at the foot of the ruined castle (13C–15C), whose towers and curtain wall of dark schist are reinforced by a firing caponier linked to the keep by a postern.

EXCURSIONS

Menhir de Pierre Frite

5km/3mi S on D 878 to la Prévière, then D 6 left and look for sign the right.

This 6m/19.5ft-high standing stone is tucked away in the heart of the woodland.

Château de la Motte-Glain

17km/11mi S. Guided tour (45min) mid-Jun–mid-Sept Wed–Mon 2.30–6.30pm. 6€. 02 40 55 52 01.

Originally built in red-stone, this château was reconstructed in granite and limestone in the late 15C by **Pierre de Rohan-Guéménée**, Counsellor to Louis XI and later one of the commanding officers of the armies of Charles VIII and Louis XII in Italy. A reminder of the château's location on the Mont-St-Michel–Compostela pilgrimage route is given by the scallops and pilgrim's staff motifs decorating the courtyard façade.

The gatehouse is flanked by two round towers. Renaissance fireplaces and 15C–16C furniture embellish the interior, together with hunting trophies, most of them of African origin.

ADDRESSES

EAT

Ferme-Auberge Théâtre de l'Herberie – *1km/.06mi W of Pouancé on D 771 towards Châteaubriant, then D 3 towards Rennes. 02 41 92 62 82. www.ferme-herberie.com.* This former stable block now houses a remarkable set-up combining horse and sheep breeding, cultivation of vegetables, flowers and aromatic herbs, regional cuisine and evenings of theatre. Dining is available with or without a show.

Château de la Motte-Glain

Craon

Surrounded by woodland and pastures devoted to arable farming and cattle rearing, Craon (pronounced *Cran*) is a quiet Angevin town on the River Oudon. It is famous for its horse racing *(Aug and Sept)*. The riverside château, one of the finest examples of Louis XVI architecture, is bordered by an English-style park. A few fine old timber-framed houses line the narrow streets of the old town, in particular the Grande-Rue.

- **Population:** 4 629
- **Michelin Map:** 310: D-7
- **Info:** 4 r. du Mûrier, 53400 Craon. 02 43 70 42 74.
- **Location:** Craon is 30km/19mi S of Laval and 19km/12mi W of Château Gontier.
- **Timing:** Allow half an hour for the château, then an hour or so to explore the village.

CHÂTEAU★

Guided tours (45min) Apr–Oct Sun–Fri 1–7pm (reserve in advance online or by phone). 7€ (château). 02 43 06 11 02. www.chateaudecraon.com.

Built in the local white tufa, this elegant château (now a hotel) has a curvilinear pediment and windows embellished with festoons characteristic of the Louis XVI period. Several 18C rooms with fine woodwork and Louis XVI furnishings are on show. Many of the trees in the **park** can be identified with the aid of descriptive labels. There is a kitchen garden with its 19C greenhouses, a laundry building where clothes were steamed over wood-ash and an underground ice house.

EXCURSIONS

Cossé-le-Vivien

12km/7.4mi N via N 171.

In 1962, the painter and ceramicist **Robert Tatin** (1902–83), gave free rein to his architectural fantasies around the old farmhouse called La Frénouse. The result has now become the **Musée Robert-Tatin**★ *(guided tours (1hr) Apr–Sept 10am–7pm; Oct–Mar 2–6pm, last admission 1hr before closing; closed Jan, 25 Dec; 5.60€ museum, 7.20€ house and museum; 02 43 78 80 89; www.musee-robert-tatin.fr)*. The museum is approached along an avenue lined with statues leading to the Giants' Gate and the figure of a dragon. Then come three major coloured structures representing Our Lady of the Whole World, the Moon Gate and the Sun Gate, which stand reflected in a pool shaped like a cross and lined by representations of the 12 months of the year. The architecture, painting and ceramics in the museum take the visitor into the fantastic world of this self-taught artist, whose naïve and visionary creations draw on Oriental, Pre-Colombian and even Celtic sources.

Renazé

10km/6mi SW.

An important centre of slate production in the early 20C, Renazé made quality fine-grained slates until 1975. Now the former slate workers, known as 'perreyeurs' demonstrate their skills in the Musée de l'Ardoise.

Château de Mortiercrolles

11km/7mi SE on D 25 and a track to the left beyond St-Quentin-des-Anges. Guided tours of the fortifications and chapel (1hr) late Jul–Aug daily 3.30pm, 4.30pm. 6€.

This beautiful moated château was built in the late 15C by Pierre de Rohan, Marshal of Gié. It is guarded by a remarkable **gatehouse**★ with alternating courses of brick and stone and fine machicolations in tufa. In the courtyard, the main apartment building (*right*) sprouts superb dormer gables. To the rear, lies an elegant chapel of brick with stone courses: note the pretty Renaissance side door and the piscina ornamented with shells.

Running southwest from Le Mans towards Angers, the Sarthe Valley traces an undulating line between the undulating curves of Normandy's hills and the straight lines of Loire Valley vineyards. Even if the high-octane thrills of Le Mans' car racing heritage leave you cold, its splendid Gallo-Roman walls, Gothic Cathédrale St-Julien and Renaissance mansions within the restored old town make it a very special place. Follow the Sarthe as it meanders between woodlands, orchards and fields, calling at ancient towns of medieval buildings, where you're never far from a Renaissance château.

Much More Than Motoring

Synonymous with car racing, Le Mans is an unmissable pit-stop in this region. Petrolhead pilgrims have flocked to Le Mans in June for the 24-hour race ever since daredevil racers strapped on leather helmets and goggles in 1923. But there is far more than high-speed thrills to this ancient walled city, as its attractive medieval centre of half-timbered houses and arcaded alleyways attests. Its centrepiece Cathédrale St-Julien rivals any of France's great Gothic monuments.

Southwest of Le Mans lies Sablé-sur-Sarthe, the main port and jumping off point for exploring the Sarthe Valley. It has plenty to detain you with its château and 18C mansions, and a lively medieval market on Sundays. Whether you choose to move on by boat, by car or by striding out on a network of walking trails designed to suit hikers of all abilities, make sure to visit the Benedictine abbey at Solesmes to hear Gregorian plainchant, then admire the Gothic murals in the church as Asnières-sur-Vègre.

La Venise de l'Ouest

Northeast of Le Mans, the canals and waterways of La Ferté-Bernard have earned the town the nickname of "Little Venice of the West" so hiring a canoe or electric-powered boat is a fun way to get around its 15C and 16C houses, market hall and the splendid flamboyant Gothic church of Notre-Dame-des-Marais.

The Perche-Gouët region to the east makes for a particularly satisfying driving tour of interesting churches and small châteaux. While in the area, visit Brou which has preserved a market square straight out of the Middle Ages.

Highlights

1. **Vieux Mans** and the legendary racetrack (p293)
2. **Sablé-sur-Sarthe**'s delicious shortbread biscuits (p305)
3. Attending a service at the Benedectine monastery of **Solesmes** (p306)
4. Architectural wealth of **La Ferté-Bernard** (p311)
5. Touring the deep lanes of **le Perche-Gouët** (p312)

Cathédrale St-Julien, Le Mans

©Yann Guichaoua/age fotostock

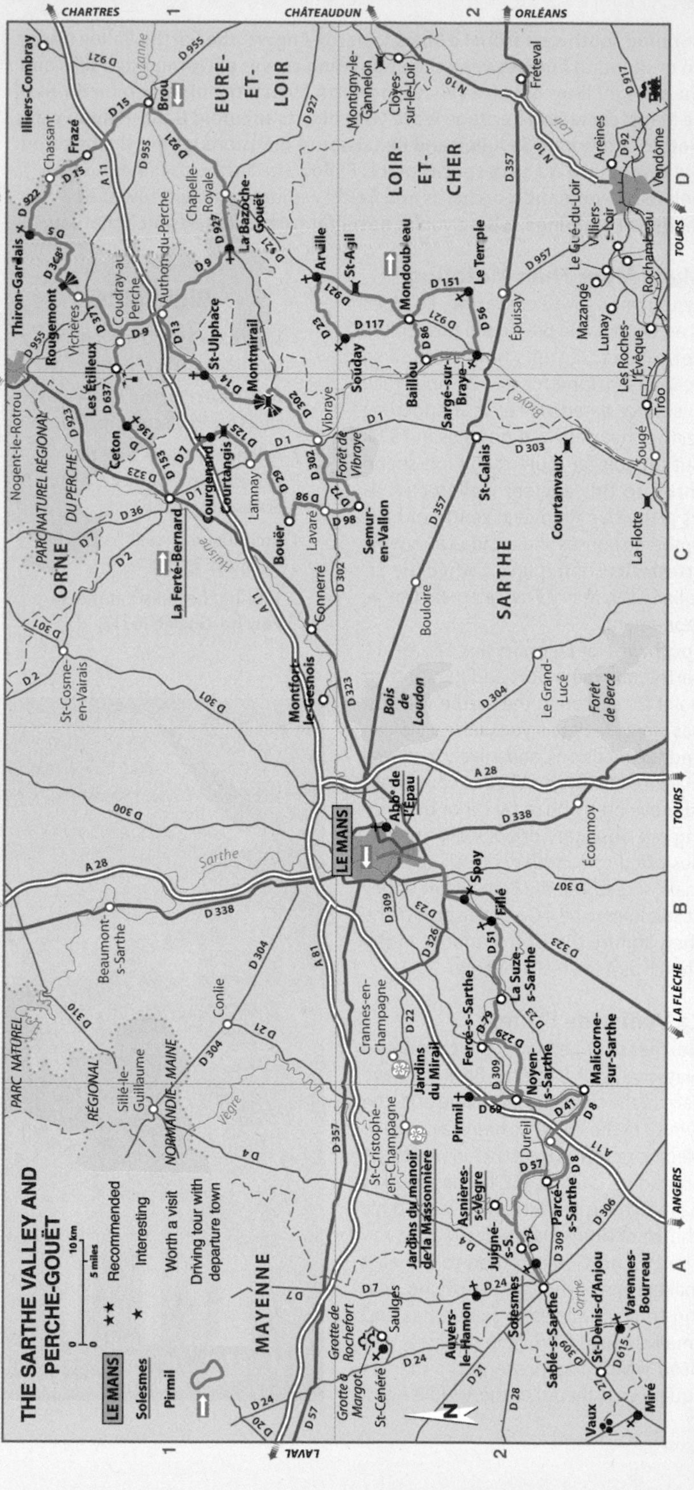
THE SARTHE VALLEY AND PERCHE-GOUËT
LE MANS
Solesmes
Pirmil
★★ Recommended
★ Interesting
Worth a visit
Driving tour with departure town
5 miles
10 km
CHARTRES
CHÂTEAUDUN
ORLÉANS
ALENÇON
TOURS
LA FLÈCHE
ANGERS
LAVAL
EURE-ET-LOIR
LOIR-ET-CHER
ORNE
SARTHE
MAYENNE
PARC NATUREL RÉGIONAL DU PERCHE
PARC NATUREL RÉGIONAL NORMANDIE-MAINE
Illiers-Combray
Frazé
Brou
Thiron-Gardais
Rougemont
Nogent-le-Rotrou
Les Étilleux
Ceton
La Ferté-Bernard
Montmirail
St-Ulphace
La Bazoche-Gouët
Arville
St-Agil
Mondoubleau
Le Temple
Souday
Baillou
Sargé-sur-Braye
Vibraye
Courgenard
Courtangis
Bouër
Semur-en-Vallon
Montfort-le-Gesnois
Connerré
St-Calais
Courtanvaux
Vendôme
Fréteval
Cloyes-sur-le-Loir
Montigny-le-Gannelon
Troo
Lavardin
Les Roches-l'Évêque
Abbaye de l'Épau
Spay
Fillé
La Suze-s-Sarthe
Fercé-s-Sarthe
Noyen-s-Sarthe
Malicorne-sur-Sarthe
Jardins du Mirail
Jardins du manoir de la Massonnière
Asnières-s-Vègre
Juigné-s-S.
Parcé-s-Sarthe
Solesmes
Sablé-s-Sarthe
St-Denis-d'Anjou
Varennes-Bourreau
Miré
Vaux
Auvers-le-Hamon
Saulges
Grotte de Rochefort
Grotte à Margot
St-Cénéré
Sillé-le-Guillaume
Beaumont-s-Sarthe
Conlie
Bois de Loudon
Forêt de Bercé
Forêt de Vibraye

Le Mans★★

Located 54min southwest of Paris by the high-speed TGV train, Le Mans stands on the banks of the Sarthe at its confluence with the Huisne. It is a thriving provincial capital renowned for good food: potted pork *(rillettes)* and poultry accompanied by sparkling cider and the famous local Reinette apple, as well as for its 24-hour motor race.

- **Population:** 194 825
- **Michelin Map:** 310: K 6-7
- **Info:** Hôtel des Ursulines, r. de l'Étoile, 72000 Le Mans, ☎02 43 28 17 22. www.lemanstourisme.com.
- **Location:** The old town, the city's centre, lies between the left bank of the Sarthe and a hill.
- **Parking:** There is plenty of parking available around pl. des Jacobins.
- **Don't Miss:** A stroll through the old town, along its narrow streets and river embankments. This is where the British Plantagenet dynasty was born.
- **Timing:** Spend 1hr in the old town and 1hr in the Cathédrale St-Julien before taking the 3hr driving tour through the countryside of the Sarthe Valley.
- **Kids:** Musée Vert Véron de Forbonnais, a museum of natural sciences with rooms reserved for children.

A BIT OF HISTORY

The Plantagenet Dynasty

When **Geoffrey Plantagenet**, Count of Anjou, married Matilda, the grand-daughter of William the Conqueror, he added Normandy and Maine to his estates. Geoffrey often resided at Le Mans and on his death in 1151 he was buried here.

His son, who in 1154 became **Henry II** of England, was the founder of the Coëffort Hospital and it was to Le Mans, his birthplace, that he retired in his old age only to be expelled by one of his rebellious sons **Richard the Lionheart**, then in alliance with the French King.

While on the Third Crusade Richard married **Queen Berengaria of Navarre** and it was to her in her widowhood that Philippe Auguste gave the county of Maine which he had reconquered from Richard's younger brother, John Lackland. Berengaria founded Épau Abbey (*see Excursions)* where she was buried.

River Sarthe at Le Mans

Studio 3Bis/MICHELIN

The Birthplace of the French Motor-Car Industry

In the second half of the 19C **Amédée Bollée** (1844–1917), a local bell-founder, began to take an interest in the incipient motor-car industry. His first car *(L'Obéissante)* was completed in 1873. Later he built the *Mancelle,* the first car to have the engine placed in front under a bonnet and to have a transmission shaft. The Austrian emperor, Franz-Joseph, went for a ride in the Mancelle.

Bollée's son Amédée (1867–1926) devoted himself mainly to racing cars; they were fitted with **Michelin** tyres and reached 100kph/62mph. After the First World War he began to produce an early form of piston rings, which became the main line of manufacture in his factory.

On 27 June 1906, the first prize on the Sarthe circuit was won by Szisz driving a Renault fitted with Michelin detachable rims.

In 1908 his brother, Léon Bollée, invited **Wilbur Wright** to attempt one of his first flights in an aeroplane at Les Hunaudières. When asked how the aircraft had performed, Wright replied, "Like a bird". In 1936 Louis Renault set up his first decentralised factory south of Le Mans in the Arnage plain.

The Drama of 5 August 1392

In the summer of 1392 **Charles VI** of France launched a campaign against the Duke of Brittany, who supported the English. On 5 August the King left Le Mans with his troops and rode westwards. Suddenly, as they approached a leper house, an old man, hideously disfigured and with his clothes in tatters, blocked the King's path and cried "Don't go any further, noble King, you have been betrayed."

Charles was deeply affected by this incident but continued on his way. A little later, when they were pausing to rest under the hot sun, a soldier let his lance fall against a helmet causing a strident clang in the silence. Charles jumped. Gripped by a sudden surge of fury and believing he was being attacked, he drew his sword and shouted out that he was being delivered to his enemies. He killed four men, gave his horse free rein and galloped wildly about for some while without anyone being able to intervene. Finally he wore himself out and one of his knights was able to mount behind and bring the horse under control. They laid the King in a wagon and tied him down; then they took him back to Le Mans, convinced that he was about to die.

Maison du Pilier Rouge

Ancien hôtel de Rouxelin d'Arcy.... **B**

Maison de la-Reine-Bérengère (musée)... **M**

Maison de la Tourelle........... **N1**

Maison de Scarron............... **N2**

Maison des Deux-Amis........ **N3**

INDEX OF STREETS

Reine-Bérengère (Rue de la).............1

St-Pavin-de-la-Cité (Rue)......................2

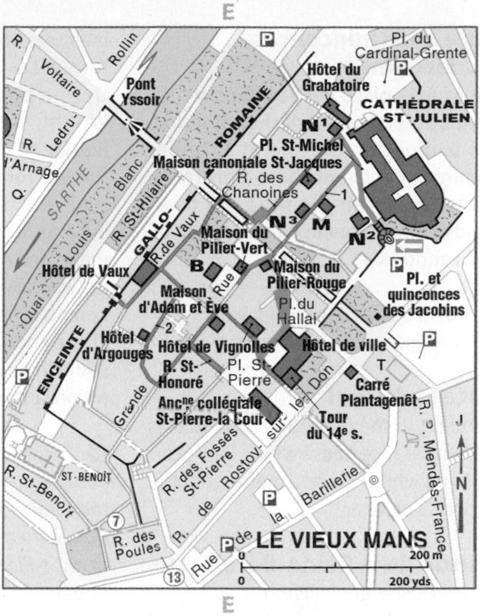

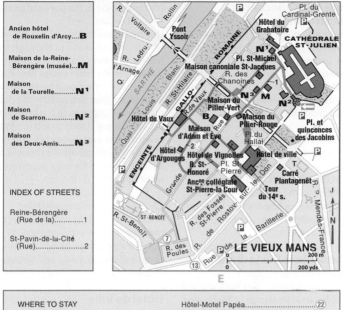

WHERE TO STAY	
Chambre d'hôte La Ferme Chauvet......	1
Chambre d'hôte La Tuffière.................	4
Chambre d'hôte Le Fresne..................	7
Chambre d'hôte Le Petit Pont..............	10
Chambre d'hôte Mme Bordeau.............	13
Hôtel du Commerce..........................	16
Hôtel Émeraude................................	19
Hôtel-Motel Papéa..............................	22
Mercure Batignolles............................	24

WHERE TO EAT	
Auberge du Rallye..............................	1
La Botte d'Asperges...........................	4
La Ciboulette......................................	7
Le Grenier à sel.................................	13
La Maison d'Élise...............................	16

This terrible onset of madness in the middle of the Hundred Years War had serious consequences. Deprived of its ruler and prey to princely rivalries, the kingdom grew weak. From time to time Charles VI would regain his senses only to lapse back into madness. Henry V of England was quick to take advantage of the situation: in 1420 he imposed the famous Treaty of Troyes by which Charles VI disinherited his son and recognised Henry as his heir. Charles VI finally died in 1422, 30 years later.

WALKING TOUR

OLD TOWN★★

Allow 1hr.

The old town *(Le Vieux Mans)* is built on a hill overlooking the Sarthe. Restaurants and craft shops enliven the pretty, winding streets, intersected by stepped alleys and lined with 15C half-timbered houses, Renaissance town houses and 18C hotels graced by wrought-iron balconies. Clearly visible from all along the quays of the Sarthe, the well-restored **Gallo-Roman ramparts**★ in their typically pinkish hues, are a truly unique landmark.

The overall impression of elegance is created by the alternating layers of brickwork and black and white ashlar arranged in geometrical patterns. This military construction, interrupted by 11 towers, is one of the longest in France.

Start from pl. des Jacobins at the bottom of the cathedral steps.

Place and Quinconces des Jacobins

The square, place des Jacobins, which is famous for its view of the cathedral, was laid out on the site of a former Dominican convent. At the entrance to the tunnel through the old town stands a monument to Wilbur Wright by Paul Landowski.

Go up the steps and follow the itinerary indicated on the town plan.

Place St-Michel

Standing in the cathedral precincts is the Renaissance house where Paul Scarron lived while he was a member of the cathedral chapter.

Maison de la Reine-Bérengère

9 r. de la Reine-Bérengère.

This elegant house was built around 1460 for an alderman of Le Mans, over two centuries after the death of its namesake Queen Berengaria, wife of Richard the Lionheart. The decoration consists of an accolade above the door, beams supported on brackets and sections of carved woodwork on the façade.

Musée de la Reine Bérengère★

Open Tue–Sun Jun–Sept 10am–12.30pm, 2–6pm; Oct–May 2–6pm. 2.80€. 02 43 47 38 51. www.lemanstourisme.com.

The Maison de la Reine Bérengère is now a **Museum of History and Ethnography**. A Renaissance room on the ground floor contains a display of regional furniture.

On the first floor, the glazed pottery of the Sarthe region (Ligron, Malicorne, Bonnétable and Prevelles) makes a lively and imaginative display, with strikingly fresh colours – yellow, green and brown – lavished onto statuettes, altarpieces, chafing-dishes, pots, roof finials, etc. On the second floor are paintings by 19C artists from the Sarthe region.

Maison des Deux-Amis

18–20 r. de la Reine-Bérengère.

The two friends *(deux amis)* are shown supporting a coat of arms. This mansion was built in the 15C and two centuries later was home to the poet and painter Nicolas Denizot.

On the opposite side of rue Wilbur-Wright, which was cut through the hillside to relieve traffic congestion, is the **Maison du Pilier rouge** (Red Pillar House), a half-timbered house featuring a corner pillar decorated with a dead man's head. Opposite, at the beginning of Grande-Rue stands *(right)* the **Maison du Pilier vert** (Green Pillar House). These coloured pillars are thought by some to be a rudimentary street recognition system.

Return to the Maison du Pilier Rouge and turn right onto the street of the same name which leads to pl. du Hallai, then continue along r. du Hallai to pl. St-Pierre lined with half-timbered houses.

Hôtel de Ville

The town hall was built in 1760, within the walls of the palace of the counts of Maine. Take the steps to rue Rostov-sur-le-Don from where there is a view of the old town's southeast ramparts; on one side of the steps is a 14C tower and on the other the old collegiate church of **St-Pierre-la-Cour** *(now an exhibition and concert hall; daily 10am–12.30pm, 2–6pm, public holidays 2–6pm; 02 43 47 38 51).*

Hôtel de Vignolles

This 16C mansion with tall French-style mansard roofs stands at the beginning of rue de l'Écrevisse on the right.

Maison d'Adam et Ève

No. 71 Grande-Rue. This superb Renaissance mansion was the home of Jean de l'Épine, an astrologer and physician.

At the corner of r. St-Honoré a column shaft is decorated with three keys, the sign of a locksmith. The street is lined with half-timbered houses. The picturesque Cour d'Assé opens opposite r. St-Honoré. From here onwards Grande-Rue runs downhill between elegant Classical mansions.

Bear right onto the less patrician r. St-Pavin-de-la-Cité.

Continue along the street and after a vaulted passageway turn left onto r. Bouquet. The Hôtel de Vaux at no. 12 is a late-16C mansion.

Farther on to the left there is a view of the Great Postern steps, part of the Gallo-Roman ramparts.

Walk back along r. de Vaux. Cross r. Wilbur-Wright and climb the steps turning left onto r. des Chanoines.

Maison de la Tourelle

In front of the cathedral.

This Renaissance mansion is named after the corbelled turret, which it features on the corner of the Pans-de-Gorron stepped alley.

Hôtel du Grabatoire

On the other side of the steps, opposite the Romanesque doorway of the cathedral, this 16C mansion stands on the site of what was originally the infirmary for sick canons. On its right stands the Maison du Pèlerin (Pilgrim's House) decorated with cockleshells, the symbol adopted by pilgrims on their way to Santiago de Compostela.

OTHER DISTRICTS

Pont Yssoir

This bridge affords a nice view of the cathedral, the old town, the Gallo-Roman fortified wall with its geometric decoration and a riverside walk past traces of medieval fortifications.

Église Notre-Dame-du-Pré

Close to the bridge on the north bank.

In a square planted with magnolia trees stands the old abbey church of the Benedictine convent of St Julian in the Fields (St-Julien-du-Pré).

Jardin d'horticulture

r. de l'Éventail.

This beautiful horticultural garden (covering 5ha/12 acres) with its rock garden and cascading stream was designed in 1851 by the [illegible] responsible for [illegible] and the parks of [illegible] Chaumont in Paris.

Église Notre-Dame de la Couture★

This church, now in the centre of the town, was originally the abbey church of the monastery of St-Pierre-de-la-Couture. The façade is 13C.

The wide single nave, built in the late 12C in the Plantagenet style, is lit by elegant twinned windows surmounted by oculi. The enchanting white-marble **Virgin**★★ (1571), on the pillar directly opposite the pulpit, is by Germain Pilon.

The 10C crypt, altered in 1838, has pre-Romanesque or Gallo-Roman columns and capitals; an inverted Antique capital serves as a base for one of the pillars.

Église Ste-Jeanne-d'Arc★

Open May–mid-Sept Sun 3–6pm, other days by request. 02 43 84 69 55.

This church was founded c. 1180 by Henry II of England in atonement, it is said, for the murder of his former Chancellor, Archbishop **Thomas Becket**. The 12C great hall or ward for the sick is now the parish church. The plain façade, pierced by an arched doorway, crowned by twinned windows, opens into a vast room divided into three naves of equal height. The elevation is elegant with slender columns topped by finely carved capitals, supporting Plantagenet vaulting.

Cathédrale St-Julien★★

This magnificent cathedral, dedicated to St Julian the first Bishop of Le Mans, makes an impressive spectacle seen from place des Jacobins, where its Gothic **chevet**★★★ (*see Architecture in Introduction*) rises in a succession of tiers supported by an amazingly intricate system of Y-shaped, two-tiered flying buttresses. The present building comprises a Romanesque nave, Gothic chancel and Rayonnant or High Gothic transept flanked by a tower.

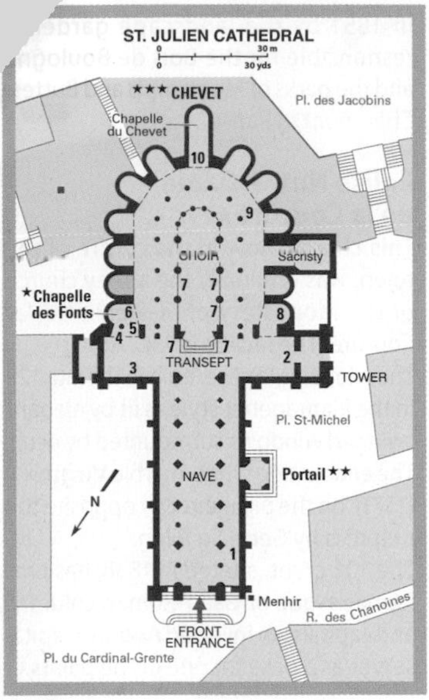

Exterior

The south porch overlooking the charming place St-Michel has a superb 12C **doorway**★★. At the right corner of the west front is a pink-veined sandstone menhir. Tradition has it that visitors should place their thumb in one of the holes to claim that they have truly visited Le Mans. Among the other scenes on the arch mouldings are the Annunciation, Visitation, Nativity, Presentation in the Temple, Massacre of the Innocents, Baptism of Christ and the Wedding at Cana.

The west front, built in an archaic Romanesque style, overlooks place du Cardinal-Grente, its sides lined with Renaissance mansions. Clearly visible is the original 11C gable which was embedded in the gable added the following century when the new vaulting was being built.

Interior

The Romanesque main building rests on great 11C round arches which were reinforced in the following century by pointed arches. The convex or Plantagenet-style vaulting springs from splendid capitals with particularly finely worked detail. In the side aisles are eight Romanesque stained-glass windows; the most famous one represents the Ascension **(1)**. The great window of the west front, heavily restored in the 19C, depicts the Legend of St Julian.

Transept

The 14C–15C transept, with its boldly soaring elevation pierced by immense stained-glass windows, has an ethereal quality in striking contrast to the nave. The south arm is dominated by the 16C organ-loft **(2)**, whereas the north arm is suffused with light transmitted through the beautiful 15C stained glass. Three 16C tapestry hangings **(3)** illustrate the Legend of St Julian.

At the entrance to the baptismal chapel *(Chapelle des Fonts)*, which opens into the north arm of the transept, are two remarkable Renaissance **tombs**★★ opposite one another. The tomb on the left **(4)**, that of Charles IV of Anjou, Count of Maine, the brother of King René, is the work of Francesco Laurana. On the right, the magnificent monument **(5)** to the memory of Guillaume du Bellay, cousin to the poet, shows the figure holding a sword and a book and reclining on one elbow in the Antique manner on a sarcophagus which is adorned with an attractive frieze of aquatic divinities. A third tomb **(6)**, that of Cardinal Grente, was erected in 1965.

Chancel

The lofty Gothic chancel (13C), encircled by a double ambulatory with a circlet of chapels, is one of the finest in France.

The massed ranks of the tall upward-sweeping columns support lancet arches showing Norman influence. In the high windows of the chancel and first ambulatory and in the low windows of the chapels, the 13C **stained glass**★★ is a blaze of colour dominated by vivid blues and reds.

Hanging above the 16C choir stalls is the famous series of **tapestries (7)** of the same period depicting the lives of St Gervase and St Protase.

Chancel precincts – In the first chapel on the right is a moving 17C terracotta Entombment **(8)**. The sacristy door

14C mural paintings, Cathédrale St-Julien

A. Cassaigne/MICHELIN

beyond used to be part of the 17C rood screen. The beautiful 16C woodwork in the sacristy originally formed the high backs of the choir stalls. The 14C Canons' Doorway features a tympanum with an effigy of St Julian **(9)**.

The 13C **Lady Chapel** *(Chapelle Notre-Dame-du-Chevet)* is dedicated to the Holy Virgin; it is closed by a delicate 17C wrought-iron grille. A remarkable series of late-14C **mural paintings**★ on the chapel vaulting was restored in recent years. Forty-seven musicians and singers portrayed as angels declare their faith to Mary; they are suffused with light and compose a magnificent tableau in which colour and perspective blend harmoniously.

Among the 27 musical instruments depicted in the fresco, note the *échiquier* (also spelt *eschiquier*), a rare occurrence indeed. Up to then, this instrument featuring a stringed keyboard, the ancestor of the piano, had never been represented in art although mention of it was made in the account books belonging to King John II the Good as far back as 1360. The stained-glass windows date from the 13C; they depict the Tree of Jesse **(10)** and the story of Adam and Eve.

ADDITIONAL SIGHTS

Carré Plantagenêt

r. Claude Blondeau. Open daily 10am–6pm. Closed Mon. 4€, Sun 2€. 02 43 47 46 45/38 51. www.lemanstourisme.com.

This new museum of Archaeology and History opened in June 2009 right by the Plantagenet city. It runs through the city's history from prehistoric times to the 15C using collections of over 1 000 artefacts. Two circuits are laid out in a fun and educational manner with modern interpretation.

Église de la Visitation

pl. de la République.

Built according to a nun's design, this former 18C convent chapel sits in the bustling centre of Le Mans. Note the classical corinthian columns of its portico and the rocaille-style door.

Musée de Tessé★

Open daily Tue–Sun 10am–12.30pm, 2–6pm; 2–6pm, public holidays 2–6pm. Closed certain public holidays. 4€. 02 43 47 38 51. www.lemanstourisme.com.

This museum, housed in the old bishop's palace built in the 19C on the site of the Tessé family mansion, contains fine collections of 19C paintings and archaeology.

Basement – This is where the **Egyptian collections** are displayed: reconstruc-

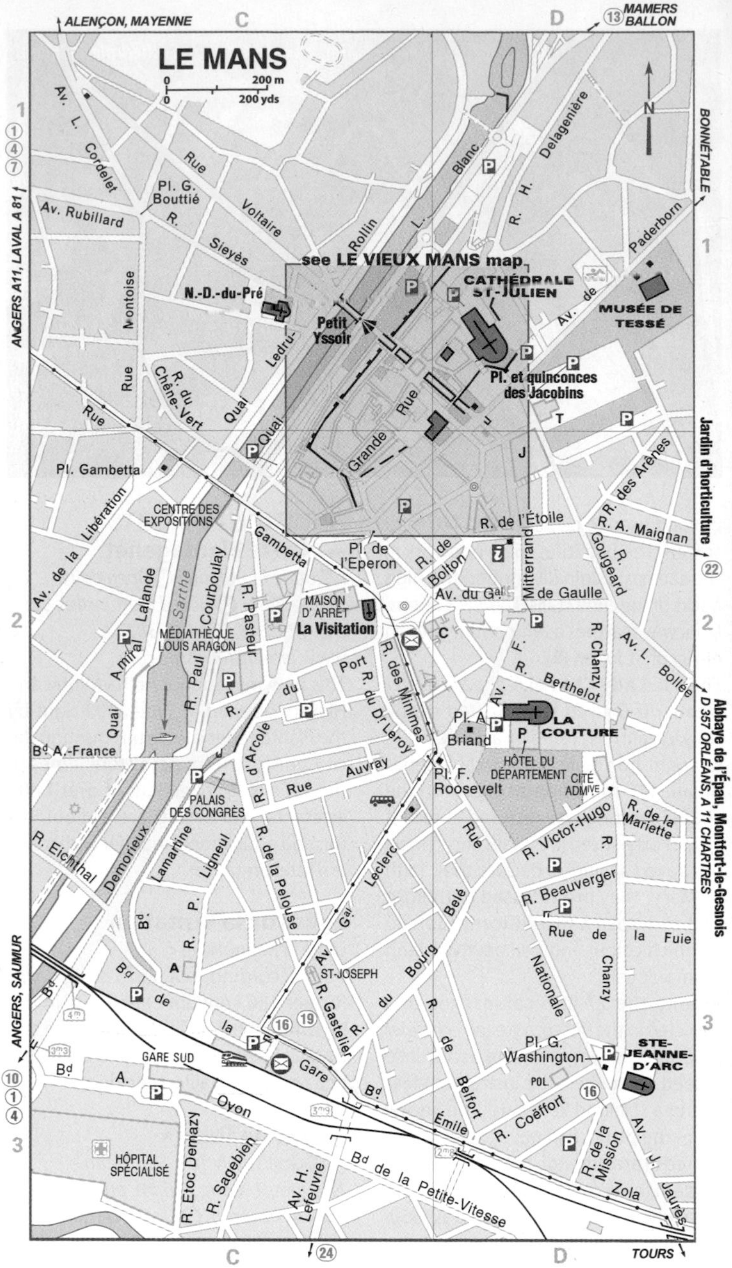

tion of the tombs of Nefertari (Ramses II's first wife) and of Sennefer (mayor of Thebes), mummy dating from 750 BC.

Ground floor – A small room *(left)* contains a superb enamelled copper plaque, called the **Plantagenet enamel**★, a unique piece depicting Geoffrey Plantagenet, Count of Anjou and Maine from 1129 to 1151, Duke of Normandy in 1144 and father of Henry II of England.

The Italian paintings include a series of 14C–15C altarpieces with gold backgrounds.

In the Renaissance Room there are two panels by the Master of Vivoin, part of an altarpiece (c. 1470) from Vivoin Priory (Sarthe).
The 18C Room displays a superb bookcase by Bernard van Risenburgh.
First floor – The Northern School of painting is represented by Van Utrecht, Kalf *(Still Life with Armour)*, several *bambocciate* (scenes of street life) and landscapes. A whole room is devoted to *The Comic Novel* by Scarron; a portrait of the author is exhibited alongside paintings by Coulom and engravings by Oudry and Pater.

Musée Vert – Véron de Forbonnais

SE, at no. 204 av. Jean-Jaurès. Open Mon–Fri 9am–noon, 2–6pm, Sun 2–6pm. 2.80€ (half price on Sun). 02 43 47 39 94. www.lemanstourisme.com.
This interesting museum houses a number of collections devoted to mineralogy, palaeontology, entomology, botany and ornithology. Two rooms are reserved for children.

MOTOR-RACING CIRCUITS

To the S of Le Mans between N 138 and D 139.

Le Mans 24-hour Race

In 1923 Gustave Singher and Georges Durand launched the first Le Mans endurance test which was to become a sporting event of universal interest and an ideal testing ground for car manufacturers.
The difficulties of the circuit and the duration of the race are a severe test of the quality of the machine and of the endurance of the drivers.
The track has been greatly improved since the tragic accident in 1955 when 83 spectators died and 100 were injured. Whether seen from the stands or from the fields or pine woods which surround the track, the race is an unforgettable experience: the roaring of the engines, the whining of the vehicles hurtling up the Hunaudières section at more than 350kph/200mph, the smell of petrol mingled with the resin of the pine trees, the glare of the headlights at night, the emotion and excitement of the motor car enthusiasts.
Every year there is also a Le Mans 24-hour motorcycle race and a Le Mans 24-hour truck race. A Grand Prix de France motorcycle race is held here regularly.

Circuit des 24 Heures

The 24-hour circuit (13.6km/8.5mi long) begins at the Tertre Rouge bend *(virage)* on N 138. The racetrack, which is about 10m/33ft wide, is marked in kilometres. The double bend on the private road and the Mulsanne and Arnage hairpin bends are the most exciting hazards on the 24-hour course. In 1972 the course was laid out to give a better view.

From the main entrance to the track on D 139 a tunnel leads to the Bugatti circuit and the museum.

Circuit Bugatti

Open for group visits only. 02 43 40 24 30.
Apart from being used by its school for racing drivers, the track is also a permanent testing ground for teams of racing car drivers and motorcyclists who use it for private trials.

Musée des 24 Heures du Mans – circuit de la Sarthe★★

Open Jun–Aug 10am–6pm; Sep–May 11am–5pm, (last admission 1hr before closing). 8€ (children 0–18 years 6€). 02 43 40 24 04. www.lemusee24h.com.
Rebuilt in 1991, the Motor Museum displays 110 vehicles and covers over a century of automotive history in an extremely modern and instructive setting. The section on racing cars, in particular those that won the Le Mans 24-hour race, presents a superb collection of outstanding automobiles. All of the following won races: a 1924 Bentley, a 1949 Ferrari, a 1974 Matra, a 1983 Rondeau, a 1988 Jaguar, a 1991 Mazda and a 1992 Peugeot.

Milestones in the Le Mans 24-hour Race

1923 – The first 24-hour race in 1923 was won by Lagache and Léonard from Chenard and Walcker; they covered 2 209.536km/1 372.942mi at an average speed of 92.064kph/57 205.917mph; the fastest circuit time was achieved by Clément in a Bentley at 107.328kph/66.691mph.

1971 – In 1971 when the track was 13.469km/8.360mi long Helmut Marko and Gijs Van Lennep covered 5 335.313km/3 315.2011mi in a Porsche 917 at an average speed of 222.304kph/138.133mph; Siffert drove the fastest lap, also in a Porsche 917, at an average speed of 243.905kph/151.555mph.

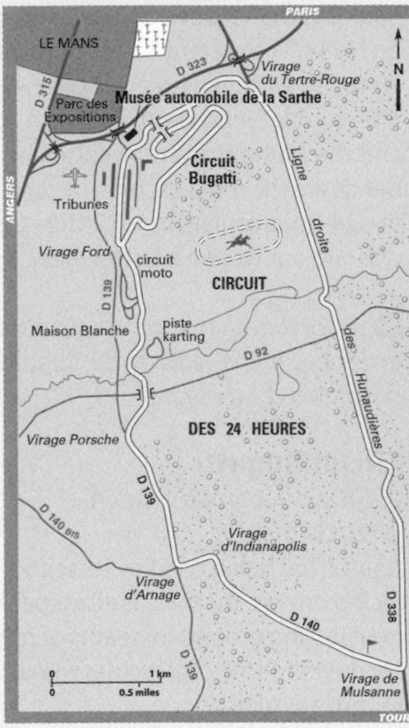

1991 – The circuit was redesigned and granted new facilities, making it the first racing track of its kind in the world. Mazda came first (unprecedented victory of a Japanese firm and a rotary engine).

1993 – Peugeot's historic hat-trick: three cars on the starting line, three cars on the finishing line, and three cars winning laurels. Moreover, they succeeded in setting a new track record on the longer circuit (13.600km/8.451mi) covering 5 100km/3 168.993mi at an average speed of 213.358kph/132.575mph.

1998 – The Scot Alan McNish and the two Frenchmen Laurent Aïello and Stéphane Ortelli celebrate Porsche's 16th triumphant arrival; their GT1 performed 351 laps (4 723.78km/2 935.22mi) at an average speed of 199.32kph/123.852mph.

2000 – The drivers Biela, Kristensen and Pirro won the 68th race. Three Audi R8s took the first three places, the first one having gone round the track 368 times!

2008 – Audi win their 9th consecutive victory.

2009 – Peugeot's third win and a double for the 908 HDI-FAP cars, which took the first two places.

Aston Martin Racing at 24 Heures du Mans in 2009

Thierry Gromik/MICHELIN

EXCURSIONS

Abbaye de l'Épau★

4km/2.5mi E via av. Léon-Bollée. Open mid-Jun–Sept 9.30am–noon, 2–6pm; rest of year 9.30am–noon, 2–5.30pm. 2.30€. Guided tours (1hr–1hr30, 4€) possible Sat–Sun in summer. Closed 1 Jan, 25 Dec. 02 43 84 22 29.

In 1229 a Cistercian abbey was founded on the south bank of the Huisne by **Queen Berengaria**, the widow of Richard the Lionheart, who spent her last days here.

On the left is the **church**, which was built in the 13C and 14C and remodelled in the 15C. The church was designed to the traditional Cistercian layout: a square east end with three chapels facing east in each arm of the transept.

L'Arche de la Nature

Near the Abbaye de l'Épau. Pony rides available Apr–Oct, and many more activities in the summer months. 02 43 50 38 45. www.arche-nature.org.

This natural site comes to life in season with activities on the theme of "rivers", "woodlands", etc. On offer are visits to the Maison de l'Eau, to a model farm, rides in horse-drawn carts (*Apr–Oct*), hikes, sports grounds and outdoor games.

Montfort-le-Gesnois

20km/12.4mi E of Le Mans along av. Léon-Bollée and N 23; after 16km/10mi bear left onto D 83.

Not far from **Connerré**, a small commercial town renowned for *rillettes* (potted meat made from pork or goose), Montfort, lies in a peaceful, site which grew around the Roman **bridge** over the River Huisne.

Jardins du Manoir de la Massonnière

In St-Christophe-en-Champagne, 35km/22mi W via A 11 (exit Le Mans Sud) then D 22. Open Jun–Sept Fri, Sat, Sun 2–6pm (last admission 30min before closing). 4.50€. 02 43 88 61 26.

Surrounding an attractive manor house, these gardens, inspired by Impressionist painting, display a splendid array of colours, perfumes and topiaries, trees and bushes trimmed in the shape of chess pieces.

Jardins du Mirail

23km/14mi W in Crannes-en-Champagne. Open Jun–mid-Sept, Wed–Sun 1–7pm. €5. 02 43 88 05 50.

Laid out in 1987, the gardens enfold a 16C château tucked against a hillside. An elegant outlook over greenery sheltering perennials and a hundred varieties of roses.

DRIVING TOUR

73km/45mi – about 3hrs.

Sarthe Valley

The Sarthe meanders peacefully southwest through the beautiful Maine countryside. The river is navigable between Le Mans and the confluence with the Mayenne along lateral canals running parallel to it. The countryside through which it flows consists of woodland alternating with meadows and fields of cereals, potatoes and early vegetables.

Leave Le Mans on N 23 heading SW.

Spay

10km/6mi on N 23 and D 51 via Arnage.

Spay is bordered by the Sarthe. Note the 12C church and **Spaycific'Zoo** (*open daily 10am–8pm; www.zoospay.com; 9€ (children under 1m/3.3ft free, over 1m/3.3ft 6€; over 16 years 9€).*

Take D 51 to Fillé.

Fillé

Guided tours possible. 02 43 87 14 10.

The village is on the north bank of the Sarthe; its **church** contains a large painted statue of the Virgin Mary (late 16C), glazed somewhat by the fire of August 1944.

La Suze-sur-Sarthe
The bridge over the Sarthe provides a good view of the river, the remains of the castle (15C) and the church.

Leave La Suze on D 79 going W through woods towards Fercé.

Fercé-sur-Sarthe
Attractive views from the bridge and from the road up to the church.

Return across the river and turn right to St-Jean-du-Bois.

The road (D 229) passes the troubadour-style castle of La Houssaye and provides several glimpses of the Sarthe before reaching Noyen.

Noyen-sur-Sarthe
The village is built in terraces on the sloping north bank overlooking the canal which at this point runs parallel to the broad Sarthe.

Pirmil
4km/2.5mi N of Noyen along D 69.
The **church**, a Romanesque building with buttresses, dates from 1165.

Malicorne-sur-Sarthe
Malicorne is pleasantly situated at the water's edge. From the bridge there is a pretty view of a mill and the poplars along the bank. Downstream, set back from the south bank of the river in a beautiful park, stands the 17C **château** where Mme de Sévigné liked to stay, which belonged to the Marquise de Lavardin. It has turrets and mansard roofs and is surrounded by a moat which is spanned by a humpback bridge.

Malicorne Espace faïence
Open Easter–Oct daily 10am–7pm; rest of year Wed–Mon 10am–12.30pm, 2.30–6.30pm. Closed 25 Dec. 6€. 02 43 48 07 17. www.espacefaience.fr.
This interactive museum, devoted to the local speciality, is housed in the renovated buildings of a former factory. Workshops help to illustrate the process of making and firing earthenware, its uses and the art of potters. On the eastern side of the town, there is a working **pottery** (*guided tours (45min) Apr–Sept Tue–Fri 9–11am, 2–4.45pm, Sat 9–11am, 2–3.45pm; 4.40€; 02 43 94 81 18; www.faiencerie-malicorne.com)* which produces pieces in the Malicorne style, as well as reproductions of period pieces.

Take D 8 W towards Parcé, making a detour along a small country track (V 1) to the right via Dureil, which provides attractive glimpses of the River Sarthe before rejoining D 8.

Parcé-sur-Sarthe
Parcé is a charming little village grouped round a Romanesque tower with a mill on the river. The cypress-girted cemetery at the entrance to the village makes a peaceful setting for the chapel with its gable-belfry.

After crossing the river and the canal, turn left onto D 57.

On leaving Avoise note, on the left, La Perrigne de Cry (*private property*), a 16C manor overlooking the river.

Bear left to Juigné.

Juigné-sur-Sarthe
Juigné is a pleasant village set on a promontory which juts south across the valley. There are 16C and 17C houses and the 18C château which belonged to the Marquis of Juigné. From the church square there is a view of the river below and of Solesmes Abbey downstream.

Solesmes
See SABLÉ-SUR-SARTHE

Take D 22 alongside the canal and the old marble quarries to Sablé.

ADDRESSES

STAY

Chambre d'hôte La Ferme Chauvet – *72430 Chantennay-Villedieu. 3km/2mi E of village. 02 43 95 77 57. www.fermechauvet.fr. 5 rms.* . All modern comforts at a reasonable price; working farm.

Chambre d'hôte Le Fresne – *72300 Solesmes. 02 43 95 92 55. www.lefresne.com. 3 rms.* . Discover the delights of a working farm; rooms are in an annex.

Chambre d'hôte Mme Bordeau – *Le Monet, 72190 Coulaines. 5km/3mi N of Le Mans. 02 43 89 45 56. 2 rms.* A chance to stay in the countryside, but not too far from town. This typical regional house has been restored but has retained its original character.

Chambre d'hôte Le Petit Pont – *3 r. du Petit-Pont, 72230 Moncé-en- Belin. 11km/6.8mi S of Le Mans on D 147 towards Arnage, then D 307. 02 43 42 03 32. www.latourdesplantes.com. 5 rms. evening meal* . The rooms are simply decorated and well equipped. The property is situated on a working farm.

Chambre d'hôte La Tuffière – *72430 Asnières-sue-Vègre. 2km/1mi NE of Asnières-sue-Vègre. 02 43 95 12 16. www.tuffiere.com. 3 rms.* On a working farm; regional cuisine.

Hotel-Motel Papéa – *RN 314, Bener, 72530 Yvré-l'Evêque. 02 43 89 64 09. www.hotepapea.com. 21 rms.* *6€.* A cross between camping and a motel, using chalets.

Hotel Le Commerce – *41 bd. de la Gare. 02 43 83 20 20. www.commerce-hotel.fr. 31 rms.* *10€.* Close to the station, this hotel has ensured it has good soundproofing. Functional, tidy rooms.

Hôtel Émeraude – *18 r. Gastelier. 02 43 24 87 46. www.hotel-emeraude-le-mans.com. Closed 26 Jul–17 Aug, 21 Dec–5 Jan. 33 rms.* *12€.* A very reasonably priced little hotel near the station. Well kept, simple and pastel coloured rooms. Breakfast served in the iner flower-decked courtyard in fine weather.

Mercure Batignolles – *r. Pointe. 02 43 72 27 20. www.mercure.com. Closed end Sept–May, Mon lunch.* Modern, practical and well-kept rooms; those to the rear are quieter. Garden with crazy golf. Dining room decorated with photographs recalling the legendary Le Mans 24-hr race. Traditional repertory.

EAT

Auberge du Rallye – *13 r. des Gesleries, 72210 Fillé-sur-Sarthe. 12km/7.4mi S of Le Mans on D 147E, D 23 towards Allones, then D 51. 02 43 87 40 40. www.aubergedurallye.com. Closed Wed eve, Thu. Reservation required for weekends.* It's good to get away from the noise of the city and eat in a country setting in the Sarthe, on a shaded terrace.

La Botte d'Asperges – *72230 Guécelard. 18km/11mi S of Le Mans on N 23 02 43 87 29 61. Closed 4–11 Mar, 5–28 Aug, Sun eve, Mon except public holidays.* A simple little restaurant, in a former staging inn. Unpretentious cooking with good menus, including one for children.

La Ciboulette – *14 r. Vieill-Porte. 02 43 24 65 67. Closed 22 Jan–6 Feb, 1–8 May, 1–15 Aug, Sun, Mon lunch, Sat lunch.* Located in a medieval house in Old Le Mans, the red prevails throughout in the bistro atmosphere of this restaurant. Traditional dishes. Menu changes daily.

Le Fontainebleau – *12 pl. St-Pierre 02 43 14 25 74. Closed 25 Feb–5 Mar, 20 Sept–8 Oct, Tue.* A rustic atmosphere with walls dating from 1720, this restaurant in Old Mans offers modern cuisine according to the season. Faultless table settings and friendly welcome.

Le Grenier à sel – *26 pl. de l'Eperon 02 43 23 26 30. Closed 2–12 Mar, 24 Aug–16 Sept Sun–Mon.* Right in the town centre, this former salt store now houses a restaurant serving modern cuisine. Menu changes daily.

La Maison d'Élise – *6 r. de la Mission. 02 43 40 00 58. Closed 15 Jul -15 Aug, 15-28 Feb, Sun & Mon.* Stylish designer furniture in the contemporary ground-floor dining room. The first floor opens onto a peaceful terrace. Fixed-

Window shopping in the Old Town

A. Cassaigne/MICHELIN

price lunch menus and a carte that moves with the times.

NIGHTLIFE

Le Saint-Flaceau – *9 r. St-Flaceau. ℘02 43 23 24 93.* This cocktail bar is something really different: the setting is an 18C apartment in the old town, complete with parquet floors and mouldings, and furnished with old sofas and chairs. Wide choice of drinks at reasonable prices, and a wonderful terrace on the old Roman walls overlooking the town – which was the main reason for converting this bar from an apartment. A real find, but get there early.

ENTERTAINMENT

L'Espal – *60–62 r. de l'Estérel. ℘02 43 50 21 50. www.theatre.espal.net. Open Tue 1–7pm, Wed 10am–7pm, Thu 2–7pm, Fri 1–7pm, Sat 10am–5pm. Closed end Jul–Aug, 25 Dec, 1 Jan.* The Espal centre is both a community arts centre and a cultural venue. It organises workshops and courses (dance, lithography) as well as putting on shows.

LEISURE ACTIVITIES

Les Croisières au Mans – *101 quai de l'Amiral-Lalande. ℘02 43 80 56 62.* Make your reservation through the tourist office for a boat trip or cruise (with a meal) on the Sarthe. A different way of discovering Le Mans and its surroundings.

MJC Jacques-Prévert – *97 Grande-Rue. ℘02 43 24 73 85. Opening hours according to events. Closed Aug.* An arts centre in a lovely 17C building where there is always something going on.

Radio Alpha (107.3) is Le Mans' latest community radio station, whose studios are open to the public. In the vaulted cellar, the Inventaire holds concerts of rock, jazz and French songs, as well as theatre performances.

TAKING A BREAK

Café Crème – *2 r. de la Barillerie. ℘02 43 14 26 29. Closed Sun.* With its upper floor, hidden corners and bench seats, this café on the corner of place de la Sirène is known as a smart place to go.

Hollyrock – *46 r. du Dr-Leroy. ℘02 43 23 00 00. Daily 6pm–4am.* Heavily influenced by the American 1950s style, this huge bar includes a sports hall and a main dance floor with DJ.

Mulligan's – *44 r. du Dr-Leroy. ℘02 43 14 26 65.* Concerts Thu and Fri. Fine Irish pub with benches and barrels for tables, and the landlord speaks the language of James Joyce with an accent as authentic as the Guinness he serves.

Reignier – *19 r. de Bolton. ℘02 43 24 02 15. www.warrain.reignier.fr. Closed Sun, Mon, public holidays.* Two floors of high-quality wines, Reignier's own-brand top-class tea and coffee, delicatessen and regional specialities.

Sablé-sur-Sarthe

Situated at a point where two tributaries, the Vaige and the Erve, flow into the Sarthe, Sablé is dominated by the austere façade of its château, which once belonged to the Colbert family and now houses the National Library's restoration and book binding workshops. Famous for its shortbread biscuits *(sablés)*, the town is the second largest economic centre in the Sarthe region. A favourable environment and pronounced dynamism have helped develop the foodstuff industry and diversify the local economy.
Nearby, art lovers will discover the fascinating Benedictine abbey of Solesmes and the church of Asnières-sur-Vègre, superbly decorated with Gothic murals.

- **Population:** 12 602
- **Michelin Map:** 310: G-7
- **Info:** pl. Raphaël-Élize, 72305 Sablé-sur-Sarthe. 02 43 95 00 60. www.tourisme.sable-sur-sarthe.fr.
- **Location:** Midway between Le Mans and Angers.
- **Don't Miss:** Gregorian chant at Abbaye St-Pierre.
- **Timing:** Half a day for the town and its surrounds.

VISIT

In the 17C the fief belonged to Laval-Bois-Dauphin, Marquis de Sablé. In 1711 Colbert de Torcy, the nephew of the great Jean-Baptiste Colbert, Louis XIV's Minister, rebuilt the château and radically changed the appearance of the town; many houses and the hospital date from this period.

Development has highlighted a fine group of 19C buildings in rue Carnot. The small port on the canalised part of the Sarthe used to receive sand-laden barges from the Loire. Nowadays it harbours about 20 craft for hire *(pénichettes)* as well as Le Sablésien, a **tourist boat** *(quai National, 72300 Sablé-sur-Sarthe; open Mar–Oct; 02 43 95 93 13; www.sablesien.com)* offering leisurely rides or luncheon-cruises along the Sarthe.

EXCURSIONS

Auvers-le-Hamon

8.5km/5.3mi N along D 24.

The chuch's nave has 15C–16C murals paintings depicting local saints and religious scenes.

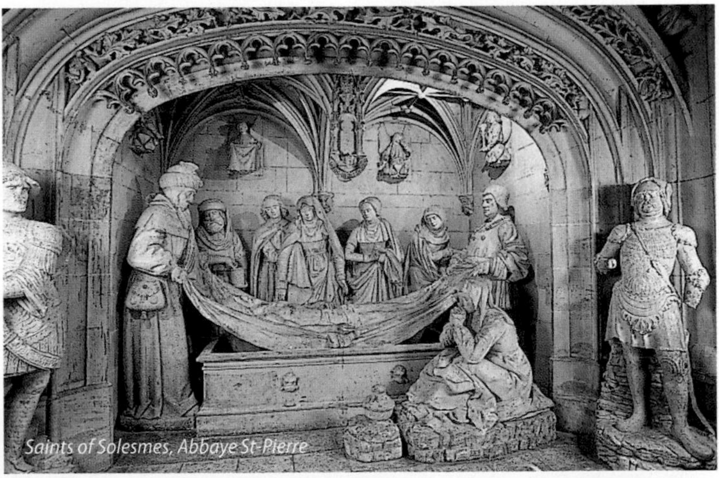

Saints of Solesmes, Abbaye St-Pierre

Ph. Gajic/MICHELIN

Wall paintings in the church, Asnières-sur-Vègre

S. Sauvignier/MICHELIN

Solesmes★

3km/2mi NE along the picturesque D 22.

A few miles upstream from Sablé lies Solesmes, which has won renown through its association with the Benedictine Order. From the north bank of the Sarthe and from the bridge there is an impressive **view★** of the north front of the abbey, a dark wall built at the end of the 19C in the Romanesque-Gothic style. The abbey buildings are reflected in the river, next to a less imposing, but rather more inviting-looking 18C priory. It expanded rapidly and by the early 16C had become very wealthy. The Revolution brought ruin, but a new community was established in 1833 by a priest from Sablé, Dom Guéranger, and in 1837 the abbey became the headquarters of the Benedictine Order in France.

The abbey **services**, to which the public is admitted, demonstrate the beauty of the liturgy celebrated in Benedictine monasteries.

Abbaye St-Pierre★

Only the abbey church is open to the public (in the main courtyard).

The **church** comprises the nave and transept which date from the 11C and 15C and the domical-vaulted chancel which was added in 1865. The famous sculpture groups, which are known as the **Saints of Solesmes★★**, are in the transept. Note in the south transept a monumental Entombment (1496) with a beautiful representation of Mary Magdalene at prayer; on the left, a terracotta Pietà from an earlier period, and, in the north transept, a remarkable composition depicting the scenes from the Virgin's life.

Asnières-sur-Vègre★

10km/6mi NE along D 4 and D 190.

Asnières lies in an attractive setting, deep in the picturesque Vègre Valley. The road *(D 190)* from Poillé gives a pretty view over the old houses with their steeply pitched roofs, the church and the Cour d'Asnières mansion.

Bridge

This medieval humpback structure provides a charming **view★** of the river, the old mill – still operational – against a backdrop of fine trees, and the elegant mansion with its turret and dormer windows on the right bank. Close to the mill stands a château known as the Moulin Vie dating from the 17C and 18C.

Church

The interior is decorated with Gothic **wall paintings★**: 13C in the nave and 15C in the chancel. The most famous, on the inside wall of the main façade, depicts Hell. On the left Christ is preparing to release the souls trapped in Limbo by attacking the three-headed dog, Cerberus, with a lance; in the centre Leviathan is swallowing up the Damned; finally, canine-headed demons are stirring a cauldron of the Damned in which the wimple of the lady of the manor and the bishop's mitre can be seen. The scenes on the north wall of the nave portray the Adoration of the Magi, the Presentation of Jesus in the Temple and the Flight into Egypt.

Cour d'Asnières

A little to the south of the church is an elongated Gothic building, with pretty windows. It was here that the canons of Le Mans, the one-time lords of Asnières, exercised their seigneurial rights, hence the name *cour* meaning court.

St-Denis-d'Anjou

10.5km/6.5mi SW along D 309. Guided tours by appointment 4€. Unaccompanied visit 8am–6.30pm. 02 43 70 69 09. www.saintdenisdanjou.com.
This village, with its numerous pretty gardens, has a 12C **fortified church** with keel vaulting and 12C and 15C frescoes that were discovered in 1947. Opposite the church, which belonged to the Chapter of Angers, stands the 15C canons' house (now the town hall), and the 16C wine market.

Chapelle de Varennes-Bourreau

10km/6mi S along D 159. Guided tours by appointment. 02 43 70 69 09.
This chapel nestles in the lush vegetation beside the River Sarthe; it is decorated with beautiful 12C and 15C frescoes: a mandorla surrounds Christ, whose hand is raised. The village of Varennes was formerly a small port engaged in the transport of wine to Angers.

Miré

16km/10mi SW via D 309 and D 27.
In this small village, the church is roofed with wooden keel vaulting decorated with 43 late-15C painted panels depicting the Four Evangelists, Angels bearing the Instruments of the Passion and the Apostles presenting the Creed.

Château de Vaux

3.5km/2mi NW of Miré on D 29 towards Bierné. Exterior and tour of moats only Jul–Aug Mon–Fri. www.chateau-devaux-anjou.com.
The picturesque château stands well back from the road to the right. The ruined curtain wall enclosed an elegant building with a stair turret and mullioned windows. This manor house was built at the end of the 15C by **Jean Bourré**, Lord of Miré, whose main claim to fame is that he introduced a delicious fruit – *bon-chrétien* pears – to the Angevin orchards.

ADDRESSES

STAY / EAT

Village Vacances nature et jardin – *53290 Bouère. 02 43 06 08 56. www.paysmeslaygrez.fr. 11 chalets for 7 pers.* A village of 11 wooden chalets (one adapted for those with reduced mobility) within a flowery village next to a 2ha/5-acre lake. Each has a fireplace and a private storage area for bicycles and fishing tackle.

Hotel Aster – *rte. de la Flèche. 02 43 92 28 96. www.hotelaster.fr. 30 rms.* An independent hotel close to the centre of Sablé. Bedrooms are functional and come with well-equipped bathrooms. The restaurant offers provençal décor and ambience, and traditional cooking at wallet-friendly prices. Staff are welcoming, professional and friendly.

SHOPPING

La Nouvelle Maison du Sablé – *38 r. Raphaël-Elizé. 02 43 95 01 72. www.le-petit-sable.fr.* The world of the sablé biscuit lies within this pleasant boutique with a sea-green Art Deco-style façade and blackcurrant-hued walls. The round golden biscuits are still hand-made according to the house's 1932 recipe. Make sure to try a Croq'Amours – a light chocolate, coffee or vanilla-flavoured meringue made with whole almonds and hazelnuts.

LEISURE ACTIVITIES

Croisières Saboliennes – *quai National. 02 43 95 93 13. www.sablesien.com.* Cruises on the Sablesien II (74 pers max) can be combined with a meal and the duration depends on the chosen itinerary. A different way to take in the fine landscapes of the Sarthe.

EVENTS

Fête Rock Ici Mômes – *End Jul in the grounds of the château. 02 43 62 22 22. www.sablesursarthe.fr/rock-ici-momes.* This child-oriented music festival brings together over 10 000 youngsters between the ages of 3 and 12.

Saint-Calais

Situated on the border between Maine and the Vendôme region, St-Calais is a market town dominated by the ruins of a medieval château. A few old gables still look down on the narrow streets.

- **Population:** 3 589
- **Michelin Map:** 310: N-7
- **Info:** pl. de l'Hôtel-de-Ville, 72120 St-Calais. ℘02 43 35 82 95. www.payscalaisien.com.
- **Location:** St-Calais lies 44km/27mi SE of Le Mans and 95km/59mi W of Orléans.
- **Don't Miss:** The Apple Turnover Festival – the Fête du Chausson aux Pommes has taken place every year since 1581 *(first weekend in September)* to commemorate the end of the plague.
- **Timing:** Allow yourself 1–2hrs to explore the town. Take a morning or afternoon to appreciate the château.

SIGHTS

The **quais de l'Anille** offer pleasant views of the riverside wash-houses, now overgrown with moss, and gardens of flowers against a background of picturesque roofs.

The district on the west bank developed round the Benedictine abbey which was founded in the reign of Childebert (6C) by Karilefus, an anchorite from Auvergne. The monastery was destroyed during the Revolution but the few 17C buildings that survived are now occupied by the library, the theatre and the museum.

Église Notre-Dame

Construction of the church began in 1425 with the chancel; the building is a mixture of the Flamboyant Gothic and Renaissance styles.

The Italianate **façade**★ was finished in 1549 and is typical of the second Renaissance. The carved panels of the twin doors portray scenes from the Life of the Virgin Mary.

The first three bays of the interior are Renaissance; the vaulting with pendentives springs from majestic columns with Ionic capitals. The 17C loft came from the abbey and the organ itself is of the same date. Restored in 1974, it is the pride and joy of the church's organists.

EXCURSION

Château de Courtanvaux

12km/7.4mi S along D 303 to Bessé-sur-Braye; from Bessé, follow the signposting. Open mid-Apr–Sept Tue–Sun 10am–noon, 3–7pm; for guided tours (1hr) call for information. Free entry to grounds all year 9am–7pm ⚭4€. ℘02 43 35 34 43. www.chateau-de-courtanvaux.abcsalles.com.

The château, a Gothic building sheltering in the valley, was the seat of a marquisate held successively by the Louvois and Montesquiou families; one of the owners was Michel Le Tellier, **Marquis de Louvois** (1639–91) and Louis XIV's Minister for War. In 1815, when Napoleon fell from power, the château came to life again after 150 years of neglect and became the residence of the **Countess of Montesquiou** who had been the governess to the King of Rome, Napoleon's son by Marie-Louise.

An avenue of plane trees leads to the charming Renaissance gatehouse. The buildings have typical 15C and 16C features: tall roofs, mullioned windows and pointed dormer pediments.

The courtyard is overlooked by two terraces. The main block, called the Grand Château, has a suite of four rooms (47m/154ft long) on the first floor, which were redecorated in 1882.

Mondoubleau

Approached from the west, Mondoubleau can be seen clustered on the east bank of the River Grenne. Perched at a precarious angle on a bluff to the south of the road to Cormenon, the ruins of a keep overlook the village where remains of the curtain wall are partly hidden among the houses and trees. Several graceful churches and properties that once belonged to the Knights Templars can be seen in the surrounding area.

- **Population:** 1 509
- **Michelin Map:** 318: C-4
- **Info:** 2 r. Brizieux, 41170 Mondoubleau. 02 54 80 77 08.
- **Location:** Between La Ferté-Bernard (30km/19mi to the NW) and Vendôme (25km/15.5mi to the SE).
- **Timing:** Allow about half a day to get the most out of your visit.

FORTRESS

Visit by guided tour only Jun–Aug (departing from the Maison du Perche, pl. du Marché) Sat 3pm; daily by appointment for parties of four. 3.60€. 02 54 80 77 08.

At the end of the 10C, Hugues Doubleau, from whom the town has taken its name, built a red-sandstone fortress over which towered a 33m/108ft-high keep. All that remains of this imposing stronghold are half a keep, the governor's house, known as the Maison Courcillon (15C), and the baronial building (16C).

DRIVING TOURS

1 NORTH OF MONDOUBLEAU

Round trip of 26km/16mi on D 921 – about 1hr.

Château de St-Agil

Guided tours of the outside only: Mon–Sat except public holidays 10am–noon, 3–5pm. 02 54 80 94 02.

This is an interesting château encircled by a moat. The part of the building dating from the 13C was altered in 1720. The early-16C gatehouse is flanked by two towers decorated with a diaper pattern in red and black bricks. The machicolations guard the sentry walk and the pepper-pot roofs. The main building has a dormer window with a medallion of the lord of the manor, Antoine de la Vove. The park was landscaped by Jules Hardouin-Mansart and transformed in 1872 in the English style complete with a fine ice house from the 16C.

Commanderie d'Arville

Open Jun–Aug 10am–12.30pm, 1.30–6.30pm; Apr–May and Sept–Oct 10am–noon, 1.30–5.30pm; Mar and Nov 1.30–5.30pm. 8€ (audioguide +6€). Closed Dec to Feb , and Wed except in Jul–Aug. 02 54 80 75 41. www.commanderie-arville.com.

The road D 921 running south from Le Gault-Perche offers a good view of the Templar Commandery which later passed to the Knights of St John of Jerusalem. The ironstone building in its rural setting makes an attractive picture.

The 12C chapel housing the Commandery is crowned by a gable belfry which is linked to a flint tower, once part of the former ramparts. The town gateway (late 15C) is decorated with two brick turrets with unusual conical roofs made of chestnut. The handsome tithe barn and dovecote have been restored and an information centre about military religious orders has been set up to retrace the history of the crusades and re-create the crusaders' life with the help of pictures, sounds and even smells (badian, anise, etc.).

Souday

The nave of the **church** is extended by an interesting 16C two-storey chancel. Two flights of stairs, with wrought-iron railings which date from 1838, lead to the upper floor which is lit by Renaissance stained glass depicting the Pas-

The Templars

The Order, which was both military and monastic, was founded in 1119 in Jerusalem. The members took vows to defend the Holy City from the Muslims and protect all Christians making a pilgrimage to Jerusalem. They built fortified commanderies along the routes to serve as banks in the 13C: pilgrims deposited money at their local commandery then drew it out on arrival in the Holy Land.

The Templars thus grew rich and powerful. Early in the 14C the Order of Templars numbered 15 000 knights and 9 000 commanderies. It had its own judicial system, paid no tax and took its authority directly from the Pope. Such wealth and independence earned it many enemies and brought the Order's downfall.

In 1307 Philip the Fair persuaded the Pope that the Templars should be brought to trial; he had every single member of the Order in France arrested on the same day. The Grand Master, Jacques de Molay, and 140 knights were imprisoned in Chinon Castle; the following year they were brought to Paris on trumped-up charges. Fifty-four of them, including Jacques de Molay, were burned at the stake on one of the islets in the Seine.

sion and the Resurrection of Christ. The elegant ogive vaulting in the 11C crypt springs from columns without capitals. The south transept is decorated with 16C paintings of St Joseph, St Joachim and four scenes from the Life of John the Baptist.

2 SOUTH OF MONDOUBLEAU

Round trip of 24km/15mi – about 1hr.

Le Temple

All that is left of the Templar commandery is a 13C church with a squat bell-tower and a square chevet nestling pleasantly by a pool.

Turn right onto D 56.

Sargé-sur-Braye

The church of St-Martin was built in the 11C and 15C. The painted wainscots date from 1549. The murals discovered in the nave are 16C (*Pietà, St Martin*) and in the chancel 14C (*Christ in Majesty* and *Labours of the Months;* note the three faces of Janus symbolising January).

Baillou

The little village is attractively clustered below a great 16C–17C château. The beautiful early-16C **church** stands alone on a mount. The Renaissance doorway is flanked by scrolled pilasters, surmounted by figures of Adam and Eve.

Take D 86 back to Mondoubleau. Fine view of the town on arrival.

ADDRESSES

STAY

Chambre d'hôte Peyron-Gaubert – *Carrefour de l'Ormeau. ℘02 54 80 93 76. Closed Nov–Mar. 5 rms. evening meal.* All of the furniture in this strangely seductive 17C property was made by the owner, a cabinetmaker and artist. Well worth staying here.

SHOPPING

Medieval market – *rte. des Templiers, 41170 Arville. ℘02 54 80 75 41. www.commanderie-arville.com.* This Middle Ages-themed market takes place at the Commanderie-Arville each Sun from Whitsun onwards. Lively and hugely entertaining, it features local craftspeople, sword fighting, jugglers, fire eaters, dancers, and **activities for children**. Great for local produce and brushing up on your French.

La Ferté-Bernard★

The Renaissance houses of La Ferté-Bernard cluster round the church of Notre-Dame-des-Marais. The lush pastures of the Huisne Valley are watered by the Huisne River, its tributary the Même and the Sarthe. La Ferté-Bernard was the birthplace of the poet Robert Garnier (1544–90), whose best-known tragedy, *The Jews*, echoes Corneille and foreshadows Racine.

- **Population:** 9 262
- **Michelin Map:** 310: M-5
- **Info:** 15 pl. de la Lice, 72400 La Ferté-Bernard. 02 43 71 21 21. www.la-ferte-bernard.com.
- **Location:** 40km/25mi E of Le Mans, 90km/56mi SW of Chartres, and 5km/3mi from autoroute A 11.
- **Parking:** There are town centre car parks as well as on-street parking around the church.
- **Don't Miss:** The St Julien gate.
- **Timing:** Allow 1–2hrs to explore the town and have a coffee.
- **Kids:** Explore the town by canoe or electric-powered boat.

A BIT OF HISTORY

The old fortified town, that grew up round the castle *(ferté)* was erected on stilts in the middle of the marshes.

It was distinguished by the name of the first feudal lord, Bernard, whose descendants held the domain until the 14C. Under Louis XI it was made the property of the Guise family; in the 16C it enjoyed a period of economic prosperity giving rise to some remarkable buildings which contribute to the charm of the town.

After siding with the Catholic League and being defeated by the troops of Henri IV, La Ferté was sold to Cardinal de Richelieu in 1642 and was held by his heirs until the Revolution.

SIGHTS

Porte St-Julien

This gate, which is protected by two round towers and machicolations, was built in the 15C under Louis XI; the moat was fed by the River Huisne. There was a postern and a double gate guarded by a portcullis and a drawbridge.

Porte St-Julien

Ph. Blondel/MICHELIN

Old houses

East of the Porte St-Julien in r. de l'Huisne are a few Renaissance houses.
There are several old houses in rue Carnot including a pilgrim inn (15C) on the road to Santiago de Compostela and a house (butcher's shop) decorated with a figure representing a pilgrim (ground floor).

Halles

The market hall *(restored)* on place de la Lice and in rue Carnot was built in 1535. The façade overlooking the square is decorated with Guise lions on each gable and an extensive tile roof pierced by dormers and supported by a splendid timber frame.

Fountain

pl. Carnot.
The granite fountain (15C–16C) is fed by a spring in the Guillottières district which is channelled beneath the Huisne.

Chapelle St-Lyphard

Thorough restoration work has revealed the chapel of an 11C feudal castle. The outbuildings *(private property)* also remain. The chapel, which was originally built against the main body of the castle and given a small side oratory, is decorated with modern stained-glass windows portraying Louis, Duke of Orléans, and his wife, Valentina Visconti, lord and lady of La Ferté-Bernard to whom the castle was endowed in 1392.

ADDITIONAL SIGHTS

Église Notre-Dame-des-Marais★★

Guided tours available; ask at the tourist office. 02 43 71 21 21.
This magnificent church is a fine example of the Flamboyant Gothic style with early touches of the Renaissance. The nave, the transept and the square tower were built between 1450 and 1500; from 1535 to 1544 Mathurin Delaborde worked on the church and between 1550 and 1590 the Viet brothers were in charge of the construction of the spacious chancel (completed in 1596).

DRIVING TOUR

Le Perche-Gouët★

87km/54mi round tour – Allow half a day.
Take D 153 via Cherreau and then the D 136 towards Ceton.

Le Perche-Gouet, which is sometimes known as Lower Perche, was named in the 11C after **William Gouet**, who owned five baronies within the jurisdiction of the Bishop of Chartres.

Église Notre-Dame-es-Marais
©Hemis/Alamy

Le Perche-Gouët lies between the Loir and the Huisne. Much of the immense forest which once covered the land has been replaced by fields and orchards. The eastern part of Le Perche-Gouët is very similar to the Beauce, but is distinguished from it by its scattered farms and the abundance of hedges and trees. The farms hidden in the deep lanes were originally built of wattle and daub or within a brick framework. Their owners raise cattle, particularly dairy herds, which have replaced the breeding of the Percheron draught horses, their coats dappled grey, roan or black.

Ceton

The **church of St-Pierre** derives its importance from the Cluniac priory to which it belonged from 1090. The tower is Romanesque, the Gothic nave and chancel were built in the 13C–16C. Each bay in the side aisles has its own roof at right angles to the nave in the Percheron manner.

Continue along D 637 towards Coudray-au-Perche.

Les Étilleux

South of the village on the D 13, take the marked path that climbs to the summit of the hillock (270m/885ft high, with a radio-relay station) for fine views across the Ozanne Valley, the Perche hills and the Huisne Valley.

Return to Coudray-au-Perche (D 124) then go on to Authon-du-Perche (D 9) to arrive at St-Ulphace on the D 13, which becomes the D 7.

St-Ulphace

Half way up the slope, the 15–16C church has an imposing façade leaning against a tower, and a Renaissance portal.

Continue along D 14.

Montmirail

The attractive little town of Montmirail, once strongly fortified, was built on a site with excellent natural defences. The **castle** (*guided tours (40min) Jul–mid-Aug Wed–Mon 2–7pm, May–Jun and mid-Aug–mid-Sept Sat–Sun and public holidays 2.30–6.30pm; 5€; 02 43 93 72 71*), built in the 15C on top of a medieval mound, was altered in the 18C by the Princesse de Conti. It still has the original underground works dating from the 11C and 14C. On 9 January 1169, the castle was the scene of a memorable encounter between the Kings of England and France in the course of which the exiled Archbishop of Canterbury, **Thomas Becket**, reaffirmed the primacy of the Church. The apartments of the Princesse de Conti (the daughter of Louis XIV and Louise de La Vallière), including the Louis XV Grand Salon, are open to the public, as are the dungeons and armouries. The Classical west façade, contrasting with the medieval south and east fronts, can be viewed from the terrace, which also gives a vast **panorama★** over the countryside of Le Perche-Gouet.

Go towards La Vibraye. The D 302, the D72 cut through part off the Vibraye forest.

Semur-en-Vallon

This is an attractive village by a man-made lake. In the valley on the western edge of Vibraye Forest stands a 15C moated and turreted castle. The entrance façade, flanked by round towers with lanterns, was altered in the 17C.

The Decauville **tourist train** (*Jun–mid-Sept Sun 2.30–6.30pm; 3.50€ (children 3€); 02 43 71 30 36 or 02 43 93 67 86; http://ccfsv.free.fr*) runs on a 1.5km/1mi long circuit.

Take D 98 towards Lavaré. At Bois Guinant slow down to enjoy the view to the left and take first left.

Bouër

Don't miss this tiny village lost among the hills dominating the Huisne Valley. Its arrow-shaped slate steeple is attached to the tower by spiral volute scrolls.

Take D 29 towards Montmirail until it meets the D 1. Go left here. At Lamnay, go right onto D 125.

Château de Courtangis

Among the tall trees in an idyllically isolated valley are the turrets, dormers and steeply pitched mansard roofs of a graceful early-16C manor house.

Leave Courtangis towards Courtenard on D 36.

Courgenard

In this small village with its pretty gardens, the door of the **church** is carved with low-relief statues in the Renaissance style.

ADDRESSES

EAT

Le Dauphin – *3 r. d'Huisne - 02 43 93 00 39 - closed 5–22 Aug, Sun eve, Mon.* A splendid restaurant near the Porte St-Julien, serving traditional and regional cuisine in a cool and atmospheric setting. You are advised to make a reservation, as this is a very popular eatery.

Auberge de la Forêt – *38 r. Gabriel-Goussault, 72320 Vibraye. 16km/10mi S of La Ferté-Bernard, towards St Calais then D 211. 02 43 93 60 07. www.auberge-de-la-foret.fr. Closed mid-Jan–1st week in Feb, 1st week Sept, Sun eve and Mon. €9.50.* Replete and content are the words to describe how you will come away from this auberge after sampling its local dishes. The art on the walls is for sale. Outdoor terrace in summer and 7 modern bedrooms for a stopover.

Brou

Although Brou was once a barony in Le Perche-Gouet, it is more characteristic of the rich and fertile agricultural region of Beauce; a town centred on its market place where poultry and eggs are the main commerce. Many old street names here have remained unchanged since the Middle Ages.

- **Population:** 3 572
- **Michelin Map:** 311: C-6
- **Info:** r. de la Chevalerie, 28160 Brou. 02 37 47 01 12.
- **Location:** 22km/14mi NW of Châteaudun, 40km/25mi S of Chartres and 45km/28mi E of La Ferté-Bernard.
- **Timing:** Come on Wed morning for the foodie market in the pl. des Halles.
- **Kids:** Let off steam in the Thiron-Gardais gardens.

THE TOWN

Place des Halles

On the corner of rue de la Tête-Noire stands an old house with projecting upper storeys, which dates from the early 16C; the timberwork is decorated with carved motifs. In rue des Changes near the market place there is another 16C house with a curved façade; the corner post bears the figures of St James and a pilgrim, since Brou lies on the old pilgrimage route from Chartres to Santiago de Compostela in Spain.

Église de Yèvres

1.5km/0.9mi E.

The **church** dates mainly from the 15C and 16C, its Renaissance doorway framed by carved pilasters and surmounted by a double pediment. The interior contains remarkable classical **woodwork**★: the pulpit which is decorated with effigies of the Virtues; the retable on the high altar; the altars in the side chapels; and an eagle lectern.

The door into the baptismal chapel (fine carved wood ceiling) is beautifully carved with scenes of the Martyrdom of St Barbara and the Baptism of Christ.

EXCURSIONS

Illiers-Combray

Illiers, on the upper reaches of the Loire, 24km/15mi southwest of Chartres and 28km/17mi northwest of Châteaudun is a market town serving both the Beauce and Perche regions.

It was under the name of Combray that **Marcel Proust** (1871–1922) portrayed Illiers in his novel *Remembrance of Things Past*. Proust spent his holidays in Illiers where his father was born; the impressions young Marcel experienced here were later to become "that great edifice of memories".

Musée Marcel-Proust - Maison de tante Léonie

4 r. du Docteur-Proust.

Guided tours (1hr) Jul–Aug Tue–Sun 11am, 2.30pm, 4pm; mid-Jan–Jun and Sept–mid-Dec Tue–Sun 2.30pm and 4pm. 7€. Closed mid-Dec–mid-Jan, 1 May, 1 and 11 Nov.

02 37 24 30 97.

Some of the rooms (kitchen, dining room) in this house belonging to Proust's uncle, Jules Amiot, are still as they were in the novel. The bedrooms have been arranged to match Proust's descriptions of them.

The **museum** evokes the writer's life, work and relationships, and has portraits and mementoes as well as a number of early photographs taken by Paul Nadar.

Pré Catelan

S of Illiers-Combray on D 149.

Designed by Jules Amiot, the gardens, which include a serpentine, a dovecote, a pavilion and some fine trees, make a pleasant place for a walk beside the Loir.

DRIVING TOUR

Le Faux-Perche

65km/40mi –allow half a day.

Although it also borders the Beauce region, the western part of le Perche-Gouët, known also as **Faux-Perche**, differs from le Bas-Perche due to its varied habitats – abundant hedgerows, trees and rolling landscapes. Farms are known locally as "borderies", and rely mainly on cattle breeding particularly dairy herds, which have taken the place of breeding dapple-grey, black or chestnut percheron draft horses. The waterways of the Ozanne, Yerre and Braye flow towards the Loir; only the Rhône meets the Huisne at Nogent-le-Rotrou.

Take the D 921 via Chapelle-Royale to La Bazoche-Gouët, the gateway to the Perche Regional Natural Park.

Le Bazoche-Gouët

The 12C–13C church was modified at the start of the 16C by adding flamboyant window bays and side aisles. Note the portal with spiral columns of the south bay. Inside is a square 16C belfry; the Renaissance stained glass in the chancel depicts the Passion of Christ as seen in German engravings – this was a gift from the local Lords, the Bourbon-Conti family. Note the realism of expression and details.

Take D 9 towards Nogent-le-Rotrou, then approx 5km/3mi after Authon-du-Perche, go right onto D 371 towards Vichères where you turn off to La Gaudaine.

Ferme de Rougemont

From D 371 at this high farmstead enjoy a sweeping view over the Ozanne basin.

Thiron-Gardais

The village has developed on the south bank of the Thironne, which flows out of the Étang des Moines (Monks' Pool) near the abbey founded by St Bernard in 1114 and dedicated to the Holy Trinity.

Château de Frazé

©A.J.Cassaigne/Photononstop

Tiron Abbey (written without the "h" in those days) was especially prosperous in the 12C and 13C. The **abbey church** is still a huge building even though the chancel collapsed in 1817.

Continue along D 922 towards Brou via Chassant.

Frazé

Frazé is a little village beside the River Foussarde. Its origins are Gallo-Roman; later it was fortified and surrounded by water. The village square provides a charming view of both the church and the château.

The **château** was first built to a square ground plan in 1493 and protected by a moat and a pool; it was completed in the 16C and 17C with the outbuildings which form an entrance porch. The surviving buildings include: a watchtower; two towers of which one stands alone and is decorated with machicolations and a moulding; a fort flanked by towers and ornamented with sculpted corbels; and an interesting chapel with historiated ornaments. An old well, gardens, canals and terraces enhance the courtyard and the park (*grounds only: mid-Apr–Sept Sun 3–6pm; 3€; 02 37 29 56 76*).

ADDRESSES

STAY

Chambre d'hôte Le manoir de Planchette – *Manoir de Planchette. 72400 Cormes. 02 43 93 24 75. 5 rms.* Tranquil 13C country manor with light and spacious bedrooms.

Hôtel le Plat d'Étain – *15 pl. des Halles. 28160 Brou. 02 37 96 05 65. www.leplatdetain.fr. 21 rms.* Completely renovated town centre hotel offering 21 comfy modern rooms.

EAT

L'Ascalier – *9 pl. Dauphin. 02 37 96 05 52. Closed Sun, Mon & Tue eves.* Simple cooking, reasonable prices, and a lovely 16C staircase. Near market hall.

LEISURE ACTIVITIES

Chemin de fer touristique de Semur-en-Vallon – *02 43 93 67 86. Wed, Sat, Sun, 14 Jul–31 Aug, 2.30–6pm – 4€ (under 12 years 2.50€).* 45min trip on a lovely old narrow-gauge train stopping off at Muséotrain.

Parc de loisirs – *rte. des Moulins - 28160 Brou - 02 37 42 02 17 - www.parc-loisirs-brou.fr - Jul–Aug 10am–8pm.* 28ha/69-acre lake, beach, watersports, tennis, fishing, etc.

Although Le Loir cannot offer the architectural splendours of La Loire, it has a more rustic charm that many find more seductive than its stately big sister, as visitors dawdle gently through a lushly verdant, lightly-wooded landscape, with little bridges straddling the waters at each village. The confusingly named tributary runs over 300km/186mi from south of Chartres to Angers, and is at its most attractive between Vendôme and Trôo, where there is a maze of troglodyte dwellings.

A Breath of Fresh Air

The Loir offers an abundance of churches, châteaux and historic towns, as well as fishing, boating, walking and cycling trails and wine-tasting. In its upper reaches, the river winds its way through hills, meadows, well-heeled towns and pretty villages. At the busy market town of Châteaudun, the Gothic and Renaisssance Château de Dunois soars dramatically from a bluff above the banks of the Loir. The next major port of call heading south is Vendôme, a captivating and picturesque town built on islands in the river. Pilgrims heading for Santiago de Compostela once stopped here; now it is a chic place to live within commuting distance of Paris, with trendy waterside restaurants to cater to an affluent clientele. Continuing west along a lovely wooded stretch of the Loir, you arrive at quaint Lavardin, a small village of restored houses and a romantically ruined château. Then comes Montoire, where Pétain and Hitler met in 1940, and the poet Ronsard was prior of the frescoed chapelle St-Gilles.

After a trip around the troglodyte houses and breathtaking Romanesque frescoes in the church of St-Jacques-des-Guérets in Trôo, wine buffs might want to explore the vineyards on the slopes around Poncé and La Chartre-sur-le-Loir, where Côteaux du Vendômois and the unique Vin Gris wine is produced. North of the river, a foray among the oak of the Forêt de Bercé awaits.

Rejoining the Loir, the impressive parkland and formal gardens of the Renaissance Château du Lude are a must. Finish at La Flèche, where the Prytanée, a military academy set up originally as a Jesuit college in the 17C by Henri IV, can be visited.

Highlights

1. **Châteaudun** and its imposing castle (p322)
2. **Old Vendôme** and la Trinité (p328)
3. **Lavardin**'s ruined château (p338)
4. Walking in the **Bercé** forest (p343)
5. Magnificent park of **Château de Lude** (p347)

Vendôme

THE LOIR VALLEY

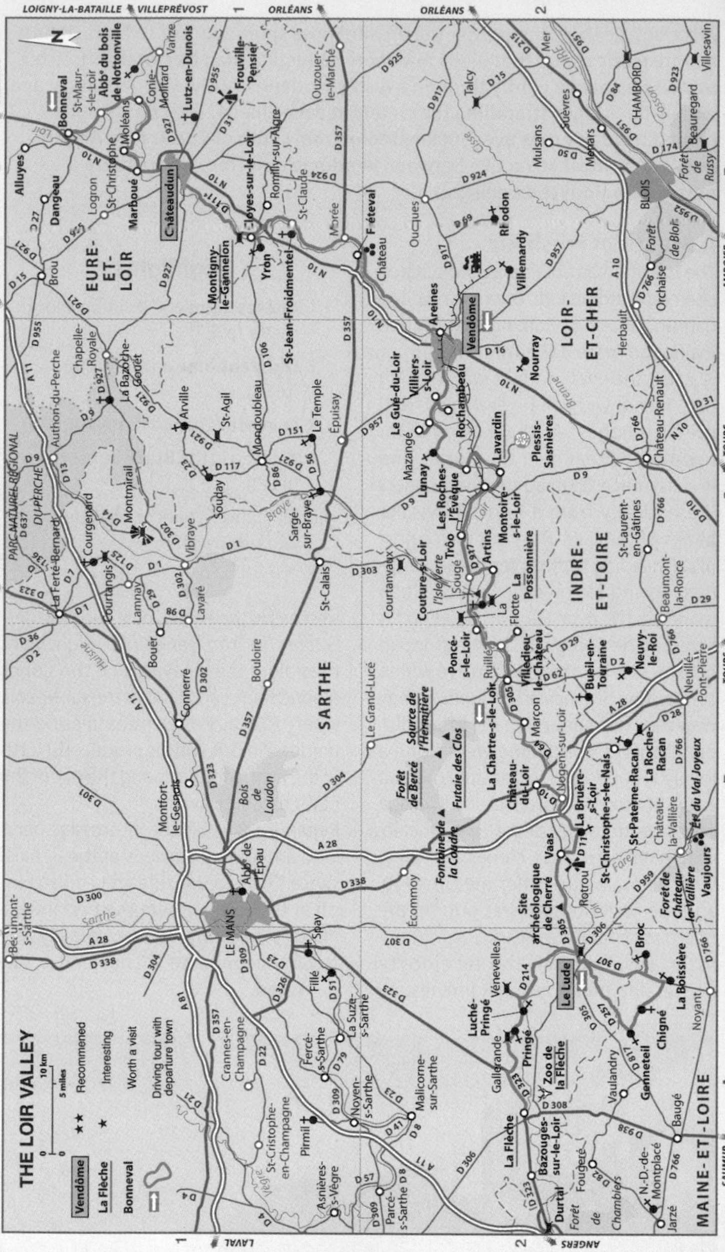

Bonneval

Bonneval developed in the Middle Ages around the 9C Benedictine monastery of St-Florentin on the River Loir. The old town walls are reflected in the waters of the surrounding moat. With its small attractive churches, often decorated with frescoes, and shaded riverbanks, the Bonneval region is an angler's paradise and a walker's dream. Inhabitants of Bonneval are called *Bonnevalais* (*Bonnevalaises* in the plural).

- **Population:** 4 161
- **Michelin Map:** 311: E-6
- **Info:** 2 pl. Westerham, 28800 Bonneval. 02 37 47 55 89. www.ville-bonneval.fr.
- **Location:** Along the N 10, between Chartres (28km/17.4mi to the N) and Châteaudun (15km/9mi to the S).
- **Don't Miss:** The Loir Valley is well worth exploring; very scenic.
- **Timing:** You can explore Bonneval in 1hr, but take a day and get to know the surrounding area.
- **Kids:** A boat trip on the canals (*see box, below*).

SIGHTS

Ancienne Abbaye

A specialist hospital centre now occupies the former abbey buildings.

The beautiful 13C **fortified gateway**★ with its pointed archway was integrated into the abbot's lodging, which was built for the Bishop of Chartres in the late 15C.

The lodge is an attractive building of chequered stonework, flanked by two machicolated towers and capped with pinnacled gables over the dormer windows. In front of the abbey stretches the **Grève**, a large shaded promenade beside the moat.

For an attractive view of the old towers and the church spire, go to the end of r. des Fossés-St-Jacques to the west of the town.

Église Notre-Dame

The early-13C church was built in the pure Gothic style: a fine rose window above the flat chevet, an elegant triforium in the nave, fine woodwork behind the font and a 17C figure of Christ.

From the nearby bridge there is a picturesque view of the fortifications and of the moat lined with washhouses.

Porte St-Roch and Tour du Roi

Several pointed arches mark the old houses that line rue St-Roch, the street which leads to St-Roch Gate

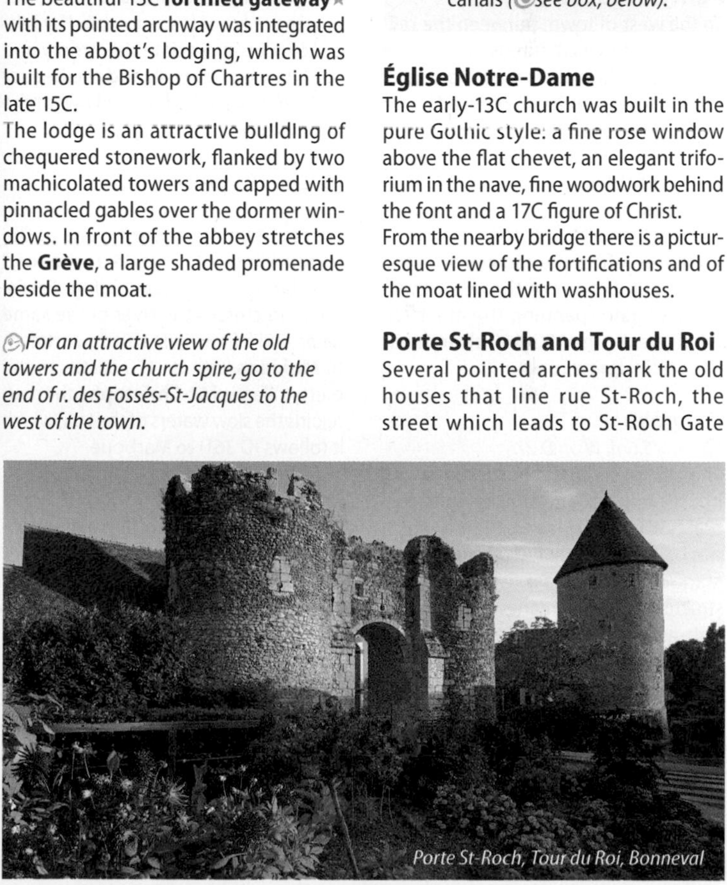

Porte St-Roch, Tour du Roi, Bonneval

Boat Tour

Board one of the small, motorised boats *(4 people)* that navigate the local canals, offering views of Bonneval's monuments and attractions from a different angle. *Jul–Aug daily 2–8pm; Apr–Jun and Sept Sun and public holidays 2.30–6.30pm. Bateau "Ruban Bleu", La Grève. 06 22 91 63 82. www.ville-bonneval.eu/visite.php.*

with its two round towers. Beside it stands the King's Tower, the old keep, pierced by loopholes and capped with a pepper-pot roof.

Porte Boisville and Pont du Moulin

To the west of town, between the railway and the bypass, stands the Boisville Gate (13C); the only remaining part of the first town wall, it was reduced in size in the 15C.

EXCURSIONS

Alluyes

7km/4.3mi NW on D 144.

All that is left of the old **castle** is the great round tower of the keep and a fortified gate spanning the moat. On the riverside, the 15C–16C **church** has two fascinating murals.

Dangeau

9km/5.6mi W on D 27.

The village square is bordered by old houses of brick and timber construction (15C). The **Église St-Pierre**, which was built in the early 12C by monks from Marmoutier, is a vast, well-balanced structure in pure Romanesque style. The buttresses and facings are in ironstone. The door in the south porch is embellished with scrolls and strange symbols carved on the lintel: the Cross appears between the Sun and the Moon, which have been given human faces. Avarice is shown as a demon holding a purse, whereas Lust is portrayed as a female figure.

The wooden ceiling in the nave is supported on archaic pillars. There are several statues in the aisles: the two figures on horseback are typical of popular 15C–17C sacred art. The baptistery contains a marble triptych of the Passion and the Resurrection, dated 1536.

DRIVING TOUR

Upper Reaches of the Loir★

77km/48mi. Allow one day.

The Loir wends its leisurely way through a peaceful landscape defined by rolling hills, green meadows, smart towns and charming villages, which have earned the region the name *La Douce France* (Gentle France). Originally the river was navigable up to Château-du-Loir, but now the only boats are occupied by fishermen who appreciate the variety and abundance of the fish and the beauty of the poplars and silvery willows at the water's edge.

Leave Bonneval to the S.

There are uninterrupted views of the surrounding countryside as the road cuts through the plateau. Before **Conie**, the road crosses the river of the same name and follows it (D 110) downstream to **Moléans** with its 17C castle. In the pretty village of **St-Christophe** the road rejoins the slow waters of the Loir, which it follows (D 361) to Marboué.

Marboué

Once a Gallo-Roman settlement, the village is known for its tall 15C bell-tower and crocketed spire and for its bathing beach on the river.

Châteaudun★★

See CHÂTEAUDUN

Montigny-le-Gannelon★

This fortress on the north bank of the Loir can be seen from afar on N 10. The name Montigny comes from Mons-Igny meaning Signal Hill; Gannelon evokes either the traitor who betrayed Roland to his enemies, or more likely the priest of St-Avit in Châteaudun who inherited the fortress in the 11C.

Château★

Guided tours (1hr) Mon–Fri Jun–Sept 10am–noon, 2–5pm, Sat–Sun 2–5pm). Park and château 8€; park only Jun–Aug 10am–6pm 3€. 02 37 98 30 03. www.domainedemontigny.com.

The château is approached through the park, in full view of the highly composite west façade. The combination of brick and stonework is striking. Two towers – Tour des Dames and Tour de l'Horloge – are the only remains of the Renaissance château that was rebuilt from 1475 to 1495 by Jacques de Renty. The château contains interesting information on the illustrious **Lévis-Mirepoix** family. To the right of a large Renaissance staircase adorned with portraits of Marshals of Lévis in medallions are the Gothic cloisters with a fine collection of 16C Italian faïence plates. The richly furnished rooms that follow contain numerous portraits and mementoes of the Montmorency and Lévis-Mirepoix families. They are the Salon des Colonnes, Salon des Dames, Grand Salon (portrait of Gilles de Montmorency-Laval, Sire of Rais, said to have inspired Charles Perrault for his character Bluebeard) and the Salle à Manger Montmorency (portraits of Louis XVIII and Charles X by the Baron Gérard). On the grounds, ostriches, emus, nandus (a South American ostrich), waterfowl and pheasants roam beneath 150-year-old trees. Hidden behind a screen of greenery stand the former riding school and stables, a vast shed on a frame of steel girders built at the same time as the Eiffel Tower in Paris. Today it contains old farm implements, carriages and stuffed animals.

Cloyes-sur-le-Loir

Cloyes, once a fortified town and staging post on the pilgrim road to Santiago de Compostela, straddles a bend in the Loir on the southern edge of the Beauce region. It is a welcoming town with several picturesque old houses and a church with a 15C belfry. In 1883 **Émile Zola** stayed in Cloyes to study the local customs for his novel *The Earth*, which is set in Cloyes and **Romilly-sur-Aigre**.

Leave Cloyes on D 81 E to Bouche-d'Aigre. Drive 1km/0.6mi S on D 35 (towards Vendôme), then turn right onto D 81; entrance in the garden of the home for the elderly.

Chapelle d'Yron

This Romanesque chapel is decorated with well-preserved **mural paintings** in red and ochre tones.

Those in the nave are 12C and depict the *Flagellation* and the *Offering of the Magi (left)*, the *Kiss of Judas* and an abbot (St Bernard) *(right)* and the *Apostles (apse)* below a gentle-featured *Christ in Majesty* (14C) on the oven vault of the apse.

Return to the D 35 and turn right when you get to the N10.

St-Jean-Froidmentel

On the west bank is the village of St-Jean-Froidmentel. Its church has an attractive Gothic Renaissance doorway.

Return to the east bank.

A row of poplars separates the road from the river. Between Morée and Fréteval there are fishing huts on the bank and one or two pretty riverside houses with flat-bottomed boats moored nearby.

Fréteval

The ruins of a **medieval** castle *(15min round trip on foot)* look down from their bluff on the east bank to Fréteval on the far bank, a favourite meeting place for fishermen. Soon after, the signed tourist road leaves the river bank.

Areines

Lying in the Loir plain, this village was an important town in the Roman era. The 12C **church** bears a plain façade, adorned by a 14C Madonna.

Châteaudun★★

On the south bank of the Loir at the point where the Perche region joins the Beauce, Châteaudun and its castle stand on a bluff, indented by narrow valleys called *cavées*.

- **Population:** 13 955
- **Michelin Map:** 311: D-7
- **Info:** 1 r. de Luynes, 28200 Châteaudun ℘02 37 45 22 46. www.ville-chateaudun.com.
- **Location:** 130km/80mi SW of Paris, between Chartres (45km/28mi to the N) and Vendôme (40km/25mi to the SW).
- **Don't Miss:** The dungeon, and the Musée des Beaux-Arts et d'Histoire naturelle.
- **Kids:** Explore the Loir by canoe or go horse-riding. Visit the Foulon caves.
- **Timing:** Summer visitors should consider reserving places at the medieval dinner; allow 2hrs to explore the town.

A BIT OF HISTORY

Dunois, the Bastard of Orléans (1402–56) – Handsome Dunois, the faithful companion of Joan of Arc, was the illegitimate son of Louis I of Orléans and Mariette d'Enghien. He was brought up by **Valentina Visconti**, Louis' wife, who loved him as much as her own children. From the age of 15 Dunois fought the English for several decades. In 1429 he rallied the army to the defence of Orléans and delivered Montargis. He took part in all the great events of Joan of Arc's career. Towards the end of his life, having won all the honours it is possible for one man to win, he retired to Châteaudun in 1457.

Dunois was buried in the church of Notre-Dame at Cléry. He was well educated and well read and Jean Cartier, the chronicler, described him as "one of the best speakers of the French language."

A heroic defence – On 18 October 1870 the Prussians attacked Châteaudun with 24 cannons and 12 000 men. Confronting them were only 300 local members of the national guard and 600 free fighters, who managed to hold out all day behind their barricades, despite heavy bombing which lasted from noon to 6.30pm. Finally, they had to admit they were outnumbered and consented to retreat. The Prussians promptly set fire to the town and 263 houses were razed. In recognition of services rendered to France, Châteaudun received the Legion of Honour and adopted the motto *Extincta revivisco* ("I rise again from the ashes").

WALKING TOUR

OLD TOWN★

Rue du Château, which is lined by overhanging houses, opens onto a charming little square with two old houses: the one with pilasters, beams and carved medallions dates from the 16C; the other, heavily restored, is a corner house with a carved corner post showing the Virgin and St Anne *(badly damaged)*.

It is prolonged by rue de la Cuirasserie (fine 16C house with a corner turret), which opens onto a square named after **Cap-de-la-Madeleine**, a town in the province of Quebec in Canada founded in the 17C by a priest from Châteaudun. On the right sits the Hôtel-Dieu, founded in 1092 and modernised in 1762; on the left rises the Palais de Justice (Law Court), housed in a former Augustinian abbey built in the Classical style.

The **Église de la Madeleine**★ is built into the ramparts; its north façade is topped by pointed gables, a common local feature. The interior is vast; the church was built in the 12C to an ambitious plan and never completed due to insufficient funds.

Continue down rue des Huileries to rue de la Porte-d'Abas; on the left, near the ruins of a Roman gate, stands the 16C Loge aux Portiers (Porters' Lodge) deco-

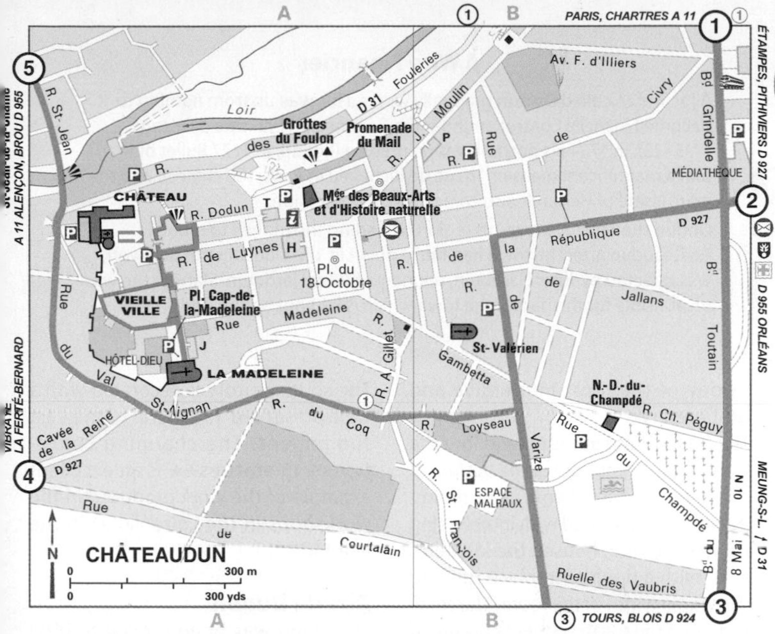

WHERE TO STAY

Etap Hôtel .... ①

WHERE TO EAT

Aux Trois Pastoureaux .... ①

rated with a carefully restored statue of the Virgin Mary.

Walk up r. St-Lubin, lined with impressive houses (nos. 2 and 12), to return to the front of the château.

Go through the arch at the beginning of rue de Luynes and onto impasse du Cloître-St-Roch, then turn right onto a narrow, winding street, venelle des Ribaudes, which opens onto a small square on the edge of the bluff; from here there is a pleasant **view** of the Loir and its valley. On the right of the square stands a 15C house with a Flamboyant door and mullion windows.

Take r. Dodun back to the château.

Promenade du Mail

The mall walk, which runs along the edge of the bluff above the river valley, has been widened and turned into a public garden. The **view**★ stretches westward across the two branches of the Loir, the suburb of St-Jean and beyond to the hillsides of the Perche region.

CHÂTEAU★★

Open Jul–Aug 10am–1pm, 2–6.15pm; May–Jun 10am–1pm, 2–6pm; Sept–Apr 10am–12.30pm, 2–5.30pm (last admission 1hr before closing). 7€.
Closed 1 Jan, 1 May, 25 Dec.
02 37 94 02 90.

Châteaudun is the first of the Loire châteaux to come into sight on the road from Paris. It stands on a bluff rising steeply above the River Loir.

There is an excellent view from the north bank at the level of an old mill near the bridge

Crude and fortress-like from the outside, the buildings resemble a stately mansion when seen from the courtyard. The keep, which is 31m/102ft high without the roof, dates from the 12C; it is one of the earliest circular keeps, as well

A Wise Financier

A local man called **Dodun** gradually worked his way up from nothing to become Financial Controller under the Régence (of Philippe d'Orléans, 1715–23). In 1724 his portrait was painted by Rigaud; in 1727 Bullet built him a magnificent mansion in rue de Richelieu in Paris; the château and the marquisate of Herbault also came into his possession.

Dodun showed loyalty to his region by finding the money to rebuild Châteaudun after the town had burnt down in 1723. Reconstruction work was directed by Jules Hardouin, nephew of Jules Hardouin-Mansart; he was responsible for the part of the town which is laid out on the grid system.

as one of the most impressive and best preserved.

The **basement rooms** extend into the Dunois wing *(entrance at the bottom of the Gothic staircase)*. Two of these rooms, beautifully decorated with intersecting ribbed vaulting, housed the kitchens, each with a double fireplace running the whole width of the room. The small rooms on the north side were occupied by the guards in charge of the cramped prison cells, some of which feature ogee vaulting.

Sainte-Chapelle

Dunois was responsible for this elegant 15C building; it is flanked by a square belfry and two oratories and the chancel ends in a three-sided apse.

The upper chapel, which was provided for the servants, has a panelled wooden ceiling; the lower chapel has ogee vaulting.

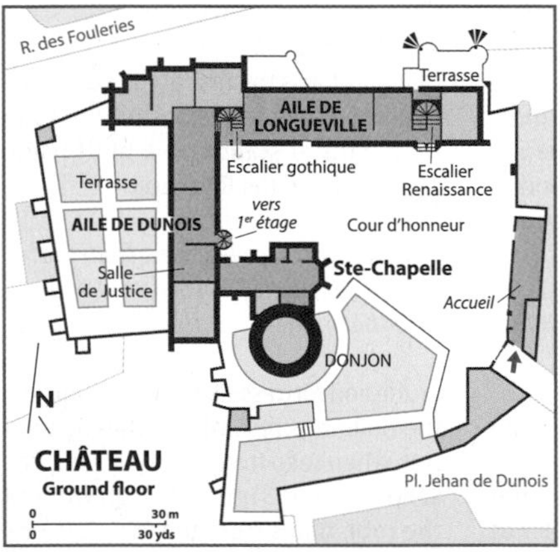

The south oratory is decorated with a well-preserved 15C mural of the Last Judgement. The charming collection of 15 **statues**★★ is an excellent example of the work produced in the workshops in the Loire Valley in the late 15C.

Aile de Dunois

This wing was begun towards 1460 and is built in the true Gothic tradition, although the interior furnishings suggest the desire for comfort which followed the Hundred Years War.

The huge living rooms have massive overhead beams and are hung with tapestries, including, on the first floor, a superb series from Brussels depicting the Life of Moses. Visitors then come to the Salle de Justice (Court Room), where the Lord of the Manor passed judgement and which was panelled in the 17C and painted with the arms of Louis XIV for an occasion when the King visited Châteaudun. This room served as a Revolutionary tribunal in 1793.

Aile de Longueville★

In completing his father's work, François I de Longueville had a **staircase**★ built in the Gothic style. The design echoes the transition between the medieval turreted staircase of the Dunois wing and the Renaissance at the east end of the Longueville wing.

The Longueville wing was built between 1510 and 1520

Châteaudun

by François II de Longueville and then by his brother the Cardinal on foundations which date from the preceding century, but it was never completed. At roof level an Italian cornice supports a Flamboyant balustrade. The staircase at the east end is richly decorated with Renaissance motifs set in a Gothic setting. The ground floor rooms, including the Renaissance gallery, are hung with 17C Paris and Amiens tapestries. In the Grand Salon on the first floor there are carved 16C chests and, facing each other, two monumental chimneypieces, one in the Gothic and one in the Renaissance style.

ADDITIONAL SIGHTS

Musée des Beaux-Arts et d'Histoire naturelle

Open Jul–Aug daily 9.30am–noon, 1.30–6pm; Jun and Sept Wed–Mon 9.30am–noon, 1.30–6pm; Oct–May Wed–Mon 9.30am–noon, 1.30–5pm; last admission 30min before closing. *Closed 1 Jan, 1 May, 25 Dec.* *3.70€. 02 37 45 55 36.*

This Fine Art and Natural History Museum is worth visiting for its remarkable **collection of stuffed birds★** (2 500) from countries all over the world. The room on the ground floor devoted to Egyptian archaeology contains funerary objects from the early Dynastic Period (3100–2700 BC) discovered at Abydos. The same room also displays mummies and sarcophagi from the Roman Antiquity. Local history is evoked by the reconstitution of a typical Beauce domestic interior, a display of artefacts excavated in the vicinity of Châteaudun and by souvenirs of the 1870 War.

On the first floor, the section on Asian and Oceanian art presents French East India Company porcelain, together with a great many pieces belonging to the Wahl-Offroy collection: weapons from the Middle and Far East, Chinese jewellery, Buddhist statuary and Islamic miniatures. The Painting Gallery presents a series of 19C Eure-et-Loir landscapes.

Église St-Valérien

The 12C building is topped by a tall belfry with a 15C stone spire. On the southern flank, admire the fine poly-lobed romanesque portal.

Chapelle Notre-Dame-du-Champdé

All that remains of this funerary chapel, destroyed at the end of the 19C, is a Flamboyant façade with finely worked ornamentation; a delicate balustrade is supported by sculpted consoles at the base of the gable which holds an effigy of the Virgin Mary, to whom the chapel is dedicated.

Birth of the Alexandrine Metre

It was at Châteaudun in the 12C that the poet **Lambert le Tort** was born. He was one of the authors of the *Story of Alexander*, a heroic poem inspired by the legend of Alexander the Great that was very popular in the Middle Ages. Its 22 000 lines were written in the heroic metre, with 12 feet or syllables to the line, which subsequently came to be known as the Alexandrine metre.

Grottes du Foulon

35 r. des Fouleries. Guided tours (1hr). Open Jul–Aug 10am–noon, 1–6pm; Apr–Jun and Sept Tue–Sun 10am–noon, 1–5pm; Oct–Mar Sat–Sun and public holidays 1–5pm. 6€. 02 37 45 19 60.

Lining the roadside like the many other caves in the area, and clearly visible, these caves owe their name to the activity of the fullers (*fouleurs*) who used to work here.

Hollowed out in Senonian limestone by the waters of the Loir, the cave roofs have flinty concretions which in places have been transformed into geodes of chalcedony or quartz by the effects of crystallisation.

Église St-Jean-de-la-Chaîne

Exit ⑤ on the town map.

In the suburb of St-Jean on the north bank of the Loir stands an early-16C ogee-arched gate at the entrance to the churchyard. The **church of St-Jean** was built mainly in the 15C but the apses date from the 11C and 12C.

From this side of the river there is a fine view of the north façade of the château.

EXCURSIONS

Lutz-en-Dunois

7km/4mi E along D 955.

Lutz has a charming Romanesque church with a low bell-tower crowned by a saddleback roof. The interior is decorated with 13C murals in red and yellow ochre: those on the oven-vault above the apse depict the Apostles and Bishop Saints; on the walls of the nave are Christ's Entry into Jerusalem, the Entombment, the Resurrection and the Descent into Limbo.

Abbaye du Bois de Nottonville

18km/11mi E; take D 927 to Varize and then follow the signs.

Guided tours (45min) Open Jul–Aug by 2-day advance reservation; May–Jun and Sept–Oct Sat–Sun and public holidays 2.30–6.30pm. 3.10€. 02 37 96 91 64.

Abbaye du Bois de Nottonville

The 11C priory (restored in the 15C) belonged to Benedictine monks from Marmoutier. Note, in particular, the fortified doorway, the barn with a roof shaped like an inverted ship's hull, and the dovecot.

Moulin de Frouville-Pensier

10km/6mi SE. Take D 31 towards Ozoir-le-Breuil, then go left on D 144 towards St-Cloud-en-Dunois. Open Apr–Sept, Sun and public holidays 2.30–6.30pm. 2€ (children under 15 years free). 02 37 98 70 31.

This is the only surviving stone windmill of the Beauce region. It dates from 1274 but was rebuilt after a fire in 1826. See it in action and admire the impressive millstones (1.9m/6.2ft and 1.3m/4.2ft in diameter), its 21m/69ft wingspan and the roof that pivots with a rudder tail.

Musée de la Bataille de 2 décembre 1870

In Loigny-la-Bataille, 34km/21mi W along the D 927 towards Janville and Pithiviers. At the Orgères-en-Beauce exit, turn right on to the D 39 for access to the church/memorial. Open Easter to Whitsun Sun 2.30–5.30pm. Closed public holidays. 4€ (children under 12 years free). 02 37 99 74 96.

The village's name and neo-romanesque memorial church next to the museum commemorate 9 000 men who died in the battle of 2 Dec 1870. The crypt holds the tombs of Generals Charette and Sonis; in the nave, paintings by Lionel Royer depict the night of the battle with the Prussian army. The soldiers' bones (1 200 French and 60 Prussians) lie in an ossuary. The museum holds a unique collection of objects, weapons and uniforms from the war of 1870.

Château de Villeprévost

At Tillay-le-Péneux 34km/21mi W on D 927. 3km/1.8mi after Orgères-en-Beauce go right onto the D 118 via Tanon. Open mid-Apr–Oct 1st, Sat, Sun and public holidays 1–7pm. €5. 02 37 99 45 17.

Surrounded by French-style gardens, this 17C–18C manor house once belonged to Amand-François Fougeron, a King's counsellor and Justice of the Peace for Orgères. Thanks to his efforts the 'Orgères scorchers' were arrested – a dreaded gang of over 300 criminals who terrorised the region by burning their victims' feet! Their trial was held in Villeprévost in the reception lounge of the château. The lovely 16C dovecote contains the horrific death masks of the condemned men.

ADDRESSES

STAY

Etap Hôtel – *Les Garennes, RN 10. 02 37 45 78 78. 50 rms. P. 6€.* Very comfortable and well equipped classical rooms, at reasonable prices.

EAT

Aux Trois Pastoureaux *31 r. André-Gillet. 02 37 45 74 40. Closed 5–21 Jul, 27 Dec–4 Jan, 15–23 Feb, Sun and Mon.* Wood panelling and local art to go with traditional or medieval menus in ancient Châteaudun *auberge*.

LEISURE ACTIVITIES

Centre Équestre Dunois *chemin de St-Martin. 02 37 66 00 00.* As well as the usual horse-related activities on-site, you can also get out and explore the area on horse or pony. Itineraries can last several days, staying in gîtes, farms or campsites. Excellent fun for all ages.

Club Canoë Kayak Dunois *4 r. des Fouleries. 02 37 45 53 36/06. Open daily Jul and Aug, rest of year by arrangement. 20€ (children under 8 years 10€).* There's nothing quite like a trip in a canoe or kayak for getting to know the Loir Valley. Various itineraries available with transport to the starting point at St-Christophe. The gently-flowing river means that all ages can enjoy a calm journey downstream.

Vendôme★★

At the foot of a steep bluff, which is crowned by a castle, the River Loir branches out into several channels which flow slowly under a number of bridges. Vendôme stands on a group of islands dotted with gables and steep slate roofs.

- **Population:** 17 029
- **Michelin Map:** 318: D-5
- **Info:** Hôtel du Saillant, 47-49 r. Poterie, 41100 Vendôme. ℘02 54 77 05 07. www.vendome.eu.
- **Location:** 30 km/18.6mi NW of Blois, between Tours (56km/35mi to the SW) and Châteaudun (40km/25mi to the NE). By TGV, Vendôme is just 45min from Paris.
- **Parking:** Large car park at pl. de la Liberté.
- **Don't Miss:** The older parts of town.
- **Kids:** Torchlight tours of town on Thursday evenings in summer.
- **Timing:** A 2hr guided tour of the town is worthwhile, but you should allow half a day or more to get the best from your visit.

A BIT OF HISTORY

A turbulent past – Although the origins of Vendôme can be traced as far back as the Neolithic periods, before the town received its name, Vindocenum, in the Gallo-Roman period, it only began to acquire importance under the counts, first the Bouchard family, who were faithful supporters of the Capet dynasty, and particularly under the son of Fulk Nerra, **Geoffrey Martel** (11C), who founded La Trinité Abbey.

Henri IV's son, César – Vendôme was given to César de Bourbon, the eldest son of Henri IV and Gabrielle d'Estrées as a royal prerogative. César de Vendôme was often resident on his feudal estate while he involved himself with conspiracies, first during the minority of Louis XIII and then against Richelieu. He was imprisoned at Vincennes for four years before being exiled. He eventually lent his support to Mazarin's cause, before dying in 1665.

SIGHTS

Jardin public

Running down to the riverside, the public garden gives a good view over the town, the abbey and the 13C–14C gateway, **Porte d'Eau** or Arche des Grands Prés.

Porte d'Eau, Vendôme

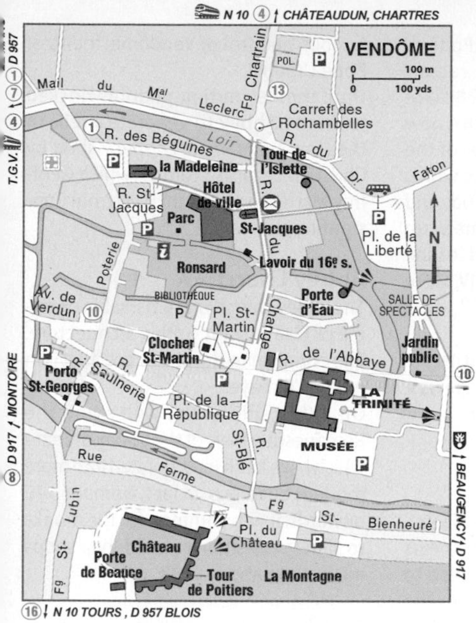

WHERE TO STAY

- Chambre d'hôte Ferme de Crislaine........ ①
- Chambre d'hôte La Borde........ ④
- Chambre d'hôte Le Moulin d'Échoiseau........ ⑦
- Hôtel Le St-Georges........ ⑩
- Hôtel Le Vendôme........ ⑬
- Mercator........ ⑯

WHERE TO EAT

- Auberge de la Madeleine........ ①
- Auberge du Port des Roches........ ④
- Le Terre à TR........ ⑧
- La Vallée........ ⑩

From the open space on the opposite bank, place de la Liberté, there are views of the Porte d'Eau from a different angle as well as of the 13C Tour de l'Islette. Together with the **Porte St-Georges** *(see p330)* these structures are all that is left of the old ramparts.

Parc Ronsard

Round this shaded park are the Lycée Ronsard (originally the Collège des Oratoriens where Balzac was a pupil and now occupied by the offices of the town hall), the late-15C Hôtel de Saillant (now the tourist information centre) and the municipal library with its important collection of old books. A 16C two-storeyed washhouse is sited on the arm of the river running through the park.

Chapelle St-Jacques

Rebuilt in the 15C, and subsequently attached to the Collège des Oratoriens in the 16C, the chapel once served the pilgrims on their way to Santiago de Compostela.

Église de la Madeleine

Dating from 1474, the church belfry is topped by an elegant bracketed spire.

Place St-Martin

Until the 19C St-Martin's Church (15C–16C) stood here; only the bell-tower remains. There is also a fine 16C timber-framed house called the Grand St-Martin; it is ornamented with figures and coats of arms and has a statue of Maréchal de Rochambeau *(see Middle reaches of the Loir, p333)*.

Porte St-Georges

St-Georges gateway was the entrance to the town from the Loir; it is flanked by towers largely built in the 14C although the front facing the bridge is decorated with machicolations and carvings of dolphins and Renaissance medallions which were added early in the 16C by Marie de Luxembourg, Duchess of Vendôme.

Château

Closed for restoration.

02 54 77 05 07.

Access by car via St-Lubin district and Le Temple, a hamlet which grew up round a Templar commandery. The ruined castle is set on the top of an outcrop – La Montagne – which overlooks the Loir. It consists of an earth wall and ramparts with 13C and 14C machicolated round towers at intervals; the great Poitiers Tower on the east side was reconstructed in the 15C. The early-17C Beauce gate leads into the precinct which is now a huge garden. There are traces of the collegiate church of St-Georges which was founded by Agnès of Burgundy and is where the counts of Vendôme were buried. Antoine de Bourbon and Jeanne d'Albret, the parents of Henri IV, were also buried here.

Promenade de la Montagne

From the terraces there are fine **views**★ of Vendôme and the Loir Valley.

ANCIENNE ABBAYE DE LA TRINITÉ★

One summer night, Geoffrey Martel, Count of Anjou, saw three fiery spears plunge into a fountain and decided to found a monastery, dedicated to the Holy Trinity on 31 May 1040. Under the Benedictine Order the abbey grew considerably, becoming one of the most powerful religious foundations in France, to the extent that eventually the abbot was made a cardinal. In the late 11C this office was held by the famous Geoffroi of Vendôme, friend of Pope Urban II.

Until the Revolution pilgrims flocked to Trinité Abbey to venerate a relic of the Holy Tear *(Sainte Larme)* – shed by Christ on Lazarus's tomb – which Geoffrey Martel had brought back from Constantinople.

Abbey Church★★

The abbey church is a remarkable example of Flamboyant Gothic architecture. The entrance to the abbey precinct is in rue de l'Abbaye.

On either side of the wall stand the Romanesque bays of the abbey granary which have been incorporated into more modern buildings. In fact, from the 14C onwards, it was common for the monks to allow tradesmen to build their shops against the abbey walls.

Exterior

To the right of the west front and set apart from it stands the 12C **bell-tower**. An interesting feature is the way the windows and arcades, which are blind at ground level, grow larger as the embrasures also increase in size.

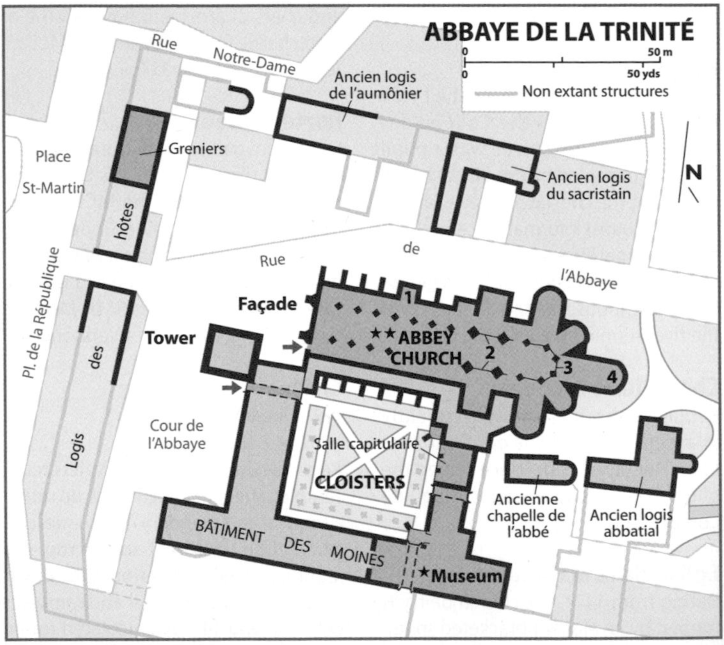

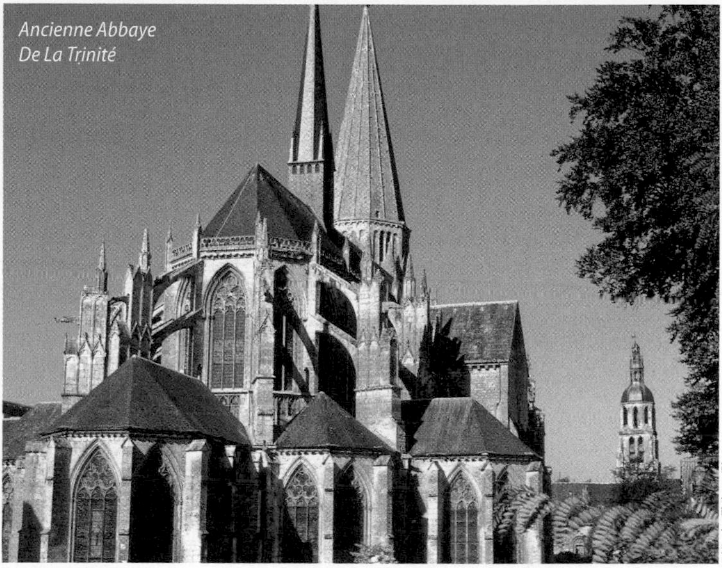

©Nicolas Thibaut/Photononstop

The transition from a square to an octagonal tower is made by means of openwork, mini bell-towers at the corners. The Flamboyant **west front**, accentuated by a great carved gable, is thought to have been built in the early 16C by Jean de Beauce, who designed the bell-tower of Chartres Cathedral. The decorative openwork, so delicate it looks like a piece of lace, contrasts with the plainer Romanesque tower.

Interior

The nave, started at the transept end in the middle of the 14C, was not completed until the early 16C; the transept, all that is left of the 11C building, leads to the chancel and ambulatory with its five radiating chapels.

The baptismal chapel **(1)** in the north aisle contains a Renaissance font in white marble supported by a carved pedestal from the gardens of Blois Château.

The primitive capitals of the transept crossing are surmounted by statues (13C) of the Virgin Mary with the Archangel Gabriel, St Peter and St Eutropius who was venerated in the abbey church. The transept vaulting was altered in the 14C in the Angevin style.

The 14C chancel, which is lit through windows from the same period, is decorated with beautiful late-15C **stalls**★ **(2)**. The misericords are decorated with naïve scenes illustrating daily life with various trades and zodiac signs. The choir screen **(3)** enclosing the chancel bears the influence of the first Renaissance. To the left of the high altar is the base of the famous monument of the Holy Tear, decorated with tears, with a small aperture through which the relic was displayed to the faithful by one of the monks.

The chapels radiating from the ambulatory are decorated with 14C and 16C stained glass which has been extensively restored: the best section, which depicts the meal in Simon's house, taken from a German engraving, is in the first chapel to the left of the axial chapel. This also contains a **window** dating from 1140 depicting the Virgin and Child **(4)**.

Conventual buildings

Only the east side of the 16C cloisters exists in its entirety. In the 14C **chapter house** (*open Apr–Oct daily 10am–6pm, rest of year Mon–Sat 10am–6pm; closed 1 Jan, 1 May and 25 Dec; 02 54 77 26 13*) a number of wall paintings have been uncovered, depicting episodes from the Life of Christ. The Classical-style buildings now house a museum.

Honoré de Balzac (1799–1850)

On 22 June 1807 the Collège des Oratoriens in Vendôme registered the entry of an eight-year-old boy, Honoré de Balzac. The future historical novelist was an absent-minded and undisciplined pupil. Balzac was to recall the severity of school discipline of those days in his writing. His general clumsiness and ineptitude at standard children's pursuits made him the frequent butt of his fellow pupils' jokes. He regularly got himself put into detention in order to read in peace. The harshness of the school regime eventually undermined his health and his parents had to take him away.

Balzac's early efforts at writing met with minimal success, so he embarked on a career in printing. However, the firm in which he was joint partner went bankrupt, leaving him with debts at the age of 30, which he was to spend the rest of his life attempting to pay off. He returned to writing and over the next 20 years produced a phenomenal number of novels (about 90), a vast collection which constitutes a richly detailed record of contemporary society, covering all walks of life and reflecting what he saw as people's overriding motivations at that time, chiefly money and ambition. Typically, Balzac's novels contain keenly observed settings, peopled by characters exaggerated almost to the point of caricature by their creator's vivid imagination. Balzac's fascination by the contrast between life in the provinces and that in the glittering French capital is also reflected in his work.

Balzac retrospectively attached the label **La Comédie Humaine** to his life's work, giving some indication of the breadth of scope of the world he had tried to evoke – an ambitious project formulated after he had already written many of his most famous novels, but which was to remain uncompleted on his untimely death from overwork, just months after he had finally married Eveline Hanska, the Polish countess with whom he had passionately corresponded for over 18 years.

Take the passage through the south range of buildings to admire the monumental south front which was built between 1732 and 1742; the pediments bear the royal fleur-de-lis, the motto (Pax) and the emblem (Lamb) of the Order of St Benedict.

Museum★

Open Apr–Oct Wed–Mon 10am–noon, 2–6pm; rest of year Mon–Sat 10am–noon, 1.30–5.30pm. Closed 1 Jan, 1 May, 25 Dec. 3€. 02 54 77 26 13.

The museum collections are displayed in the abbey's monastic buildings which are reached by a majestic stairway.

Rooms on the ground floor are devoted to **mural painting**★ in the Loire Valley and to **religious art**★ in the Vendôme area from the Middle Ages to the Renaissance.

On the upper floors are sections on archaeology and natural history. Certain rooms are devoted to 16C–19C paintings and furniture and to earthenware; there is a superb late-18C **harp**★, the work of Nadermann, Marie-Antoinette's instrument maker, together with contemporary sculptures by the artist **Louis Leygue** (1905–92).

EXCURSIONS

Nourray

12km/7.4mi S on D 16, then right onto D 64 in Crucheray.

The little **church** which stands alone in the square has a row of Romanesque arcades beneath carved corbels. Inside, the oven-vaulted apse is surrounded by arcading with carved capitals.

Villemardy

14km/9mi SE on D 957; turn left to Périgny and bear right to Villemardy.

The **church** dating from the 12C has a simple nave ending in a Gothic chancel. The interior decoration in carved oak is remarkably uniform; the high altar and tabernacle, which are surmounted by an altarpiece, are in the Classical style, as are the two small symmetrical altars in the nave.

Rhodon

20km/12.4mi SE on D 917 (towards Beaugency), then turn right in Noyers.
The internal walls and Gothic vaulting of the church bear traces of 14C and 15C mural paintings: *Christ in Majesty* in the apse and the *Months of the Year* on one of the transverse arches of the nave.

DRIVING TOURS

Middle Reaches of the Loir★

1 FROM VENDÔME TO LA CHARTRE

78km/48.4mi. Allow one day.
Route marked in purple on map p335.

Villiers-sur-Loir
The village overlooks the sloping vineyards opposite Rochambeau Castle. Numerous outdoor activities are available: swimming, rambling, fishing, volleyball, boules, table tennis, sailing, archery and more. In Riotte, special courses offer an introduction to the local fauna and flora.

Take the road towards Thoré. Immediately after crossing the Loir turn left.

Rochambeau
The road runs along the foot of the cliff through the semi-troglodyte village up to the castle where **Maréchal de Rochambeau** (1725–1807) was born; he commanded the French expeditionary force in the American War of Independence and was buried in Thoré.

Return to the west bank of the river and turn left onto D 5.

Le Gué-du-Loir
The hamlet was built where the Boulon joins the Loir amid lush meadows and islands ringed by reed-beds, willows, alders and poplars.

On leaving the hamlet the road (D 5) skirts the wall of **Manoir de Bonaventure**, which was probably named after a chapel dedicated to St Bonaventure. In the 16C the manor house belonged to Henri IV's father, Antoine de Bourbon-Vendôme who entertained his friends there, including some of the poets of the Pléiade. Later Bonaventure came into the possession of the De Musset family. The poet, **Alfred de Musset**, whose father was born at the manor, used to spend his holidays as a child with his godfather, Louis de Musset, at the Château de Cogners, since the manor had by then been sold.

Continue W on D 5 towards Savigny; then take the second turning to the right (C 13) at a wayside cross.

A wooded valley leads to the picturesque village of **Mazangé** clustered round its church.

Return to Gué-du-Loir; turn right onto D 24 towards Montoire-sur-le-Loir, then right again onto D 82 to Lunay.

Lunay
Lunay is grouped in a valley round the main square where a few old houses have survived. The huge, Flamboyant Gothic church of St-Martin presents an attractive doorway.

Les Roches-l'Évêque
The village occupies a long narrow site between the river and the cliff. The troglodyte dwellings are a well-known feature of the region, their hen houses and sheds half-concealed by festoons of wisteria and lilac in season.

Cross the Loir (D 917 – follow the signposts); turn right to Lavardin.

Lavardin★
See LAVARDIN

Take the pretty minor road along the south bank of the river to Montoire.

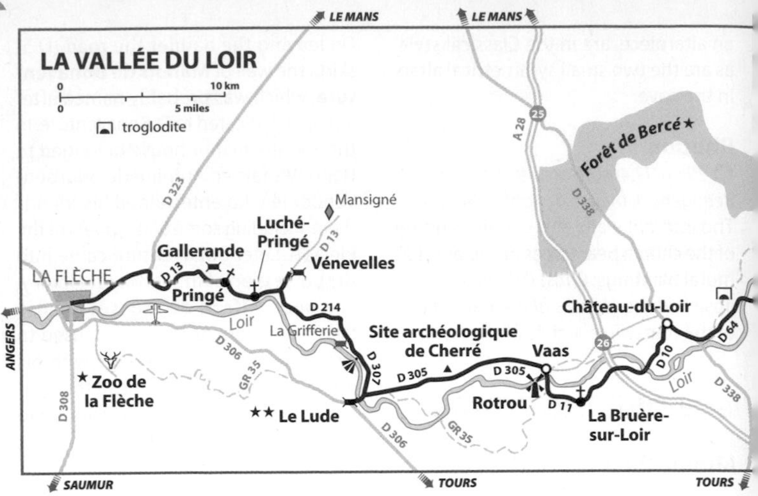

Montoire-sur-le-Loir
See MONTOIRE-SUR-LE-LOIR

Soon Trôo and its church appear on the skyline. Continue to Sougé where you turn left onto the signposted tourist road to Artins.

Vieux-Bourg d'Artins
The village is situated right on the river bank. The church has Romanesque walls with Flamboyant Gothic windows and a pointed-arched doorway.

From Artins take D 10 E; then turn right to L'Isle Verte; shortly turn left onto a road which runs in front of the Château du Pin.

From the bridge opposite the château L'Isle Verte (Green Island) can be seen a little way upstream where the Braye joins the Loir. It was here, where the row of poplars sway in the breeze and the willows mark the edges of the meadows, that the poet Ronsard wanted to be buried; nowhere is more evocative of his genius.

Couture-sur-Loir
The church has a Gothic chancel with Angevin vaulting and 17C woodwork in the Rosary Chapel.

In Couture-sur-Loir take D 57 S to La Possonnière.

Manoir de la Possonnière★
Open mid-Jun–mid Sept, Wed–Mon, 10am–1pm, 2.30–7pm; Apr–mid-Jun and mid-Sept–end Oct, Thur–Sun and public holidays 2–6pm. Guided tours. 6€; gardens only 4€. 02 54 72 40 05. www.pays-de-ronsard.fr.
When Louis de Ronsard, soldier and man of letters, returned from Italy in the early 16C he undertook to rebuild his country seat in the new Italian style. The result was La Possonnière, characterised by the profusion of mottoes engraved on the walls.

Manor★
The name comes from the word *posson* (*poinçon*, a measure of volume) and has sometimes been altered to Poissonnière under the influence of the Ronsard family coat of arms – three silver fishes (*poisson*) on a blue ground – which can be seen on the pediment of the carved dormer window at the top of the turret.
The manor house is built against the hillside on the northern fringes of Gâtines Forest and enclosed with a wall. The main façade has mullioned windows in the style of Louis XII on the ground floor but the windows on the first floor are

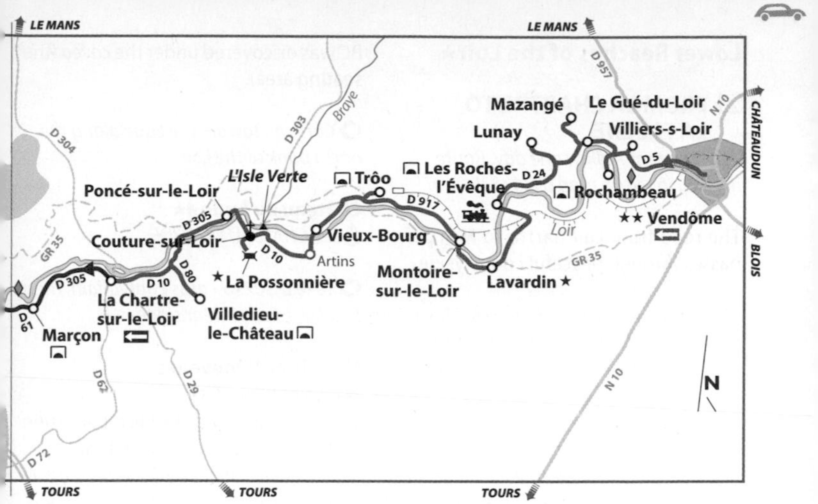

flanked by pilasters with medallions, in the Renaissance style. Projecting from the rear façade is a graceful staircase turret adorned with an elegant doorway capped by a pediment decorated with a bust.

Return to Couture and continue N (D 57), crossing the Loir at the foot of the wooded hill on which Château de la Flotte stands.

Château de Poncé-sur-le-Loir

Open Apr–May and Sept 2–6.30pm; Jun–Aug 10.30am–6.30pm. 6.50€. 02 43 44 24 02.

This originally consisted of two pavilions flanking a central staircase tower, one of which was destroyed in the 18C and replaced by a more austere wing.

The stone **Renaissance staircase**★★ is one of the most remarkable in France; in front of it are the remains of a loggia. The coffered, white-stone ceilings of the six straight flights are sumptuously sculpted, executed with refinement, fluidity and a mastery of the art of perspective rarely to be found. Over 160 decorative motifs portray real-life, allegorical and mythological subjects.

The well-tended **gardens**, with their symmetrical layout, are a pleasant place for a stroll: beyond the flower beds prettily edged with boxwood, the arbour leads to several clearings where the leafy branches meet overhead to form a ceiling of foliage, a maze and a long vaulted path.

The dovecote with its 1 800 nesting holes and revolving ladders for gathering the eggs is still intact. The outbuildings house the local folklore museum, the **Musée départemental du Folklore sarthois.**

In Ruillé turn left onto D 80, which crosses the Loir.

Villedieu-le-Château

This village has a pleasant **setting** in a valley with troglodyte dwellings. Houses, gardens, crumbling remnants of the old town wall and the ruins of the belfry of St-Jean priory all add to its charm.

Return to Tréhet and left onto D 10.

La Chartre-sur-le-Loir

On the north bank of the river, opposite this village, are Bercé Forest and the Jasnières vineyard which produces a white dessert wine which ages well.

Lower Reaches of the Loir★

2 FROM LA CHARTRE TO LA FLÈCHE

75km/46.6mi – allow one day. Route marked in red on map p334–335

The road from La Chartre to **Marçon** passes through peaceful countryside.

In Marçon turn right onto D 61. Turn left onto D 64, which skirts the hillside with its numerous troglodyte dwellings.

Château-du-Loir

The keep in the public gardens is all that remains of the medieval castle, to which this town owes its name. Underneath it are the old cells occupied briefly by convicts who passed through here bound for the penal colony of Cayenne.

Leave Château-du-Loir on D 10 going S towards Château-la-Vallière. After crossing the bridge in Nogent turn right immediately onto C 2.

La Bruère-sur-Loir

The **church** here contains elegant chancel vaulting in the Renaissance style and 16C stained-glass windows.

Leave La Bruère on D 11 towards Vaas and turn right onto D 30.

Vaas

On the left, just before the bridge, stands an old corn mill, the **Moulin à blé de Rotrou** *(guided tours year round, phone for times; 3.20€; 02 43 46 70 22)*. The riverside, with its houses, tiny gardens and church makes a delightful scene.

Follow D 305, then turn right to Cherré archaeological site.

Site archéologique de Cherré

The Gallo-Roman settlement comprises a temple, baths, two other buildings and a theatre of pointed reddish sandstone, which has been completely excavated. During the digs a necropolis from 8C–5C BC was discovered under the *cavea* (the seating area).

Carry on towards Le Lude along the north bank of the Loir.

Château du Lude★★

See CHÂTEAU DU LUDE

Take D 307 towards Pontvallain, then first left towards Mansigné.

Manoir de Vénevelles

No public access.

15C–17C manor with a wide moat sitting in the hollow of a sleepy small valley. Before reaching the Château de la Grifferie there is a view over the valley which is laid out in fruit orchards, asparagus beds, potato fields and maize plantations.

Bear left onto D 214 to Luché-Pringé.

Luché-Pringé

The exterior of the **church** (13C–16C) is unusual, with many gables decorated with crockets and the row of tiny musician figures sitting on the edge of the roof on either side of the façade.
The interior contains an early-16C *Pietà (right)* carved in walnut. The wide chancel (13C) ends in a square chevet; the Angevin vaulting is supported on tall slim columns in the Plantagenet style.

Pringé

An arched romanesque portal opens through the façade of the small **church**. Inside are 16C murals depicting Saint Hubert, Saint George and Saint Christopher.

Château de Gallerande

No public access.

The D 13 skirts the moats around the romantic grounds where cedars, lime trees and oaks border sweeping lawns. Walk up to the gateway of the courtyard for a good view of the northeast façade, which is divided by round towers with machicolations and a curious octagonal keep.

ADDRESSES

STAY

Chambre d'hôte Ferme de Crislaine – *41100 Azé. 11km/7mi NW of Vendôme. ℘02 54 72 14 09. ⌧. 5 rms. Evening meal* €€ Staying here is an excellent way to discover an organic farm. An ideal stopping place for families and walkers. Bikes and swimming pool for guests' use.

Chambre d'hôte La Borde – *41100 Danzé. 2km/1mi N of Danzé. ℘02 54 80 68 42. www.la-borde.com. ⌧. 5 rms. evening meal* €€. Situated in the middle of a 10ha/XX-acre park, this manor house dates from the 19C.

€€**Hôtel-Restaurant Mercator** – *rte .de Blois. ℘02 54 89 08 08. www.hotelmercator.fr. 53 rms.* Close by a roundabout but surrounded by plenty of greenery, this family-run hotel's welcoming little rooms are done out in an up-to-date style. The restaurant goes for a pared-back modern look and serves traditional dishes.

€€**Chambre d'hôte le Moulin d'Echoiseau** – *Le Gué-du-Loir, 41100 Mazangé. 1km/0.6mi S of Mazangé. ℘02 54 72 19 34. www.moulin-echoiseau.fr. ⌧. 4 rms.* You will long remember the calm atmosphere staying at this former mill.

€€**Hôtel le St-Georges** – *14 r. Poterie. ℘02 54 67 42 10. www.hotel-saint-georges -vendome.com. P. 28 rms. ☕8€.* Located in the centre of town, with functional rooms in a modern style.

€€**Hôtel le Vendôme** – *15 faubourg Chartrain. ℘02 54 77 02 88. www.hotel vendomefrance.com. 35 rms. ☕10€.* Practical and efficient, a good location in the town centre.

EAT

€**Le Petit Bilboquet** – *On the old Tours road. ℘02 54 77 16 60. Closed 16 Aug–7 Sept, Thu eve in winter, Sun eve, Mon. Reservation required weekends.* This little restaurant was once an officers' mess. The cooking is well presented and simple, as is the décor.

€€**Auberge de la Madeleine** – *pl. de la Madeleine. ℘02 54 77 20 79. Closed Feb, 8–17 Nov, Wed.* There is a real family atmosphere in this town-centre inn, with its smart, split-level dining room.

€€**Le Terre à TR** – *14 r. du Maréchal-du-Rochambeau. ℘02 54 89 09 09. www.le-terre-a-tr.com. Closed 15–30 Aug.* It may be out in the suburbs, but what makes this restaurant stand out is tucked inside a troglodyte cave. There's also an outdoor terrace in summer. Set menu and à la carte deal in up-to-date dishes.

€€**Auberge du Port des Roches** – *Le Port-des-Roches, 72800 Luché-Pringé. 2.5km/1.5mi E of Luché-Pringé. ℘02 43 45 44 48. Closed 28 Jan–10 Mar, Sun eve, Tue afternoon, Mon.* A splendid restaurant serving traditional dishes with a smile.

€€**Auberge du Val de Loir** – *3 pl. Marcel-Morand, 72500 Dissay-sous-Courcillon. 5km/3mi SE of Château-du-Loir. ℘02 43 44 09 06. Closed 23 Dec–8 Jan, Fri, Sun eve out of season. Reservation required.* This restaurant, with its creeper-covered façade, serves tasty regional cuisine. Rooms available.

€€€**La Vallée** – *34 r. Barré-de-St-Venant. ℘02 54 77 29 93. www.restaurant-la-vallee.com. Closed 2–8 Jan, 7–13 Mar, 20 Jul–3 Aug, 26 Sept–9 Oct, Sun eve, Mon–Tue.* A splendid find with exposed beams, serving seasonal cuisine.

LEISURE ACTIVITIES

Pland d'Eau de Villiers-sur-Loir – *41100 Villiers-sur-Loir. ℘02 54 72 90 83.* Take your pick from swimming, walking, fishing, boules, sailing, archery, or hire a pedalo or mountain bike. Learn about the local fauna and flora at Riotte.

SHOPPING

Verrerie d'Art Gérard-Torcheux – *27 r. des Côteaux, 72340 Poncé-sur-Loir. ℘02 43 79 05 69. www.torcheux.com. Closed 10–30 Jan.* In the workshop beneath the château visitors can see the traditional art of the glassmaker in action.

Lavardin★

The crumbling ruins of Lavardin Fortress are perched on a rocky pinnacle towering above the village and the Loir, which is spanned by a Gothic bridge, forming a picturesque scene.

- **Population:** *788*
- **Michelin Map:** 318: C-5
- **Info:** Office du Tourisme de Montoire. 16 pl. Clemenceau 41800, Montoire. ☏02 54 85 23 30. www.lavardin.net.
- **Location:** 22km/14mi SW of Vendôme (via the D 917 or N 10 and then the D 108).
- **Timing:** Allow 1hr, or more if you take a guided tour.

A BIT OF HISTORY

The principal stronghold of the counts of Vendôme in the Middle Ages, Lavardin's strategic importance greatly increased in the 12C owing to its location half way between the kingdom of France under the Capets and the possessions of the Angevin Kings. In 1188 Henry II of England and his son Richard the Lionheart besieged the castle, but in vain.

In 1589 the troops of the Catholic League captured the castle but the following year it was besieged by Henri IV's soldiers under the Prince de Conti and surrendered. The King ordered the castle to be demolished.

SIGHTS

Old houses

One is 15C and half-timbered whereas the other is Renaissance with an overhanging oratory, pilastered, mullioned dormer windows and a loggia overlooking the courtyard.

The **mairie** (town hall: *Open Wed and Fri 4–7pm, Thu 8.30am–noon; ☏02 54 85 07 74; www.lavardin.net*) contains two beautiful 11C rooms with handsome 15C vaulted ceilings.

The 13C **bridge** offers an attractive view of the lush green river banks.

A lane behind the church climbs up to a group of cave dwellings.

Castle

Open Jul–Aug Tue–Sun 11am–noon, 3–6pm; May–Jun and Sept Sat–Sun and public holidays 11am–noon, 3–6pm. 3€. ☏02 54 85 07 74.

Although well worn by the weather and the passage of time, the ruins are still impressive and give a good idea of the three lines of fortified walls, the gatehouse (12C–15C) and the rectangular 11C keep (26m/85ft high), which was

Gothic bridge, Lavardin

S. Sauvignier/MICHELIN

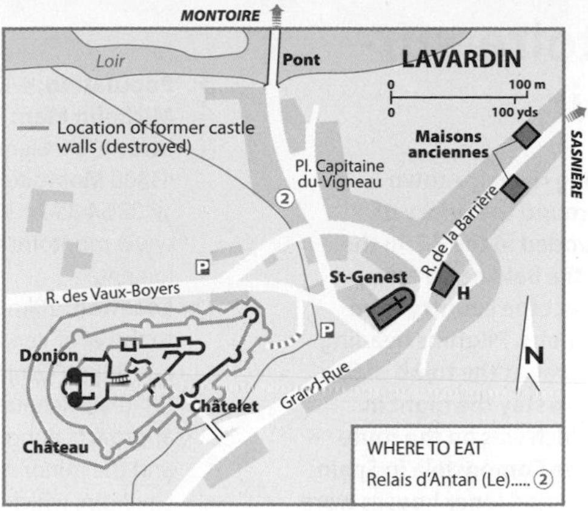

reinforced in the following century with towers of the same height. The innermost defensive wall is best preserved.

Église St-Genest★

The priory was built in an archaic Romanesque style with a square belfry-porch. Low-relief sculptures have been reused in the structure; those in the apse represent the signs of the zodiac.

Interior – The church is divided into three parts by square piers capped by delicately carved early 12C imposts. The chancel, which is entered through a triumphal arch, ends in an oven-vaulted apse, where curious Romanesque pillars, probably part of an earlier building, support roughly hewn capitals. The windows in the north aisle are framed by delightful twisted Romanesque colonnettes.

The **mural paintings** date from the 12C to 16C. The oldest, most stylised and majestic ones are on the pillar at the entrance to the left apsidal chapel, depicting the *Baptism of Christ* and a *Tree of Jesse*. The well-conserved group in the chancel and apse shows scenes from the *Passion (on the right)* and the *Washing of the Feet (on the left)* on either side of a *Christ in Majesty* surrounded by the symbols of the *Evangelists*.

In the right apsidal chapel note a *St Christopher* and *Last Judgement* (15C) where *Paradise (above)* and *Hell* are colourfully portrayed. On the pillars in the nave and aisles are 16C figures of saints venerated locally.

Note the *Martyrdom of St Margaret* on the wall of the south aisle and the *Crucifixion of St Peter* on a pillar on the north side of the nave.

EXCURSION

Parc et jardin du domaine de Sasnières

6km/3.7mi SE by D 108.

Open Easter–Oct Thu–Mon 10am–6pm. 7€. Guided tour (1hr30min). 02 54 82 92 34. www.jardin-plessis-sasnieres.fr.

This attractive 3.5ha/8.5-acre English-style garden enhanced by clumps of trees and shrubs surrounds a pretty lake laid out at the foot of a hill. It presents a wide range of plants belonging to many different species and is particularly appealing in spring and summer on account of its blossoming roses and magnolias.

The autumn season too is a feast for the eyes, when the foliage takes on superb shades of russet.

ADDRESSES

EAT

Le Relais d'Antan – *6 pl. du Capitaine-Vigneau, 02 54 86 61 33. Closed 19 Feb–6 Mar, 22 Oct–6 Nov, Mon eve, Tue.* A really lovely old inn. After visiting Lavardin, enjoy a meal in the comfortable little dining room or on the lovely terrace overlooking the Loir. The menu changes weekly.

Montoire-sur-le-Loir

This charming riverside town developed round the priory of St-Gilles founded in the 7C. In the 9C, Charles the Bald had a fort built to protect the country from Viking incursions. Pilgrims heading for Tours to pray at the tomb of St Martin used to stay the night in Montoire, which was on the route to Santiago de Compostela in Spain. During this period leper houses were set up in Montoire and Trôo.

- **Population:** 4 127
- **Michelin Map:** 318: C-5
- **Info:** 16 pl. Clemenceau, 41800 Montoire-sur-le-Loir, ✆02 54 85 23 30. www.montoire-sur-le-loir.net.
- **Location:** 20km/12.4mi to the W of Vendôme and 19km/12mi N of Château-Renault. Try to approach along the D 108 and the minor road from Lavardin, which runs alongside the river.
- **Parking:** You will find only on-street parking.
- **Timing:** Allow 1hr to explore the village.

SIGHTS

Castle

A stone fortified wall encloses the 11C keep which stands on a spur of rock.

Bridge

There is a beautiful **view**★ of the Loir flowing past old houses covered with wisteria where weeping willows trail their tendrils in the water among the fishing boats moored to the banks.

Renaissance houses

Two Renaissance houses stand side by side on place Clemenceau; the larger, with mullioned windows and high dormer windows, is also the older. There are two others: the 16C Antoine-Moreau Hospital in rue St-Laurent and, in rue St-Oustrille, the Maison du Jeu de Quilles, which owes its name, the "Skittle-game house", to the columns decorating the façade.

Chapelle St-Gilles★

The main gate opens on to the apse of an elegant Romanesque chapel which belonged to a Benedictine priory

Fresco in Chapelle St-Gilles

The Meeting at Montoire

In mid-October 1940, convoys of German soldiers swarmed into the region and set up anti-aircraft batteries on the hills. Patrols searched houses in Montoire and barricaded the roads. Electricity and phones were cut off. French SNCF railway workers were replaced by Germans, and people whose houses overlooked the railway were ordered to close the shutters and stay indoors. A Messerschmitt squadron scared cattle in the fields, and two armoured trains bristling with cannons criss-crossed the line from Vendôme to Tours, Bordeaux and Hendaye

On 22 October, Hitler met up with Pierre Laval at Montoire station; in case of emergency his train could shelter in the tunnel near to St-Rimay. Two days later, the infamous meeting between the Führer and Marshall Pétain took place, a black day during which the German word *zusammenarbeit* (cooperation) was translated as collaboration.

founded in the 7C. The chapel and the prior's lodging are set against a pleasant backdrop of lawns and yew trees. In the 9C an envoy of Charles the Bald oversaw the building of a fort on the hilltop to defend against Norman raids.

The poet Pierre de Ronsard set off from St-Gilles in October 1585 to visit the priories of St Madeleine de Croixval and St Cosme, where he died two months later.

Frescoes★★ decorate the three apses laid out in a cloverleaf shape with the chancel and transept. The spherical vaults each diplay a Christ from a different era.

The oldest, dating from the early 12C, is to be found in the main apse: seated on a rainbow, he holds the Book of the Seven Seals surrounded by four angels and four animals symbolising the evangelists. In the southern transept arm, a Byzantine-influenced Christ in majesty (1180) passes keys to St Peter (now effaced). In the northern transept arm, a 13C Christ sits with the apostles.; the tormented attitudes, whites, ochres and sky blues show the nascent style of the local school of artists.

Railway Station: Musée des Rencontres

av. de la République. May–Aug Thu–Sun and public holidays 10.30am–12.30pm, 2.30–6.30pm, Wed 2.30–6.30pm ; Apr, Sept and Oct Wed–Sat 2–6pm. Closed Nov–Mar, Mon, Tue and Wed morning. 4€ (children 12–16 years 2€). 02 54 85 23 30/ 33 42. www.montoire-sur-le-loir.net.

On the site of the famous meeting of 24 Oct 1940, the Musée des Rencontres portrays the event by means of a large-scale model, photos and period film footage.

Musikenfête

Espace de l'Europe, quartier Marescot. Open Tue–Sun Mar–Sept 10am–noon, 2–6pm; Oct–Dec 2–6pm. 5.80€. 02 54 85 28 95. www.musikenfete.fr.

In this show-museum of traditional music from all across the globe, many instruments – often left by musicians who have performed at festivals in Montoire – are brought to life.

Summer street music – *During the 2nd week in July, it is the turn of violins, double basses and other instruments; then from mid-August onwards, the International Folklore Festival takes over.*

ADDRESSES

STAY

Camping municipal Les Reclusages – *41800 Montoire-sur-Loire. 02 54 85 02 53. Leave town on rte. de Tours, then rte. de Lavardin, on the left after the bridge. Open May–end Sept, advance reservation advised.*

Trôo

A picture book 900 years old, yet still extraordinarily fresh awaits on the walls of the delightful church in St-Jacques-des-Guérets. Make sure to explore Trôo thoroughly (it is pronounced "tro") and discover a tangle of tiny streets with tiered houses, staircases and mysterious underground passageways.

- **Population:** 323
- **Michelin Map:** 318 B-5
- **Info:** La Poste, 39 r. Auguste-Arnault, 41800 Trôo. 02 54 72 87 50. www.troo.com.
- **Location:** 26km/16mi W of Vendôme and 16km/10mi SW of St-Calais.
- **Kids:** Visit the petrifying caves.
- **Timing:** About an hour to see the town.

THE TOWN

The Mound★

From the top of this feudal hillock there is an excellent view across the coiling Loir and its valley. Spot the little church of St-Jacques-des-Guérets opposite Trôo.

Ancienne collégiale St-Martin

Founded in 1050, and remodelled a century later, the church is dominated by a remarkable square tower pierced by Angevin-style window bays. The interior features convex vaulting, historied romanesque capitals, and 15C stalls and communion table; also note the 16C statue of St Mamès whose name is invoked to cure stomach pains.

Mural paintings, Église St-Jacques-des-Guérets

Grands Puits (The Great Well)

Also known as the Talking Well, thanks to its 45m/148ft depth which gives an excellent echo.

Lazaret of Ste-Catherine

Located on D 917 at the far end of town, this quarantine hospital for pilgrims on the routes to St-Martin de Tours and Santiago de Compostela features lovely romanesque arcatures. A leper hospital used to exist outside the walls to the west of Trôo.

Grotte Pétrifiante

39 r. Auguste-Arnault. Open May–Sept Wed–Mon 10am–noon, 2–6pm; Jul and Aug open daily; rest of year phone for times. 02 54 72 87 50.

Water streams abundantly into the cave to form stalactites and petrified shapes.

Église St-Jacques-des-Guérets

On the left bank of the Loir.

The splendid **murals**★painted between 1130 and 1170 were influenced by Byzantine art and have preserved an amazing freshness of colour. The most lovely are to be found in the apse, and show the *Crucifixion, Day of Judgement, Christ in Majesty* and the *Last Supper*. Elsewhere, the martyrdom of St James, beheaded by Herod, the Garden of Paradise, the Nativity and the Massacre of the Innocents are depicted.

Forêt de Bercé★

Bercé Forest is all that remains of the great Le Mans Forest that once reached from the Sarthe to the Loir. The magnificent sessile oaks mixed with chestnuts and beeches, provide cover for a herd of deer. The Forest is now carefully exploited for high quality oak.

- **Michelin Map:** 310 L-8
- **Info:** Hôtel des Ursulines, r. de l'Étoile, 72000 Le Mans. ☎02 43 28 17 22. www.lemanstourisme.com.
- **Location:** The vast forested region of 5 377ha/13 287 acres lies 30km/19mi SE of Le Mans, and 11km/7mi N of Château-du-Loir.
- **Kids:** There's a special children's mountain bike trail.
- **Timing:** Allow a whole day for outdoors action, hiking and biking in the forest.

SIGHTS

Guided tours (2hrs) mid-Jul–Aug (depart from the Chêne Boppe car park). For information ☎02 43 24 44 70. Free maps available on request. Several waymarked mountain bike itineraries of varying lengths criss-cross the forest, many of which are ideal for beginners.

Fontaine de la Coudre

The spring, which is the source of the River Dinan, a tributary of Le Loir, flows slowly under the tall oaks known as the Futaie des Forges. An educational trail explains the workings of the forest to children, including "hammering", the system whereby trees due to be felled are carefully marked and numbered.

Sources de l'Hermitière★

A deep valley thick with towering oaks and beeches hides the pure waters of these springs.

This is the finest stand of oaks in the forest. Two violent storms in 1967 caused gaps among the trees. While some of the giant oaks (300 to 350 years old) are very decrepit, others are splendid specimens.

A path leads to the Boppe oak, or rather to its stump, protected by a roof, since the ancient tree was struck by lightning in 1934 at the venerable age of 262. Its neighbour, Roulleau de la Roussière, is still flourishing after more than 350 years.

Forêt de Bercé

©S. Sauvignier/Michelin

Roadsign in Forêt de Bercé

Carnuta

2 r. du Bourg Ancien, 72500 Jupiles. Carnuta is in the village of Jupilles approx 35min drive SE of Le Mans. Take exit no. 25 or 26 on A 28. Open Jun–Sept daily 10am–6pm; Oct–May Wed–Sun 2–6pm. 6€. 02 43 38 10 31. www.carnuta fr.

The Carnuta centre is a cross between an interpretation centre and an informative and fun way for children to learn about the Bercé Forest and the men and women who have lived and worked with it for centuries. Using pictures, sounds, slide shows and games it brings to life the forest experience in a modern and engaging manner.

ADDRESSES

EAT

L'Hermitière – *In the lieu-dit l'Hermitière in Bercy Forest. 72150 St-Vincent-du-Lorouër. 02 43 44 84 45. www.lhermitiere.fr.* Atmospheric country restaurant built around a 400-year-old pear tree. Lovely terrace by lake and garden. Perfect peace.

SPORT

Mountain biking – *02 43 38 16 60. www.vallee-du-loir.com.* A total of 315km/197mi of marked trails between 8km/5mi and 41km/26mi in length. No climbs above 100m. Good for beginners as well as experienced bikers. Ask for map of trails.

An historic destiny

The remaining tracts of the ancient forest of the Carnutes, where the annual gathering of the Druids of Celtic Gaul once took place in the 1C BC, acquired the name of Burçay under the rule of the Counts of Anjou.

The forest came under the ownership of the Crown in the 16C and supplied oaks for shipbuilding for many years, while its beeches were in great demand for making clogs. Nowadays, the Bercé Forest is managed by the ONF (Office Nationale des Fôrets) – the French Forestry Commission – and produces top-quality oak. The trees are felled when they are between 200 and 240 years old to produce pale yellow, fine-grained timber which is prized as a veneer by cabinet makers and exported widely throughout Europe.

St-Paterne-Racan

St-Paterne stretches out along the Escotais, which is bordered by riverside washhouses and weeping willows.

- **Population:** 1 637
- **Michelin Map:** 317 L-3
- **Info:** 02 47 96 58 22. www.tourisme-langeais.com.
- **Location:** Between Le Mans and Tours, you approach the village by pretty roads along the banks of the Escotais river.
- **Don't miss:** The polychrome statues in the church.
- **Kids:** Outdoors activities by the Val Joyeux lake.
- **Timing:** Allow 2–3hrs for the village and surrounds.

CHURCH

The church contains interesting works of art, some from the abbey of La Clarté-Dieu. The 16C terracotta group to the left of the high altar portrays the *Adoration of the Magi*; at the centre is a charming **Virgin and Child**★.

EXCURSIONS

Château de la Roche-Racan

2km/1mi SE on D 28. Guided tours (45min) Jul–mid-Aug 9.30am–12.30pm, 2.30–5.30pm. 5€. 02 47 29 20 02.

The Château de la Roche-Racan stands perched on a rock overlooking the Escotais Valley which, together with the Loir, was a constant source of inspiration to the first owner and poet, **Racan**.

Born at Champmarin near Aubigné, Honorat de Bueil, Marquis de Racan (1589–1670), was a member of the well-known local family, the Bueils. Not really cut out for the life of a soldier and following a number of unlucky love affairs, Racan retired to his country seat for the last 40 years of his life, a period described in his work, *Stances à la retraite*.

There he was quite content to stroll by his fountains or hunt game or visit Denis de la Grelière, the Abbé de la Clarté-Dieu, who invited him to put the Psalms into verse. He brought up his children, pursued his lawsuits, grew beans and rebuilt his château.

In 1635 Racan commissioned a local master mason, Jacques Gabriel, a member of a long-established family of architects, to build this château. The main building was originally flanked by two pavilions, only one of which remains, pedimented and adorned with a corner turret and caryatids. Long balustered terraces, above arcades decorated with masks, overlook the park and Escotais Valley.

St-Christophe-sur-le-Nais

Also lying in the Escotais Valley, this village is the scene of a pilgrimage in honour of St Christopher. The **church** is composed of two separate buildings, an old 11C–14C priory chapel and the parish church with its 16C nave and belfry.

On the threshold of the nave a gigantic St Christopher welcomes you. To the right is a reliquary bust of the saint. To the left of the chancel, the door leading to the prior's oratory is surmounted by a fine 14C statue of the Virgin and Child. Two Renaissance medallions adorn the church's timber roof.

Neuvy-le-Roi

9km/5.6mi E on D 54.

The **church**, which dates from the 12C and 16C, has a Romanesque chancel and a nave covered with Angevin vaulting.

Bueil-en-Touraine

8km/5mi NE along D 72 and D 5.

Set above the valley of the River Long, this village is the cradle of the Bueil family which has supplied France with an admiral, two marshals and a poet, Honorat de Bueil, Lord of Racan.

At the top of the hill stands a curious group of buildings formed by the juxta-

position of the church of St-Pierre-aux-Liens *(left)* and the collegiate church of St-Michel, founded in the 14C.
In the church of St-Pierre-aux-Liens is a remarkable Renaissance baptistry decorated with statuettes of Christ and the apostles.

Château de Vaujours

17km/11mi SW.

Closed to the public.

The fortified barbican is visible among the remains of more romantic round towers and a chapel of this 15C château, which welcomed Louis XI on several ocassions.

Étand ge Val Joyeux

17km/11mi SW.

A vast expanse of water at the foot of a pleasant wooded hillside offers the possibility of swimming and even sailing.

Forêt de Château-la-Vallière

17km/11mi SW.

Vast woodlands of pine and oak dotted with marshes extend for around 3 000ha/7 413 acres around Château-la-Vallière. Come in autumn and you may hear the sounds of a hunting horn and the barking of the pack.

ADDRESSES

STAY

Hôtel-Restaurant Bar des Voyageurs. *r. Lezay Marnesia, 37330 Château-la-Vallière. 02 47 24 04 56. 8rms.* Unfortunately, the hotel section suffers from noise from the route nationale passing nearby. The restaurant is more inviting than the bar and offers a selection of unfussy fixed-price menus. The easygoing ambience and simple cuisine will delight.

Chambre d'hôte Le Clos de Launay *rte. de Tours, 37330 Souvigné. 02 47 24 58 91. www.chambres-touraine.fr. . 5 rms.* Nothing disturbs the peace in this lovely modern house set in 7ha/17..3 acres of gardens. The cosy set-up includes a comfy guests' lounge and a fish pond for pleasant walks.

Chambre d'hôte Domaine de la Bergerie *On D 959, 37330 Braye-sur-Maulne. 02 47 24 90 88. www.domaine-bergerie.fr. 5 rms.* An unforgettable stay is guaranteed at this 19C château set in immense grounds with ponds and woodland. Romantically rustic rooms and independent gîtes. Warm welcome with a glass of wine, and table d'hôte dining available.

Château du Lude★★

This magnificent château, on the south bank of the Loir and surrounded by a beautiful park, offers visitors a fascinating mixture of Gothic, Renaissance and Louis XVI styles. The 11C fortress of the counts of Anjou was replaced in the 13C–14C by a castle, which withstood several assaults by the English before it fell in 1425; it was recaptured two years later by Ambroise de Loré, Beaumanoir and Gilles de Rais.

- **Michelin Map:** 310: J-9
- **Info:** pl. François-de-Nicolaÿ 72800, Le Lude. 02 43 94 62 20. www.tourisme-bassinludois.fr.
- **Location:** In a wooded area midway between La Flèche and Château-la-Vallière along the D 959.
- **Don't miss:** The annual Fête des Jardins held in the grounds.
- **Timing:** You will need 2hrs to visit the château and explore the grounds, but up to half a day if you want to explore more widely.

A BIT OF HISTORY

In 1457 the castle was acquired by Jean de Daillon, a childhood friend of Louis XI. His son built the present château on the foundations of the earlier fortress: it kept the traditional square layout with a massive tower at each corner, but the large windows and the delicate decoration make it a country house in the fashion of its age.

VISIT

Open mid-Jun–31 Aug daily 10am–noon, 2–6pm; Apr–mid-Jun and Sept Thu–Tue 10am–noon, 2–6pm. Château and gardens 7€. 02 43 94 60 09. www.lelude.com.

Exterior

Facing the park is the François I wing. Its façade is a combination of the fortress style, with its round medieval towers, and Renaissance refinement. Overlooking the river, the Louis XVI wing exemplifies the Classical style; it is sober and symmetrical, its façade broken only by a central projecting section topped by a carved pediment.

Interior

The Louis XII wing houses a large 19C library with 2 000 books that belonged to the Duke of Bouillon. The 18C building contains a fine suite of rooms including

Château du Lude

©Nicolas Thibaut/Photononstop

A Thousand Years of History

The 11C fortress of the Counts of Anjou was replaced by a fortified château in the 13C and 14C, which stood up to several assaults by the English before it was taken in 1425, then re-conquered two years later by Ambroise de Loré, Beaumanoir and Gilles de Rais.

Jean de Daillon, a childhood friend of Louis XI acquired the château in 1457, and his son built the current edifice on the foundations of the old fortress. It was further modified during the Renaissance period and in the 18C, and has stayed in the same family until today. Unusually, most of its furniture survived the Revolution. Famous guests include Henri IV, Louis XIII and Madame de Sévigné.

a splendid oval salon in pure Louis XVI. In the François I wing a small library contains a 17C Gobelins tapestry; in the dining room, where the window recesses reveal the thickness of the medieval walls, there is a vast chimney-piece with a carved salamander and ermine.

EXCURSION

Maison des Architectes

3 r. du Marché-au-Fil, near the château entrance. No public access.

Built in the 16C by the architects who designed the château, it displays Renaissance features such as transom windows, pilasters with corinthian capitals decorated with circles and lozenges, and a frieze underlining the first floor.

DRIVING TOUR

The Quest for the Cross of Anjou

Round trip of 28km/17.4mi – about 1hr 30min. Drive S out of Le Lude on D 257.

Genneteil

The Romanesque **church** has a 13C bell tower with a stair turret and a 11C doorway; note the arch stones, which are carved with the signs of the zodiac and human faces.

Take D 138 E to Chigné.

Chigné

The **church** (12C–15C) features an interesting façade flanked by a round tower.

Continue via Les Quatre-Chemins to La Boissière.

La Boissière

Guided tours (30min) by request mid-Jul–Aug 10am–noon, 3–6pm; Easter 10am–noon, 3–5pm. 02 41 89 55 52.

The name of La Boissière is linked with a precious relic: the **Cross of Anjou** (*see BAUGÉ*). The cross was brought from the Middle East in the 13C and during the Hundred Years War was kept in Angers. It returned to La Boissière in about 1456 and remained there until 1790 when it was transferred to Baugé.

Drive back towards Le Lude on D 767; in La Croix-Beauchêne turn right onto D 138.

Broc

The **church** has a Romanesque tower and apse decorated with 13C frescoes.

Return to Le Lude via La Croix-Beauchêne then turn right onto D 307.

ADDRESSES

STAY

La Renaissance *2 av. de la Libération, 72800 Le Lude. 02 43 94 63 10. www.renaissancelude.com. 8rms.*

Stay right by the château in this hotel-restaurant serving up-to-date cuisine. Modern dining room, or eat in a courtyard terrace in summer.

La Flèche★

Pleasantly situated on the banks of the Loir, this charming Angevin town is renowned for its Prytanée, a military school that has trained generations of officers.

- **Population:** 15 321
- **Michelin Map:** 310: I-8
- **Info:** Office du Tourisme, bd. Montréal, 72200 La Flèche. ℘02 43 94 02 53. www.tourisme-paysflechois.fr.
- **Location:** Students tend to group around the Henri IV fountain (on the square of the same name); a stroll along boulevard Latouche and Carmes gardens is a pleasant way to orient yourself.
- **Kids:** Zoo's sea-lion show.

A BIT OF HISTORY

Henri IV – La Flèche was given as part of a dowry to Charles de Bourbon-Vendôme, grandfather to Henri IV of Navarre, of "Paris is well worth a Mass" fame. It was here that the young Prince Henri spent a happy childhood and where in 1604 he founded a college.

A breeding-ground for officers – The Jesuit college grew rapidly and by 1625 there were 1 500 pupils. Over the years it has produced a great many celebrities who have distinguished themselves in the service of their country: Charles Borda, René Descartes, Marshalls Bertrand, Clarke, Pelissier, Gallieni and, more recently, astronauts Patrick Baudry and Jean-François Clervoy and the actor Jean-Claude Brialy – not to mention more than 2 000 generals and a number of government ministers.

Missionaries in Canada – **Jérôme le Royer de la Dauversière**, a native of La Flèche, was one of the founders of Montreal. Another old pupil of the college in La Flèche, **François de Montmorency-Laval**, became the first bishop of Nouvelle-France in 1674.

Unhappy exile – Under the monarchy La Flèche was a peaceful town with nothing to offer by way of entertainment but a hairdresser's, two billiard halls and a café. The witty poet **Jean-Baptiste Gresset** (1709–77) composed the heroic-comic masterpiece on the adventures of the parrot Ver-Vert, for which he is famous, while in exile in La Flèche for the indiscreet use of his tongue and his pen.

SIGHTS

Prytanée National Militaire★

Guided tours (1hr) Jul–Aug 10am–noon, 2–6pm. 3.50€. ℘02 43 48 59 06 (weekdays).

This military academy educates more than 900 male and female students, housed in two pavilions, named respectively after Henri IV and Gallieni. This State establishment offering an all-round education is open to any French youths wishing to prepare for entrance to the national service academies *(grandes écoles militaires)* such as the École Polytechnique, the École Spéciale Militaire in Coëtquidan, the École Navale in Brest, the École de l'Air at Salon-de-Provence and academies specialised in engineering. The school boasts an excellent library containing around 45 000 volumes, some of which date back to the 15C.

Église St-Louis★

Housed within the Prytanée National Militaire with same visiting conditions and contact details.

The layout is typical of the Jesuits with its single well-lit nave. This is a remarkable example of Baroque decoration, from the main altarpiece to the magnificent **organ casing★**. Tucked away in the left transept, the gilded heart-shaped urn contains the ashes of the hearts of Henri IV and Marie de' Medici.

Library, Prytanée National Militaire

Chapelle Notre-Dame-des-Vertus

In av. Rhin-et-Danube in the direction of Laval, go right into Impasse des Vertus.

A delightful romanesque edifice with a semicircular archway above the portico. Note the wooden vaulting entirely covered with 17C painting and superb Renaissance **panelling★** taken from the château du Verger, and don't miss the so-called **muslim warrior★** carved into the leaved door.

Château des Carmes

The 17C buildings erected on the ruins of a 15C fortress now house the town hall. The façade facing the Loir consists of a steep gable flanked by two machicolated turrets.

The **Parc des Carmes**, which is open to the public, stretches down to the river; from the bridge there is a fine view of the calm water reflecting the garden and the château.

EXCURSIONS

Zoo de la Flèche★

5km/3mi E. Leave La Flèche on D 104; the zoo is 1km/0.6mi after the third-level crossing. Open Apr–Sept 9.30am–6pm (Jul–Aug 7pm); Oct–Mar 10am–noon, 1.30–5.30pm; school holidays 10am–5.30pm. 17.50€ (children 3–11 years 14€). 02 43 48 19 19. www.zoo-la-fleche.com.

The zoo covers 7ha/17 acres in a forest setting. There are mammals (big game, monkeys, deer, elephants, etc.), many birds and numerous reptiles housed in two vivariums (pythons, boas, crocodiles, tortoises, etc.). Sea-lions appear at scheduled performances. The **Musée de Sciences naturelles** displays a diorama on regional fauna. The 600 stuffed animals in the collection of the naturalist Jacques Bouillault are on show in reconstructions of their natural habitats.

Bazouges-sur-le-Loir

7km/4.3mi. Drive W out of La Flèche and follow N 23.

From the bridge there is a charming **view★** of the river with its wash-houses and river gate, of the castle and the mill, of the church and its tower in the square and of the gardens climbing towards the roofs of Bazouges.

Château de Bazouges-sur-le-Loir

Guided tours (45min) mid-Jun–mid-Sept Thu–Sun and public holidays 3–6pm; Easter–mid -un and public holidays 3–6pm. 3€. 02 43 45 32 62.

The Château de Bazouges, together with its watermill, was built on an attractive site on the banks of the Loir in the 15C and 16C by the Champagne family, one of whom, Baudoin (Baldwin), was chamberlain to Louis XII and François I. The entrance is flanked by two massive towers, with machicolations and pepper-pot turrets; one of them contains the 15C chapel decorated with Angevin vaulting and two old statues portraying St Barbara and St John. The guard room over the gateway leads to the sentry walk. Another more imposing guard room, with a stone chimney-piece, is on view as well as the 18C State Rooms and the formal French park, which is planted with cypresses and yew trees and circled by water.

Chambiers Forest

This forest on the southern edge of the town provides 1 300ha/5sq mi of walks among the oak and pine trees; broad rides radiate from the Table au Roy (King's Table).

Château de Chambiers

15 pl. des Terrasses, Durtal. Guided tours hourly (45min) Jul–Aug Fri–Mon 10.30am, 11.30am, 2.30–5.30pm; rest of year varies 6.50€. 02 41 69 92 60. www.chateau-durtal.com.

This grand stronghold on the Loir belonged to François de Scépeaux, Marshal of Vieilleville, who was host to Henri II, Charles IX and Catherine de' Medici. It came through the Revolution relatively unscathed. The 15C wing is flanked by round towers with machicolations and pepper-pot roofs. The highest one (five storeys) affords a good view of the Loir Valley. The Renaissance Gallery, lavishly decorated with paintings, overlooks the river.

The Schömberg Pavilion, characterised by string courses, cordons and cornerstones with vermiculated bossage, prefigures the Classical period. A tour of the interior will take you through the guard room, the kitchen quarters, the dungeons, the Renaissance Gallery and the Great Tower *(Grande Tour)*.

Porte Verron

This 15C gate flanked by two turrets is part of the original curtain wall of the castle.

Vieux Pont

This old bridge commands a nice **view** of the River Loir, the watermills, the pointed roofs of the town and a medieval round tower upstream.

ADDRESSES

STAY

Camping municipal de la Route d'Or – *allée du Camping. 02 43 94 55 90. www.camping-laroutedor.com. Open Mar–end Oct - 250 pitches. Reservation advised.* € Ample space on this well-run campsite, as well as renovated sanitary blocks and newly-installed mobile homes. In the centre of the site is a kids playground, 2 swimming pools and, next door, a canoe centre.

Le Vert Galant *70 Grande-Rue. 02 43 94 00 51. www.vghotel.com. 21 rms. €12.* This former 18C post station lies in the town centre not far from the Prytanée. A mix of traditional and contemporary furniture in the rooms, and breakfast is taken in a pleasant veranda.

EAT

Restaurant des Plantes *54 av. d'Angers. 49430 Durtal. 02 41 76 41 57. www.restaurantdesplantes.com. Closed Sun, Mon and Tue eves.* Hidden in a quaint building on the edge of the village, this popular spot is often full thanks to its lunchtime fixed-price menu which brings in the happy locals. Advance booking is a good idea.

Le Moulin des Quatre Saisons *r. Gallieni. 02 43 45 12 12. www.moulindesquartresaisons.com.Closed 2–25 Jan, Wed and Sun eves, Mon.* Your first impression upon arriving at this 17C watermill in summer will be the scent of wisteria that overhangs the front path. The restaurant overlooks the Loir and features cooking from the south of France; the décor is Alsatian.

D

STAY

EAT

MAPS AND PLANS

THEMATIC MAPS

MAPS AND PLANS

MAP LEGEND

	Sight	Seaside resort	Winter sports resort	Spa
Highly recommended	★★★	⚲⚲⚲	✳✳✳	⚕⚕⚕
Recommended	★★	⚲⚲	✳✳	⚕⚕
Interesting	★	⚲	✳	⚕

Additional symbols

🄸	Tourist information
═══ ═══	Motorway or other primary route
➊ ➊	Junction: complete, limited
▭══ ═══	Pedestrian street
⊏═════⊐	Unsuitable for traffic, street subject to restrictions
▦▦▦ - - - -	Steps – Footpath
🚂 🚉	Train station – Auto-train station
🚌 S.N.C.F.	Coach (bus) station
───────	Tram
⊙	Metro, underground
🅿	Park-and-Ride
♿	Access for the disabled
✉	Post office
☎	Telephone
✉	Covered market
⚔	Barracks
△	Drawbridge
∪	Quarry
✗	Mine
Ⓑ Ⓕ	Car ferry (river or lake)
⛴	Ferry service: cars and passengers
⛵	Foot passengers only
③	Access route number common to Michelin maps and town plans
Bert (R.)...	Main shopping street
AZ B	Map co-ordinates

Selected monuments and sights

◉ ➡	Tour - Departure point
▮ ♱	Catholic church
▮ ♱	Protestant church, other temple
✡ ▭ ☪	Synagogue - Mosque
▰	Building
■	Statue, small building
♱	Calvary, wayside cross
◎	Fountain
●━■▬	Rampart - Tower - Gate
⋈	Château, castle, historic house
⁑	Ruins
∪	Dam
☼	Factory, power plant
☆	Fort
∩	Cave
▭	Troglodyte dwelling
⊓	Prehistoric site
▼	Viewing table
₩	Viewpoint
▲	Other place of interest

Map Legend continued overleaf

Abbreviations

A	Agricultural office (Chambre d'agriculture)
C	Chamber of Commerce (Chambre de commerce)
H	Town hall (Hôtel de ville)
J	Law courts (Palais de justice)
M	Museum (Musée)
P	Local authority offices (Préfecture, sous-préfecture)
POL.	Police station (Police)
	Police station (Gendarmerie)
T	Theatre (Théâtre)
U	University (Université)

Sports and recreation

- Racecourse
- Skating rink
- Outdoor, indoor swimming pool
- Multiplex Cinema
- Marina, sailing centre
- Trail refuge hut
- Cable cars, gondolas
- Funicular, rack railway
- Tourist train
- Recreation area, park
- Theme, amusement park
- Wildlife park, zoo
- Gardens, park, arboretum
- Bird sanctuary, aviary
- Walking tour, footpath
- Of special interest to children

COMPANION PUBLICATIONS

REGIONAL AND LOCAL MAPS

To make the most of your journey, travel with Michelin maps at a scale of 1:200 000: **Regional maps nos 513, 518 and 519** and the new local maps, which are illustrated on the map of France below.

MAPS OF FRANCE

And remember to travel with the latest edition of the **map of France no 721**, which gives an overall view of the region of the Châteaux of the Loire, and the main access roads which connect it to the rest of France. The entire country is mapped at a 1:1 000 000 scale and clearly shows the main road network. Convenient Atlas formats (spiral, hard cover and "mini") are also available.

INTERNET

Michelin is pleased to offer a route-planning service on the Internet: **www.travel.viamichelin.com** or **www.viamichelin.com or**
Choose the shortest route, a route without tolls, or the Michelin recommended route to your destination; you can also access information about hotels and restaurants from *The Red Guide*, and tourists sites from *The Green Guide*. There are a number of useful maps and plans in the guide, listed in the table of contents.

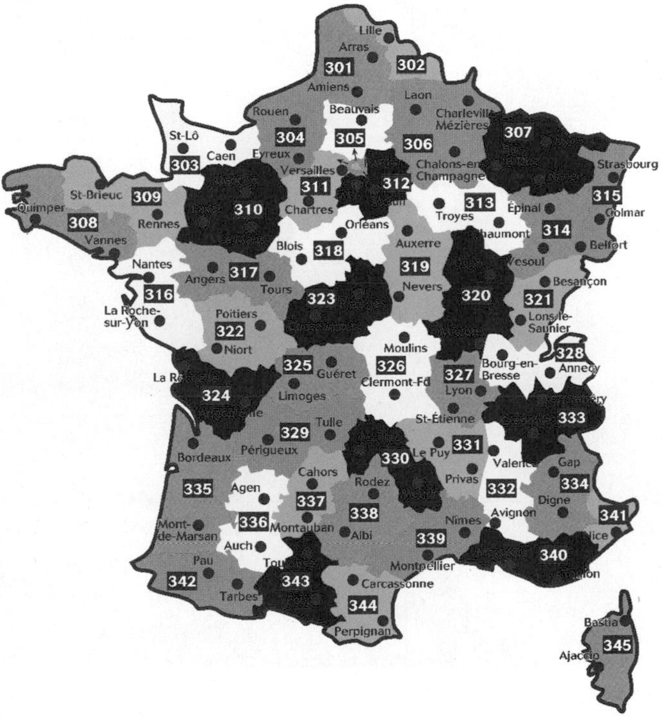

The Michelin Adventure

It all started with rubber balls! This was the product made by a small company based in Clermont-Ferrand that André and Edouard Michelin inherited, back in 1880. The brothers quickly saw the potential for a new means of transport and their first success was the invention of detachable pneumatic tires for bicycles. However, the automobile was to provide the greatest scope for their creative talents.

Throughout the 20th century, Michelin never ceased developing and creating ever more reliable and high-performance tires, not only for vehicles ranging from trucks to F1 but also for underground transit systems and airplanes.

From early on, Michelin provided its customers with tools and services to facilitate mobility and make traveling a more pleasurable and more frequent experience. As early as 1900, the Michelin Guide supplied motorists with a host of useful information related to vehicle maintenance, accommodation and restaurants, and was to become a benchmark for good food. At the same time, the Travel Information Bureau offered travelers personalised tips and itineraries.

The publication of the first collection of roadmaps, in 1910, was an instant hit! In 1926, the first regional guide to France was published, devoted to the principal sites of Brittany, and before long each region of France had its own Green Guide. The collection was later extended to more far-flung destinations, including New York in 1968 and Taiwan in 2011.

In the 21st century, with the growth of digital technology, the challenge for Michelin maps and guides is to continue to develop alongside the company's tire activities. Now, as before, Michelin is committed to improving the mobility of travelers.

MICHELIN TODAY

WORLD NUMBER ONE TIRE MANUFACTURER

- 70 production sites in 18 countries
- 111,000 employees from all cultures and on every continent
- 6,000 people employed in research and development

forward together
where mobility is safer

It also involves helping motorists take care of their safety and their tires. To do so, Michelin organises "Fill Up With Air" campaigns all over the world to remind us that correct tire pressure is vital.

WEAR

DETECTING TIRE WEAR

The legal minimum depth of tire tread is 1.6mm. Tire manufacturers equip their tires with tread wear indicators, which are small blocks of rubber moulded into the base of the main grooves at a depth of 1.6mm.

Tires are the only point of contact between the vehicle and road.

The photo below shows the actual contact zone.

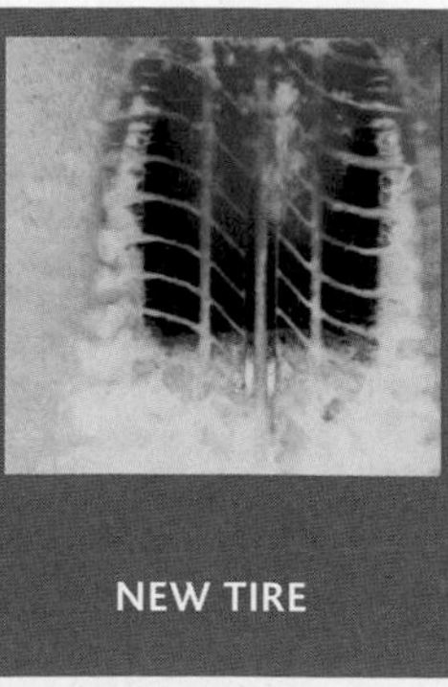

NEW TIRE

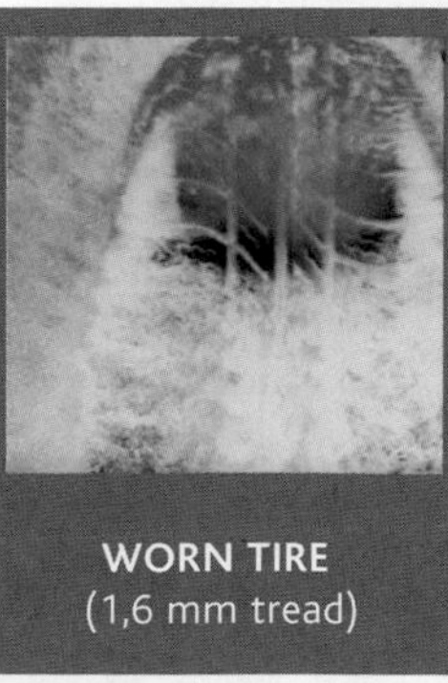

WORN TIRE
(1,6 mm tread)

If the tread depth is less than 1.6mm, tires are considered to be worn and dangerous on wet surfaces.

Moving forward
means sustainable mobility

INNOVATION AND THE ENVIRONMENT

By 2050, Michelin aims to cut the quantity of raw materials used in its tire manufacturing process by half and to have developed renewable energy in its facilities. The design of MICHELIN tires has already saved billions of litres of fuel and, by extension, billions of tons of CO2.

Similarly, Michelin prints its maps and guides on paper produced from sustainably managed forests and is diversifying its publishing media by offering digital solutions to make traveling easier, more fuel efficient and more enjoyable!

The group's whole-hearted commitment to eco-design on a daily basis is demonstrated by ISO 14001 certification.

Like you, Michelin is committed to preserving our planet.

Chat with Bibendum

Go to
www.michelin.com/corporate/en
Find out more about
Michelin's history and the
latest news.

QUIZ

Michelin develops tires for all types of vehicles.
See if you can match the right tire with the right vehicle…

Solution : A-6 / B-4 / C-2 / D-1 / E-3 / F-7 / G-5

Michelin Apa Publications Ltd

58 Borough High Street, London SE1 1XF, United Kingdom

ISBN 978-1-907099-50-2
Printed: December 2011
Printed and bound in Germany